Praise for *The Unfinished Presidency*

"Carter has enjoyed a full share of other triumphs. Among them, surely, is the fortune of attracting Douglas B   a fairminded and thoroughly readable biographer. His accou   ultimate antipolitician' offers as full an answer available to the   t's Jimmy Carter been up to? Much, it turns out."
— *The Washington Post*

"Douglas Brinkley, one of our   citing historians, not only provides a richly textured narrative of   r's amazing postpresidency, he also uses the story to explore the relationship between realism and moral values in American foreign policy."
—Walter Isaacson, author of *Kissinger*

"*The Unfinished Presidency* is an unauthorized biography, not a hostile one . . . Until Carter authorizes a biography, this rigorously footnoted text gives a thoroughly sourced intimate portrait of one of the country's most respected ex-presidents."
—*USA Today*

"This excellent study of Carter's life and activities since 1980 is not an 'authorized biography' but is, withal, a very well-informed portrait of the ex-president."
—*Foreign Affairs*

"Jimmy Carter has given the role of ex-president new luster; and Douglas Brinkley's excellent book records the possibilities and perils of an activist ex-presidency with candor, insight, and readability. A fine history!"
—Arthur Schlesinger, Jr.

"This superb book shows how broad, sustained, and controversial were Carter's efforts in Panama, Nicaragua, Haiti, the Middle East, the Gulf War, and Korea. Every chapter is filled with insight and revelation."
—Gaddis Smith, Larned Professor of History, Yale University

"It is widely agreed that Jimmy Carter is among the greatest if not *the* greatest of all ex-presidents in U.S. history . . . this thorough and authoritative work will be of keen interest to students of the presidency and foreign affairs."
—*Library Journal*

"Brinkley's research into Carter's personalized diplomacy is first rate (helped by special access to Carter's papers); his prose is insightful about the religious convictions underlying Carter's tenacious will to find peace wherever the parties to a conflict seem stymied and intransigent."
—*Booklist*

"Brinkley captures Carter's sometimes maddening authenticity . . . a rich, energetic American story. His account of Carter's behavior during the run-up to the Gulf War is especially fascinating."
—*Time*

"Truly impressive . . . Brinkley presents a compelling picture of Jimmy Carter as an individual driven by stubborn righteousness and missionary zeal." —*New Orleans Times-Picayune*

"With its astonishing detail and subtle insights, it is hard to imagine that this definitive account will ever be surpassed."
—Peter G. Bourne, author of *Jimmy Carter: A Comprehensive Biography from Plains to Postpresidency*

"*The Unfinished Presidency* should help redeem the man whom both Republicans and Democrats for two decades have kicked around like a political football . . . [it] should be given to Clinton as a going-away present to inspire him as he begins his post-presidential odyssey in 2001."
—*Commercial Appeal* (Memphis, Tennessee)

"Jimmy Carter is the most active and influential former president since Teddy Roosevelt. He has earned everyone's admiration and become a model of how to not just carry on but to contribute after leaving the White House. Doug Brinkley, the best of the new generation of American historians, tells us in vigorous language the story of Carter's quite amazing range of activities, at home and around the world. As a bonus, Brinkley's *The Unfinished Presidency* offers marvelous portraits of a wide range of world leaders, as seen from the unique perspective of Jimmy Carter. Highly recommended!"
—Steven Ambrose, author of *Undaunted Courage*

PENGUIN BOOKS

THE UNFINISHED PRESIDENCY

Douglas Brinkley is professor of history and director of the Eisenhower Center at the University of New Orleans. He has written award-winning books on James Forrestal, Dean Acheson, and Franklin Roosevelt, as well as *Rise to Globalism: American Foreign Policy Since 1938*, with coauthor Stephen E. Ambrose. He is a regular contributor to National Public Radio, and has written for *The New York Times*, *Foreign Affairs*, *The Washington Post*, *The New Yorker*, *Foreign Policy*, and *The Atlantic Monthly*. His book *The American Heritage of the United States* was deemed by Walter Cronkite the "best of recent decades' one-volume histories of the United States."

The Unfinished Presidency

Jimmy Carter's Journey to the Nobel Peace Prize

~∞~

Douglas Brinkley

PENGUIN BOOKS

PENGUIN BOOKS
Published by the Penguin Group
Penguin Putnam Inc., 375 Hudson Street,
New York, New York 10014, U.S.A.
Penguin Books Ltd, 27 Wrights Lane,
London W8 5TZ, England
Penguin Books, Australia Ltd, Ringwood,
Victoria, Australia
Penguin Books Canada Ltd, 10 Alcorn Avenue
Toronto, Ontario, Canada M4V 3B2
Penguin Books (N.Z.) Ltd, 182–190 Wairau Road,
Auckland 10, New Zealand

Penguin Books Ltd., Registered Offices:
Harmondsworth, Middlesex, England

First published in the United States of America by Viking Penguin,
a member of Penguin Putnam Inc. 1998
Published in Penguin Books 1999

3 5 7 9 10 8 6 4

Grateful acknowledgment is made for permission to reprint
"Chris" by Garry Trudeau. By permission of the author.

ISBN 0-670-88006-X (hc.)
ISBN 0 14 02.7616 5 (pbk.)
(CIP data available)

Printed in the United States of America
Set in New Caledonia
DESIGNED BY BETTY LEW

To Patricia Cimalore and
Thomas Cimalore
for Tammy

To help mend the world is true religion.

—*William Penn*

Contents

PREFACE

CITIZEN CARTER

~~∞~~

In a few days I will lay down my official responsibilities in this office
to take up once more the only title in our democracy superior to that
of President: the title of citizen.

— Jimmy Carter, Farewell Address, January 14, 1981

T*he Unfinished Presidency* is not the book I set out to write. My plans began to change in late 1994 when I was interviewing Georgians who knew Jimmy Carter for the first in a projected three-volume biography of the thirty-ninth president, a comprehensive undertaking modeled on Stephen Ambrose's *Nixon* and Taylor Branch's books on Martin Luther King Jr. I had already written the first eleven chapters of volume 1 and was ready to begin chapter 12 when my subject suddenly appeared on the evening news and the covers of *Time* and *Newsweek*—and then reappeared. His postpresidency had become the talk of the globe.[1]

At that point my research on Carter, including a half-dozen long interviews with him at his home in Plains, had been focused primarily on his early years—peanut harvests from the fields of his family's farm, a distinguished stint in the U.S. Navy, another on the Sumter County Board of Education in the wake of *Brown v. Board of Education of Topeka*, and yet another as a Georgia state legislator.[2] I monitored Carter's postpresidential foreign policy work with great interest, but it all seemed a long way off from the period I was writing about, 1970, when my subject had been elected governor of Georgia. I was looking forward to writing up some fresh 1976 campaign anecdotes I had collected, which illuminated how Carter had become president after spending only four years in the Georgia Senate and another four as governor of the nation's fourteenth-largest state—putting him in the White House with the briefest public record of any president since Woodrow

Wilson. Yet wherever I went, few seemed interested in Carter's early years; people were far more curious about the political resurrection that had turned 1980's malaise-ridden loser into 1994's distinguished global peacemaker.

Carter had not been media shy in the previous thirteen years, but never in the history of America had an ex-president captured as many international headlines as the seemingly omnipresent Carter did in 1994 for his peripatetic peace missions to troubled and suffering nations from Sudan to Haiti to North Korea to Bosnia. Since he had "involuntarily" left the White House in January 1981, as Carter liked to put it, the dark-horse presidential aspirant journalists had dubbed "Jimmy Who?" early in 1976 had become "Jimmy Everywhere." It was nothing new: to the various Secret Service details who had protected Carter during the presidency, globetrotting with him to European palaces and West African shantytowns, he had always been "Dasher"—a grinning Georgia overachiever blessed with a tinkerer's restless mind and a zealot's near-messianic confidence in his own abilities.[3] Ever since he was a boy nicknamed "Hot," for "Hotshot," Carter had been goal oriented. Whether the objective was becoming a respected officer in Admiral Hyman Rickover's nuclear navy, marrying the prettiest girl in Plains, winning a softball game, or engineering a new hybrid peanut, Jimmy Carter attacked everything with supreme self-confidence and dogged determination. "Jimmy just hated to lose," recalled Francis Hertzog, one of his closest friends at Annapolis. "He wanted to be the best at whatever he did. When he fixed that steely, pale-blue-eyed gaze on something . . . man, look out."[4] As fellow graduate (and later Bill Clinton's first ambassador to Great Britain) Admiral William Crowe succinctly put it, "Carter was never lazy and certainly never trivial."[5]

If anything, he was even more vigorous at seventy than at forty. Between July and December 1994 Carter had stopped a U.S. military invasion of Haiti, possibly prevented war with North Korea, and journeyed to Bosnia to procure a four-month cease-fire. As President Bill Clinton's foreign policy floundered, Carter didn't hesitate to dash into the void, proselytizing for peace in troubled lands and criticizing State Department and White House policies with stark candor all over CNN International. Many applauded, but the former president was excoriated by some who felt he was blurring America's foreign policy into his personal agenda and complicating U.S. diplomacy with his unorthodox assumptions of authority. During the autumn of 1994 not a week went by without a reporter from the Associated Press or Reuters or USA Today calling me to ask what Carter was up to. Why did he seem to be undercutting Clinton? Was he really trying to be a one-man UN? Was he after the Nobel Peace Prize?

According to Carter's critics, his freelance diplomatic gambits and public good works were just ego-driven attempts to redeem his failed presidency by reminding everyone of the remarkable Camp David accords that should have won him the prize already. These harsh assessments stung Carter. One particularly bad blow came when he was dubbed "a menace" by the *New Republic*, a magazine he once respected.[6] And that was the supposed liberals; far from viewing Carter as a shrewd practitioner of post-cold-war diplomacy, most conservatives regarded his self-styled peacekeeping efforts as the equivalent of unleashing a blind dog in a butcher shop. When *George* magazine asked the right-wing radio commentator Rush Limbaugh to list the top ten things he would do if elected president, number two was, "Never send Jimmy Carter anywhere."[7] Even many more objective observers thought it looked as though Carter wanted to make peace at any price—embracing thugs, if necessary. How, they wondered, could a genuine human rights activist be willing to kowtow to dictators and despots as brutal as North Korea's Kim Il Sung, Haiti's General Raoul Cédras, and Bosnia's Radovan Karadzic? Columnist William Safire offered a plausible answer in the *New York Times*: Carter *did* lust in his heart for the Nobel Peace Prize.[8]

Carter himself insisted his objectives were more altruistic: to end suffering even if it meant forgoing judgments as to which side in any civil war could be considered guiltier of past abuses. "The problem with Carter is that he prefers stability to justice," a spokesperson for Amnesty International noted, and Carter agreed—but there was more. The former engineer honestly believed that democracy could thrive and justice prevail only where order was firmly established; as he put it, "The Nuremberg trials could not have taken place while the Second World War was raging." What's more, Carter took exception to the way American foreign policy tended to mandate the demonization of one faction in every conflict the United States took an interest in. "We select a favorite side in a dispute and [the other] side becomes satanic," Carter lamented. "This all-white or all-black orientation is usually not true. In most cases, both sides are guilty of atrocities."[9]

He was well aware that his diplomatic principles might appear at cross-purposes; after all, he championed international human rights while judging the morality of political actions according to cold-blooded reality. The truth is simpler: Carter thought like an empirical scientist, focused only on results. He followed an apparently contradictory approach to peacemaking because he believed it was the only way to put an end to human rights abuses and civil wars—and the end always justifies the means. To say that Carter was only out to win the Nobel Peace Prize with his last-resort diplomacy may actually say more about America's languid post-cold-war foreign policy than it does about Jimmy Carter. "The news analysts who have to rationalize a change in

attitude toward me assume that I have changed, not that they have erred in
the past," Carter explained—adding, "I don't see any change."[10]

Carter's single term as president had not run smoothly, but from the
broader perspective time affords, his administration's foreign policy
record looked better and better. First among many notable diplomatic
accomplishments were the Camp David accords he'd brokered in September 1978, a personal triumph that made an unprecedented peace between
Egypt and Israel. In addition, his negotiating skills brought about the
Panama Canal Treaties to defuse a volatile Central American controversy—
and enabled him to assemble a bipartisan majority to ensure their ratification by Congress. Diplomatic relations with the People's Republic of China,
which Richard Nixon had jump-started in 1972, were normalized by President Carter in 1979. Similarly, his support for Nixon's SALT II agreement
with the Soviet Union, although never ratified, demonstrated Carter's very
real commitment to détente and arms control. He made a strong statement
on South Africa, denouncing apartheid, and he also helped oversee the
peaceful transition of white-ruled Rhodesia into black-controlled Zimbabwe.
And he supported an agency on human rights to deal with misfortunes such
as the missing persons in Argentina.

While in office Carter also achieved a host of less showy but still signifi-
cant diplomatic-military goals, including restoring stable relations with
Greece and Turkey, NATO's southeast flank; reducing U.S. ground troops in
South Korea; pardoning Vietnam War draft resisters; concluding the Tokyo
Round trade agreement; providing U.S. assistance to the resistance in
Afghanistan; making diplomatic overtures to Cuba and Vietnam; welcoming
refugees from Indochina; scrapping the B-1 bomber; and canceling plans to
develop a neutron bomb. The Carter administration's "sheer level and range
of activity, if not the results, suggested a foreign policy equivalent of the domestic activity of the first year of Franklin D. Roosevelt's New Deal," wrote
historian Gaddis Smith.[11]

Instead of praising Carter for his many significant successes, however,
most newspaper columnists reviewing his presidency in the 1980s credited
Carter only for what he didn't do, such as abandon civil rights or send
American soldiers to war. As veteran newspaperman Haynes Johnson observed, no matter what Carter did, "He received credit for almost nothing,"
and even Henry Kissinger recently admitted that "Carter never really got a
fair shake."[12]

But he went on, undaunted. Equipped with an unusual combination of
spiritual strength, organizational skills, and international experience, Jimmy

Carter spent the years after he left the White House tackling intractable problems in the world's most volatile trouble spots: observing nascent democratic elections, mediating potentially murderous conflicts, listening to those whose cries would otherwise go unheard, bringing aid to the afflicted, peace to the beleaguered, and hope to the despairing. He led efforts to eradicate medieval-sounding diseases such as guinea worm and river blindness and to make sure the world's children were immunized against polio and measles. He directed programs to make harvests more bountiful in countries facing agricultural ruin; he preached around the globe about the importance of religious tolerance; and he launched an imaginative urban rehabilitation program in Atlanta. These endeavors, all pursued under the auspices of the Carter Center, will stand as Jimmy Carter's ongoing legacy well into the next century.

Along with his steadfast wife, Rosalynn, Carter has become a true citizen of the world, working to build societies in which the human spirit can prevail and where freedom and democracy can flourish. A pioneer in election-monitoring techniques, he has contributed to the transition to democracy in nations as diverse as Panama, Guyana, Haiti, Nicaragua, and Jamaica. And without Carter's high-profile, hands-on carpentry, it is doubtful that Habitat for Humanity, a nonprofit Christian organization devoted to building houses for the poor, would have grown into such an international success. "Jesus, whom Carter worships, was said to have conducted his ministry among the downtrodden, among lepers and prostitutes," Curtis Wilkie wrote in the *Boston Globe Magazine*. "As a private citizen with no rank other than former President, Carter deals regularly with inhabitants of godforsaken villages and renegade leaders whom American officials ordinarily refuse to touch."[13]

Of course, Carter was not the first ex-president to continue working toward the public good after relinquishing the official reins of power. Thomas Jefferson founded the University of Virginia. John Quincy Adams spent seventeen years in the House of Representatives speaking out against slavery; known as "Old Man Eloquent," he dutifully died at his desk in the U.S. Capitol. Martin Van Buren sought the presidency again as a Free-Soiler, as did Millard Fillmore on the Know-Nothing ticket. Seven years after escaping impeachment by a single vote, Andrew Johnson returned to Washington as a U.S. senator from Tennessee, while Ulysses S. Grant traveled incessantly in search of enough sympathetic citizens to get himself renominated for president.

Only Grover Cleveland, the sole Democratic chief executive between 1860 and 1912, made the ultimate comeback, regaining the White House in 1892 after having lost it in 1888. William Howard Taft taught law at Yale University, served as chairman of Woodrow Wilson's War Labor Board, and ultimately attained his lifelong goal, becoming Chief Justice of the United States Supreme Court. The indomitable Theodore Roosevelt, in addition to exploring African jungles and Brazilian rivers, split the Republican ranks by forming the Bull Moose party, which handed the presidential election of 1912 to Democrat Woodrow Wilson. Herbert Hoover proved a particularly vigorous ex-president, writing dozens of books, working at Stanford University's Institution of War, Revolution and Peace, and leading two eponymous commissions aimed at reorganizing the federal government. In his eighty-fifth year he traveled 14,000 miles, delivered 20 speeches, accepted 23 awards, and answered 21,000 letters.[14]

Only the even more peripatetic Jimmy Carter, however, used the White House as a stepping-stone to greater *global* achievement. The only comparable figure may be Eleanor Roosevelt, who continued after her husband died to do humanitarian work internationally, earning the popular title "First Lady of the World."[15]

When Carter left the White House in 1981 at the relatively young age of fifty-six, logic dictated that he continue to be politically active, although he promised he would never try to regain the presidency. The question was how he wanted to spend the rest of his life. He knew he wanted to do a lot more than build a museum-library in tribute to himself and give a lot of after-dinner speeches. What Carter really wanted was to find some way to continue the unfinished business of his presidency, and he made this no secret from the start. "Without attempting to represent the government of my own country as a former President, there was, perhaps, a worldwide forum I might address which could influence the actions of political leaders," Carter explained in *Keeping Faith*, the memoir he wrote at home in Plains during his first eighteen months out of office. "I had the same kind of thoughts about alleviating tension in the troubled areas of the world, promoting human rights, enhancing environmental quality, and pursuing other goals which were important to me. These were hazy ideas at best, but they gave us something to anticipate which could be exciting and challenging during the years ahead."[16] These "hazy ideas" evolved into a grand design: the Carter Center in Atlanta, which has become his lasting institutional legacy to peace, democracy, health, and human rights.

Every facet of Carter's personality—his sky-high energy level, his willpower, his humanitarianism, his need for accomplishment—made it obvious to all who knew him that there was no way he would settle back into the role of gentleman farmer like a latter-day George Washington. The self-serving pursuits of his extant successor and predecessors appealed to Carter even less: Ronald Reagan had sold the cachet of his U.S. presidency to the

Japanese for $2 million in speaking fees; Gerald Ford spent much of his time in Palm Springs working on his golf swing while collecting director's fees from corporate boards; and Richard Nixon was holed up in New Jersey with his Dictaphone in an endless quest to remake his image from dirty crook to international sage. Moral considerations did not seem to weigh heavily upon these men.[17]

The opposite was true of Jimmy Carter. In *Everything to Gain: Making the Most of the Rest of Your Life* (1987), Jimmy and Rosalynn had written about their post–White House partnership, and he had detailed the goals of his Carter Center in *Talking Peace: A Vision for the Next Generation* (1993), but neither these books nor the endless press coverage of the former president told the whole tale. By 1994 media reports on Carter came in two varieties: one mythologized him as a seventy-year-old "peace outlaw," prevailing through personal wisdom, inner drive, selflessness, and uncanny timing; the other derided him as a vain, sanctimonious, born-again interloper seeking political redemption via the Nobel Committee. But no matter what the American press said, most other nations revered Jimmy Carter as the most trustworthy American politician alive.

Carter's critics too often overlooked the underpinnings of his diplomatic efforts. Using his administration's Camp David accords as a model of successful conflict resolution, Carter had worked diligently to master the arts of two-track diplomacy and election monitoring, digesting mountains of information from an array of foreign policy and economic experts, many of whom the Carter Center later hired. In addition, the Atlanta-based center's wide-ranging projects were made possible by the former president's substantial talent for fund-raising, which was usually ignored in the continuing analyses of his quixotic personality.

Since leaving office Carter had been involved in mediating an impressive list of foreign disputes, civil wars, and political transitions in such troubled lands as Ethiopia, Sudan, Somalia, North Korea, Haiti, and Bosnia. He had also monitored elections in Panama (1989, 1994), Nicaragua (1990, 1996), Haiti (1987, 1990, 1995), the Dominican Republic (1990), Zambia (1991), Guyana (1990–92), Paraguay (1993), the West Bank/Gaza (1996), Liberia (1997), and Jamaica (1997).[18] Why had Jimmy Carter been invited to these places? Why did he believe so fervently in democracy promotion?

Some of the reasons were obvious: his appeal as an international mediator grew from his Baptist missionary sensibility and the honest-broker integrity it implied. What's more, Carter had the ability to disarm dictators and rebel leaders alike with his empathy, lack of pretense, and in the eyes of critics, his willingness to grant respect even where it might not be merited. (For instance, amid tense negotiations over the transfer of power in Haiti, Carter invited ousted lieutenant general Raoul Cédras to address his Sunday school class in Plains.)

During every diplomatic mission he undertook after leaving office, Carter had made it clear in public remarks that he favored neither side in any dispute and that his sole objective was to end or avert war. This scrupulous neutrality was the key to his negotiating strategy, and for the most part it worked well. In fact, it worked even better when Carter was wrong. For example, in 1989 when George Bush's State Department announced its opinion that Panamanian president Manuel Noriega would not hold fair elections, Carter publicly disagreed, saying he took the corrupt general at his word. Once it became clear that Noriega's cronies had indeed tampered with the election, however, Carter denounced the contest as fraudulent. His credibility soared throughout Latin America, precisely because he hadn't disparaged the election before the fact.

Nothing about the White House so became Carter as his having left it. I told a number of people at the Carter Center that I was considering interrupting volume 1 of the complete biography to write a short book on Carter's postpresidency and his work on the likes of Habitat for Humanity, Global 2000, the Council of Freely Elected Heads of Government, and the International Negotiating Network. I received hearty encouragement to tell the public about the thirty-ninth president's continuing achievements. I asked the Carter Center if they would cooperate with me if I wrote such a book. I soon received a note from President Carter saying that if I could "squeeze it into my already full schedule," he would offer me chances to observe him at work, close range.[19]

It was hard to resist the opportunity to watch the ex-president operate up close, travel with him to Jerusalem and Port-au-Prince, and observe his wide-ranging pursuit of human rights. I did however have two conditions for taking on the project: that I would have full access to Carter's postpresidential papers and trip reports, and that the biography would be unauthorized, so I would be free to draw my own conclusions. Carter agreed.

The obvious quickly became apparent: but being president was a necessary step in becoming an ex-president. I had recently touted such presidential accomplishments as the Camp David accords, the Panama Canal Treaties, the Alaska Lands Act, and the progress that had been made on human rights matters. I wrote in an essay that it was an insult to call Jimmy Carter a "great ex-president"—that if he had not promoted human rights from the White House, he would not have been embraced everywhere he went in South America in 1983. If he had not denounced apartheid in South Africa, pushed for the creation of Zimbabwe, or visited Nigeria and Liberia while president, he would not have been invited to set up Carter Center programs throughout Africa. If he had not overseen the Camp David accords that made peace between Israel and Egypt, he would not later have won the attention of the PLO's Yasir Arafat, Syria's Hafez al-Assad, or Jordan's King Hussein. If he had not invited Nicaraguan president Daniel Ortega and his Sandinista cabinet to the White House in September 1979 and told them, "If you don't hold me responsible for everything that occurred under my predecessors, I will not hold you responsible for everything that occurred under your predecessors," his voice would have gone unheard during the 1990 Nicaraguan election. If he had not championed the withdrawal of U.S. troops from South Korea when he was president, North Korean dictator Kim Il Sung would not have been willing to establish relations with the Carter Center. And the list goes on.[20]

Some observers have suggested that Carter used the White House as a stepping-stone to the status of elder statesman. It is more accurate to say that instead of abandoning his agenda when he lost badly to Ronald Reagan in 1980, he chose to continue working toward programs and policies he believed in, in office or out of it. That he has tried to complete his unfinished agenda with such vigor and such success is a testament to his stubborn will and tenacious refusal ever to throw in the towel. Jimmy Carter may be many things, but a quitter is not among them—so this book, like his presidency, will remain unfinished as long as he's alive.

> Douglas Brinkley
> The Eisenhower Center
> University of New Orleans
> December 3, 1997

ONE

ELECTION DAY 1980

∽◦∾

On November 4, 1980, at 9:01 P.M. Eastern time, President Jimmy Carter telephoned former governor Ronald Reagan at the Republican's imposing home in southern California; he added to the courtesy with a short telegram congratulating the president-elect on his decisive victory. An hour later at the Sheraton Washington Hotel ballroom—only an hour and a half after the first network projections of Reagan's victory—Carter announced the verdict officially. It was the earliest concession by a presidential candidate since 1904, when Alton B. Parker had bowed before Theodore Roosevelt. "I promised you four years ago that I would never lie to you," Carter told his weeping supporters, echoing the best-known line from his 1976 campaign. "So I can't stand here tonight and say it doesn't hurt."[1]

White House press secretary Jody Powell had tried to get the soon-to-be ex-president to delay his speech until eleven o'clock Eastern time, when the California polls would close, but Carter didn't want anyone to think he was sulking in the White House and insisted, "It's ridiculous. Let's go and get it over with."[2] Many in the Democratic establishment were furious with Carter for conceding more than an hour before the polls closed on the West Coast, thus hurting other Democratic candidates in the Pacific time zone. "What in God's name is wrong with you people?" Speaker of the House Thomas P. "Tip" O'Neill fumed by phone from Boston to Carter's congressional liaison, Frank Moore. When Moore told O'Neill that Carter just wanted to "get it over with," damn the western Democrats, the speaker exploded with rage, yelling, "You guys came in like a bunch of jerks, and I see you're going out the same way."[3] Representative Tom Foley of Washington State put it more succinctly: "It was vintage Carter at its dead worst."[4]

To some, such as Democratic congressmen Al Ullman of Oregon and James Corman of California, Carter's unconscionable act seemed an apt metaphor for everything that had been askew with his presidency, from bad public relations to political fatuity. Both Ullman and Corman blamed Carter's early concession for their own narrow defeats, and they were hardly alone in their disgust; even those who had come to expect such slights from the "partyless president" were appalled.[5]

Of course, robust cheer was in short supply anywhere Democrats were assembled. A profound numbness had settled over the White House even before 8:15 P.M., when John Chancellor of NBC News first announced to the nation that Carter had become the only elected president to lose his bid to stay in the White House since Republican Herbert Hoover in 1932. An office on the second floor of the West Wing contained the loyal but exhausted foot soldiers who had moaned when their greatest fear became inescapable fact: the swashbuckling, government-hating Reagan had been chosen in place of their boss. "I had been convinced for at least six months that we were going to lose," then thirty-seven-year-old White House staffer Stuart Eizenstat recalled. "But it was like preparing yourself for the death of a family member: when it comes, it's still devastating."[6] The grim mood caused former White House counsel Robert Lipshutz to dub the mournful occasion "The Wake in the White House," as evidenced by the funeral mien of everyone in the official photographs.[7] "A part of my soul died that night," campaign manager Hamilton Jordan confessed later.[8] Despite a coast-to-coast campaign to muster last-minute support, the light at the end of the tunnel, as poet Robert Lowell once put it, was the light of an oncoming train. Carter had come to power four years earlier with an expansionary economic platform and a fresh face full of political promise; now he was about to exit Washington as perhaps the most conservative Democratic commander in chief since Grover Cleveland, who was also done in by a recessionary economy.

During the frenetic last days of Carter's desperate quest for reelection, he pleaded with the throngs out to glimpse a real live president at rallies and town hall meetings, repeating "I need you! I need you!"[9] But Americans turned a deaf ear. With inflation in the double digits, oil prices triple what they had been, unemployment above 7 percent, interest rates topping 20 percent, fifty-two American hostages still held captive in Iran, and unsettling memories of the Soviet invasion of Afghanistan lingering, it's hardly surprising that there was no election day surge to the Jimmy Carter–Walter Mondale ticket. Having gone four years without projecting a unifying vision or instituting a sweeping program like FDR's New Deal, Truman's Fair Deal, JFK's New Frontier, or LBJ's Great Society, Carter was judged inept and uninspiring, and voters rejected him in no uncertain terms.[10]

Jody Powell, all of thirty-six years old, tried to take a stoic view of the imminent debacle. Nonplussed by the idea of losing, like the last Confederate soldier he spent election day spinning visions of victory to skeptical newsmen. Until he got home, that is—then he had to inform his thirteen-year-old daughter, Emily, that Jimmy Carter was going to lose. "She was just devastated," Powell sighed much later. "I had a hard time telling her the game was over."[11]

Apathy characterized the 1980 election—only 52.4 percent of eligible voters participated, the lowest turnout since 1948 (and the beginning of a downward trend)—but those who did vote clearly shifted to the right. When all was said and done, Reagan—the sixty-nine-year-old conservative Carter had pronounced "untruthful" and "dangerous"—had won a commanding 51 percent (43,899,248) of the popular vote to Carter's sorry 41 percent (35,481,435). Dark-horse alternative John Anderson, a liberal Republican congressman from Illinois who had run as an Independent, managed to pull in 7 percent (5,719,437), primarily from upper-middle-class libertarians and disgruntled liberals. The electoral vote looked even better for Reagan: 489 votes to Carter's 49, with none for Anderson. The Sun Belt and Rocky Mountain regions came in so overwhelmingly Republican that billboards were erected overnight in Oklahoma and Wyoming: WELCOME TO THE REAGAN REVOLUTION. Far worse for Carter, the ex-Confederate states, with the exception of Georgia, also went Republican.[12]

Carter had entered the White House believing that the failures of Lyndon Johnson and Richard Nixon had been moral ones, and that he had been elected to reestablish a government "as good and honest and decent and compassionate and filled with love as are the American people."[13] So it stung all the more that he had lost to a man he thought immoral to the core: an unprincipled but telegenic B-grade Hollywood cowboy who had ridden into the White House on such "patriotic" themes as abhorrence of government, xenophobia, and massive tax cuts. "Reagan is different from me in almost every basic element of commitment and experience and promise to the American people," Carter had said at a town hall meeting in Independence, Missouri, two months earlier.[14] Years later he would go further and state that "allowing Ronald Reagan to become president was by far my biggest failure in office."[15]

✦

Almost immediately, commentators began comparing Carter's clobbering with what Richard Nixon had done to George McGovern in 1972. Some even raised the specter of Herbert Hoover, who had failed to provide the forward-looking leadership the nation craved during the Great Depression. Of course, Carter was used to that charge; throughout the campaign Republicans had mocked him as "Jimmy Hoover," another well-intentioned engineer-president who deserved to be ousted from office for a lack of vision. History, as usual, would repeat itself: just as the Democrats made meat of Hoover's "prosperity is just around the corner" well into the 1950s, the Republicans would campaign against the ghost of Carter's "malaise" for the next decade and beyond.[16]

As bad as the rest were, the worst moment for Carter that election day was when he broke the bad news to his wife. "Don't say anything yet to Rosalynn," Carter had instructed his staff. "Let me tell her."[17] First Lady Rosalynn Carter, whose soft-edged toughness had earned her the nickname "Steel Magnolia," simply refused to believe the lopsided verdict. "I was in such denial," she admitted years later. "It was impossible for me to believe that anybody could have looked at the facts and voted for Reagan."[18]

When voters were asked why they chose Reagan, most said it was "time for a change." The 1980 election indeed marked a true sea change in American history. Reagan was FDR in reverse, and made it clear that as president he intended to dismantle the welfare state created under the New Deal. Like his Republican predecessors Warren Harding and Calvin Coolidge in the 1920s, Reagan planned to lower taxes on the rich in order to stimulate America's productive energies. But where Harding and Coolidge pressed for disarmament, Reagan vocally wanted to accelerate the arms race enough to beat the Soviet Union in the cold war.

Apparently that's what Americans wanted too. Riding Reagan's coattails and a surging tide of conservatism, the Republicans also captured the Senate for the first time since 1952 and managed to reduce the Democratic majority in the House by 33 votes. Leading liberal senators including Frank Church of Idaho, George McGovern of South Dakota, John Culver of Iowa, and Birch Bayh of Indiana suffered upsets largely because they were associated with Carter's policies. Even reelected Democrats such as Senator Edward Kennedy of Massachusetts were jeered in the press for a 1960s-style "sideburn liberalism" as passé as Woodstock and the lava lamp. "If I had realized more fully what would follow us in Washington, I would have listened more carefully to your good political advice concerning how to deal with the Democratic liberals, the grain embargo, draft registration, and an overload[ed] agenda," Carter later confessed to Walter Mondale. "Perhaps we could have spared the country a lot of suffering and embarrassment."[19]

Carter's drubbing extended even into the left wing of the Democratic party. One postelection poll reported that fewer than a third of those who described themselves as liberal voted for him; the rest opted for Independent candidate John Anderson or stayed home. This came as no surprise to Carter, who had confided in his White House diary on January 19, 1978, "In many cases I feel more at home with the conservative Democratic and Republican members of Congress than I do with the others."[20] In fact, the penny-pincher in Carter had always considered the so-called liberal coalition little more than a smug coterie of money-hungry interest groups. He saw himself, by contrast, as a New South populist morally above party allegiance who had been elected to serve "the people directly." He prided himself on having little to do with the Wall Street, Washington, or Hollywood Democratic establishments, which he regarded as elitist private clubs for the rich. "I do not condemn the cocktail circuit," Carter noted. "It's just not natural for me to be a part of it."[21]

But in the end, being the consummate outsider proved fatal. Carter never fought in the trenches alongside his fellow Washington Democrats in the great battles of the era—over the Vietnam War, Medicaid and Medicare, civil rights legislation, Nixon's Supreme Court appointments, or Watergate—and therefore he could only be viewed as a political fluke by his own party. Carter mistakenly assumed that he could compensate for lacking the requisite battle scars by devising rational policies to show his presidential leadership. On top of that naïveté he failed to understand that making policies was just the beginning—then he had to sell them to the American people, and "selling" seemed such dirty business.

Tales of Carter's contempt for and ineptitude at politicking were legion on Capitol Hill throughout his term in office. "When it came to the politics of Washington, D.C., he never really understood how the system worked," Tip O'Neill wrote in his memoirs. "And although this was out of character for Jimmy Carter, he didn't want to learn about it either." In fact, O'Neill couldn't escape the feeling that Carter was working against fellow Democrats—including the Speaker himself. "Once, when the city of Boston applied for a government grant for some roads, I called the Carter people to try to speed it along," O'Neill wrote. "Instead of assisting me, however, they did everything possible to block my way."[22]

Other perceived slights were more subtle. Indiana congressman John Brademas, the Democratic whip who said he had to spell his name to the receptionist every time he called the Carter White House, got an even sharper slap in the face when Carter visited his district and made his landmark human rights speech at Notre Dame University. Brademas felt exultant that Carter had come to South Bend as he and Senator Birch Bayh introduced

the chief executive to Notre Dame's distinguished president, Reverend
Theodore M. Hesburgh. The thrill didn't last long; later that afternoon,
Carter delivered his speech without either recognizing or thanking the two
leading Democratic politicians of Indiana, both of whom were sitting right
behind him on the platform. Brademas felt snubbed and humiliated. "When
a president comes to your district, addresses your constituency, and doesn't
even mention your name when you're standing right beside him . . . something is wrong," Brademas declared later. "I was on Nixon's enemies list, but
he never treated me that way." When Brademas lost his congressional seat in
1980—after having won eleven straight terms—he didn't hesitate to pin part
of the blame on Carter.[23]

But to Carter, many Democratic senators were at best little more than
celebrity lobbyists. Oregon senator Mark Hatfield, a Rockefeller Republican
who had befriended Carter in the early 1970s, was startled by the president's
inability to connect with other Democratic politicians. "Carter was so much
smarter than most of the Democrats in Congress—and he let them know it,"
Hatfield explained: Henry "Scoop" Jackson of Washington State and Edward Kennedy of Massachusetts in particular were known to "grind their
teeth" as they walked out of White House meetings, livid that Carter had
"talked down to them."[24]

More than any other president in memory, Carter had turned his back on
money lenders and influence peddlers. He believed that even private conversations with senators, for example, might cause him to compromise—or
look as though he were compromising—his principles. "Carter invited my
husband and me to the White House for a private dinner only once," remembered Bethine Church, widow of the former Senate Foreign Relations
Committee chairman Frank Church, "and he just refused to talk politics. It
was so odd. He really believed his 1976 outsider campaign."[25] In a December 1980 postmortem on Carter's presidency, Newsweek commented that he
had "shown Reagan how not to do business in an insider's city" by acting
"standoffish" toward "the lords and ladies of Washington society."[26]

Carter never fit in the capital because his leadership style was essentially
religious in nature, more preacher than politician. Among American presidents only Carter peppered his speeches with the word "love" and earnest
Christian entreaties for "tenderness" and "healing." As commentator Eric
Severeid once quipped, Carter was a "wheeler-healer" who simply refused
to become a "wheeler-dealer." As president he spoke openly of his Christian
faith and all it entailed: daily prayers, abhorrence of violence, the belief that
the meek shall inherit the earth, the courage to champion the underdog.
Most of all, his faith taught him that a clear conscience was always preferable

to Machiavellian expediency—a pretty healthy attitude that proved both Carter's greatest strength and his bane.[27]

Shortly after the 1980 presidential election Kenneth Kline, a politics buff from Mogadore, Ohio, took it upon himself to send two hundred notable personages a questionnaire asking why Jimmy Carter had lost so overwhelmingly to Ronald Reagan. Kline's cover letter pointed out that it had been only four years since Carter had been anointed the perfect elixir to assuage the political ills during the 1970s, when Americans still raw from the trauma of Vietnam sat transfixed before their television sets watching the Nixon administration unravel. By 1976, America's bicentennial year, a nation disheartened by political corruption capped by a suspicious presidential pardon wanted to believe in something—and there was Jimmy Carter, a devout evangelical Christian who promised "to make government as good as its people." So what happened?[28]

Nearly every U.S. senator Kline polled, from William Proxmire on the left to Barry Goldwater on the right, attributed the Carter presidency's implosion to the prolonged Iran hostage crisis and the stagnant U.S. economy. Republican senator Jesse Helms of North Carolina put it in grander terms, boasting that Carter's defeat was part of a paradigm shift that "marked the decline and fall of the public's faith in statist liberalism . . . the idea that the solution to all our problems as a nation and as individuals is to be found in some sort of intervention by [the] federal government."[29]

Even those who were not overtly hostile were melancholy over what might have been. Responding to Kline's survey, Father Hesburgh wrote, "I have always had the feeling that [Carter] is a good man, but somehow was not able to bring his vision to reality. That is not unusual on this earth."[30] This benign assessment was shared by many, including Jesse Jackson and Billy Graham. Veteran NBC News commentator David Brinkley summed the matter up crisply in 1981:

- He had no base in the Democratic party and few friends in the federal government, making it difficult for him to achieve his purposes.
- Despite his intelligence, he had a vindictive streak, a mean streak, that surfaced frequently and antagonized people.
- He became so absorbed in detail he never was able to articulate a coherent public policy, foreign or domestic.
- Several failures during his term were not his fault, but neverthe-

less hurt him politically: inflation, the hostages, the blundered
rescue attempt. . . .

- The extravagant promises in his campaign generally were not
kept. Many could not have been kept and he should never have
made them.
- And [he exhibited some] examples of excruciatingly bad taste,
such as telling an insulting and unfunny joke [about Mon-
tezuma's revenge] at a dinner in Mexico City.[31]

To Brinkley's corrosive litany the political historian might add that the
public's repudiation of Carter was in line with a broader post-Vietnam tendency: faced with myriad domestic and international quagmires, the people
simply evicted their president—again. Lyndon Johnson, Richard Nixon,
Gerald Ford, and now "outsider" Jimmy Carter had all been either forced
out by public outrage or rejected by the voters. Polls in 1980 may have rated
Carter as the least popular president since Truman, but they also showed
that Ronald Reagan was the least popular *candidate* to win the White House
since Truman. After Vietnam and Watergate, the power of Congress grew
while that of the White House dwindled. The presidency had become the
"fire hydrant of the nation," as Carter's vice president, Walter Mondale, had
phrased it, if indelicately, during the 1980 campaign.[32]

The appeal of king-making-and-breaking fueled this next round of media
reassessments. The same reporters who had helped propel peanut farmer
"Jimmy Who?" from political obscurity to the Oval Office just because it was
a good story turned on him only days after his arrival in the nation's capital.
When Carter actually assumed the role of citizen-president and acted on his
disdain for artifice—selling the presidential yacht *Sequoia*, carrying his own
luggage, abolishing limousine service for top White House staff, banning
"Hail to the Chief"—the Washington press corps lit into him as a sanctimonious hick. It was too easy, what with the Christian moralizing, beatific grin,
and treacly Georgia drawl, and journalists took to brutalizing the president's
Calvinistic quirks largely for the fun of it. But Carter ignored their mockery
and stuck to his moral certitude that a people's president had no call to be
putting on airs. If the Protestant Reformation had taught Carter anything it
was that pomp and circumstance were not smiled upon favorably by God.
"By 1980 the press was very much against me," Carter maintained. "But I
still thought I could beat Reagan."[33]

There were good reasons why Carter was confident Ronald Reagan
could be whipped as easily as Senator Edward Kennedy in the Democratic
primaries. Once described as "an amiable dunce" by Lyndon Johnson's secretary of defense, Clark Clifford, Reagan seemed an easy target.[34] His daily

rhetorical gaffes on the campaign trail on matters from the national security
to the cost of bread neatly offset Carter's piety as something for the press to
have fun with. It seemed impossible for Carter's team to believe that Americans would really elect a president who blamed trees for smog, who expressed doubts about evolution and favored teaching "creationism" in the
public schools.[35] It wasn't much of a stretch to assume that the idea of Hollywood's "Gipper," whom Carter portrayed as a kind of "mad bomber," with
his finger on the nuclear button would give the public pause. On August 11
Reagan had a commanding lead of 27 percentage points in the polls, but just
a week later "Comeback Carter" had trimmed it to 7 points. "If Reagan
keeps putting his foot in his mouth for another week or so, we can close
down campaign headquarters," a cocky Pat Caddell snickered in a memo to
the president.[36]

What the Carterites underestimated was the advantage Reagan gained
by operating from a strict ideological framework. His positions were always
clear: if it was a tax, he was against it; if it was a new weapons system, he was
for it. Carter, on the other hand, was always mired in specifics, trying to explain why he was against the B-1 bomber but for the Stealth fighters, and it
confused people.[37]

And Carter had problems beyond Reagan: he had secured only a small
portion of the organized-labor support that had backed Ted Kennedy, and
he could not stanch the steady flow of liberals to John Anderson's third-party
candidacy. Millions of anti-Reagan liberals lashed out at Carter for his "va-
pidity," as novelist E. L. Doctorow later put it, which was allowing "the electorate to bring in the wolves on the right who had all the time been pacing
back and forth fitfully, baying in the darkness beyond the campsite."[38] As
poet Allen Ginsberg noted, "Any soul with even a mild streak of progres-
sivism in their bones felt betrayed by Carter."[39] The litany continued.
Economist John Kenneth Galbraith, who ended up voting for Carter, concluded that it was his economic advisers who doomed his hopes of reelection. "Carter was an admirable man," Galbraith maintained, "subject to far
from admirable advice on how to control inflation."[40] To historian Arthur
Schlesinger Jr. the born-again president was a "narcissistic loner" who
should never have been elected in 1976 and whose performance in the Oval
Office certainly didn't merit a second term. "It was the only time in my life
that I voted for anyone but a Democrat for president," Schlesinger admitted. "Carter's handling of the Iran hostage crisis and the economy had been
disastrous."[41]

Even the Democrat's most stalwart constituency—women—felt by and
large betrayed that Carter had given only lukewarm support to the Equal
Rights Amendment, opposed a constitutional amendment to legalize abortion,

fired the popular Midge Costanza as presidential assistant, clashed with the indomitable Bella Abzug, and failed to mention women at all in his plan to stimulate the economy. Carter's cultural retardation certainly didn't help matters: feminists found it hard to believe that a born-again Southern Baptist known to address women as "honey" and "beautiful" could be on their side. In fact Carter had appointed more women, including a handful of genuine feminists, to federal agencies and the White House staff than any president in history. But in 1980 nobody—particularly liberals—felt like giving Jimmy Carter a break.[42]

L ooking back at the 1980 election, it does seem possible that the Democrats could have ironed out their interparty squabbles had the crisis in Iran been resolved. But fifty-two of the Americans who had been taken hostage when Iranian militants stormed the U.S. embassy in Tehran exactly a year before the election remained in captivity. And Walter Cronkite of the *CBS Evening News* and Ted Koppel of ABC's *Nightline* reminded their viewers of the sad fact daily.[43]

The crisis had erupted after Iran's exiled shah Mohammed Reza Pahlavi arrived in New York on October 22, 1979, and was admitted to New York Hospital–Cornell Medical Center to be treated for cancer and gallstones. Under the influence of Ayatollah Ruhollah Khomeini—an aged fundamentalist fanatic who had returned to Iran from Parisian exile in February 1979, hoping to launch an Islamic revolution throughout the Middle East—the militants had seized the embassy to demand the shah's return to stand trial. Carter refused to extradite him, making for a long stalemate—and every day those fifty-two Americans remained hostage, the Carter administration looked more confused and ineffective. "To the public, Iran became a metaphor for everything," as media adviser Gerald Rafshoon remarked years later.[44] For nearly a year the crisis handcuffed the administration, which tried everything it could think of to end the standoff: suspending oil imports, freezing Iranian assets, expelling Iranian diplomats, imposing economic sanctions, even conducting clandestine negotiations. Iran was looking more and more like an Achilles' heel that would cripple the Democratic ticket on election day if a face-saving remedy were not found—and soon. Carter had made a fatal error to state at the outset that his primary concern was bringing the hostages home alive. The Iranians used this to blackmail the Carter administration.

Angry and desperate, Carter finally made the most unfortunate decision of his presidency: on April 24 he sent a team of commandos to attempt to rescue the hostages. Six C-130 transport planes carrying ninety commandos landed on a remote airstrip in Iran's Dasht-e Kavir desert. Eight helicopters were sent for the assault on the embassy, but only six made it to the rendezvous site and one of those developed hydraulic problems. The ground commander said the rescue could not be effective with only the remaining helicopters. Carter agreed to recall the rescue team. As they were departing, however, one of the helicopters struck a transport plane that was refueling on the ground, setting off a series of mishaps that would have been comic had the outcome not been so tragic: eight American servicemen died, and four others were badly burned in the fire and explosions that ensued. The surviving commandos did get out of Iran in the remaining planes, but the militants later put the charred bodies of the other eight commandos on display in the square of the occupied U.S. embassy. Carter went on TV to disclose the attempted rescue and its failure, taking full responsibility for the debacle, which the *New Republic* dubbed "The Jimmy Carter Desert Classic."[45]

After the aborted rescue attempt, many believed that Carter had not only tarnished the nation's honor but lost control of his own administration in the process. Critics condemned him for failing to mount a rescue operation sooner, for not putting enough military hardware into it once he did act, and then for retreating at the first sign of hazard. "Let's face it," foreign policy sage Paul Nitze remarked years later, "Carter's rescue mission was a flop before it was even conceptualized."[46]

In June 1980 the shah, then in Cairo, died, prompting speculation that the crisis might end. Khomeini, however, had other ideas, demanding the return of the shah's assets, the release of Iranian assets in the United States, and a U.S. pledge not to interfere in Iranian affairs. When that wasn't forthcoming, on September 9 the Iranian government informed Carter through the West German foreign minister, who was in Tehran, that Khomeini was ready to discuss a resolution of the hostage situation. A breakthrough finally occurred on September 22, 1980, when Iraq and Iran went to war; suddenly Khomeini realized his nation could not take on two powerful enemies at once.[47]

Diplomatic headway toward resolving the crisis began inching forward hour by hour. Newspaper editorials and television commentaries insisted that Carter and his chief crisis negotiator, Deputy Secretary of State Warren Christopher, had an "October Surprise" up their sleeves. Other media reports intimated that the Reagan team was so worried the Carter administration would procure the release of the American captives before election day that Republican campaign manager William Casey had made a secret deal with Iran to hold on to the hostages until after November 4. Speculation aside, it was plain that a Carter failure to bring the hostages home alive would hand Reagan the White House. "Unless the hostage yo-yo suddenly stops, the 1980 campaign is over," a *New York Times* editorial declared the Sunday before the election.[48]

Fifteen years after the fact, Carter said he still believed he could have been reelected if he had bombed Tehran until the hostages were released or incinerated along with the entire Iranian government. But that kind of ground-zero solution, favored by some Republicans, was too morally repugnant for Carter even to consider at the time. So was selling arms to the ayatollah, as Khomeini wanted, so Carter held his ground. "There were a lot of grumbles about my handling of the hostage crisis," he said looking back, "but not a single responsible politician offered a more realistic alternative."[49]

The Carter administration's strategy toward Iran had revolved around two fundamental objectives: protecting America's vital petroleum interests and finding the quickest possible route to the hostages' safe release. But when asked by a college student in 1987 what one thing he would have done differently as president, Carter only half-jokingly replied, "I would have ordered one more helicopter."[50]

In the end, of course, it's not campaign clichés or hostage situations or nuclear arms control that get presidents elected and reelected; it is, in James Carville's famous dictum, "the economy, stupid"—and that was where Carter was most vulnerable. Ronald Reagan made sure everyone knew it, too; the Great Communicator made an art of attacking the administration's economic weaknesses, painting Carter as a spendthrift liberal responsible for sending America into a "depression." When economists criticized Reagan's upgrading of the actual recession, he began telling audiences, "I'm told I can't use the word *depression*. Well, I'll tell you the definition. A recession is when your neighbor loses his job; depression is when you lose your job. Recovery is when Jimmy Carter loses his."[51]

Writer John Updike captured the mood of the Carter years perfectly in his 1981 novel *Rabbit Is Rich*, set in 1979: "The people are out there getting frantic, they know the great American ride is ending. Gas lines at ninety-nine cents a gallon and ninety percent of the stations to be closed for the weekend. People are going wild, their dollars are going rotten."[52] Just days before the election Reagan played to Rabbit Angstrom's economic anxieties in a speech in Des Plaines, Illinois: "Jimmy Carter's persistent double-digit inflation has made it almost impossible for many families to properly feed and clothe their children. High unemployment has brought fear of job loss as the silent visitor at the dinner table each evening. And his near-record interest rates have all but ended the dream of buying a decent home for millions of American families."[53]

Carter's promises that his second term would bring greater productivity and higher employment through tax cuts gave voters scant hope. Carter tried to showcase on the campaign trail his success at deregulating transportation industries, but few working-class voters were impressed. Shortly before election day, a poll including such traditional Democratic constituencies as blue-collar workers and inner-city residents showed that 31 percent of Americans had concluded that the economy would be irretrievably damaged if Carter remained in the White House. "The reason for Carter's horrible failure in economic policy is plain enough," Schlesinger wrote during the 1980 campaign. "He is not a Democrat—at least in anything more than the Grover Cleveland sense of the word."[54]

When it was all over, pundits reviewing Carter's White House tenure applauded him most for what he didn't do. In a January 10, 1981, article entitled "Not to Worry, Jimmy," *New York Times* humorist Russell Baker imagined high-school students in the year 2081 preparing for a test on twentieth-century U.S. presidents by asking their teacher to tell them what Jimmy Carter had accomplished in the White House. "I fancy the teacher will have to reflect a minute before saying something like, 'Well, he really didn't do anything dreadful at all,' " Baker wrote. "For the era of 1961–1981 that is not a bad notice from the history critics."[55]

This sentiment was articulated even more succinctly by Carter speechwriter Hendrik Hertzberg, who used to tell his liberal friends that "Jimmy Carter is the first president of my adult life who is not criminally insane." Both Lyndon Johnson and Richard Nixon had continued the war in Vietnam even though they knew it could not be won, just to save political face with the electorate. These presidents also taped associates' telephone conversations, sponsored covert assassinations by the CIA abroad, and harassed any number of citizens, including great civil rights leaders such as Martin Luther King Jr. and Ralph Abernathy. Even the relatively benign Gerald Ford had sent eighteen U.S. servicemen to their deaths in the *Mayaguez* incident, all in the name of patriotism. "It is wrong to kill people for no reason other than political gain or political fear," Hertzberg explained. "Jimmy Carter never did anything like that."[56]

Presidential scholar James David Barber made a similar assessment of Carter's tenure: "It was four years without war or social unrest. Considering our recent record, that is no small achievement." In other words, at best Carter was damned with faint praise by East Coast opinion makers and students of presidential politics.[57]

Public opinion paralleled that of the experts. In the final Gallup Poll on Carter's performance as president, only 3 percent of respondents thought history would regard him as an "outstanding" president, while 46 percent expected him to be rated "below average" or "poor." Where Carter's immediate predecessor, Gerald Ford, had left office with an approval rating of 53 percent, Carter could muster only an anemic 34 percent. Dismissing the zeitgeist problem, Lyndon Johnson's White House counsel Harry McPherson lay the blame squarely on the man: Carter "never displayed that 'fire in the belly' quality that people want in a political leader. . . . This is not the stuff of history."[58]

Throughout the campaign, whenever Reagan asked the powerful question, "Are you better off now than you were four years ago?" most Americans answered with a resounding no. As McPherson pointed out, Carter ignored the blue-collar, populist resentment that had sprung up toward big government, affirmative action, the welfare state, and Keynesian economics, which advocated government spending to create jobs. A master at reading the pulse of the nation, Reagan—who on the campaign trail had once referred to Carter as "a little schmuck"—understood, embodied, and benefited from the post-Vietnam hunger for a renewed sense of America's greatness and global mission. "Reaganomics was a fraud," Carter would tell *Time* magazine in October 1982, "but [Reagan] is a persuasive speaker, and the American people bought it."[59]

The day after the election, Carter held a meeting with reporters to assert that he wanted a "good, positive relationship" with Reagan—but the president-elect turned out to have other ideas. In contemporary memory only the celebrated animosity between Truman and Eisenhower after the 1952 election reached the level of bitterness between Carter and Reagan.[60]

This was hardly surprising—Reagan had won the White House in part by pounding on Carter's approach to foreign affairs, such as his human rights advocacy, his decidedly strict Soviet grain embargo, and his boycott of the Summer Olympics in Moscow—the latter two levied against Soviet premier Leonid Brezhnev for ordering the invasion of Afghanistan in December 1979. All in all, Reagan considered Carter "too soft." While Carter spoke of controlling the cold war proliferation of nuclear weapons as "the most important single issue in this campaign," Reagan scarcely mentioned it. And where Carter championed the Panama Canal Treaties that would relinquish U.S. control of the passageway to the Panamanians in December 1999, no influential American politician was as vehemently against the notion as Reagan. Even surprising pleas from Reagan's right-wing friend John Wayne to support the legislation for the sake of hemispheric harmony had no effect on the president-elect's opposition.[61]

In the same vein, Reagan also ridiculed the Camp David accords, which Carter considered his greatest presidential legacy. In September 1978 Carter had brought together Israeli prime minister Menachem Begin and Egyptian president Anwar al-Sadat to renew the stalled Middle East peace talks at Camp David, where the two leaders hammered out two documents— a Framework for Peace in the Middle East and a Framework for the Conclusion of a Peace Treaty. In March 1979 Begin and Sadat formally signed the unprecedented peace treaty; Reagan, with the Jewish vote in mind, claimed Carter had gotten too cozy with the Arabs.

On the campaign trail, Reagan also chastised Carter for developing the SALT II treaty, which would have limited the number of offensive nuclear weapons stockpiled in both the United States and the Soviet Union. Met with stark opposition by conservatives in Congress, the treaty was never sent to the full Senate for ratification after the Soviet Union invaded Afghanistan. The criticisms didn't end there: disgusted that Carter had continued Richard Nixon's work and normalized relations with China, Reagan made a series of campaign statements about the need to restore "official" dealings with Taiwan—the implied message being that if elected president, he would repudiate recognition of China. (In fact, he promised to turn the People's Republic into "a land of laundromats.")[62]

The irony of Reagan's attacks on Carter's foreign policy was that so much of it were just continuing ideas and efforts that had been initiated by Carter's Republican predecessors. The SALT process, for example, picked up where Gerald Ford had left off in Vladivostok. The Panama Canal Treaties grew out of a negotiating framework begun by Lyndon Johnson and resumed by Richard Nixon in 1973. The dramatic transformation in Washington's relations with Beijing, symbolized by the official recognition and exchange of ambassadors that took place under Carter, had been set in motion by President Nixon's trip to China in 1972. Carter's human rights program built on the "Final Act" of the Helsinki Accords. And even in the Middle East, after having failed to organize a general peace conference in Geneva, the Carter administration had returned to Kissinger's step-by-step approach, including some very productive shuttle diplomacy in the form of Carter's walks back and forth between the Camp David cabins occupied by Menachem Begin and Anwar al-Sadat.[63]

If one had to sum up Carter's leadership style in a phrase, it would be "hands-on engineering." Among Carter's greatest flaws as president—and one the Republicans exploited without mercy—was his excessive micromanagerial style. For better or worse, Carter was a control freak who wanted to know exactly what was happening around him at all times. The Panama Canal Treaties, for example, probably would never have been executed without the president's direct involvement in everything from seeing that CBS anchor Walter Cronkite pronounced Panamanian names correctly on the ·evening news to making sure that dictator Omar Torrijos was treated as a political equal. Carter may have wanted to be a great chief executive, Republicans argued, but he was blind to the fact that great presidents are so because they build great teams. The charge was valid: Americans had put an obsessive micromanager in the White House. Uninterested in assembling a dynamic squad of surrogates, Carter wanted to do it all himself from beginning to end. He would be a one-man band; there would be none of Eisenhower's "hidden-hand" advisers, FDR's "brain trust," or JFK's "best and brightest."[64]

Instead, Carter approached the presidency like a family farmer: plow the fields, spread the fertilizer, harvest the crop—and keep an eye on every detail the whole way. You hire help, of course, but sharecroppers, migrants, or day-wagers just don't have the same stake in the work as the farmer; a good harvest depends on his devotion and God's will. But while that philosophy may work down on the farm, it is hardly sensible for governing the world's strongest nation. For proof one need only compare the results achieved by hands-on farmer Carter with those of "show me my mark" actor Ronald Reagan.

The "Gipper" from Hollywood recognized the importance of star power to box office success, but he also understood that there would be no movie without a director, producer, cinematographer, makeup artist, sound engineer, and scores of other experts. Still, there was a certain advantage in being the leading man in the White House: you could stay above the fray while Cabinet staff and members scurried about to make you look good. The motto of Carter's Oval Office had been Truman's The Buck Stops Here; Reagan's was Ignorance Is Bliss, as the Iran-Contra affair demonstrated. Where Carter stood at the podium dryly preaching austerity, Reagan bounded onstage waving the American flag, delighted to be starring in his greatest role. Carter may have known all the nitty-gritty details of every policy, but Reagan understood intuitively what the modern American presidency demanded, and it wasn't facts and figures. Image mattered even more than outcomes: Reagan ran on slashing government, but the presidential transition that ushered him into office was one of the biggest and priciest in American history—because the public preferred a little pomp to the sight of a president toting his own luggage down Pennsylvania Avenue.[65]

Given the vigorous policy disagreements between the outgoing and incoming presidents, it was no surprise that Carter decided to devote much of

the eleven-week interim to making sure Reagan could not undo his administration's accomplishments. Nevertheless, out of a sense of obligation Carter
invited Reagan to the Oval Office on November 20 for a detailed briefing on
twenty top-secret subjects, chiefly national security and nuclear policy.
Carter discussed the hostage crisis, Nicaragua and El Salvador, and the war
between Iran and Iraq. "Reagan listened without comment while I covered
each point," Carter recalled years later. "Some of [the issues] were very sensitive, involving such matters as the management of our nuclear forces in
time of attack on our nation."[66] Much of the ninety-minute briefing focused
on Poland, where the Solidarity movement was making the Soviets uneasy.
Both men agreed that stern U.S. warnings should be issued constantly, and
that any Soviet invasion of Poland would have to be met head-on by a U.S.
military counteroffensive. Richard V. Allen, soon to be Reagan's national security adviser, used the opportunity to ask Carter to postpone selling
AWACS aircraft to Saudi Arabia until Reagan and his team had time to consider the ramifications of the deal. The president agreed.[67]

According to Republican transition director Ed Meese, who would soon
become attorney general, Reagan left the meeting impressed by Carter's
"graciousness" and "mastery of detail." Although he took few notes, Reagan
came away concerned about a possible Soviet invasion of Poland and convinced that it would be best to let the Carter administration extract America
from the Iran hostage crisis by themselves before his inauguration. After the
briefing Reagan, Meese, and Allen reviewed the essence of what Carter had
said in a private, forty-five-minute meeting. "Reagan recalled verbatim
everything Carter had told us," Meese remembered, defending his old boss
against accusations from the Carter camp that the president-elect had been
inattentive. "He didn't take notes because he didn't need to." Meese believed that Reagan had felt sorry for Carter at the White House that day—
that the Gipper was just not a good hater. "Though he profoundly disagreed
with Carter on policy issues, Reagan harbored no mean-spiritedness toward
Carter," Meese insisted. "It's usually the loser that is full of sour grapes."[68]

GOP adviser Richard Darman, who later became President George
Bush's director of the Office of Management and Budget, later laughed
about the awkwardness of the Carter-Reagan transition meeting. "We've
both been governors," Darman remembered Carter telling Reagan, like a
concerned Sunday school teacher. "But let me tell you—it's different in the
White House. The day begins early. A CIA officer briefs you at 7:00 A.M."
According to Darman, at that moment Reagan smiled and interrupted,
"Well, he's sure going to have to wait a long while for me." Carter just stared
at the president-elect, unamused.[69]

Personal styles aside, there was one issue that cropped up during the transition on which Carter and Reagan did see eye to eye: a pressing human rights violation in South Korea. Carter's personal devotion to individual human rights matters had always made him a rarity among politicians, but the case of Kim Dae Jung, a political opposition leader who had been sentenced to death on charges of sedition, caught the attention of the president-elect as well. At Carter's request, Reagan ordered Allen to send word to South Korean president Chun Doo Hwan that relations between Washington and Seoul would be "strained" should Kim be executed. The tactic worked: Kim's life was spared, and in the bargain Carter finally found something positive to say about Reagan. When Kim Dae Jung visited America in December 1982, he contacted Carter personally to thank him.[70]

Apart from that moment of cooperation, however, the transition was marked by an exchange of barbs between the Carter and Reagan camps, much to the delight of the media. In addition to all the policy disagreements, a stir was created over Nancy Reagan's "gentle hint," reported to Rosalynn Carter by seasoned UPI White House correspondent Helen Thomas, that the Carters move into Blair House a few weeks before inauguration day so Mrs. Reagan could redecorate the executive mansion. With her swank California tastes for red dresses and David Hockney paintings, Nancy Reagan looked down her nose at Rosalynn Carter, such a drab bumpkin whose White House was so, well, *beige.* One tabloid reported that the Reagans' interior designer from Los Angeles couldn't wait to "get the smell of catfish out of the White House." Nancy Reagan quickly called the First Lady with assurances that these remarks had been taken out of context. But the very next day the president-elect's son Ronald, a dancer with the Joffrey Ballet, told reporters that he would refuse to shake President Carter's hand at his father's inauguration because the Georgian had "the morals of a snake" and "would have sold his mother to get reelected."[71]

To attack Carter's morals was mean-spirited and ridiculous. A deeply ethical man full of good intentions, Carter could have bombed Tehran to stay in the White House, but his Christian belief in the sanctity of life wouldn't let him. In fact, although his critics saw him as self-righteous, Carter was the most principled American president since Harry Truman— and nowhere was his morality on clearer display than in his insistence that human rights be a cardinal principle of global governance. "Because we are all free, we can never be indifferent to the fate of freedom elsewhere. . . . Our commitment to human rights must be absolute," Carter declared in his inaugural address.[72] And these weren't just pretty words; human rights became the hallmark of his administration, or as he put it, "the soul of our foreign policy."[73] As he prepared to leave office, it was little wonder that Carter wanted his work for human rights to be remembered above all else.

As president, Carter had been realistic enough to recognize that human rights policy could never be completely pure and good, and thus could not be "based on a blind adherence to consistency."[74] But at the same time he believed that the United States should denounce, with varying degrees of vehemence, authoritarianism wherever it held sway, particularly in the form of government-sanctioned kidnappings, torture, and murder. Thus Carter became the first American president since Woodrow Wilson to try actively to reform repressive regimes in other nations. "This does not mean that we can conduct our foreign policy by rigid moral maxims," Carter stated in May 1977. "We live in a world that is imperfect, and which will always be imperfect; a world that is complex and confused. I understand fully the limits of moral suasion. We have no illusion that changes will come easily."[75]

Presidential moralizing during the cold war was often written off as just a variation on the usual hard-nosed anti-Soviet rhetoric. But for Carter—whose soul still sang "We Shall Overcome" in spiritual sympathy with the civil rights movement that had inspired the Supreme Court to smash the nation's shameful Jim Crow laws—it was a guiding principle. Although it's true that as president he pressed harder for human rights on the Soviet Union, Argentina, and Chile than he did on such stalwart American allies as South Korea, the Philippines, and the shah's Iran, Carter's approach to world affairs did focus across the board on international human rights and the importance of building democracy. Under Carter's direct orders the Agency for International Development and the United States Information Agency began making human rights a priority in every project. Carter cemented this thrust in early 1977 by establishing a State Department bureau of human rights headed by Assistant Secretary Patricia Derian, a well-known Mississippi civil rights activist.[76]

Under Carter, human rights considerations became the litmus test for deciding which governments—left- or right-wing—received American aid and political support. The State Department was ordered to document the human rights standards of all governments receiving American foreign aid and to make its annual assessments public. This meant that some of the rightist regimes that had grown used to getting substantial economic and military assistance from the United States, including El Salvador, Guatemala, Uruguay, Nicaragua, and Ethiopia, suffered major cutbacks. The Carter administration's human rights policy hit hardest in Latin America, where U.S. military assistance was slashed from $210 million in 1977 to only $54 million in 1979.[77]

If Carter's new emphasis on human rights bolstered America's credibility in criticizing the Soviet bloc countries, it also undermined such traditional anti-communist allies as Nicaraguan president Anastasio Somoza, a West Point graduate and longtime friend of conservative Americans, who imprisoned those who dared disagree with his authoritarian policies. In 1979 Somoza was overthrown in a popular revolt led by the left-wing Sandinistas. "The virtue of the Carter [administration] so far as liberal democratic internationalism was concerned," political scientist Tony Smith wrote in *America's Mission*, "was its unambiguous conviction that authoritative governments were poor custodians of American security interests abroad."[78]

In essence, the Carter administration had championed a post-cold-war foreign policy before the cold war was over. Predictably, this policy— dubbed "resurgent Wilsonianism" by Smith—met with staunch resistance from many of the more hawkish Washington establishment types. In 1979 Georgetown University professor and Reagan's future ambassador to the UN Jeane Kirkpatrick derided the Carter administration's human rights policy as not only too soft on the Soviet Union but too hard on what she termed "moderately repressive regimes" on the right. But then her first act as UN ambassador was to meet with the Argentine military junta that had been responsible for the disappearance of 9,000 citizens, children and adults alike; she followed up by calling on Chilean dictator Augusto Pinochet. Kirkpatrick wasn't an anti-human-rights loose cannon: the first foreign leaders invited to the Reagan White House were Ferdinand Marcos of the Philippines and South Korea's Chun Doo Hwan. "This was a deliberate signal sent out by the Reagan administration that the so-called Carter human rights era was over," Carter complained.[79]

Not everyone mourned its passing. In fact, some foreign leaders thought Carter's focus on human rights had been naive all along; West German Chancellor Helmut Schmidt, for example, said the American president had acted like an evangelist formulating "policy from the pulpit." Carter's relationships with other First World European leaders such as Valéry Giscard d'Estaing of France and Margaret Thatcher of the United Kingdom were equally frosty. It is telling that his closest leader-to-leader friendships developed with such non-Europeans as Egypt's Anwar al-Sadat, China's Deng Xiaoping, Japan's Masayoshi Ohira, and Panama's Omar Torrijos. Unlike the Europeans, all these leaders flattered Carter, stressing the importance of personalities.[80] In any case, Carter's human rights agenda never quite worked as a coherent strategy, largely because he failed to comprehend that it was impossible to "combine support for our more authoritative allies and friends with the effective promotion of human rights within their countries."[81]

By the end of Carter's term and in the wake of the Soviet invasion of Afghanistan, human rights were eclipsing on the American foreign policy screen. Ronald Reagan had promised that if elected he would usher back in the traditional cold war trinity that dated to Harry Truman: containment, realpolitik, and anti-communism under the banner of "peace through strength." Yet no matter what Reagan said on the campaign trail, Carter's human rights policy had given the United States moral credibility around the world—no small feat after Vietnam—while putting the Soviet Union on the defensive by exposing the Kremlin as "evil," just like Reagan said. Due to his Christian belief in redemption—and the power of positive thinking—Carter was pro-democracy, not anti-communist. He wanted to wean Russians away from communism and toward the Bible.

In sharp contrast to the general public's perception, human rights champion Jimmy Carter was no pacifist. It should not be forgotten that the only twentieth-century American president who had a longer military career than Carter's in the U.S. Navy—from 1943 to 1954—was four-star general Dwight D. Eisenhower, supreme Allied commander in World War II. Carter abhorred only the unnecessary use of military force, and as president he worked to modernize the armed forces, not weaken them. "I'm a military man by training and background, and the statistics are there," he pointed out years later to rebut Reagan's claim that his predecessor had left America's armed forces in shambles.[82] After all, it was the hard-line Carter administration defense policies Reagan inherited and built on that led to the end of the cold war. "I believe historians and political observers alike have failed to appreciate the importance of Jimmy Carter's contribution to the collapse of the Soviet Union and the end of the Cold War," Bush administration CIA director Robert M. Gates has maintained. "He was the first president during the Cold War to challenge publicly and consistently the legitimacy of Soviet rule at home. Carter's human rights policy . . . by the testimony of countless Soviet and East European dissidents and future democratic leaders challenged the moral authority of the Soviet government and gave American sanction and support to those resisting that government."[83] Martin Walker, U.S. bureau chief of Britain's *Guardian*, in his book *The Cold War* (1994) laments the fact that a mythology has been created that "Reagan arrived to find a West half-disarmed and thoroughly demoralized, and wrought a great transformation." As Walker made clear, this Tory view of America's later cold war history was nonsense, as the facts bore out. Carter strengthened and modernized the U.S. military during a very difficult post–Vietnam War period, when the Pentagon was unpopular.

Just months after he became president, Carter began badgering the NATO allies to rearm; in fact he demanded solid commitment from every member to increase their defense budgets by 3 percent a year. When the Soviets started deploying SS-20 missiles, it was Carter who countered by proposing that NATO cruise and Pershing missiles be based in Western Europe. And far from slashing American armed forces in Europe, Carter deployed an additional 35,000 troops to boost the American NATO contingent above 300,000, which more than compensated for the cuts the Nixon and Ford administrations had made under détente. Besides modernizing NATO, Carter approved deployment of both nuclear cruise missiles and the Pershing II IRBMs—intermediate range nuclear forces—in Europe.[84]

Carter had no intention of appeasing the Soviets; in fact his very concentration on human rights was in part intended to weaken the Kremlin. Where Gerald Ford had refused to welcome exiled Russian author Aleksandr Solzhenitsyn to the White House, Carter had embraced political dissidents Vladimir Bukovsky and Andrei Sakharov with open arms. Perhaps the most moving document on display at the Carter Presidential Library in Atlanta is the February 5, 1977, note he sent to Sakharov: "Human rights is the central concern of my administration," Carter wrote. "You may rest assured that the American people and our government will continue our firm commitment to promote respect for human rights not only in our country, but also abroad." This epistle, which the Nobel Prize–winning physicist proudly waved in President Leonid Brezhnev's face, prompted the Soviet leader to pronounce Sakharov an enemy of the state.[85] As Robert Gates noted, "Whether isolated and little-known Soviet dissident or world-famous Soviet scientist, Carter's policy encouraged them to press on."[86]

More to the point, it was Carter—not Reagan—who first exploited the human rights provisions of the Helsinki Accords in order to allow movements such as Czechoslovakia's Charter 77, Poland's Solidarity, and the Helsinki Watch groups in East Germany and the Soviet Union to flourish. Czech Republic president Vaclav Havel went so far as to claim that Carter's human rights agenda so undermined the legitimacy and self-confidence of the Warsaw Pact's chieftains that dissidents across Eastern Europe regained the hope that carried them on to democracy. Lech Walesa claimed that it was Carter's tough December 3, 1980, statement—which warned the Soviets about the consequences of their military building on the Polish border— that sent a signal that, unlike Czechoslovakia in 1968, the United States would not abandon "anti-Socialist" forces in Poland. And that wasn't all: Carter's human rights policy also created an environment that allowed 118,591 Soviet Jews to emigrate during his presidency, and encouraged Indonesia alone to release some 30,000 political prisoners from jail. Under Carter's direct order, the CIA began covertly smuggling into the Soviet Union and Eastern Europe literature about democracy and books like Aleksandr Solzhenitsyn's The Gulag Archipelago. Perhaps even more inspired, Carter had the CIA infiltrate the Soviet Union with thousands of books promoting the heritage of ethnic minorities. All in all, the Carter administration's insistence on human rights, no matter how inconsistent in practice, saved thousands of lives and put the Soviets on the defensive to boot. And, before long, Soviet-style communism collapsed more or less peacefully within and without, thanks in part to Carter's promotion of human rights.[87]

Few would argue that Carter had not made a sincere effort to coexist with the Soviets—and Reagan claimed that this pusillanimity made it possible for the Soviets to invade Afghanistan. Yet that brutal incursion proved a fatal miscalculation on Brezhnev's part and the final turning point in the cold war. The Soviet Union's actions in Afghanistan revealed what it had been all along: truly expansionistic and utterly unconcerned with human rights. After that, whoever took the harder line against the Soviets was bound to look better to the American people, and during the 1980 presidential campaign Carter had pledged to increase defense spending by a full 5 percent, compared with Reagan's proposed 7 percent hike. This difference hardly qualified Carter as a dove. Meanwhile, it was Carter who first imposed economic sanctions on the Soviets, outraging U.S. farmers and businessmen; Reagan would continue punishing Moscow with economic measures.

Thus as Reagan prepared to take office, it was far easier for him—thanks to Carter—to rally a consensus behind his strident policies for winning the cold war. Carter tried peaceful coexistence with the Kremlin and had been betrayed. The stupidity of the Soviet invasion of Afghanistan turned Carter into a hawk. As journalist Martin Walker later wrote, "Americans should recall the steel beneath the gentleness; the real historical legacy of Jimmy Carter is [as] one of the men who won the Cold War."[88] Yet it was the compassion of the human rights program that had freed political prisoners across Latin America and the Soviet Union that Carter wanted to be his lasting legacy—and that is what he set his mind to upon leaving the White House.

TWO

PASSING THE TORCH

❦

Nobody likes failure, but Jimmy Carter was "the world's worst loser," according to Hamilton Jordan—who added that few could rebound as well.[1] "I have always believed that it is a sign of weakness to show emotion, giving in publicly to despair, frustration, or disappointment," Carter wrote in his 1982 memoir, *Keeping Faith*. "I try to hide my own feelings, to reassure others by emphasizing the positive aspects of the situation and to pray for strength and wisdom. Privately, I commit myself to overcoming obstacles or to figuring out a new course of action."[2] Thus Carter seized upon the fact that he still had eleven weeks to maneuver bills through Congress, including hot-potato ones regarding toxic waste, energy conservation, and the Alaskan wilderness. "I knew these were controversial congressional issues that the victory-high Republicans were eager to deal with before Reagan came to office," Carter explained years later.[3]

An avid outdoorsman particularly keen on canoeing and fly-fishing, from his first day in the Oval Office Carter championed environmental causes. Known for his staunch opposition to pork-barrel federal dam projects, he made full use of his presidency to help the planet, issuing executive orders to protect wetlands, floodplains, and desert ecosystems. A true believer in alternative energy sources, especially natural gas and solar power, Carter expended enormous political capital during his first year in the White House trying to coordinate a comprehensive long-range energy policy. He did get somewhere, creating the Department of Energy that year and later initiating

"Superfund" legislation, which mandated collecting on chemical manufacturers' insurance policies to clean up toxic-waste dumping grounds.[4]

Superfund was developed in the wake of reports about a highly toxic, abandoned chemical-waste site in the Love Canal neighborhood near Niagara Falls, New York. With horror stories about "radioactive" houses all over the airwaves, Carter led the crusade to pass the Comprehensive Environmental Response Compensation and Liability Act that created Superfund—with a price tag of $1.6 billion. "Superfund is landmark in scope and in its impact on preserving the environmental quality of our country," Carter announced as he signed the legislation on December 11, 1980. But as his term drew to a close, Carter felt Superfund wasn't enough of an environmental legacy and became fixated on protecting the north Alaskan wilderness—which was 99 percent "untapped" by industry—from resource-hungry oil and mining concerns. The Superfund legislation responded to existing environmental destruction; the Alaska Lands Act aimed to prevent future degradation. This landmark wilderness legislation put Jimmy Carter in the pantheon of conservation-minded presidents, right alongside the two Roosevelts.[5]

On November 12, 1980, just a week after losing his bid for reelection, President Carter at last sent Congress the most sweeping environmental legislation in U.S. history, and after a few compromises saw the bill signed into law at a White House ceremony on December 2. The Alaska Lands Act more than doubled the size of America's national parks and wildlife refuges and almost tripled the amount of U.S. land designated as wilderness. It also protected twenty-five free-flowing Alaskan rivers in their natural state, doubling the size of the wild and scenic river system. "I physically cried when that legislation went through," former secretary of the interior Walter Hickel said years later, adding that he could recall the precise moment when he received the horrendous news at his bank office in Anchorage. "In my lifetime," the Republican sighed, "I knew I wouldn't be able to get it undone."[6]

Carter's compromises to get the bill passed included provisions allowing seismic exploration of the oil-rich parts of Alaska's North Slope as well as limited offshore drilling. Overall, however, the legislation was hailed as a miracle by environmentalists while Hickel complained "That total of 171 million acres is just twice over the size of Norway. It's just ludicrous." Fifteen years later Carter averred, "While most sane Americans consider this environmental act an important step in saving some of our nation's most pristine land, a movement to overturn it still exists. In Fairbanks even today workers in bars still throw objects at my photograph for sport."[7] In 1867 Congress had ridiculed Secretary of State William Seward for purchasing Alaska from Russia for $7 million; 113 years later, the president believed

that "regardless of Republican chatter about 'Carter's folly,' " future generations would view the Alaska Lands Act as one of the great conservation laws
of all time. Carter also sent to the Senate a treaty to protect Antarctic
wildlife.[8]

In addition to the Alaska legislation, Carter also pushed other items on
his agenda in his last days as president: he vetoed a controversial amendment approved by the House and Senate that would have prohibited the
Justice Department from intervening in lawsuits over busing schoolchildren
to achieve desegregation; he issued an executive order strengthening the
government's ability to administer its fair-housing programs; he signed into
law another amendment to the national historic preservation program; he
signed into law the Pacific Northwest Power Planning and Conservation Act,
increasing by $1.25 billion the Bonneville, Washington, Power Administra-
tion's borrowing limit to finance conservation and energy projects; he signed
legislation establishing a grain reserve to help alleviate world hunger; and he
set aside funds for research into whether methane gas could become a practical automobile fuel. The legislative frenzy helped replace the postelection
pall over the White House with a sense of accomplishment.[9]

A few weeks before Thanksgiving, Israeli prime minister Menachem Begin visited the White House for purely nostalgic purposes. "Begin had
already written me off and discounted my input completely," Carter recalled. "He was no longer even indicating friendship or cooperation or mutual dependence on me. It was tough."[10]

Things had not been comfortable between Carter and Begin for some
time. During the 1978 Camp David meetings Carter had become disgusted
with Begin, particularly by the way he treated Sadat as an inferior, refused to
take the Palestinian issue seriously, and rejected the notion that Middle East
peace was impossible so long as Israel continued to build settlements on the
disputed West Bank. Begin had taken advantage of Carter's sincerity, but he
had never taken real risks as Sadat had done by visiting Jerusalem in November 1977, a bold act that turned the entire Arab world against him.

In sharp contrast, Carter considered Anwar al-Sadat, with his omnipresent pipe, dapper dress, and encyclopedic knowledge of the Middle East,
a "blood brother" and the "best friend" he ever had. Carter admired Sadat's
ability to stay sympathetic to people who shared his peasant background, to
make the poorest soul feel like an equal. "I don't know of anyone who has
ever contributed more toward peace on earth in my lifetime—perhaps this
century—than has President Sadat," Carter said.[11]

The feeling was mutual: Sadat truly admired Carter and thought he should have been better rewarded for his forceful efforts at Camp David. The two leaders shared a belief in the power of prayer, often discussing together the New Testament and the Qur'an. Once Carter was out of office, Sadat set about spearheading a campaign to win the soon-to-be-ex-president the 1981 Nobel Peace Prize. In a letter to Nobel committee members in Oslo, Sadat nominated Carter for the prize, citing his "genuine dedication to the cause of human rights," his "unwavering commitment" to Middle East peace as evidenced at Camp David, and his efforts to find a solution to the Palestinian problem.[12] "It was touching for Sadat to nominate me," Carter later admitted.[13]

Those sympathetic to Carter believed he should have shared the Nobel Peace Prize—an honor he clearly deserved—with Begin and Sadat for his dazzling diplomatic efforts at Camp David, thereby joining the rarefied ranks of Theodore Roosevelt and Woodrow Wilson as the only American presidents so honored. Some thought that receiving civilization's most august award surely would have imbued Carter with the dignity, gravitas, and statesmanlike aura he so desperately needed to win the 1980 election. Former secretary of state Henry Kissinger, however, dismissed this line of thinking, saying that "Even if Carter had won a Nobel Peace Prize for Camp David, it wouldn't have made a difference. The combination of inflation, the hostage crisis, and his own demeanor did him in. I don't think the American people want a president who wears a sweater. They want someone who is a little more majestic."[14]

Watching from her bathroom window, Rosalynn Carter broke into tears the morning of Begin's last visit, as her husband and the Israeli prime minister embraced on the White House lawn to the sound of a lone trumpet.[15] Begin, though icy toward Carter in private, praised him publicly as a "shining example of a true democrat" and offered his lasting adherence to the Camp David accords. "We shall continue our efforts to be faithful to what we have achieved, written, and signed at Camp David," Begin asserted. Carter, worried that Reagan would try to dismantle his Middle East peace efforts, stressed that the accords were also "permanently binding on us."[16]

Carter's favorite partner in peace, Sadat, was warmer in expressing his personal regards via phone calls and letters—as well as his concerns about what Reagan's victory might mean for Middle East peace. Saying that he loved Carter deeply, Sadat promised to visit him in Plains, which he did ten months later.[17] But the transition period wasn't all valediction: on December 6 the American special representative to the Middle East, Sol Linowitz, informed a relieved Carter that Reagan intended to keep the Camp David framework in place.[18] On the heels of Begin's visit and Sadat's messages, Congress appropriated economic assistance to the tune of $750 million for

Egypt and $785 million for Israel in 1981. Maintaining peace in the Middle East was truly an expensive endeavor for the American taxpayer.[19]

A ccording to press reports, Carter had a wonderful time at his seventy-fourth and final Cabinet meeting on December 3, which was marked by "many bursts of laughter." Secretary of Education Shirley Hufstedler remembered that "the mood was optimistic, in terms of a review of the accomplishments of the administration." With Secretary of State Edmund Muskie seated at his right and Secretary of Defense Harold Brown on his left, Carter spent only a few minutes discussing the unfinished business in the Middle East. This was a time for swapping stories from the trenches and whooping at the prospect of letting somebody else deal with the country's problems and Sam Donaldson for a while. Carter gave everyone present a few minutes to reflect aloud on his or her service; Vice President Walter Mondale's turn came last, and he summed up the Carter administration's accomplishments nicely: "We told the truth. We obeyed the law. We kept the peace. And that ain't bad." As Carter recalled, "It was a bittersweet last get-together."[20]

Lightheartedness held sway at the farewell reception for the White House staff. Carter took the occasion to tweak one of his chief campaign advisers, Robert Strauss, quipping that "Bob is a very loyal friend. He waited a whole week after the election before he had dinner with Ronald Reagan." Presenting Strauss with a framed reproduction of a Norman Rockwell painting called *The Defeated Candidate*, Carter gibed, "I intend to inscribe it 'TO BOB STRAUSS—THANKS FOR MAKING IT ALL POSSIBLE.' " Continuing on his roll, Carter quoted the old maxim, "Victory has a hundred fathers, but defeat is always an orphan"; then he described a recent interview in which an embarrassed Strauss had supposedly, like the apostle Peter, said of his boss to a reporter, "Well, I understand he did a fair job as president, but of course I never knew the man personally."[21]

It was a telling moment. Although most considered Carter a kind, amiable man, he could turn nasty in an instant. At times he was downright vicious; in fact, his trademark steely, laser-sharp stare usually preceded a hurtful put-down. This brusqueness—a lot like that of his old boss in the U.S. Navy and father of the nuclear submarine, Admiral Hyman Rickover—kept Carter's subordinates on their toes and made others take him seriously. But it did not tend to inspire deep friendships. Even in the most informal of settings, Carter had to let everybody know he was in charge.[22]

Despite his lone-wolf tendencies, Carter actually chose not to go it alone in anything: he always had Rosalynn, who was his partner in the fullest sense. Not since Eleanor Roosevelt had a First Lady exercised such profound public influence on the shape of her husband's administration, regularly attending Cabinet meetings and crusading for her particular interest, mental health reform, wherever she went. "When we decided to enter politics," Carter wrote in his 1975 autobiography *Why Not the Best?*, "Rosalynn helped me from every standpoint. We have been full partners in every major decision since we first married."[23]

The president and the First Lady would often pull rocking chairs out onto the White House's Truman Balcony and sit there dissecting Washington's political personalities, her biting observations on the likes of Ted Kennedy and Ronald Reagan usually right on the mark. Zbigniew Brzezinski, Carter's national security adviser, befriended Rosalynn, and revealed that he was impressed by her "clear involvement in everything" the president did. Most of the time, though, even after heated discussions the Steel Magnolia would graciously defer to her stubborn husband in the end.[24]

Rosalynn was Carter's best friend, but hardly the only one. In south Georgia hundreds of people considered Carter kinfolk. In truth, friendship came easily to him—he was just usually too busy to nurture it. "To be involved with Carter as a friend," Hamilton Jordan maintained, "you have to be involved in his work. He is not the type to shoot the breeze for three hours or spend an afternoon golfing for the purpose of forging bonds."[25] But he did enjoy spending free time with his four children, preferably in his beloved outdoors. Carter preferred his office at Camp David to the Oval Office; the solitude allowed him to get more work done, and the woods were perfect for jogging, and for clearing his mind.

After Christmas in Plains, the Carters headed back to Camp David to ski cross-country one last time in the wintry Catoctins. Skimming down a hill, Carter lost his balance, fell, and broke his collarbone. "The accident was a sad but somehow apropos end to a difficult year," Rosalynn Carter said later.[26] That New Year's Day a national television audience saw a crippled Jimmy Carter, flanked by twenty-two of his closest friends, cheering on his University of Georgia Bulldogs as they defeated the Notre Dame Fighting Irish in the Sugar Bowl.[27]

Over the holidays, the president had been devastated to hear from his lawyer and longtime friend Charles H. Kirbo that the peanut warehouse business he had inherited from his father and built into a substantial enterprise—and which he had placed in a blind trust when he headed to Washington—was $1 million in debt. Returning to Plains would hardly be an escape from his troubles. But just about everybody else around Carter was anxious for Reagan's inauguration day so they could get on with their lives after the White House.[28]

On January 4, 1981, Jimmy Carter taught his last Sunday school class as president of the United States from the balcony of the First Baptist Church in Washington, D.C. His lesson was taken from Luke 9:46–48, and he began by addressing the definition of accomplishment. "Is greatness being a president?" he inquired. "An emperor?" The answer, of course, was no, for Jesus taught that "the foundation of greatness is service to others." Carter ended his lesson by intoning: "If you act like Jesus, you'll be good Christians." None of the hundred people packed into that balcony had any doubt that the president meant what he said. Even through a long, hard-fought reelection campaign, his Republican opponents had been unable to tarnish the image of Jimmy Carter as a man of personal integrity with a deep and abiding commitment to Christianity who, having been "born again," tried wholeheartedly to live by the tenets of his faith.[29]

As Washington prepared for the inauguration, Carter still had his hands full of foreign policy, as the Reagan transition team had given him carte blanche to negotiate the release of the hostages. As far as Ed Meese, Alexander Haig, and other Reaganites were concerned, Iran was Carter's responsibility. They refused even to read the outgoing president's "final" compromise proposal on the grounds that the incoming administration should not be contaminated by problems inherited from its predecessors. Thus Carter also submitted his final budget for 1982 to Congress without consulting the Reagan team. The budget called for cuts in many programs, although none in defense spending. Nevertheless, Carter was well aware while putting the document together that Reagan was likely to alter it drastically with higher defense allocations and deeper cuts in social programs such as welfare and education.[30]

A few of the Carterites—notably Jordan, who was hired as a visiting fellow by Emory University, and Jack Watson, who rejoined the prestigious Atlanta law firm of King & Spalding—left Washington, but most stayed in town in new jobs as consultants or lobbyists. "The administration doesn't have the commercial potential of the Nixon people," Hertzberg joked, referring to the cottage industry of writing books on Watergate. "Our crowd is more likely to produce scholarly, relatively unreadable tomes, and memoirs published overwhelmingly by university presses."[31] But Stephen Glass of the *New Republic* was closer to the mark, writing in 1997, "They didn't get speech offers. They didn't get NPR gigs. They didn't get rich off K Street."[32] In fact, throughout the 1980s, having worked for Jimmy Carter was in Washington the mark of a loser.

At a January dinner with some of his favorite journalists, Carter spoke with startling frankness—during the sort of loose, off-the-record banter he had always avoided before—about some of the members of his departing administration. He called his State Department spokesman Hodding Carter III a "creep" for constantly leaking news and said Secretary of State Cyrus Vance was "too reticent," making headline news on both counts the next day.[33] Meanwhile, Rosalynn asked the White House photographer to take pictures of every room for the Carter archives, and spent a day cataloging the paintings she and Jimmy so loved in the family quarters. Filled with melancholy, she wandered around the White House one last time. "I walked through the Lincoln Bedroom where my mother had always stayed; the Queen's Bedroom, which Miss Lillian had as her own; and Amy's bedroom, my favorite," Rosalynn Carter wrote in her memoirs. "We had completely redecorated it and now everything would probably be sent to the warehouse to become just another relic from a past administration."[34]

Carter spent the second week of January focused on his farewell address. Eisenhower had left office with a famous valedictory warning about the growing military-industrial complex; Carter wanted to deliver a comparable speech alerting the nation to its present dangers. With the help of speechwriters Hendrik Hertzberg, Achsah Nesmith, Christopher Matthews, and Gordon Stewart, he took on his three greatest concerns: controlling nuclear weapons, conserving natural resources, and protecting human rights. Carter and his writers put more man-hours into the farewell address than any other speech of his presidency. "I think he unconsciously equated rhetoric with lies and wanted no part of it," Nesmith noted. "But in the farewell address he broke his own rules and did great."[35]

Hertzberg, who would go on to become an editor at the New Republic and later at the New Yorker, had been a liberal influence on Carter's speeches since he first joined the White House staff in 1977 at the request of James Fallows, the administration's first chief speechwriter. But slowly he had soured—not on Carter but on the bulging bureaucracy it takes to run a government and on the hawkish approach Brzezinski brought to Carter's foreign policy. Hertzberg wanted his president to stay the earnest, blue-jeaned populist candidate of yore: "If Carter approached society at large the way he approaches reorganizing the government, he would be a real radical," Hertzberg sighed to his diary on March 11, 1977. The speechwriter felt strongly about showcasing Carter's humanistic side, and after years of deferring to senior staff, on June 8, 1980, he had finally spoken out at a high-level policy meeting as the president was considering how best to approach his re-election campaign. "I thought," Hertzberg recorded in his diary, "that he would have to find a much higher plane for his themes in the general election, starting with the acceptance speech; that the Global 2000 study [issued in July 1980 by more than a dozen federal agencies], which predicts all sorts of horrors for the world if there aren't some big changes, might be the basis for thinking about those themes; that we ought to say that yes, we have to be strong, but that we must realize that arms races and quarrels between East and West are games that the planet cannot afford to play much longer."[36]

At the time, no one had listened to Hertzberg, but after the election the Global 2000 report to the president and its January 1981 sequel, from the State Department and Council on Environmental Quality, became the starting point of Carter's farewell address. "The Global 2000 warning made it clear that we could no longer take the planet's ecological resiliency for granted," Carter explained. "Furthermore, it projected that if the present trends continued unabated, the gap between rich and poor would be so unbridgeable and dangerous."[37]

The address turned out to be the philosophical blueprint for Carter's own postpresidential activities. Bursting with moral passion, he exhorted the Reagan administration to continue emphasizing human rights and environmental conservation, giving his more progressive side full voice and reprising the ideas and ideals he had premiered on the campaign trail in 1976. According to speechwriter Matthews, when Rosalynn Carter first read a draft of the farewell address, she exclaimed, "Why, Jimmy! These are the reasons you lost."[38]

The central themes of Carter's farewell address were stewardship of the environment, nuclear disarmament, and human rights. The speech, which juxtaposed the title of citizen over the role of president, never even mentioned Reagan. The outgoing president did, however, denounce the proliferation of "single-issue groups and special-interest organizations," a slighting reference to such right-wing lobbying outfits as the Moral Majority and the National Rifle Association, which he contended exerted a disproportionate and unhealthy influence on the political process. "The national interest is not always the sum of all our single and special interests," he warned.[39]

Carter went on to emphasize the peril of nuclear arms buildups, especially in unstable nations such as Iran and Pakistan, both of which he considered likely to acquire their own nuclear arsenals in the near future. "It may be only a matter of time before madness, desperation, greed, or miscalculation lets loose this terrible force," Carter warned. But optimism stormed back into the address in language provided by astronomer Carl Sagan, who had been asked to contribute. "Nuclear weapons are an expression of one side of our human character," Carter recited. "But there's another side. The same rocket technology that delivers nuclear warheads has also taken us peacefully into space. From that perspective, we see our Earth as it really is—a small and fragile and beautiful blue globe, the only home we have. We see no barriers of race or religion or country. We see the essential unity of our species and our planet, and with faith and common sense, that bright vision will ultimately prevail." Carter then enumerated some of what had to be done to justify this hopefulness, pleading for higher environmental standards for air, water, and "the land, which sustains us." There was no mention of the hostage crisis, the economy, or his defeat.[40]

Although conservative political columnist William Safire was clearly more impressed by Carter's farewell speech's language than with its substance, even he had to write, "As one who rarely ingratiated himself at the Carter White House by commenting on Carter oratory, I am impelled to cough up a bit of praise for his farewell address."[41] Likewise former senator Eugene McCarthy, Democrat from Minnesota, who had once referred to Carter as an "oratorical mortician," believed the farewell address was masterful, brimming with purpose and principle.[42]

"Not bad for a tenth draft," Carter wrote to Hertzberg. "Maybe we should have been more careful on earlier speeches and saved this one four more years."[43] Carter later noted, "As a global citizen it seemed important to act on these reports, not just stick them in a drawer and wish the problems away. My farewell address was an attempt to issue a warning about the insanity of the nuclear arms race, the horror of international human rights violations, and the need for tougher worldwide environmental cleanup and preservation efforts."[44]

Contained in his farewell address and the two global reports were the intellectual underpinnings of Jimmy Carter's remarkable postpresidential career; together with the lessons in negotiating he had learned by working on the Camp David accords, they provided much of the impetus for his eventual creation of the Carter Center in Atlanta. But before he could act seriously on his humanitarian impulses, Carter had to deal with a host of existing responsibilities, from overseeing the dramatic release of the hostages to handling the foreclosure on his peanut warehouse. It would be a full year before Jimmy and Rosalynn Carter would become emotionally and financially solvent again—and able to accept their defeat at the hands of the voters.

J immy Carter's boyish exuberance may have taken a beating during his four years in the White House, but he never threw in the towel. Even his final days as president of the United States were a frenzy of diplomatic activity in a desperate, round-the-clock effort to free the fifty-two American hostages in Iran before their fate become the responsibility of Ronald

Reagan. After he lost the election, Carter was even more determined to persuade the terrorists to release their captives. Finally, after fourteen months of grueling, behind-the-scenes negotiations through intermediaries, Carter thought a workable deal had been struck. At 4:55 A.M. on January 19, 1981, a haggard and hollow-eyed president who had not slept for two days appeared in the White House Press Room to announce that an agreement had been reached with Iran. After 443 days, the harrowing ordeal was about to end.[45]

The turning point was the American election; Ayatollah Khomeini may have decided it would be wiser to deal in earnest with the Georgia devil he knew than with the hawkish Republican he didn't. Just before Christmas, the Iranian government demanded that the United States deposit a $24 billion "ransom" for the hostages in an Algerian bank. Carter refused to bend to extortion. Nevertheless many in his administration, Deputy Secretary of State Warren Christopher among them, considered the "Algerian formula" an opening for future discussions.[46]

When Iran dropped its demand to $20 billion on January 6, Carter sensed that the dynamic of the crisis had shifted for the first time since the hostages had been captured. Further negotiations involving a tangle of international bankers and multilingual lawyers whittled the figure to $8 billion of the $13 billion in Iranian financial assets then frozen in the United States. Of that, $5 billion was to be set aside to pay Iran's debts to U.S. and European banks. In the end, Carter's last official act as president would be signing a dozen executive orders implementing the elaborate agreement, which included an end to the trade embargo against Iran; apart from that the only advantage Khomeini got under the settlement was a largely symbolic American promise not to interfere in Iran's internal affairs.[47]

Ed Meese, who headed the Reagan transition team, supported the negotiations with a stern warning to Iran not to expect a better deal from the Republicans. The day before the inauguration, when negotiations for the release of the hostages were still going on, Carter called Reagan to give him a detailed report on the matter. Afterward Hamilton Jordan asked, "What did he say, Mr. President?" Everyone in the Oval Office gathered around to hear. Completely deadpan, Carter replied facetiously: "Well, I briefed him on what was happening to the hostages. He mostly listened. But when I finished, he said, 'What hostages?' "[48]

Later that night Iran accused the U.S. government and American banks of reneging on the agreed-upon details of transferring the shah's foreign assets to an escrow account in London. The hostages were once again in limbo, and whether by design or coincidence, Iran's action had dashed Carter's hopes for a triumphant last act as president: greeting the freed

Americans on the eve of Reagan's inauguration. So it wasn't until inauguration day itself, January 20, that the hostages were finally herded onto two Algerian 727s that had sat idling on the runway at Tehran's Mehrabad Airport.
Moments after Ronald Reagan was sworn in as the fortieth president of the
United States, the planes took off.[49]

Reagan was informed of the release as he was en route to Capitol Hill for
his first luncheon as president with the congressional leadership. It was a
glittering premiere: raising a glass of white zinfandel with his patented avuncular ease, Reagan announced to the assembled legislators that "some 30
minutes ago the Algerian planes bearing our prisoners left Iranian airspace,
and they're now free of Iran."[50]

Khomeini may have thought that by delaying the release he had stuck
one final knife into Carter's back, but in truth he had provided him at least a
somewhat graceful exit. The news reached Carter as he was en route to Andrews Air Force Base. A short time later, on the flight home to Georgia,
Warren Christopher phoned Carter from Algiers to officially inform him
that the two jetliners carrying the hostages had cleared Iranian airspace.
Cheers erupted on the plane that only a day before had been Air Force One.
The reporters and former White House staffers accompanying the Carters
were ecstatic.[51]

Anne Wexler, whose White House job had been to build political support
for President Carter, felt triumphant for the first time in more than a year.
"The 1984 Iowa caucuses are exactly three years from today," she reminded
the press on the plane. When reporters asked Jody Powell what Carter
thought of Reagan's inauguration, the outgoing press secretary didn't miss a
beat: "He liked the release of the hostages better."[52] Whatever criticism
Carter had endured during the hostage crisis, he had managed to bring all
fifty-two captives home alive.

On the flight home Jimmy and Rosalynn Carter sat together and offered
prayers of thanks. The usually animated couple looked ashen and drawn; the
reckless pace of a life in politics that had begun in 1962 was now over. But
despite the bruises, Jimmy, fifty-six, and Rosalynn, fifty-three, were returning to Plains with their souls intact. The next few months presented an array
of quotidian chores: enrolling their youngest child, Amy, in a new school;
finding a buyer for the bankrupt peanut warehouse; building an addition to
their house to store the papers and memorabilia they had collected over the
years; paying off the $1.4 million campaign debt; and starting a drive to raise
$25 million to build a presidential library. Their final task was to review the
highs and lows of their White House years for the memoirs each was writing.
The struggle to reorder their lives was just beginning, but the humiliating

election loss had brought Jimmy and Rosalynn Carter even closer together. Their devotion to family and faith had always meant more to them than high office, and still inspired them to public service. After all, with a combination of grit and circumstance they had risen to pinnacles undreamed of by most activist couples. They had suffered the indignation of defeat before and had always bounded back as champions through a tenacity in the face of adversity that was their most remarkable trait as a couple.

Jimmy Carter made his first mark on Georgia politics in 1962, when the thirty-eight-year-old peanut farmer and chairman of Sumter County's School Board had decided to run for the state senate from the Fourteenth District. Old-style politics still flourished in rural Georgia back then, maintained largely by a county-unit system of voting that kept conservative white Democrats in power at the expense of blacks and liberal whites. But the U.S. Supreme Court had changed all that in March 1962 with its famous "one man, one vote" decision in *Baker v. Carr*, which invalidated the county-unit system. A new, more democratic era dawned in Georgia politics, but unfortunately for Carter the entrenched and all-powerful county political boss Joe Hurst had no intention of abiding by any new rules; he won the election for his candidate, hardware store owner Homer Moore of Richland, through bribery and intimidation.[53]

Carter had initially lost the election to Moore by 139 votes, but he demanded a recount when his friend John Pope of Americus witnessed Hurst tearing up the ballots of an elderly couple who had voted for Carter in Georgetown, a small town in Quitman County. Hurst had also stuffed the ballot box with votes cast by people who had moved from the county or were dead. When *Atlanta Constitution* investigative reporter John Pennington discovered these votes, the newspaper published an editorial cartoon depicting a Quitman County politician campaigning in a cemetery, saying, "And I owe it all to you, my public-spirited friends." The injustice of the election galvanized Carter into launching a successful legal battle to overturn the fraudulent results. "I was mad as hell," he wrote in his 1992 book *The Turning Point*.[54]

This time around—eighteen years later—Jimmy Carter was mad as hell about losing to Reagan, but there wasn't much he could do about it. Democracy had prevailed: the American people had voted, fair and square, to cast him out. So now he was leaving the brutal furnace of Washington to return to Plains, where his neighbors knew the real Jimmy Carter—the stubborn peanut farmer who never gave up, the pious Christian who believed absolutely in the infallible will of God. It was this bedrock faith that kept him going. Prayer had always been the Carters' way of analyzing their problems, and it was through prayer that they learned that God was simply testing them, strengthening them, defying them to do better, reminding them that they were servants of the Lord. Jesus Christ had not abandoned them, even if the Democratic voters had. And the son of God urged them to press on, to abandon despair for love, and to turn defeat into victory.[55]

THREE

EVERYTHING TO GAIN

❧⚬❧

The Carters' plane landed at Warner Robins Air Force Base near Macon, Georgia, and they were whisked by motorcade to Plains. Despite a steady winter drizzle three thousand friends and supporters awaited them on Main Street, the block-long town center lined with century-old red-brick stores. Carter described what he was coming home to: "Here in all the world were people who loved us for ourselves and not for whatever power or influence we might have had, who had known our names when the rest of the world still said 'Jimmy Who?' and remembered our fathers and still cared about our mothers just as they would have if we remained peanut farmers."[1]

John Pope, the now ex-president's intimate friend, epitomized Carter's paean to his hometown. Raised in Coffee County, Alabama, Pope, a silver-haired man with twinkling blue eyes, four years older then Carter, was by trade a manufacturer of burial vaults. Since 1953, when Carter returned home from the navy to run the family peanut business, the men had been friends. Together with their wives they attended the Elks Club dances, shoveled peanuts until dark, built a cement swimming pool, rode the City of Miami train to the first Daytona 500 auto race, and often lunched together at the peanut warehouse until Jimmy became state senator. Pope, who had never spent a day of his life in college, embodied Sumter County's notion of a Renaissance man. He understood everything, could fix just about anything that broke, and became a multimillionaire by dint of hard work, business acumen, and wise investments.[2]

John and Betty Pope helped lead the 1976 Peanut Brigade and the 1980 Club, and were always generous contributors to all of Jimmy Carter's endeavors. The Popes occasionally were overnight guests in the White House, sleeping in the Lincoln Bedroom—the south Georgian friends the Carters loved and trusted most. "It was terrible that they lost," Betty Pope recalled. "But all of us in Plains were excited to have Jimmy and Rosalynn back home again."[3] Plains had become as synonymous with Carter as Lincoln's Springfield or Truman's Independence. It was a place almost frozen in a more Norman Rockwell–like era, when family farms flourished and collective institutions like church, school, and social clubs cemented the community. After they lost the 1980 election, it was clear that Jimmy and Rosalynn would return to Plains. "I never doubted that this is where I belong," Carter stated in no uncertain terms.[4]

Plains town officials, led by Mayor Linton "Boze" Godwin, hoped Carter would decide to put his presidential library in his hometown rather than in Atlanta (at Emory University, Georgia Institute of Technology, or Morehouse College), Macon (at Mercer University), Athens (at the University of Georgia), or Americus (at Georgia Southwestern College)—all of which had made alluring overtures. Two universities even offered him presidencies. But metropolitan Atlanta, with its excellent transportation system and budding international reputation, clearly had the edge. Back in mid-December Jody Powell had announced that Carter's papers would be stored for "the immediate future" at a United States Post Office annex in Atlanta, where twenty-four moving trucks from Washington, D.C., were already headed.[5]

When the Carters wanted advice on building a presidential library, they went straight to someone who spoke their language: Lady Bird Johnson. They spent the evening of April 1 with her at the LBJ Ranch in Stonewall, Texas, and the following afternoon at the LBJ Library in Austin. Carter had long identified with President Johnson in having to put up with both the high-and-mighty Kennedys and the Washington media bias against anyone who hailed from Dixie. Thus Carter instinctively understood LBJ's direction to Lady Bird toward the end of his life: "When I die," he told her, "I don't just want our friends who can come in their private planes. I want the men in their pickup trucks and the women whose slips hang down below their dresses to be welcome too."[6]

Six months later Carter announced that he would accept a consortium offer put forth by the presidents of all the institutes of higher learning in Atlanta; but it ended up being associated only with Emory University. His presidential library would be erected at the Great Park, 219 acres of abandoned state land east of downtown that had been the center of a political battle between pro-highway and local NIMBY forces for more than a decade. Plains would have to settle for becoming a National Historic Site in early 1987.[7]

But as he stood in the light rain addressing the gathering of citizens who had come from all over Georgia to greet him that January, Jimmy Carter's voice quavered with emotion. In the rain on a makeshift stage in front of the old train depot, Carter voiced his gratitude to all those who had supported him since he first sold bags of hot boiled peanuts in town as a boy, and then broke to the joyous news of the hostages' release. "It is impossible for me to realize—or any of us—how they feel on that plane because they recognize that they are hostages no more, that they are prisoners no more, and they are coming back to the land we all love," Carter said. Following a moment of silence for the eight men who had perished in the failed rescue attempt in Iran, a local country-western band launched into a dirgelike version of "Dixie," a song suppressed during Carter's campaign and presidency because of its identification with the Confederacy.[8]

Jimmy and Rosalynn then danced a slow Tennessee waltz for the photographers and well-wishers, and the Carters' welcome home ended with a potluck feast billed as "the world's largest covered-dish dinner" featuring clog dancing by the Muckalee Mudstompers. After their fill of casseroles, the Carters waved good-bye to the crowd and walked the few blocks to their modest ranch-style home at 1 Woodland Drive, located at the west city limits off Highway 280, and built in 1961 with the profits of two successive bumper crops. A freshly painted sign in front advised motorists "No Stopping, Keep Moving." Over the span of twenty years the house itself had changed little, but now the grounds were surrounded by a high wrought-iron fence—the same fence that had once protected Richard Nixon's house in Key Biscayne, Florida. Then, as his brother Billy put it, Jimmy Carter began the job of "living the rest of his life."[9]

A t President Reagan's request, Carter had agreed to travel from Plains to West Germany the day after the inauguration as a special envoy to greet the hostages. "This arrangement," former secretary of state Alexander Haig admitted in his memoir Caveat, "had the virtue of giving Carter public credit for the deliverance of the hostages while separating him from the nearest media center by the width of the Atlantic and Rhine."[10] At 5:00 A.M. January 21 Carter rose, said his morning prayers, and headed to the muddy Plains softball field where a helicopter waited to take him to a presidential plane bound for Wiesbaden. Accompanied by Walter Mondale, Harold Brown, Edmund Muskie, Hendrik Hertzberg, Hamilton Jordan, former treasury secretary G. William Miller, and former White House counsel Lloyd Cutler, Carter arrived in West Germany at 8:30 P.M. The delegation planned to stay only five hours before heading home. "The president looked as old and tired as I had ever seen him," Jordan recalled.[11]

In Frankfurt the delegation was met quite unexpectedly by throngs of people waving American flags and the yellow ribbons that had come to symbolize the hostages' plight. After a short but polite conversation with Chancellor Helmut Schmidt and Foreign Minister Hans-Dietrich Genscher, Carter was off to the U.S. Air Force Hospital with two columns of motorcycles as escort. Sheldon Krys, the State Department official who had been responsible throughout the 444-day-long crisis for communicating with the hostages' families and preparing for their return, briefed Carter. "Mr. President," Krys began, "I am sorry to report to you that the mistreatment and abuse of the hostages was more comprehensive and severe than we had anticipated." He went on to details of specific mental and physical cruelty.[12]

That evening Carter met with the hostages, fifty men and two women, who were attired in baggy hospital gowns and blue robes, in the hospital's sterile third-floor conference room. Former hostage Bruce Laingen, who had been the U.S. embassy chief in Iran and thus the ranking diplomat among the captives, led Carter into the room where the other fifty-one hostages were seated in three concentric circles of folding chairs. Trying to dispel the tense atmosphere, Carter held up that day's copies of the *Americus Times-Recorder* and *Warner Robins Daily Sun*, headlined "Carter Efforts Bring Freedom to Hostages" and "Free At Last—Hostages Leave Iran," pointing out that the hostage-release stories had bumped Ronald Reagan's inauguration to below the fold. Carter's attempt at levity fell flat, so he adjusted his tone to the serious frame of mind of his listeners and briefed them accordingly.[13] For fifty minutes Carter offered the group a startlingly candid summary of the rationale behind his roller-coaster diplomacy during the crisis; then he fielded questions. "Carter identified with every one of us," Laingen recalled. "He knew all of us by name, knew our backgrounds, our families. It was obviously an emotional moment for him."[14]

Most of the hostages displayed respect for Carter and his commitment to bring them all home alive, although some peppered him with hostile questions ranging from why the rescue mission was not attempted sooner to whether the United States had lost honor by paying the Iranians a "ransom" for their release. Once Carter explained that no ransom had been paid, that only $3 billion had been returned out of the $13 billion in Iranian assets frozen in the United States, the group broke into thunderous applause with plenty of high fives. Carter continued with an emotional diatribe against the Iranian terrorists and urged those present, no matter how anxious they were to go home, to follow their physicians' orders for the next couple of days. Finally he posed for photographs with each former hostage, as did Mondale, and then Carter and Laingen hugged. "It was apparent from the strained look on his face," Laingen recalled, "that he had agonized during the crisis as much as we had—perhaps more."[15]

At bottom, the hostages knew they owed their lives to Carter's tenacity and restraint. "Jimmy Carter, I suspect, by many of us, is considered a very stolid individual with less than an affable personality," outspoken hostage Barry Rosen later reflected at an academic conference devoted to studying Carter's presidency, "but he was warm, gracious, sensitive, apologetic—unnecessarily so, in many ways—a fine and decent human being."[16]

After the meeting Carter, his voice on edge, told the press that the hostages had suffered abuse "much worse than has been previously revealed," including mock firing squads, Russian roulette, and periodic beatings. He then headed directly back to his plane, where he phoned President Reagan to brief him before taking off for home. Carter, always dead serious when discussing the hostage ordeal, has said that the meeting was "one of the most gratifying experiences of my life."[17]

The failed rescue mission continued to haunt Carter in the same way Watergate did Nixon, and Vietnam, LBJ. Nixon took to blaming everybody but himself; LBJ found redemption by foregoing a reelection bid in favor of bed rest, long hair, beads, and hand-rolled cigarettes. Carter externally adopted the stance followed by Truman after ordering the dropping of atomic bombs on Japan: he claimed he never lost a night's sleep revisiting decisions made during the crisis. In Carter's case, this the-buck-stops-here decisiveness did not really bring peace of mind. "I am still haunted by memories of that day," Carter would write in 1982.[18] The entire series of events constantly flashed through his mind like a slide projector carousel that never stopped playing, image after image in a Sisyphean replay. Yet from that time onward Carter put the crisis behind him, refusing to let it become a central memory of his presidency. "I regret," Laingen has said, "that Carter has distanced himself from us, refusing to have much to do with any of us." It was the death of the eight servicemen during the rescue attempt—victims of bad luck and unpredictable mishaps—that plagued him, and he privately prayed for their forgiveness.[19]

Later, as the plane began its descent into Warner Robins AFB, there was nothing more to be said than good-bye. "You clowns don't forget about coming down to Plains," Carter instructed Jordan and Powell, the two young members of his administration he loved like sons. "We've been through too much together not to be close."[20]

Back in Washington, the Reagan administration had issued notice that it "fully intended" to carry out the financial commitments made by the Carter administration to Iran. But at the new regime's first National Security Council meeting on January 21, just-appointed secretary of state–designate Alexander Haig was stunned to hear the new president raise the possibility of abrogating the agreement. "I was appalled that such a cynical action could even be considered," Haig wrote in *Caveat*. "The agreement, however bitter, however deeply flawed, was a binding contract."[21] As time went on, U.S.-Iran relations were seriously strained by what Zbigniew Brzezinski called "a residue of bitterness," but on February 18 Reagan did announce publicly that he would observe the terms of the Carter agreement—although he also made clear that he would not have negotiated with Iran to obtain the hostages' release.[22] Many others at the time denounced the Carter deal as paying ransom, pure and simple. William Safire was completely disparaging in the *New York Times*, calling the deal a "surrender to terrorism" and demanding an investigation into what he called "the disaster and dishonor that was the dreary Carter record in Iran."[23]

The hostage crisis lingered on in the national consciousness, and soon with fresh impetus. Not long after the captives' release, unsubstantiated rumors surfaced to the effect that senior aides to candidate Reagan had met secretly in Europe with Iranian government officials before the November 1980 election to bargain for a delay in the hostages' release. The Reagan operatives purportedly sought a delay to keep Carter from reaping any political gains to be had by resolving the crisis.

A decade later, on April 15, 1991, these allegations were given a full airing in the *New York Times* by Gary Sick, a former Iran specialist on Carter's National Security Council staff who from 1981 to 1990 had investigated the circumstances of the hostages' release. During the 1980 presidential campaign, Sick claimed, representatives from Reagan's team made secret deals with Tehran to hold on to the hostages until after the election. Once Reagan took over, the Iranians were to release the hostages—in exchange for large quantities of U.S. arms.[24] "I personally have no doubt that William Casey secretly met with the Iranians," Sick has asserted, basing his charge on computerized databases he compiled on the crisis.[25] His research suggested "a curious pattern" of events, Sick claimed. Without a smoking gun, however, or the evidence to prove exactly what happened at each stage, Sick's astute analysis of the Iranian revolution, detailed in his 1991 book *October Surprise*, was dismissed as rumor-mongering by President George Bush, whom Sick implicated in the alleged hostage deal.[26] Carter, who abhors the clandestine approach or conspiracy theories, nevertheless believes that Sick's assertions are probably correct. "If you try to dig further into Gary's *October Surprise* revelations, and are successful, you may not like what you find," Carter has stated.[27]

Keyed up by the publicity surrounding Sick's allegations, a number of Democrats and eight former hostages eventually called for a congressional investigation. In October 1991 the Senate voted to conduct an inquiry, but a few weeks later Republican senators succeeded in blocking financing for the investigation. The Senate inquiry was deemed insufficient by Democrats because it had a budget of $75,000, limited subpoena rights, and prohibitions on overseas travel. Inquests by the House continued and eventually resulted in a November 23, 1992, 968-page bipartisan report debunking the charges, although it did note that Reagan's top campaign aides—Richard Allen and Robert McFarlane—came perilously close to improper conduct by meeting at a Washington hotel with questionable characters who claimed they could deliver hostages to the GOP team. More than 230 people were interviewed in several countries by ten lawyers and six investigators working for the House "October Surprise Task Force."[28]

Sick remained convinced that his original research was valid and that documentary evidence confirming his allegations would eventually be produced.[29] The congressional report did state that Casey was "fishing in troubled waters and that he conducted informal, clandestine, and potentially dangerous efforts on behalf of the Reagan campaign to gather intelligence on the volatile and unpredictable course of the hostage negotiations." The House panel also said it had undertaken its inquiry because, if Sick's charges were true, it would be "wholly beyond the wildest excesses in our constitutional history." But until more evidence surfaces, Sick's assertions must be considered a theory based on purely circumstantial findings.[30]

Carter returned from West Germany to Plains completely exhausted. He slept for nearly twenty-four hours, then awoke to what he characterized as "an altogether new, unwanted, and potentially empty life." As an entourage of White House staffers and political advisers who had come to Plains prepared to leave, Carter succumbed to a spell of real depression, exacerbated by his bleak financial situation. Mere days ago he had been the most powerful man in the world; now his immediate concern was whether the brick sidewalk he was laying in front of his home was crooked.[31]

Since George Washington relinquished power to John Adams in 1797, there has never been an official role for former presidents. William Jennings Bryan once suggested that all former Presidents become ex officio members

of the Senate, an idea lampooned by William Howard Taft at New York's
Lotus Club shortly after his defeat in the 1912 election. In essence, all ex-
presidents were curiosities, sideshow attractions who drew constant gawks
wherever they went. And while Thomas Jefferson founded a university upon
retirement, James Monroe, forced by debt to sell his Virginia estate, lived
with his daughter in New York; Franklin Pierce endured the pro-Union
taunts of his New Hampshire neighbors; and Calvin Coolidge retired to a
$32-a-month duplex in Northampton, Massachusetts. The most important
thing for an ex-president was to keep busy and exude a dignity befitting a
member of what Herbert Hoover called an "exclusive trade union."[32]

As it happened, former White House appointments secretary Phil Wise,
a twenty-nine-year-old Plains native who would work for Carter intermit-
tently throughout his postpresidential years, had gotten together with a
group of White House staffers and Cabinet officers to surprise the boss with
the ideal retirement gift: hand and machine tools to outfit a complete home
woodworking shop. Long ago Wise and Jody Powell had noticed that whenever Carter was at Camp David he would often drift over to the compound's
woodworking shop to craft a hickory chair or an oak chess set. With that in
mind, shortly after the 1980 election Wise called Sears, Roebuck corporate
headquarters in Chicago, whose head of equipment helped him assemble a
basic woodworking kit to be delivered to Plains for setup in one of the
Carter warehouses.[33] "It was the perfect gift," Carter recalled.[34]

His first full day back in Plains, Carter, dressed in blue jeans and a plaid
work shirt, rolled up his sleeves and moved the woodworking equipment
from the warehouse to his two-car garage. Then he headed ten miles away to
Americus in a chauffeured limousine to purchase two-by-fours from a
lumberyard. The incongruity didn't faze Carter, who stayed focused on his
humble first project: laying down a tongue-and-groove floor in the attic to
make space for storing the memorabilia and gifts he had collected in twenty
years in politics. "It was a difficult job," Carter remembered, "carrying all
the long boards up a rickety folding ladder, working in the cramped spaces,
chiseling and planing the uneven joists to provide a smoothly finished surface, notching out and fitting each board snugly around the ceiling braces
and other obstructions, and nailing them in, often with little room to swing
the hammer."[35]

Miss Lillian, Carter's mother, still on the mend from a hip broken in
September and about to undergo breast-cancer surgery, had grown tired
of "holding court" in town and had moved to the more secluded and modern Pond House, a gift from her children in the late 1960s upon her return from Peace Corps service in India. Once she returned to the woody
outskirts of Plains, Miss Lillian's two-story brick house on Church Street

just across the road from Jimmy's place became his postpresidential office. Phil Wise and Carter's secretaries Lori Fossum and Susan Clough were the only full-time staffers, and they were inundated with approximately 68,000 letters—many sent to the Atlanta office—from citizens praising Carter's handling of the hostage crisis and his presidency in general. Madeline Edwards, Rosalynn Carter's devoted White House personal assistant, also stayed on.[36]

As things turned out, Carter visited the Church Street office infrequently, preferring to work out of his study so he could beat the boredom of writing his memoirs or frustration in answering his mail by walking thirty feet and switching to crafting a wooden handsaw for his old friend John Pope or a rosewood cigar box for P. J. Wise or a collection plate for Maranatha Baptist Church. When Rosalynn tried to rekindle her interest in playing the keyboard, Jimmy made her a beautiful music stand, and over the ensuing weeks Carter crafted wooden thank-you gifts for various friends around town who had helped him prosper in politics over the years. "The woodworking shop proved very therapeutic for Carter," Phil Wise avowed, "for it gave him useful hours to put his presidential years behind him and to think about the future."[37]

The other members of Carter's transition team, soon to be led by postpresidential chief of staff Dan Lee, occupied five thousand square feet of the seventeenth floor at the Richard B. Russell Federal Building in Atlanta. Every week Carter, escorted by his Secret Service guards, made the three-hour drive from Plains to the Atlanta office, where the main focus became planning for his presidential library. Carter did not keep an apartment in Atlanta; sometimes he stayed at the Colony Square Hotel, where he spent many evenings stewing over how to fund-raise for a library.[38]

Over the years former presidents had been chastised by a number of Congressmen and political pundits for indulging in post–White House extravagance, complete with Secret Service protection for widows and children, seven-figure book deals, ostentatious offices, bloated staffs, and presidential libraries that were more shrine than research center. A financially strapped Carter did not feel like he was being pampered with taxpayer generosity. His annual federal pension of $69,630 (plus $150,000 a year for staff expenses during a thirty-month postpresidential adjustment period) was far too little to pull him out of his dire financial situation.[39]

When his personal counsel and financial trustee, Charles H. Kirbo of Atlanta, told Carter in November 1980 that the peanut warehouse operation— put four years earlier into a blind trust to be managed by Billy Carter—was more than $1 million in the red, it came as a shock. The only chance he had to regain solvency and keep the farm was by selling the entire commercial enterprise. "No one could accuse me of becoming rich in the White House," Carter pointed out.[40]

At sixty-two, Kirbo was not much older than Carter, but the former president had come to rely on him as a surrogate father. Kirbo, the crafty cracker-barrel lawyer who spoke in a clipped, monotonous drawl, was, as columnist Jack Andersen put it, Carter's "one-man kitchen cabinet." Ever since he successfully challenged the 1962 State Senate election outcome in Carter's favor, he had become his most trusted adviser. A single yes or no from "Mr. Kirbo" carried more weight than the most articulate spiel of anybody else. Like John Pope, Kirbo never used Carter for his own advancement. He turned down Governor Carter's 1971 offer to fill a U.S. Senate vacancy due to the death of Richard Russell. In 1976, Carter had depended heavily on him to screen potential vice presidential candidates. Refusing to move to Washington as an official part of the Carter administration, Kirbo stayed in Atlanta, talking with the president almost daily, flying into Washington so often that he earned the nickname "Overnight Kirbo."[41]

Kirbo, embarrassed by his uncharacteristic negligence of the warehouse record, immediately set off to find a buyer for the family firm that Carter had toiled to build from the day he inherited it from his father in 1954 to the day he was elected president in 1976. Within a few months the Carters found a buyer in the politically savvy Archer-Daniels-Midland Company of Decatur, Illinois. Its bipartisan chairman and CEO, Dwayne Andreas, had made a fortune in feed grain and had a hobby of extricating politicians from Thomas Dewey to Ronald Reagan out of financial jams. In 1972 he walked into the Nixon White House with an envelope stuff with one-hundred-dollar bills. (Andreas later gave the Carter Presidential Center more than $300,000; he also hired the Carters' oldest son, Jack, as a broker for his company on the Chicago Stock Exchange.) Although unprovable, there is circumstantial evidence that Andreas intentionally overpaid the former president for his peanut warehouse to help him out of his financial jam. "It just lucked up that we found a purchaser," Carter noted. "Had we not, we would have had to do something to make money to pay off those debts."[42]

Liquidating the family business embarrassed Carter, who felt he had let down his ancestors as well as the Plains agricultural community. Thus it's little wonder that Carter did hang onto more than 2,000 acres outside town. "Selling off our family's business holdings was painful," he confessed, "but to have lost that land would have been a devastating blow."[43]

Just as archetypal southerner Scarlett O'Hara always had Tara, Jimmy Carter always revered "the land," the flat red-clay country of his native southwest Georgia, part of the balmy Coastal Plains region, which had once been covered by the Atlantic Ocean. His ancestors' simple headstones, many dating to the early 1800s, can be found in the tiny and well-kept Carter family cemetery, where many unnamed slaves lie haphazardly below in an unmarked mass grave. For Carter, as for his English and Scotch-Irish forebears, owning and maintaining land had been an essential part of life, and the relationship between man and soil a deeply personal one. To labor in the heart of the barren Georgia redlands, to let the slightly sandy, iron-fraught vermilion soil slip through his fingers, was for Carter an intense and spiritual experience.[44]

To him, there is no sight prettier than an overcast gray sky bearing a light rain. With a farmer's faith and a Christian's prayer he knows to wait for the warm Gulf front to sweep in the sharp sunshine that makes the land burst into a thousand shades of green. Throughout his entire political career Carter honestly, if romantically, viewed himself as just a struggling small farmer. He even once characterized his burgeoning friendship with then–Soviet premier Mikhail Gorbachev by saying, "Two farmers can't be antagonistic toward one another."[45]

But bucolic pursuits didn't generate any income, and even with the warehouse sold, the family was short of cash. They turned therefore to that time-honored pastime, the memoir. Washington lawyer Lloyd Cutler had introduced Jimmy and Rosalynn to literary agents Marvin Josephson and Lynn Nesbit back in January, and all parties had gotten along immediately.[46] Carter would have preferred to write a book about his diplomatic efforts at Camp David, but Josephson and Nesbit convinced him that a larger advance would be offered for a presidential memoir. Jimmy acquiesced, with the stipulation that he would devote only one year to the project. That set the agents shopping, and in early March they scored a multimillion-dollar deal with Bantam Books. "I hope to make it highly personal in nature, not a definitive history," Carter said about what would become *Keeping Faith: Memoirs of a President*. "I'm not going to try to write an apology or rationalization of what we did."[47]

Rosalynn Carter, after consulting with Edmund Morris, the Pulitzer Prize–winning biographer of Theodore Roosevelt, likewise decided that she did not need to set the record straight or settle scores. Instead she accepted Morris's advice: "Don't try to make your place in history. It's already made." Constantly interrupted by house chores, telephones, and a high-maintenance husband, and in pain from muscle inflammation caused by a polymyalgia rheumatica, Rosalynn had great difficulty finishing *First Lady from Plains* (1984) for Houghton Mifflin. But the two-and-a-half-year struggle paid off: her autobiography rocketed to number one on the *New York Times* best-seller list and remained there for eighteen weeks, all the while garnering unanimously positive reviews.[48]

On March 18 Carter announced his publishing deal in New Jersey, at Princeton University's Woodrow Wilson School of Public and International Affairs, during a student lecture, supposedly closed to the press, where he also advocated a single six-year term for the U.S. presidency. Book deal and lecture aside, Carter's primary motive for visiting the Garden State was to consult with scholars of the presidency, particularly distinguished American historian Arthur Link, editor of the multivolume Woodrow Wilson papers and author of several seminal works on Wilson. Buoyed by Link's encouragement, Carter left Princeton ready to write and so stimulated by his interaction with students that he gave serious consideration to becoming a university professor—like William Howard Taft, who went on to teach law at Yale University after leaving the White House in 1913.[49]

Of course, Carter was already a published writer with a gift for clear, unadorned prose—what he called "peanut farmer language."[50] In 1975, as he was crisscrossing the country to muster support for his presidential campaign, Carter had written *Why Not the Best?*, which was published by Broadman Press, a Southern Baptist inspirational-literature firm based in Nashville. Carter brought his yellow scratch-pad scrawlings, composed longhand in airports and hotels, country kitchens and community centers, home to Plains at night and kept going on his portable typewriter on weekends. Bantam bought the paperback rights to the autobiography in 1976, when Carter moved ahead of the Democratic pack in the presidential primary race; by the time he left the White House, the book was in its twelfth printing, having sold almost a million copies. Along with John F. Kennedy's Pulitzer-winning *Profiles in Courage*, *Why Not the Best?*—which has sold more than one million copies—proved to be one of the most effective campaign devices ever used by a presidential aspirant, affording an intimate introduction to the relatively unknown Georgian.[51]

As the last president allowed by law to keep the documents created during his tenure, Carter had a wealth of material for *Keeping Faith*. (The Presidential Records Act of 1978 stipulated that all presidential papers after Carter's term would become the property of the federal government, would fall under Freedom of Information Act provisions, and would be subject to public disclosure after twelve years.)[52] Carter also had been diligent about keeping a diary. At Brzezinski's suggestion he had tape-recorded lengthy entries, usually once a day, while serving as chief executive, often focusing on his impressions of the world leaders who visited the Oval Office. A secretary would then immediately transcribe them, putting the entries into large black binders to offer a running commentary on life in the White House. "No president ever left office with such a meticulous and voluminous record of official papers," journalist James Reston reported.[53] Papers, but not tapes;

mindful of what befell Richard Nixon, Carter never recorded conversations while president without the permission of those involved.

The Carter diaries, which fill some 6,000 double-spaced pages, are as compelling and near-comprehensive a look at White House life as any president recorded. "I was exceedingly disciplined and meticulous about my diary," Carter has declared. "No matter the circumstances, I recorded my observations." Due to their highly personal and subjective nature, Carter has not yet allowed scholars to study his presidential diaries, which he keeps tucked away in a cabinet in his Plains study. But when it came to writing *Keeping Faith*, the diaries proved his most valuable resource. "I can vouch for the advantages of hindsight," Carter noted ruefully after reliving the events of his presidency as they unfolded in his own diary.[54]

Carter took on as a research assistant Steve Hochman, a reflective thirty-five-year-old historian and protegé of Dumas Malone who had just assisted the near-blind University of Virginia professor with *The Sage of Monticello*, the final installment of Malone's six-volume, Pulitzer Prize–winning study of Thomas Jefferson. Carter and Hochman labored away eight to ten hours a day for thirteen months, and reflected how Jefferson had occupied himself after his White House service in tending his elaborate gardens, drafting documents, corresponding with friends, and founding the University of Virginia.[55]

Keeping Faith—written by Carter on a Lanier word processor— appeared in bookstores in October 1982. The public and scholarly communities had high expectations for the White House memoir, and their reactions were mixed. Carter emerged as a highly intelligent and competent president, a peacemaker with an abiding commitment to honesty. Clearly he had a more probing, retentive mind than most of his recent presidential predecessors. The passages from his diary make for often intimate and absorbing reading; yet at almost six hundred pages of largely pinched and wary prose, *Keeping Faith* lacks passion, is singularly self-absorbed, and omits any anecdotes of life in the Washington fishbowl that might indicate that Carter understood what was going on around him. What Carter omitted attracted more attention than what he left in. Many felt the book proved that he had failed to grasp the political dynamics of his own presidency or to appreciate how his behavior influenced others. "*Keeping Faith* ought to be taken more as a warning for the future than as an illuminating assessment of the recent past," concluded Richard Barnett in the *New Yorker*.[56] The *Washington Post* went one further, trashing the book as disingenuous and filled with errors.[57]

The book's real contribution lies in Carter's detailed, at times pedantic analyses of historic events and policies—how the Panama Canal Treaties squeaked through the Senate, or why he responded to the Soviet invasion of Afghanistan by boycotting the Olympics. As the reviewer for *Time* noted, *Keeping Faith* offers an "intimate and detailed narrative of Camp David— the intense arguments, the searing animosity." The *New York Times*, in a decidedly mixed review, applauded Carter's report on Camp David as "absolutely riveting," singling out a passage that described Carter's blocking the door to keep Sadat and Begin from walking out on the peace process— certainly the first time in American diplomacy that a president had to play bouncer.[58]

China's Deng Xiaoping and Leonid Brezhnev of the Soviet Union emerge in the memoir as world leaders Carter came to understand well, while West German chancellor Helmut Schmidt comes across as pompous and arrogant. And while he couldn't claim to fully understand the fates that conspired against him, Carter did not shy away from analyzing such incomprehensible obstacles as Khomeini and Kennedy. *Keeping Faith* stayed on the *New York Times* best-seller list for eleven weeks, although it never ranked above Jane Fonda's first workout book, which became a joke of his on the lecture circuit.

Carter's six-city promotional tour was his first real public exposure since leaving the White House, and Carter asked his longtime media adviser, Gerry Rafshoon, to accompany him. "Carter was unusually reflective during our travels," Rafshoon recalled. "He spoke about how much he missed his father."[59] The tour included the usual appearances on all the major TV networks. In Washington, D.C., Carter held a candid press conference. Asked how it felt to be back in the capital as a private citizen, Carter smiled and said, "It's fine, but I'd still rather be president." The *Washington Post* reported Carter's sarcastic retorts to questions about Ronald Reagan's leadership, Menachem Begin's Lebanon policy, and Ted Kennedy's possible bid for the presidency in 1984. Carter also used his Washington appearance to tout Mondale but added, "It's obvious that he wants to put some distance between us. There's a lot of baggage that goes with having served in my administration, and I don't want to drag him down."[60]

No presidential author had ever made himself so available to the media. Harry Truman, Dwight Eisenhower, and Lyndon Johnson were aloof, and Richard Nixon was downright reclusive. The biggest self-promoter of the lot, Gerald Ford, did only a few television interviews from New York and Washington. "I would think that this is much more than a promotional tour for a book in Jimmy Carter's mind," syndicated columnist Carl T. Rowan commented. "I think he would like to refurbish his image with the public and take a more prominent place in the Democratic Party."[61] Nevertheless

Carter avoided the White House and kept his return to Washington brief: he was anxious to finish his book tour and get back to Plains in time to teach his Sunday Bible class.

Faith has deep roots in the American South. Religious beliefs may appear to run along many different roads, but the basis for all remains the same: Christian faith. Carter was a true native son. "If you don't understand the Bible, the Southern Baptist Convention, and what it means to be saved by Jesus, you'll be hard-pressed to understand Jimmy Carter," according to President Bill Lotz of the World Baptist Alliance, which has 200 million members worldwide.[62] The Southern Baptist Convention (SBC) was formed in 1845 in downtown Augusta, Georgia, by Christians below the Mason-Dixon line who wanted to uphold the "peculiar institution" of slavery, and for the next hundred years was plagued by accusations of institutionalizing racism in the name of Jesus Christ.[63]

But the SBC, boasting more than 15 million members in 1998, underwent a radical transformation during and after the civil rights movement of the 1960s. Most churches accepted integration with an odd mix of reluctance and compassion.[64] Jimmy Carter's own Plains Baptist Church, founded in 1848 with twenty members, had at last voted to permit blacks to join after the 1976 election, but the Reverend Bruce Edwards, the pastor who had orchestrated the change, was forced to resign. As a result, a group of liberal-minded locals retreated from Plains Baptist late in February 1977 and formed the Maranatha congregation less than a quarter mile away, welcoming black members and tourists with open arms. Jimmy and Rosalynn, who lived in the White House at the time, avoided the Plains church riff by joining the First Baptist Church of Washington, D.C., where the president occasionally taught Bible class. On their visits home, the Carters straddled the schism by worshipping at Maranatha and attending Sunday school at Plains Baptist. But after the 1980 election, when Carter returned to Plains as a permanent citizen, he could no longer have it both ways: a decision had to be made. "There was never really a question of how he would decide," Hugh Carter recalled.[65]

On January 25, 1981, Jimmy Carter's first Sunday as ex-president, those milling in front of the Plains Baptist Church watched with disappointment as their auspicious neighbor's limousine drove past and pulled into the parking lot of the white-columned, redbrick Maranatha Baptist Church. As the welcoming hymn, "There Is a Fountain Filled with Blood," sounded from a small Rodgers organ, the congregation of eighty-four, singing along as best they knew how, nodded supportively to the Carters as they walked arm in arm into their new sanctuary. "Mister Jimmy and Mrs. Rosalynn, we welcome you," said local agriculturalist Tim Lawson, as he presented them for membership.[66]

Maranatha Baptist Church has continued to serve not only as Carter's house of worship but also as his combination lyceum–lecture hall. Journalists doing stories on Carter inevitably found themselves there on a Sunday morning in Plains to witness the odd spectacle of a former president discoursing about Galatians and Ephesians and raising such themes as "Suffering for Jesus's Sake" (I Peter 1:1–9) and "Overcoming the Barrier of False Religion" (Acts 17:15–18:4). Every Sunday Carter was in Plains he taught an adult Bible class to anywhere from ten to five hundred listeners. With a small microphone attached to his lapel, he would update the congregation on his activities, be they monitoring an election in Zambia or fishing in the Okefenokee Swamp.[67] "It's a minister's dream to have non-church members from fifty states and a hundred countries fill up the seats on any given Sunday," Dr. Daniel Ariail of Maranatha Baptist has noted. "People come to see a world leader and end up learning about the Bible. It's a beautiful thing."[68]

Carter's religious convictions did not suddenly appear when he decided to run for president in 1976. Ever since he was a boy, Carter had studied and taught the Bible. His classmates at the U.S. Naval Academy remembered that on Sundays, while other midshipmen enjoyed a few hours respite from the strict Annapolis regime, Carter would hold impromptu Bible classes, sometimes teaching Scripture to the officers' daughters. Later, while stationed on the USS *Pomfret* in Hawaii and the USS *New York* in Norfolk, Virginia, Carter maintained his devotion to Jesus Christ.[69] "We never swore around Jimmy," remembered Francis Hertzog, a close Carter friend at Annapolis. "It would have been like cussing in front of your grandmother or the Lord."[70]

When he returned to Georgia after twelve years in the navy, Carter immediately answered a "calling" to teach the Bible at Plains Baptist Church. He made a commitment then—and openly admitted it to voters when he ran for president of the United States—that Jesus would always come first in his life. Carter's born-again experience came not long after losing the 1966 election for governor to arch-segregationist Lester Maddox, a man he disdained as a hateful bigot. Carter, feeling betrayed by God, reached out in despair for his kid sister Ruth, who had recently gone through a profound religious experience. As they walked together through some woodlands on the outskirts of Plains, Ruth shared with her brother her "total commitment" to Jesus Christ. At that frozen moment Jimmy turned over his spirit to Jesus and his body to the work he now fervently believed God wanted him to perform. Being born again made an optimist of him—it "mind-cured"

Jimmy Carter, as philosopher William James described the Christian conversion experience. Ruth, who went on to write a book about inner healing, began traveling the world talking with other lost souls, hoping to bring them God's love. Her ministry of excoriating the five basic negatives—fear, frustration, inferiority, guilt, and loneliness—out of one's life brought her thousands of converts besides her brother.[71]

From that walk in the woods onward, Jimmy Carter promised to put religion ahead of politics, never again to feel the desolation of a life rooted in personal selfishness void of Christian good works. Carter went door to door witnessing for Jesus in Pennsylvania and Massachusetts, and passed out Bibles in Mexico, initiating lifelong travels in less-developed nations to demonstrate his visceral empathy with the downtrodden of the world. Even as president Carter, who prayed regularly, witnessed for Christ by inviting others to take the savior into their hearts.[72]

Carter naturally adopted Billy Graham, a fellow Southern Baptist, as a Christian model of faith put into direct, uplifting action. Both Carter and Graham fervently believed that Southern Baptist congregations should be integrated. Although Graham was a close friend of Nixon and Ford, he took a shine to Carter when he ran for president in 1976, and their friendship, occasionally strained, blossomed over the years. When Republicans sniped at Carter, Graham took to defending him. Asked during the 1976 presidential campaign whether Carter wore his religious commitment on his sleeve, the Reverend Billy Graham replied, "I don't believe it is on his sleeve, I believe it is in his heart."[73]

Reverend Ariail first became Jimmy Carter's pastor in October 1982, when Ariail moved to Plains. This community of seven hundred supports eight churches, including the Pentecostal "Church of God, the Living God, and the Pillar and Ground of Truth." At the more mainstream Maranatha Baptist, "President Carter and I hit it off from the start," Ariail recalled. "I was surprised by the depth of his Christian commitment." It helped that Ariail and Carter shared an affinity for the loose-knit local congregation over the hierarchy of the Southern Baptist Convention as well as a preference for the modernist New Revised Standard Bible over the more traditional King James version.[74]

In an account of his experiences as the former president's pastor, *The Carpenter's Apprentice* (1996), Ariail explains Carter's religious devotion. "His faith is not a department of his life," Ariail noted, "but really it is the superstructure that holds his whole life together. Miss that metaphor and you miss who he is."[75] Detractors may mock Carter's religious zeal, label him self-righteous and sanctimonious, accuse him of a Christ complex born of the initials J. C., and raise their eyebrows at his pious carpenter act, but to people in the Bible Belt Jimmy Carter makes perfect sense: he is simply a good Christian, an unashamed exemplar of the simple values taught in American Sunday school. "The closest fellowship Rosalynn and I have with those outside our family is through the Maranatha Baptist Church," Carter wrote in *Living Faith* (1996). "But *church* does not mean 'Maranatha' or 'Baptist' or 'Protestant'; it is the totality of those united in the love of Christ."[76]

Those unfamiliar with Carter's brand of open-minded Southern Baptist Christianity sometimes equated him with convulsive trial-by-ordeal Christians who handle rattlesnakes to test their faith, or with right-wing fundamentalists such as the Reverend Jerry Falwell, who rail against homosexuality and abortion. Carter's beliefs were much more inclusive. Carter assailed the religious right as political propagandists more interested in the accoutrements of worldly power than in the love of Jesus Christ. Outraged that these activists— many of them Southern Baptists—tried to justify racist, xenophobic, or militaristic views by quoting Scripture, Carter preached ethnic tolerance, the waging of peace, social justice, and nuclear arms control as the goals compatible with the true Christian mission. "A true Christian loves everybody," Carter says. "Blacks, Mexicans, gays, you must feel compassion for everybody."[77]

The tourists who attended services at Maranatha Baptist Church more often had cameras than crucifixes dangling from their necks, but most came away from Carter's Bible class commenting on what a devoted and humble servant of Jesus Christ he truly was. "The church is the center of our social life," Jimmy told *New York Times* reporter Wayne King in 1989. "It's like breathing for us."[78] It took only one encounter with Deacon Jimmy Carter, usually clad in a golf shirt and blue blazer, at Maranatha—where he mowed the lawn, hand-carved the four wooden collection plates, and served as chairman of the finance committee and member of the deacon board in addition to teaching Scripture—to recognize that he is an authentic religious man of principle.

FOUR

INTERREGNUM

❧

Before leaving office Carter had told Democratic National Committee leaders that he planned to play a "quiet" role in party affairs once he stepped down, and he remained true to his word. The Carters took a sabbatical from politics as they worked on their memoirs. Instead of monitoring the news and keeping up with the Washington grapevine, they rode their bicycles, unearthed arrowheads, and collected old bottles.[1]

Any real effort to draw Carter back into politics—Mark Rosenberg's *New York Times* op-ed piece "Carter for Congress," for instance, which appeared on March 14, 1981—he brushed aside.[2] After all, most Democrats now distanced themselves from Carter. He was labeled a has-been, a former shooting star with not even a tail left to fizzle. "As a political personality, even as a mouthpiece, Jimmy Carter evaporated after his defeat," *Time* magazine senior White House correspondent Laurence Barrett wrote. "History may rehabilitate his record, but to his party in 1981, he was a non-person."[3]

During this time Carter tried his best to keep from commenting on national party politics, but he did dabble now and then. He used his limited influence with the Reverend Jesse Jackson to urge the civil rights leader to exercise his presidential ambitions within the Democratic Party and not as an Independent. Occasionally he supported a friend running for office—his former United Nations ambassador Andrew Young in his successful 1981 bid to be mayor of Atlanta, and his former White House chief of staff Jack

Watson in his failed attempt at governor of Georgia in 1982—but Carter made few endorsements outside his own state.[4]

Not that he was asked to. His own former vice president, Walter Mondale, downplayed his role in the Carter administration when he ran as the Democratic presidential nominee in 1984. Mondale stressed his relatively few policy clashes with Carter: his vehement disapproval of the July 1979 "malaise" speech, in which the president admitted a crisis of confidence; the decision to sell equipment to Saudi Arabia to enhance the offensive capabilities of their F-15 fighter planes; the abortive scheme to deploy the colossal MX missile in a revolving "racetrack" mode at enormous expense; and the final Rose Garden strategy of postponing active reelection campaigning in deference to the hostage crisis. Mondale essentially adopted the position— which wounded Carter—that he would gladly talk about his role as vice president but in no way wanted to be labeled a Carterite.[5] "Mondale was a great vice president," Carter noted, "but in 1984 he felt that for political reasons it was best to keep a distance from me."[6]

Although he generally remained aloof from Democratic politics, Carter did not long refrain from lashing out at Reagan administration policies. The former president did give his successor the customary criticism-free honeymoon through Reagan's first four months in office; after all, Carter was shrewd enough to understand that, given his own low public opinion rating at the time, an attack against Reagan was likely to backfire. The president no doubt would dismiss any disapproval with a nod and a "There you go again."

The spring of 1981 was a disagreeable time for Carter. Day after day the programs and visions of his White House were diluted, eliminated, or reversed by the Republicans as he could only sit idly by and feign indifference. "It was incredibly frustrating watching Reagan's people undermine so much of my agenda," Carter recalled.[7] The list of affronts seemed endless: for instance, the Reagan administration permitted the environmentally unconscionable sale of oil and gas leases on eighty-one tracts off the coast of California; developed closer ties with South Africa's white minority government and reversed the policy of threatening South Africa with sanctions if it did not relinquish control over southwest Africa; denounced Carter's proposed budget for 1982; ended the fifteen-month curb on U.S. grain sales to Russia, imposed on human rights grounds; instituted a new foreign aid program that would send arms to Pakistan and Morocco while greatly reducing economic aid to Zimbabwe; supported international development-bank loans to Argentina, Paraguay, and Uruguay, despite flagrant human rights abuses in those nations; supported Secretary of the Interior James G. Watt's proclamation that he would try to expedite oil and gas exploration on the

Arctic Wildlife Range of Alaska's northeast coast; attempted to cut government grants to the Comprehensive Employment and Training Act Program (CETA); requested a $38 billion increase in military outlays; lifted a ban on export-import bank loans to Chile and embraced that nation's military dictatorship; reappointed Nuclear Regulatory Commission chairman Joseph M. Hendrie, who had been dismissed by Carter for his bungled handling of the Three Mile Island accident; proposed a 50 percent cut in appropriations for the National Endowments for the Arts and Humanities (NEA and NEH); drastically cut housing and development aid; eliminated federal subsidies to help states and cities buy land for parks; dismissed all but one of the Carter administration's thirty politically appointed ambassadors (the exception being Mike Mansfield in Japan); and under Secretary of Education Terrell H. Bell, dismissed proposed regulations that public schools teach foreign-speaking students in their native tongues, and reduced federal spending on education, including curtailing Basic Educational Opportunity Grants and student loans.[8]

It was no surprise that during his eight years in office Reagan never invited Jimmy and Rosalynn to the White House for a state dinner. Carter was infuriated by Reagan's treating him as a nonentity. On one trip to Turkey in 1982 Carter was even given the cold shoulder by Reagan's ambassador Robert Strausz-Hupe, who went so far as to cancel some of his prearranged appointments with the former president, according to the *Chicago Tribune* and *Washington Post*.[9] "We were not even invited to go to the White House when they hung our portraits," Carter informed his Maranatha Baptist Bible class one postpresidential Sunday. "We got no invitation to participate in the ceremonies. They never did tell us that it happened. So I guess President Reagan and Nancy stood around and watched them hang Rosalynn and mine's portrait."[10] He could understand why Herbert Hoover had wept when President Truman called on him for advice after twelve years spent unheeded "in the wilderness."

As president, Carter himself had frequently briefed his Republican predecessors Gerald Ford and Richard Nixon, and had consulted them on such familiar and important matters as the Greek-Turkish NATO dilemma, SALT II negotiations, and the normalization of relations with China. Carter had even personally invited the disgraced Nixon to be his guest at his inauguration; Nixon graciously declined. At one point Nixon kindly told Carter, whom he considered "very tough, very shrewd," that he did not need to be briefed by Hugh Carter Jr., the president's cousin, so often.[11] "Reagan was too petty to consult with Ford, Nixon, or myself," Carter has noted. It did not take long for Carter to develop friendships with Ford and Nixon based on mutual disgust at Reagan's disregard of all of them.[12] "Carter attracted a curious blend of Nixon's admiration and aversion," Monica Crowley wrote in *Nixon Off the Record* (1996). "He respected Carter's integrity, idealism, and sincerity; he disdained his politics, naïveté, and what he perceived as haughty self-righteousness."[13]

Carter spent four months demanding a briefing from the Reagan administration to no avail.[14] Pushed to the limit, he sent word to Zbigniew Brzezinski and Jody Powell in Washington to notify National Security Council adviser Richard V. Allen that he was going to hold a press conference to announce that he had been refused briefings from the White House. The threat worked. Two days later Allen, accompanied by an aide, made his way to Plains. There he found the former president in a surly, no-nonsense, mood.

"He did that strange bulging-of-the-eyes routine with me," Allen recalled, "either consciously to stress a point or unconsciously to reveal his intense frustration at our administration." Allen apologized to Carter for his tardiness in holding the briefing, offering the crisis of the attempted assassination of Reagan by way of explanation. "My guess is that Carter thought Reagan was some movie-star doofus who could only read four-by-six cards," Allen conjectured. "What he failed to understand is that the cards were six by eight and he wrote all the words himself."[15]

After Allen gave the Reagan administration perspective, Carter voiced disagreement over a number of policy issues. Then he specifically asked the NSC adviser to urge Reagan not to attend an upcoming Northern-Southern Hemisphere summit on grounds that the United States would be subjected to a barrage of attacks from the less-developed nations. "Reagan disregarded this advice and was a big hit at the summit," Allen boasted.[16]

The NSC continued to brief Reagan's predecessor on occasion—as it did Nixon and Ford—but the exchanges were never substantive or frequent enough for Carter. "They used to send me this nicely bound pamphlet that was really nothing more than a regurgitation of recent Reagan speeches that had already appeared in the *New York Times*," Carter recalled. "Then they would stick in one or two satellite photographs marked Top Secret, of a Russian IBM site or something like that. The entire charade was insulting and superficial."[17] When told of Carter's lingering hard feelings, Allen dismissed him as a "brooding Democrat repudiated by a Reagan landslide."[18]

Unable to maintain his self-imposed moratorium on criticizing Reagan, on May 17, in an address before the New York Board of Rabbis at the Waldorf-Astoria Hotel, Carter attacked his successor's anti–human rights policies. Naturally, this speech made front-page news in the *New York Times*.[19] Having been urged by members of his erstwhile administration to be candid, Carter came out swinging on July 3, stating in a three-page letter to his former Cabinet officers and senior staff members that the Reagan administration's budget cuts threatened "the poor, the sick, and the unemployed." Sales of conventional weapons abroad were, he opined, "serving, unfortunately, to restore our former reputation as arms merchant to the world." On the human rights front, Carter expressed outrage at an administration official's claim that the Argentine publisher Jacobo Timerman had exaggerated the inhumane treatment he suffered as a political prisoner of the brutal military junta that ruled Argentina from 1976 to 1983. "Most of us felt more comfortable with the good old days when the American government attacked the torturers and sympathized with the tortured," Carter sneered in the letter. Nowhere, however, in this fusillade did Carter mention the president by name.[20]

Jody Powell, at the time acting as Carter's unpaid press secretary, reported that the first draft of the letter had been even more stinging, but friends had convinced the ex-president to tone it down. Even in the bowdlerized version, Secretary of the Interior James Watt took a few gut punches. After excoriating his policies, Carter quipped that Watt thought wilderness was a parking lot with no yellow lines. Carter ended his open missive by letting it be known that when it came to public issues of national security or the environment, he would not keep quiet.[21]

Of all Jimmy Carter's experiences his first year out of office, the visit of Egyptian president Anwar al-Sadat to Plains on August 9, 1981, was the most rejuvenating.[22] The lowland hamlet spruced itself up for the arrival of the Nobel Peace Prize laureate, with Wise and Hochman doing everything from sending out lunch invitations to constructing a dais. Their efforts were rewarded: as soon as he embarked from his helicopter on the Plains softball field, the Egyptian leader kept his promise to pray with Carter on the red-clay soil that afforded his friend such spiritual strength. Carter, beaming all day long, took Sadat on a walking tour of Plains, then hosted a private southern lunch for his colleague at his home. "It was quite an experience," John Pope recalled. "All of Jimmy's friends got to meet Sadat, a real man of peace."[23] Mantels all over Sumter County still boast farmers' souvenir pictures of themselves with Sadat. The visit even had an unintended happy aftermath. "Deen" Day Smith, the widow of Georgia residential builder and Days Inn motel developer Cecil B. Day, who died in 1978, met her future husband Charles O. Smith at the reception Carter gave for Sadat. A supporter of Billy Graham's brand of evangelism, "Deen" Day Smith— who in 1984 would sell her holdings for $600 million—would become one of the principal founders of the Carter Center, donating millions to it over the years.[24]

"Sadat liked three things about Jimmy Carter aside from political considerations," explained Tasheen Basheer, a longtime spokesperson for the Egyptian leader. "First, that he was a small-town farmer type. Sadat did not like slick city boys. Second, that he was a religious man of principle. He has a spiritual core uncontaminated by crude politics. Third, he was a military man. So was Sadat."[25] And aside from the personal gratification, Sadat's visit offered Carter, who was eager to remind the public of his successes, occasion to revisit the Camp David accords—and to accuse the Reagan administration of failing to build on them.

Shortly after Sadat's visit, the Carters headed to China and Japan for two weeks, their first foreign journey since the quick trip to Wiesbaden.[26] The former president intended to talk seriously with Deng Xiaoping, whom he described as a "small, tough, intelligent, frank, courageous, personable, self-assured, friendly man."[27] Carter wanted to reassure Chinese officials that Reagan was not as zealously pro-Taiwanese as his campaign rhetoric may have suggested. Deng knew that as president Carter had taken on the powerful Taiwan lobby, as well as that Carter had recently spoken to high Reagan administration officials about their plans to sell arms to Taiwan. While he was in no sense an official emissary of the Reagan administration, Carter did go to China as a knowledgeable conduit ready to explain U.S. policy.[28]

This postpresidential journey was not Carter's first exposure to China. As a navy lieutenant aboard the USS *Pomfret* in 1949 he had spent a few weeks dockside in the port city of Shanghai, just when the Communist revolution was raging.[29] "Whenever we went to port we would tie up our submarine with the bow pointed out to sea so that we could crank up our engines and take off fast without having to turn around," Carter recalled of those momentous months before Chiang Kai-shek and his nationalist forces fled defeated to the island of Taiwan. One of his most vivid memories was of watching one night from his submarine as the silent city of Quindao, surrounded by the blazing campfires of Mao Tse-tung's army, prepared for the Communists' expected conquest in the morning. "Being in China as Mao was about to take over was quite an experience for a young naval lieutenant," Carter recounted. "But I've always been fond of the Chinese people."[30]

As a boy Carter had heard stories about China from itinerant Baptist missionaries and from his uncle Tom Gordy, a Navy radioman who made frequent port calls to Shanghai and Tsingtao, and he retained an intense fascination with the most ancient of modern civilizations. "Once when we [a group of his Cabinet appointees] were discussing the Far East, I remarked that the people of our country had a deep and natural affection for the people of China," Carter wrote in *Keeping Faith*. "When most of the group laughed, I was perplexed and a little embarrassed. It took me a few, moments to realize that not everyone had looked upon Christian missionaries in China as the ultimate heroes and had not, as youngsters, contributed a penny or a nickel each week, year after year, toward schools and hospitals for little Chinese children."[31] When Deng Xiaoping, an atheist, made his dramatic journey to the United States in January 1979 to celebrate the normalization of relations and discuss the resulting trade issues, he and President Carter had a friendly debate over whether Christian missionaries had had a positive influence on Chinese society. During the course of the conversation Deng promised Carter that under his leadership freedom of worship would be respected and that Bibles would be made widely available throughout China.[32]

On August 24, 1981, Prime Minister Zhao Ziyang and Carter met privately for nearly two hours. Zhao expressed apprehension at reports that the Reagan administration was poised to authorize the sale of advanced fighter planes to Taiwan, but the two men also discovered common interests, including a mutual obsession with daily jogging. That day the two established a friendly rapport that proved lasting, and that night Zhao held a state dinner at the Great Hall of the People to honor Carter's "outstanding contribution" to the U.S.-China reconciliation. "We will never forget it," Zhao said. In response, Carter rose and proclaimed that the Nixon-Kissinger-Carter efforts at cementing Sino-American relations were "of such obvious value" that "the process would be irreversible and able to withstand the inevitable shocks of changing political times."[33]

As the Chinese people warmed to Carter, their press began calling his visit the "Great Reassurance Mission," as he was repeatedly trying to ease Chinese worries about Reagan. Leaving Beijing for Xian to visit the ancient Chin dynasty ruins, Carter admitted that Reagan's campaign slant toward Taiwan had been a "deviation from normalization commitments," but added that "recent developments and explanations of the Reagan policy have been very reassuring to me." All of China's newspapers published front-page photographs of Carter jogging along the 1,500-mile Great Wall. During his private talks with Communist party chairman Hu Yaobang, Prime Minister Zhao Ziyang, Deputy Party Chairman Deng Xiaoping, and Deputy Prime Ministers Huan Hua and Bo Yibo, Carter even swallowed hard and praised Secretary of State Alexander Haig for his understanding of the importance of Sino-American relations. "When it came to harmonious Sino-American relations," Carter noted, "Haig was for it."[34]

The Taiwan arms issue clearly was the most significant problem outstanding between the two nations. Over and over Carter explained to Deng Xiaoping that the Reagan administration's policies toward his country, including the sale of defensive weapons to Taiwan, were compatible with the agreement they had reached in 1979. Deng Xiaoping "never deviated," Carter told reporters, from being "unalterably" opposed to any kind of U.S. military aid to Taiwan.[35]

From his delegation's point of view, Carter's visit was a success. As Jody Powell noted, "The China trip was standard Jimmy Carter—do everything, see everybody, pack in as much work and fun as you could in a sixteen-hour day."[36]

Before he left Georgia, Amnesty International had supplied Carter with the names of Chinese dissidents they considered unjustly imprisoned. Carter pleaded with top officials for their release. "I have brought these things up to let them know I continue to be interested in the degree of human rights protection in China," Carter told the press in Shanghai. He was also able to raise the issue of American scholars routinely being denied access to research materials as well as to interactions with Chinese citizens, and was assured these restrictive policies would be relaxed in the near future. After an initial showdown with Chinese authorities over his freedom of movement, Carter was left unfettered to take daily jogs, bicycle rides, and walks when and wherever he felt like it. His only complaint about modern China, he joked to reporters, was that he couldn't find any peanut butter in Beijing. The next morning a jar was delivered by special messenger to Carter's hotel room.[37]

In Japan as in China, Carter was seen as a peacemaker, not as a failed American ex-president. Appearing on Japanese television in Osaka for a ninety-minute interview, a tanned and congenial Carter discussed everything from his fear of another rise in OPEC oil prices to his dislike of the "weak" and "unpredictable" Ayatollah Khomeini of Iran. None too shy about his administration's geopolitical successes, Carter also asserted that it was the West's unflinching stand against Brezhnev's 1979 invasion of Afghanistan that had kept the Soviets from occupying Poland.[38]

A couple days later Carter spent much of an afternoon discussing trade issues with Japanese prime minister Zenko Suzuki.[39] Respect was accorded to the former president unofficially as well: everywhere he went, the Japanese treated him with the honor due a global statesman. "The Japanese have always been enthusiastically fond of Jimmy Carter," Nobel Prize–winning novelist Kenzaburo Oe explained. "Not only because he was president, but because he is a humble wise man of deep honesty and integrity unusual in the world of politics."[40]

Of course, Carter's interest in Japan predated his presidency. In addition to his work with the Trilateral Commission promoting economic cooperation among the United States, Japan, and Western Europe, Carter was the first Georgia governor to go out and lure Asian businesses to invest in the Peach State. Under Carter's initiative Tokyo (and Brussels) opened trade offices in Atlanta, the new crossroads of the South so determined to transform itself from an old railroad town into an international business mecca worthy of holding global economic summits or even the Olympics.[41] The relentless "pro-Japan" campaign paid off. On October 18, 1974, Governor Carter presided at the groundbreaking ceremony for a YKK Zipper plant in Macon, Georgia, a pants-zipper and extruded-aluminum operation that would eventually expand to more than 2 million square feet of highly automated manufacturing facilities. Carter had unleashed a flow of Japanese investment in the American South.[42]

The owner of YKK, Tadao Yoshida, was a bootstrap industrialist outsider from Japan's business elite who soon became one of Jimmy Carter's closest and most trustworthy counselors as well as his personal guest at the White House on three separate occasions. "The root of my friendship with Tadao Yoshida," Carter noted, "is a firm base of almost identical philosophies about the dignity of man, the spirit of fair play, tenacity in the face of insurmountable odds, loyalty to family, friends, and colleagues, the sanctity of one's world, and the lack of fear of the unknown." Carter continued approvingly, "All of these things were part of Tadao's philosophy, and he often expressed them when speaking about his 'Cycle of Goodness.' "[43]

The two men's bond grew out of the "perfect marriage" of Georgia and YKK. Already impressed with the company he called a "model corporate citizen of Georgia," Carter took Yoshida's warmth and integrity as assurance that YKK would bring "far more than jobs and money to our state." He proved right, and the success in Macon—a city of 53,000 pulled out of a recessionary spiral—encouraged other Japanese companies to invest in Georgia. Before long, only New York, California, and Hawaii enjoyed more Japanese investments than Georgia.[44] Speaking at the Japan Society in New York in 1982 to inaugurate the Ohira Memorial Lecture Series, ex-president Carter stated that "it was my relationship with Tadao Yoshida and YKK that gave me the confidence I had as president in the importance of our country's partnership with Japan."[45]

So citizen Carter, desperate for financial help to build the Carter Center, turned to Yoshida and his son Tadahiro during his September 1981 visit to

Japan. "I felt that they had done so much for our society by bringing a good, solid business to our state, when we needed that so much, that I was hesitant about asking them for support of the center," Carter recalled. "The response I received was typical of Tadao Yoshida, who felt that he was in my debt for having encouraged YKK to come to Georgia." Yoshida agreed to become a founder of the Carter Center, eventually not only providing the exquisite Japanese strolling garden but also donating $2.5 million and spearheading the center's Pacific Basin fund-raising drive. Deeply grateful, Jimmy Carter would communicate with Yoshida regularly throughout his post–White House years, attending YKK's fiftieth-anniversary celebration in May 1984 and personally involving his friend in the Carter Center's July 1985 ground-breaking ceremonies and the grand opening in October 1986.[46]

Upon returning from the Far East, Carter was delighted to learn that Israeli prime minister Menachem Begin would be making a pilgrimage to Plains on September 15. But Carter's misgivings about Begin became apparent when he boldly used the prime minister's visit to criticize recent Israeli air raids on an Iraqi nuclear reactor and on the Lebanese capital of Beirut. Once Begin had grown visibly nervous, Carter pulled back and said that, of course, the attacks were in response to the threat of terrorist strikes against Israel. "We have all been concerned that bloodshed has returned to the area, precipitated by terrorism and suffered primarily by the innocent," Carter elaborated. "The situation is serious, but it is not hopeless, because the people of Israel and your neighbors both want peace."[47]

After lunch Carter and Begin had a private chat, during which the Israeli prime minister revealed that he would soon be ready to discuss the principles for Palestinian self-rule that the Carter administration had proposed a year before. With policy out of the way, Begin turned to politics, signing autographs, kissing babies, and handing out commemorative ribbons before he headed home. For all their pronounced differences, Begin and Carter shared a grudging mutual respect. Still, Carter admitted to a perverse joy that Begin was Reagan's problem now.[48]

The visits of both Sadat and Begin to Plains renewed Carter's involvement with the Middle East, a region he had studied almost all his life. As a reward to himself for finishing *Keeping Faith*, Carter had been planning a trip to Israel and Egypt in the near future. He looked forward to walking the foothills around Capernaum with Begin and to sipping mint tea with Sadat at his boyhood home of Mit Abul-Kum, northwest of Cairo along the main route to Alexandria, which he read about in the Egyptian president's autobiography *In Search of Identity* (1978).[49]

Carter was working in his Plains study on October 6, 1981, when a reporter called to ask his response to the attempted assassination of Sadat. The former president broke out in goosebumps. This was the first he had heard about the hail of automatic gunfire at a military parade in Cairo that left eleven dead and forty wounded. Reassured that his Egyptian friend had "only suffered minor injuries" in the shooting, Carter gave the reporter a short statement denouncing terrorism, then quickly ended the conversation so he could try to reach Sadat in Cairo. Unable to do so, Carter talked to the American ambassador in Egypt, who reassured him that Sadat was alive and that the failed assassins—an Egyptian army major and two enlisted men— had been apprehended. Carter monitored CNN news reports all that afternoon, expecting to hear upbeat updates, when suddenly the tragic news of Sadat's death was announced, the assassins having been identified as religious fanatics opposed to Sadat's peace treaty with Israel and to his recently ordered arrest of 1,500 Coptic and Muslim extremists. Carter sat alone in his study and wept.[50] "It was a great personal loss for me and a severe blow to the prospects for peace in the Middle East," he lamented.[51]

Shortly after the grim announcement, Sadat's widow, Jehan, called Jimmy and Rosalynn and invited them to stay at her Cairo home for the funeral. The Carters were, after all, close to Sadat's entire family, including his children and grandchildren. Shortly thereafter, however, the State Department called. On the grounds that government security agencies deemed it "too dangerous" for Reagan or Bush to make the journey to Egypt, State officials formally requested that Carter join ex-presidents Richard Nixon and Gerald Ford in the official U.S. delegation to the funeral.[52]

This was Alexander Haig's brainchild, and Carter refused. Incensed that Reagan was afraid to make the journey, he was determined to go to the funeral on his own. The State Department mounted a relentless campaign to change his mind: "Ed Muskie and Cy Vance and Jody Powell and Hamilton Jordan and financial contributors to my campaign all called to say I should go with the official delegation," Carter recalled. "So after about the tenth call I decided I would go with Nixon and Ford. I was really aggravated about it, though."[53] Reagan did apologize for staying home at an interfaith memorial service for Sadat at the National Cathedral, where the Reverend John T. Walker, Episcopal bishop of Washington, eulogized the Egyptian president as a "great prophet" for global peace. Before attending the service, Reagan had signed a proclamation instructing that all American flags on government buildings, embassies, and naval ships be flown half-staff. The only foreign citizens previously accorded such an honor were UN secretary Dag Hammarskjöld in 1961 and Winston Churchill in 1965.[54]

Stricken with grief, Jimmy and Rosalynn Carter flew to Washington, D.C., where they met Nixon and Ford for a helicopter ride at dusk to the South Lawn of the White House.[55] Once inside, they traded stories about Sadat with President Reagan in the Blue Room for more than half an hour. "We had a short but necessary meeting with Reagan," Ford recalled. "It was a very wise decision on his part to have us former presidents attend the funeral as a display of continued American support of Egypt."[56] Reagan, in a low-key mood, wished his three predecessors good luck with a toast: "Ordinarily I would wish you happy landing, but you're all navy men, so I wish you bon voyage."[57]

Carter was impressed neither by the occasion, by Reagan's remarks, nor by his own return to the White House. "The only reason Reagan greeted us was to have a photograph of four presidents together," Carter quipped.[58] And the shot would be a rarity: this was the first time in the twentieth century that three former presidents had met with an incumbent. What's more, not since Harry Truman, Dwight Eisenhower, John Kennedy, and then–vice president Lyndon Johnson attended the funerals of former Speaker of the House Sam Rayburn in 1961 and Eleanor Roosevelt in 1962 had so many presidents appeared in the same frame.

It was clear who was in charge on the flight from Andrews Air Force Base to Cairo: Alexander Haig, the official leader of a delegation that included a handful of congressmen and senators, Secretary of Defense Caspar W. Weinberger, ambassador to the UN Jeane Kirkpatrick, army chief of staff General Edward Meyer, former secretary of state Henry Kissinger, Motown singer-composer Stevie Wonder, and a fourteen-year-old boy from Liberty, South Carolina, who had become pen pals with Sadat. Haig claimed the large compartment in the front of the plane for himself, leaving the three former presidents, Rosalynn, and Kissinger to fight for elbow space in the small press compartment.[59]

Nixon noticed that there was some initial tension between Carter and Ford, so he played the icebreaker. "We were all former presidents who served our country well, so there was no reason for any residual bad blood between us," Ford recalled. "Nixon brought us all together."[60] As for the incumbent administration, throughout the flight Reagan's chief of protocol, Lee (Mrs. Walter) Annenberg, continually interrupted the former presidents' conversations and naps with firm instructions from General Haig as to his rules once they arrived in Egypt. "One of the instructions was that when we arrived in Cairo, no one was to get off the plane before Secretary of State Haig," Carter recalled. "He was to get off first, and he was to be the only one to speak to news media. It was ridiculous. He treated us like children."[61]

Upon landing Haig strode off the plane like Douglas MacArthur returning to the Philippines and addressed the press pool assembled at the airport as the three former presidents stood muzzled on the tarmac. When he was finished, Haig waved the former commanders in chief into armor-plated limousines flown in from Washington, which whisked them first to their hotel and then to meet Hosni Mubarak at the Al-Tahara Palace. Cairo was quiet, its streets empty due to the four-day feast of Eld al-Adha, a traditional Muslim observance that not even Sadat's assassination could disrupt. At the palace Mubarak assured the American presidential delegation that he would carry out Sadat's policies, including the Camp David peace accords. Carter felt fully confident of Mubarak's ability to govern Egypt and his own mission to create a Palestinian homeland, as determined at Camp David, in memory of "Brother Anwar."[62]

Immediately after the funeral all the international dignitaries who had descended on Cairo dispersed. Haig stayed on to hold more detailed conversations with Mubarak while Nixon flew to Saudi Arabia to discuss with the Arab monarchs the Reagan administration's proposed sale of AWACs radar-surveillance aircraft to the kingdom. With most of the other notables who had flown over drifting to Europe or lingering in the Middle East, Gerald Ford and Jimmy Carter found themselves with private time on the flight home to discuss everything from Nixon's attempted rehabilitation to reminiscences about life in the White House.[63]

Like Carter four years later, in 1977 Ford had found himself faced with the dilemma of how to begin his private life after losing the presidency. Having spent thirty years as either a member of the House of Representatives, vice president, or president, he considered the Washington, D.C., area home but had to start a new life as a unemployed "former," dividing his time between Grand Rapids, Michigan; Beaver Creek, Colorado; and Palm Springs, California. Ford had telephoned Carter on election night 1976 to concede defeat and promise the incoming Georgian, whom he decidedly disliked, that he could expect a smooth and accommodating transition. "Ford stayed true to his word," Carter noted. "He is a high-caliber man of honor."[64] At Carter's inauguration his first words were directed toward Gerald Ford: "For myself and for our nation I want to thank my predecessor for all he has done to heal our land."[65] Years later Carter would even admit that Ford did the right thing for the country in pardoning Nixon.[66]

An easy camaraderie would develop between Carter and Ford, sustained in the coming years as their wives, Rosalynn and Betty, also became friends,

lobbying together on such worthwhile causes as alcohol and drug prevention, the Equal Rights Amendment, and health care policies toward the
mentally ill. But in October 1981, for a few animated hours aloft, Jimmy and
Jerry traded political war stories, compared their appetites for alpine skiing,
and made plans to collaborate on future projects. "We've made an agreement never to discuss domestic policy issues because the gulf between us is
so wide," Ford recalled. "But on foreign policy our views are similar, so we
can work together on joint projects very effectively."[67]

Carter accepted Ford's offer to cohost an upcoming two-day conference
at his presidential library in Ann Arbor, Michigan; in turn, Ford offered to
cochair Carter Center programs in Atlanta. Later they coauthored articles in
leading periodicals and issued numerous joint statements on everything
from supporting the ERA to criticizing the tobacco lobby. Perhaps presaging
their future cooperation, midway through the Cairo-to-Washington flight
the two ex-presidents held a joint news conference, taking turns answering
questions about the Middle East. The Carter-Ford team even made international news by boldly stating that the United States had to start talking with
the Palestine Liberation Organization (PLO) if any meaningful peace settlement was to be reached in the Middle East. This simple remark—so obvious
in its logic—triggered a swarm of denunciations from the State Department,
not to mention from citizens who considered the PLO a mob of unshaven,
murderous lunatics. "To characterize Palestinians as a body as terrorists is a
fallacious thing to do," Carter said. "This stigmatizes a race of people and is
a racist approach which does damage to the process."[68]

The next day Reagan was forced to clarify his administration's policy.
"There has never been any refusal to talk with the PLO," he noted in annoy-
ance at the Carter-Ford pronouncement. "There has only been a single condition: until they would recognize the right of Israel to exist as a nation,
which they still have never done."[69]

The PLO seized upon the former presidents' remarks to further lend
credibility to its cause. Zehdi Labib Terzi, the PLO's UN observer in New
York, praised Carter and Ford for finally realizing that "there is no way to
peace without discussing the question of Palestine, dealing with the Palestinian people through their representatives, the PLO." Claiming that both
Carter and Ford had been under Zionist pressure not to talk to the PLO
while serving in the White House, Terzi praised them for at last finding the
courage to speak their minds. When news of the Carter-Ford comment
reached PLO leader Yasir Arafat on a trip in Tokyo, he immediately issued a
statement welcoming their intervention and added that he hoped President
Reagan would heed the counsel of these wise elder statesmen. Both Arafat

and Terzi sidestepped reporters' questions about whether the PLO would ever agree to the Reagan administration's condition that it recognize Israel's right to exist.[70]

U pon their arrival at Andrews Air Force Base, Carter and Ford fielded media questions about Sadat's funeral, then parted. Ford headed to Vail, Colorado, while the Carters made their way to downtown Washington for a three-day visit, their first extended stay since leaving office nine months earlier. Making their headquarters in the townhouse across from Lafayette Park reserved for ex-presidents, the Carters experienced the odd sensation of viewing 1600 Pennsylvania Avenue through iron bars.

Carter was ostensibly in town to lobby senators to support the sale of AWACs radar surveillance aircraft to Saudi Arabia; to denounce Reagan's decision to build the B-1 bomber, which he had cancelled, as a "gross waste" of money; and to attend a Democratic fund-raiser at Esther Coopersmith's Potomac, Maryland, mansion.[71] Coopersmith's theme was a nostalgic re- union for the Carter administration: there were peanut-shaped cakes, and green-and-white Carter-Mondale buttons were pinned to every dinner guest. The fund-raiser gave Jimmy and Rosalynn a chance to catch up with friends like pollster Pat Caddell and former White House assistant Anne Wexler. "The style of the evening, which would have been in fashion here just a year ago, was noticeably at odds with President Reagan's Washington," Lynn Rosellini reported in the New York Times. "No limousines were in evi- dence. Unlike their clean-cut Republican counterparts, some of the Carter men had shaggy haircuts. And not only was Mr. Carter the centerpiece of the evening, he was also the centerpiece on the tables—each was decorated with a pumpkin drawn with a grinning Carter face."[72]

The real Jimmy Carter was also in a smiling mood. After suffering through four years of what he considered "biased and unfair reporting" on his administration by the Washington Post, he was planning to sue the news- paper for libel, and many legal analysts believed he had a good chance of winning his case.[73] "Jimmy Carter's declared intention to sue the Washing- ton Post for libel has piqued the public appetite for a great case," New York Times columnist Anthony Lewis wrote just as the matter started heating up.[74] The only other ex-president to file a libel claim against a newspaper was Theodore Roosevelt, who sued Michigan editor George Newett in 1913 for publishing erroneous allegations that Roosevelt was a drunkard.[75]

The controversy began over an item in "The Ear," a popular gossip column the Post had picked up from the defunct Washington Star. On Octo- ber 5—the day before Sadat was shot—"Ear" columnist Diana McClellan reported that the Carter administration had bugged Blair House, the president's official guest residence since 1942. "The Ear" claimed that after Carter lost the 1980 presidential election, he offered Blair House to Ronald and Nancy Reagan as a transition headquarters. Shortly after the Reagans unpacked, Helen Thomas of UPI reported that Nancy wanted the Carters to vacate the White House early so she could start redecorating. Nancy denied any such lèse majesté, and the story died until "The Ear" resurrected it with a "hot new twist" nine months later: "They're saying that Blair House, where Nancy was lodging—and chatting up First Decorator Ted Graber—was *bugged*. And at least one tattler in the Carter tribe has described listening to the tape itself."[76]

The day after the column appeared, an outraged Jimmy Carter asked his able young Washington-based attorney, Terrence Adamson, to slap a seven-figure libel suit on the *Washington Post* for "scurrilous, irresponsible falsehoods," regardless of whether the paper issued a public apology.[77] "I don't want to sound maudlin, but as a former president I don't have much money, just my privacy and my reputation," Carter explained in a public interview at the time. "It really hurt me in this country and throughout the world to say I would stoop so low as to eavesdrop on the conversations of my successor."[78] The next day a front-page headline of the *Miami Herald* read: "Gossip Item Has Carters in Mood to Sue."[79]

What transpired over the next nineteen days was soap-opera-cum-brinkmanship. Ever since the *Post*, with a circulation of 730,000, had broken the Watergate burglary story that eventually led to Nixon's resignation, many perceived a new brashness in the paper. "The *Post* is suffering from radiation, or smart-ass sickness after overlong exposure to Nixon & Co.," British commentator Alistair Cooke put it in 1978. David Halberstam, in *The Powers That Be* (1983), mused that "perhaps Watergate had brought the paper too much glamour, too much success."[80] Just prior to the Carter libel suit Sally Quinn of the *Post* had published an erroneous account of Zbigniew Brzezinski's purported lewd sexual misbehavior—the retraction of which *Post* employees called "The Erection Correction"—as well as a totally fabricated, if Pulitzer Prize–winning, story by reporter Janet Cooke about an eight-year-old heroin addict, a gaffe that called for an eight-page correction. The public was ripe to see the prestigious paper taken to the woodshed, and Carter seized the moment.[81]

Understandably indignant over the false report—which if true deserved to be front-page news—Carter demanded a public apology. The *Post*'s executive editor, Benjamin C. Bradlee, refused. "How do you make a public apology?" he said in response to Carter. "Run up and down Pennsylvania Avenue bare-bottomed shouting, 'I'm sorry'?"[82] Adamson told CNN that he replied, "I would like to present that proposal to my client." While the *Post* "began to trap themselves in this huge box," Adamson made plans to file Carter's libel suit against the newspaper in U.S. District Court in Americus, where a jury of Georgians would decide the case.[83] In a letter seeking a retraction and an apology from Katharine Graham, chairman of the Washington Post Company, Adamson wrote that the bugging report was "false, defamatory, and libelous *per se.*"[84]

Larry Speakes, then deputy White House press secretary, aided Carter's case by announcing that the White House knew of "no evidence" that the Reagans' conversations at Blair House had been secretly taped.[85] Washington superlawyer Lloyd Cutler (Carter's former White House counsel and sometime legal defender of the *Post*) stepped into the fray as mediator, urging Bradlee to make amends with an editorial.[86] "The whole damn thing was getting out of hand," Bradlee recalled. "The Grahams did not feel like getting sued by a president."[87]

On October 14, after relentless cajoling by Cutler, the *Post* ran an editorial meant to placate Carter. The page-leading piece stated that, upon further examination, the paper's editors found it "utterly impossible to believe" the bugging rumor they had carelessly printed two weeks before.[88] To Cutler's dismay, Carter felt "baffled" by this "feeble attempt at apology," which he claimed only compounded the offense.[89] "It's clear that the *Washington Post* has decided not to retract its original story and not apologize for it," Carter told reporters outside a townhouse at Jackson Square as he prepared to leave for Pennsylvania for a fishing trip while Rosalynn headed back to Plains to work on her autobiography. "The matter is certainly not closed," he warned.[90] The *Post* was now in a murky legal situation. Because the editorial, composed by Meg Greenfield, explicitly stated that the *Post* did not believe Carter had bugged Blair House, the newspaper had foolishly exposed itself to a finding of "actual malice": publishing a defamatory report about a public figure "with knowledge that it was false or reckless regardless of whether it was false." Greenfield's editorial, which she later conceded was "badly thought out and badly written," was an outright admission that the *Post* considered the Blair House bugging rumor false but went ahead and published it as a rumor anyway.[91]

Refusing to duel with Carter any longer, *Post* publisher Donald E. Graham hewed to the line, "The editorial speaks for itself."[92] Carter, meanwhile, was finding helpful allies for his libel suit in journalists all over town, and among editorial writers nationwide. Carl Bernstein, half of the *Post*'s Pulitzer Prize–winning Watergate investigative team, denounced "The Ear" as "a gossip column where there is no attempt by the people who write the column to check the facts, one of the most basic reporting tools."[93] On his

Washington-based political TV chat show, *Agronsky & Company*, Martin Agronsky asked his four panelists from the press—Hugh Sidey, James J. Kilpatrick, Carl Rowan, and George F. Will—if *they* would have passed along the rumor that Carter had bugged Blair House. Naturally, they responded with a stinging chorus of nos. What made this nationally syndicated moment so remarkable was that *Agronsky & Company* was produced and owned by the Washington Post Company, and all the panelists except Sidey wrote columns for the *Post*. Will vented the most outrage, declaring that "printing gossip is pandering to the voyeurism of a celebrity-struck public. When you combine [this] with the doctrine that says we are not responsible for the factual nature of the rumor at all, only for the fact that it is a rumor, then you have given your gossip columnist a license to disseminate lies."[94]

Under siege or not, the *Post* held firm on the bugging story, insisting McClellan got it firsthand from two members of Carter's immediate family: his wife, Rosalynn, and his faith-healing sister, Ruth Carter Stapleton. "I've been hearing from the highest principled people in the world," Bradlee argued. "They raise the question: is a gossip column fit for human consumption in Washington, D.C.? Gossip is the biggest industry in town! I don't want to edit the dullest, stuffiest, intellectualist paper around."[95] A line had been drawn, and a long legal battle was sure to ensue.

At issue was the question of whether the reporting of gossip could be considered news. The *Post* stonewalled on a direct apology for the item for two and a half weeks, while Carter, as Bradlee put it, "picked us off first base."[96] An abrupt change in attitude occurred when Bradlee ventured to Princeton, New Jersey, to confer with his source, Dotson Rader, a freelance writer who had recently done a postpresidential profile of the Carter family for *Parade* magazine. Rader remembered Bradlee telling him that "his tail was in a crack and I had to get it out" by divulging his sources in an affidavit for the court. Rader refused, adding that he would go to jail before revealing such information. Bradlee turned another shade of pale when the reporter mentioned that his sources had never actually used the word "bugging"; rather, they had heard that tapes existed of a conversation between Nancy Reagan and her interior decorator. "He said he didn't see any difference— 'bugged' or 'taped'—but there was a *big* difference," Bradlee concluded, realizing for the first time that his newspaper was in the wrong.[97]

A dejected Bradlee now wondered if he *would* have to streak down Pennsylvania Avenue to end "Gossipgate." He returned to Washington and moved swiftly. Famed lawyer Edward Bennett Williams was despatched to resolve the matter. He called and then went to Adamson's Pennsylvania Avenue office, where the two of them, with an occasional call to their clients, worked out the terms of resolution. The next day, October 22, the *Post* ran a front-page news story describing the letter of retraction and apology *Post* publisher Donald Graham had just written the Carters. Without naming Rader, Graham confessed that the *Post's* information had come from "a source whom we believed to be credible and reliable. We now believe the story he told us to be wrong and that there was no 'bugging' of Blair House during your Administration." The Graham letter, as Carter had requested, also included a repudiation of the policy contained in the editorial that rumors believed to be false could be published.[98]

Vindicated, Carter accepted the *Post's* tardy apology, announcing that he would drop his libel suit. "The *Post* learned a much-needed lesson in journalistic responsibility," Carter later noted proudly.[99] Terrence Adamson, who had done an effective job of presenting Carter's case, offered Meg Greenfield, who had got caught in the middle of something larger, an olive branch in the form of a letter on November 13 saying he had "very high regard" for her.[100]

While *Jimmy Carter v. "The Ear"* was not likely to vie for space in the history books with *Marbury v. Madison* and *Brown v. Board of Education*, it was an important case with far-reaching implications. Because Blair House is also Washington's official residence for foreign dignitaries, any bugging there would be a gross violation of protocol and a stain on the image of the U.S. government around the world. Foreign visitors would be afraid to speak openly in their quarters. Carter had never forgiven the *Post* for attacking Bert Lance's ethics, falsely accusing Hamilton Jordan of using cocaine in a New York discotheque, continually humiliating his brother Billy for public amusement, and insinuating that he played martyr during the Iran hostage crisis to attract votes. The popular victory over Bradlee was thus something to savor.

The momentous events of Carter's October—Sadat's assassination, forging a friendship with Ford, journeying to the Middle East, establishing a fund for the Carter Library, whipping the *Washington Post*—helped inspire Carter to formulate an activist agenda for the following year. While in Washington in October he also met briefly with Reagan in the Oval Office to discuss the proposed deal to sell AWACs to Saudi Arabia, and once again came away astonished that anyone so stupid could become president.

For the first time since leaving it, Carter seemed to be relishing life outside the White House, with its freedom to comment at will. "This administration and what it stands for, in my judgment, is an aberration of the political scene," Carter told staff members of the Democratic National Committee in Washington, grinning like his own caricature. In December, during a talk in New York before the Council on Foreign Relations, Carter lambasted the Reagan administration again for its "one-sided attitude of belligerence toward the Soviet Union." He also voiced deep concern over "radical changes" in American foreign policy in Poland, Latin America, Africa, and the Middle East. Rosalynn even got into the act, labeling the Reagan administration's repeal of the Mental Health Systems Act a "tragedy."[101]

What the Carters had learned during the fall of 1981 was that they had a role to play in both national and international affairs: there *was* life after the White House. Suddenly, they saw that it had meaning to be the opposition, to serve as voices in protest crying for human rights and democracy building abroad and for compassion toward the less fortunate at home. And, thanks to modern communications by computer, satellite, and WATTS lines, the Carters could speak out on the business of Jimmy Carter's unfinished presidency from their Atlanta offices and even from their home in Plains. "I have found every aspect of Plains life better than I anticipated," Carter told the press that October.[102] The despair and drifting were over.

FIVE

BUILDING FOR PEACE

❦

As Rosalynn Carter tells the story, the "grand notion" of the Carter Center came to her husband in the course of a fitful night's sleep early in January 1982. Plains had been hit with an unusual cold spell, and Jimmy was focused painfully on the looming deadline for *Keeping Faith*. After tossing and turning for hours, he suddenly sat up in bed. "What's the matter?" Rosalynn asked. "Are you sick?" He answered "no" in a euphoric tone, the same one she had heard in 1972 when her husband had told her he intended to run for president. "I know what we're going to do with the library," Carter continued decisively. "We're going to make it a place to resolve conflicts. There is no place like that now. If there had been such a place, I wouldn't have had to take Begin and Sadat to Camp David. There have been a lot of new theories on conflict resolution developed since that time, and we might put some of them to work."[1]

This folksy account of the Carter Center as "a germ of an idea born in the middle of the night" belies the institution's complex origins. Since the waning days of his presidency, Jimmy Carter had wanted to create a nonprofit "global action institute" completely distinct from his presidential library. As his longtime political mentor Charles H. Kirbo recalled, "Jimmy became interested in establishing some kind of public policy institute in the immediate wake of the 1980 election. What perplexed him was the precise mission it would take—how it would be structured."[2] In search of ideas, the Carters visited more than fifty benevolent foundations and spoke with conflict resolution specialists at Harvard University and democracy theorists at George Mason University. His former deputy secretary of state, Warren Christopher, was soon to become president of the board of trustees at Stanford University and gave Carter a detailed analysis of Stanford's connection with the Hoover Institute. Carter was intrigued by this model, although he saw his center as less academic and more result oriented.[3]

What Carter really wanted to do was duplicate Camp David in Atlanta, creating a center that would serve as a neutral forum within which hostile groups could meet to explore common approaches to problems. Since the U.S. government was constantly involved with managing the larger international conflicts, Carter wanted to resolve civil wars and legal disputes between the poorest countries in the world, those forgotten places like Ethiopia and Sudan. Carter wanted to be a peacemaker, even if it meant inviting African warlords or Latin American despots to Atlanta. After all, when Anwar al-Sadat visited the White House for the first time, most Americans viewed all Arabs, including the Egyptian president, as Islamic fanatics and petroleum thieves. Sadat changed that image forever at Camp David, where he became a heroic martyr to peace. As Carter envisioned it in 1982, his conflict resolution center would be a place where adversaries courageous enough to sit down with their enemies could search for common ground.[4]

First, however, Carter needed to raise millions to construct the center. "Asking for money is excruciatingly painful," Carter later commented. "It's just the worst task in the world."[5] Nevertheless, he proved to have quite a gift for unearthing donors over the next few years, with the constant assistance of Tennessean Jim Brasher III, the development officer who had directed the $60 million 1979 United Negro College Fund campaign and who would eventually help the center library amass $28 million. An early $5 million gift from Robert Woodruff, the Coca-Cola Company's philanthropic CEO, provided a fast start.[6]

Most of the individuals who had given generously for Carter's 1980 campaign, however, still felt cheated by his loss and were not interested in investing in the whims of a defeated candidate. This cold political reality hurt Carter; more than a little naively, he had assumed these big contributors were his friends. The harshest blow came from Tom Watson Jr. of IBM, who stiffly refused to serve as chairman of the fund-raising campaign. "When 'Mr. Tom' turned him down, Carter was embarrassed to talk to others," Brasher recalled.[7] In fact, Hamilton Jordan had advised Brasher to "throw that campaign-contribution list away," because "the people who gave money to President Carter the winner were not interested in ex-president Carter the loser."[8] Brasher took Jordan's sage advice and pointed Carter away from political cronies and toward the foundation world, where he appealed for funding from forty-three grant-giving institutes from the spring of 1982 to early 1983.[9]

Meeting with a number of foundation executives forced Carter to further conceptualize and clarify his mission. David Hamburg at the Carnegie Corporation of New York and Frank Harris of the Ford Foundation made particular impressions, listening with interest as Carter spoke of using Camp David as a model for a conflict resolution center.[10] In 1982 thirty major civil wars (a designation indicating at least a thousand battle-related deaths annually) as well as more than eighty "lesser" conflicts raged. The foundation pros convinced Carter that, provided he didn't duplicate the efforts of such other institutions as the World Bank and the United Nations, he could fill a niche with an organization aimed at breaking international logjams through back-channel mediation. In the end, after Coca-Cola it was America's Big Six foundations—Carnegie, Ford, Rockefeller, MacArthur, Mott, and Hewlitt—that had the faith in ex-president Carter to turn on the money spigot so he could start institutionalizing his vision.[11]

While Carter still had to kowtow to the corporate and foundation worlds, for consolation he had carte blanche to be rude to the press. On one fundraising trip to Chicago, as he disembarked from the commercial flight at O'Hare, still carrying his own bag, he was greeted by a swarm of reporters, photographers, and television crews clamoring to interview him about Reagan's first hundred days. One TV reporter anxious to start filming said, "Mr. President, you're too close. Could you step back a couple of feet?" Carter, his face red, shot back, "Hell, no. *You* step back two feet!" The incident led, as Carter recalled, to "a delightful realization that I didn't need to let reporters push me around anymore."[12]

After securing corporate and foundation support, Carter hosted a well-publicized and creative fund-raising event that took place at Sotheby Parke Bernet's haute auction house in New York. The evening included the auction of three hundred eclectic lots of items donated by the rich and famous. The event was conceived by Carleton Varney, the interior designer who had planned the decor for White House parties during the Carter administration, and it netted $320,000. The auction dinner was fully underwritten by Saudi Arabian businessman and arms dealer Adnan Khashoggi, then among the world's richest men. "I intend to spend the rest of my life working in this place," Carter told the Sotheby's crowd. "But it's not a monument to me. I consider it to be my contribution to my state and the nation for allowing me to serve as president of the United States."[13]

Jordan understood, better than anyone else, Carter's burning ambition and stout dedication to continue to be a world peacemaker. In a February 25, 1982, memorandum Jordan essentially laid out the necessary

parameters for establishing a conflict resolution center, and warned Carter
to somehow try to contain his ingrained penchant for overbooking, over-
committing, and overshooting. "It would be a big mistake for the institute to
be all things to all people," Jordan warned. "Fifty or one hundred years from
now, the work of that same institute will be significant not because your
grandchildren sit on the board of governors. It will be significant because of
the standard of work and excellence created at the outset and sustained."
Echoing Ralph Waldo Emerson, Jordan reminded Carter that "an institution
is the lengthened shadow of one man."[14]

Carter's proposed site for his conflict resolution center covered 219 vacant
acres between downtown Atlanta and Emory University, on the small
crest from which General William Tecumseh Sherman watched Atlanta
burn to the ground in 1864. But Carter was suddenly blindsided by a chorus
of complaints from residents who opposed the construction of the 2.4-mile
parkway through their neighborhood, which was needed to make the library
and policy center easily accessible to three major interstate highways for the
anticipated 600,000 visitors a year. To Carter's consternation, more than
eight hundred Emory faculty and staff members signed a petition in support
of the antiroad coalition, which called itself Caution. The four-lane parkway,
these opponents said, would not only harm the environment right away but
would also eventually lead to an extension through nearby Druid Hills, destroying the posh Atlanta neighborhood where many of them lived. "Jimmy
was so upset about the highway dispute that he told me he was considering
just not having a library or policy center," Rosalynn recalled.[15]

Acrimony over the access road continued even after the Georgia Department of Transportation officially approved it on July 15, 1982. Shortly thereafter a neighborhood coalition called Road Busters convinced the city
council to halt Presidential Parkway construction temporarily due to a number of irregularities surrounding the approval of the road and the bids to
build it from construction companies. Eventually, bulldozers and concrete
mixers appeared on the site, and it was clear that the road would go through.
Nevertheless, throughout 1985 attempts at sabotage by the neighborhood
antiroad groups became so frequent that the Shepard Construction Company, which had won the road-building contract, was forced to hire private
security officers to protect survey sticks from being pulled up and sand from
being poured into construction vehicles' gasoline tanks.[16]

Carter, nettled to the extreme, decided to fight back like a rough-and-
tumble ward politician. He lobbied the Atlanta City Council, Judge William
Clark, and even White House Chief of Staff James A. Baker III—initiating

what would soon become a highly efficacious working relationship—to make sure the federal Council on Environmental Quality approved the parkway. Andrew Young, then mayor of Atlanta, also came to Carter's defense, arguing that the road would benefit the entire city. By the time the Carter Presidential Center officially opened in October 1986, Caution had the proposed roadway tied up in the courts. It was not until 1996, as the Olympics loomed, that the Department of Transportation and Caution finally agreed to compromise. The result, the Freedom Parkway, was completed before the games began.[17]

The Carter Presidential Center consists of two distinct but adjacent entities: the Carter Center (a private, nonprofit, nongovernmental organization affiliated with Emory University) and the Jimmy Carter Library and Museum (owned and operated by the U.S. National Archives and Records Administration).°[18] Congress had stipulated in 1955 that once a presidential library was built and its records deeded, it would be turned over to the National Archives, which would process the documents, make them available to scholars, and curate a museum. Carter abided by this mandate with scant enthusiasm. "Unlike the Carter Center, I never took much direct interest in the library," Carter noted, "yet I was deeply involved in selecting the appropriate architectural firm to design the building complex."[19]

A procession of representatives from four top architectural firms had presented Jimmy and Rosalynn with possible visions for the Carter Presidential Center complex: one was a towering spire topped by a cross, a Star of David, and a Muslim crescent, heavy-handedly symbolizing the Camp David accords; another planned a glass atrium similar to the John F. Kennedy Presidential Library in Boston. Carter grimaced at them all. "When he said he didn't want a monument, he clearly meant it more than I imagined," Rosalynn noted.[20] The problem was solved by Christopher Hemmeter, a flamboyant developer from Hawaii.

By the early 1980s Hemmeter had become known as the Walt Disney of the Hawaiian luxury resort world, having amassed a fortune upward of $200 million in destination resort hotels, earning him a spot on *Forbes* magazine's list of the four hundred richest Americans.[21] Jimmy and Rosalynn took an immediate liking to Chris and Patsy Hemmeter when they met the developer at a CEO convention in late 1981, and were impressed by the distinctive, opulent architectural style of the couple's Hawaiian properties. Carter

---

°The original Articles of Incorporation for the Carter Center were registered in the State of Georgia in October 1981 under the name "Carter Presidential Library, Inc." but in April 1987 were changed to "The Carter Center, Inc." No wonder the public has been confused as to the difference between the Carter Center and the Carter Library.

asked Chris Hemmeter if he would come to Plains to help judge the architectural designs being submitted for his presidential center. Hemmeter agreed, assuming he would never hear from the former president again.[22] But Jimmy Carter did contact him, and a week later the venture capitalist found himself in Plains with the disgruntled former president: "I would never set foot in any of them," Carter said about the first round of designs.

After listening carefully to why Carter was disenchanted with the work of the four architecture firms, which had each spent six months on the project, Hemmeter offered to try his hand at a draft. "Give me a week," he asked Carter, then left Plains to hole up for the next six days at his small office in downtown Aspen, Colorado.[23]

Fusing classical and contemporary design with some clear influence of Frank Lloyd Wright, Hemmeter's blueprint showed four saucer-shaped one-story buildings arranged in a graceful semicircle and linked by walkways surrounded by gardens of azaleas and sunflowers. Set in the shadow of Atlanta's shiny downtown skyscrapers, so symbolic of the New South, the similarly significant Carter Presidential Center would include an exquisitely landscaped arboretum complete with a 2.5-acre lake, a double-colonnade entranceway to give the impression of a cloister lined with all fifty state flags, an elegant reflecting pool and fountain, and inviting wooden benches placed beneath weeping willows and crepe myrtles. (Ultimately, the wealthy Yoshida family—who owned businesses in Georgia—donated a garden designed by Japan's "national treasure" Kinsaku Nakane, who personally placed the seven hundred tons of stone needed to create the distinctive garden.)[24]

In addition to ample museum display space and a full-scale replica of the White House Oval Office, the library would hold a glass-walled research room where the general public could see firsthand how 27 million presidential documents—a staggering 13,500 cubic feet of paper—are preserved. As Hemmeter envisioned it, the Carter Library would also be a teaching center, complete with interactive technology that would allow schoolchildren to participate in town hall meetings with a Max Headroom–style video image of President Jimmy Carter, which would give prerecorded responses to a user-friendly menu of questions. The idea was that the museum would provide general history lessons about Carter and bring to life the institution of the presidency.[25]

What Hemmeter envisioned, and ultimately created, was a futuristic architectural piece for cosmopolitan Atlanta—and it took some time for urban traditionalists to warm to the ultramodern structure. Atlanta magazine, for example, later opined that the Carter Center complex looked like a "stack of dinner plates knocked askew across the top of Copenhill."[26]

The Carters loved Hemmeter's innovative design from its unveiling, but they had one concern: that they would be insulting first-rate Georgia architecture firms by signing with an outfit based in Hawaii. Hence, a collaborative deal was struck between the Atlanta architecture firm Jova-Daniels-Busby and Hemmeter's Honolulu-based Lawton-Unemura-Yamamato to build the Carter Presidential Center, with all construction jobs going to AFL-CIO-card-carrying Georgians.

Over the next few years Carter and Hemmeter would travel together to the Middle East and Asia, attend Super Bowls, backpack in the Rockies, and discuss politics in Bonn with Chancellor Helmut Kohl and economics in Britain with Prime Minister Margaret Thatcher.[27] Hemmeter was flying high—perhaps too high. In many ways an unrealistic, impractical man full of grand visions but with modest financial savvy, Hemmeter began making outlandish business investments, funded by junk bonds, to build casinos in Colorado and New Orleans. The developer who had the magic touch with Hawaiian megaresorts and with Jimmy Carter found himself nearly bankrupt by 1995.[28]

B y 1985 Jimmy Carter had a physical model of the complex but had yet to delineate how to operate his Camp David–like nongovernmental institute. To formulate its mission, the former president drew from a variety of feelings: the optimism of the Camp David peace process and the pessimism of the *Global 2000 Report* he had commissioned as president; his evangelical Christian-activist philosophy and his scholarly approach to the Bible; the civil rights legacy of Dr. Martin Luther King Jr. and the spiritual resolve of Anwar al-Sadat; the economic lessons learned by serving on the Trilateral Commission and the engineer's approach to problem solving acquired from his mentor, Admiral Hyman G. Rickover. Behind all these influences lay the example of his resolutely independent mother, Miss Lillian, known in the late 1970s at "First Mother of the World."

"More than anyone else, my mother made me see the inequities around us," Carter has noted.[29] A longtime civil rights activist, liberal admirer of the Kennedys, and registered nurse and director of a nursing home in Blakely, Georgia, Miss Lillian spent her life aiding the impoverished and championing the needy regardless of race, social status, gender, religion, or nationality. One night—at age sixty-seven—she had been watching television when she saw a public service announcement recruiting Peace Corps volunteers with the slogan "Age Is No Barrier." She determined to sign up then and there. "I wanted to work with people who were the underdogs," she said at the time.[30] Without hesitation she quit her job, turned Carter's peanut warehouse over to her sons Billy and Jimmy, and prepared to take Peace Corps training courses in Chicago before moving to Bombay.

Miss Lillian left for Vikhroll, India, in September 1966 and did not return for almost two years. She looked frail but was filled with impassioned tales of her relief work in a land she previously had known only through the stories of Rudyard Kipling. "My going to India strengthened my faith in God, and made my relationships with other people take on real meaning," she had written to Gloria.[31] One of her primary tasks had been to inoculate Indian children against polio, measles, and tuberculosis while simultaneously working with a missionary zeal at an unsanitary makeshift clinic for lepers. She was also responsible for "family planning," teaching contraception to male workers and assisting with vasectomies.[32]

Jimmy Carter, then waging his first campaign for governor of Georgia, had given his mother a Phillips Bible as a going-away gift, which she used in reading New Testament passages aloud to curious Hindus, who then shared with her the wisdom of the Bhagavad-Gita. Deeming jewelry an arrogant insult to the poor, the white-haired matriarch usually wore a simple light green nurse's uniform, occasionally draping a cashmere shawl around her slight shoulders during the rainy season. She walked four miles through city slums almost every day, sometimes passing out candy and clinic supplies to eager children. Some in the Peace Corps began referring to her as "Mother India." While she was there, Miss Lillian wrote to Gloria that "Hinduism is seeping into my dormant mind," and she began attending lectures by a local swami. She learned about the life of Mahatma Gandhi, met the great Swami Chinmayananda, learned how to speak Marathi and some of the Gujarati dialects, and tried to teach the local populace about the need for proper sanitary conditions, to help prevent dysentery and other dreaded diseases.[33] "My time in India meant more to me than any other thing in my life," Miss Lillian noted some years after her return to the United States.[34]

Jimmy Carter had always been fascinated by Christian missionaries, and he was extremely proud of his mother's Peace Corps service. When her peers were playing canasta in Boca Raton, she was making a real difference in a neglected corner of the world. Although he realized that his policy institute could never sponsor a program as large as the Peace Corps, Carter hoped it would be able to tangibly improve the lives of those suffering in less-developed nations. "If I had one wish for my children, it would be that each of you would dare to do the things and reach for goals in your own lives that have meaning for you as individuals, doing as much as you can for everybody, but not worrying if you don't please everyone," Miss Lillian had written Gloria from Bombay. Jimmy, very much his mother's son, never forgot those wishes.[35] While Jimmy was in the White House his mother, building on her Peace Corps work, toured five African nations promoting public health and global love to the world's neediest people. "Hunger and poverty are things I cannot live with, and I cannot live with myself unless I work to do something about them," she told the press upon her return.[36] And after Jimmy lost to Ronald Reagan in 1980 she encouraged him to have the Carter Center of Emory University help Africans advance from poverty to prosperity.

Founded in the town of Oxford on the edge of the Appalachian wilderness by an act of the Georgia Assembly in 1836—when Texas was still part of Mexico and before Atlanta even existed—Emory College was originally a postsecondary school where students could combine farmwork with a college-preparatory curriculum. By the mid-1980s Emory University ranked among the top twenty-five institutions of higher learning in the United States. Modeled after England's venerable Oxford University, over the years Emory, a Methodist school, had attained a global reputation for innovation and excellence. Alumni include Harry Truman's vice president, Alben Barkley; eminent historian C. Vann Woodward; Thomas Jefferson scholar Dumas Malone; Booker Washington biographer Louis Harlan; Speaker of the House Newt Gingrich; and Senator Sam Nunn. But never in its illustrious history had an event at Emory generated as much national attention and local commotion as the announcement in April 1982 that a former president would be teaching courses on campus.[37]

Carter was to hold seminars and give lectures in classes on ethics, theology, government, and international affairs—in short, he would be a wandering sage. Emory president James T. Laney introduced the former president to the press in April 1982, triggering Carter to use for the first time what would become one of his favorite opening lines: "Hello. My name is Jimmy Carter. I'm a professor at Emory University—only four years sooner than I wanted."[38] Over the ensuing years, and despite often difficult circumstances, particularly their searing disagreements about building what became the Freedom Parkway, the bond between Carter and Laney would continue to grow.

Laney had first met Carter in 1972 when he invited the Georgia governor to address a Yale alumni seminar in Atlanta. "I was incredibly impressed with Carter's style and grace in sophisticated company from the East," Laney recalled.[39] The next time they met was in 1979, when Emory conferred an honorary doctorate upon President Carter. Laney was subsequently invited to the White House on two occasions in 1980, and in 1981 he cleverly arranged for Hamilton Jordan to spend a year on campus as a visiting faculty member while he wrote his book, *Crisis: The Last Year of the Carter Presidency*, which would become a best-seller. So it was that when other universities tried to lure Carter to join their faculties, his close confidant Jordan sang the praises of Emory from personal experience. "I think that I am the only person that understands the depth of your own interests in this institute and also has some appreciation for Emory's assets, interests, and special needs," Jordan wrote Carter in February 1982. "I know that you and Jim Laney share the same dream for the institute which will be affiliated with both the Carter Library and Emory University."[40]

As Jordan inferred, a certain commonality of experience joined the two men. Laney was from the hardscrabble cotton town of Wilson, Arkansas, moving to Memphis during World War II, where in high school he became very interested in the Bible. Laney won a scholarship to Yale University, but his Ivy League education was interrupted by a stint in the Army Counter-Intelligence Corps in Korea from 1947 to 1948. A Korean War veteran, he earned his degree in divinity at Yale in 1954 and then, influenced by his Methodist minister grandfather, became determined to study how the life of Christ could be applied to the modern daily grind. Eventually he returned to South Korea in 1959 for a five-year stint teaching theology at Yonsei University.

Laney was appointed president of Emory in 1977, initiating a sixteen-year era of unprecedented growth and development for the university in myriad areas. Within two years of his appointment, Coca-Cola heirs Robert W. Woodruff and his brother George—Atlanta's premier moguls and the South's wealthiest philanthropists—donated $105 million to the university, at the time the largest gift ever made to an American educational institution. The conscientious new president wanted to make sure the Woodruffs' munificence was allocated "solely to promote greater excellence in the academic programs of the university." Over the next fifteen years Laney would administer Emory's endowment as it grew from $178 million to $1.76 billion, the sixth largest in the country. Determined to make Emory the "Harvard of the South," Laney appointed to the faculty such world-renowned scholars as translator and classicist William Arrowsmith and James Joyce specialist Richard Ellmann, who won the Pulitzer Prize for his biography of Oscar Wilde. It was Laney himself who seized the opportunity to have ex-president Carter teach on campus and work there to establish his policy center.[41]

Carter made himself readily available, and Emory professors quickly seized the opportunity to have the president lecture to their classes. Thus students in a course on Soviet politics, for instance, might one day see Jimmy Carter, Secret Service officers in tow, pick up a piece of chalk and start lecturing on nuclear arms control or his personal impressions of Leonid Brezhnev. Throughout the 1980s he averaged approximately thirty lectures a year, discussing everything from politics of national health care with students at the nursing school to environmental degradation with biology classes. The student-run newspaper, the *Emory Wheel* (which earlier had published anti–access road editorials that caused the former president much grief), gave students running updates on Jimmy Carter "happenings" around campus, as if he were a rock star on tour—or Billy Graham on crusade.[42]

Dean Jim Waits, who had succeeded Laney at the Theology School, arranged for a number of his graduate students to intern at the Carter Center, writing reports on an array of issues as well as performing the sort of unpaid gofer work that keeps nonprofit institutes running. One afternoon Carter lunched with the interns at Emory's Cox Hall cafeteria. As Rob Townes, one of "Dean Waits's boys," recalled, "All was going well, the conversation flowing nicely, until Carter learned that out of the seven theology graduate students none was going into the ministry." This boggled Carter's mind. "Don't *any* of y'all want to preach?" he asked, incredulous that the discipline of theology had become so theoretical. "No, sir," was all the interns could manage, to the ex-president's dismay. For all the Niebuhr and Tillich he had read, Carter believed in that old-time religion and didn't fully approve of the more modern, less evangelical variety.[43]

Laney understood this sentiment, and his friendship with Carter was in large measure due to the fact that each was a sharp-minded Christian activist with a burning social conscience and an ingrained integrity of purpose. Once a month for the next ten years they breakfasted together, addressing such matters as Zen Buddhism and Kierkegaardian existentialism over yogurt and toast. But it wasn't all airy talk: the pair also worked on turning innovative ideas into reality. One such notion was to have Carter hold regular "town hall" forums on campus to allow him to reach the greatest number of people. "The students just loved him," Laney recollected about Carter's first packed forums. "He never dodged a question."[44] At another breakfast, this one in early 1982, Carter confessed some uncertainty about how to organize his public policy institute. "James Laney was one of the first to understand that the public policy center I had in mind would be activist-oriented," Carter recalled.[45] And in response to Carter's early uncertainty, Laney convened a "working group" of Emory administrators and faculty who would meet monthly to draft "mission papers" on how best to structure this new institution to serve the academic community.[46]

Headed by physics professor John Palms, who would later became president of the University of South Carolina, the academic task force bickered about everything from what to call the institute ("Center for Conflict Resolution" and "Institute for Multi-Tract Diplomacy" were popular but abandoned) to whether it should offer advanced degrees like Harvard's John F. Kennedy School of Government. No ringing decision was ever handed down: instead the generic moniker "The Carter Center" evolved, and the group reached a consensus that the center would not have the faculty resources to offer degrees, an assessment with which Carter agreed. In fact, Carter told Laney he found hands-on institutions such as the University of Georgia's Southwest Branch Agricultural Experiment Station in Plains more worthwhile than "self-satisfied" think tanks and "book factories" like the Brookings Institute and Harvard's JFK School. The model he had in mind was the Southwest Branch Agricultural Experiment Station, which had given a tremendous boost to the farmers of Sumter County; what's more, it was clearly a wise investment for taxpayers, returning eight dollars for each one spent.[47]

In some sense, the Southwest Branch Agricultural Experiment Station was a Carter family legacy to Plains. During the Great Depression, Earl Carter had been one of the first local farmers to grasp the advantages of investing in scientific farming techniques: replacing the mule-drawn plow with a tractor, eliminating the insatiable boll weevil with insecticides, rotating crops to combat soil erosion. By the time Jimmy left Georgia for the U.S. Naval Academy in Annapolis in 1943, "Mr. Earl" had become Plains's undisputed agricultural leader due to his dedication to innovation and experiment. "Daddy was a scientist as well as a farmer," Carter noted, betraying an admiration that has grown with the years.[48] Whenever a new peanut seed or herbicide or curing technique became available, Earl Carter would be first in line to try it out. Eventually his keen interest in scientific farming prompted him to take the lead in raising the funds and purchasing the land for the University of Georgia to construct the agricultural experiment station. There, from its opening in 1951, local farmers could learn how to reap larger harvests from Georgia's heavy red-clay soil and how to make raising livestock more efficient.[49]

In 1953, when Earl Carter was dying of pancreatic cancer, Lieutenant Jimmy Carter sat at his father's bedside as hundreds of local farmers and small businessmen came by to pay their final respects. It was then that Jimmy realized the impact of his father's work, both as a state legislator and as an advocate of scientific farming. "I decided shortly after Daddy's death that I could help more people as an active community citizen in Plains than as a naval officer," Carter recalled. The young lieutenant quit the navy and took his wife and three young sons back to his hometown to run the family farm.[50]

With his mother, Miss Lillian, Carter set up a modest agribusiness enterprise in the disastrous year of 1954, which saw one of the worst droughts in Georgia's history. "We had a total profit of less than $200," Carter recalled. "I was my one and only employee during the season and sold about 200 tons of fertilizer in 100-pound paper bags."[51] Carter then realized that he was operating on old-fashioned assumptions from his boyhood days, and that he needed to learn more about scientific farm management. Thus the Annapolis graduate went back to school while still running the peanut business. His main teachers were the state scientists who ran not only the Southwest Branch Station in Plains but also the University of Georgia Station in Tifton, although he also took classes offered only at Abraham Baldwin Agriculture College in Tifton, Georgia. Carter's coursework included cow-fence building; farm record keeping; peanut, cotton, and corn growing; weed killing; fish and pond management; and grain storage, especially the art of aerating. These courses, cost-free to Carter as a Georgia resident, enabled him to become a self-sufficient agribusinessman.[52]

This education still inspired Carter twenty years and a governorship later. In August 1976 the Democratic presidential candidate returned to the Southwest Branch Station to pay homage to Dr. Clyde Young, a food scientist who had developed a remarkable new technique for determining the maturity of peanut crops. Farmers from all over Georgia sent samples from their fields so Young could tell them the exact date their crop should be harvested. "Sometimes farmers will spend a whole season—a very expensive season—preparing land, planting, cultivating, controlling insects," Carter told the reporters assembled on a peanut field. "Then just because of an error of a week or two in harvesting, they can lose maybe 15 to 20 percent of their gross profit, which might be 30 to 40 percent of their net profit, just by harvesting at the wrong time."[53] Dr. Young's breakthrough—the Arginine Maturity Index (AMI)—produced an average increase in yield of 600 pounds per acre. Sumter County farmers were soon tripling their peanut crops, and before long other peanut-producing states such as Alabama and Texas adopted the method. "Before Dr. Young developed his Arginine Maturity method, I had to decide when to dig peanuts, as other farmers did, by pulling them up and looking at them," Carter explained. Another major breakthrough in peanut productivity was provided by Dr. Vernon Broyles, who recommended minimal cultivating once the nut began to develop.[54] As president, whenever he was confronted with the reality of famine, whether from photographs of malnourished children in Ethiopia or in meetings with starving villagers in Sudan, Carter wished he could put innovations like these Southwest Branch Station methods into practice everywhere.

These then were Carter's postpresidential models—Miss Lillian's Peace Corps experience, the conciliatory atmosphere of Camp David, and Georgia's agricultural programs: worldwide health care, international peacemaking, hunger relief, and agricultural efficiency were the matters at hand. Some, of course, were more pressing than others, and Carter had also decided to use the *Global 2000 Report*, which he had commissioned as president, as an additional resource for tackling world problems. And it was the Middle East where Carter first wanted to put his shoulder to the peace wheel. Thus, in an April 1982 interview in the joint Sunday editions of the *Atlanta Journal* and *Constitution* the former president, cheerful that the last Israeli soldiers were pulling out of the Sinai Desert, announced that he planned to join negotiations on Palestinian autonomy in the West Bank and the Gaza Strip as the second phase of the peacemaking begun at Camp David. "I'll use my influence, whatever it is, to continue the process," Carter announced. "Particularly in Egypt, and I think to a major degree in Israel, I'm still trusted. As a private citizen working in a proper way, I'll use my influence if a time of trouble comes."[55]

A s Carter began looking again at the Middle East peace process, deciding how he could best become a mediator in the region, he continued his planning for the center, and in July he rounded up a panoply of his closest associates for a weekend meant to transmute his still vague ideas for the center into something more concrete. To facilitate creative thinking, Carter chose Sapelo Island, an isolated, twelve-mile-long strip of land off the Georgia coast, accessible only by ferry and known for its pristine Atlantic beaches, tall-grass savannahs, wind-gnarled oaks draped in Spanish moss, and salt marshes teeming with waterfowl and other wildlife. The Carters invited an inner circle of advisers and selected Emory administrators and faculty including Laney, Waits, Kenneth Stein, a leading authority on Arab-Israeli and Palestinian matters, and Ellen Mickiewicz, a recognized authority on diplomatic relations between Washington and Moscow and particularly on Soviet media and communications.[56]

When Stein, then a thirty-five-year-old assistant professor of history, received a phone call from Carter chief of staff Dan Lee, inviting him to Sapelo Island, he agreed to attend with some trepidation, sure to be out of his league among the heavy hitters who doubtless would be there. After hanging up the telephone, Stein told his wife, "We better head over to Brooks Brothers so I can get some slacks and sports coats." A few days later Jimmy Carter's personal secretary, Nancy Koiningsmark, called to tell the freshly wardrobed young professor that the dress code for Sapelo Island would be "jeans and sneakers." Stein, struggling to make ends meet on an nontenured salary, was furious with himself for going on such a giddy spree. "Being summoned by a president does strange things to you," Stein confessed.[57]

When the day of reckoning came, Stein traveled to the secluded resort and headed straight for the meeting room. He entered and froze in astonishment. Sitting informally around a conference table, chatting amiably among themselves, was a cabal of exalted political and diplomatic figures whose faces he knew only from the evening news: Cyrus Vance, Zbigniew Brzezinski, Warren Christopher, Sol Linowitz, Hamilton Jordan, Jody Powell, and Andrew Young, not to mention Rosalynn and Jimmy Carter. Carter broke the tension with a lighthearted "Don't be *too* impressed, Professor. Go put your bag in your room and come back down."[58]

Waits and Laney led into the brainstorming with an overview of the Carter Center's relationship to Emory University, followed by comments from the former president's most trusted advisers. Just as he had at nearly every meeting he attended in the Carter White House, Brzezinski did the most talking and thereby shaped the discussion. Over and over, he repeated that the Carter Center had to be "action-oriented," that it had to "problem-solve." Echoing Carter's own views, "Zbig" explained the pitfalls the center would face if it became too academic or pretentious. "Forget the academic Globalony," Brzezinski exhorted Carter. "With your enormous depth and energy you can achieve results." Linowitz seconded this opinion, but cautioned that it would be essential not to duplicate able peacekeeping or diplomatic efforts already being made by the United Nations, World Bank, State Department, or any other significant organization, in or outside government.[59]

Brzezinski and Linowitz understood that what Carter wanted was to practice "track-two diplomacy." Former U.S. foreign service officer John Montville had coined the term in a spring 1981 *Foreign Policy* article, coauthored with psychiatrists, to describe such informal and unofficial meetings as were then taking place between the United States and the Soviet Union. A student of the psychology of international mediation, Montville believed that open-minded and high-level consultations outside formal ("track one") diplomatic channels could advance dialogue, dispel misunderstandings, enhance communication, provide cover for military movement or retreat, prepare the ground for formal negotiations, and even humanize the enemy, at least to the negotiators. By definition unable to commit to contracts and unencumbered by clear-cut official instructions, a track-two diplomat has maneuvering room to explore possibilities. According to Montville, the key assumption underlying track-two diplomacy is that "actual or potential conflict can be resolved or eased by appealing to common human capabilities to respond to good will and reasonableness."[60]

Carter, in fact, had a plan already. In preparation for the Sapelo Island meeting, Carter had digested huge amounts of information from an array of foreign policy and conflict resolution experts, some of whom he would eventually hire. Those at the conference agreed with his premises: that the Carter Center's primary goals should be to promote international human rights and to make peace among warring factions, wherever they may be, using the Camp David accords as a model of successful negotiation. "The center would stand on the humanitarian principle that everyone on earth should be able to live in peace," Carter proclaimed to his brain trust, harking back to his farewell address. He intended nothing less than to create an institute broad enough in scope to carry on his unfinished presidency.[61]

"It was hard to believe," fellow Georgian and former secretary of state Dean Rusk commented in 1990; "Carter wanted to create a mini–United Nations in downtown Atlanta."[62] Carter insisted the center be bipartisan, allowing Democrats and Republicans to work in tandem on forums and field projects. The ex-president spoke passionately about what can be accomplished when people and resources are marshaled to resolve conflict, to foster democracy and development, and to fight hunger, disease, and human rights abuses. He believed that as a former U.S. president, he would have easy access to world leaders and so could act as broker for peace. That, however, was far from evident at the time. As *Atlanta* magazine later admitted, "In the center's early years . . . it seemed that Carter was only barking at the moon, that perhaps he really didn't intend to take on world problems, that he just wanted to chat about them."[63]

In fact, Carter's far-reaching vision for the center made Laney gulp even as they forged ahead at Sapelo Island. "I didn't think what he wanted to create was impossible," Laney recalled, "but my goodness—it was awful ambitious."[64] As Sol Linowitz noted, "It frightened me to think that Carter really believed it when he said he could have a bigger impact with his center than if he had been reelected."[65]

Once he had described his big picture of "waging peace," Carter turned to specific current events in the Middle East and asked Stein, who had remained silent so far in the session, "What do you think we can do in the region?" Carter had mentioned earlier that soon, in 1983, he wanted the center to sponsor a "consultation"—a euphemism for an unofficial but more than academic conference or meeting. Stein suggested the center focus this first event on the Middle East, revisiting the Camp David accords the next fall—a nice, round five years after the historic event—to evaluate its successes, shortcomings, and lessons for future negotiations. In the fifteen months before the anniversary, Carter would meet Arab and Israeli leaders in the Middle East, discuss the Palestine issue with scholars, and invite representatives of the relevant parties to Atlanta. Stein added that perhaps the Carter Center, as an academic institution, could serve as an informal meeting place for representatives of Israel and her Arab neighbors while they were officially not communicating with one another.

Carter embraced the assistant professor's ideas without the slightest hesitation. Brzezinski's hyperactive and imaginative mind also seized upon Stein's plan, and he immediately detailed which countries Carter should visit and how the first Atlanta consultation should be organized.[66]

A t Sapelo Island, Carter and Cyrus Vance maintained a congenial if strained relationship. Carter and Brzezinski had never fully forgiven Vance for resigning over the failed Iranian rescue mission in April 1980, convinced that even a successful attempt would have led to the death of many hostages, posed grave risks of drawing the Soviet Union into the situation, and created other, even greater risks in the Middle East.[67]

With hindsight, Carter had come to believe that he should have appointed George Ball, undersecretary of state during the Kennedy and Johnson administrations, to the post. "Only Ball's outspokenness on Middle East issues" prevented his selection, Carter remarked later.[68] He had become increasingly impressed with Ball for his willingness during the 1980s to challenge America's "passionate attachment" to Israel, although the tough-minded Ball, the first member of the Johnson administration to challenge LBJ's Vietnam policy, did criticize Carter for his handling of the hostage crisis. But overall Ball's assessments of Carter as foreign policy practitioner were glowing: "When it came to understanding the political situation in those regions, Carters grasped the arcane minutia and comprehended historical tensions between opposites as well as anybody in Washington. That's saying a lot about a one-term southern governor."[69]

Diplomatic historians have argued about Brzezinski's confrontations with Cyrus Vance over foreign policy during the Carter years. Most believe that Vance's principled, détente-minded approach to the Soviet Union, grounded in Yankee pragmatism and perseverance, was preferable to Brzezinski's bitter realpolitik, with its "primacy of power" stance toward communism. If only the president had listened more to Vance, the cautious establishmentarian, and less to the Polish-born Brzezinski, the argument goes, Carter's foreign policy agenda would have been more coherent. Carter does not see it that way. While he liked to listen to their diverse perspectives—and even play Vance and Brzezinski off each other—Carter says he was uncomfortable with Vance almost from the start, because Vance's worldview too closely mirrored his own.[70]

Carter's inability or unwillingness to put an end to the squabbling within his administration, particularly between Vance and Brzezinski, continued to dog him even after the 1980 election. While still head of the NSC, Brzezinski sparked a furor among liberal Democrats in late November when he appeared to embrace Reagan's choice for secretary of state—General Alexander Haig, the hawkish former NATO commander, Nixon chief of staff, and NSC deputy to Kissinger—by seconding Haig's view that it was necessary to deal toughly with the Soviets. "I think the Democratic party damages itself when it moves excessively to the left, and if it becomes excessively preoccupied with what might be called the do-gooder agenda in international affairs," Brzezinski stated in December 1980, an obvious swipe at Vance.[71] Yet Brzezinski still remained fiercely loyal to, even downright defensive of, Carter, whom he considered a hawk. The two men had, after all, shared a vision of infusing American foreign policy with a new realpolitik concern for human rights that would confound the Soviets, even if it was only partially successful.[72]

The Polish-born Brzezinski, a respected professor of international affairs, had been Carter's eager tutor. Both men believed in promoting a post-cold-war foreign policy based on democracy building, although Brzezinski was always more skeptical of the Soviets than his presidential pupil. Their professional bond was reinforced by a personal bond: Brzezinski and Carter got along famously. The Eastern European and the southern American, workaholics both, were Washington outsiders, impatient with the ceremonial side of governing and blessed with a stunning ability to absorb and retain mounds of raw foreign policy data. "Dining with Carter and Brzezinski was an interesting experience," journalist James Reston once remarked. "They were both so intense that their knives cut into their plates."[73]

Since 1980 Carter's relationship with Brzezinski had ripened into an enduring bond on a par with that between Harry Truman and Dean Acheson or George Bush and Brent Scowcroft. Carter's relationship with Vance, on the other hand, never healed beyond a surface cordiality. Carter did stay overnight at Vance's New York apartment while on his *Keeping Faith* book tour, but a tenseness permeated their relationship which would never fully mend. Meanwhile Carter, who saw himself more philosophically aligned to Vance than to Brzezinski, had come to see his former secretary of state as a well-meaning creature of the Council on Foreign Relations, where erudite rhetoric was preferred to concrete results. In 1995 Carter canceled his membership to the council because he wasn't getting enough for his money.[74]

Buoyed by a sense of accomplishment, the Sapelo participants shared an unspoken understanding that Jimmy Carter's real postpresidential political career was now under way. Only the residual tension between Vance and Brzezinski marred the celebratory mood. At one point Brzezinski noted that he had received a proof of Vance's forthcoming memoir, *Hard Choices*. "Congratulations on your book," Brzezinski offered his sparring partner: "It's fascinating." Vance, fully cognizant that his version of Carter's presidency was light-years from Brzezinski's, just smiled and said, "It's amazing we were in the same administration."[75]

But the ebullient former president, tanned and trim, was too busy celebrating to pay attention to any bad feelings lingering between his advisers. Rather, as Carter later recalled, "Thanks to Ken, Zbig, Sol, and the rest, Rosalynn and I left Sapelo Island with a bolstered sense of purpose. It was clear that there was a vacuum we could fill."[76]

Ellen Mickiewicz came away equally fired up. A Yale University Ph.D. and editor of the journal *Soviet Union*, Mickiewicz was dean of Emory's graduate school at the time of the Sapelo Island meeting. "Carter," she explained years later, "was never going to conform to typical qualified bureaucratic speech or bureaucratic modes of behavior." The conference also showed Mickiewicz what a pivotal role Rosalynn Carter played in every aspect of her husband's life. "Ever since Sapelo I've had enormous respect for the cohesiveness and fruitful partnership the Carters have," Mickiewicz recalled. "It's one of the most perfectly complementary relationships I've ever encountered."[77]

After Sapelo Island, Jimmy and Rosalynn fled Plains's oppressive late-summer heat and spent a few weeks at their just-completed vacation cabin in idyllic Turnip Town Creek, near Ellijay (population 1,327) in the cool mountains of northwestern Georgia. Here they had waterfalls, rapids, and air perfumed by mountain laurel and rhododendron. The hand-hewn, new yellow-pine cabin, co-owned with their closest friends, John and Betty Pope, became the Carters' shelter from the steady rain of public scrutiny.[78] Even in Plains they had a host of obligations, from throwing barbecues to raising school library funds to hosting private dinners for international dignitaries on tour. But on their ten-acre piece of Walnut Mountain, in a cabin hidden behind a dense thicket of alders and groves of towering white oaks, the Carters could relax undisturbed. "It is the second home that almost all people say they want and almost no one ends up with, usually because simplicity gives way to the temptation of adding just a little bit here and there," Carter noted. In Turnip Town Creek Jimmy read Gandhi and Thoreau; crafted furniture; painted scenes of rural Georgia life; and wrote highly personal poems about everything from his admiration of Dylan

Thomas to possum hunting in Plains. Perhaps most important, at their retreat Jimmy and Rosalynn could present a proper fly to a rising trout just
fifty feet from their front door.[79]

It's not really exaggerating to say that fly fishing was a spiritual endeavor
for both Jimmy Carter and his wife. Most modern presidents have dabbled
at some sort of angling—trolling lures from yachts or hauling in majestic
blue marlin for the photographers—but Carter is a serious fly fisherman.
With the possible exception of Dwight Eisenhower, not since Herbert
Hoover (who wrote *Fishing for Fun*, a book about his quest for the perfect
trout) had the White House harbored an angler as obsessed as Carter, who
called fly fishing a "high art form." A devotee of Izaak Walton's seventeenth-
century treatise *The Compleat Angler*, Carter even decided to try his hand at
outdoor journalism, penning a seven-page lead article for *Fly Fisherman*
magazine in 1983. The favorable reception of "Spruce Creek Diary," an account of Carter's times fishing a Pennsylvania limestone creek with his dairy
farmer friend Wayne Harpster (who each year jointly celebrates his birthday
and the annual hatch of fish-seducing Green Drake mayflies), inspired the
former president to write half a dozen more sporting articles. These were
collected along with essays on hunting in his 1988 *An Outdoor Journal: Adventures and Reflections.*[80]

Whether it was going after salmon on Quebec's Matapedia River with
their friend Curt Gowdy or chasing the perfect rainbow trout in New
Zealand (where a minister at a Sunday church service asked the Lord to
"guide the rod and the line of Brother Jimmy"), the Carters never passed up
an excuse to don chest waders, slosh to midriver, and cast. "Besides the
sporting aspect itself, fly fishing and hunting have enriched our lives in so
many other ways," Carter has noted. "Many of our closest friends are outdoor enthusiasts like ourselves."[81] In fact, it was fly fishing that firmed up
Carter's very useful friendship with Atlanta's freewheeling media and sports
mogul Ted Turner.

Turner had first met Carter early in the 1976 campaign when the presidential candidate held a fund-raiser at the Heart of Atlanta Motel. Turner
immediately deemed Carter "bright, bright, bright." Still striving then to
make his name a household word, Turner enjoyed being seen in the company of a former governor and fellow Georgian with the "cast-iron balls," as
Turner put it, to believe he could be president of the United States.[82] "I just
love it when people say I can't do something," Turner explained. "There's
nothing that makes me feel better, because all my life people have said I
wasn't going to make it."[83]

Determined to fulfill his father's ambitions, Turner aimed to become
something like a latter-day robber baron. "I'd like to own everything!" he

once proclaimed. He grappled with two divorces and bouts of depression. But somehow Turner had bet on the right business, and before long his Cable News Network (CNN) began not only to turn a handsome profit but also to enter the world's collective consciousness with its all-day, up-to-the-minute, on-site live news broadcasts. By 1989 Turner owned TNT, WTBS, and Headline News, in addition to CNN—approximately a third of all U.S. cable broadcasting—as well as major league baseball's Atlanta Braves and the National Basketball Association's Atlanta Hawks.[84]

During Carter's presidency the embryonic Turner Broadcasting Company—the first on-air offering of which was an exclusive interview with President Carter in June 1980—had led the corporate fight to minimize regulation of the cable industry. Although he was invited to several state dinners during the Carter administration and was even appointed to the president's Council on Energy Efficiency, Turner was reputed to be a Republican, and in truth was anxious not to seem too close to any political party. "In the news business," as he put it, "you can't play party favorites." Turner felt differently after Carter lost to Ronald Reagan. He well knew the depression that can gnaw at the psyche of a thwarted optimist. "So I called Jimmy Carter and asked him out to lunch," Turner recalled, with pride. "He was really down, and I lent him a sympathetic ear." He did more than give an ear: Turner also gave Carter a check for $100,000, a welcome contribution to the presidential library. "At that time it was the most money I had ever donated to a single cause," Turner recalled. "But a friend in need is a friend indeed."[85]

A tireless promoter of Atlanta as a cosmopolitan city, Turner thought the Carter Center complex would be a "wonderful educational addition to town." The commonality between the two Georgians made them easy friends. They both were ambitious and idealistic, and shared a naval background, a love of outdoor sports, and a preference for informality.[86]

The two men's relationship developed into true symbiosis. The ex-president was a die-hard Atlanta Braves fan, and Turner owned the team. Before long the Carters could be seen munching popcorn and doing the Braves' tomahawk chop next to Turner in his Fulton County Stadium box, a scene brought into millions of homes courtesy of national superstation WTBS. From time to time Jimmy and Rosalynn also visited Ted and his wife, Jane Smith Turner, at Avalon, their $6 million, 8,000-acre estate just outside Tallahassee, Florida. Together the couples hunted quail and turkey in the tangled underbrush. "Avalon is beautiful!" Carter wrote Turner in February 1987. "You can be proud of the general atmosphere of the place, its warmth and hospitality. It deserves to be owned by someone like you."[87] While Turner gained gravitas being seen in Carter's company, the former president found the tycoon's unbridled behavior refreshing and enjoyed his Atlanta boosterism. "Ted and I became very close friends," Carter recalled.[88] Both men had been jarred by the environmental warnings sounded in June 1980 in the *Global 2000 Report*. One of Turner's friends claimed the report "hit him like a ton of nonrecyclable bricks." Sharing his friend's concern for such topical environmental issues as acid rain and the ozone hole, Carter joined the board of directors of Turner's Better World Society, which operated under the credo Harnessing the Power of Television to Make a Better World.[89]

Thus it was no surprise that Carter began popping up more regularly on CNN, both his foreign missions and his Atlanta consultations receiving extensive coverage. With CNN as his forum, Carter could address a global audience on human rights and environmental policy or speak directly to Palestinians in Gaza City or to the Chinese in Beijing. Asked at one point in 1995 whether CNN had a pro-Carter bias, Turner responded with characteristic bluntness: "Unconsciously, sure. I like showing off Georgians. Why not? New Yorkers do it all the time. A lot of my top people are good ol' Georgia boys. Jimmy Carter is a great man, the best former president America has ever seen, and I have twenty-four hours of programming to fill every night. You're damn right I favor Carter. Good for me."[90]

After divorcing his second wife in 1988, Turner began dating the actress and aerobic workout queen Jane Fonda, to whom Jimmy and Rosalynn grew quite close. The former "Hanoi Jane" reminded the Carters of their equally radical-minded daughter, Amy, and the two couples themselves were all save-the-earth activists with sophisticated understandings of the politics of ecology. Together they would lobby against mining in Antarctica and clear-cutting in Brazil. In 1991 Fonda and Turner married, and the Carters made regular visits to the newlyweds' 3,500-acre Flying D Ranch in Montana and to their 300,000-acre Ladder Ranch in New Mexico. Wading in the Yellowstone or Gallatin River, the Carters and Turners reeled in trout together under the big sky and exulted in the success of two southern overachievers amid the Yankees.

"Do you want to know what I like about Jimmy Carter?" Turner asked, barely pausing before answering himself. "He is extremely competent, a fabulous fly fisherman, a crack shot, possessed with an uncanny intelligence, well versed in international affairs, and like any good self-made man built the Carter Center from nothing into a first-class institution—a real asset to Atlanta, America, and the world."[91]

Without exception Ted Turner would become Carter's most valuable postpresidential ally. Not only would the Atlanta-based news organization cover Carter Center consultations, but a camera crew followed the ex-president as he globetrotted for peace in such remote places as Rwanda and Sudan. CNN International became Carter's global soapbox, his reliable media outlet for his expansionary peace agenda. If Billy Graham was America's first reputable televangelist, Jimmy Carter would become our first telediplomatist, courtesy of CNN. So what if the State Department sneered at Carter's track-two diplomacy: millions of world citizens could be educated to the virtues of nonviolence by watching CNN. TV news viewers became Deacon Carter's international congregation.

While Reagan was further polishing his reputation as the Great Communicator in the mid-1980s, using television to frighten the Soviet Union with boasts of American technological prowess and moral superiority, Carter was quietly mastering the art of conflict resolution and telediplomacy. When Carter learned the symbiotic relationship between the two, during the Bush years, he once again became a high-profile actor on the world stage, a self-styled peace outlaw whose Christian message was constantly beamed into the palaces of the rich and the shantytowns of the poor.[92]

SIX

SEARCHING FOR MIDDLE EAST PEACE

⌒∽o∽⌒

The chaotic legacy of foreign domination in the Middle East, exacerbated by the British when they discovered oil in Persia in 1908, had become Jimmy Carter's primary intellectual focus as he began teaching at Emory University in September 1982. Great Britain had made a succession of promises to the Arabs between 1914 and 1918 concerning independence, self-government, and the principle of the consent of the governed. Among the dozens of territorial disagreements that regularly flared into acts of violence, the most grievous occurred after World War II. Borders had been arbitrarily imposed by the Europeans, resulting in constant disputes, turmoil, and war. In the thirty-five years since Carter had graduated from the U.S. Naval Academy in Annapolis, he had witnessed six armed confrontations between Arabs and Israelis: the War of 1948, the 1956 Suez War, the June 1967 Six-Day War, the 1969–70 War of Attrition, the October 1973 Yom Kippur War, and the June 1982 war that ensued when Israel invaded Lebanon in an attempt to destroy the PLO infrastructure there.[1]

With the assistance of Emory's Middle East expert Ken Stein, Carter hoped to travel to the region, meet with leaders like Saudi Arabia's King Fahd and Syria's Hafez al-Assad, and weigh in on the Palestinian homeland quagmire. Campus life was too slow and incestuous for his temperament: academics work by the calendar: Jimmy Carter worked by the clock. Now as an Emory professor, a private citizen, he was anxious to build on his unfinished presidential legacy in the Middle East.[2]

As president, Carter had placed high priority on Middle East peace, building on Henry Kissinger's remarkable shuttle diplomacy. "Peace in the Middle East was a major concern for me and my administration," Carter later noted, "and our work in this area gave me much of my early experience in negotiation." He spent thirteen days relentlessly in September 1978 mediating with Israeli prime minister Menachem Begin and Egyptian president Anwar al-Sadat in the Maryland mountains to convince them to sign two landmark agreements: a framework for peace between Israel and Egypt of March 1979 (the terms being restoration of the Sinai to Egyptian sovereignty accompanied by normalization of the Palestinian problem), and a commitment to find someday a solution to the Palestinian homeland issue. While the first accord was precise in its terms and could be successfully executed, the second—which promised "full autonomy" to Palestinians living in the West Bank and Gaza—was intentionally ambiguous. At question was what to do with the territories set aside for Palestinian Arabs by the UN in its 1947 partition plan that were militarily occupied by Israel in 1967.[3]

Because the Camp David agreement spoke in terms of people rather than land, Arab nations could view the plan as a sly way for Israel to maintain its hegemony over the occupied territories and to withdraw its consideration of a Palestinian homeland. And indeed, by 1982 more than half of the 4 million Palestinians (85 percent of them Muslim, 15 percent Christian) lived under Israeli administration either in Israel as citizens (approximately 650,000), or in the occupied West Bank and Gaza (approximately 1,370,000). This suspicion was further reinforced by the Israeli government–assisted movement of Jewish settlers into the West Bank and Gaza, which to Palestinians meant jeopardy for their Palestinian state.[4] Israeli Labor party leader Yigal Allon took a swipe at Begin's Likud government for its sponsorship of the settlements, remarking that "only in Marc Chagall's paintings do people float in midair, free from the laws of gravity."[5]

On September 1, 1982, President Ronald Reagan issued his plan for Middle East peace.[6] It called for the withdrawal of all foreign troops from Lebanon and for Palestinian home rule in the West Bank and Gaza in association with Jordan—not an independent Palestinian state. After serious consideration, Menachem Begin rejected the Reagan plan.[7] His purpose in invading Lebanon had been to destroy the PLO, in order to weaken Palestinian national identity and resolve. For its part the PLO dismissed Reagan's proposal as "pro-Israeli propaganda" and just another ploy to dismantle the organization. At a summit meeting in Fez, Morocco, a week after the Reagan plan was put forth, the Arab League announced its own proposal for a settlement of the Palestine question; it was scoffed at by Israel, Libya, and the PLO. Carter publicly gave the Reagan plan his approval, acknowledging

that it was in line with the Camp David accords. With his characteristic optimism and determination, he privately concluded that a freelance former
U.S. president who was still respected in the region might be the best candidate to end the long cycle of war and mistrust.[8]

In Lebanon bloody chaos erupted. President-elect Bashir Gemayel was
assassinated in a bomb explosion, and in retaliation barbarous Christian Mar-
onite militia forces (the Phalangists) launched a savage two-day massacre of
hundreds of Palestinians and Lebanese Muslims in the Sabra and Shatila
refugee centers. Most journalists, including prominent Israeli reporters,
blamed Israel for the atrocity: the previous June, Begin had ordered troops
into Lebanon with the support of the Phalangists and the seeming acquies-
cence of the Reagan administration. At the time Begin had promised that Israeli forces would not penetrate far into the country, but within weeks they
had surrounded Beirut. "At no time in recent [Middle East] history," Carter
lamented, "has human misjudgment been so tragically the cause of pain as
in September of 1982, when hundreds of defenseless people were slaughtered in the Sabra and Shatila refugee camps in Lebanon."[9] It was a reminder that 750,000 Palestinian Arabs, or approximately half the Palestinian
population in 1948, had been made refugees.[10]

Egypt, in an embarrassing position as signatory of a March 1979 peace
treaty with Israel, immediately withdrew its ambassador from Tel Aviv. The
peace process was at a stultifying impasse. Carter refused to give up hope,
still thinking he might be able to find common ground between the Israelis
and Palestinians. Many international mediators had gone before him since
Israel's establishment in 1948, seeking a flexible partition of historic Palestine—
the territory between the Jordan River and the Mediterranean Sea—into
two states where both Israeli security and Palestinian political rights would
be assured. Unlike the period of his term as president, Carter's time was
now his own, and he spent it immersed in intensive study of every aspect of
the conflict. Stein began churning out monthly ten-page analytical reports
for Carter on the situation in the Middle East, in effect doubling as shadow
NSC adviser and State Department desk officer. "I quickly learned," Stein
recalled, "that Jimmy Carter loved numbers."[11]

Carter approached the ancient feuds among Christians, Jews, and Muslims with the combined focus of an astute international affairs analyst and a
biblical scholar. "In my discussions of these religious conflicts with President
Anwar Sadat of Egypt," he recollected, "he mentioned frequently, and most
casually, the brotherhood of Arab and Jew and how they are both the sons of
Abraham. His references to the patriarch caused me to reexamine the ancient biblical story of Abraham and his early descendants, looking at their
adventures for the first time from a Jewish, a Christian, and an Arab point of

view simultaneously."[12] The more Carter learned about the Palestinian problem, the more angry he was at Begin for refusing to allow a Palestinian representative to attend Camp David.[13]

The former president sought the counsel of one of his former NSC hands, Brookings Institution analyst William Quandt. Carter pored over Quandt's January 1, 1983, memorandum, "Prospects for Peace in the Middle East," a summary of how negotiations might be jump-started in the absence of positive developments in Beirut and the West Bank.[14] Carter's regional education was not confined to policy issues; he also began studying the Qur'an and the Torah, and consulted with experts on Islam and Judaism in preparation for his planned tour of the Middle East early in 1983. The ever-faithful Zbig Brzezinski made travel arrangements with the State Department on Carter's behalf. "I have been in touch with all of the embassies," Brzezinski informed his old commander in chief on January 13, 1983, "and needless to say all have responded very positively."[15]

Convinced the Reagan administration's policy of inaction failed adequately to address the complexities of the region, Carter established his own contacts with controversial Palestinian scholars who, he thought, could help guide him through the byzantine maze to peace. Palestine became a preoccupation: as his education progressed, Carter began to sympathize with the destitute refugees who longed for a homeland and could only reminisce about the sand dunes of Ashdod, the orange groves of Ramle, and the port bustle of Jaffa. As he became more knowledgeable, he began to marvel at the resilience of Palestinian society despite the mass violence that sometimes was directed against it. He saw more clearly how the establishment of present-day Israel in 1948, while resolving the problem of vulnerability and statelessness for Jews, had created a new set of problems for the Palestinian Arabs, whose land and houses had been taken by Israelis.[16] The October publication of *Keeping Faith*, with its detailed chapters on Camp David, prompted many leading Democrats to urge Reagan to consult with Carter on the Middle East. Even Richard Nixon recommended that Reagan seek his predecessor's input. "I think consultations with Carter would be useful," Nixon told the *New York Times* on November 13, 1982, particularly, he noted, because Carter knew obdurate Israeli prime minister Menachem Begin "better than Reagan does."[17] Gerald Ford also began working closely and avidly with Carter on the Palestinian question, taking it up as his primary foreign policy concern as well.

The remarkable Ford-Carter partnership produced tangible results that November, when the two ex-presidents issued a joint statement warning of the disastrous economic consequences of protectionism in world trade. They followed this statement with a collaborative article, published in the

February 1983 *Reader's Digest*, that stated they had come to "the painful conclusion" that Israel was not living up to various commitments as outlined in the Camp David accords. Israel "has shown little inclination to grant real autonomy to the Palestinians in the West Bank and Gaza areas," Ford and Carter wrote. "It has continued to confiscate properties in occupied territories and to build settlements as if to create a *de facto* Israeli ascendancy there. It has publicly repudiated the Reagan peace plan, which calls for a freeze on Israeli settlements. This has caused both of us deep disappointment and a sense of grave concern that is shared by many other stalwart supporters of Israel."[18]

Recommending that Israel open negotiations with King Hussein of Jordan, Ford and Carter cautioned that lasting peace in the Middle East could come only if Tel Aviv abided by the Camp David agreement and embraced the Reagan plan. Not without cause, the *Reader's Digest* article was construed in Israel as an outright attack on Begin. Indeed, both Carter and Ford objected to the prime minister's continuing militaristic leadership as manifested, among other ways, in the 1981 Israeli air strike that destroyed an Iraqi nuclear reactor, in the deployment of Israeli troops to Lebanon, in Begin's announced "annexation" of the Golan Heights, and in his escalating effort to construct Jewish settlements on the West Bank.[19]

Just after the February 1983 *Reader's Digest* hit the stands, the bipartisan former president led a two-day conference on public policy and communications at the Gerald R. Ford Presidential Library in Ann Arbor, Michigan. The February 9–10 gathering was sponsored by the Domestic Policy Association, a group devoted to improving America's infrastructure.[20] Hobbling on crutches due to recent knee surgery, Ford opened the conference by observing, "To my knowledge this was the first time two former presidents ever cooperated in such a tandem fashion."[21] Although their ostensible purpose was to hold a public policy forum on such domestic issues as Social Security, inflation, and employment policy, Carter and Ford used the high-profile opportunity to browbeat Begin again for stalling on the withdrawal of Israeli troops from Lebanon and for continuing to rush the construction of Jewish settlements on the West Bank. "Having two former presidents—one Democrat, the other Republican—criticizing Begin for errant behavior created a mild stir in Israel," Carter recalled. "It put extra heat on him."[22]

A little more than two weeks later Carter joined Ford and Richard Nixon at a $1,000-a-plate dinner honoring retired U.S. admiral Hyman G. Rickover in order to raise funds for the Rickover Foundation, which the admiral had created to provide college scholarships in science and technology. In a dinner speech he lauded the eighty-three-year-old admiral as "omnipotent, omniscient, and omnipresent." Carter also conferred with Ford and Nixon one last time before he headed off on a five-country tour of the Middle East, a "peace mission" to the Holy Land that he had been planning in earnest since Sapelo Island. The next day's *New York Times* reported that Republican senator Bob Dole of Kansas, upon seeing a photograph of Carter, Ford, and Nixon posed in line, had quipped that it was a classic portrait of "see no evil, hear no evil, and evil."[23]

An embarrassing flap occurred even before Carter arrived for a week-long stay in Cairo in March 1983 as a guest of the Egyptian government. It had all begun in January when he had granted Russell Warren Howe, a free-lance journalist, an interview, ostensibly for *al-Majalla*, an influential Arab newspaper. Howe instead sold the Q&A to *Penthouse*, the cover of which promised "Jimmy Carter's Frankest Interview" inside. Clearly, *Penthouse* publisher Bob Guccione was hoping for something along the lines of the "lust in my heart" interview Carter had granted *Playboy* during the 1976 campaign, much to the magazine's profit. Carter's Middle East commentary in *Penthouse* did prove controversial, but for quite different reasons.[24]

When Howe asked if he planned to meet with Yasir Arafat during his up-coming Middle East trip, Carter had replied that it "would be an option that I would pursue." This simple comment, trumpeted in a *Penthouse* press release the evening before Carter's departure, put both the Reagan administration and the Israeli government on notice. Suddenly urgent State Department messages began streaming to Carter, asking him not to speak to Arafat on grounds that his doing so would create difficulties for the U.S. government. Reluctantly Carter caved in, but he made it clear that he would meet with other representatives of the PLO.[25]

Carter traveled to Cairo in a private jet loaned to him by Christopher and Patsy Hemmeter, who accompanied the former president on the first two weeks of the mission. Arriving at the terminal, Carter was greeted by a pool of anxious journalists with only one question on their minds. "I won't see Arafat," Carter answered. "I think it would be improper for me to speak to Arafat until the PLO is willing to recognize Israel's right to exist, but," he continued, "I will see other Palestinian leaders in Gaza and the West Bank, and they might very well be members of the PLO."[26]

Carter spent eight eventful days in Egypt, all the while emphasizing that he was there as an Emory University professor and not "representing my country in any way." He made a courtesy call on Reagan's special envoy to the Middle East, the venerable Philip Habib; he paid a solemn visit to Sadat's grave; he had a leisurely tour of Cairo's museums and the Great Pyramids; he held long policy sessions with President Hosni Mubarak (whom Carter thought lacked the "boldness and perhaps strategic concepts" of Anwar al-Sadat); he embarked on a calm cruise up the Nile River, stopping at ancient sites and inspecting fertile fields along the way; and he held meetings with PLO officials on the need to curb terrorism.[27]

There was a personally bittersweet undercurrent, of course. It had been seventeen months since Sadat's assassination, and his friends from Plains thought about him constantly as they traversed his homeland. Carter's well-known rapport with Sadat, along with his celebrated efforts to solve Middle Eastern conflicts without a pro-Israeli bias, led many Egyptians to regard him as an ally and a visionary. When the former American president jogged by on the dusty roads in the early mornings, field hands and artisans would smile and wave at him, thrilled to have caught a glimpse of "Jimmee," Sadat's peacemaking friend. "In each place along the river I tried to talk to as many of the local officials and other Egyptian people as possible," Carter recalled. "In private homes there were often photographs of [Gamal Abdel] Nasser, a few of Sadat, and occasionally one of me."[28]

One afternoon Carter stopped to worship at an ancient Coptic Orthodox church in a remote Egyptian village. The priests there offered him tea, then began frantically telling him how their leader, Pope Shenouda III (the 117th pope of Alexandria), had been charged with inciting Christian-Muslim strife and placed under house arrest by President Sadat just a month before he was assassinated. The Coptics, a Christian denomination of eight million whose patron is Saint Mark, had begged Mubarak to release Pope Shenouda, to no avail. Carter promised the priests he would study the matter closely and would intervene personally if he found their account of Shenouda's bogus political arrest was correct. Once back at Emory, Carter learned that Pope Shenouda indeed had been unfairly imprisoned by Sadat. He embarked on a relentless twenty-one-month campaign, lobbying Mubarak by mail and messenger. Eventually Carter's persistence paid off: one day in December 1985 Ken Stein received a telephone call from one of Mubarak's advisers. "Tell your boss all of his letter writing has finally reached success," the Egyptian spokesperson said. "Pope Shenouda will be released tomorrow." Two years later the Alexandrian pope, one of Carter's letters to Mubarak in hand, journeyed to Atlanta to thank the former president for his perseverance.[29]

Pressing for the release of Pope Shenouda was a prime illustration of Carter putting his moral conviction to work. Foreign leaders knew that once Carter was on their soil he would discuss human rights with them and bring up the plight of prisoners of conscience, with names of specific incarcerated individuals provided to him by Amnesty International. It was the beginning of Carter's international pastorship of promoting the basic freedoms of speech, assembly and worship, or the right to move from one job to another or one home to another, or to emigrate to another country. He did not invent human rights, but human rights did in a way reinvent Jimmy Carter, giving all his postpresidential journeys a distinct missionary aura.[30]

In addition to diplomatic meetings and human rights promotion, Jimmy and Rosalynn Carter had a personal engagement to attend in Egypt. Among their first destinations was Mit Abul-Kum, Sadat's serene boyhood town northwest of Cairo in the Nile Delta, for lunch with his widow Jehan and her rather large and impressive family. After an hour of warm conversation with the family over mint tea, the Carters, accompanied by Sadat's son-in-law as well as Christopher Hemmeter and Ken Stein, took a stroll through the quiet village and its surrounding orange groves and cotton fields. Hundreds of farmers gathered to see them, shouting heartfelt greetings to Jimmy Carter as if he were a latter-day Mahatma Gandhi.[31]

Later, after a traditional Egyptian meal at the Sadat home, Jehan cleared her throat, bringing a hush to the table. "Jimmy," she intoned, "I was cleaning out my husband's desk, putting his papers in order, and I came across one of the things he wrote about you just before his death. Would you care to hear it?" Carter would. Jehan cleared her throat again and read: "Jimmy Carter is my very best friend on earth. He is the most honorable man I know. Brilliant and deeply religious, he has all the marvelous attributes that made him inept in dealing with the scoundrels who run the world." Silence fell over the room. Then Carter smiled, somewhat awkwardly, and nodded his head.

"Well, maybe," he said softly and graciously. "But I'll never change."[32] That Sadat had considered him his closest friend meant more to Carter than mere words could express. When asked ten years later how often he thought about Sadat, his answer was, "Every day," and he pointed to a picture of the Egyptian peacemaker prominently displayed on his desk next to that of Rosalynn.[33]

At a press conference toward the end of the week Carter predictably praised Sadat's protégé Mubarak, touted the Camp David accords as "still the best formula for peace," and made front-page news in Cairo by saying, "The problems of the Palestinians should be resolved in all their aspects, and the principles expressed by the United Nations in many resolutions should be honored."[34] Carter had learned something crucial from Mubarak and others: that Egypt deemed the PLO leadership not terrorists but symbols of freedom in the Arab world—even the controversial Yasir Arafat, perennial dark glasses, army uniform, stubble, houndstooth kaffiyeh, and all. "I was starting to see that Arafat had been, to a substantial degree, unfairly maligned in the Western press," Carter said later.[35]

A s the Carters headed to Jerusalem, they asked the pilot to take them
over Mount Sinai so they could see the spot where Moses had received
the Ten Commandments. Down below, meanwhile, speculation raged
as to exactly what the former president was up to. Although he made it clear
he was not in the Middle East "to bring people together or negotiate in any
way," and that he had no intention of legitimizing the PLO, it seemed to
many in Israel that that was precisely what Carter was doing.[36] And it certainly didn't help that in Brzezinski's just-published memoir *Power and Principle*, given wide circulation in the Israeli press, he recalled that during the
tense days of Camp David President Carter had referred to the Israeli prime
minister as a "psycho."[37]

Carter was coming to a far more troubled land than that he had visited
ten years before as governor of Georgia. "The sense of unanimity among the
Jewish citizens and the carefree confidence of 1973 were gone," he noted,
nostalgic for tranquil days before the constant presence of armed military
personnel.[38] In 1973 Prime Minister Golda Meir had embraced the ambitious and curious American from Georgia who referred so often to the Bible.
Chain-smoking Chesterfield cigarettes with Jody Powell, Meir expressed
concern over the ultra-orthodox Jewish religious parties that wielded political influence far beyond their numerical strength. As leader of the right-
wing Herut (later Likud) party, which held only 22 percent of the Knesset
seats, Begin was considered by many an extremist; by 1977 he would replace
Meir as prime minister of Israel.[39]

By his 1983 trip, self-determination for the Palestinians had become
Carter's chief interest in the region—and the mention of the issue raised the
tempers of Herut party members. Almost from the moment Carter stepped
off the plane and was greeted by U.S. ambassador Samuel W. Lewis, things
in Tel Aviv were off to a rocky start. Carter's initial consultation with Begin,
at an unremarkable office in the Israeli parliament building, went as well as
could be expected: courteous, if forced, nostalgia alternated with profound
disagreement over many aspects of U.S.-Israeli relations. "It was not a warm
exchange," Carter recalled. Accustomed to Begin's headstrong moods and
intransigent postures, however, Carter insisted on pressing his points
advising the prime minister point-blank, for example, to "pull out of Lebanon
now." Jimmy Carter was still a burr under Begin's saddle, now as a former
American president sympathetic to the plight of the Palestinians and openly
critical of America's "special" relationship with Israel.[40]

Following this unproductive session with Begin, Jimmy and Rosalynn
toured East Jerusalem and the West Bank and Gaza, which they had not

been free to do during their official trip in 1979, as the United States did not recognize Israeli control over those areas. Just an hour before the Carters were scheduled to begin a walking tour of the walled Old City of Jerusalem, gangs of teenage Palestinians congregated at Damascus Gate and at Herod's Gate. They threw bottles and demolished a police van; chants of "Carter is a Zionist" and "Carter, go home" were quelled only when police fired shots in the air to disperse the mob, in the process arresting thirteen youths. In response, a wild horde of yeshiva students took to smashing the windows of Palestinian-owned stores in the Old City, turning its narrow streets into rivers of shattered glass and prompting an additional nine arrests.[41]

Wherever they went in the Israeli-occupied West Bank and East Jerusalem on March 9, the Carters were met by angry demonstrators waving vituperative placards in front of buildings festooned with similar banners. Protests erupted at Jimmy Carter's lunch meeting with Bethlehem's Palestinian mayor, Elias M. Freij; at the local university, where protestors were teargassed, then arrested; in the West Bank town of Hebron, where five Israelis were injured by rocks thrown by Arabs, and at the Dheishe refugee camp, where Jewish settlers fired machine guns over the heads of a gang of rampaging Palestinians. Secondary schools were ordered closed in hopes of dispersing the young protestors, and Defense Minister Moshe Arens urged Jewish settlers to refrain from violence against Palestinians.[42] "The riots were scary," Hemmeter recalled. "Our motorcade had to take circuitous routes to avoid getting stoned or fired upon. As we entered Bethlehem with all this violent commotion, the president just stared introspectively out the limousine window, visibly upset and biting his lip, but not saying a word."[43]

Carter sympathized with the frustrated Palestinians and their demand for the basic rights of citizenship. To him, the most distressing sight on the West Bank was not the Palestinian hooliganism but the high-rise cities being erected by Jewish settlers. After a day in the occupied Gaza Strip—where he met separately with a cross-section of Palestinians and a group of Israeli scholars—Carter took two public occasions to criticize the Begin government: for taking a "narrow" view of the Camp David accords and their application to the West Bank and Gaza, and for failing to adhere across the board to the terms of UN Resolution 242, which called for withdrawal from territories seized in conflict since 1967. Begin, as ever, saw things his way, and maintained that agreeing to pull out of the Sinai meant he did not have to withdraw Israeli armed forces from the biblically significant Judea and Samaria.[44]

Begin shed no tears when Jimmy and Rosalynn Carter, refusing a State Department request that their passports be left without Israeli stamps, crossed over the Jordan River and headed to Amman on March 13 for the third leg of their Middle East journey. Once in Jordan they were escorted by a complement of meticulously uniformed Bedouin guards to lunch with the thirty-six-year-old Crown Prince Hassan ibn-Talal. Later that day the prince urged his brother, King Hussein ibn-Talal, to play a forceful role in future talks with Israel about Palestinian autonomy. The Carters were greeted warmly by King Hussein and Queen Noor (the American-born former Lisa Halaby), and given accommodations in a guest house within the royal compound. Although he resisted Carter's attempt to engage him in peace talks based on the Reagan plan without the consent of the PLO as well as the rest of the Arab world, Hussein was nevertheless sympathetic to the former president's efforts—and behind closed doors encouraged him to keep them up.[45]

Hussein had never recovered from what he later admitted was a regrettable decision to side with Syria and Egypt in their ill-conceived military offensive against Israel in 1967. Israeli troops triumphed in a matter of days and had occupied East Jerusalem and the West Bank—then under Jordanian jurisdiction—where they remained firmly rooted at the time of Carter's trip. Jordan had been the biggest loser in the Six-Day War: gone, practically overnight, were almost half its population, East Jerusalem, the Holy Land tourist draws of Jericho and Bethlehem, and vast tracts of agriculturally productive land. A quarter million Palestinian refugees had fled the now-Israeli-occupied West Bank for Jordan's side of the river. Retaliation intensified, including some of this century's worst acts of terrorism, especially in the years 1968 to 1973. "Despite Hussein's efforts to control them, the increasingly powerful and militant Palestinians used some of the refugee camps as commando bases for their almost constant attacks on Israel," Carter noted after his meeting with the Jordanian leader. "Many of these militants were perfectly willing to accept the retaliatory raids on Jordan because they weakened Hussein's political power by making him unpopular. One of the objectives of the militant Palestinians was to replace Jordan's monarchy with a republic like that of Nasser's Egypt."[46]

Discussing the Palestinian question face to face with King Hussein helped Carter realize for the first time how imperative it was for Jordan to be involved in the peace process. At a press conference he held just before departing Amman for Saudi Arabia, Carter declared that Israeli settlements in the West Bank were "a direct violation of international law and the most serious adverse development [in the region] in the past two years." Carter also reiterated his hope that "King Hussein and the Palestinians on the West Bank would enter into negotiations with Israel." Carter's peace-minded trial balloons were making him Arab friends at Israel's expense.[47]

Jordan may have been an unstable nation fraught with political difficulties, but as the Carters found, it was also a delightful place to explore. The couple mingled with farmers, chatted with journalists, and met with professors at the University of Jordan; they inspected impressive agricultural projects on the East Bank, and were taken in jeeps to the ancient Nabatean city Petra in the Valley of Moses, where, according to the Bible, God blessed the Israelites with water that flowed when Moses struck his staff upon a rock. "It was breathtaking," Carter reminisced. "It seemed as if many eons and thousands of miles separated us from the current problems of the Middle East."[48]

The next stop was Saudi Arabia, where Carter was met at the airport by U.S. ambassador Richard Murphy and conducted through a full day of lukewarm consultations with Crown Prince Abdullah, defense minister Prince Sultan, foreign minister Prince Saud al-Faisal, and other leaders of the Saudi government, including many more members of the royal family. King Fahd sent his regrets that he had been unable to greet Carter in Riyadh as he was in the desert meeting with tribal leaders, but added that he wanted the former president to join him the following day at his encampment 250 kilometers north of the capital.

The Carters flew by helicopter to his remote desert camp. After a spectacular flight over vast expanses pocked only occasionally with signs of life in the form of black goat-hair tents and recently sprouted wildflowers, the Carters spotted King Fahd's retreat shimmering in the desert like a mirage. "As we circled closer, we noticed that immediately behind each of the main tents was an elaborate mobile home perched on a large Mercedes truck chassis, modern additions to the traditional tent dwellings of Saudi chieftains," Carter recorded in his notebook at the time. "Just beyond the periphery of the camp was a group of portable diesel electric generators and an elaborate array of satellite dish antennas to provide power for the several hundred desert homes, international communications for the nation's ruler, and television entertainment for those at the campsite."[49]

Upon landing Jimmy was immediately taken to see King Fahd, while Rosalynn, not permitted under Saudi custom to participate in a meeting with men, was bustled to an isolated area of the compound reserved for women. The traditionally second-class status of women in the Arabian Peninsula was so ingrained in the culture that Carter refrained from commenting on it, afraid that it would be perceived as an insult. "They were in a different camp entirely," the former president noted, "over the sand dune and out of sight." Carter met the king at his central tent, which was filled with ancient heirlooms and extravagant oriental rugs. In three hours of wide-ranging talks, Carter found the king, a compulsive all-night CNN viewer, cordial and anxious to learn about his recent sessions with Mubarak, Begin, and Hussein. "King Fahd was so very grateful for my selling his nation F-15 airplanes in 1978," Carter recalled, "and for supporting the sale of AWACs so he could protect his people from unwarranted attack initiated across the Persian Gulf."[50]

The king unleashed all his charm upon Carter. He detailed the advances his nation had made in everything from agriculture to women's rights, even as he stressed that Saudi Arabia was bent on "modernization" rather than "Westernization." Distressed that the Qur'an's high moral standards were often ignored in late-twentieth-century Saudi Arabia, Fahd was equally perturbed by American stereotypes of Arabs either as camel-racing Monte Carlo sheiks made decadent by oil money or as unshaven terrorists toting bombs onto airplanes. Instead he portrayed a people struggling to adopt old ways to new realities; so it was that protecting Islam's holy cities, Fahd said, was his primary military interest. Given Saudi Arabia's current situation— the Iran-Iraq war raging along its border, the Persian Gulf heavily mined, the possibility that Soviet troops could turn the country into a Russian satellite, and the propinquity of a formidable, highly armed Israel as antagonist— Carter could sympathize with the king's obsession over self-defense. That made it all the more gratifying for Carter to learn that the circumspect and patient King Fahd, a vehement supporter of the Fez declaration, felt there were only differences in nuance regarding the Palestinian question between the Arab resolution and the Reagan plan.[51]

After a lavish ten-course dinner with Prince Abdullah, head of the Saudi National Guard, the Carters and Ken Stein were escorted to an elaborate recreation area. While Carter and Prince Abdullah engaged in deep political discussion, Stein diplomatically lost a game of eight ball to Prince Bandar.[52] Carter was then introduced to two PLO leaders, and their discussion carried on throughout the night. "We left the desert camp reassured that King Fahd wanted to resolve the Palestinian issue even though he certainly was no admirer of Israel," Carter said.[53] And he put his money where his mouth had been: King Fahd not only pledged Saudi Arabia's participation in an upcoming Carter Center Middle East "consultation," but he also donated $1 million in order to be counted among the founders of the new non-governmental organization. It was clear that private chats with Arab leaders—as with so many others—could reveal much more than their public statements.[54]

∽∘∾

On March 16, even as the Damascus press denounced him as a hateful mouthpiece of the U.S. State Department, Jimmy Carter prepared for a series of "constructive talks" with President Hafez al-Assad. "I reviewed [the] news summaries from our embassies with some concern," Carter recalled. "Syria and the United States were aligned against each other in Lebanon, and the newspaper articles and radio broadcasts in the state-controlled media had to mirror Assad's feelings." Undeterred, Carter proceeded as planned. He had met Assad six years earlier in Geneva, Switzerland, and found him "shrewd and flexible," an observation that annoyed many in the Reagan administration. "In Assad," Carter noted, "I observed a man who spoke simply for himself and his country, without self-doubt and with little consideration for how his views might conflict with those of anyone else."[55]

It was this curious ability of Carter to understand, and at times sympathize with, brutal dictators such as Assad that caused him to be denounced by Washington officialdom as naive at best, and a menace at worst. How could a man who preached human rights so passionately out of one side of his mouth praise nefarious criminals out of the other, even in the name of peace? It had not gone unnoticed by the Reagan administration that in the Middle East Carter seemed more comfortable dealing with autocratic rulers like King Fahd and President Assad than with the avowedly pro-American leadership of Israel's chaotic democracy. Ignoring such criticism, Carter went on consorting with international pariahs. "I've seen Carter sit for an hour with Assad and listen patiently, not saying a word," Stein has noted. "Then he would finally speak up, summarizing brilliantly and offering workable solutions to aspects of the inflammatory issue at hand."[56]

Throughout his postpresidential career Carter was caricatured in two ways: as an international "peace outlaw" prevailing through personal wisdom, inner drive, selflessness, and uncanny timing, or as a vain and sanctimonious interloper ("pacifist-aggressive," quipped one commentator) seeking political redemption in the form of a Nobel Peace Prize. Carter philosophically answered his detractors: "The rain falls on the righteous and unrighteous alike." On this occasion, American ambassador to Syria Robert P. Paganelli was happy with Carter's visit, as it provided him an occasion to meet the aloof President Assad for the first time.[57]

During the four-hour meeting Assad—who had then been president of Syria for fourteen years—argued against the Camp David accords and the Israeli-Egyptian peace treaty as horrendous mistakes that undermined pan-Arab unity. Entrenched distrust of Israel underlay his conviction that only a continued demonstration of solidarity among Arabs would force Jewish settlers to withdraw from the West Bank, Gaza, and the Golan Heights. Yet it was clear that Assad wished to be asked to participate in any negotiations between the Palestinians and Jordanians.[58] "I think one of the reasons that President Assad wants to see you is the sense of isolation he now feels from the Arab world and the United States," Stein had written Carter in a prescient memo before the trip. "He needs to be wanted."[59]

Thus encouraged, Carter sought an opening in Assad's prejudices through which forward-looking dialogue could flow. "I decided to push Assad on some sensitive issues," he recalled. Along these lines Carter asked about Syria's contingency plans for a variety of possible crisis situations. No matter what the question, however, and no matter how brilliantly based on probing analysis, Assad's answers all rested on the simple assumption that Syria's actions were always justified, Israel's always suspect. So when Carter chided him for purchasing Soviet airplanes and munitions, Assad shot back, "Will you sell me any arms with which to defend my country, even a pistol?" Scoffing at Secretary of Defense Caspar Weinberger's recent statement that Syria, a direct supporter of the PLO revolution, was a Soviet puppet, Assad made it clear that his ultimate dream was not a Communist Syria but a united and fortified Arab nation extending along the southern and eastern shores of the Mediterranean Sea all the way to the Persian Gulf.[60] Stein, who sat in on part of the meeting, found Assad to be a surprisingly "thoughtful, intelligent, and pragmatic fellow."[61]

Ever the optimist, Carter left Syria feeling that somewhere down the line Assad could play a positive role in the region rather than his usual obstructionist one. "Although he has so far demonstrated only a negative influence," Carter later noted, "under circumstances to his liking Assad could even be a prime catalyst in achieving an overall peace agreement in the Middle East."[62] Looking forward to that day, the former president extracted a promise from Assad that Syria's foreign minister would participate in the Carter Center's upcoming consultation on the Middle East. What's more, he received a special gift from Assad: a rare gold sword, which Carter later gave to Christopher Hemmeter to "ward off lawyers."[63]

Carter believed he had taken the first small steps toward pulling Syria out from the Soviet sphere of influence. For years outside the Arab world Assad, with a well-documented history of torturing his enemies, had no real friends except in the Soviet Union, which supplied Syria with military aircraft and other sophisticated weaponry. The idealistic Carter wanted to change that, and succeeded in building a permanent "open channel" to Assad in Damascus. From 1983 onward Assad communicated by telephone with Jimmy Carter, the American who had shared pigeon soup at his table. Although he might disagree strongly with the former U.S. president, Assad believed he was a man of his word, a man he could trust. Carter felt the same way about Assad.[64]

The sojourn in Syria was not, of course, all business. While in Damascus the Carters made a point of walking down "the Street called Straight," the lane where the Apostle Paul's sight had been miraculously restored after his conversion from Judaism to Christianity. "The entire trip brought the Bible to life for us," Rosalynn recalled.[65] "It would have been senseless to have made this educational journey and skipped Syria," Carter noted. "If you are going to forget Syria you can forget permanent peace."[66]

The last major stop on the Carters' Middle East tour was Lebanon, which Jimmy Carter called "the most ravaged, the most shattered country on the face of the globe."[67] After a circuitous flight around Lebanese territory, Carter landed at Beirut International Airport, a virtual fortress manned by 1,500 American soldiers. A large contingent of them formed a circle around the jet to protect it on the tarmac; inside the plane Tom Benedict, the head Secret Service agent, passed out bullet-proof vests for everyone to wear. Carter's delegation sped through the desolate, decimated streets of Beirut in an armored limousine surrounded by an escort of five U.S. Marine HumVees, part of a multinational peacekeeping force. Their destination was the presidential palace, where they were to be hosted by Amin Gemayel, thirty-four-year-old brother and successor of recently slain President Bashir Gemayel. Carter wrote in *The Blood of Abraham* (1985), "Our haste could not hide the devastation of war-bombed-out buildings with people still living in them; telltale scenes of soldiers in all kinds of uniforms standing guard at machine-gun stations all along the sidewalks with guns slung over their shoulders; and little children playing around them, some with miniature weapons of their own, others running their wagons and race cars down tracks cut into the sides of the earthen bunkers."[68]

As the motorcade passed Christian-dominated East Beirut into Muslim- and PLO-controlled West Beirut, which had been devastated by Israeli bombs, the Carters saw Lebanese marines holding RPG launchers, ready to blow up an apartment building. Along the highway were signs of the multilateral force—Italian, French, and American flags interspersed among Lebanese contingents and even an Israeli group. At the airport Carter had spoken with Colonel James Mead, commander of the U.S. unit. He registered his unhappiness that his soldiers had to carry unloaded weapons (to the scorn of the Israelis) and that regardless of provocation or disruption they were under orders to continue to stand at attention and avoid fights. "It was difficult," Carter noted. "Our marines were placed in the unenviable position of ignoring abusive comments, doing everything possible to avoid an international incident."[69]

Meticulous in his double-breasted suit and pointed Italian shoes, President Gemayel greeted Carter at his palace, unruffled by fears for his safety—nor was he openly critical of Israeli actions. His one complaint to Carter was about interference from Israel in his effort to reconstruct the Lebanese army: Begin, he said, had been insisting that a Lebanese colonel who had become a de facto adjunct of the Israeli army monitor the southern portion of Lebanon for Israel. The young Gemayel, Carter thought, was just a puppet in a deadly power game he did not fully comprehend.[70]

His visit to Lebanon disturbed Carter more than he had anticipated; it was clear that when the foreign troops pulled out, which he hoped would happen soon, civil war of major proportions would break out again. The situation in Lebanon, Jimmy Carter realized, could not easily be rectified.

The trip back to the airport was frightening. The Secret Service had discovered that several renegade individuals with hand grenades had been apprehended by the Israeli military before Carter reached the palace. Toting Uzis, Tom Benedict and the other agents climbed into the backseat of the limousine, with Stein and Carter's secretary Faye Dill serving as decoys while Jimmy and Rosalynn were escorted to a nondescript automobile. Before departing Carter addressed a group of American soldiers at a well-lighted airport hangar, and the rest of his unnerved delegation hoped his remarks would be brief. "I wanted so much to be gone from Lebanese air space," Stein wrote Hemmeter the next day from the haven of a café in Fez. "I have read all the dispatches which the Secret Service had received detailing the security problems in and around the airport; all I could think of was some hand-held piece of equipment that would disintegrate the Bac 1-11."[71]

"The trip gave [Carter] a renewed sense of self-worth," Stein noted.[72] Carter's fellow Democrats—for instance, presidential hopefuls Walter Mondale and John Glenn—may not have been eager for his distilled wisdom, but the king of Saudi Arabia and the president of Egypt had been. Caspar Weinberger and Reagan's new secretary of state, George Shultz, may have disdained Carter's Middle East trip as deliberate and unwelcome meddling in official policy making, but midlevel foreign service officers and even Reagan's ambassadors had welcomed and catered proudly to the former president in each of the seven countries he had visited. "I want once again to emphasize what a success for Moroccan-American relations you and Mrs. Carter's visit to the Kingdom was," U.S. ambassador to Morocco Joseph Verner Reed wrote. "Bravo! Your audience with his Majesty King Hassan II remains a highlight of my tenure as President Reagan's envoy."[73] The message Carter left wherever he went was that he was still a force to be reckoned with—a peacemaker without portfolio, perhaps, but one filled with conviction and stamina.

After reporting privately on his trip to the secretary of state, Carter also made an excruciatingly candid presentation at a meeting of the Council on Foreign Relations in New York. He strongly criticized the Israeli government, Moshe Arens and Menachem Begin in particular, arguing that on the key issues—Palestinian self-determination and withdrawal from the West Bank and Gaza—there were no substantial differences among the positions of Egypt, Jordan, the Palestinians, and the United States. "Israel is the problem toward peace," Carter informed the council.[74]

Carter's blunt council speech raised eyebrows, and word of it reached Atlanta courtesy of Brookings Institution fellow William Quandt. Stein threw up his hands: his boss was sounding like the openly anti-Israel former undersecretary of state George Ball. "Are you being too brutally candid?" Stein wrote to Carter. "I am afraid that people will focus ultimately on your tone and not the content of your remarks on Israeli settlements, Palestinian rights, etc. And again, I reiterate what I said to you in the notes prepared for the Council on Foreign Relations talk, criticism of Israel can be even understood as long as it is put into the context of what supporters of Israel (not Begin) want to hear—namely Israeli security, territorial integrity, and independence."[75]

After a dinner in Atlanta with Kenneth Bialkin, president of the Anti-Defamation League of B'nai Brith, Stein was even more concerned that Carter was losing the honest-broker status he had earned at Camp David. "I believe you carry a standard into this conference as an adversary of Israel," Stein wrote Carter on August 5 in reference to the upcoming Emory consultation. "Rightly or wrongly, you are not trusted by Menachem Begin or supporters of Israel in this country." Stein feared that the media would make it look as though "*we* are out to fry Israel and Begin." Carter laughed Stein off, telling him the freedom to speak candidly served as pressure release from the odious chore of fund-raising.[76]

And it was quite a chore: over the next six months the ex-president traversed the world with Christopher Hemmeter in pursuit of the $28 million needed to build the Carter Center complex. The most productive stop on the campaign for cash proved to be Japan. In July Carter consulted with Prime Minister Yasuhiro Nakasone, then gave TBS a live television interview from Tokyo in which he chastised the Reagan administration for making public demands on the Japanese government to alter their trade and defense policies. Such arrogance, Carter proclaimed, was "not only ill-advised, but counterproductive."[77]

Social and diplomatic efforts aside, there was still business to be done. Carter had just been named—along with Gerald Ford and two former Japanese prime ministers, Takeo Fukuda and Nobuskue Kishi—an honorary adviser to the grant-making board of the United States–Japan Foundation. The resourceful Carter used the honor to gain direct access to Ryoichi Sasakawa, the ultrarightist Tokyo tycoon who had created the foundation in 1981 with $45 million from his Japanese Shipbuilding Industry Foundation. Emory's president James Laney accompanied Carter and Hemmeter to their meeting with the octogenarian, in which they hoped to convince Sasakawa to collaborate with the Carter Center. They succeeded. Over the next two years Sasakawa—who in his lifetime gave $4 billion to the cause of world peace— became a Carter Center benefactor, contributing more than $1.7 million to programs for providing health care and alleviating social problems in less-developed nations.[78]

Stein had stayed behind to put together the inaugural Middle East consultation, scheduled to be held on campus November 6–9. Prominent scholars and policy makers from most of the Arab countries had promised to attend, but Israel was letting Carter down. Prime Minister Begin, who had promised to send his close advisor Eli Rubenstein, resigned in early September. Israel's ambassador to the United States, Meir Rosenne, called Carter on October 10, less than a month before the conference, to relay the message that Israel was boycotting the event because Palestinian historian Dr. Walid Khalidi of Harvard University had been invited to participate. Khalidi, the Israelis maintained, was the "intellectual spine" of the PLO (an assertion the U.S. State Department refuted). With that telephone call, Jimmy Carter's five-year-old hope of rekindling the spirit of Camp David was extinguished. The usually self-assured Carter suddenly began to question whether this grand "meeting of the minds" was going to work at all.[79]

Only a week earlier, Ruth Carter Stapleton—the sibling to whom Carter felt closest—had died of pancreatic cancer in Fayetteville, North Carolina, having refused chemotherapy. It was Ruth's support that had helped Jimmy Carter use his Christian strength to continue in politics after his defeat in the 1966 governor's race by arch-segregationist Lester Maddox, and her loss hit hard. Only three weeks later Miss Lillian also died of pancreatic cancer. Her funeral was held in Plains on November 1, All Saints' Day. Hundreds of people attended the funeral, and flowers poured in from admirers as diverse as George Wallace and Loretta Lynn. "This woman was full of good works," the Reverend Fred Collins told a mourning assemblage.[80]

With the pain of his double loss still raw, Carter felt oddly abandoned and unsure of himself, even though his faith reassured him that he would meet his mother and sister again in heaven. His personal distress cast a pall over his work as well, leaving doubts where enthusiasm had been. "Is this consultation really going to work? I have my doubts," he told Stein. Among Carter's concerns was the potential damage the media could do. In June Stein had sent Carter a note asking, "How involved in the conference do you want representatives of the media to be?" The former president wrote back, "Maximum at their expense."[81] Sol Linowitz had advised against allowing the press into what they were already dubbing "Camp Carter." He worried that with reporters and cameras around, "the government designates would be playing to home audiences, posturing, taking extreme positions." As the event neared, Carter began to think Linowitz had been right. And security was much on Carter's mind after October 23, when a truck loaded with TNT had been driven kamikaze-style into U.S. Marine headquarters in Beirut, killing 241 Americans.[82]

On the morning of November 6 the Woodruff Medical Center Auditorium at Emory University was brimming with noteworthy diplomats, statesmen, and scholars of the Middle East. Also in attendance were sharpshooters on the roof, sixty police officers, a team of explosive-sniffing German shepherds, and a small battalion of Secret Service agents.

The four-day consultation, cochaired by former presidents Carter and Ford, turned out to be an unprecedented gathering of international experts from ten nations, including the Soviet Union. Among the participants were Usamah al-Baz, the Egyptian president's adviser on political affairs; Meron Benvenisti, former vice mayor of Jerusalem; Zbigniew Brzezinski, at that time with the Center for Strategic and International Studies; Philip Habib, senior research fellow at the Hoover Institute; Walid Khalidi of the Center for Middle Eastern Studies at Harvard; Prince Bandar ibn-Sultan, Saudi Arabia's ambassador to the United States; the crown prince of the Hashemite Kingdom of Jordan, Hasan ibn-Talal; and former U.S. secretary of state Cyrus Vance. A symposium at this level was usually sponsored by the United Nations or the World Bank.[83] "At this stage in the cold war this sort of track-two diplomacy was unusual," recalled William Quandt. "Carter deserves credit for making this type of useful back-channel diplomatic exchange more acceptable."[84] But by his own outspokenness on the Palestinian question, Carter had denied himself the role of Middle East peacemaker he so desired: no high-profile Israelis attended.[85]

Opening the consultation with the timeliest issue, Carter and Ford stated their shared opinion that the United States should forgo military retaliation for the deadly attack on the marines in Beirut. That morning the press had reported that President Reagan was ordering thirty U.S. Navy ships, carrying three hundred planes, to the Mediterranean. Carter warned that such saber rattling would prove counterproductive to the recessed Geneva peace talks between Lebanon's government and the nation's rival factions. "To guess who is responsible, or to base a military action on unsubstantiated allegations, would be a very serious mistake," he declared.[86]

For the next four days Emory University became a media mecca. Television crews filmed members of royal families sipping coffee next to blown-up photographs of the Camp David meetings. Stretch Cadillacs lined up in front of the medical center auditorium. The *Atlanta Journal & Constitution* ran daily front-page accounts of the event—exactly the sort of hometown support for the center Carter had craved. Various Arab newspapers covering the spectacle, including Kuwait's *al-Oabas*, dubbed the consultations the "Atlanta Initiative."[87]

As for results, the talks produced a consensus that the Camp David accords should be used as the basis for future formal discussions. That and the fact that nobody stormed out in a rage were enough for the event to be deemed a success by CNN. "The consultation's most significant contribution," Carter noted later, "was the informality that allowed face-to-face discussion."[88]

Not all was warm and fuzzy. The passions surrounding these decidedly nonacademic issues erupted now and then, such as when Walid Khalidi was joined at the podium on the last day of the consultation by Israeli scholar Haim Shaked in what became a wrenching (if at times humorous) demonstration of political differences. Khalidi castigated the United States for treating the Palestinian people as a "nonentity" and the PLO as a "leper," then called on the Reagan administration to recognize Palestinian rights to a homeland. To the dismay of the Israelis present, Harold Saunders, who had been a State Department adviser on the Middle East in the Carter administration, concurred: "I don't see why the United States just can't come out and say it . . . in so many words that the Palestinian people have the right of self-determination."[89]

Impressed by the general cordiality among antagonists, Alexander Zotov, a political counselor at the Soviet embassy in Washington, predicted that the consultation "could be a substantial contribution to peace in the long run."[78] In part, he was referring to a suggestion Egypt's Usamah al-Baz put forth for a "new approach": simultaneously putting on the table the Camp David accords, UN Resolution 242, the Fez declaration, and Reagan's September 1982 proposal. If common ground could be found among these initiatives, the idea went, delegates from each involved nation could attempt to negotiate the differences into one comprehensive plan for peace. The only negative feelings that seemed to remain among the participants were toward Israel, for boycotting the talks.[90]

If Israel was the consultation's loser, Jimmy Carter was its winner. Glowing reports appeared in the *New York Times*, the *Washington Post*, *Newsweek*, *USA Today*, and dozens of other newspapers and periodicals.

Carter had proven that his conflict resolution center could indeed fill a significant vacuum. Atlantans seemed proud to have had such an important and visible event in the city's backyard, so far from the usual power centers of Washington, New York, Los Angeles, and Chicago. "We are impressed by this first endeavor of the new Carter Center of Emory University," the *Atlanta Journal* pronounced in its November 11, 1983, lead editorial.[91] Carter's preconference apprehension that the media might disrupt honest dialogue had proved unfounded: all the participants had been on their best behavior and eager to display their reasonableness. "We should make every effort to have C-SPAN or CNN carry our public programs gavel to gavel," Stein told Carter. He also passed on numerous statements from Arab governments, as reported by the Foreign Broadcast Information Service, boasting that they had mustered the courage to talk peace while Israel cowered alone.[92]

Carter may not have been able to make the United States' Middle East policy from Georgia, but he could isolate the problems and identify the players who wanted to make peace. One of these was King Hussein's brother, Crown Prince Hassan of Jordan, who began to form a significant personal relationship with Jimmy Carter as a result of the Emory consultation. Hassan took a scholarly approach to the Middle East's complex political issues, studying the literature and participating in international forums, where his elegant manners never failed to impress less regal scholars. When the Carter delegation had visited Jordan in March 1983, Hassan had been delighted to show off his expertise in the history of his nation. Not long after the "Atlanta Initiative," Hassan began corresponding with Carter, using the former president as his interpreter of American politics and as a sounding board for his own ideas. It was a relationship Carter relished, for it gave him a direct channel to the mind of King Hussein—something neither George Shultz's Middle East experts nor the CIA's operatives could establish, no matter how they sought to infiltrate the power circles in Amman. When King Hussein gave a particularly relevant political speech, Prince Hassan would dispatch a transcript addressed to Jimmy Carter, "friend of Jordan," always with a personal note attached. Hassan even wrote the former president confidential reports from time to time, such as a March 9, 1984, memo detailing various intrigues in the Arab world that previously had been unknown to Carter and were possibly still unknown to the Reagan administration as well.[93]

On one occasion Prince Hassan wrote to Carter of his worries about a forthcoming vote on the Moynihan Bill (Senate 2031), which called for the U.S. embassy in Israel to move from Tel Aviv to Jerusalem. Muslims construed this proposed gesture as an encouragement to Jews to settle in Arab East Jerusalem which Israel had annexed during the Six-Day War. Carter replied to Prince Hassan on March 23, taking the precaution of having his letter hand-delivered in a sealed envelope through the Jordanian embassy in Washington. Carter wrote:

> As usual, your analysis of the disturbing circumstances in the Middle East is very helpful to me. The reconstitution of Jordan's parliament and your role in the increasing acceptance of Egypt back into the Arab fold attest to the moderate and responsible efforts of your nation's leaders. My presumption is that the P.L.O. leaders did not agree to a more dynamic role for King Hussein in joining the peace talks, and I realize that there has not been any help forthcoming from Washington. The cancellation of the arms sales proposals by the President and the strong move in Congress to shift our Embassy to Jerusalem are counterproductive and somewhat embarrassing. Unfortunately—even tragically—our Middle East foreign policy seems to be debilitated by presidential election year concerns on incumbents and candidates, which means that other officials here and abroad will have to initiate whatever action might prove to be feasible. With limited means and influence, President Ford and I will do what we can to maintain some semblance of balance in these matters, and it will be very helpful to us to know about any tangible moves that may be possible among those like you who are directly involved.[94]

Carter immediately began spearheading a campaign to stop the embassy move, keeping Prince Hassan informed of its progress. Having lined up Ford and Nixon, Carter wrote and called important legislators, urging them to derail Moynihan's "shameless bill," which he described as a cheap ploy to get political support from American Jews. Carter believed, as he wrote to Democratic representative Lee Hamilton of Indiana, that "such a decision by our country would be a devastating blow to the prospects for further progress toward peace in the region, would seriously damage relations between the United States and all Arab countries, and would be counter to the best interests of Israel."[95] On this issue George Shultz was in full agreement with Jimmy Carter, and he lobbied Capitol Hill with all the vigor he could muster to kill the Moynihan Bill. The concerted effort succeeded, and the American embassy remained in Tel Aviv.[96]

After the Middle East conference the PLO also praised Carter for seeming to understand their plight. Hoping eventually to meet with Yasir Arafat face to face, Carter began to establish a back channel to the

Palestinian leader, thinking they might communicate by messenger on a monthly basis. Understanding that in his position at Emory, Stein could not help put this private conduit together, Carter began sounding out his longtime friend and former Peace Corps director Mary King—whom he knew was trusted by the PLO—about how best to structure a secret dialogue with Arafat.[97]

Naturally, as Carter gained adherents in the Arab world, more Israelis began to regard him as an unwelcome meddler who talked too much and could pose a threat to Israeli security. The Israeli leaders saw Carter as cavalierly pursuing his own political rehabilitation rather than sincerely working for peace. When Carter was lobbying against the Moynihan Bill, Teddy Kollek, the mayor of Jerusalem, wrote him a blistering letter condemning derogatory remarks Carter had recently made about the city as well as his open-mouth policy in general. "It was sad to read your interview in the Kuwait *el-Anbaa*, which contained the statement that Jerusalem has become 'a home for killing, hatred, provocation, and misunderstanding,'" Kollek wrote. "*Never* in the history of Jerusalem has such freedom existed, and we are making every effort to ensure that this situation is maintained. It is difficult to understand how you who observed this from close by could describe our city in such terms."[98] He enclosed an anti-Carter editorial that had just appeared in the *Jerusalem Post*. Carter was stung by Kollek's reprimanding tone, but wrote back simply that he had been misquoted; he had "never made such a statement."[99]

Ignoring the critics as usual, Carter continued his efforts on behalf of the Palestinians, occasionally conferring with Assistant Secretary of State for Near Eastern Affairs Richard Murphy or with Shultz himself, although never with Reagan directly. Appearing on CBS's much-watched *60 Minutes* early in 1985 to promote his book *The Blood of Abraham*, Carter summed up his views in one unequivocating sentence. Asked by Mike Wallace what "bold move" he might make if he still resided at 1600 Pennsylvania Avenue, Carter answered, "There is no reason why George Shultz can't sit down with Yasir Arafat." In the same interview Carter utterly disparaged the Republican administration, offering that he "could not think of a single international or diplomatic achievement that's been realized by Ronald Reagan."[100]

Given his harshness, Carter was taken by surprise later that year when a letter he sent to Ronald Reagan explaining the importance of including Jordan in the peace process evoked a long, warm, and extremely coherent response from the president himself. "Dear Jimmy," Reagan's letter began. "Forgive the informality, but since we are both members of a somewhat exclusive club, I thought maybe we could forgo protocol." After explaining that he was trying to bring King Hussein and Prime Minister Shimon Peres to the negotiating table, the president acknowledged Carter's suggestion that he could be of use as Middle East mediator. "You are kind to offer your personal support," Reagan wrote. "I remain hopeful that the next few months will see a convergence of the Israeli and Jordanian approaches that could provide a sound basis for more direct and active U.S. involvement in the process. At that point these two courageous leaders will need all the good will possible. In the meanwhile, if you would like a more detailed reading of the status of this process, I would only be too pleased to make available Ambassador Richard Murphy, who has been my representative in these sensitive discussions."[101]

Murphy did speak with Carter on occasion, but there was never any serious attempt to bring him into the administration's peace process. In truth, it didn't matter. Carter had created a unique role for the Carter Center and for himself in the Holy Land. When Ken Stein traveled to the Middle East in early 1986, he found that *all* of the Arab leaders—and moderate Israelis as well—admired Jimmy Carter. "It is important for you to know that the November 1983 consultation gave us credibility," Stein wrote Carter. "The Israelis realize, particularly [Ezer] Weizman, that you and the Center have a role to play."[102] Carter agreed—and had already expanded his new bailiwick far beyond the Middle East and into arms control.

SEVEN

THE POLITICS OF RENEWAL

∽∘∾

Jimmy Carter's 1984 began with a New Year's declaration calling on the world's governments to end hunger within a decade.[1] It was the first of many utopian proclamations Carter would make over the next several years: the elements of both courage and guilt in his compassion for the downtrodden. The press, uninterested in platitudes, instead tried to draw Carter into commenting on the upcoming Iowa caucus and New Hampshire primary—where Walter Mondale, Alan Cranston, George McGovern, John Glenn, Jesse Jackson, Gary Hart, and Jerry Brown, among others, would be battling it out for the Democratic presidential nomination. But the former president refused to chime in on the campaign gossip, preferring to spend the next few months talking about the Carter Center's new extragovernmental role in arms control and health care policy. "Jimmy Carter has been about as visible in Democratic politics as a rabbit in a cane thicket," the *New York Times* noted in May.[2]

The Carter Center, meanwhile, was moving into high gear. In February 1984 Carter and James Laney had made Ken Stein the center's first executive director, succeeding interim head Jim Waits. "In retrospect," Stein said later, "it may have been a punishment for my success."[3] A history professor first and foremost, he had accepted the administrative position with some trepidation. As executive director, he would be responsible for coordinating programs in a host of areas, including Latin American democracy building, conflict resolution, human rights, and health care policy. The next major

Carter Center event, in May, was to be a forum on the state of U.S.-Soviet détente given the failure to ratify SALT II, the derailment of the Reagan-Brezhnev START talks, and the subsequent hardening of relations between the superpowers. The time was ripe for looking at nuclear issues, as the end of 1983 saw the Soviet delegation walk out of the INF and START negotiations after Washington began deploying Pershing II and ground-launched cruise missiles in Europe. Even though the *Bulletin of the Atomic Scientists* recently had moved forward the hands on the symbolic clock they used to show how much time they felt was left to prevent nuclear destruction (noting that the United States had stockpiled more than 9,000 nuclear warheads to the Soviet Union's 7,000), Carter believed that sane diplomacy could completely eradicate atomic weapons in his lifetime.

Carter put Ellen Mickiewicz, dean of Emory's graduate school and an expert on Soviet media, in charge of the conference. A new kind of Kremlin specialist, fluent in Russian, Mickiewicz had devoted her career to trying to understand Soviet culture and politics, and she had focused astutely on mass media as the bellwether of the views of both government and populace. Monitoring Soviet radio and television around the clock, Mickiewicz would become one of the first American scholars to recognize Mikhail Gorbachev as a revolutionary figure whose calls for glasnost (openness) and perestroika (restructuring) were not empty slogans but dramatic policy initiatives that could soon end the cold war. Thus Jimmy Carter became one of the first influential Americans to publicly state that glasnost was not cosmetic but a real change.

With Carter's enthusiastic support, Mickiewicz brought Russian television to Emory University via a giant satellite dish, a specially equipped monitoring room, and research grants for student staff trained to scan news programs from Leningrad to Siberia. Eventually, at Mickiewicz's insistence, the Carter Center created a Commission on Radio and Television Policy, whose U.S. members included ABC News president Roone Arledge; NBC News president Michael Gartner; CBS News president Eric Ober; and naturally, Ted Turner.[4]

The death of vaguely progressive Soviet leader Yuri Andropov on February 13, 1984, and the succession of the hard-line seventy-two-year-old Konstantin Chernenko, brought uncertainty to the Carter Center's arms control project. An ex–propaganda chief and thirty-year confidant of former general secretary Leonid Brezhnev, Chernenko hardly seemed likely to usher in an era of radical reform in Moscow. Still, Carter was heartened by Chernenko's call for peaceful coexistence with the United States. "We need no military superiority," Chernenko had declared upon assuming power in his first address to the Central Committee of the Communist party. The new

Soviet leader's apparent open-mindedness encouraged Carter to believe that honest arms reduction talks could be reopened.[5]

Carter found his defining arms control focus on March 23, 1983, when Ronald Reagan announced his plan to use the latest technology to build and deploy an invulnerable shield against missiles—the infamous "Star Wars."[6] Strategic Defense Initiative (SDI) was supposed to take the place of the threat of massive nuclear retaliation. Almost immediately, SDI became known in the press as Star Wars—the title of a Hollywood science fiction blockbuster. Carter decided that his center's May 1984 arms control symposium should aim to discredit Star Wars while publicly acknowledging Chernenko for his seeming willingness to renew SALT or START talks.

Everything Reagan did drove Jimmy Carter crazy, but Star Wars was just too much. The former president set out deliberately to challenge his successor's "one-sided attitude of belligerence toward the Soviet Union."[7] After all, even before the Grenada invasion on October 25, 1983—when more than 1,900 U.S. Marines stormed the shores of that tiny Caribbean island to "rescue" American medical students, restore democratic institutions, and vanquish a governing band of what Reagan called "Cuban thugs"—Carter had been painting the president as an irresponsible warmonger. Reagan had sent marines to Beirut to protect U.S. interests, only to withdraw them after 241 troops were killed in a terrorist raid. The day after the terrorist attack in Beirut, Reagan invaded Granada.

In truth, with the exception of their positions on SDI, there were few and slight differences between the defense policies of the Carter and Reagan administrations. The neoconservative editor of *Commentary*, Norman Podhoretz, would seize upon this point late in 1985. In articles in *Foreign Affairs* and the *New York Times*, Podhoretz wrote that after the Soviet invasion of Afghanistan, Jimmy Carter, like Ronald Reagan, believed it was essential to negotiate with the Kremlin from a position of strength. Thus Carter had pledged, if reelected in 1980, to increase defense spending by 5 percent—compared with Reagan's proposed 7 percent hike. For all of Reagan's militaristic talk, the B-1 bomber was the only additional nuclear system deployed during the Reagan years.[8]

There is no doubt, however, that Jimmy Carter both in and out of office was more committed to arms control than was Reagan and less inclined toward military intervention. When the streets of Manhattan swelled with 80,000 demonstrators rallying against nuclear proliferation on June 12, 1982, Carter added his voice to Coretta Scott King's clarion call on the generals of war to turn their swords into plowshares. It was a call he could justifiably make, since Carter while president had used U.S. armed forces only twice—in Zaire in 1978 in the form of military aircraft sent to provide logistical support to Belgian/French rescue operations, and in 1980 in Iran, to which he dispatched six transport planes and eight helicopters in the failed attempt to free the American hostages—while Reagan deployed military forces eighteen times and often much more aggressively. In his 1993 book for young adults, *Talking Peace: A Vision for the Next Generation,* Carter lists all of the Reagan military initiatives in a chapter about the insanity of making war. If Armageddon was really imminent, as Reagan warned on a number of occasions, Carter was prepared to be the last Christian soldier battling the prophecies of the Book of Revelation. "Under Reagan, military madness had taken hold," he exaggerated later.[9]

To Carter, this insanity peaked with SDI. He recognized its chilling potential to spark an unnecessary new race to build defensive systems in space and high-tech offensive weapons on land and sea. His vehement opposition to Reagan's initiative was fully consistent with his presidential rejection of the B-1 bomber and other weapons he deemed unnecessary or unworkable. But this does not mean Carter had been a proponent of disarmament for disarmament's sake: as president, he had been determined to gain a technological edge on the Soviet Union. In fact, his policies had worried the Soviets long before Reagan announced Star Wars, as evidenced by Soviet army chief of staff Nikolai Ogarkov's candid revelation of genuine distress in the Kremlin over the accelerated pace of U.S. military science during the Carter years.

The point man on these programs had been Assistant Secretary of Defense William Perry, who would later become President Clinton's secretary of defense. A mild-mannered managerial type, Perry had convinced the Carter-era military brass to embrace radar-defeating Stealth technology, microcircuitry, smart bombs, satellite communications, and laser-targeting systems. The Soviets were shocked—far more so than they were later by Reagan's Star Wars program or the B-1 bomber—by the spectacular first display of the West's technological superiority in June of 1982, when the American-equipped Israeli air force destroyed its Syrian counterpart over Lebanon's Bekaa Valley.[10]

Mickiewicz found that the former president had a physicist's understanding of the major weapons of the day. As a naval nuclear engineer Carter had studied blueprints, so he would know exactly how a piece of military hardware worked before he could approve or disapprove of it. And now he knew that SDI—with its lasers, microwave devices, and satellite particle beams zapping Soviet missiles before they could strike American territory—was a science fiction pipe dream. Carter was convinced that the Reagan administration itself—with the possible exception of the president—did not believe Star Wars was feasible, but it never occurred to him to think that the

Republicans were simply devising a bargaining-chip hoax to get a psycho-logical upper hand on the bankrupt Soviet government.[11]

The Carter Center's May 31 symposium, chaired by Carter himself, was the first of three public forums on international security and arms control cosponsored by Emory and UCLA. Mickiewicz had secured four of the era's best-informed experts on American security: Ambassadors Gerard C. Smith and Ralph Earle II, who had headed respectively SALT I and SALT II nego-tiating teams; former secretary of defense Harold Brown, and former State Department counselor Helmut Sonnenfeldt. Admittedly, the deck was somewhat stacked: with the exception of Sonnenfeldt, the big-name partici-pants generally shared Carter's views on defense policy. Nevertheless, the president emeritus behaved more like a bright student than a policy maker, scribbling notes and raising his hand when he wanted to ask a question. As the Soviet Union had opted not to send a representative to the conference, there was no need for the nicety of "nonjudgmental objectivity," and Carter's questions were of a decidedly caustic bent. But it was clear Carter had an unfinished presidential agenda item up his sleeve: relaunch SALT II.

Carter and Sonnenfeldt dominated the dialogue. Between them they raised such troublesome questions as how a president could sell arms con-trol agreements like SALT II to Congress and whether it made sense for more than half of the U.S. defense budget to go to NATO while the Euro-pean allies' contributions were so disproportionately small. Some disagree-ment emerged over the merits of the neutron bomb and the proper response to the Soviets' unconscionable attempt to subdue the uprising in Afghanistan with chemical weapons, but there was little dissension when it came to Star Wars: most of the assemblage thought it a delirious lark. After all, it was pointed out, in 1972 Washington and Moscow had agreed to limit antimissile defense systems on the grounds that they were both destabilizing and futile.[12]

A few weeks after the symposium Carter joined an illustrious anti–Star Wars coalition of former government officials, including Dean Rusk, Cyrus Vance, Edmund Muskie, Robert McNamara, and Stansfield Turner. Their announced goal was to stop the Reagan administration from spending $24 billion in the 1980s alone to develop a system of high-technology weapons capable of intercepting ICBMs, an imperious but pie-in-the-sky notion of a strategic defense that would supposedly render nuclear weapons impotent and thus obsolete. As Carter summed it up, "Star Wars was a scam," a Rea-gan slush fund for defense contractors, and "an absolute stupid waste of money."[13]

The day after the arms-control coalition announced a national campaign to save the Anti-Ballistic Missile treaty of 1972, Defense Secretary Caspar

Weinberger claimed in a Boston speech that Carter and his followers were spreading "a wealth of misinformation." Although he admitted that the 1972 treaty forbade certain kinds of deployment, Weinberger insisted that it was nonetheless "designed to permit research—which is exactly what we plan to do—and what the Soviets have been doing for the last decade."[14]

Convinced that Reagan and Weinberger were intentionally deceiving the public, Carter decided to speak out at the Democratic Convention in San Francisco that July. Whether many Americans cared what he had to say was another matter entirely.

Although Carter never publicly endorsed a candidate until after the Iowa caucus and the New Hampshire primary, at Mondale's request, the ex-president lobbied George Wallace in January 1984 to support his former vice president. "You and I know from experience how difficult it is for a Democrat to hold on to a favorite's spot—since our strong suit has been in knocking the favorites off their perches," Carter wrote Wallace in a letter hand-delivered to the governor in Montgomery by his son Chip. "I also know from my intense relations with him in the White House that he is dedicated to good solid Southern Principles which you have always espoused." Carter even went so far as to offer Wallace his "personal admiration" for the way he ran Alabama. Flattered by Carter's lobby efforts, Wallace did not break rank with the Democrats, and he publicly endorsed Mondale.[15]

When Carter supported Mondale in the Georgia presidential primary in March 1984, he phrased the endorsement vaguely, allowing his former vice president to stake out new policies and show the voting public that he was his own man. Throughout the year Carter maintained that Mondale could win the election, though sometimes with the disclaimer that he was "not good on giving advice on how to run against Ronald Reagan." Carter accurately perceived that he could serve Mondale best by keeping a low profile, doing what he could to deliver Georgia's twelve electoral votes but nothing more. The only concrete advice Carter offered Mondale, in a meeting before the convention, was to "expedite the process" of selecting a running mate but "not to make a token selection."[16] (Mondale didn't listen: he took a long time to select Congresswoman Geraldine Ferraro of New York from a shortlist that included two other women, San Francisco mayor Dianne Feinstein and Kentucky governor Martha Layne Collins.)

Democratic leaders in Washington viewed Carter as an obstacle rather than an asset. "The Kennedy types tried to keep Dad from speaking at the convention," Chip Carter recalled. "They thought he should be banned from attending."[17] After much debate, Democratic National Committee (DNC) chairman Charles T. Manatt reluctantly concluded that it would be smarter politics to invite Carter to speak at the San Francisco convention than to have his absence dominate the news coverage. Manatt's hope was to slot him in on opening night, before the television networks began their live prime-time coverage. Diplomatically, the DNC chairman asked the former, president to be brief and noncontroversial. Carter, in fact, not at all anxious to attend, essentially agreed but made it clear that his speech would be on topics of his own choosing: arms control and human rights.[18]

"Here I go again," Carter began, playing on the line Reagan had famously taken against him in 1980. "And I'm still talking about the same things: about economic and military security; about peace backed by American defense forces but derived from diplomacy and statesmanship; about simple human justice and basic human rights." Hendrik Hertzberg had helped draft the speech, but the boldest and most poetic passage was pure Carter, an antiwar statement centered on his recent visit to Hiroshima. "The nuclear shadow still darkens this city where an atomic weapon was exploded in anger for the first time," Carter lamented to the assembled Democrats. "The survivors of the next world war, if any, would merely scratch for existence in the poisoned ruins of a civilization that has committed suicide."[19]

For all the vivid imagery, Carter's delivery was unemotional, his soft voice hard to hear over the restless commotion of the 3,944 delegates. The boisterous straw-hatted conventioneers in Moscone Center waved cardboard placards that read "John Glenn Has the Right Stuff" and "Women Power—Ferraro for VP" and scarcely noticed Carter during his time on the stage. Most were waiting for the headline act: that evening's keynote address by New York's fiery governor, Mario Cuomo. Four years earlier President Carter had been the Democratic party's nominee, the most sought-after interview in America. Now, with his media adviser Gerald Rafshoon at his side, he left the convention platform to a smattering of polite applause; reporters walked straight past him, often without even a casual nod or gesture of acknowledgment. As the DNC had hoped, few television stations even showed a film clip of his speech on their evening news.[20]

In truth, the San Francisco convention was just a diversion for Carter. Just a week after his speech, for example, he and Gerald Ford headed a bipartisan group crusading for spending cuts and tax increases to reduce the federal deficit. The chief architect of the group—called Proposition One— was Governor Richard Snelling of Vermont, a longtime Republican who was planning to leave office in January 1985 to devote his energies to eliminating the deficit. Snelling had told the press that Proposition One's goal was to balance the federal budget by 1989 by cutting military and social expenditures and increasing taxes. "National solvency and stability," Snelling had said, "is the number-one proposition for any nation." Snelling had already raised $200,000 for Proposition One. It was just the beginning: he hoped to net a total of $10 million and to recruit 10,000 volunteers to put pressure on both Reagan and Mondale. "If we can explain what the deficits are doing to people, how they impact on their lives and dreams," Governor Snelling announced, "we can build a constituency for making decisions about defense spending and revenue measures which recognizes that the whole cannot be more than the sum of its parts." This was one of the rare times the two former presidents had worked in tandem on a domestic issue. Throughout the late summer and early fall Carter stayed in touch with Ford as they prepared to cochair the second round of the Carter Center's arms control consultations at the University of Michigan in Ann Arbor that November.[21]

Throughout the campaign, the Republicans ran full throttle against Mondale as Carter's vice president in the "Reign of Error."[22] The Democrats had to work overtime to distance themselves from what had become a commonplace charge. At a press conference in Pittsburgh, Geraldine Ferraro, "her eyes glittering with anger," chided a reporter for associating her with Jimmy Carter. "It's not Carter-Mondale," she growled. "It's Mondale-Ferraro. It's four years later. It's not 1980. That's what Ronald Reagan wants to rerun. We're not going to let him do it."[23]

Vilified by Reagan and denied by Mondale, the former president was happy to head to Latin America in October 1984. Carter's original plan was to travel to Brazil to address a convention of the Friendship Force, an international people-to-people exchange program he had initiated in 1977, but he decided to widen the scope of his trip and convinced his former director of the National Security Council Office of Latin American and Caribbean Affairs, Robert Pastor, to make up an itinerary and accompany him on a four-nation tour. He was also anxious to recruit the thirty-seven-year-old Latin America expert for the Carter Center and to teach at Emory University.[24]

Bob Pastor had rocketed from Hillside, New Jersey, to the top of his profession. As a Phi Beta Kappa undergraduate at Lafayette College in Easton, Pennsylvania, he had written his honors thesis on the U.S. response to the revolution in Guatemala from 1944 to 1954. In order to really understand the circumstances that precipitated the covert activities in Guatemala of Allen Dulles's CIA—which helped to overthrow the legitimate government of President Jacobo Arbenz during Eisenhower's first administration— Pastor had hoisted a backpack in December 1968 and boarded a banana boat headed to Central America out of Tampa, Florida. He arrived in Guatemala soon after U.S. ambassador John Gordon Mein had been assassinated.

After three months spent interviewing leftist politicians who were hiding from the military and CIA agents who had retired in Guatemala after directing the operation against Arbenz, Pastor was hooked on a life of adventure in foreign lands. After graduation he moved to Washington, D.C., to work for the Congressional Research Service. In 1970, still unsure of his career path and opposed to Nixon's Vietnam policy, Pastor joined the Peace Corps and spent the next two and a half years working in the most remote areas of Borneo (Malaysia), training farmers and forging a development plan for the area. Imbued with these experiences, Pastor headed for Harvard to begin studying international affairs and U.S. foreign policy in a serious way in September 1972.[25]

Pastor's big break came in 1974, when as a graduate student he wrote a pair of case studies on U.S. policy toward Latin America for the Murphy Commission, a joint initiative of the White House and Congress to evaluate the government's foreign-policy-making machinery. When Argentina initiated a conservative new economic recovery program reversing longstanding Peronist policies, Pastor had an analysis ready for Sol Linowitz, the well-regarded Johnson administration ambassador to the Organization of America States (OAS) and a former chairman of the Xerox Corporation, before the news item appeared on the AP wire. And when Panama blocked two U.S. vessels in the canal for illegal fishing in 1976, it was Pastor who instructed all the Democratic presidential candidates not to comment.[26]

Carter, who prided himself on his fluency in Spanish, had a deep interest in Latin American affairs and had planned as president to pursue controversial new policies toward the region. Topping his White House agenda were two Panama Canal treaties: the first transferring operational responsibility for the canal to Panamanians by the year 2000, and the second guaranteeing the permanent neutrality of the canal and providing for its defense. Undeterred by public opinion and Republican attacks, Carter pressed on, and so did his minions: Pastor coordinated the National Security Council's administrative efforts, and his behind-the-scenes role was helpful in getting the Panama Canal treaties passed by a single Senate vote. While many respected him for his negotiating abilities, Carter appreciated Pastor most for his top-notch briefings on Latin America. And it was Pastor who crafted the 1978 and 1979 speeches Carter gave in Spanish to the national assemblies of Mexico and Venezuela—the first major addresses delivered by a U.S. president entirely in a foreign language.[27]

But Pastor's biggest supporter was First Lady Rosalynn Carter. In the

late spring of 1977 the president had asked his wife to undertake a special
mission to six Latin American and Caribbean countries in order to highlight
his new policies and genuine interest in the region. Few took her assignment
seriously except for Bob Pastor. For a couple of feverish months Pastor
briefed Rosalynn on every aspect of Latin American and Caribbean affairs,
bringing in more than thirty experts to elaborate on everything from the role
of the OAS to the subtleties of U.S. nonproliferation policy. "I was impressed by her tremendous determination to learn," Pastor recalled.[28]

In the end, the May–June 1977 trip Rosalynn Carter and Pastor took to
Jamaica, Costa Rica, Peru, Ecuador, Brazil, and Venezuela proved a smashing success. An admirer of open-minded approaches to hemispheric relations such as FDR's Good Neighbor Policy and JFK's Alliance for Progress,
Pastor found in Rosalynn an invaluable ally capable of hacking shortcuts
through the bureaucratic jungle of Washington decision making. Every
morning of their journey Pastor briefed Rosalynn at 6:00 A.M. sharp. In
those cases where U.S. policy had not yet jelled, she telephoned the Oval
Office, posed the issue at hand, and waited as her husband quickly made a
decision as to how she should proceed. Despite his youth, Pastor was one of
the first Washington insiders to understand that Rosalynn Carter had the
sort of political influence on her husband the White House hadn't seen since
Eleanor's last dinner with Franklin Roosevelt. "By the end of our trip Mrs.
Carter had been responsible for clarifying or making new policies to Latin
America on a number of issues," Pastor recalled. She returned the enthusiasm. "Bob is a walking encyclopedia of Latin American affairs," Rosalynn
explained.[29]

Jimmy Carter was still convinced that Pastor was far and away the best
choice to put together an activist Latin America program at the Carter Center, and the former president persisted in his overtures. Pastor finally agreed
to accompany the Carters on their October 1984 ten-day trip to Peru, Brazil,
Argentina, and Panama.

All of Lima, Peru, accorded the Carters a welcome befitting the pope: after all, President Carter's efforts at promoting human rights and democracy had helped lead to the election of Fernando Belaunde Terry as
president in 1980 in the first honest political contest in Peru since 1968. In
Brazil Carter was embraced again for having curbed human rights violations
and contributing to the end of a military dictatorship. Brazilian president
João Baptista Figueiredo, a general who three months later would oversee the indirect election of a president, the first civilian to hold the office
in twenty years. He saluted Carter as a champion of democracy, and his

countrymen chimed in. "Millions of Brazilians are delighted that Jimmy Carter should come here so that they can publicly express their immense gratitude for everything he did," said Leonel Brizola, governor of the state of Rio de Janeiro. Brizola added that President Carter's quiet diplomacy had saved his life when Uruguay's military junta expelled him from refuge there in 1977.[30]

Carter was gratified by this warm reception; when he had visited Brazil in March 1978 he had been treated coolly by General Ernesto Geisel's military government, which viewed his advocacy of human rights as interference in Brazil's internal affairs. On the 1980 campaign trail Ronald Reagan and Jeane Kirkpatrick had berated Carter for criticizing an anti-Soviet ally like Brazil just for having an "authoritarian" government that violated human rights, but by 1984 Brazil was actively cleansing itself of political repression: democracy was the rage, and Carter was in vogue. "Now Brazil has a total absence of persecution and a totally free press," Carter crowed to the Friendship Force in Rio de Janeiro, particularly praising his old friend Wayne Smith, under whose leadership the organization had opened chapters in more than forty countries.[31]

The highlight of the former president's visit to Brazil was his reunion with Paulo Evaristo Cardinal Arns, the archbishop of São Paulo. During an official state visit to Brazil in 1978 Carter had insisted on meeting the archbishop and other human rights activists, even though the State Department advised strongly against it. Pastor had arranged a secret—albeit soon to be public—meeting between Carter and the cleric, a gesture that electrified the democratic resistance movement against Brazil's military regime. In 1984, with the archbishop at his side and the television cameras rolling, ex-President Carter chastised current President Reagan for trying "to refute our national commitments" to human rights in Latin America. "The first major trip by Jeane Kirkpatrick was to Chile and Argentina to meet their dictators," Carter lamented. "It sent a clear signal that the human rights policy had been abandoned. But the hunger for human rights is strong. The fact of the reversal in the White House won't stop it. You can't undo what's being done in Argentina, Peru, and other countries."[32]

In Argentina, Martin Andersen of the Washington Post wrote, Jimmy Carter "found the praise and official expression of gratitude for his activist human rights policy that have often eluded him at home."[33] Only nine months earlier, Argentina's civilian leadership had ripped power from a far-right military junta, thus ending eight years of military dictatorship. Argentines had not forgotten that throughout his presidency Jimmy Carter had kept pressure on their military to end human rights violations—not a small matter at a time when thousands of people were being murdered and tens of thousands were "disappearing" into the night, presumably to their deaths at

the hands of the merciless government security forces. As president, Carter
had cut off U.S. military aid to Argentina and had instructed American
diplomats around the world to denounce the systematic terror being per-
petuated there; by 1984 newly elected Argentine president Raul Alfonsin
embraced Carter and his policies, which had saved the lives of thousands of
innocent people. "Thank you, Jimmy," trumpeted the *Buenos Aires Herald*
lead editorial, continuing: "It was Jimmy Carter's government that did more
than any other group of people anywhere for the cause of human rights in
Argentina."[34]

At a private meeting Alfonsin and Carter discussed the Reagan administration's callous disinterest in human rights, where being anti-Soviet was the
only criteria needed to be a U.S. friend. But most of the conversation centered on Alfonsin's decision to dispose of the amnesty law that would have
protected the nine generals and admirals who comprised, at different times,
the junta that ruled Argentina. The Argentine leader, anxious for any hemispheric democracy-building program, offered to help Carter develop a Latin
American program at his Atlanta public policy center that could assist democracy. The two men's interests clicked: "Alfonsin is a true democrat,"
Carter later noted. "He is moderate and honest."[35]

On October 11 Carter enjoyed a moment of true bliss. At a lunch at the
U.S. ambassador's residence he met with six of Argentina's best-known human rights activists, including former Buenos Aires newspaper publisher Jacobo Timerman, Nobel Peace Prize winner Adolfo Perez Esquivel, and
ambassador-at-large Hipolito Solari Yrigoyen. Timerman—whose lyrical
1981 plea for justice, *Prisoner Without a Name, Cell Without a Number,* had
become a best-seller in America—toasted Carter for saving his life when he
was in jail being tortured by the fascist military. "It was very emotional; there
were tears and much embracing and we all wanted to thank him," Timerman
told reporters covering the lunch. "He kept saying he had risked very little,
that there was no reason to thank him. I told him there were many who ran
less risks than he—the head of the most powerful country on Earth—but
who said nothing."[36]

The Reagan administration clearly wanted little to do with Carter's successful tour through Latin America: although the Timerman luncheon was
held at his residence, U.S. ambassador Frank Ortiz had deliberately left
town before Carter's arrival. As the swearing-in of Nicolas Ardito Barletta as
Panama's first democratically elected president in sixteen years, Carter met
Secretary of State George Shultz on his own three-day sweep through Central America. "It was like vinegar meeting oil," one reporter recalled.[37] The
Reagan administration's Latin America policies were almost diametrically
opposed to the Carter-Pastor view of things. But as Pastor toured the

Panama Canal, he was filled with pride at Carter's past accomplishments, a feeling only enhanced when he heard the thunderous ovation Carter received at Ardito Barletta's inaugural ceremony.[38]

On the flight home, Pastor told Carter he would seriously consider the ex-president's offer to direct the Carter Center's Latin American Program if Mondale lost the election. Several months later Pastor accepted a one-year Fulbright professorship at the prestigious El Colegio de Mexico; after that, in September 1986, he and his family moved to Atlanta, where he became a tenured professor in Emory's Political Science Department and Latin American Fellow at the Carter Center. With Pastor on board, Carter could now make Latin America and the Caribbean a major focus of the Carter Center.[39]

Jimmy Carter took Mondale's loss that November in stride. During the campaign's homestretch he had contributed only by calling certain Reagan foreign policy moves "extreme" or "crazy" and their perpetrator misinformed, a verdict on Reagan that Carter happily offered to anyone who asked. Mondale wrote Carter a dejected note after the election, lamenting that his political career was probably over.[40]

Mere days after Reagan's reelection, Carter left Plains to join Gerald Ford in Ann Arbor for their second arms control conference. During the meeting, unsurprisingly, Carter spent little time with the big names: *Foreign Affairs* editor William Hyland; Reagan's assistant secretary of state for European and Canadian affairs, Richard Burt; and General Brent Scowcroft, Ford's national security adviser—all, from the former president's perspective, "Washington political types." Instead he sought out physicists Michael May of the Lawrence Livermore Laboratory and Richard Garwin of the Thomas J. Watson Research Center for information about recent breakthroughs in advanced weapons technology; while others at the meeting focused on nuclear politics and the ramifications of a second Reagan administration, Jimmy Carter was looking for blueprints of the newest radar-surveillance systems.[41]

Although Carter despised journalists' quips that the Carter Center was becoming a shadow government, there was a dash of truth to the gibe. He clearly regarded his own administration as unfinished, and took it upon himself not so much to repudiate Reagan as to tackle pressing issues he thought the Republican incumbent was avoiding. Far from the White House in every sense, Carter was freed from the Washington roundabout of what Dean Acheson called "that foul word—'comment' "—and set loose in the realm of direct results.[42] Oblivious to political norms or the expectations of anyone else, after his presidency Carter just plunged headfirst into whatever issue moved him. At any given moment he might announce that he was about to start a task force on the national debt, or to fly to a Latin American capital in need of financial aid, or to launch a campaign demanding the release of a political prisoner from a foreign tyrant.

From the Century Club in New York to the Metropolitan Club in Washington, the rap on Carter was that he remained a bright but politically naive loner, now one who had not come to grips with his electoral defeat. But Jimmy Carter's direct approach was not politics as usual: he was operating under his own rules, a born-again joker who had never quite fit into Washington's playing deck. An acerbic, anti-Republican speech by the Democratic former president at the Waldorf-Astoria or the National Press Club was one thing—but inviting the Soviet Union's leading scientists and diplomats to Atlanta to discuss nuclear-arms-reduction issues six months before President Reagan was to head to Geneva for a major superpower summit on the same pressing issue was another matter entirely.

Some Democrats thought that Carter's preliminary track-two diplomacy with the Soviets might illuminate differences that could be ironed out before the Geneva talks commenced. To many Republicans, however, it seemed that private citizen Carter was deliberately undercutting the official American position by behaving like some sort of proxy president. Neither interpretation told the whole story. A key to understanding Carter's postpresidency is to realize that he seldom tested the waters: he made bold pronouncements and followed them with blitzkriegs of supposed empiricism, letting others scramble to react. Even Carter's close associates saw him as all offense and no defense, like a star basketball forward who scores 40 points while his team loses. But Carter proved that when a former president of the United States starts playing aggressive offense—beckoning world leaders to Atlanta, for instance—the powerful will accept the challenge.

The discussions in Washington, D.C., in 1983 with Harold Brown, Gerard C. Smith, Marshall Shulman, and William Hyland had convinced Carter that the Russians were ready for a dramatic disarmament initiative. Carter had asked Shulman, whose opinion he respected, "Would the Soviets really like to see real reductions?" Columbia University's resident Russian expert had answered, "Yes, for their economy's sake. They have profound problems. They have two ways out. There is economic reform, but their large and aging bureaucracy resists that. But there is another approach—reductions—and they would take this chance." Carter had been heartened, but the session also convinced him that for his arms con-trol consultations to make a real difference, he would have to get high-ranking Soviet officials to participate.[43]

As Mickiewicz and Carter began planning their final consultation, they realized that this time they had to succeed where they had failed previously. The initial results were disappointing: neither Andrei Gromyko nor Nikolai Ogarkov would attend the April 1985 meeting. Finally Carter was able to secure the USSR's worldly ambassador to the United States, Anatoly Dobrynin. Carter arranged to meet him for two private sessions, in Washington and Toronto, before the session in Atlanta. As it turned out, the two men shared an utter disdain for Star Wars; furthermore, Dobrynin said he fully supported Carter's track-two diplomatic efforts and commended his pursuit of disarmament accords.[44]

The Carter Center's final arms control consultation spanned the last week of April 1985 and could not have come at a more opportune moment. In meetings the previous January 7 and 8, U.S. secretary of state George Shultz and Soviet foreign minister Andrei Gromyko had forged an agreement to initiate nuclear- and space-arms-control talks in Geneva on March 12. On March 15, following Konstantin Chernenko's death and a short power struggle, Mikhail Gorbachev became the new Soviet premier. "We're ready to work with the Soviet Union for more constructive relations," President Reagan declared in a speech in Quebec on March 18. "We all want to hope that last week's change of leadership in Moscow will open up new possibilities for doing this." Speculation was rampant as to what Gorbachev's policies of economic reforms at home and easing tensions abroad would mean for the future of U.S.-Soviet relations.[45]

Again, the Carter Center had seized the moment. Unlike the previous two, this arms control consultation was attended by eight high-level Soviets, including Dobrynin; Evgeny Velikhov, deputy director of the Kurchatov Institute of Atomic Physics; and Sergei Tarasenko, deputy director of the U.S. Department of the Soviet Union's Ministry of Foreign Affairs. "Gorbachev's stamp was on whatever the delegation said," Mickiewicz recalled. "This was the first time the U.S. got to discuss arms control issues openly with Gorbachev's government." Delegations also attended from the other nations with nuclear arms—France, Great Britain, and China—as well as from countries technically capable of producing nuclear explosions, such as Israel, Canada, East and West Germany, Argentina, Brazil, Pakistan, and India.[46]

Mickiewicz had convinced an enthusiastic Ted Turner to air the center's final consultation live on CNN: eleven hours total, in addition to late-night rebroadcasts. Thus Carter and Ford briefly held sway on cable TV as cohosts of panels—on "Weapons, Strategy, and Doctrine," "Alliances, Proliferation, and Regional Conflict," and "Negotiations and Diplomatic/Political Aspects," among others, all concerned with reversing the nuclear arms race. Emory president James Laney turned Lullwater House, his elegant residence, over to working groups attended by such luminaries as Cyrus Vance and Henry Kissinger, who asserted with his customary Prussian logic that "we are essentially out of ideas on arms control that make any major contribution except in the symbolic field of having made progress." Cynicism aside, Kissinger—who always had a good relationship with Carter—noted years later that the consultation was important not only as a contribution toward détente, but also because "it provided a fresh way to look at foreign affairs issues."[47]

Given that some very important Soviets were attending and that Gerald Ford was cochairing the conference, Reagan decided military affairs adviser Ken Adelman and Secretary of the Navy John Lehman should participate. "The Reagan administration was fully cooperative," Ellen Mickiewicz recalled.[48]

Partisan posturing aside, what made the New York Times's front page was a verbal showdown at the consultation between Dobrynin and Kenneth Adelman, head of the U.S. Arms Control and Disarmament Agency. Even with a Reagan-Gorbachev summit slated to begin in November, each accused the other side of impeding the preliminary arms control talks that had begun in Geneva on March 12. Reports from Switzerland indicated deadlock over SDI, with both sides eager to place blame elsewhere. Taking the offense, Adelman announced that the Soviets' recent public comments on the Geneva talks breached the confidentiality of the negotiations and thus threatened their progress. Dobrynin countered that it was the United States that was jeopardizing the Geneva talks by refusing to disclose scientific information about the so-called Star Wars program. The tug of war continued for some time, the only point of agreement being that SDI had become the primary sticking point in arms reduction talks.[49]

Senator Sam Nunn, the ranking minority member on the Armed Services Committee, entered the fray, claiming that both Pravda and Soviet television had violated the confidentiality of the Geneva talks by complaining about U.S. intransigence on SDI. Dobrynin shrugged him off, expressing astonishment that Nunn would make such a petty charge. For the USSR's part, Dobrynin insisted that Reagan intended SDI to ensure American arms superiority, to prevail in the event of a nuclear war, and thus to win the cold war in space. He ended on a terse note, describing current U.S.-Soviet relations as "tense, complicated, and unstable." Other GOP conference participants interviewed on CNN—including Senate majority whip Ted Stevens of Alaska and former Senate majority leader Howard Baker of Tennessee—agreed that arms control talks were unlikely to go anywhere until the respective hefts of the superpowers' offensive and defensive forces were determined and compared.[50]

Carter managed to end the contentious consultation on an upbeat note in the form of five goals: continued adherence to the Interim Agreement on Offensive Nuclear Weapons to SALT II; retention of the 1972 ABM treaty; achievement of a comprehensive test ban through gradual reduction of permissible levels under the Threshold Treaty; continued meetings among top political leaders and frequent new meetings of military leaders from both sides; and minimization of diplomatic linkage between Washington-Moscow arms disagreements and conflicts elsewhere in the world. The Soviets showed what Carter called "a surprising flexibility" with their agreements to stop nuclear testing and to permit on-site inspection of some of their radar and missile facilities, if necessary, to end the Reagan administration's fretting over verification. Carter concluded the consultation by endorsing former Joint Chiefs of Staff chairman General David Jones's suggestion that in addition to continuing high-level political meetings between the United States and the USSR, the top military brass from each side should hold bilateral retreats to seek common ground.[51]

Carter truly believed that the gaping differences between the two superpowers had narrowed—perhaps because pessimism had no place in his approach to diplomacy. But even Secretary of State George Shultz, on a mission to Japan, publicly commended the Carter Center's efforts, although he did mention administration grievances about recent Soviet behavior, including their radar scrambling of U.S. missile flight-test data. Pleased that the Soviets had seemingly softened their hard line on weapons inspections, Sam Nunn saluted Jimmy Carter: "We thank you for what you've done for our country and what you are doing here with your center. This program is certainly not the beginning, but is, from my perspective, the highlight so far of your endeavors, and they are going to pay dividends."[52]

The three Carter-Ford arms control forums had not directly affected policy making but they had helped raise issues that Washington and Moscow studied in preparation for Geneva. To some degree Carter achieved his goal of exposing Star Wars as a "scam" by providing the forum in which two former secretaries of defense—Harold Brown and James Schlesinger—denounced SDI as infeasible and ridiculous. Jimmy Carter himself deviously elaborated to the CNN audience that Brown and Schlesinger were "aligning themselves with the Soviet delegation and attacking the American delegation." But while Carter meant the consultations to sound Star Wars's death knell, his efforts only wounded it.[53]

For the rest of the year Carter continued to lash out against the expensive SDI program and to cultivate an international constituency behind his pro-SALT compliancy. Conversations with various United Nations diplomats in Geneva and with NATO leaders in Corfu further impressed him that the November U.S.-Soviet summit would be unproductive. The Soviets had made it clear that SDI had to be scrapped, and Carter knew that Weinberger would never let Reagan take it off the table. In September, in a speech heralding the opening of the Edmund S. Muskie Archive at Bates College in Lewiston, Maine, Carter once again denounced SDI. The program was not, he said, a bargaining chip, as some advocates were claiming; it was the key obstacle to success in Geneva.[54] On this point the former president was strategically blind. "Carter was just incapable of comprehending that SDI was largely a ploy," Paul Nitze stated.[55] The Reagan "bargaining chip" approach was beyond his moral scope.

Given Gorbachev's domestic initiatives, prospects for a dramatic new era of détente and military cuts seemed bright. Yet as Carter had predicted, Reagan followed Defense Secretary Caspar Weinberger's advice not to agree to the terms of SALT II, not to negotiate on a single aspect of SDI, and not to make any arms reduction treaty, period. Thus, despite six hours of private conversation the two leaders failed to reach agreement. Gorbachev warned at a news conference that the Soviet Union could build a better missile-defense system than SDI: "Mr. President, you should bear in mind we are not simpletons," he chided. Reagan for his part treated Geneva as a triumph, telling his countrymen by radio upon his return that Gorbachev had failed in his "main aim" at Geneva, "to force us to drop SDI." Reagan and Gorbachev, however, did agree to the goal of a 50 percent reduction in their respective nations' strategic arsenals. Two months later Gorbachev proposed a phased transition to a nuclear-free world by the year 2000—an idealistic vision to match Reagan's of a world without the threat of nuclear weapons courtesy of an impervious Star Wars shield.[56]

Carter's disagreements with Reagan extended well beyond SDI. On two occasions in 1985, for example, Carter telephoned Reagan to ask him to stop falsely maligning his predecessor's administration. "I asked Reagan to please stop saying I had left our armed forces in a state of shambles," Carter recalled. Both times Reagan assured Carter that what he had said was not what he meant, and vice versa. Carter reluctantly gave Reagan the benefit of the doubt. The final straw, however, came in February 1986, when Reagan gave a speech again misstating the Carter administration's record on national security and defense, claiming that it had gutted the military. Carter's friends warned him to dismiss Reagan's remarks, but he took the opposite route on March 1, 1986, lambasting Reagan's dishonesty from Plains.

Carter accused Reagan of habitually misstating his administration's record, persistently making statements "he knows are not true and which he personally promised me not to repeat." To substantial publicity, Carter assaulted Reagan for falsely taking credit for developing the MX and Trident missile programs actually initiated in his administration. What's more Carter pointed out that as president he had *increased* defense spending, despite Reagan's claims that he had slashed it. Carter went on to accuse Reagan of lying to the American people about the Nicaraguan Contras and about administration efforts to undermine the Sandinista government; he also resuscitated his outrage from 1983, when 241 U.S. Marines were killed in Lebanon and Reagan blamed the tragedy on degradation of intelligence services under the Ford and Carter administrations. Carter brought up several other specific misrepresentations as well, regarding El Salvador, SALT II, and of course Star Wars. The former president had kept a scorecard since leaving office.[57]

EIGHT

THEOLOGY OF THE HAMMER

∽o∾

On January 20 1977, as Jimmy Carter thrilled the nation on inauguration day by shedding imperial pretensions and hopping out of his limousine to walk down Pennsylvania Avenue, Millard and Linda Fuller were shingling the roof of a house at a Christian commune only ten miles from Plains. They met Carter only twice during his presidency: for a courtesy handshake at a physician's house near Plains and ten words one Sunday morning at Fellowship Baptist Church in Americus. But their lives would soon be forever linked.[1]

Carter had first learned about the Reverend Millard Fuller's new house-building program, Habitat for Humanity, when longtime Plains neighbors Ralph and Jane Gnann visited the White House in 1978 proudly pronouncing that they had decided to build houses in Zaire for two years.[2] While Carter was president, Habitat initiated projects in Zaire, Zambia, Uganda, Guatemala, Peru, Haiti, and Kenya, not to mention affiliates in a dozen states, with the Americus office providing funding and on-site training of overseas volunteers and general guidance for all projects. When the Carters returned to Plains after the 1980 election, they were surprised to see Habitat for Humanity volunteers who had moved to Americus filling the pews in Maranatha Baptist Church. "We were impressed with their dedication and enthusiasm," Carter recalled. "Also, Millard Fuller was very eager for us to become actively involved in his project and provided us with a flood of information, invitations, and requests—much more than we wanted."[3]

In truth Carter was skeptical of Fuller, worried that he was some holy roller trying to use a former president to further his personal agenda. This gut feeling was exacerbated during his last few weeks in the White House when he began reading the *Americus Times-Recorder*, anxious to catch up on the local news and gossip. Most of the offerings were "Welcome Home Jimmy and Rosalynn" stories except for one sour note. A fellow named Millard Fuller, founder of Habitat for Humanity, was intimating that Carter was a fake humanitarian, unconcerned about the plight of the poor in his own hometown. What had goaded Fuller was Carter's refusal to attend a Plains house-dedication ceremony. "The invitation had been one of hundreds we had received at the White House, and had been routinely declined by staff members," Carter recalled. "However, the Habitat people had taken the negative response as a personal affront, and made loud complaints to the regional and national press."[4]

For a year after returning to Plains, Carter tried to ignore anything with the name Habitat for Humanity imprinted on it; but the steady flow of volunteers filled Maranatha Baptist every Sunday, and their idealism and Christian commitment was infectious. In early 1982 Phil Gailey, a friend of Fuller and reporter for the *New York Times*, wrote a small article about how both Reagan and Carter refused to build houses for the poor. Reagan had the excuse of being president; Carter, on the other hand, could only offer indifference.[5] Painted into a corner, Carter accepted an invitation to greet Habitat's board of directors for their fall 1982 meeting in Americus; "Declining the request would have just caused more negative sniping," as Carter recalled.[6]

Millard Fuller, a six-foot-four-inch, mild-looking but ambitious son of an Alabama grocer, exuded infectious enthusiasm, ineffable charm, and stubborn determination even as an adolescent. Born January 3, 1935, in Lanett, Alabama, Fuller always had a knack for selling. Starting with a scrawny pig his father gave him, Millard became a livestock trader during his teens, earning enough to pay his way through Auburn University. He got his entrepreneurial start early, delivering with his classmate Morris Dees personalized birthday cakes and holly wreaths on campus as he studied law at the University of Alabama in 1957.[7]

During his last year of law school he forged a business partnership with Dees—later to become the founder of Montgomery's Southern Poverty Law Center—ostensibly to practice law, but mail order catalog sales proved more lucrative. From 1960 to 1964 the Fuller and Dees Marketing Group, Inc., a direct mail publishing company that sold everything from rat poison to tractor seats, doormats, and cookbooks, became the small commercial success story of Montgomery.[8] "Millard had a genius for the opening," Morris Dees recalled.[9] They were Willie Lomans of the first magnitude, convinced you had to work hard and dream big to get rich, gleefully counting their substantial profits as they came pouring into their east Montgomery office headquarters, where they employed 150 people.

At age twenty-nine Fuller had become a millionaire, and he and his wife, Linda Caldwell, a twenty-three-year-old from Tuscaloosa, Alabama, lived the full lives of the rich—mansion, Lincoln Continental, maid and nanny, 2,000 acres of farm, horse stables, and cattle, private fishing lakes, and a bank account where the yearly interest alone was enough to buy a medium-sized town in North Dakota. It was the American dream, but after six years of marriage Linda Fuller wanted a divorce. She felt Millard had become a workaholic void of personal integrity and caring.

By 1965 Fuller was emotionally devastated and physically exhausted. Linda had fled Alabama for New York City, and Millard impulsively flew to Niagara Falls; a quick nature fix, he thought, would help straighten out the jumbled puzzle of his existence. Once in Niagara Falls he rented a nondescript hotel room on the Canadian side, sulked over dinner, and watched an old late-night movie on television. Out of nowhere a line in the movie, which was about Chinese missionaries, triggered in Fuller a rare moment of introspection: "A planned life can only be *endured*."[10]

"That's what I was doing—enduring life," Fuller concluded. "My plan was to get richer and richer, until finally I'd be buried in the rich section of Montgomery Cemetery. And right then, by all indications, I was headed there."[11] At that frozen moment he telephoned his wife and begged her to let him come visit, to hear about his self-realization. She agreed to a meeting in Manhattan. "Linda," he said, "we should make ourselves poor again, give our money away, and start over. What do you think?" She embraced the idea without the slightest hesitation. They would liquidate their financial assets and give all their money away to charities. The Fullers had no further need for marriage counseling or financial advice. They had made their cathartic decision to be poor, to embrace a life of voluntary simplicity, ecstatic as newlyweds. To the Fullers, it was as if God was ordaining their life-affirming decision. Their marriage had been born again.[12]

Once back in Montgomery, the Fullers loaded their kids in the station wagon and took a two-week vacation to Florida, anxious to enjoy each other as a family for the first time in years. On their way home, his mind heavy with how he would fend for his family once he abandoned all his earthly possessions, Millard stopped for eggs and grits at an Albany, Georgia, roadside restaurant. Suddenly, the name of Reverend Al Henry popped into Millard's head. Instead of continuing on Highway 82 west over the Chattahoochee

River to Montgomery, Fuller veered forty miles north of Albany on Highway 19 to the town of Plains, hoping to track down "Reverend" Al, who had been dismissed from the Pilgrim Congregational Church of Birmingham in 1963 for advocating racial integration. "I'd felt sorry for him at the time," Fuller recalled. "Old Al had battled the forces of evil and lost—and then gone into the wilderness, never to be heard of again." It seemed the ideal moment to reconnect.[13]

Only a few miles from where the Fullers were headed, a forty-year-old state senator named Jimmy Carter would within the year lose his long-shot 1966 election bid to become governor of Georgia, and would subsequently take his infamous "walk in the woods" with his faith-healing sister Ruth. As Fuller found simplicity, Carter was "born again" as a Christian.

The Fullers found Henry living on a Christian commune just outside of Plains called Koinonia (pronounced "coin-uh-NEE-uh") Farms, a fully integrated community founded in 1942, and committed to nonviolence and economic sharing. Koinonia was a 1,400-acre Christian haven for the battle-scarred who wanted to escape the bustle of modern society and commune in interracial peace. Henry introduced the Fullers to the renegade founder of Koinonia Farms, a high-flying Christian visionary named Clarence Jordan, who had earned a Ph.D. in New Testament Greek from the Southern Baptist Theological Seminary in Louisville, Kentucky.[14]

Farmer-theologian Jordan had stared down members of the Ku Klux Klan eyeball to eyeball on any number of occasions, exhibiting the grit that comes only with intense conviction. Jordan was most famous, however, for his "Cotton Patch" translations of the New Testament, which took Christianity to a new place of earthly relevance, with Jesus born in red-dirt Georgia. He had translated the Bible into the contemporary American context, peppered with slang and populated with backwoods Georgia characters. In Clarence's book series Atlanta was Jerusalem, Valdosta was Bethlehem, and the road from Jerusalem to Jericho started in Atlanta and ended in Albany. *The Cotton Patch Gospel Musical*, based on Jordan's version of the Gospel of Matthew, became a Broadway musical in 1982, performed on stages all over the world, with a score by folksinger Harry Chapin.[15]

But trouble had struck Koinonia Farms in the late 1950s as the Klan, the White Citizens Council, and the John Birch Society earmarked the integrated community as a Commie threat to the virtues of white supremacy. Night Riders made Koinonia Farms a drive-by shooting gallery, often with human targets. The roadside markets where the communitarians sold boxed pecans and homemade fruitcakes were repeatedly bombed and eventually torched to the ground. Not only did Sumter County impose a boycott on all Koinonia products, but often members of the commune would get bloodied up if they dared to venture into Americus. One evening a group of hooded men called Jordan from his house, telling him, "You'll be out of Sumter County before the sun goes down." Preacher Jordan, so the story goes, stared back and replied mockingly, "I'm mighty proud to meet a man who can control the sun." This civil rights showdown occurred only twelve miles from Jimmy Carter's home.[16]

The Fullers were immediately taken by Jordan's optimistic magnetism and his contradictory nature: a dirt-farming aristocrat, a gentle soul who thundered when he preached, a humble Christian who entered the home of an affluent person with the greeting, "Nice piece of plunder you have here." For a month the Fullers stayed at Koinonia Farms, packing pecans and talking about Jesus. They admired Jordan's bold efforts to help black sharecroppers and tenant farmers stay on the land and avoid the even greater destitution that they would find in the crime-ridden cities. "Clarence Jordan had more integrity and sheer guts than any man I ever met," Fuller would note twenty years later. When the KKK and White Citizens Council bombed Koinonia's roadside pecan stand, Jordan abandoned direct sales and turned to mail ordering fruitcakes and pecan logs. His controversial new slogan was "HELP us ship the Nuts out of Georgia."[17]

Millard and Linda left Koinonia at Christmas in 1965 and in the summer of 1966 visited Christian missionaries in Africa, searching for a way they could directly help the poor. It was in Mbandaka, the capital of the Equator region of Zaire, located 412 miles upriver from Kinshasa, that the Fullers encountered squalid living conditions unimaginable in America. The Fullers had met some Disciples of Christ missionaries who had just purchased a block-and-sand project from a nervous Belgian businessman who had fled the country at independence in 1960; they were anxious to convert what was essentially a block-making operation to a nonprofit house-building enterprise for the poor. "As we drove around the dusty streets of Mbandaka looking at thousands of mud shacks and incredible living conditions, I wondered what we could do to help," Fuller would later write in *Bokotola* (1977), his moving memoir about their attempts to launch a poverty housing project in the Third World.[18]

Upon returning to America, Fuller spent the next two years canvassing the country for Tougaloo College, while also trying to sensitize people to the dire needs of poor people in Tanzania, Ghana, and Zaire. During this time Clarence Jordan was never far from Fuller's mind. He had just hatched an alternative living plan he was calling Koinonia Partners—a well-thought-out scheme to develop what he called "Partnership Housing." Taking the Scripture to heart, Jordan viewed landlords and real estate dealers as vipers, unChristian people who milked humans' basic need for shelter for profit. The

Bible, he would say, teaches that profit should not be made on the backs of the poor—meaning no interest should be charged when lending money. All around Sumter County tenant farmers were being forced off the land by mechanization, left with nowhere to go. The shanties they lived in lacked heat and plumbing, and they couldn't afford repairs. "What the poor people need is not charity but capital," Jordan proclaimed, "not caseworkers but co-workers."[19]

The "Fund for Humanity," as they called it, would not be based on welfare or capitalism. Jordan, along with the Fullers, would solicit gifts and no-interest loans from benefactors to construct houses for poor rural families, charge no interest, and make no profit from the new homeowners—the authentic "economics of Jesus."[20] Building would start at Koinonia, on land the community already owned. Fuller laid out forty-two half-acre lots and began touring to raise money and recruit volunteers. The Fullers never forgot the joy they experienced when they picked up hammers and built unemployed tenant farmers Bo and Emma Johnson, uneducated and landless descendants of slaves, the first dwelling they ever lived in that was not a shack. As Fuller recalled, it was "a solid, concrete block house built at a cost of six thousand dollars to be repaid each month for twenty years with no interest. It included a modern kitchen, a good heating system, and an indoor bathroom. Their monthly mortgage payment was twenty-five dollars, paid to the Fund for Humanity." Bo, unable to write, signed the mortgage with an X.[21]

When Clarence Jordan died suddenly on October 29, 1969, of a heart attack, the Fullers suddenly inherited the Partnership Housing initiative. All forty-plus people who lived at Koinonia worked with them to make Clarence Jordan's vision a reality. Before long Koinonia Village maintained a handful of community houses, and an evangelical success story had been launched. Restless, the Fullers were now ready to test the Koinonia housing program out in Zaire, where the stark poverty and overcrowded settlements they had encountered seven years ago had reached the deepest wellsprings of their Christian consciousness. The Christian Church (Disciples of Christ), headquartered in Indianapolis, sponsored the Fullers from 1973 to 1976 in Zaire. With no resources or money, and as idealistic foreigners in a Third World country hampered with a "ludicrous bureaucracy" and "capricious arrests," the Fullers started building simple, decent cement-block houses for the downtrodden who had been living in vermin-infested stick-and-mud shacks. "No one in America or Europe would have lived in our houses," Fuller admits, but by Mbandaka standards the Fund for Humanity dwellings were palaces for the poor, windproof shelters that stood up to the torrential rains and kept pestilence at bay.[22]

The Zairean experience of building 114 houses confirmed the Fullers' belief that partnership house-and-community building not only worked from a social point of view but also triggered a spiritual awakening in the builder. Zairean president Mobutu Sese Seko may have made it unlawful for citizens to use their Christian names, but by the time the Fullers left Mbandaka the city of 150,000, by and large, was singing the praises of the Disciples of Christ. "We showed them that real Christians were there to build, not pillage like the colonial powers had done," Fuller noted.[23]

The Fullers returned to Georgia in July 1976, just as native son Jimmy Carter was about to capture the Democratic nomination for president at Madison Square Garden amid a frenzy of bicentennial celebrations. They were indifferent toward Carter, but the candidates' mother, Miss Lillian, was well liked by the communitarians at Koinonia Farms for her racial integrationist views. She stood up for her son numerous times when arch-segregationist merchants in Sumter County boycotted the Carter family's peanut warehouse. On August 26, 1976, Christians from all over the United States, called together by the Fullers, met at a Koinonia chicken barn to form a new international organization, founded on the pioneer house-building program in Zaire. That summer the United Nations was holding an international "Habitat" conference in Vancouver to discuss the problem of inadequate Third World housing. "The word 'Habitat' perfectly described what we wanted to provide," Fuller recalled. "Not just a house but a sense of community." Habitat for Humanity was officially born.[24]

The first operating premise has not changed for over twenty years. Each local Habitat project would be totally ecumenical; each would keep the overhead as low as possible and would be financed by a revolving Fund for Humanity. Money would be raised from private sources—individuals, churches, and corporations. Volunteers would do the majority of the building to keep the cost down and to provide people an opportunity to do hands-on work as an expression of faith. Houses would always be simple, but they would be solid and of quality construction. They would be sold to needy families with no profit added and no interest charged. And the families would be involved through "sweat equity," required to contribute several hundred hours of work toward building their own houses and houses for others.[25]

On October 16, 1982, Carter arrived at the First Presbyterian Church in Americus to a thunderous standing ovation, the sanctuary packed with Habitat volunteers. Low-key as usual, Carter spoke about the difficulties in the modern world of putting theory into practice, providing affordable housing for the homeless and poor. As president he had grappled with the problems of refugees from Haiti, Thailand, and many other nations, and it haunted him that these children of God had no place to call home. Then, to the surprise of everyone present, he not only embraced Habitat for Humanity but the ghost of Clarence Jordan, the eccentric Christian neighbor he had avoided like the plague when running for political office. "I am proud to be a neighbor of Koinonia . . . and to have seen, from perhaps too great a distance, the profound impact of Clarence Jordan on this country . . . and to have known this quiet man who demonstrated in his own life an image of Christ . . . with human fallibility, yes, but with the inspiration of Christ," Carter noted. "I think I will be a better Christian because of Clarence Jordan, Koinonia, and Habitat. And I hope to grow the rest of my life, along with you."[26]

Millard Fuller grabbed on to the last line, hoping to parlay it into a fund-raising gambit. With the persistence of Job, Fuller, the king of spin, started plotting. At Christmas he hit Jimmy and Rosalynn up for a personal donation and got $500 in return. As Fuller preached around the country, he began quoting Carter's October 1982 First Presbyterian comments incessantly. In August 1983 he had organized a long fund-raising trek—on foot—from Americus to Indianapolis, 700 road-weary miles, as if he were some latter-day Vachel Lindsay, handing out copies of Clarence Jordan's "Cotton Patch Gospels" and "Sermon on the Mount," raising money, and enlisting volunteers. Rosalynn and Amy Carter walked with the Habitat folks from downtown Americus to the city limits, a ninety-minute jaunt, and Millard Fuller was right there between them, their arms interlinked, the closest thing to a civil rights march Sumter County would experience in the age of Reagan.[27]

The theme song for the walk that day was "We're Marching to Zion," which Fuller claimed had special meaning because in Clarence Jordan's "Cotton Patch" books, Jerusalem—known as Zion in the Bible—was Atlanta. "So we're marching to Zion," the lanky Fuller enthused, wearing his customary denim overalls and Habitat baseball cap, squinty eyes darting about under his wire-rim glasses, which rested upon large ears. "What could have been more exciting?" Fuller was getting to know the Carters intimately by following his simple philosophical instinct that it is better to "ask" than "not ask," because "more good things happen" that way. "Yes is a much more Christian word than No," Fuller maintained. As December 1983 rolled around, the tireless Fuller was able to lure Jimmy and Rosalynn to speak at the dedication of Habitat's expanded office building in Americus.

Carter did not mind being used for a good cause, and the more he learned about Habitat, the more impressed the engineer in him was with the net results. But to Millard Fuller kind words at board meetings and building dedications were not enough. The former president should swing a hammer for the poor. And at a private meeting in Plains on January 23, 1984, Fuller pressed his point. "President Carter," he said, "I'm here as a neighbor, because you and Mrs. Carter have expressed interest in Habitat for Humanity." The neighbor gambit was a perfect ploy—the surest angle to get Carter to do just about anything. Fuller then cut to the chase: "Are you simply interested in Habitat for Humanity, or are you *very* interested?" His entire strategy for using Carter was based on this one question. Carter flashed his famous grin, knowing full well what Fuller was up to, looked at Rosalynn, and softly answered, "We're very interested." The conversation now turned to specifics, with Carter recommending that Fuller go back to his office, ponder how they could be most useful, and write him a detailed letter, adding: "And don't be bashful."[28]

Many adjectives had been used to describe Millard Fuller over the years, but *bashful* was never one of them. Fuller sent Carter a long flowing letter on February 8, detailing in fifteen points how he could be of service to Habitat, including serving as director and making various media appearances and appeals. The most important point was number thirteen: "Be a volunteer. If you would work on the Americus construction crew for one day, it would set a great example. You, Rosalynn, could help either in the office or on the construction crew—we don't discriminate against women! We could document your volunteer work on film and let your example inspire others."[29]

A month later in early March, Jimmy Carter, dressed in blue jeans and a plaid work shirt, joined the Habitat construction crew in Americus for morning devotions and a day of house building. "I already knew the president was a talented carpenter who had crafted beautiful furniture for his own home and for friends," Fuller said. "But to have him working here beside our Habitat crew, putting up framing for Dorothy and Willie Solomon's new house on Habitat Street, was just fantastic."[30] As an amazed *New York Times* reported stated, "Mr. Carter has been toiling in a callus-raising enterprise that may be unheard of for a former Commander in Chief."[31]

The Americus house building hooked Carter on Habitat. A few weeks after his initiation to building, the ex-president left a speaking engagement in New York City, meticulously dressed in a gray suit, and visited a Habitat project at 742 East Sixth Street, where a six-story tenement between Avenues C and D was being gutted for renovation. Out of this rubble Habitat planned to make twenty apartments for the poor. As with all Habitat projects, the price of the apartments would be the prorated cost of the renovation, and Habitat would offer no-interest loans. Those purchasing the apartments had to help with the renovation, putting in at least thirty-two hours a week from the time they were accepted. To be eligible you had to already live in the neighborhood and earn no more than $21,750 for a family of four.[32]

Surrounded by Secret Service agents, Carter toured the building on April 1, 1984, pausing at a cinder-block window with "WAR" graffitied on it, and worked his way up a temporary wooden stairway, past piles of unsightly rubbish and splintered boards. "Well," Carter said to Rob DeRocker, director of the New York project, as they stood together on the half-collapsed rooftop, peering out over the vast cluster of Manhattan skyscrapers, "I can see you've got some work ahead of you here. Let Millard know if there's anything I can do to help you. He's my boss." DeRocker seized the opening: "Why don't you come back with a group from your church for a work week?" Breaking into a smile, Carter replied, "We'll think about it."[33]

When Carter returned to Plains, Fuller pounced like a cat: Jimmy and Rosalynn should lead a group of Georgia volunteers to New York for one week to renovate those apartments. Somewhat reluctantly Carter agreed, a little annoyed that Fuller had seized upon his casual New York aside as if it had been an ironclad agreement. Rosalynn was not thrilled about taking part in such an oddball adventure. The Carters would be responsible for signing up volunteers, everyone would have to bring their own tools, and for a week they would all sleep on cots inside the Metro Baptist Church, a 1911 sanctuary in Hell's Kitchen. Most worrisome of all to Jimmy was that the folks they were most likely to recruit "probably would never have used a saw, mixed mortar, laid a brick, put up a stud, or used a hammer except to hang a picture on the wall."[34]

But Mayor Ed Koch's disdainful attitude to the renovation spurred them on. "Koch told Habitat to get lost," Carter recalled. Habitat for Humanity follows the practice of never buying the land on which it builds homes, relying instead on the generosity of local authorities to provide it. Yet when Habitat approached Koch, he refused to donate property or even offer it at a token price. Habitat was forced to pay $28,000 to the city of New York for a piece of overlooked, dilapidated real estate on the Lower East Side. Carter, who still remembered the way Koch showboated on Middle East politics during his presidency, would tell anyone who asked that the mayor was a "jerk." As ex-president, Carter felt free to talk bluntly about whomever he wanted.[35]

The Carters' nearly twenty-four-hour Trailways trek from Americus to New York was memorable, as a real camaraderie developed among the thirty-six volunteers. Most of the people came from Atlanta, Americus, Ellijay, and Calhoun, and Esther Fein of the New York Times joined them, publishing a front-page story about the journey on Labor Day.[36] Jimmy Carter sat next to Florence "Sister" Sheffield, a wise, graceful Americus woman who owned an elegant boutique, for the entire journey. "There are things I told Sister that I hadn't told anybody," Carter would confess years later.[37] Deen Day Smith was also along, ecstatic that she was about to sell her Days Inn Motel chain for $300 million. John and Betty Pope, the Carters' closest friends, sat in the front, retelling stories from the Peanut Brigade years and passing around baked goods made especially for the journey. Ted Swisher, who had moved to Koinonia Farms from New Jersey in 1970 to find Christ, was upbeat, amazed that a former president was now part of their ministry. Of course, Millard Fuller was also on board, talking a blue streak and commanding the bus to stop in Columbia, South Carolina, for a fried-chicken buffet supper courtesy of the local Habitat affiliate.[38]

After dinner Fuller introduced Carter to say a few words. Shyly the former president began by pointing out that the Habitat board of directors was the only one he served on, having turned down corporate offers and hundreds from other nonprofit groups. This was followed by a moving oration in which the former president pledged his lifetime commitment to the organization. "Habitat for Humanity can make a profound impact on Christendom," he said. "I am proud to be part of it."[39]

That evening the Georgians departed Columbia in good cheer, dozing off in their seats to the lonesome sounds of the highway at night. In the morning they awoke to find themselves on the New Jersey Turnpike, exiting in the little town of Bellmawr to worship at the Conservation Baptist Church, where the congregation was delighted to have a former president in their pew. A few hours later they emerged out of the Lincoln Tunnel and drove to the Metro Baptist Church on Fortieth Street near the Port Authority Bus Terminal, where hundreds of people had congregated to welcome Jimmy and Rosalynn Carter to New York City. "We never could have expected such a grand welcome," said volunteer Betty Pope. "But in truth, we were zonked out from the long bus ride."[40]

The euphoria quickly dissipated as the Habitat group arrived in New York and went to see the shell of a building they were supposed to transform into liveable human quarters. "It looked much worse and more fragile now with the structure more fully exposed than it had been in April, when it was full of trash," Carter recalled. "Our hearts sank . . . discouraged almost to the point of resentment that anyone—they all looked at me—could have thought of bringing them so far to be part of an absolute fiasco."[41] Carter and the handful of other skilled carpenters held an impromptu summit meeting to devise a realistic strategy for success. Work groups were formed, a list of additional needed supplies drafted, and a declaration made that a good evening's rest be had by all.

Spartan dormitory-style bunk beds for women were on the third floor, quarters for men on the fourth floor; the Carters were given the only private room (dubbed "the presidential suite") to share. But Carter said no. "Rosalynn and I have been sleeping together for over forty years," he told Fuller. "We can survive quite well separated for a week."[42] Instead, the Carters turned their designated suite over to Phyllis and Tom Wheeler, newlyweds who had journeyed with them from Georgia on the bus. "The Suite was just a Sunday School room with a mattress on the floor," Phyllis recalled. "But the Carters amazingly gave up their only chance at privacy to show support for our new marriage."[43]

To deal with the myriad press requests, Fuller had scheduled a press conference for Carter the next morning in front of the eighty-year-old, fire-damaged Lower East Side building they were going to revamp. Carter had long grown accustomed to gawkers and crowds swirling about him, but he was startled to find so many Manhattanites crowded around 742 East Sixth Street, hoping to catch a glimpse of him prying up rotten flooring or sweeping shattered glass off the tenement floor. The notion of a former president dressed in overalls and work boots, with a red bandanna tied around his neck, actually doing menial labor of the most unpleasant and backbreaking kind seized the public's imagination.

At the press conference reporters fired questions at Carter about the upcoming Reagan-Mondale presidential election. Carter would have none of it; Habitat was what he had come to discuss. Trying to blend the two, one clever reporter asked, "Isn't this kind of project exactly what President Reagan is talking about in terms of self-help, with private citizens doing things to build up the country and help those in need?" Carter replied: "Yes, I think it is, but talking about doing is one thing. Doing is something else."[44]

That entire week did wonders for Jimmy Carter's morale and Habitat for Humanity's bank account. As the volunteers sawed and hammered away, crowds gathered in front of the dilapidated tenement chanting, "Go, Jimmy, Go." All the network morning shows did stories on the carpenter-president. "My wife has never been more beautiful than when her face was covered with black smut from scraping burned ceiling joists and streaked with sweat from carrying sheets of plywood from the street level up to the floor where we were working, cutting subflooring with a power saw, and nailing it down with a few hard hammer blows," Carter later claimed.[45]

Habitat's New York office was going crazy with a flurry of requests and offers from everybody imaginable. Donations of money were offered, free labor pledged, and building materials delivered. Local churches were providing hearty hot lunches. The Silver Palace Restaurant in Chinatown fed all the workers a complimentary six-course meal. Free Broadway tickets were handed out like flyers for evening performances. The president of the New York District Council of the Limited Brotherhood of Carpenters and Joiners of America paid homage to the work site, presenting Carter with a $500 check, a gold union card, bundles of sheetrock, and the assistance of several apprentice carpenters. The Sub-Contractors Trade Association gave $2,000 to Habitat, and the Hittner Truck Rental Company offered free use of moving vans until the renovation was complete. Office workers on coffee breaks would stop by and contribute a box of nails or a liter of soda to the cause.[46] One elderly woman from the Bronx took a subway to the Lower East Side to offer Carter a flowering plant. "It was placed on the fire escape in front of the building, symbolizing the new hope that had blossomed in the blighted neighborhood," Fuller noted.[47]

Carter seemed liberated by the whole intoxicating experience. Every morning he was the first up, often jogging three miles from the church to the work site to get an hour's head start on everybody else. Working in the building was treacherous, but Carter, with hard hat on, paid the danger little mind. When the Reverend James Holt of the First Baptist Church of Ellijay, Georgia, slipped coming up the makeshift stairs, tearing the flesh in his right leg so badly that forty stitches were required, Carter led a prayer session for his recovery. Danger was everywhere.[48] "That week our block experienced a drug raid, a fire, a shooting, and a stabbing," Betty Pope recalled. "But never mind. . . . We just kept hammering away."[49]

As the week ran down Carter also was the star attraction of Fuller's Habitation fund-raiser, held at Saint Bartholomew's Episcopal Church at Fiftieth Street and Park Avenue. A master at the art of generating publicity, Fuller had the Habitat workers sing before a packed congregation of president watchers, then passed hard hats down the pews for the offering. The collected $10,000 was then dumped into wheelbarrows and rolled down the aisle, providing the churchgoers with an offbeat memory, something to differentiate Habitat from all the other nonprofit organizations begging for funds. Carter jarred some in attendance by announcing that Habitat's next project would be to build homes for landless peasants in Nicaragua, a nation whose Sandinista government the United States refused to recognize. "We've got a lot of friends in Nicaragua," Carter told the congregation. "We want the folks down there to know that some American Christians love them and that we don't hate them."[50]

Carter's New York work camp had been an astounding success for Habitat. As the same Trailways bus pulled up to Metro Baptist the Sunday after it first arrived and the Georgians boarded for the 989-mile return drive home, Millard Fuller prayed to the Lord on his hands and knees for blessing his ministry with the Carters, Habitat for Humanitarians for life.

ᏊᎧᏊ

Jimmy and Rosalynn Carter became devoted Habitat volunteers, going anywhere, doing just about anything they could to help out the Fullers. On October 1—Jimmy's sixtieth birthday—he asked friends to write Habitat for Humanity a check instead of buying him a gift. (The *New York Times* reported that Walter Mondale did just as his former boss requested.)[51] Carter also began soliciting funds from philanthropic New York friends like Malcolm Forbes Sr., making hard-hitting, direct, personal appeals that were hard to ignore. World leaders like James Callaghan of Great Britain and Bishop Desmond Tutu of South Africa wrote Carter, congratulating him on his efforts to help the poor. UN general secretary Javier Pérez de Cuéllar praised the former president for setting a humanitarian example for the world. The Nicaraguan leader Daniel Ortega, as part of his New York visit to the UN, made a controversial pilgrimage to 742 East Sixth Street, curious to see the quality of the renovation, particularly because Habitat planned to build about one hundred homes for residents of Pomares, a small Nicaraguan village in the province of Chinandega. With its distinctly Christian message, Habitat was becoming popular throughout Latin America. As Fuller structured it, all U.S. Habitat affiliates were expected to give at least 10 percent of their undesignated income to Habitat International headquarters for the work in developing countries. On the average, a house in Latin America then cost 10 percent of what a Habitat house cost in America.[52]

The Carters ventured that October by airplane to Puno, Peru, a community 13,000 feet above sea level overlooking Lake Titicaca, the highest navigable lake in the world, to spend an inspired day hammering at a work site and to hold a special meeting with President Fernando Belaunde Terry to discuss how to expand Habitat for Humanity in his country. In order to have fresh springwater in Puno, Habitat volunteers helped villagers dig a two-mile-long ditch from the mountain source to the building site. Having few tools, many of the women got in the pipeline trench and dug with tin cans. "They worked from sunup to sundown, so thankful they were to have water and homes," Carter noted, impressed by the dedication of the Habitat volunteers he encountered.[53]

When dealing with Carter Center matters, the former president always let those around him know he was in charge. In contrast, at Habitat meetings Carter behaved in the most humble manner imaginable, seeing himself as just another ordinary member of the Christian flock, a good samaritan anxious to help the poor. Those who worked for "President Carter" in Atlanta seldom heard their boss evoke Christ as a motivation for his conflict resolution and human rights agenda. A lot of the Carter Center staff worried that the organization's reputation would be diminished if word got out that the ex-president prayed to Christ that particular diplomatic endeavors would work. Carter recognized the dilemma, and so he behaved in Atlanta as he did during his White House years, with his religious motivation remaining largely a personal thing, keeping his Bible, as it were, close to his chest. But at Habitat he was "Brother Jimmy," deacon of Maranatha Baptist Church and an unashamed, born-again Christian. Much of Carter's personal correspondence to members of Habitat are signed "In Christian Partnership," "In Fellowship with Christ," or "In Christ Forever," salutations he would never consider penning for anything related to the Carter Center.[54]

At the first Habitat Board meeting, in Amarillo, Texas, on October 11, 1984, "Brother Jimmy" and "Sister Rosalynn" were among fellow evangelicals, leading a two-hour workshop on how the theology of the hammer could be spread globally through an astute media campaign and offering to use their notoriety to dedicate homes and host fund-raisers. For although the Carters' primary focus was to raise cash for their Atlanta center, at Amarillo they magnanimously offered to chair Habitat's two-year, $10 million fund raising campaign. To start the ball rolling, Carter pledged thousands of dollars from honoraria given to him for speeches and lent his machine-reproduced signature for their solicitation letter, which was mass mailed to over 2 million homes.[55]

Carter was determined to raise the $10 million for Habitat if that was the last thing he did. On February 21, 1985, he invited twelve Georgia-based leaders to serve on his $10 Million Campaign Committee, including the reliable Deen Day Smith, who wrote out a check for $1 million, and Andrew Young. They would do whatever it took—including making the rich feel guilty—to find money to put roofs over the heads of the poor. In Haiti, for example, it cost only $1,500 to construct a Habitat house to shelter a family of four—the price a businessman paid for three nights lodging at a five-star hotel like the Waldorf-Astoria. They flashed heartrending pictures of Haiti's poor across the desks of CEOs. Carter had made it his mission to bring corporate angels to Habitat, believing he was intervening on Christ's behalf. As one Habitater summed it up, "Carter was a one-man, red-carpet door opener to the rich."[56]

By the spring of 1985 Carter had, by his own admission, become "addicted" to Habitat. The farmer-engineer instinct in him didn't like starting projects without completing them. Almost weekly he got in touch with the New York Habitat chapter to monitor the progress being made at 742 East Sixth Street. Upon learning that the project was going slowly, with most of the construction being done by weekend volunteers, Carter announced that in July he would bring a bus load of Georgia Habitat volunteers back to the Big Apple to finish the job. "Jimmy reinvigorated us all," said John Pope, recovering from a cardiac arrest. "We got the old gang back together and headed north."[57]

That July 29, with the hot summer sun blazing down on their blue-and-white Habitat for Humanity T-shirts, Carter and thirty-two sweltering others boarded the same Trailways bus they had a year earlier, full of anxious chatter, ready to once again grind up I-95 to Washington, D.C., where a Sunday doughnut-and-coffee breakfast was promised them at the Trailways bus station on Connecticut Avenue. They devoured the sunrise meal, groggy and blurry-eyed, and then filed back on board the bus, which groaned onward toward Manhattan. After a few more road hours, Carter, who had failed to send the Secret Service in advance of him to find a sanctuary for his fellow Christians to worship in, directed the driver to take Exit 10 off the New Jersey Turnpike to Edison, where they would hear the gospel at a random church.

Carter asked at the Edison fire station for a local church with an 11:00 A.M. service. Astonished to be giving road directions to a former president, the firemen directed the Habitaters to a tiny Lutheran church only a couple blocks away. As the bus pulled into the driveway, they saw a sign posted: "St. Stephen's Evangelical Lutheran Church—Sunday Service, 10:30 A.M." Unfortunately, it was then 10:55. Carter and Fuller huddled to discuss options, deciding that they were at least in time for the sermon, so all thirty-three of them poured out of the bus. Quietly they entered the Norwegian-style church, but were surprised to find it silent and empty, void of even a flickering candle.[58]

One of the volunteers noticed that some local boys were tossing a football around outside an adjacent, flat-roofed cinder-block building, so Carter, Fuller, and others stalked over to learn that the entire congregation was inside celebrating the birthday of eighty-five-year-old Magnus Johnsen, who had been brought over from a local nursing home. As the hundred dumbfounded parishioners looked over to see Jimmy Carter standing in their social hall, they burst into spontaneous applause, standing in wonderment. The first reaction of many was that these were presidential impersonators hired to perform at Magnus's birthday.[59]

E. Walter Cleckley Jr., the young pastor—who coincidentally hailed from Augusta, Georgia—informed Carter that their service had actually begun at 9:30 A.M.; they were done praying for the day. Disappointed, Carter asked if they could use his house of worship to put together their own service, since they had a couple of preachers on board their bus. "Of course you may use the sanctuary," Bob Lynd, the church council president, interjected.

Cleckley added, "But if you'd like us to, we'll be glad to repeat our service for you." A minute later Deacon Jimmy gave Pastor Cleckley the presidential thumbs-up. Everybody filed back into the church, the organist played "We're Marching to Zion," on Fuller's request, and Reverend Cleckley asked everybody to open their Bibles to the second chapter of Ephesians. To the amazement of Carter and the Habitat volunteers, the sermon for the day concluded with a verse from Paul:

> You are not foreigners or strangers any longer; you are now fellow-citizens with God's people and members of the family of God. You, too, are built upon the foundation laid by the apostles and prophets, being the corner stone, Christ Jesus himself. He is the one who holds the whole building together and makes it grow into a sacred temple dedicated to the Lord. In union with him you too are also being built together with all the others into a place where God lives through his Spirit.[60]

"Corner stones" and "foundations" and "buildings"—Fuller embraced the sermon as ordained from heaven. "The Lord had prepared a sermon especially for us," Fuller later noted, with a lingering sense of awe.[61]

Cleckley, nervous beyond belief, asked Carter to give an extemporaneous prayer and the benediction, which he did. "This was the highlight of my life," Cleckley recalled ten years later. "It was such a shock." Over birthday cake and Danish cheese sandwiches, Rosalynn invited the pastor and his wife to visit them at the New York renovation. "Rosalynn was fantastic," Cleckley recalled. "When we showed up at the Habitat building, she screamed, "Oh Jimmy, look, it's the Cleckleys." The young pastor was stunned that Jimmy and Rosalynn Carter actually remembered who they were.[62]

The bus departed Edison, its passengers spiritually aglow, and headed into New York City. On East Sixth Street the nineteen families that were going to live in the refurbished building worked side by side with the Carters, paying off their sweat equity. The Carters were particularly happy to see Jessica Wallace, an unskilled New York kitchen worker whom they had befriended on their 1984 visit. Jessica had great news for the Carters: she had been accepted as an apprentice carpenter in the local union. "Now she had learned a new trade—on the job," Carter enthused.[63] More than anything else, Carter enjoyed mingling with the needy, intervening on any number of levels to help the downtrodden meet their Christian potential. Fuller surmised, "Habitat has made Carter an authentic friend of the poor."[64]

By rolling up his sleeves and working hard, Carter had reminded New

Yorkers once again about the meaning of Christian charity. For a full week the Georgia Habitaters hammered nails and sawed boards on East Sixth Street. "This is about the best way I can spend my vacation," Carter told the press. Governor Mario Cuomo stopped by to watch Carter at work, praising his dedication to uplifting the downtrodden.[65] Meanwhile Fuller had hatched another idea: Why not have Carter invite Pope John Paul II to Americus and Plains to lend his support to Habitat for Humanity during his scheduled 1987 U.S. tour, which was also "The International Year of Shelter for the Homeless"? Carter just laughed. "Sure, why not?" he told Fuller as they left the work site after a week of labor. And then he dozed off on the Trailways bus as they headed back south.[66] A month later the Carters were back in New York for the building dedication ceremony at 742 East Sixth Street, welcoming the new tenants to their new apartment homes.[67]

NINE

THE WORLD'S HEALTH

⌒⌒

J ust as the 1984 Democratic National Convention was opening in San Francisco, Jimmy Carter and James Laney received the first semiannual report on the Carter Center from its executive director, Ken Stein. The eighty-nine-page document assessed the progress of the Carter Center as it moved from concept to reality. Leaving the roadway controversy and architectural developments for Carter's chief of staff, Dan Lee, to comment on, Stein praised Carter for his active participation in academic classes and other university programs, reporting that the former president had convinced "a vast majority of those skeptical faculty that his presence on campus is special, unique, and substantive."[1]

Stein's report was not, however, all puffery. He noted the lingering problems of insufficient staff and especially physical space. At the time the center operated out of three locations: the development office on Marietta Street, Stein's study in Emory's history building, and the Woodruff Library's crowded sixth-floor operations center. Jimmy Carter had kept his plush Atlanta headquarters downtown in the Richard B. Russell Building. These varied locations caused administrative confusion. Nevertheless, Stein wanted to expand the center's activities by producing a newsletter with a circulation of 2,000 and by opening the center to daily participation by Emory students. Stein soon acquired even more space for the center in the form of a rambling old two-story house at 1641 North Decatur Road, just across the street from Emory's main campus.

Stein stressed in his report the importance of continuing high-profile international consultations as well as appointing distinguished fellows who would attack major issues boldly enough to command worldwide attention. He suggested that the Middle East, arms control, and the newest concern, health care policy, become the Carter Center's priorities for the next year. As prospective fellows, Stein recommended the eminent scholar and East-West trade expert Harold J. Berman of Harvard Law School and the world-renowned creator of the polio vaccine, Dr. Jonas Salk. Stein felt confident the Carter Center could attract people of that caliber; after all, the opportunity to work with a former president gave the center a "magnetic attraction."[2]

Amid the good news, Stein's report made clear that the Carter Center lacked infrastructure. Its biggest asset contributed to the failing, of course: the center's activities revolved around the specific interests of one man, whose well-honed work ethic made him want to tackle everything at once. Far from a textbook example of how to build a public policy institute, the center sprouted in all directions like the kudzu that blankets rural Georgia. Carter did things his way, and some around the center joked that his way was "Ready, Fire, Aim." But however unorthodox, even eccentric, his approach, Carter also was astonishingly good both at integrating himself into the Emory community and at raising huge sums of money for the center. "My relations with Emory and Atlanta have been quite pleasant and gratifying," Carter wrote to Stein after reading his report, "and our fundraising efforts have been surprisingly successful."[3]

Still, much work remained to be done if the Carter Center was to flourish. A fair amount of the $28 million needed to construct the presidential center remained to be raised, as did the extra funds required for the constantly expanding public policy center. Emory was paying only 3 percent of the annual operating expenses out of its own unrestricted endowment. Even more disappointing, the university did not raise money for the center. And though Carter was spending 85 to 90 percent of his time raising money, there never seemed to be enough capital to outfit the center's ambitious agenda. The finances probably could have been brought into balance if Carter had slowed down, but as Jody Powell put it, "Nobody reels Jimmy Carter in."[4]

Carter's solution to the mounting commitments was to hire more top-flight professionals to help him implement each new initiative. He saw himself, correctly, as the hub of the Carter Center, and was determined that its spokes be the sharpest people he could find, to keep him spinning in dozens of different directions. And as Carter began to focus more attention on his plans for a public health initiative, he proposed to Dr. William Foege—a longtime medical missionary described by the *Harvard Public Health Re-*

view as a "knight errant in the crusade against human suffering"—that he set up shop at the Carter Center. In the coming years they would together strive to eradicate disease, inoculate the poor against polio and tuberculosis, teach preventive health care, take on the powerful tobacco lobby, and end world hunger. They would work with—or around—the World Health Organization, the World Bank, the U.S. Agency for International Development, and other United Nations programs to combat neglected sicknesses that came to their attention. Carter believed that this center could be a unique institution, a health-care problem-solving workshop. This forceful, can-do philosophy dovetailed with that of William Foege, an obstinate man who specialized in bucking contemporary wisdom and producing astonishing results. Foege, who had been associated with the Carter Center since 1982, signed on full-time as fellow for health policy in November 1985. In time, this appointment would prove to be among the most fortunate choices of Jimmy Carter's post-presidency.

William Foege (pronounced "FAY-ghee") was born in 1936 in Decorah, Iowa, an agricultural town about the size of Americus. When he was seven, his family moved to rural Washington State, where William's father became a respected Lutheran minister. Young William, athletic and lanky even before he reached six feet seven inches, enjoyed exploring the cool streams and timberlands of the northeastern Rockies. Then, when he was fifteen, he fractured his hip during a basketball tryout. Faced with the choice of undergoing risky surgery to mend his separated femur or remaining immobilized in a body cast for three months, Foege took the second option. "It was one of those difficult decisions that ultimately worked in my favor," he reflected many years later.[5]

Propped up in a hospital bed, the convalescing teenager devoured books about exotic, faraway lands. Eventually bored with Edgar Rice Burroughs's Tarzan fantasies, Foege latched onto *Out of My Life and Thought*, the 1933 memoir of Nobel Prize–winning medical missionary Albert Schweitzer, and never let go. The Alsatian-born Schweitzer, also the son of a Lutheran pastor, had moved twenty years earlier to French equatorial Africa. Schweitzer's medical adventures along the banks of Gabon's Ogowe River thrilled Foege, and he adopted the multifaceted doctor as his role model.[6]

An unassuming and likable young man, Foege earned an M.D. from the University of Washington Medical School in 1961. While at UW, Foege took a course on preventive health care taught by Dr. Reimert Ravenholt, then the King County public health officer. He decided to follow in his esteemed footsteps before he caught up to Schweitzer's, beginning with an internship at the U.S. Public Health Service Hospital on Staten Island. He then spent two years at the Epidemic Intelligence Service branch of the federal Center for Disease Control (CDC) in Denver. The Atlanta-based CDC sent him on his first medical missions overseas, to India in 1963 and to the South Pacific island-chain nation of Tonga in 1964, where Foege traveled to the outlying islands to help vaccinate 60,000 people against smallpox. The starving babies and disease-ravaged villages he encountered in India and Tonga tempered his romantic view about the Third World. This experience, in fact, led to Foege channeling his disillusionment with the American Medical Association's ignoring Third World despair into a sense of societal obligation to expand public health programs based on modern medical techniques in order to alleviate some of the misery found in the poorest pockets of the globe.

Foege had accepted a commission from the Lutheran Church Missouri Synod to serve in an eastern Nigerian medical mission, where he could help that impoverished nation's 51 million people develop preventive health care habits.[7] Based at an outback missionary hospital in Yahae, Nigeria, which was funded by a consortium of U.S. Lutheran churches, his ambition was to eradicate smallpox, a fierce killer: death claimed about a quarter of those infected with the virus; the rest were left with permanent scars. The disease was a hemorrhagic, causing bleeding from the gums and tissues and acute pain from just moving a limb. "There is a smell to smallpox," Foege maintained. "I could walk into a ward and one whiff would tell me if there was smallpox in the house." Yet with just two small bottles of vaccine Foege could inoculate 1,000 people against the hated virus in an hour. Once, at a vermin-infested penitentiary, he inoculated 1,600 prisoners in just over sixty minutes; in the inoculation game, seconds mattered.[8]

The audacious Foege, following the lead of Dr. D. A. Henderson, initiated his pivotal tactic for fighting smallpox, known colloquially as "search and contain," while in Nigeria. In December 1966, when the virus broke out in a rural region with a short vaccine supply, Foege and his team improvised a plan of attack: search for the incidence of disease, calculate scientifically where it would strike next, and use the limited stock of vaccine to contain its spread. The quick, positive results surprised even Foege.[9]

Yet just as he was starting to feel encouraged about his medical mission, Foege found himself trapped in the middle of a bloody, eighteen-month civil war. The Nigerian state of Biafra declared its independence, and the new state, which included Foege's hospital, was surrounded by a federal Nigerian army numbering some 250,000 soldiers. Biafra's remaining territory was home to 8 million people—a third of them refugees, many dying of starvation in squalid temporary camps. The Biafran police captured Foege at machine-gun point, declared him a political prisoner, and threw him in a cell.

Released within a few days, Foege drifted to northern Nigeria, his hydraulic foot-pump inoculator always at his side. Local authorities there soon arrested and imprisoned him on a false charge of inciting riots. On his release a week later, he returned to Yahae to find his clinic a smoldering ruin. Foege had finally had enough of life in a war zone; he journeyed back to the United States, where he accepted a position as an epidemiologist in the CDC's Smallpox Eradication/Measles Control Program—even though he planned, once the civil war ended, to return to Nigeria and reestablish his smallpox mission.

Part of the U.S. Public Health Service (PHS), the CDC had grown out of a unit created during World War II for the express purpose of protecting military bases below the Mason-Dixon line against malaria. Mosquitoes, the pesky transmitters of the disease, were everywhere in the swampy South, which was experiencing an influx of soldiers and war-related industry workers, most of whom had never been exposed to malaria. When in 1939 the disease became widespread at his Ichuaway Plantation hunting preserve in Baker County, Georgia, the deep-pocketed Coca-Cola tycoon Robert W. Woodruff purchased enough quinine tablets to distribute throughout the state and donated money to the federal government to construct a medical research facility adjacent to Emory University. This became the Malaria Control in War Areas Unit.[10]

When the war in the Pacific ended, Woodruff's malaria-prevention unit was rewarded for its success with a broader mission and new name: the Communicable Disease Center (CDC). It kept the acronym despite further name changes over the years, first to the Center for Disease Control (1970) and then to the U.S. Centers for Disease Control (1980). Led in the immediate postwar period by Dr. Joseph W. Mountin, an assistant surgeon general in the PHS, the CDC worked closely with state health departments. When it was founded, many of America's best medical minds were invited to Atlanta in an unprecedented effort to study and experiment with new methods for limiting the spread of communicable diseases.

Whether controlling a diphtheria outbreak on a Sioux reservation or immunizing children against polio in Appalachia, the CDC was fighting a full-blown war against infectious disease. Arriving at the CDC in 1966, the maverick Dr. William Foege, still armed with his trusty hydraulic foot-pump inoculator, became the CDC's "evangelist" in the West and Central African Smallpox Eradication/Measles Control Program. Like his hero Albert Schweitzer, Foege saw the faces behind the numbers.[11]

During the Eisenhower and Kennedy administrations the CDC grew even broader in scope, administering federal grants to the states for disease control and launching national venereal-disease-control and immunization-assistance programs. Throughout the 1960s the CDC and NASA were among the American public's favorite government programs. The ever-increasing frequency of international air travel had increased the likelihood that exotic viruses would reach the United States; Vietnam War veterans had contracted venereal diseases previously unknown in America; even the science-fiction-created notion of killer germs arriving from outer space gained currency as the Apollo missions headed to the moon, and Michael Crichton's chilling novel *The Andromeda Strain* was adapted into a box-office-smash movie. Americans began to fret about biological or germ warfare as well as nuclear holocaust. In this atmosphere the CDC seemed a wise investment of tax dollars.

A major medical breakthrough occurred in 1975 when William Foege's "Target Zero Pox" program in India demonstrated that a disease that had ravaged millions of people since ancient times could be stamped out.[12] "It's now been more than fifteen years since the last smallpox case anywhere in the world," Foege confirmed in 1995. "When I was back in India last year, I consciously looked at children in the streets. You no longer see pockmarks on anyone." His taste of victory over smallpox whetted Foege's appetite to abolish other diseases, including polio, rubella, measles, yaws, leprosy, and guinea worm disease.[13]

As a reward for his work in Africa, the Carter administration appointed Foege as director of the CDC in the spring of 1977. "With his consuming interest in disease eradication, Foege was hands-down the best person for the job," former Health, Education and Welfare (HEW) secretary Joseph Califano recalled.[14] In the next six years Foege completely reorganized in order to provide "well-conceived and exceedingly effective prevention/control services for the American people."[15] Foege confronted three major health crises during his regime: toxic shock syndrome, a woman's sometimes fatal reaction to tampon use; Reye's syndrome, a dangerous fever caused by aspirin in some children with chicken pox or flu; and the appearance of AIDS, which first came to Foege's attention in the summer of 1981 through reports trickling into the CDC of young men with aberrant pneumonia or a rare form of skin cancer called Kaposi's sarcoma.

While most other health organizations at first ignored AIDS, hoping it would just go away, Foege and his staff at the CDC were convinced that this deadly virus, although in these early cases it had only shown up in homosexuals, Haitians, intravenous drug users, and hemophiliacs, was a new plague almost beyond the scope of medical reason. Although the CDC sounded a warning, nobody bothered to listen. The agency's recent boy-who-cried-wolf alarmism over swine flu and Legionnaires' disease afforded the Reagan administration and the World Health Organization (WHO) some cause to scoff at Foege's dire prognosis. "I found out that there is an incubation period for ideas as well as for viruses," Foege sighed.[16] With no funding allotted for AIDS research, Foege was forced to borrow from the CDC's existing venereal disease program. He put out much of the first "safe sex" material printed about AIDS prevention before medical science had even isolated the virus.

Curious about the AIDS virus, in 1984 ex-president Jimmy Carter visited a CDC laboratory to study it under an electron microscope. As the epidemic grew in proportion, Carter became increasingly angry at the Reagan administration for ignoring a serious health crisis because it purportedly afflicted only homosexuals, minorities, and drug users. "What did Christ do with lepers?" Carter asked his Bible class in Plains. "He had love for them. Even if we condemn what causes AIDS, we should have compassion for the victims." In years to come Carter would cohost conferences with the AIDS National Interfaith Network with such titles as "AIDS—The Moral Imperative."[17]

But this newest deadly ailment was far from Foege's only concern: as CDC director he also initiated the international Combating Childhood Communicable Diseases Program. As First Lady, Rosalynn Carter had taken an interest in his activist global health agenda when he accompanied her and U.S. Surgeon General Julius Richmond in 1979 on an inspection tour of Cambodian refugee camps in Thailand, where malaria, dysentery, tuberculosis, and starvation had turned human beings into little more than bare skeletons. "I felt momentarily paralyzed by the magnitude of the suffering," Rosalynn recalled. The death rates in the gruesome camps were astronomical, even higher than those in Leningrad during the brutal winter of 1942. Desperate to stay alive, thousands took to eating tree bark and grass just to delay the inevitable.[18]

Rosalynn Carter and Notre Dame University's president, the Reverend Theodore Hesburgh, convinced Carter to grant UNICEF $2 million for the immediate purchase of rice and to use an additional $4 million in U.S.-allocated UN funds for more relief work at the refugee camps. "Carter impressed me by his heartfelt concern for these refugees," Foege recalled. "And having Mrs. Carter actually visit the camps changed my view of public health care policy. From that trip on I also understood the value of having a high-profile politician along when visiting the less-developed nations."[19]

Foege did not meet personally with the president again until after Carter had lost the 1980 election. At that time Carter telephoned Foege to quiz him about the CDC's myriad health programs and to explain his own plan to create an Atlanta-based policy center that would promote global human rights and conflict resolution. "President Carter told me that he would take a personal interest in developing health programs overseas, which he thought was a critical part of the equation," Foege remembered. The energetic but sensible Foege would be an ideal director for the Carter Center. "It took me a while to decide if I wanted the job," Foege explained. "I'm not an ambitious person in the usual sense. You don't run off to Nigeria and live in a mud hut if you are." But stubborn as he himself was, Foege soon learned that the willful Jimmy Carter was a difficult person to refuse.[20]

Carter's unique combination of access, activism, and academic credentials did the trick. Never keen on bureaucratic procedure, Foege had grown tired of constantly lobbying official Washington for help. "By capitalizing on Jimmy Carter's global network of contacts, decisive bureaucratic shortcuts could be made in the campaign to eradicate diseases," Foege realized. Although he still declined the directorship, he did agree to organize a three-day national consultation for the Carter Center on preventive health policy.[21]

Closing the Gap: The Burden of Unnecessary Illness," held at Emory November 26 to 28, 1984, was intended to convince Americans to alter their poor health habits; provide knowledge about how they could do so; and identify how the Carter Center could most effectively disseminate this preventive health care information. Few new facts emerged; the issue was how to get Americans to finally pay attention. Among the consultation's findings was the unsurprising fact that tobacco, which killed more than 300,000 Americans annually, was the leading preventable cause of morbidity and mortality. The issue was an emotional one for Jimmy Carter: his parents, Mr. Earl and Miss Lillian, and his sister Ruth had all been heavy cigarette smokers, and all had died of pancreatic cancer. (Within two years his brother Billy and sister Gloria would become victims of the same disease.) Concerned about his own health, every three months Carter received a CAT scan to check for any signs of pancreatic cancer.[22] "Everybody in Jimmy Carter's family has died of cancer," Andrew Young pointed out. "And I think he's always felt that he lives under that constraint; of course all of us do. But it means that he approaches life like it's not an end in itself, but that this life is part of a whole that extends beyond this life, and we're not prepared for that kind of religion or politician."[23]

Some years later, when Carter learned that long-term smokers have twice the risk of developing pancreatic cancer as nonsmokers, he banned smoking in the Carter Center offices and set off on a crusade against the tobacco lobby. Elimination of cigarette smoking would eventually prevent approximately 27 percent of pancreatic cancer cases, saving 6,750 lives annually in the United States. "All tobacco money is lethal," Carter told his friends. "And nicotine is an addictive drug pure and simple."[24] As Carter wrote Japanese billionaire Ryoichi Sasakawa's son, Yohei, he would dedicate the rest of his life to warding off "the terrible ravages of tobacco."[25]

Carter had not always been against smoking. Although tobacco was not grown in Plains, the Peach State was America's fourth-largest producer of the leafy crop. Thus, like any other Georgia politician anxious for votes, Carter had refrained from criticizing tobacco in years past. In fact, when running for president in 1976 he told a North Carolina audience that "cigarettes should be made even safer"—the implication being that they were already safe. It was HEW secretary Joseph Califano, before his dismissal, who pressed President Carter to lend Oval Office clout to the antismoking crusade. Once converted to the cause, Carter planned if reelected in 1980 to support a major increase in federal tobacco taxes "to $2 per pack," believing that action would save hundreds of thousands of lives while simultaneously raising billions for health care reform and deficit reduction.[26]

Now Carter studied pages of statistics from the American Cancer Society and the American Lung Association; in fact, he became something of a walking encyclopedia about the health risks of smoking. Smoking was a contributing factor in half of all deaths in the United States. Even more alarming, individuals who smoked a pack of cigarettes a day were three times more likely than nonsmokers to have heart attacks. Not only did smoking cause 90 percent of all lung cancer; it also served as a catalyst for cancers of the larynx, mouth, throat, bladder, pancreas, and cervix. Smoking also lowered the body's resistance to viruses and influenza.[27]

Carter began to denounce the tobacco companies as government-sanctioned drug pushers. He would often quote the fact that in 1985 alone 375,000 Americans had died from cigarette-related causes, compared with 3,562 whose deaths could be traced to cocaine, heroin, and other drugs *combined*. "More Colombians are killed in a single year by tobacco they import from the U.S. than there are Americans killed by cocaine from Colombia," Carter told *Christian Century* magazine. His antismoking sermon, whether in an editorial for the *New York Times* or on a television newsmagazine program, always preached it straight: "Curb cigarettes in the name of public health."[28]

The Carters sat transfixed throughout the "Closing the Gap" consultation as America's top physicians discussed unintended pregnancy, youth homicide, infant mortality, and chronic depression.[29] The session on alcohol dependence and abuse perhaps hit home the hardest—Billy Carter, father of six, was still struggling desperately with his excessive drinking. After eight weeks of hospitalization in Long Beach, California, Billy returned to Plains, joined Alcoholics Anonymous, and fought his way to sobriety. "I never loved Billy more than during those difficult times," Carter confessed. To Jimmy Carter, "Billy Beer" and his brother's drunken benders with reporters were never jokes, but the sad follies of a very sick man.[30]

The consultation affected the Carters profoundly. Once they learned that two-thirds of the deaths of people under sixty-five are potentially preventable, they felt obliged to let the public know. The Carter Center released an urgent summary report for popular consumption. It listed nine basic rules for longevity, rule one being "Do not smoke." Working in conjunction with the CDC, the center devised a "health risk appraisal" test. People filled in their personal histories; then an elaborate computer program analyzed the medical information and spat out advice on how the individual could curb everything from obesity to high blood pressure.[31]

Medical matters would soon weigh even more heavily on the Carters' minds for another reason. On August 24, 1985, Hamilton Jordan had visited his physician for a routine examination, which turned up cancer. "Dazed," Jordan recalled, "I felt like someone had suddenly pulled a plug and all the energy and feeling was flowing from my body." Diagnosed with non-Hodgkins lymphoma (DHL), aggressive cancer that originates in the lymphatic system and spreads quickly, Jordan tried to beat back the cancer with "industrial-strength" experimental chemotherapy. Close to ten years later, however, Jordan succumbed again, this time diagnosed with prostate cancer. But this time he knew a lot more about cancer and was ready to fight. Along with his wife, Dorothy, a pediatric oncology nurse, he organized Camp Sunshine, one of the first nonprofit camps in the country for children with cancer. "When you have cancer you can't feel sorry for yourself," Jordan maintained. "You've got to form friendships with others who are afflicted."[32]

Jimmy and Rosalynn were proud of Hamilton for keeping his chin up and combating the disease. And Jordan's health struggles couldn't help but keep the Carters' minds focused on medicine.[33] The center held a second "Closing the Gap" consultation in early 1986 at the Colony Square Hotel in Atlanta. This time physicians from all over the world were invited to discuss preventive health care issues on a global scale. The symposium placed particular emphasis on how developing countries could provide smoke-free public places and get rid of what Carter called "slick advertising companies, which were having a suicidal effect" on people everywhere. When Nigerian president Ibrahim Babangida forbade cigarette companies from advertising anywhere in his country a few years later, Carter immediately congratulated him for his "courageous outlawing," adding that Babangida's precedent should be "emulated by other enlightened leaders."[34]

The Carters' *Everything to Gain: Making the Most of the Rest of Your*

Life (1987) was a Norman Vincent Peale–ish compendium of sensible advice that spent ten weeks on the *New York Times* best-seller list. The *Houston Chronicle* perfectly summed up *Everything to Gain* as "Jimmy and Rosalynn Carter's recipe book for good health—emotional and spiritual as well as physical, written particularly for those facing retirement." For this book, the Carters took to writing under their respective initials, J. and R., in the form of back-and-forth insights into how each had learned to maintain a mentally and physically happy life. Interestingly, collaborating on what was essentially a self-help book put a strain on their previously stable marriage. "We've been married forty years, and this is the worst thing we've been through," Carter admitted. Using separate word processors at opposite ends of their ranch house in Plains, Jimmy and Rosalynn turned into gladiators, often not speaking to one another for days. "There was no possible way we could have worked in the same room," Carter revealed. "That would have been lethal." Nevertheless, the Carters somehow found a way to muddle through their differences and produce a warm and personal book.[35] Working through their arguments while writing *Everything to Gain,* Jimmy and Rosalynn, forced to air long-suppressed feelings, had rediscovered one another.

Over the years Rosalynn Carter had developed endurance and toughness to match her husband's. Jimmy constantly pushed her to the brink of exhaustion, to work harder and help more people, to live the tireless existence of a Christian soldier, and she responded to the call to duty with barely a murmur of complaint, always at his side, not as a passive companion but as his eyes and ears and his most trusted private counsel. While his trip reports were technically accurate, hers brimmed with rare insight, dead-on intuition, and sparkling descriptions. "It's hard to get all the names and political players straight sometimes," Rosalynn confessed. "My life as a note-taker is easier when there is a translator; it gives me more time to frantically write." When country-hopping, which the Carters would soon be doing monthly, Rosalynn filled her time in the air reading Carson McCullers or Michael Crichton, while Jimmy wrote letters or enjoyed a Louis L'Amour novel or a Stephen Jay Gould essay. Together they jogged almost every day, usually at sunrise when the towns they visited were just awakening.[36]

Rosalynn had also branched out on her own with a number of projects. Georgia's university system had asked her to head an institute, completely distinct from the Carter Center, that would be dedicated to the study of caregiving. The Rosalynn Carter Institute for Human Development opened in October 1987 just fifteen miles from her home in Plains on the campus of her alma mater, Georgia Southwestern State University. Almost overnight it became a leading national source of practical solutions to caregivers' exasperating quandaries. Housed on the shady campus in the former university president's residence, the institute held symposia and sponsored educational programs around the country. "I think that almost every family sooner or later is going to have to take care of someone—a loved one in the family, if not physically or mentally handicapped, then an elderly person," Rosalynn Carter explained, hoping her institute would help awaken the nation to recognize that for a society to be great it must value those who care for others less able.[37] To the same end, in 1995 she and Susan K. Golant wrote *Helping Yourself Help Others,* an easy-to-read guidebook for caregivers.[38]

By traveling around the country to bring attention to neglected health care concerns, Rosalynn Carter became—as Lady Bird Johnson had with her environmental beautification efforts—an acknowledged spokesperson for those with mental illness. Her efforts brought many honors, including the Volunteer of the Decade Award from the National Mental Health Association, the Dorothea Dix Award from the Mental Illness Foundation, and the Outstanding National Leadership Public Service Award from the American Mental Health Fund. "Nobody has done more to lobby for the equitable inclusion of mental health in health care reform," claimed Dr. John Gates, head of the Carter Center's task force on the subject. The record bears him out.[39]

After Miss Lillian died, in November 1983, Jimmy and Rosalynn, deep in mourning, took solace in their children and grandchildren. Their little brick Plains home, tucked among the oak and hickory trees on the 170-acre compound, became the center of family activities in the next few years. Chip, Amy, Jeff, Jack, and their families stopped by Plains whenever possible, and Jimmy and Rosalynn talked to all their children by telephone every week.

The oldest boy, Jack, born in Portsmouth, Virginia, was now thirty-seven and a stockbroker for the Chicago Board of Trade. A veteran of the Vietnam War, Jack had earned degrees from the Georgia Institute of Technology and the University of Georgia Law School, married Judy Langford, and moved to Calhoun, Georgia, where he practiced law, operated a grain-storage business, and had two children. Later Jack divorced, and eventually remarried.

Chip, thirty-four, the Hawaiian-born middle son, who was most like his father, never finished college. He was the most politically involved of the boys, even considering a run for Congress after he remarried in 1982. In the early 1990s he entered a business venture with Bert Lance, which ultimately turned sour. More so than any of his siblings, however, Chip worked with the Carter Center, occasionally traveling to Africa on his father's behalf.

Jeff Carter, born in New London, Connecticut, in 1952, was a shy technology wizard who had graduated from George Washington University with a degree in computer cartography. Living in Atlanta with his wife, formerly Annette Davis, and avoiding politics completely, Jeff cofounded a company called Computer Mapping Consultants while his father was president. Conducting business in the Philippines, the firm soon became a leader in its field.

The irrepressible Amy had entered Brown University in September 1984, becoming an outspoken activist against South African apartheid and CIA recruitment efforts on campus.[40]

In a town as small as Plains, everybody pretty much has to get along. It was not unusual in the 1980s to see the Carters strolling down Main Street in search of peanut brittle, riding their bikes down Highway 280 to hunt for wild plums, or eating breaded catfish in the Kountry Korner Café. Sometimes Jimmy sat with cousin Hugh at his antique store to chat about their shared genealogy; other times he visited the Lake Blackshear Regional Library in Americus to study the history of southwest Georgia and of the Creek Indians who lived in the region until General Andrew Jackson marched them to Oklahoma along the Trail of Tears. Family history grew increasingly important to Jimmy Carter, and talking about his roots or reminiscing about his parents became favorite pastimes. Both Carters also became active in the successful effort to have Plains designated a National Historical Site, in recognition not only of their own political rise but also of Plains as a small town architecturally unchanged since the Great Depression.[41]

The Carters enthusiastically agreed to participate in all the Plains centennial celebration activities from May 17 to 19, 1985. They were on hand for the crowning of the Peanut Queen as well as for an old-fashioned pig roast, a best-mustache contest, and clog dancing on Main Street. Jimmy dutifully wrote a $6 check to enter the five-mile run and recorded a radio advertisement for his buddy Willie Nelson, who was slated to croon the afternoon away on the softball field, proceeds to benefit Plains. Asked by Rudy Hayes of the *Americus Times-Recorder* for his view of Willie Nelson, Carter answered, "One of America's true heroes. Has a sure and certain style, which has never needed many radical changes because his music is based on integrity. A longtime personal friend."[42]

Tourists flocked to Plains to hear Jimmy and Willie sing "On the Road Again" while Rosalynn autographed *First Lady from Plains*. But many of the shops on Main Street were closed, as was the *Plains Monitor*, while unsold Carter campaign memorabilia gathered dust by the crateful in two forlorn gift shops. Even on this reunion day in Plains, the visitors' center just east of town was nearly deserted, and weeds choked the old softball field where Billy Carter once reigned. "We used to get as many as 30,000 people a day here," Hugh Carter said in his antique and souvenir shop. "Now we get 200 to 300."[43] But the entire town pulled together for the Centennial, which culminated in the burial of a time capsule in a small park across the street from Billy Carter's old gas station. When Maxine Reese, chairman of the town's Centennial Celebration Committee, was asked by a *New York Times* reporter what the capsule contained, her answer came with a wink: "Republicans."[44]

Spurred by the Centennial's rousing success, Jody Powell got the idea to hold a Carter administration reunion in Plains over Labor Day weekend. The tenor of the homecoming illuminated just how far Jimmy Carter had come psychologically since his 1980 election defeat: the former Leader of the Free World happily flipped hamburgers, pitched softball, and sang hymns around the swimming pool at the Americus Best Western. He also challenged his erstwhile employees to a game of trivia about White House and campaign-trail happenings. "What journalist attempted to set fire to Hamilton Jordan's motel room?" the ex-president asked. (Answer: Hunter S. Thompson of *Rolling Stone*.) As the *New York Times* noted, "Jimmy Carter and his faithful were able to laugh again." The self-deprecating humor went on for two days. When some former administration members arrived in Plains, Carter remembered quipping, "We didn't know what the schedule was, but that was typical of the Carter administration." Dale Liebach, a former White House press assistant, avowed that "I think most of us have a deep sense of pride for having worked for Jimmy Carter"; the ex-president himself wore a T-shirt reading, "Politicians are always there when they need you." A broken oar and large stuffed hare representing the notorious "killer rabbit" were set up at the reunion motel where most of the two hundred guests stayed. Carter good-naturedly posed for pictures in front of it.[45]

Similar perhaps to the case of Gerald Ford—arguably our nation's greatest presidential athlete, who was ridiculed as a bumbling oaf just because he took a few accidental spills coming off Air Force One—Carter's genuine skills as an outdoorsman had been eclipsed by the "killer rabbit" story. The apocryphal tale had taken root one afternoon when President Carter was fishing in Plains to escape the tedium of paperwork, and his dogs chased a rabbit into the pond. The rabbit jumped in, swam within fifteen feet of Carter's boat, and hopped out on the other side. "Any outdoorsman knows any animal can swim well when it has to," Carter shrugged. It wasn't much of a story—until six months later, when his press secretary was putting in some extra hours at a Washington tavern and told a few of his reporter buddies about the rabbit that had swum across the front end of the president's boat, to a well-lubricated chorus of disbelief. "They doubted whether rabbits could swim, and that a killer rabbit had attacked me," Carter remembered, somehow able to smile at a bogus story that contributed to his public persona as something less than a commanding presence. "It's one of those things that you don't know whether to let ride and treat as a joke, which we did, or to call a press conference and announce officially that a rabbit did *not* attack the president of the United States." Still, in his 1988 book *Outdoor Journal* Carter told dozens of field-sport tales, but his most famous animal encounter was nowhere to be found.[46]

Physical fitness formed an essential part of the Carters' regime: Jimmy jogged four miles daily, usually down U.S. 280 through the center of Plains, while Rosalynn stayed trim with a little help from Jane Fonda. In the Carter household low-fat milk had become the beverage of choice, and dry cereal with a scoop of unflavored yogurt plopped on top made for breakfast. "Mom and Dad graze every morning," Chip Carter joked. "If it's got fat in it, you'll not find it in our refrigerator." Rosalynn, an excellent cook, made sure every meal was strictly low calorie, low salt, and low cholesterol.[47]

The Carters were self-improvement zealots to the bone, the kind who treated fast-food eaters like sinners to be saved. Maintaining a strict high-fiber diet came naturally to them, particularly to Jimmy, who thrived on the sort of regimen most people find repugnant. At five feet eight, he had a medium build, and his U.S. government–recommended body weight was 165 pounds; so come hell or high water, that is what he would weigh. If he gained a couple of pounds by indulging in delicacies on a trip abroad, he would fast until the bathroom scale bent to his will. The Carters also monitored their caffeine intake, stopping after a cup of instant coffee in the morning, and Jimmy seldom indulged in more than a glass of homemade wine or the occasional Scotch when entertaining.

But life wasn't all hair shirts and self-abnegation. When Carter tired of the appointments and the public appearances, he often headed to his 2,000 acres of pine-brambled farmland just outside Plains, where he stomped through the woods with his L. C. Smith quail gun, looking for fowl in a Zen-like trance. And every Thanksgiving Day he rose at the crack of dawn, headed over to his spread, and shot his family's holiday turkey. When his nephew Earl turned thirteen, Carter gave him three boxes of shotgun shells for Christmas, his own ammunition to use on their regular quail hunts. Hunting had become Carter's way to bond with his grandchildren, as it had been a way for him to bond with his father, and with potential contributors to the Carter Center.[48] "It is always a pleasure to come to Arkansas to enjoy the woods and fields, and to consort with characters in waders [and] foul-weather gear and carrying deadly weapons," he wrote to Harryette Hodges, who played hostess during some of the former president's visits to the

Razorback State's hinterlands.[49] Often Carter would write friends about the best guns and tackle on the market, filling his letters with technical commentary.[50]

Although Carter talked about hunting as a leisure activity, those who took to the field with him saw the pursuit of game as just another expression of his intense competitive streak. Foege recalled one incident that, for him, summed up Carter's less attractive qualities. It was one afternoon near Plains, and Carter was hunting wild turkey. "You know how competitive Carter is," Foege began. "He thought *he* could call *better* than a real turkey." Indeed, Jimmy's impression of a turkey in heat worked, and before long two specimens appeared within close range. Carter shot a single bullet through both birds, killing them instantly. "How cheap," Foege laughed. "One bullet for two turkeys."[51]

Rosalynn's main complaint about her husband during these years was his taskmaster attitude. Particularly annoying to her was his obsession with punctuality, a trait he had acquired in the navy. If a reporter or lobbyist showed up even a minute late for an interview, he would cancel it. Close friends and working associates tardy for scheduled appointments would be met with icy stares. Unfortunately for Rosalynn, she was often the target of Jimmy's ire. "Rosalynn has always been adequately punctual except as measured by my perhaps unreasonable standards," Carter admitted. "All too frequently, a deviation of five minutes or less in our departure time would cause a bitter exchange, and we would arrive at church or a friend's house still angry with each other. For thirty-eight years, it had been the most persistent cause of dissension between us."

Things changed on August 18, 1984. That morning Carter went into his study to draft a speech and heard the date mentioned on National Public Radio. Anxiety shot through him—it was Rosalynn's birthday, and he had forgotten to buy or make her a gift. Thinking fast, Jimmy grabbed a sheet of paper and wrote: "Happy Birthday! As proof of my love, I will never again make an unpleasant comment about tardiness." He signed the note, put it in an envelope, and delivered it to her in bed with a kiss. It was the perfect present.[52] From that moment, every time Rosalynn ran late, Jimmy—always true to his word—bit his lip and paced but refrained from making any remark. "He kept to his word," Rosalynn joked, "but he does tap his foot impatiently on occasion."[53]

The arrival of Dr. William Foege at the Carter Center, heading various health task forces part-time, had an immediate effect throughout the global health care community. The presence of Foege transformed the center into a sort of medical Pony Express. Never before had an ex-president taken such a direct interest in health issues. Carter made it clear he would walk the plank for anyone in the medical profession who was visionary but whose ambitious agenda was dismissed routinely as over-reaching by WHO or the World Bank. "WHO should be the ministry of health for the world," Foege often lamented. "But since the mid-1980s, they've been a disaster."[54]

Carter was not afraid to expose what he saw as the hypocrisy of such bu-reaucracies, including the U.S. Agency for International Development, which, he once wrote, "was supposed to be designed for sustainable devel-opment in the Third World" but had become "almost totally incompetent."[55] Of course, Carter wanted direct results almost overnight. A Peter Bourne–and–William Foege–inspired relief program called Project Africa was stillborn because Carter deemed it "too USAID" in approach—that is, "un-productive." Writing to a Foege staffer, Jeffrey Clark, who had been hired to run Project Africa, Carter railed against his center's turning into a fudge fac-tory. "By the end of September will we have planted a grain of wheat/corn, delivered a bushel to a hungry family, or initiated an African government policy change?" his angry letter inquired, accompanied by an inked-up copy of the Project Africa update report. "Conferences and committees are not an end in themselves. I need something a peanut farmer can A.) Understand and B.) Do."[56] It was in this spirit that the Carter Center had become per-manent home to a new organization dedicated to children's health problems, which clearly met Carter's peanut-farmer test.

Dr. Jonas Salk and former secretary of defense Robert McNamara had organized a conference on health in Bellagio, Italy, in March 1984 to discuss ways to immunize children worldwide against polio, measles, tetanus, diph-theria, and whooping cough. Thirty-three world leaders and public health experts attended, their sole mission to find a way to save young lives. For in-stance, dehydration caused by diarrhea—which was killing 1,000 children a day in dozens of less-developed nations—could be prevented by administer-ing a simple mixture of sugar and salt dissolved in water. Every year 3.5 mil-lion children died from six vaccine-preventable diseases: measles, pertussis, tetanus, polio, diphtheria, and tuberculosis. Was there a coherent strategy to prevent these needless deaths?[57]

After much discussion, the Salk/McNamara group decided to create a new umbrella organization called the Task Force for Child Survival (TFCS). Consideration then turned to who could best oversee such an ambitious health initiative, and Jim Grant of UNICEF and Halfdan Mahler of WHO agreed on the obvious answer: William Foege, Dr. Eradication. Formally of-fered the position of executive director of the task force, Foege agreed on one condition: that the organization be headquartered in his hometown of Atlanta. Thus, when the Carter Center opened its new Copenhill facilities in October 1986, TFCS set up shop there.[58]

In June 1984, under the moniker "Shot of Love," Foege launched one of the most impressive vaccination programs in history. The results were staggering. In the program's first five years, children immunized in developing nations jumped from 20 to 80 percent. Playing on the African proverb, "It takes an entire village to raise a child," Foege wrote of the movement toward international health care, "It takes an entire world to raise a child." But it was Tom Ortiz, TFCS's director of operations, who best explained its mission: "To put ourselves out of business."[59]

Foege was the first to acknowledge that the real heroes of the task force were the thousands of volunteer health workers in the field. Realizing that the immunization project would have to start in just a few nations, Foege selected Colombia, India, and Senegal as his first targets. He recruited his boss, Jimmy Carter, to help with the massive immunization effort in Colombia. An honorary chairman of UNICEF's U.S. Committee, Carter always liked to be of use in furthering good causes. A telephone call from Colombian president Belisario Betancur Cuartas was the only prompting he needed to board a plane to Bogota, bringing other members of the task force with him.

As it happened, shortly before Carter's arrival a volcano erupted in Colombia.[60] The volcano, 120 miles northwest of Bogotá in Ruiz, erupted for the first time in 400 years on November 13, 1985. Hot lava and mud slides killed more than 20,000 people, while another 50,000 were left homeless. President Betancur quickly recognized that the very popular former U.S. president's presence in his capital in dungarees and guyaberra shirt, with a jet vaccine injector in hand, made for a powerful symbol. Betancur invited Carter to the presidential palace, where he administered the Sabin polio vaccine to two infant boys on national television.[61]

The volcano's eruption was not the only cause of chaos in Colombia. Only a week before the eruption, the Palace of Justice had been seized for twenty-eight hours by a vicious guerrilla group called M-19. They had murdered 115 people, including 11 judges, one of whom was president of Colombia's Supreme Court. The nation was in turmoil; to the outside world, the Medellín and Cali drug cartels appeared to be running Colombia. Nevertheless, Carter had praised Betancur as one of the region's best leaders. He was particularly effusive about the Colombian president's outspoken opinions on events in Central America, on efforts to combat the illegal-narcotics traffic, and most important, on pioneering efforts in child health care. Even before the task force's arrival, Betancur had overseen an immunization program that had reached 85 percent of his country's children through 10,000 posts manned by more than 100,000 volunteers. Wisely, Betancur actively involved the Roman Catholic Church, to which 95 percent of Colombians belonged. On the Sunday preceding each monthly vaccination day, priests in each of the nation's 2,280 parishes urged parents to make sure their children got their "shot of love."[62]

While Betancur attended a funeral service for the victims of the Ruiz volcano, Carter traveled by helicopter to three villages, accompanied by Colombia's First Lady, Dina Rosa Helena Betancur. In the temporary hospitals set up to deal with the injured, sanitation was almost nonexistent. Blood-soaked bandages, mud and flies clinging to the living and dead alike, the stench of decaying flesh, and mournful cries surrounded Carter, who was moved to bitter tears.

Working with church groups and the Red Cross, he inoculated villagers and helped move debris in search of bodies. In the village of Mariquita, Carter asked a man holding a baby where the child's mother was. "She is lost, with all our other children," he replied. "My mother and father were also killed, as were my only brother and two sisters. My baby girl and I are the only ones left in my family." Carter managed to ask if the man planned to return to his hometown, where a mud wave had buried his family. The reply was immediate: "No, nunca. Todos mis recuerdos son malos." (No, never. All my memories are bad.)[63]

The missionary zeal in Jimmy Carter caught fire. He had lent his hands to the relief effort, but as a former U.S. president who prized unremitting sacrifice, surely he could do more. Carter wanted health care to become a serious priority at his center, which would work closely with its CDC neighbor to attack diseases with a ferocity that WHO seemed to lack. Now all Carter had to do was convince William Foege to join the center on a permanent, exclusive basis. A personal note did the trick: Foege wrote back, "The Carter Center has opportunities in International Health which are probably unique. I look forward to exploring the contributions which the Carter Center can make to life quality throughout the world." Foege made it clear, however, that he was signing on only as health policy fellow—not as director—and he inked in a caveat at the bottom of his acceptance letter: "I will have to clear this officially with the CDC but expect no problem." Foege also telephoned James Laney to make sure that he would not be reporting to the dean of Emory's Medical School; years of experience had taught him that even the best meaning academic institutions tend to put roadblocks in the way of pioneers.[64]

Carter was understandably excited by Foege's decision to join his team, writing him on December 4 to express his hope "that you will be aggressive in helping to expand our beneficial relationship." After all, Foege was not just a legendary physician but also an adept administrative juggler. So, still a high-level consultant to the CDC, Foege was now also health policy fellow of the Carter Center, director of the Task Force for Child Survival and Development, and executive director of Global 2000 Inc., an organization founded to increase agricultural yields in underdeveloped countries. "What is so exhilarating about working with Jimmy Carter," Foege learned, "is that you never know where the ripple stops."[65]

TEN

AFRICA'S GREEN REVOLUTION

❧

I f there is one place in the world in which American presidents have shown almost no interest, it is sub-Saharan Africa. Unless they're protecting U.S. corporate enterprises, particularly mining and oil concerns, presidents traditionally have treated the impoverished half-continent as little more than a gargantuan drain on U.S. development funds and as an occasional pawn in the cold war—that is, until Jimmy Carter.

When Jimmy Carter had stepped off Air Force One onto the hot tarmac of Murtala Muhammed Airport in Lagos, Nigeria, in April 1978, the first American president to visit sub-Saharan Africa, he realized that this was a place where a devout Southern Baptist with a missionary bent could make a difference. He was received warmly by President Olusegun Obasanjo, just one of a number of African leaders with whom he would establish intimate working rapport as ex-president.[1]

With passion for human rights came his stouthearted support for majority rule, which made Carter ready to denounce South African apartheid. He equated Ian Smith's Rhodesian followers with the Ku Klux Klan and the White Citizens Council, which had once threatened his life for selling produce to local blacks. His appointment of Andrew Young as U.S. ambassador to the United Nations—the first African-American to hold such a high diplomatic post—also had favorably impressed Africa's black populations. Young was outspoken in condemning racism in international affairs and supporting black nationalist movements in Africa, notably the African National

Congress in Johannesburg. "Carter is widely admired throughout Africa," Young stated in 1995. "He is trusted almost across the board."[2]

The Carter administration had seen Africa as the ideal place to demonstrate the president's passionate commitment to human rights; they amassed a record of good intentions with mixed results. Because of his support for self-determination based on majority rule in Rhodesia, which became the nation of Zimbabwe in April 1980, Carter was heralded in Africa for helping to break the shackles of white supremacy. The establishment of independent Zimbabwe also brought to an end the fifteen years of international economic isolation that had begun when the United Nations imposed sanctions on Rhodesia after its Unilateral Declaration of Independence from Great Britain in 1965. The creation of Zimbabwe was the first great achievement in the long struggle for majority rule in southern Africa. "Carter's attraction to Africa and his empathy for its people," Peter Bourne would observe, "was a natural outgrowth of his childhood relationships with African Americans and the central role that their struggle for social justice had played throughout his political career."[3]

Once out of office Carter began championing the cause of Nelson Mandela, constantly looking for ways—through Andy Young and Amnesty International—to get the South African leader out of prison (he was released in 1990). Eventually, in 1985, Carter connected with District of Columbia Congressman Walter E. Fauntroy, who urged him to write the president of South Africa, Pieter W. Botha, to allow Mandela to come to Howard University for the purpose of receiving medical care.[4] Carter gladly took up the cause, both writing and telephoning Botha to free Mandela and allow him to become an expatriate in America. South African government doctors had determined that Mandela was suffering from an enlarged prostate gland and had a cyst on his liver and right kidney, and that surgery was required to alleviate the condition. "I am aware that South Africa possesses adequate medical resources to treat Mr. Mandela," Carter wrote Botha. "However, any misjudgment in the application of medical services by the South African medical establishment could be perceived as calculated, especially if serious harm comes to Mr. Mandela." Carter, not mincing words, appealed directly for Botha to allow Mandela to be transported to Howard University at once for both "moral and humanitarian purposes."[5]

Apartheid was not the only African agony—it was joined by famine and disease. As ex-president, Carter founded Global 2000 in 1985 to demonstrate how truly concerned he was about Africa's future. Global 2000 Inc. grew out of the pessimistic June 1980 *Global 2000 Report*—the result of an exhaustive study conducted by the Council on Environmental Quality and the State Department—which predicted that environmental changes and

trends in developing countries' population growth and resource management would result in continued poverty and social conflict. Eventually, the
report warned, these stresses could escalate into global catastrophes. Global
2000 set itself quite a goal: to transform sub-Saharan Africa from an agricultural wasteland into a thriving breadbasket. As more than 100 million
Africans were malnourished, and the population of Africa was expected to
triple in the next fifty years, the staff of Global 2000 had their work cut out
for them. Carter's business partner in this humanitarian undertaking was the
Japanese Shipbuilding Foundation (now the Nipon Foundation), which has
given more money to western and central Africa in recent years than any
other private organization in the world.[6] Before long, Global 2000 would
boast another heavy hitter as senior consultant: agronomist Norman Borlaug, winner of the 1970 Nobel Peace Prize for breeding the high-yield
dwarf wheat that triggered Asia's Green Revolution in the mid-1960s, which
cut deeply into world hunger. "Norman Borlaug," the *Atlantic Monthly*
noted in a 1997 profile, "has saved more lives than any other person who
ever lived"—a perfect humanitarian colleague for Jimmy Carter.[7]

The grandson of Norwegian immigrant settlers, Norman Borlaug was
born in Cresco, Iowa, just fifteen miles from the Minnesota border, on
March 25, 1914. The Borlaugs prospered until the market price for
foodstuffs bottomed out during the Great Depression. Norman attended
the University of Minnesota on a wrestling scholarship, and after college he
worked for the Du Pont Corporation during the 1940s as the head of its research on industrial and agricultural bactericides, fungicides, and preserva-
tives.[8] Drawing lessons from history and current events, Borlaug grew
determined to become a progressive voice calling for a "Green Revolution"
in the Third World. Applying his knowledge of plant genetics, plant pathology, entomology, and cereal technology to the task, Borlaug aimed to develop better, faster-growing varieties of maize, wheat, rice, and other food
crops.

Modern agricultural science made this possible: a World War II innovation in plant genetics allowed farmers to breed and grow artificially short,
stiff-stemmed wheat, rice, corn, and other grains that could absorb and
properly utilize large quantities of nitrogen-based fertilizers. This increased
tolerance for fertilizer and a shorter maturation period (120 days compared
to 180 for most other species) could, Borlaug believed, make these new
seeds three times more productive than older varieties—particularly in the
tropics, as long as the plants received enough fresh water. By adding a
"dwarfing gene" to the Mexican wheats he was studying, Borlaug felt certain

that he could develop a shorter, fertilizer-friendly wheat stalk that would not fall over and die even if overfed or buffeted by high winds. "You've got to make things happen," Borlaug would say, perennially dressed for action in khakis, work boots, and baseball cap. "They don't just happen by themselves."[9]

Borlaug's great scientific breakthroughs came during the Kennedy years, when he served as associate director of the Rockefeller Foundation, assigned to the Inter-American Food Crop Program. There between 1960 and 1963, he successfully grew a field of dwarf wheat, known as Norin 10–Brevor hybrid, that absorbed large quantities of fertilizer without toppling over—a feat that went unremarked in the press at the time. Shortly after Kennedy's assassination, Borlaug became director of the International Center for Maize and Wheat Improvement, known by its Spanish acronym CIMMYT, located just outside Mexico City on the very site where Texcoco Indians had once created the garden capital of the Aztecs. It was here that Borlaug was able to see his new crossbred wheats really deliver: before Norin 10–Brevor, Mexico produced an average of 11 bushels of wheat per acre and was forced to import half the wheat it needed; by 1969, the adoption of Borlaug's short varieties had more than tripled the average yield to 39 bushels per acre, and Mexico had become self-sufficient in wheat.[10]

Field results and dwarf wheat in hand, Borlaug headed to the Indian subcontinent. In 1966 alone, Indian farmers, using his Mexican wheat crossed with local strains, increased their yields from 11 to 56 million tons. A dozen foreign aid programs had tried to help Indian agriculture, but it was Borlaug who engineered an agronomic miracle. Lionized as "The Grain Man," he and his Green Revolution eventually enabled India and Pakistan to produce not only enough disease-resistant grain to feed their own people, but also large quantities for export. "The courageous decisions that were made during the middle 1960s by late President Auyab Kahn of Pakistan and the late Prime Minister Indira Gandhi of India were decisive—changing the course of events on the food front," Borlaug wrote Carter in 1986. "The results of these decisions gave rise to the so-called Green Revolution which during the last two decades quadrupled wheat production in India and tripled wheat production in Pakistan."[11]

Winning the Nobel Peace Prize in 1970—and delivering a widely quoted address on world hunger in Oslo—hardly put a dent in Borlaug's life.[12] He continued to divide his time between Mexico and Asia, always fiddling with new genetic hybrids of wheat seeds. In fact, he was on an evangelical mission. "You don't stand in the hot sun for twelve hours a day if you're not wildly committed," the world-renowned biologist Garrison Wilkes remarked of Borlaug.[13] His Mexican-bred semidwarf wheat varieties became the envy of the Third World, and before long the Communist government in Beijing was begging Borlaug to help China launch an agricultural revolution.

With some hesitation, he agreed. Understanding that China, the world's most populous nation, was a cold war minefield, the mild-mannered midwesterner quietly attended to his business and started experimenting in the rice paddies of northern China. He soon saw firsthand that the alleged reform periods, the Great Leap Forward of 1958–60 and the Cultural Revolution of 1966–76, had failed miserably. Machinery hardly figured in agriculture; most of the work was done by hand with hoes and sickles, without the help of so much as a plow. In addition to new agricultural methods, the Mexican-bred wheat seeds, and tons of white-nitrogen fertilizer pellets, China also thirsted for accessible water.

When the market-savvy Deng Xiaoping ascended to power in mid-1977, the family farm was restored, peasants were given incentives to grow more food, and agriculture took off the way Borlaug had predicted it could. When Borlaug launched his program in 1979, China was producing 41 million tons of wheat per year. By 1984 the yield had more than doubled. "Reflecting on the state of food shortages of the early and middle 1960s and the predicted disasters the Cassandras of that period were certain would follow for China, India, and Pakistan, it is amazing that all three of these countries are now self-sufficient in basic food grains," Borlaug wrote Carter in 1986. "This change, in a large part, resulted from difficult economic and political decisions that were made by heads of government in the 1960s which encouraged the adoption of the wheat and rice technologies that had been developed by the International Agricultural Resource Centers in Mexico and the Philippines respectively."[14]

China was meant to be Borlaug's last hurrah. Frustrated by critics of genetic uniformity, antifertilizer environmentalists, and the bureaucratic red tape that inhibited fair distribution of the Green Revolution's bounty, and with funding from the Rockefeller Foundation cut off, he returned to his wheat center in Mexico City while continuing to teach agronomy part-time at Texas A&M University. "Some of the environmental lobbyists of the Western nations are the salt of the earth, but many of them are elitists," Borlaug told the *Atlantic Monthly*. "They've never experienced the physical sensation of hunger. They do their lobbying from comfortable office suites in Washington or Brussels. If they lived just one month amid the misery of the developing world, as I have for fifty years, they'd be crying out for tractors and fertilizer and irrigation canals and be outraged that fashionable elitists back home were trying to deny them these things."[15]

The 1980s were not, however, a good time for the leader of the Green Revolution to retire: disease and famine were rampant in Africa as images of starving Ethiopian children filled television screens and front pages. The overpopulated African continent lacked effective surveillance or prevention programs for communicable diseases, including meningitis, yellow fever, cholera, malaria, and AIDS; nor could it produce enough food to feed its people. The World Bank, World Health Organization, and other United Nations agencies seemed unsure what to do. Then Ryoichi Sasakawa, the billionaire Japanese philanthropist who had become a friend of Jimmy Carter, came calling.

A small, amiable native of Osaka who often spoke in the philosophical maxims of a Zen master, Sasakawa personally donated more money to good causes each year than the Ford Foundation. Despite—or perhaps because of—a generosity almost beyond comprehension, Sasakawa was always shrouded in political and financial controversy, with critics claiming his aggressive charity was just a public relations gimmick to veil his unsavory activities. "All my critics are Red, or jealous, or else spiteful because I didn't give money to them," Sasakawa told an interviewer in 1978.[16]

A proud promoter of fascism during World War II, Sasakawa was elected to the lower house of parliament in 1942 and served Prime Minister Hidek Tojo loyally throughout the war. After Japan's unconditional surrender to the Allied Powers in August 1945, the right-wing Sasakawa was imprisoned as a war criminal by General Douglas MacArthur's occupation forces. For three years Sasakawa awaited trial, but prosecutors were unable to find him guilty of helping finance the war or of profiting from Japan's wartime occupation of Manchuria. Ironically, aiding his cause was General MacArthur, who had come to believe that a new democratic Japan could take root only if leading industrialists—such as Sasakawa—were allowed to rebuild their defeated nation's economic infrastructure.

While Sasakawa was in prison, an American soldier had given him a tattered copy of *Life* magazine that contained an advertisement for new-model U.S. motorboats. The ex-prisoner was anxious to grow richer, and speedboat racing had for quite some time been popular in Japan, so Sasakawa approached the authorities about setting up gambling concessions for the water sport, offering the government half of whatever net income he generated. To sweeten the deal, Sasakawa promised to put a percentage of his gambling profits toward charity in the honored Japanese tradition. Before long Sasakawa had more than twenty motorboat racing courses operating in eighteen prefectures, and gambling proved even more lucrative than he had imagined.

In October 1962 Sasakawa created the Japanese Shipbuilding Foundation, an organization committed to making the island nation a maritime trading powerhouse while assisting peace efforts worldwide. A staunch anticommunist, Sasakawa became a devotee of South Korea's Reverend Sun Myung Moon, and together they created the Unification Church in Japan in 1963.

By the 1970s Sasakawa had reconstructed the Japanese shipbuilding industry—his main business objective—and was determined to disprove the endless round of harsh accusations in the Tokyo press to the effect that he was, as a 1979 U.S. State Department memorandum put it, "intimately involved in the underworld activities of Japan's gangster clans—the Yakuza." Thus the mediagenic industrialist began giving away his newly acquired fortune to promote international peace under the motto, "The world is one family: all mankind are brothers and sisters." And give money away he did. Sasakawa soon became the United Nations' most consistent benefactor, financing such worthy projects as bringing birth control to less-developed countries, cleaning up oil spills, resettling Palestinian refugees, and helping the governments of West Africa confront myriad social ills. Some in Tokyo crowed that old man Sasakawa was an ego-driven self-promoter not to be trusted, pointing out that pictures of himself usually accompanied cash gifts. While some groups such as the University of Hawaii and the Foreign Correspondents Club in Tokyo refused to accept what they considered Sasakawa's tainted money, most nonprofit organizations—including the Carter Center—were glad to have it.[17]

It was Sasakawa who first sought Jimmy Carter out on a sojourn to Plains in early 1981. All Carter knew about Sasakawa at the time was that he was a Japanese tycoon who wanted to donate money to the Carter Presidential Center. "I am amazed to see the former president of the United States living in such a humble cottage," Sasakawa said upon entering Carter's modest, ranch-style home. Then, before he was even seated, he pledged $1.7 million to the future presidential library, telling Carter that it was his great honor to aid America's premier peacemaker.[18]

This was the easiest money Carter had ever raised; in fact it was all just *too* simple. Carter had his development officer Jim Brasher III do a background check on Sasakawa, learning only then that the dynamic Japanese industrialist had been giving millions to the United Nations, particularly WHO's smallpox eradication effort. As for Sasakawa's supposed ties to the Yakuza, Carter scoffed at the notion, particularly once he discovered that the Ford Foundation, the Rockefeller Foundation, Harvard University, and others had also accepted grants from the Japanese octogenarian. "People are overly critical of Mr. Sasakawa," Carter was quoted in the journal *The Chronicle of Philanthropy*. "Motorboat racing is just as legal as horse racing is in our country."[19]

Carter's bond with Sasakawa would prove to be the most financially fruitful of his postpresidency's many business partnerships. Understandably proud to have as a peace partner the former U.S. president who had brokered the Camp David accords, late in life Sasakawa hung pictures of Carter in his Tokyo office, telling journalists that together they were going to wipe out world famine. Thus when Sasakawa put together a Geneva conference on global hunger with checkbook in hand, Jimmy Carter made sure to attend.[20]

A fter their meeting Sasakawa had a public relations representative call Borlaug with a straightforward question: Why was there no agricultural initiative going on in central Africa similar to Borlaug's efforts in India and Pakistan? The seventy-one-year-old's answer was equally to the point: "I don't know anything about sub-Saharan Africa," he told Sasakawa's associate, "and I'm too old to do anything about it." The next day the phone rang in Borlaug's Mexico City home again, this time with Sasakawa's response: "I'm thirteen years older than you are, Dr. Borlaug. The central African initiative should have been done much sooner. No excuses; let's get to work."[21]

Against his better judgment, Borlaug agreed to organize a world hunger conference in Geneva in July 1985. It would be a small affair, just thirty or so of the world's experts on fighting famine. Borlaug planned to offer the group his advice on plant hybrids, wish them well, and then bow out gracefully. He was just too old for the grim rigors of reversing Africa's ghastly slide into starvation. About a month before the Geneva meeting, Sasakawa called Borlaug to ask whether his friend Jimmy Carter could attend the meeting to be financed by the Japanese Shipbuilding Foundation. Borlaug, naturally, had no objection.

The timing was perfect. Live Aid concerts, organized by musician Bob Geldof to benefit famine relief and featuring performances by such Carter friends as Bob Dylan and Willie Nelson, were being planned in Philadelphia and London. Carter and William Foege, who had just taken over for Ken Stein as director of the Carter Center in Atlanta, arrived in Geneva after the proceedings had begun. Both quickly assumed leadership roles, chairing sessions on overpopulation and insisting that the symposium produce results. Invited guests included agricultural scientists, outspoken statesmen, Islamic and Christian religious leaders, Third World agronomists, and tropical disease specialists. The Reverend Theodore Hesburgh, president of Nòtre Dame University, took part to offer the delegation encomiums on the Catholic Relief Service's desire to help alleviate Africa's misery.[22]

Thinking small was not Sasakawa's way. At the conference he announced that he would spend $3 million annually to sponsor a five-year agricultural initiative aimed at ending famine in two African countries, and he wanted the Carter Center as cosponsor. A few months later, at a small meeting in Atlanta with Borlaug in attendance, Global 2000 Inc. was created: Carter would serve as cochairman with Sasakawa, Foege would head the health care initiative, and Borlaug would function as senior agricultural consultant. George Schira, an expert in fund-raising, was tapped as executive director to handle financial arrangements with the Japanese Shipbuilding Foundation, which maintained offices in both Tokyo and Geneva.

But which two countries should they start in? Ethiopia was in such a drastic state that it was not considered for the time being. After some debate, Carter and Borlaug appraised four finalists: Ghana, Sudan, Tanzania, and Zambia. They planned a January 1986 trip for themselves and Sasakawa to meet the leaders and assess each nation's potential for setting up agricultural field stations and subsistence-farming workshops. "Today, the chaotic situation in food economic policies in African countries is similar to that which prevailed in India and Pakistan in the early 1960s and China in the middle 1970s," Borlaug wrote Carter in 1986. "The courageous decisions made in these three countries by political leaders should be a model for solving African food deficiencies at present in those countries where appropriate technology is available but not being applied because of unrealistic economic policies." At stake were the lives of millions of people.[23]

The trip to Africa had a startling effect on Carter. Before the journey, the ex-president had assumed that what each African nation would need was a small research center where farming information, from hoeing techniques to fertilizer usage, could be made readily available. Carter, Sasakawa, and Borlaug found that there was plenty of agronomy literature in these countries already, but instead of being put to good use, it was piling up on bureaucrats' desks in Khartoum, Dar es Salaam, Accra, and Lusaka. What was lacking was a way to bring modern farming techniques from the capitals out to the rural districts. Thus Global 2000/Sasakawa Africa Association (together dubbed "SG 2000") was established as a hands-on agricultural technology-transfer organization that would demonstrate new planting and cultivating methods to small farmers.

In the mid-1980s farmers in the five countries the groups visited used hand-held hoes and machetes to tend their crops; there was little animal power to be had anywhere in western or central Africa, because cows and mules died of sleeping sickness transmitted by the tsetse fly. Even had modern conveniences been available, farmers were not trained to use tractors or motorized plows. Global 2000 planned to change that and to teach African farmers environmentally sound growing techniques as well. In place of the slash-and-burn method—torching an area of forest, planting it for one year, and then moving on to fresher soil—farmers would be taught to plant in contoured rows to stave off erosion and to use enough fertilizer so they could grow crops repeatedly on the same plot of land. These simple procedures would help Africa avoid the disaster of deforestation. Fertilizer had its environmental risks, too, but they couldn't compare with destroying the forests outright. The group's plan was to first "show the farmers how to triple or even quadruple production of grain per acre," Carter explained. "When we show a direct benefit to the people, that gives them enough confidence to listen to environmental discussions."[24]

A successful pilot program was crucial. Borlaug championed Ghana as the likeliest candidate. Mineral-rich and blessed with a tropical climate as well as a manageable population of 15 million, Ghana, in Borlaug's estimate, had the best chance to implement new agricultural technology. Flight Lieutenant Jerry Rawlings, Ghana's charismatic president, wisely saw the advantages of having a Green Revolution begin in his homeland. And Borlaug knew from his Asian experiences that winning farmers over with new seeds and fertilizer was only part of the process: it was also essential to gain political backing for fair prices, a subsidized transportation system, and equitable distribution of food.

Carter agreed that Ghana was perfectly suited to launch Global 2000, but he was adamant that the second target be Sudan. This choice made no sense to Borlaug: Sudan was the most desperate and disorganized nation he had ever seen, and it was in the midst of a bloody civil war. Sandstorms were commonplace, droughts an accepted reality of life. The Nubian Desert, covering much of northern Sudan and separated from the Red Sea by low coastal hills, rarely saw rain. At least 75 percent of the people were illiterate. Parasitic diseases were endemic, and a large influx of refugees from Chad and Ethiopia in the 1980s had further burdened an already inadequate health care system to the point that yellow fever and cholera raged through the countryside unimpeded.

But Carter wanted Sudan—Africa's largest nation, with a land mass almost a third the size of the continental United States—precisely because it *was* in such dire straits. Sudan was also where Anwar al-Sadat's mother hailed from, and Carter wanted to bring prosperity to this troubled country, as homage to "Brother Anwar." Besides, Global 2000 might be able to bring the large Islamic population in the northern part of the nation into cooperation with the Christian and tribal peoples of the rural south. This fit Carter's

idea of agricultural diplomacy: conflict resolution by joining warring factions
into a concerted effort to feed *all* their people.[25]

I n June 1986 the Global 2000/Sasakawa Africa Association opened its first
office, in Accra, Ghana. Its first task was to identify respected local farmers and offer them free agricultural advice, seeds, and fertilizer at harvest
time. Each farmer was responsible for a one-acre plot using traditional techniques and for another one-acre plot using improved seed and a moderate
quantity of nitrogen fertilizer. It was crucial to let the farmers cultivate their
own land; otherwise, the highly superstitious Africans might have deemed
any agricultural success the result of a U.S.-inspired miracle instead of hard
work. By the same token, had the planting been done at an experimental station village, skeptics would have insisted there was some difficult trick
involved.

The Borlaug-inspired demonstration plots did more than succeed—they
tripled the yields of forty farmers in a single season. "I was most impressed,
but more important, the farmers were impressed," said Ghanaian agricultural secretary Steve G. Obimepeh, who visited the fields at harvest time in
the fall of 1986. "I want to give Global 2000 maximum support," he added.
Word of the bounty spread throughout Ghana, and by 1987 the number of
farmers participating in the program had swelled from 40 to 1,200.[26] In 1988
Global 2000 had 16,000 Ghanaian farmers participating, and by 1989 an unbelievable 85,000 had adopted what was being called "the Borlaug-Carter
method."[27]

"Ghana has the potential at some point to become a net exporter of
grain," Borlaug told the *Atlanta Journal & Constitution* in March 1988. "If
we can get one real success story, it will put pressure on other African nations to do something about their own food problems instead of just talking
about them."[28] A mini–Green Revolution had indeed arrived in Ghana—and
with the exception of a handful of foreign employees headquartered at a
small office in Accra, Ghanaians oversaw the entire effort. By the five-year
project's end in 1991, Ghana had become a self-sufficient food-producing
nation. Rawlings had even abolished controls on food prices, turning his nation, with help from the International Monetary Fund, the World Bank, and
the Carter Center, into a model for African development.[29]

This dramatic reversal occurred largely due to Quality Protein Maize
(QPM), which had been developed at CIMMYT in the 1960s but had never
been introduced to sub-Sahara Africa. A nutritionally charged, easily grown
and processed staple, QPM showed tremendous potential to boost the growth

and enhance the well-being of infants, children, and the malnourished throughout the Third World. "QPM not only tastes good," Carter has maintained, "but it is nutritionally complete enough to serve as a major weaning food, for it contains all of the necessary amino acids." Both Carter and Borlaug believed that QPM could become an important commodity in relief operations, better than current rehydration remedies for diarrhea in children of weaning age. Moreover, QPM could replace milk for the many young children whose mothers die of AIDS in Africa. "The prospects for fighting famine are fantastic," Carter exulted. "Ghana's QPM is a key to Africa's future."[30]

And indeed, when Ghana's Crops Research Institute released a new high-yield variety of QPM in March 1992, Ghanaian farmers dubbed the maize *obatanpa,* which in the Akan language means "good nursing mother." Obatanpa seed production and sales reached 317 tons in 1993–94, enough to plant 45,000 acres in the latter year. Supply now met demand; in fact, the grass-roots agricultural initiative had triumphed to the point that the Rawlings government sought foreign aid to build something Ghana never needed before: grain and sorghum storage silos.

The irony of Ghana's success is that politically it seemed like one of the least obvious nations for the attentions of Carter and company. President Rawlings had come to power during Carter's administration, on June 4, 1979, by helping to depose Edward Akuffo-Addo, then president, in a bloody coup undertaken by a group of junior and noncommissioned officers known as the Armed Forces Revolutionary Council (AFRC). Under Rawlings's chairmanship, the AFRC summarily executed eight senior military officers, and through special tribunals secretly and without due process tried dozens of military officers, other government officials, and private individuals for corruption. The preordained "guilty" were then sentenced to life imprisonment and their property confiscated. Through a combination of force and exhortation, the AFRC attempted to rid Ghanaian society of graft and profiteering. On December 31, 1981, Rawlings and a small group of former soldiers known as the Provisional National Defense Council launched yet another coup, this one giving the thirty-four-year-old revolutionary the presidency of Ghana. "Ghana's leading economic, social, moral and political deterioration during the seventies was largely due to the greed of vicious exploiters and politicians and their allies, the privileged elite," Rawlings wrote Carter in 1988, responding to a letter from Plains about why seven political opponents were in jail. "This minority benefitted unjustly at the expense of the majority of Ghanaians." Carter wrote back that he was pleased to learn that Rawlings had already released four of the seven political prisoners.[31]

What Carter had liked about Rawlings, though, was not his path to power but his stalwart efforts to usher in multipartisan democracy after he attained it. Carter took Rawlings at his word that in a few years he would oversee democratic elections and would even legitimize them by allowing nonpartisan international organizations to monitor the historic event. Rawlings also responded positively when Carter intervened on behalf of the Church of Latter Day Saints to allow Mormon missionaries in Ghana. Furthermore, the young president's embrace of Global 2000—including promises to extend credit to participating farmers before harvest and to build roads so that seeds and fertilizer could be delivered efficiently at planting time—set an example for other African nations. "Carter, Sasakawa, and Borlaug, wielding political, financial, and scientific power, have used it to do great good," Rawlings stated at a 1989 Global 2000 workshop in Accra.[32]

Rawlings did eventually lift the ban on political parties, and he held general elections on November 4, 1992. He won 58 percent of the vote in Ghana's first democratic contest in thirty years, with polls monitored by the Carter Center in association with the African-American Institute and the NDI.[33] It was a classic Carter initiative: win entry into a country with public health or agricultural assistance, and then, once you earn trust, push for democratic elections. Here it worked, and Ghana became a haven of stability amid the political and economic chaos of Nigeria, Ethiopia, Togo, Sierra Leone, and Liberia. More than with any other African leader, Carter formed a personal friendship with Rawlings, corresponding with him frequently on everything from Ghanaian cuisine to fertilizer technologies.[34] "I am very proud of the effective and courageous actions you have taken in dealing with your nation's economic crisis," Carter wrote Rawlings. "Also, of course, it is very gratifying to share responsibility with you for Ghana's remarkable progress in increasing food production."[35]

Sudan was another story. The enterprise there began with the opening of an office in Khartoum in August 1986. Working solely in northern Sudan—populated mostly by Sunni Muslims, who comprised 70 percent of the nation's 25 million inhabitants—Global 2000 made significant inroads. The program had less success among the Christian population, who lived chiefly in the south and were routinely persecuted by Muslims: their villages were burned to the ground, and reports circulated of priests being crucified. A heinous government Islamization program in the early 1980s had sought to impose the suffocatingly orthodox law of *sharia* on the entire nation, which rekindled civil war. The result, thanks to internal bloodletting, was that almost half the population was under age fifteen.

Carter had regarded the military overthrow of Sudan's Islamic government in 1985 as an opening for Global 2000. The officers involved in the coup fulfilled their promise of free parliamentary elections in 1986, although the new government of Prime Minister Sadiq al-Mahdi proved unable to end the civil war or improve economic conditions. Because of continuing fighting, in 1988 UN relief supplies destined for drought victims went undelivered, and at least 250,000 people died as a result. Another bloodless coup in 1989 deposed the elected government and put the military back in power.

Carter had toured Sudan extensively in October 1986. Not long after the visit, however, Sasakawa withdrew his funding and asked Carter to close down the Khartoum office: a U.S. embassy employee there had been shot in protest of Reagan's bombing of Tripoli, a punishment against Libyan terrorists. Carter refused to throw in the towel. He obtained funding from the governments of Sweden and Norway and managed to keep the operation going until its five-year plan was completed.

The Christians in the south may have failed to reap agricultural benefits, but they were elated that America's born-again Christian ex-president was trying to negotiate an end to their religious persecution with the Islamic leaders in the north. It had become apparent to all sides that if a cease-fire were to occur in the Sudanese civil war, Jimmy Carter would be its broker. He did briefly convince the warring sides to lay down their arms for two months beginning in April 1995, and to this day continues his efforts to produce a permanent end to the war. And while Carter tirelessly worked to obtain a cease-fire, Sudan's wheat production rose from 157,000 tons in 1986–87 to 831,000 tons in 1991–92—an increase that enabled Sudan to meet about 93 percent of its 1992 consumption needs.[36] "If they stop killing each other," Carter maintained, "Sudan could once again become the breadbasket of Africa."[37] Meanwhile Global 2000 was getting Carter tangled in a political maze of African briar patches, particularly in Zimbabwe.

A s president, Carter had played an active role in producing the formula that led to the transition to majority rule in Zimbabwe. Since that time the United States had been Zimbabwe's chief source of aid—more than $350 million—but relations between the two nations had steadily deteriorated. In 1983 Zimbabwe had refused to vote in the UN Security Council to denounce the USSR for shooting down the South Korean civilian airliner KAL 007; as punishment the United States had cut aid to Harare from $75 million yearly to $40 million. Far from chastened, Prime Minister Robert Mugabe, a former guerrilla leader who had headed the liberation movement that created independent Zimbabwe, mounted tirades against President Reagan. In April 1986 the U.S. ambassador to Zimbabwe, David C. Miller

Jr., resigned in a huff. The post temporarily stayed vacant, and charge d'affaires Edward Lanpher, a career foreign service officer, was left to sort things out.[38]

Lanpher—who later became President Bush's ambassador to Zimbabwe and President Clinton's deputy assistant secretary of state for South Asian affairs—was responsible for hosting ex-president Carter's July 1986 visit to Harare. Carter was in Harare under the auspices of Global 2000, which hoped to launch an agricultural initiative similar to the one in Ghana, and he was by all accounts considered a valued friend of Zimbabwe. Nevertheless, Lanpher was quite aware of the brashness of Zimbabwe's leaders, and he negotiated an understanding that there would be only brief toasts at the reception, no lengthy orations or political grandstanding.

Carter's meeting with Mugabe went well: Global 2000 was invited to start an agricultural program in Zimbabwe. But trouble erupted at the embassy reception, where Carter was the honored guest among 350 attendees. Instead of using the occasion to congratulate the United States on its 110th birthday, Zimbabwe's minister of youth, sport, and culture, David Karimanzira, read a speech on behalf of Foreign Minister Witness Mangwende in which he denounced the Reagan administration for refusing to levy harsh economic sanctions on South Africa that might affect U.S. corporate investments—even though the United States was already imposing sanctions on Nicaragua, Poland, and Libya. Mangwende's proxy also chastised the United States for bombing civilian targets in Libya under the pretext of combating terrorism while choosing to ignore the results of apartheid policies in South Africa. "It was the standard dyed-in-the-wool, nonaligned left-wing diatribe," Lanpher recalled. "Not only an insult but a real bore."[39]

Jimmy, Rosalynn, and Amy Carter, along with diplomats from several other Western nations, stalked out of the embassy five minutes into the twenty-five-minute harangue. "This was a social affair celebrating the independence of my nation, and the speech made by this minister was entirely inappropriate and an insult to my country and me personally," Carter proclaimed at a news conference. "I do not know who approved the speech, but whatever official of the Zimbabwe government did approve it should apologize to the people of my country and government."[40]

The Reagan administration supported the walkout. No apology was forthcoming from Zimbabwe, so the United States suspended disbursement of $13.5 million in economic aid. "This is seen by the United States as an insult both to the United States and to former President Jimmy Carter," State Department spokesman Bernard Kalb said. "This type of behavior by Zimbabwean leaders has led to further review of U.S. aid efforts and overall cooperation with that country." Carter wrote Mugabe on July 5, making it clear that, from his view, the Global 2000 Zimbabwe program should continue regardless of the recent flap. Mugabe wrote back, apologizing to Carter for his minister's "vituperative" language, but did not express any regrets to the Reagan administration. Mugabe had overplayed his hand: Reagan got tough.[41]

On September 2 a State Department spokesperson announced that no new U.S. economic aid would be given to Zimbabwe in the foreseeable future due to the Mugabe government's lack of "diplomatic civility." The *New York Times* reported that this was the first time in memory that aid had been terminated because of poor diplomatic behavior rather than policy. Clearly the Reagan administration was making Zimbabwe feel the painful ramifications of seeking U.S. aid while spitting on the giver. Not by chance, the announcement came just as the so-called Nonaligned Movement's leaders, including Libya's Muammar Qaddafi and Cuba's Fidel Castro, were meeting in Zimbabwe to dissect the dangers of Pax Americana.[42]

Carter, who considered the erratic Mugabe the most arrogant man he knew, still thought the Reagan administration had gone too far.[43] "If I had known it would have cost Zimbabwe aid, I would have been much more reluctant to leave the place," Carter made clear in a *New York Times* interview. Furthermore, he agreed publicly with the Mugabe government that the Reagan administration should pressure South Africa to end apartheid.[44] Once again Carter was at odds with Reagan, even though this time his successor had backed up his own defiant action. The July 4 walkout proved, however, to be a turning point in U.S.-Zimbabwe relations. "It was a maturing event," Lanpher insisted. "The government in Harare learned that there was no such thing as a free lunch."[45] And by the time George Bush became president, dialogue between the two nations had improved dramatically. Mugabe became a genuine ally, supporting the U.S. presence in Somalia. The friendliness continued: early in Clinton's presidency U.S. Army special forces from Fort Bragg began training the Zimbabwean army.

The Carters returned to Zimbabwe a number of times in the ensuing years, although the former president's relationship with Mugabe never jelled. On one occasion the prime minister asked Carter if he wanted to meet a peasant who twice had been named outstanding farmer of the year. Always eager to inspect crops, Jimmy and Rosalynn agreed, journeying 100 miles east of Harare to congratulate the farmer. After cordial greetings, Carter asked him for a tour of his land. Reluctantly the farmer brought Carter to a field. "What kind of corn do you plant?" Carter asked. The man shrugged. "When did you plant that sorghum?" Carter inquired. Again, no reply. Instead, he turned to his wife and asked her to answer Carter's questions. Not only could she talk about the crop, but she went on at great length about her special hoeing technique. Carter would say he learned a lesson that day that would help Global 2000 grow over the years: in Africa women were often master farmers, and it was vital to teach them as well as men the techniques of agricultural efficiency.[46]

Meanwhile, Carter's legend continued to spread throughout the rest of Africa. With Sasakawa's financing and Borlaug's scientific genius, Carter had become the global statesman, making a real difference in real people's lives.[47] "My work in Africa gives me the most satisfaction of all my endeavors," Carter would attest.[48] Throughout his postpresidency the eternal optimist remained hopeful that Africa's horrific triad of hunger, undernutrition, and malnutrition could finally be eased. Just about every developing nation on the map wanted Global 2000 to launch a Green Revolution in their country. Bridges, small hospitals, and schools were named in Carter's honor. In Burkina Faso, Carter visited the village of Boussé, sister city to Decatur, Georgia. After inspecting some crops, the Carters made their way to the local hospital to comfort some patients afflicted with guinea worm. When Jimmy was prepared to leave, Rosalynn was nowhere to be found. A frantic search ensued, and eventually she was discovered in the maternity ward, holding a newborn. The baby's name was Jimmy Carter Ouedraogo.[49]

ELEVEN

CENTRAL AMERICA AND
THE POLICY OF PROTEST

⇛❦⇝

The United States' relationship with Nicaragua has been, throughout the century, murky at best. During the early decades of the century U.S. armed forces occupied Nicaragua and controlled its political apparatus. When President Franklin Roosevelt pulled U.S. troops out of Nicaragua in 1933, they left behind a "national guard" to maintain order, commandeered by the right-wing strongman Anastasio Somoza Garcia. By 1936 Somoza had become dictator of Nicaragua, ruling with an iron fist until he was assassinated by poet Rigoberto Lopez Perez twenty years later. Authoritarianism had become a Somoza family dynastic endeavor, as his two sons ruled Nicaragua with authoritarian ferocity until July 17, 1979, when Anastasio Somoza Debayle relinquished power. Three days later, the Sandinista National Liberation Front (FSLN or simply Sandinistas) seized control. Within a year after the Sandinistas had assumed power, a group of former national guardsmen, who had fled to Honduras and would later be called Contras, organized raids against the Sandinista government.[1]

As president when the Sandinista revolution occurred, Carter found himself between a rock and a hard place. He was very critical of the right-wing Somoza government because of its abysmal human rights record, but he also opposed the Sandinistas because of their close ties with Moscow and Havana. Carter tried to foster a peaceful democratic transition in Nicaragua and thus avoid supporting either Somoza or a violent takeover by the Sandinistas, but the mediation failed, Jeane Kirkpatrick got her job as ambassador to the UN by lambasting the Carter administration in *Commentary* for bringing down the Somoza regime and coddling the Sandinistas, while William LeoGrande of American University chided Carter in *Foreign Affairs* for not trying to bring Somoza down. But by inviting Daniel Ortega and other Sandinista leaders for White House discussions on September 2, 1979, and providing them with $118 million in aid, Carter forever earned the disdain of the Reagan right.[2]

By the time Carter left office, the Sandinistas had been in power for eighteen months. While their record on human rights was far better than Somoza's, they had grown close to both the Soviet Union and Cuba, which was providing them with millions of dollars annually; Ronald Reagan quipped that Jimmy Carter was turning the Caribbean into a "Soviet Lake." Even more ominous, the Sandinistas' armed forces were treating all political adversaries as criminals or thieves. The Reagan administration grew worried in 1982 that the domino theory would fall into play—that with Sandinista Nicaragua a proxy of Moscow, soon El Salvador, Honduras, and other Central American countries would fall into Communist clutches. If the Carter administration had tolerated the Sandinistas, the Reagan administration was determined to discredit Daniel Ortega's regime. Immediately the Reagan administration began increasing its military involvement in Central America, in part by supporting the Contras' attempts to roll back the Sandinista revolution.[3] "During this conflict and an accompanying economic embargo," Carter later complained, "the nation's economy was severely harmed and thirty-five thousand casualties occurred. While the war was going on, the U.S. government rarely communicated with the Sandinistas."[4]

It was this disdain for dialogue that infuriated Carter. Peace could be had, even in Nicaragua, if the Contras and Sandinistas would sit down—Camp David style—and work out their differences. The Reagan administration was in his opinion fanatically pro-Contra. Carter had met Ortega and found him reasonable. "If you don't hold me responsible for everything that occurred under my predecessors, I will not hold you responsible for everything that occurred under your predecessors," Carter told Ortega in September 1979, and the young revolutionary agreed. Democracy could be had if an outside mediator—like Carter—could bring the warring parties together and get them to agree to hold an election.[5]

From February 3 to 13, 1986, Jimmy and Rosalynn, accompanied by Robert Pastor and his twenty-three-year-old assistant Eric Bord, traveled throughout Central America. Bord had never traveled with Carter before, and he marveled at the former president's frenetic energy, his ability to be so focused, to get to the kernel of every question while always looking for an opening for dialogue. The search would take four years of constant Central American shuttle diplomacy.

The real work of the trip began in Costa Rica, where Carter's old allies, former presidents José "Pepe" Figueres and Daniel Oduber, served as the group's special guides. Fourteen years earlier, when Carter was governor of Georgia, Figueres had been so impressed with his Christian conviction, his ability to hold press conferences in Spanish, his knowledge of Latin American history, and his "common touch" with the poor of Costa Rica that he had compared Carter to President John F. Kennedy: "truly a man of action— close to the people." Oduber, Costa Rica's president during the Carter administration, thought highly of his American counterpart from Carter's frequent consultations there.[6]

Carter learned from president-elect Oscar Arias Sanchez fresh information about the negotiations that had begun in 1983 as a result of a meeting on Contadora Island off Panama, where representatives from Colombia, Mexico, Panama, and Venezuela had convened to search for a diplomatic solution to the fighting between Nicaragua's Sandinistas and Contras. The Contadora group, joined in 1985 by the Lima Group (Argentina, Brazil, Peru, and Uruguay), went on to attempt to mediate civil conflicts in El Salvador as well as Nicaragua. Building on this process in 1986, Arias and Vinicio Cerezo, the president of Guatemala, decided to put the peace initiative in a Central American framework, calling for democratization and internal reconciliation throughout the region. "Arias was extraordinarily cautious and soft-spoken," Bord recalled as he outlined his own peace proposals for the ex-president, including the need to hold free and fair elections throughout Central America. Both Carter and Arias agreed that it was not a matter of democracy being exported to Central America from the United States: the power of the democratic idea was desired by the people. But it was important to establish conditions where democracy could take root.[7]

The former president's lengthy discussions in Costa Rica with Contra leaders Arturo Cruz, Alfonso Robelo, and Alfredo César, along with his plans to travel to Nicaragua to meet with Sandinista leaders, led to press speculations that Carter himself was trying to broker a peace agreement. "I've come here with no official capacity at all in my government or even in the Democratic party," Carter assured reporters at a press conference upon his arrival in Managua. Yet his disclaimers did nothing to curb continuing reports that Carter was carving out a mediation role for himself—which he was.[8]

Wherever he went in Nicaragua, people viewed Carter as the American who had presided over the White House during the fall of their hated late dictator, Anastasio Somoza. Escorted about Managua to see the showcase

Sandinista marketplace and introduced to peasants working the fields, Carter took care not to be taken in by the Potemkin Village prosperity. After all, high on his Managua agenda was the release of political prisoners that Amnesty International assured him were being held in clandestine jails. Tired of the sanitized tour, Carter asked Interior Minister Tomas Borge to release José Altamirano and Luis Mora, two political prisoners unjustly being held in solitary confinement. After a moment's hesitation, Borge denied the existence of the prison where they were held—an answer Carter refused to accept.

The Sandinista government was anxious to please Carter, worried that he might hold a CNN press conference denouncing them for human rights abuses. Within twenty-four hours Borge located the prisoners and released them as a gesture of goodwill toward Jimmy Carter. Two years later Altamirano wrote Carter, "The fact that the government gave me freedom is thanks to you."[9] That Sunday the Carters sang "Amazing Grace" in English and Spanish with the freed men at the First Baptist Church in Managua. Emotion ran high in the congregation after a sermon filled with praise for the former president's human rights approach to global governance. "It's amazing how many leaders will release someone about to be executed rather than be condemned as a human rights violator," Carter remarked.[10]

That same day Carter also participated in a Catholic mass celebrated by Bishop Bosco Vivas at Iglesia de Santo Domingo, providing the controversial cleric with enhanced personal security just by being photographed with him. The Sandinista government would never arrest a bishop who had been embraced by Carter in full view of the international press corps. "The vibrancy and the vitality of your service and your congregation are evidence of the life and passion which exist in the Nicaraguan Catholic Church," Carter wrote Bosco Vivas on February 9. "Your commitment to human rights and dignity for the people of your country is inspirational."[11] The ex-president was eventually able to convince the Sandinistas to release other political prisoners, including some convicted national guard war criminals and Contra POWs, before the elections in 1990.

Much of Carter's time was spent just getting to know President Daniel Ortega and his less dogmatic brother Humberto, the minister of defense. The Ortegas had convincing evidence that the Reagan administration was awarding political refugee status and green cards to Nicaraguans who agreed to serve as soldiers or covert agents of the CIA—powerful economic incentives for poor campesinos to join the Contras. In addition, Carter had constructive meetings with Ortega's cabinet on these and other matters.

A day trip was scheduled for a visit to a Habitat for Humanity Project near the village of Chinandega, north of Managua. Daniel Ortega insisted he drive Carter to the site in his jeep so he could show off his country's banana plantations, roadside attractions, and natural wonders. Never had Carter seen such dust as their jeep convoy threw up on the way to the house building site, making it difficult to see a few feet ahead. Eventually they made it to Chinandega, where Carter embraced American volunteers at the work site, signed autographs, and posed for pictures. These were his people, and he glowed with pride as he explained to Ortega how Habitat for Humanity operated. He also made time to lay some bricks and attend the dedications of a few houses. Soon there would be eleven Habitat communities in Nicaragua, allowing Carter a legitimate inroad, a base from which to push for democratic elections.[12]

As president, Carter had found that openly discussing his Christian faith with world leaders was beneficial. During the summit for the Camp David accords the first thing Carter did was draft a prayer, a simple one for peace. Sadat thought it was fine; Begin went over it for several hours and made semantic changes, acceptable to all. A unifying religious tone was thereby set between a Christian, a Muslim, and a Jew. Carter also had talks about his devotion to Christ with Deng of China, Park of South Korea, Torrijos of Panama, and many others. This mixing of his Christian faith with diplomacy became more pronounced during his postpresidency. Carter never tried to convince world leaders of Jesus' salvation plan, but he did describe to them "the teachings and examples of Christ," pointing out that "Jesus reached across boundaries that separate people because of differences in race and status and so forth." In Nicaragua he spoke to Ortega about Habitat's Christian message, and found him surprisingly sympathetic.[13]

With his longish hair and dark mustache, Daniel Ortega—all of forty years old—reminded Carter of his son Chip: an honest, well-intentioned leftist who refused to understand that at some point political idealism had to translate into reality to work. Wearing sloppy khakis and dropping the names of celebrities—like Kris Kristofferson, Bianca Jagger, and Vanessa Redgrave— who had taken to promoting his cause, Ortega acted like the Marxist revolutionary in an old B movie. "When I first met him in 1979, he was like a college kid who had won a revolution and didn't know a darn thing about running a government," Carter recalled. "He was a young revolutionary who knew how to fire an AK-47 and overthrow a dictator but didn't know how to run anything."[14]

But Eric Bord, who had come to Nicaragua enamored of this Ortega image, was soundly disappointed: "My idealism was shattered by the cultlike status of Daniel Ortega and the way the Sandinista tendrils of government reached into so many aspects of private life. He seemed less interested in

Welcoming the hostages released from Iran, in Wiesbaden, Germany, January 1981. *(Courtesy of the Carter Center)*

Conferring with his intimate friend and ally in peace, President Anwar al-Sadat of Egypt. *(Courtesy of the Carter Center)*

Singing the National Anthem with his mother, Miss Lillian, and Atlanta Braves owner Ted Turner, at a baseball game in 1982. *(AP LASERPHOTO)*

Dr. William Foege, who led the effort to eradicate smallpox, holding the Carter Center's 1984 report on health care. *(Courtesy of the Carter Center)*

Ronald Reagan attends the dedication of the Carter Center, October 1, 1986. *(Courtesy of the Carter Center)*

Architect's model of the Carter Presidential Library and Museum and the Carter Center at Emory University. *(Courtesy of the Carter Center)*

South African archbishop Desmond Tutu joins Carter for the presentation of the first Carter-Menil human rights prize in Houston, Texas, December 10, 1986. *(Courtesy of the Carter Center)*

The Global 2000 campaign comes to Ghana, 1988. *(Courtesy of the Carter Center)*

Jimmy Carter on duty for Habitat for Humanity at a New York City apartment renovation. *(Courtesy of Habitat for Humanity)*

There's more than one construction worker in the Carter family. (*Robert Baker, courtesy of Habitat for Humanity*)

By learning prevention techniques such as filtering their drinking water, African villagers are working to eliminate the deadly disease caused by the guinea worm parasite. (*Billy Howard, courtesy of the Carter Center*)

James A. Baker III with presidents Carter and Gerald Ford at the Carter Center's Hemispheric Agenda conference in March 1989. *(W. A. Bridges Jr., courtesy of the Carter Center)*

Jimmy and Rosalynn Carter and Daniel Ortega during the Nicaraguan elections, February 1990. *(Ben Serrato)*

Carter meets with President George Bush and Cabinet members, March 27, 1990. Middle East fellow Ken Stein is second from the left. *(The White House)*

Democratic presidential candidate Bill Clinton speaks at a news conference at the Carter Center, after being endorsed by the former president, May 20, 1992. *(AP/Wide World Photos)*

Craftsman Jimmy Carter working on chairs he made that were later sold at Sotheby's to raise money for the Carter Center. *(Christopher Hest, courtesy of the Carter Center)*

Launching the Atlanta Project: Carter and Flossie Mae Grier take information on immunization status. *(© Michael A. Schwarz)*

political or social egalitarianism than I thought." After spending the afternoon at the Habitat site, and witnessing firsthand their nation's stark poverty,
all the Ortega brothers seemed interested in was having an elaborate, private surf-and-turf dinner at an officers' club that evening. "Never in my life
had I ever seen such beef, sides of beef, beef filets, beef by the kilos," Bord
attested. Tomas Borge gave the Carter delegation special, if unsubtle gifts:
strange pink masks out of Nicaragua folklore, a takeoff on the red-black ban-
dannas the original Sandinista guerrillas wore. "It was eerie," as Bord later
described.[15] But Bord's disappointment aside, Carter left the war-torn nation believing Ortega was somebody he could trust. "It was a pleasure and
an honor to visit you in Nicaragua," Carter wrote Ortega on February 8, a
correspondence noteworthy because the Reagan administration failed to
recognize the legitimacy of the Sandinista government.[16] "So Carter thought
it was all right to drive Ortega around in a Jeep," Reagan's former assistant
secretary of state for inter-American affairs Elliott Abrams would later scoff
in disbelief. "Could you imagine the outcry on the left if, say, George Shultz
did the same with Pinochet in Chile?"[17]

In addition to the Ortega brothers and Borge, Carter also met with Violeta Barrios de Chamorro, owner of the opposition newspaper *La Prensa*
and widow of the martyred Pedro Joaquín Chamorro. He made it clear in
the *La Prensa* interview that he supported the Contadora peace process,
adding that outside negotiators acceptable to all sides—the Carter Center,
for example—might prove useful. While he refused to denounce the Reagan
administration directly, Carter acknowledged that he did not support even
U.S. humanitarian aid to the Contras. The peace process, he maintained,
had not yet been given a fair chance.[18]

From Nicaragua, Carter headed to El Salvador, where his U.S. Marine
helicopter landed in an isolated soccer field to an angry greeting from a
crowd of extreme rightists, including some who controlled some of the
nation's newspapers, waving placards that read "El Salvador Hates You,
Carter" and "Carter Is a Communist." These mostly upper-class protesters
blamed Carter for the civil war that had started in 1979, when he was president. The Secret Service accompanying Carter, fearing for his life, asked
that he stay at the American ambassador's residence rather than a hotel so
they could protect him. At one point a jeering mob five hundred strong
gathered in front of the American embassy, becoming so vociferous that
guards fired tear gas and water cannons at them. Given this atmosphere, Secret Service agent Bill Bush pleaded with Carter not to lay a wreath on the

tomb of Archbishop Oscar Romero, who had been murdered by a right-wing death squad in 1980. Carter capitulated, reluctantly promising to make the symbolic gesture on a later journey.

The highlight of Carter's Salvadoran visit was spending time with President José Napoleon Duarte—whom he had first met as president in December 1980 and considered "a courageous Democrat"—to discuss his country's political turmoil. Duarte, a graduate of Indiana's Notre Dame University who remained proud of his mestizo ancestry, impressed both Carter and Pastor as a sincere and competent leader. Duarte was a survivor. After he had won the 1972 El Salvadoran election, the military tortured him before exiling him to Venezuela. When révolution broke out in October 1979, the Carter administration had encouraged Duarte to return and play a role in trying to steer his country toward democracy. That he had done, but with mixed success. Duarte was in the middle of a bloody civil war between right-wing military and the leftist Marti National Liberation Front (FMLN). Carter desperately wanted to bring peace to El Salvador, embarrassed that as president he had sold arms to the ruling government. But this was unrealistic, considering the degree to which the right wing hated him. Of all the leaders in Central America, Carter felt the closest to Duarte.[19] "I have great admiration for you and true affection as well," Carter wrote Duarte upon returning to Plains. "I know how much you love your country, and how desperately you want peace for your people." Yet Carter sensed no genuine opening for the Carter Center in El Salvador.[20]

Soon after he arrived back in Mexico City, Carter held a press conference at the Camino Real Hotel to discuss his trip to Central America. "I must say that in all my conversations with opposition groups I found their responses," he claimed, "much more moderate and reasonable than their opponents had been led to believe."[21]

The Mexican stop turned out to have a comical dimension that also illustrated just how deep the rift was between the former president and some in the Reagan administration. Carter had scheduled a private meeting with Mexican President Miguel de la Madrid Huerta to discuss such issues as the debt crisis and the Nicaraguan imbroglio. The U.S. ambassador in Mexico, Reagan crony and Hollywood movie actor John Gavin, insisted that he be present for the Carter-Madrid meeting. Carter refused. Furious, Gavin sought revenge, canceling the embassy dinner he had scheduled in the former president's honor on the alleged grounds that his mother was sick. As far as Gavin was concerned, Jimmy Carter was persona non grata in Mexico.[22]

Left on his own, Carter met with numerous other influential leaders ranging from Nobel Prize–winning author Octavio Paz to Secretary of Finance Jesus Silva Herzog. "Carter was determined to find a peaceful solution to the Nicaraguan situation," Paz recalled. "Nobody in Latin America had use for Gavin."[23] In the coming years Carter would consult with Paz on everything from how to end the Contra war to whether the North American Free Trade Agreement (NAFTA) was beneficial to poor people. "I have tremendous respect for your insight and intellect," Carter wrote Paz on February 13, the day after they breakfasted. "If ever there was a person who could claim to have his fingers on the pulse of a nation, it is you and Mexico."[24]

Laughing off Gavin as just another indication of the Reagan administration's crude lack of professionalism, Jimmy and Rosalynn Carter took Pastor and Bord to dinner at El Refugio, a Mexico City restaurant, and even picked up the tab—a rarity for the tight-walleted former president. "What shocked me about the dinner," Bord admitted, "was not that Carter paid but that he used a green American Express Card. Every other American leader would have had a gold or platinum card." Carter sent Gavin a note before leaving Mexico offering his condolences to the ambassador's sick mother. Gavin, anxious to tweak Carter further, wrote back: "She never was sick."[25]

Carter had accomplished a number of his objectives on the 1986 swing through Central America, all aimed at promoting democracy and peace in Nicaragua. Using his clout as an honest broker to gain access, he then played the good listener, letting the Contra and Sandinista leaders vent their frustrations while constantly gathering information himself. Carter managed to gain agreement from several Contra leaders that if the Sandinistas would enter into a dialogue, they would call for a suspension of U.S. aid to the Contras. These leaders said they wanted Carter to mediate, but as Pastor later noted, "We thought that could only work if the UN or OAS secretary general would ask both sides to nominate a mediator." Nothing ever came of this Contra proposal because the Ortega brothers, after some tough conversations with Carter, never accepted it. The Sandinistas decided that the inflexible Reagan would not be moved; even more importantly, why consider compromise when they were winning the war anyway?[26]

Pastor remained in Mexico for the rest of the academic year, and on the flight back to Atlanta, Carter decided to go straight to New York to see Secretary General Javier Pérez de Cuéllar. Feeling certain that peace was possible in both Nicaragua and El Salvador, he wanted to inform Pérez of the Contra offer and get himself designated the UN mediator for the Nicaraguan civil war. Rosalynn tried to restrain her husband's impulse; it was better, she thought, to let the Contras and the Sandinistas reflect on the plan before dashing off to Turtle Bay. The dispute continued even as the group waited for their luggage at Hartsfield International Airport in Atlanta. Bord, on the phone with Faye Dill to make new flight arrangements for his boss and the Secret Service, would never forget overhearing Jimmy and Rosalynn Carter still bickering back and forth, the red-faced former president utterly determined to go to New York. "But Rosie," he exclaimed, "it is my duty to keep at it until peace is achieved." Carter seemed to be operating on emotion rather than prudence.

Bord was taken aback. It was the only time during the trip that Carter's Christian motivation was on display. A year later Bord passed the U.S. Foreign Service exam and waited anxiously to learn where he would be posted. Because of his specialty, Bord says his papers had been sent to the State Department's Bureau of Inter-American Affairs, which was then headed by Carter archenemy Elliott Abrams. He kept waiting. But no posting ever ensued. Bord went to law school instead.[27]

Because Carter's trip to Central America had been covered by CNN, ABC, CBS, NBC, the *Washington Post*, the *New York Times*, the wire services, and even the BBC, he came home to a desk full of mail, mostly supportive, from people opposed to the Reagan administration's backing of the Contras. Writers complained about Reagan's mining of Nicaraguan ports and about the recent disclosure that the CIA had prepared a manual for the guerrillas that advocated the "neutralization" of Sandinista political targets. "You have restored our faith in your brand of Christianity . . . that allows you to feel Jesus's quiet presence with the suffering Nicaraguans victimized by our own nation's arrogance," wrote one couple. Similarly, the Reverend Grant Gallup of Indiana sent a letter saying, "I have been very glad and heartened to read of your visit to Central America, and especially of your openmindedness with regard to the Sandinista government of Nicaragua. Your leadership of the nation outside the White House may ultimately be more significant than your years inside it." Still, many conservatives such as syndicated columnist Robert Novak, chastised Carter for exhibiting such profound naïveté that he had been "duped" by the Sandinistas.[28]

Carter and Pastor tossed such criticisms aside. They were convinced the Carter Center could play a major role in bringing peace to Central America, and they began plotting their strategy to do so, taking care not directly to cross swords with the Reagan administration, although they were working at cross-purposes. Carter, reaching his pinnacle as a self-styled future mediator, was regarded as perhaps the most respected U.S. citizen in the hemisphere. His anti-interventionist foreign policy pronouncements carried a weight not granted to the statements of Richard Nixon or Gerald Ford. But Carter had his own audience, who harked to his voice especially for its moral incantations to talk peace, not incite division. They, like he, just could not understand why the Reagan administration was so obsessively anti-Sandinista, and like him they applauded the June 27 verdict of the International Court of Justice, which found the United States in breach of international law for helping the Contras. But for all his diplomatic intentions of staying above the fray, the ex-president was soon forced into the open on the Reagan administration's activities in Nicaragua.

Just ten days after Carter returned from his Central America excursion, he found himself besieged by reporters asking him to comment on the activities of his eighteen-year-old daughter. It seemed that the bespectacled little girl who had spent her White House years with her freckled nose in a book from state dinners to Air Force One had grown up and was making news of her own. Amy was arrested for the first time in April 1985 at the South African embassy in Washington for protesting Johannesburg's apartheid government. She used the opportunity to make it clear that she despised injustice to the point that she would engage in acts of civil disobedience in the interest of righting societal wrongs. On February 25, 1986, she was among more than a hundred students who occupied Brown University's administration building for two hours to protest the school's $35.2 million holdings in companies that dealt with South Africa. The demonstrators demanded that Brown divest itself of South Africa–tainted investments. A week later the New York Times ran a picture of Amy taking part in a mock funeral at the university, also in protest against the apartheid regime. Over the next year America's "newspaper of record" ran no fewer than thirteen stories about Amy's collegiate struggles to affect U.S. policy in South Africa and Nicaragua as well as in regard to world hunger.[29]

Amy Carter was, and remained, the conscience of the Carter family. Extremely bright, although shy and self-effacing, she always acted out of old-fashioned conviction and heartfelt compassion. Enamored with the sixties, Amy preferred the uncompromising politics of leftists like Abbie Hoffman and Noam Chomsky to the watered-down rhetoric of modern liberals worried about expediency. Amy and fourteen of her friends lived in a vegetarian cooperative near Brown, dressed in thrift-shop finds or ripped army fatigues, and quoted Henry David Thoreau and Gil Scott Heron. Civil disobedience became their way of doing things.

On March 19, 1986, Amy and fourteen other students performed an anti-apartheid sit-in at an IBM Corporation branch office in Providence, Rhode Island. Taking a page from the tactical manual of civil rights organizations such as the Student Nonviolent Coordinating Committee (SNCC) and the

Congress of Racial Equality (CORE), they issued an ultimatum: Divest from South Africa or have us arrested. Thirty minutes later they were hauled away in a police van, fingerprinted, and booked for trespassing. The next day, however, the IBM branch manager declined to press charges, for "business reasons." Clearly IBM wanted to avoid the negative publicity that attends taking a former president's daughter to court.

Although she was just one of a band of New England college students with the moxie for hard-core political activism, it was Amy who grabbed all the headlines, whether by taking part in "Hands across America" on the U.S. Capitol steps or by presenting Congress with an eighteen-foot, 4,000-pound plaster foot meant to "Stamp Out Hunger."[30] Amy's second arrest was on November 24, where, as the Boston Globe put it, she "put the CIA on trial." Protesting CIA recruitment at the University of Massachusetts-Amherst, Amy and a hundred or so other activists refused to leave Munson Hall, which housed the university's public relations department. Police in riot gear descended on the building as if they were preparing to reenact Kent State in 1970. "There were, I would say, sixty or eighty cops in riot gear, billy clubs, Mace, with four or five police dogs—it was really terrible," Amy remembered of the afternoon. Among the apprehended was fifty-year-old Abbie Hoffman, the prominent Vietnam War opponent and professional Yippie showman. The arrests of two such well-known, if faded, public figures guaranteed that the trial, scheduled for April 1987, would be a media circus. The fifteen defendants hired attorney Leonard Weinglass, one of the Chicago Eight's counsel in 1968, to argue their case.[31]

Weinglass cleverly staged his presentation as a case against the CIA, promising to detail "heinous acts and other criminal activities that included murder and killings." He called witnesses including former Attorney General Ramsey Clark; former Defense Department official Daniel Ellsberg, who had released the Pentagon Papers to the New York Times; former Nicaraguan Contra leader Edgar Chamorro; and former CIA agent Ralph McGhee, who had been the chief United States adviser to the South Vietnamese secret police during the Vietnam War. Each of these experts testified that the Central Intelligence Agency had been and continued to be involved in torture, assassinations, and other illegal activities of varying enormity. Rarely in the United States do legal cases technically comprising only misdemeanors attract so much public scrutiny.

When Amy Carter—who had been put on limited probation at Brown— took the stand on April 13, the courtroom was filled with reporters, photographers, and the curious. Poised and well-prepared, she explained under prosecution questioning that she had left Munson Hall early that November afternoon because she did not want her family name to overshadow weeks of preparation on the part of her fellow protestors. But, she continued, she had decided to be arrested when she saw the arrogance of the police in their riot gear. "Every time a person sacrifices themselves for a larger injustice, it aids in the cycle of change," Amy stated calmly, as Weinglass nodded in approval. When the judge and six-member jury broke for lunch, the audience gave nineteen-year-old Amy a standing ovation.[32]

Back home in Plains, Jimmy and Rosalynn Carter were also cheering their daughter on. "My parents told me they were proud of me," Amy told the press. "They said they were surprised we had accomplished this much and gotten this far." The *Boston Globe* covered the case as if it were the Red Sox in the World Series, while ABC's Ted Koppel devoted a *Nightline* program to anti-CIA sentiments on American college campuses. Abbie Hoffman, the wisecracking warhorse of American protest, offered Amy pointers on how to manipulate the media.

A celebration erupted at Northampton's Hampshire District Courthouse on April 15 when the fifteen protestors were acquitted of trespassing and disorderly conduct. "The case showed that on occasion state courts and juries would effectively act to protect First Amendment rights," Ramsey Clark concluded. "And by supporting his daughter against the CIA, Jimmy Carter proved that he had an independent mind and spirit."[33]

After the verdict was announced, the defendants appeared on the courthouse steps, clad in red T-shirts that showed a gavel smashing the letters *CIA*. Hundreds of supporters chanted "CIA Go Away" and "Langley, Langley" (in reference to a protest action planned for CIA headquarters in Langley, Virginia, on April 27). "Everyone out there should be at Langley," Amy Carter shouted through a megaphone to a cheering crowd. "Tell your parents to come."[34]

Jimmy Carter was in Atlanta when news of his daughter's court victory reached him. Ever since Amy had begun protesting in earnest, he had set about conducting his own investigation into CIA activities in Nicaragua. When the results came in, he found himself siding more with Ramsey Clark than with William Casey, the agency's director. Those who thought a former president would shun association with an outlaw figure like Abbie Hoffman, whose arrest record was thicker than the Atlanta phone book, were surprised. "Abbie Hoffman is a folk hero," Carter maintained, adding that he himself was a "very proud father tonight." Pressed to comment on Amy's claim that the CIA was corrupt to the core, Jimmy Carter stood by his daughter: "Amy's been arrested four times, three times for protesting apartheid and this last time for what she considers, and I consider, illegal activity of the CIA in Nicaragua."[35]

TWELVE

THE CARTER CENTER OPENS

✑

By October 1, 1986, the day that the Carter Center's new facilities opened at One Copenhill, Jimmy and Rosalynn Carter had assembled an ideal team of fellows and senior staff. Dr. William Foege was firmly ensconced as director: his slogan "Shot of Love" was becoming known in twenty languages. Nobel laureate Norman Borlaug had brought a mini–Green Revolution to Ghana and Tanzania. And, with Robert Pastor in Latin American and Caribbean affairs, Carter had the perfect partner to help him find a solution to the Nicaraguan civil war. In Soviet media and arms control Ellen Mickiewicz was cultivating connections in Gorbachev's government, conducting the first national public opinion survey ever carried out simultaneously in the U.S. and the USSR and beginning to analyze the decision-making process in Soviet television programming. Middle Eastern affairs still were the domain of Ken Stein, who, freed of administrative duty, was concentrating on teaching history and working on the Palestinian problem.

Dayle Powell, a tough former federal prosecutor in Alabama, was now running the center's pioneering conflict resolution program. Jimmy Carter had recruited her in 1984, and soon she was conducting on-the-spot studies of some of the world's most contentious social conflicts, including those in Northern Ireland, Cyprus, and South Africa. Together, Powell and Carter created the Conflict Resolution Program (CRP) and the International Negotiating Network (INN) to study and monitor the civil wars, then numbering over thirty, that raged around the globe.[1] Catherine Rudder, executive director of the American Political Science Association, described the CRP/INN as "an international mediation consortium of high quality people committed to peace, willing to take on almost insolvable problems."[2] The construction of the Carter Center facilities had been funded entirely by $28 million in private donations from individuals and corporations. Steve Hochman continued to assist Carter with his teaching and writing. Emory president James Laney would help address theological issues. Rosalynn was as active as anybody in the center, running symposia and consultations on mental health issues, excited with Jimmy about their shared vision come true. Charles F. Kirbo still offered wise counsel from his law office high above Peachtree Street.

The umbrella concept under which all of these programs operated was human rights, what Carter once called the heart and soul of U.S. foreign policy. More than any other previous American political figure—save perhaps Eleanor Roosevelt—Jimmy Carter promoted, protected, and championed human rights at home and abroad. "In everything that I do concerning domestic or foreign policy," Carter had said in a speech in 1977, "I like to try to make other people realize that our system works, that freedom of elections, freedom from persecution, that basic human rights being preserved, that a move towards peace, reduction in weapons, prohibition against suffering from inadequate health care and so forth are part of our national consciousness and that we can demonstrate that it works in this country and serve as an example to others."[3]

Warren Christopher, serving on the center's board of advisers, had urged Carter early on to make human rights its focal point. In a lengthy memorandum submitted to Carter on December 20, 1984, Christopher outlined the need for a U.S.-headquartered center that would monitor global human rights violations and pressure leaders to release prisoners. "The emergence of human rights as a principal element of American foreign policy is one of the most important and enduring accomplishments of your Administration," Christopher wrote. "Thus, it would be especially fitting for the Center to play a major role in the field."[4]

Carter, with Christopher's urging, wanted to put the center on the front line of the crusade for global human rights alongside with Amnesty International, the Lawyers Committee for Human Rights, Physicians for Human Rights, Americas Watch, Helsinki Watch, Africa Watch, and some European organizations. "Jimmy Carter, at the time of the official opening of his center, was anxious to bring us back to the early optimism of Eleanor

Roosevelt and her Declaration of Human Rights," former State Department official Patricia Derian recalled. "As president he harbored this attitude; as ex-president it came gushing out of him."5

Yet while Christopher, Derian, Powell, and others wanted Carter to develop a human rights resource center, to travel the world making speeches and waving lists of political prisoners in front of CNN and other news media, the ex-president demurred. His approach would not be frontal; it would be more quiet and behind-the-scenes. More than anything else Carter believed that approaching world leaders directly, asking for the release of prisoners as a personal favor, was where direct results could occur, how he could best save lives. "I prefer to take up problems directly with Heads of State."6

Human rights was not just a slogan to the president emeritus. On all his global missions in the coming years he would use his access to power to campaign for the release of prisoners of conscience in every country from Nigeria to Thailand, Israel to South Africa. Whenever Jack Healy of Amnesty International heard that Carter was about to use his passport, he would send the former president a detailed letter, always with specific names of political prisoners, many subject to torture, to raise with world leaders. While it's difficult to garner exact numbers, from 1981 to 1997 Carter was directly responsible for the release of approximately 50,000 political prisoners whose human rights had been violated. This was always done without fanfare or media hoopla. Carter would raise with leaders a specific human rights case, and follow up his initial inquiry with telephone calls and pestering letters. "I hold Amnesty International in high regard and in particular endorse its work on behalf of prisoners of conscience," Carter would typically write to world leaders, then ask for prisoners to be released.7

In coming years Healy pressed Carter to convince General Henri Namphy in Haiti to assure the physical integrity of all the candidates in the 1987 election; save ninety religious activists in Tunisia from the death penalty; have Hafez al-Assad release five Syrian Jews; have Pope John Paul II denounce the U.S. death penalty; and strive for the release of over 100,000 prisoners in Africa.8 He raised the stakes in Thailand. "I know that Thailand is planning to celebrate Your Majesty's sixtieth birthday in December and my hope is that this will be the occasion of a general Royal pardon of prisoners of conscience," Carter wrote King Bhumibol Adulyadej in 1987. "I am actively associated with Amnesty International, and we would like to insure that such a pardon be given maximum worldwide attention if it does occur. At the same time, we would like to be able to draw attention once again to the sharp comparison between the benevolent activities of Thailand and the continuing human rights violations of Kampuchea." The ploy worked: the king released thousands of prisoners.[9]

When it came to the Israeli mistreatment of Palestinians, the tables were reversed, and Carter would send Amnesty International reports of human rights violations committed by the Israeli General Security Services (GSS). Known as Shin Bet, the GSS allegedly detained Palestinians, sometimes committing such torturous acts as hooding, beating, choking, sleep deprivation, subjection to freezing cold showers, threats to family, and other forms of humiliation. Carter wanted Amnesty International to pressure the American ambassador in Tel Aviv to implement U.S. Law 98-447, which mandated that the State Department officially oppose torture and report back to the Congress on its efforts in this direction. Carter also sent Healy a series of reports on the ill-treatment of children in Israeli military prisons, asking him to make this an international issue.[10]

Carter, given reports of human rights violations through his PLO underground connection, often confronted leading members of the Israeli government himself, demanding answers. "I am writing concerning the recent administrative detention of Faisel Husseini, Jamal Salama, Massoud Al Masli, Musa Al Dwidi, and Ma'amoun Al Sayyid," Carter wrote Defense Minister Yitzhak Rabin in May 1987. "I would appreciate you having someone investigate this situation and informing me of the charges and the status of their detention."[11] Rabin fired back an angry missive pointing out that all the Palestinians mentioned were active in "subversive activities" with the PLO, and operated a "network of coordinated terror aimed at totally disrupting peaceful daily existence, causing loss of life to innocent victims."[12] Undeterred, Carter continued to write to Tel Aviv about individual Palestinians he believed to be prisoners of conscience. Word of his human rights efforts spread throughout the Middle East, and almost all the Arab leaders of the region wrote Carter to congratulate him on the work of his new center.

No world leader was ignored, not even Secretary General Mikhail Gorbachev. Starting in 1985, Carter began pressing Gorbachev to free specific dissidents. It continued to irritate Carter that one could be jailed in the Soviet Union for reading the New Testament. By early 1988 he upped the ante, asking Gorbachev to give all Christian and Jewish dissenters a blanket amnesty. "The celebration commemorating the 1000th anniversary of the Russian Church will focus special attention on the importance of religious freedom," Carter wrote Gorbachev. "It is my profound hope, therefore, that you will find a way to bring about the release of all detained religious believers as a humanitarian gesture, tied to the millennium celebration of the Russian Church and your own efforts to foster human rights. The world will be gratified."[13]

In early 1986 the Carter-Menil Foundation was established as a partnership between Jimmy Carter and Dominique de Menil, a Texas champion of human rights around the globe, to promote the protection of individual freedoms in two ways: by supporting the work of the Carter Center's human rights program, and by awarding an annual prize. Each year on December 10, the anniversary of the proclamation of the UN Universal Declaration of Human Rights, the foundation would present an award of $100,000 to one or more individuals or organizations for courageous and effective work in furthering the crusade for justice. "The Carter Center might serve as a nerve center to orchestrate high level appeals to heads of government on behalf of prisoners in energizing human rights situations," Carter wrote de Menil after they had dinner together in New York.[14] An advisory committee of representatives from various human rights organizations voted to award the first prize jointly to Soviet dissident Yuri Orlov and the Group for Mutual Support, an organization of families of disappeared persons in Guatemala.[15]

Without question, Carter's postpresidential years had caused former critics on both the left and the right to concede that, at the very least, he was a superb president emeritus. "It is as if Carter had decided to take the most liberal and successful policies of his failed administration— human rights, peacemaking, and concern for the poor—and make them the centerpiece of a campaign for his own political resurrection," Kai Bird wrote in the *Nation*.[16] "The present writer has long tended to twitch uncontrollably any time somebody speaks warmly of Jimmy Carter, so he has been more spastic than usual lately," a *Fortune* magazine columnist noted in a piece titled "Mr. Nice Guy." "Esteem-wise—there is no denying it—Jimmy Carter is making a comeback."[17]

Corporations—in particular, the Coca-Cola Company—came on board too. The Carter–Coca-Cola connection had deep roots. While he was campaigning for the White House in 1976, Coca-Cola had been Carter's most important ally; in fact, he modeled his campaign on the way the Atlanta-based company sold soft drinks. In the homestretch of the campaign, when Carter's ambiguous position on issues was pulling down his popularity ratings, he hired Tom Schwartz, a New York media consultant who had developed hundreds of Coca-Cola commercials. "Whether it's Coca-Cola or Jimmy Carter," Schwartz explained, "we don't try to convey a point of view, but a montage of images and sounds that leaves the viewer with a positive attitude."

Coca-Cola continued to offer Carter help after 1980, including office services for Global 2000 in some African countries, hosting receptions for him in various out-of-the-way locations. In return, Carter's loyalty to Coca-Cola over the years has been unwavering.[18] One small example occurred in the 1990s, when Jimmy and Rosalynn went out for dinner with John and Betty Pope at a country café in south Georgia. As the waitress took the couples' food order, a tad apprehensive serving a former U.S. president supper, Carter asked for the broiled catfish platter and a Coke. "Mr. President," the waitress nervously interjected, "I'm afraid we don't have Coke; will Pepsi do?" Glaring at her, Carter asked, "Why not?" She had no satisfactory answer. "Well," Carter said, more angry than disappointed, "then bring me water."[19]

Even the Democratic party seemed to be courting Carter that fall. In mid-September the Democratic National Committee headed to Dixie to discuss the possibility of holding their 1988 convention in Atlanta. Carter offered use of the Carter Center complex, making it clear, however, that he did not plan on campaigning much for the Democratic nominee, but also telling the press that "without the South" the White House would be "impossible for the Democrats to win."[20]

Meanwhile, Carter had developed a patchwork constituency of miscellaneous organizations that claimed the former president as one of their own— whether the Brotherhood of Joiners and Carpenters of America or the No Nuke coalition, Trouts Unlimited or the American Poetry Association, the Stock Car Racing Association or the Willie Nelson Fan Club. Young people found his idiosyncrasies appealing, amazed that he could talk with authority about the nouveau country group Cowboy Junkies or the spirituality found in John Coltrane's jazz. To ensure that he did not remain completely out of the Washington loop, Carter had retained Terrence Adamson, the crack lawyer of the *Washington Post* "gossipgate" case, as his beltway defender, ready to set the record straight on everything from the historical facts surrounding the 1791 Logan Act to the ethics behind spending Sasakawa motorboat-racing money for peace programs. Jody Powell, Zbig Brzezinski, and Sol Linowitz, among others, could always be counted on to provide the Carter Center with insider information about congressional bills or State Department intentions, grist for the mill as their former boss plotted his global strategies. And of course it was impossible to hold a conversation with Carter and not have him mention his "equal partner" Rosalynn, who in the coming years would travel to over one hundred countries with him. When the ex-president spoke, it was almost always, "We did this," hardly ever "I."[21]

For all its accomplishments, the Carter Center was also hampered by the president's ingrained habits. Compassionate to everybody, Carter at times was unable to distinguish the trivial from the important: monitoring an election in the Dominican Republic carried the same moral imperative as helping a single Haitian refugee get into a good graduate school. The ex-president had never forgotten the outpouring of affection his father, Earl Carter, received from common folks all over Georgia as he lay dying of pancreatic cancer. Due to the everyday Christian favors he had done over the years for broke dirt farmers, disabled sharecroppers, bankrupt merchants, and the rural destitute—just about whomever you ask—all of Sumter County came to his funeral.

His son Jimmy, once out of government, continued the family tradition of giving. Baptist missionaries would write "Brother Jimmy" to help them get the Bible into China, keep the Second Baptist Church open in Romania, and set up an AIDS clinic in San Francisco. Common citizens would ask him to help relatives get visas to America, elementary schools to get sports equipment, the Atlanta zoo to get Panda bears. The requests were endless, and Carter disliked saying no. Letters requesting humanitarian favors went out to Mobutu Sese Seko of Zaire and Prime Minister Rajiv Gandhi of India, Emperor Hirohito of Japan and Fidel Castro of Cuba. When a family wrote to ask for his help in adopting a twenty-two-month-old baby from Romania, Carter, to their everlasting surprise, wrote President Nicolae Ceauşescu directly: "In May 1986 the Gundersons signed papers in Bucharest, Romania, commencing adoption proceedings for a 3-month-old baby boy. At that time, they were told that the normal processing time was 8 to 10 months, after 19 months, they were still waiting for their new son's adoption." The Gundersons got the child a week later.[22]

Miracles, it seemed, could happen when Carter—using letterhead with the U.S. presidential seal on top—wrote directly to world leaders. Pretty soon word of the ex-president's generosity toward common requests spread as every Sudanese or El Salvadoran exile driving a taxi pleaded for a green card, not something that Carter could obtain for them. Among the thickest files in Carter's postpresidential papers collection are labeled "Personal Favors," all stuffed with letters from American citizens in Boise or Tempe or Knoxville asking for help, all embraced by Carter, a solution-driven Ann Landers who by writing a letter or picking up a telephone could deliver dramatic results.

Certainly this desire to save specific individuals at the expense of grand strategy was heartfelt and noble, but it had its downside if you worked at the Carter Center. Over the duration of Carter's postpresidential career, Robert Pastor wrote Carter hundreds of memoranda on Latin American affairs dealing with strategic imperatives pertaining to debt and drugs, elections and democracy. Carter would return them without detailed comments—only "OK" or "No" to specific points—but laced with grammatical and punctuation corrections. Yet everybody at the Carter Center was amazed that the former president knew so much about so many varied topics. His closest associates did worry, however, that Carter had little sense of priority. A meeting with the head of Dekalb County's Chamber of Commerce was given the same preparation as a visit from the national security adviser: once a meeting was scheduled, Carter found it embarrassing to cancel no matter the circumstances. This was admirable in its authentic populism but it left full-time employees of the Carter Center confused as to visitors' rank on the ex-president's priority list. The fact was, he had no list. An hour of his time was just that—an hour of his time. In the eyes of God all were equal, and Jimmy Carter was not about to give preferential treatment to anybody simply because he or she had a Harvard Ph.D. or headed one of his own center initiatives.[23]

The Carter Center complex officially opened in October 1986, and the National Archives opened the adjoining Jimmy Carter Presidential Library to researchers in January 1987. The initial reaction of the scholars who combed through the first Carter administration documents—only a fraction of the 27.5 million had been catalogued—was how hands-on our thirty-ninth president had been, how personally engaged he was in almost all policy-related matters, scrawling comments and questions in the margins of just about every document he handled. Carter was one of the most prolific memo writers ever to live at 1600 Pennsylvania Avenue, although his notes to subordinates were usually sentence fragments written in the margins of the papers he received. Researchers also discovered that Carter's public statements completely corresponded with the written record. Decency and integrity, it seemed, were consistent traits of the Carter White House years.

Carter's chief domestic policy adviser, Stuart Eizenstat (later to become President Bill Clinton's ambassador to the European Union and undersecretary of state), had been the first political figure bold enough to proclaim, in December 1980, that "Jimmy Carter was ten years ahead of his time." He cited as primary evidence his boss's attempt to move the Democratic party toward the center by proposing to balance the federal budget and cut government spending. He also thought Carter deserved great credit for the deregulation of trucking, railroads, airlines, banking, and communications.[24] Republican senator Howard Baker of Tennessee had predicted in 1981 that "history will be kind to Jimmy Carter." Florida congressman Claude Pepper likewise was an early revisionist: "As history has evaluated the administration of President Truman much higher than he was evaluated by his contemporaries, I think history will evaluate the administration of President Carter far above the evaluation of his contemporaries' administration."[25]

Historians began to take these assessments a bit more seriously and by

1987 when the Carter Library opened, the Carter presidency was ripe to undergo what historian John Lukas called in *American Heritage* the three R's—"reviewing and revising and rethinking of the past" due largely to Carter's unique postpresidential career.[26] "The longer [Carter] stays out of office the better he is going to look," Barry Goldwater, often an outspoken critic, admitted. Benjamin Hooks of the NAACP believed that "history will be far kinder to president Carter than his contemporaries." The journalist Anthony Lewis seconded this opinion, commenting that "as historians seriously study Carter's presidency their fairminded appraisal will add up to a big plus."[27] Regardless of such upbeat revisionist assessments almost everybody agreed on one point: Carter was a better ex-president than he was president.

The morning of the grand opening (October 1, 1986), also Carter's birthday, offered typical Georgia autumn weather, hazy skies and mild temperatures. The Emory professors in attendance were dressed in full academic cap-and-gown regalia, as if for commencement ceremonies. Everywhere in the excited crowd of five thousand well-wishers were family and friends of Jimmy and Rosalynn. Their young grandchildren had been designated the official ribbon cutters. The international press corps was on hand in full force, elbowing for prime spots near the platform as the Atlanta Symphony Orchestra played Brahms, and in turn, the Fort McPherson Military Band played Sousa.[28]

The choice of Warren Christopher as keynote speaker on the momentous occasion of the Carter Center opening surprised many of Carter's closest friends. Unlike other statesmen Carter admired—Averell Harriman, Dean Rusk, George Ball, Elliot Richardson—Christopher was still a rising star. Chairman of the prestigious California law firm O'Melveny and Myers, the meticulously groomed Christopher—to whom Carter awarded the Presidential Medal of Freedom on January 16, 1981, calling him "the best public servant I ever knew"—would be a serious candidate for secretary of state if a Democrat could recapture the White House from the Republicans.[29] Due to his tireless work as the number-two man in Carter's state department, most around America who had heard of Warren Christopher considered him a Carterite—it was an inescapable rap. Serving as keynote speaker would deepen Christopher's connection to the center and instill in the public mind the notion that he was a protégé of the former president. Carter also wanted to atone for having bypassed Christopher in favor of Edmund Muskie as secretary of state when Cyrus Vance resigned. "I was surprised and stunned to be asked to deliver the keynote address," Christopher admitted.[30]

An elegant assembly of low cylindrical buildings—the impossible dream— housed the office of the former president, the Jimmy Carter Library and Museum, the Carter Center of Emory University, Global 2000, the Task Force for Child Survival and Development, and the Carter-Menil Human Rights Foundation. The Carter Center complex, said the *Arizona Republic*, embraces its thirty-acre site "in a manner reminiscent of the low, earth- hugging architecture of Frank Lloyd Wright," adding that "it bespeaks the 'understated elegance' that the Carters sought."[31] Only the hundred or so neighborhood roadway demonstrators, still outraged about what they deri- sively referred to as "Ex-Prez Way," put a damper on the gala event.[32]

Carter, who had personally invited Reagan to Atlanta, was surprised that he had accepted while Richard Nixon and Gerald Ford, also asked to partici- pate, declined due to more pressing obligations, promising to visit the com- plex sometime in the near future. After all, Reagan was already in countless books of quotations for his 1980 comment, "Recession is when your neigh- bor loses his job. Depression is when you lose yours. And recovery is when Jimmy Carter loses his."[33] But it was the audience that spoke first, as activists held up banners that read "Free Nelson Mandela" and heckled the presi- dent before being restrained by security.

Reagan delivered a warmhearted and inspired address that afternoon. He began by candidly acknowledging his political differences with Jimmy Carter. "From the time of Thomas Jefferson and Alexander Hamilton, frank debate has been part of the tradition of this republic," Reagan stated. "To- day, our very differences attest to the greatness of our nation. For I can think of no other country on earth where two politicians could disagree so widely, yet come together in mutual respect."

Reagan then spoke of Carter's peanut farmer upbringing, commendable family values, and bedrock belief in the Main Street virtues of American life. Praising his Camp David breakthrough and his efforts to bring the American hostages in Iran home safely, Reagan added, "For myself, I can pay no higher honor than simply this: You gave of yourself to your country, gracing the White House with your passion and intellect and commitment." Follow- ing Reagan's gracious remarks, Carter rose to thank him. "I think I under- stand more clearly than I ever had before why you won in November 1980, and I lost," Carter said, straight-faced, then burst into a broad grin.[34]

Warren Christopher was unsettled by the prospect of having to follow Ronald Reagan's bravura performance. Only twenty minutes earlier Christo- pher had been amazed to see Reagan scribbling his remarks—by himself—

on a notecard while Andrew Young and Georgia governor Joe Frank Harris were making brief speeches. Christopher had worked on his meticulously prepared speech for a month, and Reagan, in a matter of a few minutes, had drafted the perfect words for the occasion. "It was an impressive performance," Christopher recalled.[35]

While writing his keynote address Christopher had read the last chapters of a dozen presidential biographies, trying to understand better how Jimmy Carter's predecessors had spent their post–White House years. "One comes away from even a cursory review of the lives of ex-presidents with the chilling sense of a wasted resource," Christopher proclaimed in his address. "On the whole, their experience was undervalued and their advice too little sought." Praising in particular the postpresidential activities of Thomas Jefferson, John Quincy Adams, William Howard Taft, Theodore Roosevelt, and Herbert Hoover, Christopher added Carter to their ranks. Christopher endorsed the notion of a nongovernmental organization like the Carter Center taking an activist part in U.S. foreign policy. "This center is devoted not to past status but present works. . . . Its purpose is not to aggrandize or justify, but to contribute," Christopher declared. "It has no object but the public good."[36]

Carter was euphoric for the entire day. The icing on the cake came in the news from Washington that the House of Representatives had passed a bill creating a national historic site in Plains; the Senate would soon also approve the legislation. The historic district would include not only the home where Jimmy and Rosalynn still lived but his boyhood residence, the Plains High School, the railroad depot that served as his campaign headquarters in 1976, and two other pieces of property.

Reagan's laudatory remarks, however, did not play a part in Carter's happiness. As the *Chicago Tribune* later reported, a White House aide who accompanied Reagan to Atlanta confessed that the president delivered his speech "with actor's skill and absolutely no conviction."[37] The television nightly news broadcasters might have been impressed by Reagan's "grandiosity," but Carter interpreted his outpouring of praise as insincere. When Carter mocked Reagan that evening for friends, he seemed to them ungracious and petty: he proved to be clairvoyant.[38]

In fact, only weeks later, as Reagan was making a campaign swing through Oklahoma and Nebraska on behalf of Republican incumbents in the Senate, he began hammering away at the dire "mess" Jimmy Carter had left America in after four years in office. At the Sun Dome in Tampa, Florida, speaking on behalf of Senator Paula Hawkins, Reagan fumed, "When it came to soaring inflation, economic stagnation, and unemployment, the liberal crowd gave us a lot of talk about how we, the American people, were to blame. They said we were suffering from malaise." When a copy of Reagan's Tampa speech was faxed to the Carter Center for comment, Carter refused to rise to the bait. Revenge would soon be his, when a month later the Iran-Contra affair hit the headlines.[39]

In early November 1986 a Beirut magazine first publicly disclosed that the Reagan administration had been selling arms to Iran and that some of the proceeds had been diverted to aid the Contras in Nicaragua. Reagan, dubbed the "Teflon president" by Democratic congresswoman Patricia Schroeder of Colorado because he seemed immune to press criticism, suddenly found himself confronted with ominous questions about whether his administration had violated its own policies first by selling arms to Iran, then by attempting to trade arms for hostages, and whether it had attempted to circumvent a congressional ban on aid to the Nicaraguan Contras through diversion of funds. As the controversy grew more heated, Reagan was forced (on November 25) to dismiss Admiral John Poindexter as national security adviser, as well as the aide, Marine Lieutenant Colonel Oliver North, who had managed the Iran-Contra deal. Desperate to contain the scandal, Reagan appointed a three-man panel headed by former Texas senator John Tower, plus Edmund Muskie and Brent Scowcroft, to examine the role of the NSC in the international mess.[40]

On December 9 Carter publicly rebuked Reagan for not being honest with the American people about what had transpired in the Iran-Contra affair and for having failed to consult congressional and military leaders, or even Secretary of State George Shultz, before taking these actions. "I never made a major decision without a thorough discussion with the Secretary of State, the Joint Chiefs of Staff, and the appropriate members of Congress," Carter said about his presidential process of making foreign policy decisions.[41] Carter had heard rumors about the arms-for-hostages deal earlier that year while he was in Nicaragua but had found it difficult to believe that Reagan would deliver aid to the Contras when the Boland Amendment had firmly forbidden it. "I should have known better," Carter later said. "Reagan was capable of just about anything underhanded."[42]

When Carter went on CBS he sharply criticized Reagan for obfuscating the truth. He touched a nerve; Reagan fired off a rare personal letter to the Democrat he trounced in 1980. "I saw your answers to Dan Rather's questions on CBS News Wednesday and realized that you apparently had not been briefed on this Iranian situation, and for that, I'm sorry," Reagan wrote Carter on December 15. "With regard to whether I'm doing all that can be done to get the truth to the public, the answer is 'yes.'" In a bizarre confessional, Reagan told Carter he was having an independent counsel get to the bottom of the Iran-Contra affair, of which he was "ignorant." The letter wound through a half-dozen points, with Reagan admitting that $12 million worth of spare parts and older TOW missiles were sent to Tehran but that they "could have no real effect on the military balance between Iran and Iraq."[43] Carter never wrote back, viewing the letter as typical Reagan gibberish, and continued to slam the president for Iran-Contra at every chance he could get. But Carter had, generally speaking, gotten over losing to Reagan, and was forging forward with bold new programs like guinea worm eradication.

In 1986 dracunculiasis, meaning "small snake," a debilitating condition that had maimed and crippled some 5 million people a year, most of them living in a band that girdles the central portion of Africa, became a primary concern of Global 2000. During annual droughts, water holes on which villagers relied became smaller, and in the remaining muddy recesses the female guinea worm laid its larvae. The tiny third-stage larvae of the guinea worm, ingested through drinking the stagnant water of ponds or cisterns, lived in the body for a year before emerging through the skin as a two-to-three-foot-long worm, causing extreme pain and sometimes permanent disability. The cream-colored worm rested just below the surface of the skin until it burst through a blister, usually emerging around the ankles and feet. As it emerged, it secreted a toxin that caused a burning blister to appear on the skin.

As sufferers of guinea worm disease incubated more worms, they developed debilitating fever and nausea. In accordance with local custom, the victim, careful not to break the worm, wound it slowly around a stick as it emerged. If the worm was broken, its remainder retracted into the body, spilling substances that caused severe inflammation. But even if the worm was not broken, complications did arise: Over half the sites became infected, causing abscesses, sepsis, arthritis, and in the worse cases tetanus, which could be fatal. In a half-dozen African nations and in some isolated areas of India and Pakistan, young and old hobbled along dirt paths haplessly with multiple sores on their feet. The disease spread as those infected walked into cool water holes to relieve the burning sensation and released more larvae into the water supply. Guinea worm's only host was Homo sapiens, and in 1986 the UN estimated 100 million people were at risk.[44]

Not only did guinea worm disease take a toll in human suffering, but it affected agricultural production, school attendance, and vocational life of the village as well, since victims were crippled for months. A UNICEF-assisted study estimated that losses in rice production attributable to guinea-worm-induced incapacitation amounted to about 11.6 percent of the annual crop alone in Anambra, Benin, and Cross River states in Nigeria. One study showed that rice farmers alone in a heavily infested part of Nigeria lost an estimated $20 million in potential profits each year because they could not work.[45]

Carter had not heard of guinea worm until an international health conference in April 1986, when his friend Peter Bourne, who had been serving as an assistant secretary general at the United Nations, gave a presentation on the terrible disease. After Bourne's lunch presentation Carter asked, "If guinea worm is so easy to eradicate, why is it not being done?" Bourne explained that it was a matter of political will. Two months later, Carter decided to lead the global eradication effort.[46] By late 1986 Carter, along with Bill Foege, had convinced the World Health Organization to select guinea worm disease as the second disease to be eradicated from the earth—after smallpox. Their first move was to enlist Dr. Donald Hopkins, a Florida-born epidemiologist and tropical disease specialist. Like Foege, Hopkins had attended Harvard's Public Health School, studied disease eradication, and took part in the CDC's anti-smallpox crusade.[47] Spurred on by his smallpox experiences in Sierra Leone—where from 1967 to 1969 he helped reduce the number of new cases in that African nation from 1,697 to 80—Hopkins began researching and writing *Princes and Peasants: Smallpox in History*, which was published in 1983 and nominated for a Pulitzer Prize in history.[48]

Since guinea worm disease was a direct result of millions consuming unsanitary water, WHO hoped to attach their eradication campaign to a UN clean-drinking-water initiative. Hopkins began a monthly newsletter called *Guinea Worm Watch* to publish medical findings and gather data. For six years he traveled the world trying to raise consciousness about the horror of guinea worm disease.[49] In a keynote address, Hopkins advocated such old-fashioned measures as digging deep wells in villages and teaching people to boil water—actions that successfully eliminated the guinea worm from nineteenth-century Russia—but he knew that these measures by themselves were insufficient for the contemporary crisis. The Peace Corps and UNICEF had done a credible job of teaching villagers to dig wells in unpolluted groundwater, but they did not have enough personnel to be comprehensive. Sterilizing water had proved both too time-consuming and too dependent on scarce fuelwood for resources. The alternative was cloth filters, thousands of them, distributed with simple instructions.[50]

"There were dozens of different health problems we could have tackled," Carter recalled. "But eradicating guinea worm was something tangible."[51] Besides, the guinea worm ailment, Carter liked to speculate, which had

been with humankind since the dawn of civilization, might be the same disaster described in the Bible as the "fiery serpent" that the Israelites suffered on the shores of the Red Sea. There is some evidence that Carter's
interpretation is correct: a Sanskrit poem from the fourteenth century B.C.
contains the words, "Let not the sinuous worm strike me nor wound
my foot." And in the 1980s scientists found a calcified guinea worm in a
thirteen-year-old girl mummified around 1000 B.C. in Egypt.

Since Pakistan was one of the most significant non-African countries afflicted with guinea worm disease, the ex-president decided to tap that
nation's billionaire banker, Agha Hasan Abedi, chairman of the Bank of
Credit and Commerce International (BCCI), for financial help.[52] Carter had
first met Abedi on August 18, 1982, in Plains. The meticulously dressed, always jovial Pakistani billionaire pulled up to Carter's Plains home in a super-
stretch limousine to suggest a collaboration on famine relief for Africa and
Asia. "I had never heard of him," Carter recalls, "but his torment over conditions in these countries was so personally intense, it was almost painful to
witness." That October Carter visited Abedi in London at a private dinner
also attended by former British prime minister James Callaghan.[53] Eventually Abedi offered Carter $4 million for feeding the global poor as a good
faith offering, a personal philanthropy that he insisted the Qur'an required
of him.[54] "Your proposed project has the potential of giving enormous assistance to the people of the Third World," Carter wrote Abedi in July 1985,
"and for helping to ensure all nations a right to live in peace."[55]

Abedi had met Carter via Bert Lance; BCCI had helped rescue the former head of the Office of Management and Budget from financial disaster
soon after his resignation in 1977. The former president had become a lobbyist of sorts on behalf of U.S. government sales of aircraft to Saudi Arabia.
The Carter Center had accepted large gifts from King Fahd, the Saudi
leader, and from Adnan Khashoggi, the scandal-plagued arms dealer, both of
whom had BCCI ties. Carter's reputation as an ally of the Islamic world was
enhanced further by his carefully worded public endorsements of Arafat.

Abedi came with endorsements from respected American statesman
Clark Clifford. The initial $4 million gift was just the tip of the iceberg. As
Carter and Abedi became friends, the Pakistani banker signed on as a
cochairman of Global 2000, and became the organization's largest benefactor. By early 1988 Abedi had committed $17 million in direct support to the
Global 2000 project. He also saw to it that the organization's British office
was located in the BCCI headquarters building in London.[56]

A month after the Carter Center's grand opening, Carter and Abedi traveled together with Ryoichi Sasakawa to Pakistan, Bangladesh, and Sudan. In Pakistan the three launched an ambitious program aimed at establishing child survival programs at the provincial level. They emphasized control of polio, measles, tetanus, and diarrheal diseases, and set up nutrition and health care information centers. Carter also persuaded then-president General Mohammad Zia-al-Haq to allow Global 2000 to work with Pakistan's public health leaders to eradicate guinea worm. Zia did not know about guinea worm, but his prime minister came from a village that suffered from the disease, and with Abedi willing to pay the cost of a five-year eradication program, there was no reason not to proceed.[57]

Carter later would be embarrassed by Abedi's support once he discovered that the Pakistani billionaire was involved in one of the biggest banking scandals of all times, emanating from the BCCI, which maintained offices in seventy-two nations. "He may have snookered me," Carter admitted, though he remained a loyal friend throughout Abedi's legal ordeal. But in November 1986, Carter was thrilled to have such a deep-pocketed benefactor helping to finance his guinea worm program.[58] A week after Carter's journey, General Zia sent two high-ranking advisers to the Carter Center to help the former president launch the guinea worm eradication project. Hopkins, who was still at CDC, attended the meeting and would never forget his joy when the Carter Center and Pakistan, using Abedi's money, joined forces to wipe out the "fiery serpent." Within the year Hopkins had left the CDC to head up the center's disease eradication program based on his strategy of filters. The first task was to conduct a nationwide census to identify endemic villages; by the end of 1987, they had found 408 afflicted communities.[59] Guinea worm had been eradicated from Pakistan by October 1993.

The Carter-Abedi united front was particularly inspiring on trips to southern Africa, where Muslims and Christians were often at odds. Impressed by Carter's success in Ghana and Sudan, Abedi volunteered to help Global 2000 broaden its humanitarian mission. And when Carter traveled to Greece and Turkey on BCCI's palatial airplane, he raved to various industrialists about Abedi's "moral and beneficent approach to the world of business and finance." As payback for Abedi's contributions to the Carter Center and use of his "flying carpet with its wonderful crew" he touted BCCI to Cypriot George Paraskevaides, owner of a large construction firm, and Turk Sakip Sabanci, a leading industrialist who owned AKBANK. "[It] may be beneficial for you to become better acquainted with both of them," Carter wrote Abedi upon returning to Atlanta, adding that "we had racletter cheese for supper . . . very good, but missed the Abedis."[60]

With the BCCI start-up money guaranteed, Donald Hopkins and Jim

Brasher III journeyed to Wilmington, Delaware, to meet with executives from the Du Pont Corporation, who agreed, in conjunction with Precision Fabrics Group—Du Pont provided nylon thread that Precision Fabrics wove into the filter cloth—to develop and donate to the center special drinking-water filters. The two companies pledged to supply over 8 million of the reusable filters, which looked like oversize tambourines, by 1995. But the cloth filter was not the only line of attack. In highly contaminated areas water was to be treated with low concentrations of Abate, a nontoxic and odorless larvicide developed to eliminate mosquitoes sixteen years earlier by American Cyanamid, which donated $2 million worth to the project. The Carter Center assigned a handful of people to work abroad on the eradication program but in the main left distribution of the reusable filters, larvicide, and related educational material to the target nations. Carter was learning how to create model NGO-corporate programs.[61]

Carter wrote to ask for the full support of the involved governments, explaining that Global 2000 would work with local health workers to identify infected villages and to teach residents how to strain their drinking water. Multiple visas would be needed for some of these workers. Proper distribution of the cloth filters and larvicide had to be guaranteed before they would be shipped abroad. Villagers, most of them illiterate, would have to be taught how the disease was transmitted and prevented. Many leaders were surprised that a former president of the United States seemed so concerned about a disease in their country. If you had guinea worm it was essential not to pull the parasite out haphazardly for if it tore in half the entire body would become infected. Carter wanted the leaders of the afflicted nations to mount a radio public relations campaign to kill off the worm. African people had to overcome their ancient superstitions that guinea worm came through goat's blood or the planets.

Carter was not the first American president to establish a tradition of helping to combat disease. Thomas Jefferson actively supported efforts to disseminate smallpox vaccine in the United States; Franklin D. Roosevelt contributed immeasurably to the battle against polio through his support for the National Foundation for Infantile Paralysis and the "March of Dimes" and his establishment of the Georgia Warm Springs Foundation; and in 1965 President Lyndon Johnson committed the U.S. government, through the Agency for International Development and the CDC, to helping twenty countries of west and central Africa eradicate smallpox. Although Carter would not see his first actual case of guinea worm until March 1988, eradication of this disease had become the main health mission of Global 2000 by November 1986. "Reagan is making $2 million in speaking fees in Japan while Jimmy Carter is working to get rid of the guinea worm in Africa," Georgia senator Sam Nunn boasted. "That's making Carter look a lot better in people's eyes."[62]

On the heels of the Carter Center opening and Carter's Pakistan-Bangladesh-Sudan trip, Robert Pastor had organized a consultation co-sponsored by the Institute of the Americas called "Reinforcing Democracy in the Americas," to be held November 16 to 18, 1986.[63] Political leaders and scholars from Central America, South America, and the Caribbean would convene in Atlanta to discuss the rise of democracy in the Western hemisphere. Since accompanying Carter to Latin America in October 1984, Pastor had pushed the idea of creating a small fraternity of Western Hemisphere statesmen committed to democracy who would meet regularly in Atlanta to discuss everything from election monitoring to human rights abuses. On December 1, 1985, when he submitted his three-year Latin American and Caribbean programs plan to Carter, Pastor proposed that he start investigating the possibility of creating a "wise-man" council for the hemisphere. Carter, lukewarm about the idea, gave Pastor the go-ahead to informally raise the issue.[64]

After more than a dozen informal meetings with leaders from various countries, Pastor was even more convinced that a group of elder statesmen, composed of respected and freely elected former presidents and prime ministers from throughout the Americas and operating outside the OAS, could significantly help to reinforce democracy in the hemisphere. Seizing the initiative, Pastor drafted a nineteen-page advocacy memorandum, submitted on October 22, 1986, for Carter's review. Titled "Nurturing Democracy in the Americas," Pastor's memorandum recommended that the Carter Center, at the upcoming consultation, establish a kind of G-10 "Paris Club" to assist democracies. "When governments find it difficult to pay their commercial debts, they meet with a group called 'the Paris Club' of commercial bankers to negotiate debt re-scheduling and the banks continue to get paid," Pastor wrote. "Perhaps the time has come to establish a 'Paris Club' to assist democracies at fragile moments."[65]

Carter had strong reservations about Pastor's scheme. He crossed out full pages of the memorandum, inking "seems presumptuous" in the margin.[66] Carter feared that the Pastor plan would be difficult to organize and impossible to maintain, and that it would tread on the jurisdiction of the UN, the OAS, or the more informal Contadora Group, which was working to resolve the conflicts and tensions in Central America. But Pastor argued his case with convincing passion. Carter slowly became converted to the merits of forming a council of former presidents—but insisted that the impetus must come from the Latin American leaders themselves. He would embrace the movement if a majority of the twelve heads of state scheduled to participate in the November 1986 consultation presented the Paris Club idea on their own initiative.

Even before the distinguished participants had arrived in Atlanta, Pastor had procured agreements to create a "council of presidents" from a number of Latin American leaders. Former Costa Rican president Daniel Oduber was Pastor's most stalwart ally. Recognizing the benefits for former leaders like himself of having regular access to Jimmy Carter and Gerald Ford, Oduber agreed to sponsor the Council of Presidents idea at the consultation, to debate the issue, and then to open it up to a floor vote. A few quick preconsultation telephone calls from Oduber led to agreement from Rafael Caldera of Venezuela, George Price, former prime minister of Belize, and Pierre Trudeau of Canada. They came prepared to present a solid front.[67]

On any number of levels the three-day consultation was productive. The twelve current and former heads of governments, joined by some of the best scholars of democratization in the world, addressed the question of why the pendulum had swung between dictatorship and democracy in Latin America and the Caribbean in the past and what could be done to stop the oscillation, to maintain, consolidate, and advance democracy. The paradoxical parallel strains of authoritarianism and constitutionalism in Latin American history were discussed candidly, with an eye toward the future. Pastor and Carter grew confident that a council of presidents made great sense. All the leaders were looking for a constructive forum through which to reinforce democracy in the region, promote multifaceted efforts to resolve conflict, and advance regional economic cooperation.

After three days of discussing everything from U.S. aid to the Contras to Jean-Claude "Baby Doc" Duvalier's departure from power in Haiti earlier that year, it came time for the closing session. Vinicio Cerezo, president of Guatemala, struck the right high note when he encouraged democrats throughout the hemisphere not to forget the historical processes that have made democratic transitions possible. "We are at a historical juncture with incredible opportunities and risks," Cerezo pointed out. "The U.S. can afford to make a mistake; Latin America cannot."[68] When Canada's Pierre Trudeau sounded a call for hemispheric solidarity, Oduber found his opening. An earnest discussion ensued on the notion of creating a permanent organization.[69]

Errol Barrow, the prime minister of Barbados, who had led his country to independence in 1966, questioned the title Council of Presidents. "What

about me?" he asked. In the end the group decided to call themselves the
Council of Freely Elected Heads of Government.[70]

Excitement rippled through the auditorium. An executive committee
was immediately formed, with Jimmy Carter unanimously chosen as chairman and Pastor appointed executive secretary. Oduber and Price were designated to explore a number of election-monitoring ideas and to organize
future meetings. Anxious to announce the creation of the council to the
world community the twelve leaders sent a fait accompli telegram about the
formation of the council to the heads of government in the hemisphere, to
the secretary general of the UN, and to the OAS. "I felt like John Hancock
at the signing of the Declaration of Independence," Price recalled.[71] Word
soon spread. American newspapers ran stories questioning just what exactly
this Council of Freely Elected Heads of Government hoped to accomplish.
"Can distinguished outsiders help ensure the survival of democracies in
Latin America?" the *Christian Science Monitor* asked. "Former President
Jimmy Carter and a number of former heads of state from Latin America
think so. They are forming a council of former heads of state to examine and
speak out on such issues as elections and human rights abuses in Latin nations. . . . They hope to be listened to and even asked for advice by nations
struggling to maintain civilian rule."[72]

If U.S. press reports were low-key, usually a small article hidden on a
back page, the Council of Freely Elected Heads of Government was big
news in Quito and Caracas, Buenos Aires and Lima, Kingston and San José.
Leaders not present at the creation wrote Carter anxious letters hoping to
get on board. Carlos Andrés Pérez, former and future president of
Venezuela, and Michael Manley, former and future prime minister of Jamaica, journeyed to Atlanta to meet with Carter and ask to have their names
added to the roster. The original twelve members grew over the next decade
to thirty. The criterion for eligibility for the council was simple: you had to
have been president or prime minister of your country and be recommended by the Executive Committee.[73]

Carter and Pastor had pulled off a clever feat that would soon pay big
dividends for democracy in the hemisphere. The Council of Freely Elected
Heads of Government spent most of 1987–88 working to define itself, conducting case studies of where their services could be used most advanta-
geously. Haiti, rife with political corruption and staggering human rights
abuses, was the first spot chosen for direct action. Due largely to Pastor's
backdoor negotiations, the council was invited to Haiti by that nation's independent Provisional Electoral Commission and the Haitian Institute for Research and Development to observe the November 1987 elections. After
Pastor laid the essential groundwork, Carter and George Price made a high-

profile two-day inspection tour of the impoverished nation in October 1987 following the assassination of Yves Volel, a presidential candidate murdered by Haitian plainclothes police.[74]

.The next month, November 1987, Price returned to observe the Haitian election, but the military slaughtered a line of voters and aborted the election. Ushering in democratic processes in such authoritarian countries was no easy task. "The Carter effort," the *Miami Herald* pointed out in an October 1987 editorial, "offers needed evidence that the New World's democracies still can provide a wellspring of idealism, compassion, and hope for the poor and oppressed."[75] Even Assistant Secretary of State Elliott Abrams saw fit to praise Carter for turning the world's attention to Port-au-Prince. "I want to express my personal thanks for your visit to Haiti, a country to which our own has paid all too little attention over the years," Abrams wrote Carter. "Your repeated emphasis on elections will help make clear U.S. attitudes on this point and increase the chances for a successful transition to democracy."[76] The missions of the council observed seventeen elections in ten countries from 1987 to 1997.

THIRTEEN

TRAVELS WITH CARTER

❧

R alph Waldo Emerson once noted that there is "no truth but in transit"—
a sentiment that the intrepid Jimmy Carter fully embraced. If Carter
had learned anything over the years, it was that if you wanted to solve a
global conflict or understand an international dilemma, it was best to board
an airplane and jet off. Increasingly convinced that the Reagan administration would bash the PLO in the upcoming election to attract Jewish votes,
Carter decided to revisit the five nations of his 1983 trip with a broad
agenda, exploring an overall approach to the Middle East situation. "Reagan
had been misleading Americans about the PLO and had abandoned the
peace process," Carter recalled later. "Unlike my 1983 trip, on this one I
spoke my mind."[1]

Requests came in early March from Foggy Bottom for Carter not to visit
Syria, talk with the PLO, or try to broker a release of the American hostages
in Lebanon (or of the Anglican envoy Terry Waite, who had disappeared on
January 20 after trying to procure their release). In November 1984 the administration had banned all high-level meetings between American and Syrian officials, along with imposing several economic sanctions in retaliation for
reported Syrian terrorist involvement in an attempt to blow up an Israeli air-
liner after it was to take off from London. The situation was serious: William
Eagleton Jr., the American ambassador to Syria, had been recalled; the size
of the U.S. embassy reduced; export-import bank credits denied; and
warnings to American oil companies in Syria issued.[2] Carter thought these

punitive measures ridiculous. "For now, we will keep the Syrian visit on hold but make room for it," Carter wrote Ken Stein, who was once again putting together the itinerary. "My intention is to go. It would be better to visit Israel next to last, just prior to Syria. That way we can size up the attitude in both Egypt and Jordan before talking to the Israeli leaders and press."[3]

On the surface Carter's Middle East sojourn would look innocuous, a series of well-intentioned stops by Professor Carter of Emory University in major cities like Jerusalem and Cairo, museum strolls with regional leaders, coffees with various academics, and wreath-laying ceremonies at three different unknown-soldier memorials. Reporters following the Carters would profile them as Holy Land tourists, flipping through dog-eared copies of Fodor's and snapping photographs of themselves in front of Abraham's tomb and Ben Gurion's home. "For diplomatic purposes the itinerary when it is shared with the State Department should show the non-political essence of our journey," Stein wrote the Carters in preparation for the trip.[4] But in fact, two separate itineraries had been drawn up—one for State Department/ press purposes, and a real one that included meeting Yasir Arafat's emissaries in Jordan and Assad's cabinet in Syria.

Once again Carter used Egypt as his operational base; in Cairo everybody from bandits to bankers treated him as a great peacemaker. Wherever Jimmy and Rosalynn went during their four-day stint thousands gathered around just to get a glimpse of the architect of the 1978 Camp David accords. A new Egyptian public opinion poll claimed that a staggering 83 percent of the population still approved of the accords eight years after they were signed by Begin and Sadat. At Carter's insistence, Sadat's loyal body guard, Colonel Sahita, shadowed him for most of his day outings. "President Carter constantly searches out people who have insights on Sadat's assassination," Faye Dill has noted. "And when he is in Egypt he wants [Sahita] with him." Rosalynn spent an afternoon with Sadat's extended family, inviting them all to visit Plains.[5] For Carter the trip highlight was seeing firsthand Israelis unloading from buses in Upper Egypt, singing "Yeveinu Shalom aleichem"; it was a sight and sound he knew Sadat would have relished.[6]

After innocent gestures, Carter played his trump card on March 18 at a speech he delivered before the American Chamber of Commerce in Egypt. Carter excoriated the Reagan administration in no uncertain terms, cloaking his criticisms by saying, "I'm not here to criticize my own government," and then doing precisely that. While praising President Hosni Mubarak of Egypt and King Hussein of Jordan as peacemakers, he denounced Reagan as a militant who preferred using force over diplomacy. In doing so he broke rule number one in U.S. foreign policy making—never undermine your own nation's president when abroad. "When I was in office I was constantly involved in negotiations," he noted. "This has not been the case in the last six years. There's been more of an inclination to form a Contra army and over-throw the Sandinistas or to inject the Marines into Lebanon and to use American battleships to shell the villages around Beirut." Perturbed that Reagan viewed Middle East mediation as a "low priority item," a discour-aged Carter agreed with the position taken by Ashraf Ghorbal, a former Egyptian ambassador to Washington, that without active U.S. participation the creation of a Palestinian homeland was "doomed for failure."[7]

The State Department, this time through Ambassador Wisner, urged Carter to refrain from denouncing American policy. If an ex-president pop-ping off abroad wasn't detrimental to official Washington positions, then what was? Professor Carter's abrupt response was to reiterate that he was "not a representative of the United States Government," then head straight for Damascus for nine hours of private talks with President Hafez al-Assad, which he deemed "very interesting, broad-ranging and pleasant." Carter con-tinued to believe that despite Assad's radical pan-Arab rhetoric, he was really only interested in Syria's national security, increasing its influence with Arab neighbors, and regaining the Golan Heights. The fact that Syria depended on outmoded Soviet military equipment and technical assistance and played host to 5,000 Soviet advisers did not overly concern Carter. Other meetings were held with Foreign Minister Farouk a-Sharaa and Vice President Abdul Halim Khaddam, along with professors from Damascus University who had attended the Carter Center's November 1983 Middle East Consultation. To the surprise of many, including the *Jerusalem Post*, Assad agreed "in prin-ciple" to participate in direct negotiations within an international conference format with the understanding that solutions would not be imposed. "Assad was slowly entering the peace process," Carter maintained.[8]

Carter's stock had skyrocketed in Damascus, a city of two million, since his last visit. Syrian newspapers had printed translations of Carter's warm, thoughtful comments about the fifty-six-year-old Assad that he had written in *The Blood of Abraham* (1985), a dictator whose face enveloped telephone poles and trucks, churches and mosques. "In Syria Carter was treated like a huge hero," Randall Ashley recalled. "It was just amazing."[9] In the streets of Damascus, where people waved at him and shouted "Salaam, Salaam," Carter had achieved celebrity status. Citizen Carter had simply ignored the Reagan administration's ban on high-level meetings with Syria. "It just didn't apply to me," Carter noted.[10] He used the warm Damascus embrace to tell the entire Arab world that it was "ridiculous" to label Terry Waite a spy and to privately lobby for the release of political activist 'Akl Qurban who, ac-cording to Jack Healy of Amnesty International, had been detained since 1970.[11]

The overriding item on Carter's agenda remained the Israeli occupation, the virtual annexation of Syria's Golan Heights, and Assad's military involvement in Lebanon. "It was my intention to get Syria's position on development plans in the occupied territories before heading to Jordan and Israel," Carter recalled. "Peace without Syria is impossible, and since the Reagan administration wasn't talking to them it was up to me to get their position straight to find out how far they would compromise."[12]

In Jordan, Carter spent time with King Hussein and Crown Prince Hassan, discussing in broad historical and contemporary terms the Hashemite regime, Palestinians, and inter-Arab politics. Once again Carter apologized to King Hussein for not involving him more directly in the Camp David talks. The nation's two leading newspapers—*Jordan Times* and *al-Destour*—wrote glowing stories about Carter, praising, in particular, *The Blood of Abraham*, copies of which the ex-president passed out all over the Middle East as gifts. Jordanians relished Carter's Amman press conference when he praised King Hussein for being "courageous," criticized Reagan for "Irangate," and minced no words about the so-called Palestinian problem: "I believe that the Israelis should withdraw from the occupied territories. I believe that the rights of the Palestinians should be granted and restored. I believe that there should be full autonomy or self-determination for the Palestinians." (A few days after his visit, speaking at a dinner hosted by Foreign Minister Shimon Peres at the King David Hotel in Jerusalem, Carter stood up for the Amman government, insisting that it was politically impossible for King Hussein to agree to direct negotiations with Israel without an international peace conference: "Hussein is not Sadat and Jordan is not Egypt.")[13]

From Jordan the Carters traveled to Israel. As usual the leading Israeli politicians, from Prime Minister Yitzhak Shamir to President Chaim Herzog, were anxious to talk to the former president. Carter may not have been perceived as "a friend of Israel," but everybody respected his encyclopedic knowledge of the Middle East. "Carter is a permanent part of Israel's drama," Shimon Peres would later note. "He is a permanent player in the region. Camp David will never be forgotten."[14]

Menachem Begin, however, refused to see the ex-president. Begin, whose health was faltering, did have a phone conversation welcoming the Carters to Israel, but those close to the former prime minister knew he didn't mean it. In return Carter, at a press conference, took some direct shots at Begin's honor. When asked whether he believed Israel had fulfilled its part of the Camp David agreement, Carter said, "No, I do not." Citing Israel's violation of the agreement on the settlements and the 1982 invasion of Lebanon, he added, "I would say the Camp David agreements have not been honored in spirit and in some cases letter." Carter wished he had "got in writing" a pledge from Begin not to build more settlements on the West Bank and the Gaza Strip.[15]

Such comments did not endear Carter to the Likud party, or even to many Israeli moderates. While *The Blood of Abraham* had been embraced in Arab nations, Abraham H. Fox, reviewing the book in the *Jerusalem Post* under the headline "A Double Standard," denounced the ex-president: "His constant criticism of Israel on settlements, on the Palestinians, on negotiations at the U.N., seemed one-sided, short-sighted and at times spiteful." Throughout the review Fox complained that Carter never held Jordan or Saudi Arabia accountable for "warfare against Israel," always treating them, instead, as peace-loving underdogs.[16]

The currency Carter brought to Israel was his series of lengthy, free-wheeling conversations with Assad. No other Western politician could say with authority, "That's not the way Assad views the situation," or "Assad is flexible on that point." As Randall Ashley of the *Atlanta Journal & Constitution* archly noted, "Assad talks only to God and Jimmy Carter."[17]

Upon returning to the United States, Carter reported on his findings (April 3) to Secretary of State George Shultz, National Security Adviser Frank Carlucci, and White House Chief of Staff Howard Baker.[18] He came away from the meeting flabbergasted about how much more he knew about Syria and the PLO than they did. The CIA—whose job it was to gather information—had become in many respects an antiquated joke. The advent of the World Wide Web, CNN, e-mail, and easy international air travel allowed an eager journalist or determined layperson to be nearly as informed as a full-time desk officer at Langley. Carter had developed his own underground railroad of unusual global contacts, a kaleidoscope of people who trusted him but not the U.S. government. The Carter Center itself, he believed, still in its infancy, received better intelligence reports from South Africa, Liberia, Haiti, and Nicaragua than the CIA—with the important exception of satellite aerial photographs. And when it came to the PLO, nobody had a more superb information channel than Jimmy Carter did in his old friend Mary King.

It is impossible to understand Jimmy Carter's postpresidency—particularly his Middle East diplomacy—without taking a long look at his working relationship with Mary Elizabeth King. The daughter of a Methodist preacher who was himself the eighth minister in six generations of Piedmont region circuit riders and clergy, King was, even as a beautiful schoolgirl, determined to smash Jim Crow laws in the American South. "When I learned as a young woman that my beloved paternal grandfather had in the 1890s dined in Franklin County, Virginia, with the family that had owned Booker T. Washington, . . . it gave me a live connection to the abstract horror of ownership of another human being," King recalled of her visceral disdain for bigotry. With the metabolism of a peregrine falcon, ready to swoop into adversities, this devoted if somewhat starry-eyed twenty-three-year-old student of Mahatma Gandhi's teachings joined one of the key organizations of the civil rights movement—the Student Nonviolent Coordinating Committee (SNCC) in 1960.[19]

As codirector along with Julian Bond of SNCC's communications, King worked in Virginia, Georgia, and Mississippi alongside such legendary activists as John Lewis and Bob Moses, always making sure SNCC press releases on atrocities or SNCC activities got covered by the mainstream press. "As important as the implements of organizing demonstrations or voter registration drives, devising mock ballots, or developing alternative political parties, was the flow of information," King would write. "Seven days a week, I grabbed for every handle I could reach in order to pump words out from the vortex of the movement and through the circuits of the news media."[20] An eye-opening experience in June 1967 caused King to view the civil rights movement as "international in scope." SNCC issued a press release after the Six-Day War that sympathized with the plight of the now militarily occupied Palestinians. "Overnight all Jewish funding to SNCC had been cut off," King recalled. "From that moment onwards I realized that the struggle for civil rights was global."[21]

Six years after being assigned to southwest Georgia to write a special report on SNCC's twenty-two projects coordinated by field organizer Charles Sherrod, in 1969 King was introduced to her future husband, Peter Bourne, a British-born psychiatrist and close associate of Governor Jimmy Carter. By 1971, Bourne was raving about the ambitious peanut farmer turned progressive politician who had hung a portrait of Martin Luther King Jr. in the state capital and had appeared on the cover of *Time* as the exemplar of the New South.[22] "In the beginning, I dismissed Carter out-of-hand," King recalls. "Sumter County was one of the most racist places in America: it seemed impossible that someone forward-looking could come from such a place. I forgot my own beliefs in the possibility of redemption."[23]

Jimmy and Rosalynn were not "movement people," but they were openminded gradualists of the first order. Carter had never met Martin Luther King Jr.—in fact, he assiduously avoided even a random photograph with the "Negro rabblerouser" for fear it would prove political suicide in Georgia. Shortly after Dr. King's assassination, however, Carter was among the first white southern politicians to deem the Nobel Peace Prize–winning preacher "a truly great man." Although Julian Bond thought Carter a "dishonest"[24] politician who ran a racist campaign for governor, Mary King recognized that proximity to the African-American struggle had brought the Carters—who allowed themselves to be touched by it—an ease in grasping the essential elements of conflict, ethnic strife, and religious animosity.[25] In 1972, when her husband-to-be, Peter Bourne, became a ringleader in promoting Carter's run for the White House, King joined the bandwagon. They were married in 1974, and by 1975 she was campaigning America for the one-term governor from Dixie. When against all odds Carter actually defeated the accidental president Gerald Ford, Mary King was appointed deputy director of ACTION in January 1977, with responsibilities that included the Peace Corps, then operating in sixty countries, and several other national service corps programs.

One of King's first agenda items was to bring the Peace Corps into the poorer Middle East countries such as Tunisia and Jordan. Using her close friendship to Carter as a calling card, she carried a letter from "Brother Jimmy" to Anwar Sadat to help get the corps established in Egypt. "Getting to know the Sadats created a new awakening in me," King recalled. Mary King soon became friends with many of the key Arab players in the region. The Arab world opened its historic and religious doors to her. She was privately escorted to the Church of Nativity in Bethlehem and the Umayyad Mosque and ancient synagogue in Damascus, and invited inside the four holy Shia shrines in Najaf, Karbala, Khadamain, and Samarrah.[26] Word of Mary King's knowledgeability on the Palestinian dilemma spread throughout the Middle East, particularly after President Carter mentioned the need for a Palestinian homeland in March 1977. "When you said 'Palestinian homeland' in Massachusetts," Arafat told Carter in 1996, "all Palestinians cheered. It was, for us, a historic moment."[27]

By 1980 King was serving on the board of Save the Children, the largest U.S. private voluntary development agency in Tunisia, Jordan, Lebanon, and the West Bank. A prize-winning author of books on political movements, she was active with a private philanthropic foundation that funded international human rights groups, served on several global commissions, and was pursuing academic research in international political science. Within a few years she had spent time and cultivated contacts in ninety developing countries. Whether meeting with heads of government or visiting remote villages, she was equally at home. "Mary developed a very close, personal relationship with Chairman Arafat," prominent Palestinian-American banker Odeh Aburdene recalled. "I feel he trusted her more than any other Westerner."[28] President Carter's seasoned Middle East policy advisers—Sol Linowitz, Harold Saunders, and William Quandt, in particular—disagreed with Mary

King's interpretations of the Arab-Israeli conflict; she always championed the perceived underdog or isolated regime. But to Mary King's chagrin, when Sadat and Begin came to Camp David to make peace, there was no Palestinian representation. "It was a real deficit, a real blunder by Carter," she believed.[29]

After 1980, as Carter closely studied the Palestinian question, he began to agree with King's analysis: perpetuating the isolation of the PLO only reinforced its worst tendencies, and peace was impossible without it. Career diplomats, he reasoned, were afraid to damage their reputations by uttering the simple truth that the Israeli government ran an apartheid state that treated Palestinians as third-class citizens. "Mary King is an outstanding person—sensitive, eloquent, strong, tenacious, and courageous," Carter soon noted. "She is a good researcher and knows people—famous and otherwise—throughout our nation and the world who can share with her a commitment to benevolent (and sometimes controversial) causes."[30]

The death of Sadat and his own journey to the Middle East in 1983 convinced Carter that at all costs he had to make amends for the grievous oversight of Camp David. "Carter's awareness around 1983 began to mature in an almost tragic sense," King recalls. "He began to understand more fully the ramifications from Camp David." The Palestinians were the central subject of the "framework" in the accords, yet they were neither consulted nor asked for their concurrence. By constructing Camp David without Palestinian representation, although he had not intended it, Carter had given occupation more enduring features. Then Begin betrayed Carter by offering a view of the accords—a day after the signing—that was narrow and limited, appearing to invalidate the U.S. and Egyptian interpretations of what had been achieved. In bending over backward to assuage Israel's fears about a Palestinian state, the accords did not recognize Palestinians as a people with rights to self-determination. The accords had called for withdrawal of Israel's political and military forces from the West Bank and Gaza, but instead Tel Aviv deepened control of the territories. Carter wanted to find a way to remedy the situation.[31]

In mid-October 1984 King traveled with Hasib Sabbagh, Abdul Majid Shoman, and Munib Masri, who took her to meet with Arafat at one of the PLO leader's villas in Tunis. Donning a fur hat and a bulky ski sweater, the nocturnal Arafat met with King at 2:00 A.M., and for ninety minutes they discussed UN Resolutions 242 and 338. Forced out of Beirut, and viewed in the non-Arab world as a dangerous terrorist organization, the PLO had hit rock bottom, and the prospects for survival, if Ronald Reagan and Yitzhak Shamir had anything to do with it, looked bleak. Arafat was eager for a trusted channel to Jimmy Carter, the one U.S. leader with clout in whom he might confide: he found it in Mary King. While in Tunis, she also met with Arafat's top lieutenants Abu Jihad (Khalil al-Wazir, or Father of Struggle) and Abu Iyad, or Salah Khalaf. "I returned to Washington and wrote Carter the first of many memoranda of our conversations," King recalled. "That started an extraordinary Carter-Arafat relationship."[32]

By the mid-1980s 3.2 million Palestinians—including the president of the largest private bank in the Arab world, owner of the Middle East's premier international construction company, and an American real estate mogul who owned the Ritz Carlton hotels in Washington and Manhattan—were living outside Israel and the occupied territories. It was largely through Mary King that Carter also got to meet a group of wealthy Palestinian entrepreneurs who were in diaspora, scattered from Amman to Los Angeles. Like Carter, these educated exiles were anxious to create a Palestinian state and to receive compensation for family land taken during the 1948 war with Israel, and they supported Palestinian schools, hospitals, and charities, as well as the *intifada*, or uprising, that began in 1987. And they were willing to provide the Carter Center with healthy donations to keep the ex-president's programs alive.

Perhaps the two most influential Palestinians to establish a relationship with Carter were Hasib Sabbagh and Said Khoury, who together formed Consolidated Contractors Company (CCC) with $30,000 of borrowed money. Both Palestinian refugees, they based their operation in Aden (South Yemen), a remote land on the Arabian Peninsula, where competitors were few. "Anybody with a homeland would never have lived there," Khoury noted. Their new company became a subcontractor to Bechtel, the U.S.-based engineering giant that was building Aden's first oil refinery. Stephen Bechtel Sr. soon became a close friend of the Palestinian entrepreneurs. "His common touch matched the Arab way of doing business," Khoury said of Bechtel Sr. The CCC soon built the $1.5 billion port city of Jubail in Saudi Arabia, a 500-mile eight-lane highway in Oman, a twenty-six-bridge causeway in Bahrain, and practically all of Kuwait's oil refineries. By the time Carter left the White House, CCC was making $500 million a year. When oil prices plummeted, CCC hit a fallow period, but from their new headquarters in Athens they became an integral link in connecting Carter to the PLO. A trusted surrogate of Arafat, Sabbagh passed through King to Carter confidential documents from the PLO chairman. Carter forged a true partnership with Sabbagh, who had homes in Athens, London, New York, and Washington. Other Palestinian executives enlisted to help the Carter Center by King included Abdul Majid Shoman of Amman and Zein Myassi of London.[33]

Meanwhile, King had become the director of the U.S.-Iraq Business Forum—a nonprofit organization whose mission was to normalize trade relations with Iraq—making frequent trips to Baghdad and once meeting Saddam Hussein, whom she found tough but insular. In June 1986 King suggested that Carter accept Hussein's invitation to visit Baghdad for "private talks" on the Persian Gulf and the Iran-Iraq War. (Likewise she lobbied Carter to meet with Fidel Castro in Cuba.)[34] In fact, Carter tried to broker a backdoor peace agreement with Khomeini and Hussein that went nowhere. Carter told King that he was working on a peace agreement based on "Iraq being declared an original aggressor, but Iran condemned for continuing the war 4 or 5 years after when Iraqis were willing to end it and have peace."[35] The U.S.-Iraq Business Forum went defunct in 1990, after Saddam Hussein's invasion of Kuwait, but it lasted long enough for King often to meet clandestinely with Arafat in Baghdad, reporting back to Carter on evolving Palestinian thinking in the diaspora.[36]

Mary King was a pro on strategies of nonviolent resistance, and she hoped to enhance the turn by the Palestinians of the occupied territories away from military mobilization to strictly civilian nonmilitary organizing. A breakthrough occurred in 1983 when a forty-year-old Palestinian-American clinical psychologist named Mubarak Awad started to run workshops on the principles and methods of nonviolent struggle in Jerusalem. A center for the study of nonviolent resistance opened there two years later and distributed Awad's booklets, Arabic translations on nonviolent struggle, and volumes by the Boston theoretician Gene Sharp. A close student of the American civil rights movement, particularly the dialectics of Martin Luther King Jr.'s "Letter from Birmingham City Jail," Awad disseminated information about revolutionary nonviolence and other movements into the West Bank and Gaza during the mid-1980s.[37]

The Carter-Awad relationship is one of the more intriguing in recent Middle East history. A firm believer in the need for nonviolent methods, Carter helped Awad rewrite passages of his pamphlets before they were distributed throughout the occupied territories and to a lesser extent in Israel. Bolstered by the Carter connection and the cross-fertilization of ideas from Awad's workshops, Jerusalem intellectuals such as Hanan Mikhail Ashrawi, Sari Nusseibeh, Faisel Husseini, Radwan Abu Ayyash, Ziad Abu Zayyad, and Hanna Siniora accelerated their redefining of concepts and challenging of old doctrines. "We knew Carter was working with us," Ashrawi recalled. "That knowledge gave us strength."[38] Their new nonviolent formulations, which Carter approved of, included the importance of mass participation, ideas on winning independence and universally accorded human rights, willingness to compromise with Israel, a redefined right of return, and most significantly the importance of direct negotiations with Israel. Awad considered his time spent with Carter at the Richard Russell

Building in Atlanta "some of the most productive hours in the history of modern Palestine." Marking up the pages of Awad's pamphlets, Carter consistently emphasized that for nonviolent struggle to work, Palestinians would have to practice "pure nonviolence," for any halfway measures would turn world opinion against them.[39] The ex-president was playing an important role in one of the streams flowing toward what would soon become the *intifada* in December 1987.

Carter also began the long process of trying to persuade Arafat to make statements that would be regarded as responsible in the United States instead of his typically more ambiguous tirades. Telephone conversations were out of the question, for if knowledge of their special relationship leaked, the negative public outcry, especially for Carter, would have been enormous. Even Ken Stein was kept in the dark of Carter's blossoming friendship with the PLO chairman.[40]

With a wary eye on the festering unresolved issue of Palestinian refugee camps, Carter believed that if world leaders did not hold some sort of global conference to address the needs of Palestinians, a showdown between the poor Palestinian teenagers of the West Bank and Gaza and the well-armed Israeli police was inevitable. In *Time*, on April 20, he wrote about the new opportunities he saw for peace in the Middle East and called for greater American involvement in the diplomatic process. Unconvinced that the Reagan administration could be part of the solution, Carter that July once again took to the skies.[41]

With Reagan, up to his neck in Iran-Contra problems, indifferent to pushing the fragile peace process forward, Carter believed the key to creating a Palestinian homeland lay with Margaret Thatcher. A Tory with a pro-Israel record who had recently become the first British prime minister of the century to win three consecutive terms, Thatcher was in "an expansive mood," according to the editor of the *Atlanta Journal & Constitution*, Bill Kovach, ready to listen to Carter's ideas on a Middle East conference.[42]

Thatcher had grown to personally respect Carter as "a man of obvious sincerity," even if she considered him "personally ill-suited to the presidency."[43] But during their ninety-minute meeting at 10 Downing on June 12, she refrained from taking a direct leadership role in his proposed peace summit. Thatcher was concerned that, for all its merits, Carter's proposal—a Middle East peace conference with all the players invited—seemed to be giving the Soviet Union and the PLO too much special standing. "My position all along has been that no superpower should hold a veto at such a conference and that any group which is willing to recognize Israel's right to exist and accept UN Resolutions 242 and 338 could participate," Carter explained to Thatcher. If Carter could convince Deng Xiaoping and Mikhail Gorbachev to participate, he hoped Thatcher, and perhaps then Reagan's successor, would come more fully around—but it would be an uphill battle.[44]

From London the Carters headed to Thailand on a private plane provided by BCCI's Agha Hasan Abedi, for the laying of a cornerstone for a Global 2000 shelter for former prostitutes and abused women. Abedi, happy to assist his new American partner, pledged 1 million Thai bahts ($250,000) for the new Carter initiative. At the Asian Institute of Technology, Abedi wrote a check for an additional $250,000 to finance a Jimmy Carter school initiative.[45]

Although the purpose of the visit to Thailand was to launch these Global 2000 projects, Prime Minister Prem Tinsulanonda used the opportunity to plead with Carter to publicly denounce the continued Vietnamese presence in Cambodia (Kampuchea). Furthermore, the prime minister asked Carter to lobby both Mikhail Gorbachev and Deng Xiaoping to force Vietnam to withdraw. "I will discuss the situation in Kampuchea with leaders in China and the Soviet Union," Carter told Prem. "I imagine Mr. Gorbachev will say that Vietnam is an independent nation over which he has little influence, but I believe the influence is significant and will urge him to use it because I believe that if the United States, China and the Soviet Union keep pressure on Vietnam, they will withdraw and the nations of the region can turn their attention to economic development."[46]

By serving as a Bangkok messenger, Carter was playing a unique, if potentially dangerous, diplomatic role. Certainly his intentions were good: to stop the violent border clashes between Thailand and Vietnam before they escalated into full-scale war and to pressure Vietnam to pull its military forces out of Kampuchea. But to the State Department, Carter was once again meddling in a sensitive foreign policy situation. If this were the only additional crisis Carter embraced on his three-week world trek, it could have been overlooked. But in the coming days Citizen Carter urged Chinese leaders to allow the Dalai Lama to return as the spiritual leader of the Tibetans; called for religious freedom and integrity of Tibetan culture; recommended the normalization of U.S. relations with Vietnam; argued against Hong Kong's policy of imprisoning Vietnamese refugees; pressured Moscow to recognize Israel; and embraced four Soviet dissidents in Moscow. "While the Middle East is central to his thoughts on the trip," Kovach wrote in the *Atlanta Journal & Constitution*, "Carter accumulates new issues and responsibilities as he moves around the world like a ship sliding through Southern seas gathers barnacles."[47]

From Thailand the Carters took Global 2000 to China, where they signed letters of intent to develop programs for the training and rehabilitation of the handicapped. Cosponsored by the China Fund, the program was expanding on a project begun by Deng Pufang, the paraplegic son of Chinese leader Deng Xiaoping. The program, which provided training for teachers of the blind, deaf, and mentally retarded, was obviously touching an issue close to Deng's heart. A second program was established that supported new technologies for the fabrication and manufacturing of artificial limbs. "There were three million amputees in China who were in need of artificial limbs (prostheses)," Carter recalled, anxious to help thousands of crippled people, many of whom begged on the streets of Beijing and Canton. "Global 2000 filled the void."[48]

A year later Carter would return to China to dedicate a Global 2000 prostheses factory and meet the trained counselors. The Tiananmen Square protest had just erupted and the world community was outraged at Beijing's brutal treatment of young nonviolent dissidents who were demanding democracy. Using the factory opening as the pretext for his China visit, Carter held an emergency meeting with Deng Xiaoping and urged him to grant amnesty to all dissidents and to forgo trials of the Tiananmen Square demonstrators. "Chinese leaders informed me that there would not be additional trials of the demonstrators and authorized me to announce to the 60,000 Chinese students in American universities that they would not be arrested or abused if they returned home to live or to visit their families," Carter proudly recalled about his back-room diplomacy. Not taking Deng's word at face value, the Carter Center closely monitored the situation and discovered that two students *were* arrested when they came home. "With our help, they were released," Carter noted.[49]

Carter, like his sister Ruth, fancied himself as a global healer, the Camp David wizard who could save dissidents, resolve conflicts, free political prisoners, and promote human rights abroad, maintaining a Gandhian demeanor of spiritual evenhandedness. In a world full of ignoble misery and unnecessary despair, Carter was the traveling Baptist deacon of democratic light, anxious to uplift the dispossessed if only God would fortify him with the healing power. Few Third World politicians really believed that Carter was just a university professor, a born-again peanut farmer from Plains flying with a Muslim billionaire in tow, trying to save the world. As Bill Kovach noted about Carter's China visit, "He and his entourage—including BCCI President Abedi, whose bank has become a major presence in China and is looked on with great favor by the ruling powers for its work in helping train Chinese bank managers—are treated as if Carter still occupies the presidency."[50]

Herein lay the inherent dilemma of Citizen Carter's activist diplomacy: the sight of a former U.S. president, flanked by Secret Service, riding a private jet, CNN cameras filming his press conferences, and accompanied by Abedi, who doled out checks with startling regularity, tended to make a big, and sometimes misleading, impression. Politicians in many underdeveloped countries naturally assumed that Carter *was* the U.S. government, that he had the power to solve border disputes or procure World Bank or USAID funds or miraculously solve their internecine civil strife.

This misimpression served Carter's agenda; it gave him the added clout of being not just a peacemaker but a master facilitator with direct access to any power broker. The Chinese could not fathom that the U.S. president who formally recognized their nation was now just a benign Emory University professor. When Abedi or Sasakawa donated millions to an impoverished country, it was always clear that Jimmy Carter had made it happen.

World leaders unaccustomed to the American system of voting out presidents and giving them no official role could only assume that Carter had a massive constituency at home. How were they to realize that the Reaganites loathed him, and most Democrats wanted no part of his legacy? The contradictory fact that Carter always told world leaders—that he was a private citizen but planned to debrief the State Department or White House upon his return home—naturally left the impression of a larger endgame. So when Carter arrived in Moscow at the conclusion of his trip, full of stories about what Thatcher and Xiaoping and Assad and Mubarak "privately" told him about the Middle East, naturally Mikhail Gorbachev was all ears.

While the Chinese viewed Carter with reverence as the U.S. president who had officially recognized their nation, the Soviets remembered him as the human rights fanatic who boycotted the 1980 Summer Olympics and embargoed grain sales. Given this general impression, the international press was slightly surprised that the Soviet troika of Secretary General Gorbachev, President Andrei Gromyko, and Communist party secretary Anatoly Dobrynin treated him with the red carpet, dedicating hours of private time for off-the-record banter. The main agenda items were the Middle East conference, Soviet recognition of Israel, a resolution of the Iran-Iraq War, withdrawal of Vietnamese troops from Cambodia, and the Carter Center's new Russian media-monitoring initiative. Carter, according to Kovach, was "exhilarated by his conversations," thrilled to be in the Soviet Union for the first time.[51] "My meeting yesterday with you and General Secretary Gorbachev was most interesting, and potentially one that offers great promise in better understanding and the easing of tensions between our two people," he wrote Dobrynin. "With the waning of the Reagan Administration and the willingness of Mr. Gorbachev to explore new approaches, this is a propitious time to access these disparities and compatibilities in a more positive fashion."[52]

Carter extracted a concrete pledge from Gorbachev: Soviet participation in a Middle East Conference, to be held at the Carter Center under the auspices of the UN Security Council. The Carters had met their main trip objective: to have the Soviet Union, China, and Great Britain, all members of the Security Council, agree to send official representatives to the Carter Center's November Middle East consultation, "A Look at the Future."[53]

Commitment from these world leaders in the bag, Carter made a farewell gesture in Moscow that reminded everybody of his powerful pro–human rights note to Andrei Sakharov and demands that Jewish dissidents be released ten years earlier. (Due to Carter's human rights policies, there was a dramatic increase in the emigration of Jews from the Soviet Union from 14,000 in 1976 to more than 150,000 in 1979.) "One of the most famous Jewish leaders was Anatoly Shcharansky, whose name was always on my list to be discussed," Carter recalled about his White House advocacy. "I remember that once, Soviet Foreign Minister Andrei Gromyko said that a Jewish dissident like Shcharansky was just like a 'microscopic dot who is of no consequence to anyone.' "[54] Despite the Kremlin's denial of interest, the Soviet leadership had been affected by Carter's private and public criticisms, and now as ex-president he was corralling together four of the Soviet Union's most infamous dissidents—a Russian Orthodox priest, the editor of an underground newspaper, and two Jews seeking full national status for Soviet Jews. Carter delivered a stirring oration on the need for global human rights crusades to forge forward: "You should know that your courage and your strength is known to the world outside and serves as an inspiration to all of us," he declared.[55]

For the rest of 1987 Ken Stein doggedly worked to put together the Middle East consultation, focused on both the Arab-Israeli conflict and tensions in the Persian Gulf.[56] The consultation's off-the-record meetings afforded members of the NSC and State Department the opportunity to meet their counterparts from the Middle East and the UN. Following the Atlanta consultation, briefings on the private discussions were given to the heads of state of the countries represented. Carter and Stein would later point out that many of the points agreed upon at the November 1987 consultation were found in the 1988 peace initiative proposed by George Shultz. "There was no easy straight line like the Norwegian channel to the Oslo Accords," Quandt recalled of the two Atlanta consultations. "But the

Carter Center events were beneficial because they had Syrians and Israelis mixing it up."[57]

Weeks later Palestinians who had worked with Mubarak Awad, Faisel Husseini, and Sari Nusseibeh took matters into their own hands, with general strikes, boycotts, noncooperation measures, civil disobedience, tax resistance, demonstrations, and the spontaneous tire burnings and stone throwing by the young. A December 1987 traffic incident in northern Gaza served as the catalyst for a wave of riots that suddenly exploded into a general uprising throughout Gaza and the West Bank. One of the people Carter had met in 1983 was Dr. Haidar 'Abd al-Shafi, who played an important role in Gaza throughout the uprising. Misjudging the depth of Palestinian anger and desperation, Israeli officials initially dismissed the unrest as merely the latest in a series of periodic teenage disturbances. When water cannons and rubber-coated bullets failed to curtail the demonstrators, Defense Minister Yitzhak Rabin initiated a policy of "force, might, and beatings" designed to intimidate the Palestinians.[58]

The tenacious, unified, and broad participation in the *intifada* dispelled Israel's claims that Palestinian nationalism in the West Bank and Gaza was PLO propaganda and ploy. The *intifada* weakened Israel's military control of the occupied territories while drawing massive international condemnation of Rabin, creating a wave of sympathy for the aspirations of Palestinians yearning for their own state. "The *intifada* exposed the injustice Palestinians suffered just like Bull Conner's mad dogs in Birmingham," Carter noted.[59]

Carter empathized with elements of the *intifada*, viewing the unarmed young Palestinians who stood up against thousands of well-armed Israeli soldiers as "instant heroes" who exhibited "an unprecedented commitment to their cause and a surprising threshold for absorbing personal pain." Seeing that there were virtually no incidents in which Palestinians used firearms, especially in the first three years, to Carter these Palestinians were the 1960s equivalent of students sitting in at a Greensboro lunch counter, the Freedom Riders, or SNCC workers in rural Mississippi, allowing themselves to be beaten and jailed. While Israeli officials termed it war, he saw that, as with Rosa Parks and Martin Luther King Jr. of civil rights lore, nothing was going to turn the children of the *intifada* around. "Without using terrorism or armed struggle, young Palestinians are appealing directly to the conscience of the world," Carter wrote in a *New York Times* op-ed piece. "They have preemptively attacked Israel's most cherished characteristic: its moral fiber."[60]

Buoyed by the *intifada*, Carter passed on to the Palestinians, through Arafat, his congratulations. The highly publicized uprising had attracted the world's attention to the Palestinian cause. "With anger and mutual recrimination at a high pitch in the region, there is an increasing need for outside efforts to initiate negotiations, most notably from the United States," he believed.[61] What worried Carter the most was that 1988 was an election year in both America and Israel, and the window for capitalizing on the media value of the *intifada* might prove elusive. Carter believed the Reagan administration needed to explore new ways to open market outlets for the manufactured goods and agricultural produce of Palestinian Arabs, freeze Israeli settlements on the West Bank, and hold municipal elections as the first move toward Palestinian self-rule. And he hoped that the Likud party of Begin and Shamir would be drummed out of power. "The main problem Carter had with Israel during his post-presidency was with the Likud leaders," Quandt believed. "He got along just fine with Shimon Peres." As excited as Carter was for the new opportunities for peace in the Holy Land, he feared the 1988 campaign politics in both Israel and the United States would hamper genuine progress.[62]

With the 1988 Democratic National Convention being held in Atlanta, Carter played energetic host to scores of film crews and politicians alike, anxious to show off Manuel's Tavern, his favorite lunch spot, and his new museum. As for the Republicans—specifically Vice President George Bush—they were once again running against the legacy of Jimmy Carter. "While he scarcely seems afraid of this year's Democratic contenders," Bernard Weinraub wrote in the *New York Times*, "Mr. Bush sometimes sounds as though he would rather be running against candidates he has faced (as a Vice Presidential candidate) in the past, and especially against Mr. Carter."[63]

It is an astounding experience to read Bush's campaign speeches from April to July and see just how vociferously he lampooned Carter, clearly stealing a page from strategist Lee Atwater's previous two successful White House attempts by Ronald Reagan. "You've got to put into perspective where the policies of the liberal Democrats got us before the Republican Administration," Bush told a Fort Wayne, Indiana, audience. "You know and I know when Carter blamed us for a malaise in the spirit of the people that the blame belonged where the voters put it—on the Carter Administration and on that liberal Democratic philosophy." The modus operandi was to paint Governor Michael Dukakis as another Jimmy Carter, reminding everybody once again what life was like with 21.5 percent interest rates, double-digit inflation, runaway unemployment, and block-long gasoline lines. "Carter hangs over the Democrats like a shadow, an unwanted reminder of the failure of their policies the last time they were in power," Bush told supporters at Cleveland State University. "Now Mike Dukakis and Jesse Jackson are trying to sell that same old Democratic bill of goods. More taxes. More spending. More government control over your lives."[64]

Dean Acheson was fond of saying that when you throw a brick down a dark alley and hear a squawk, you know you hit a cat, and after the relentless Republican attacks on Carter, Dukakis was squawking. "This campaign is not about the seventies, it's about the nineties, it's about the future," a defensive Dukakis said at a May 1 news conference. And then, in an awkward effort to seize the economic offense, he added that "the Reagan Administration has piled more red ink on the national debt than all the administrations from George Washington to Jimmy Carter combined."[65]

Clearly Dukakis was in an uphill struggle for his political life. A conservative cycle had hit the country, and the notion that the liberal son of a Greek immigrant from Massachusetts could carry the Deep South, which the Democrats desperately needed, was far-fetched. The politics of racism played a big part of Campaign 1988, as Dukakis nervously dealt with his interparty rival Jesse Jackson, and George Bush ran the infamous Willie Horton ads across the nation, intimating that his Democratic opponent, if elected, would let black murderers out of jail.[66]

Carter was for his part extremely sympathetic to Jesse Jackson's run for the White House. When the reverend decried economic violence caused by "the merger maniacs" and "corporate barracudas," Carter was all Amens. Jackson might have been a fast-talking opportunist, Carter noted, but when it came to helping the disadvantaged of America, he was a Christian champion in the mold of Martin Luther King Jr., a man of peace like Anwar al-Sadat, an outspoken citizen brimming with goodwill like himself. Both Carter and Jackson, men of the South, shared the Baptist belief in Christian compassion as the springboard for uplifting social change. There was an inclusive spirit to Jackson's Rainbow Coalition that Carter admired—the reaching out to family farmers and destitute oil workers and underpaid maids.[67]

Carter had known Dukakis for a while and felt lukewarm about him; in fact, he was miffed that the Massachusetts governor was publicly promoting a move of the American embassy in Israel from Tel Aviv to Jerusalem. "That's just a really bad idea," Carter told Dukakis at a June 10 meeting in Boston. In this particular case Carter agreed fully with Secretary of State George Shultz, who called Dukakis's proposal "shocking" and detrimental to the peace process. Carter tried to dissuade Dukakis, along with New York senator Daniel Patrick Moynihan, from making the Jerusalem embassy a campaign issue.[68]

Meanwhile Jesse Jackson, a defender of the Palestinians, also was dismayed by Dukakis as the Democratic National Convention approached. And he did not stay quiet about it. When Dukakis failed to telephone Jackson at an appointed time, the civil rights leader turned prima donna. The grim situation worsened when Dukakis selected Senator Lloyd Bentsen of Texas as his vice presidential running mate, pointing to a clear rightward tilt in the party platform.

Bert Lance, a top aide in the Rainbow Coalition, recommended that Jackson ask Jimmy Carter to mediate his fracas with Dukakis or else consider bolting from the Democratic party. After all, Jackson had won 7 million votes in the primary and was now being treated as a pariah in Dukakis circles. Carter sympathized with Jackson but wisely avoided getting mired in the dispute, recommending DNC chairman Paul Kirk as better suited for the task. But in a forthright *New York Times* interview he added that New Englanders like Dukakis didn't understand how to deal with blacks. "I have lived and worked among the black people all my life, and I feel at home with blacks, who were my most loyal supporters in the nation," Carter said just a week before the Atlanta convention. "It was an integral part of my life." Racism, Carter believed, was more rampant in the North, where African-Americans were subjugated to the "invisible man" syndrome. He went on to acknowledge that Jackson and Dukakis were "quite different people," and asked that the civil rights leader be treated with respect by the DNC. The Dukakis team, Carter said, needed to reach out to African Americans in a meaningful way; and he spoke of the important roles the Reverend Martin Luther King Sr., Andrew Young, and Donald McHenry had played in both his 1976 and 1980 campaigns.[69]

Political reconciliation of another sort was occurring in Atlanta as the July convention convened. Paul Kirk had flown to Plains in February 1985 to try and patch up the bad blood between Ted Kennedy and Jimmy Carter. "If I couldn't bring them together, how was I to bring the party together?" Kirk asked himself.[70] A few years and a dozen phone calls later, Kennedy and Carter met at the Carter Center's Japanese strolling garden just before the convention, in what Curtis Wilkie of the *Boston Globe* called "a gracious encounter." Smiling gamely for cameras, Kennedy acknowledged their past difficulties but praised Carter's record on human rights and the "truly historic" Camp David accords. Carter, with great difficulty, tried to return the compliment. "I went to the dedication of his brother's library, and it was one of the nicest days of my life," was all he could manage. It was a reconciliation of sorts, particularly considering that earlier that afternoon Carter, in a feisty mood, had called Vice President Bush "effeminate" and "silly."[71] Still, despite an exchange of friendly notes after their Atlanta meeting, Carter and Kennedy remained distant from each other; and Rosalynn, unlike her husband, remained unwilling to forgive the Massachusetts senator for Chappaquiddick and his challenge in 1980.[72]

In contrast to the San Francisco convention, where Carter was treated like an uninvited guest, Atlanta proved to be a happy occasion for the ex-president. "I was delighted to have him play a key role," Kirk recalled.[73] Conspicuous throughout the political gala, he hosted Dukakis at his presidential library, gave an opening day prime-time speech, and was seen hugging Jesse Jackson from time to time. He praised Lloyd Bentsen for his sensitivity toward Hispanics. He even signed up as cochairman of the Georgia Dukakis campaign. When asked about the unprecedented DNC fellowship accorded Carter, Kirk said, "After eight years of 3 × 5 cards and hands-off government—if not disdain for government—people understand the sincerity and enlightenment that President Carter brought to his administration."[74]

But the good feelings came and went. When the confetti cleared, George Bush was still out on the campaign trail, hammering away at both Carter's presidential legacy and his "sorrowful son" Mike Dukakis from "Taxachusetts." Yet unlike the 1984 election, when Reagan's criticisms really stung, there was a cheeky, liberated feeling to all of Carter's anti-Bush retorts during the campaign, a cool confidence he had not exhibited in politics since the heyday of 1976. When Bush made reciting the Pledge of Allegiance a campaign issue, Carter scoffed in Trumanesque fashion, telling students at an Emory University town hall meeting that he respected Old Glory but would refuse to recite the pledge if ordered to do so by the government. As for the blatantly racist Willie Horton ads, Carter called them "reprehensible," a sign of gross impropriety and gutter ethics.[75]

In truth, it was hard for Carter to take Campaign 1988 seriously; his brother Billy, despite an experimental chemotherapy treatment, died of pancreatic cancer on September 26; he was only fifty-one years old. As his brother was laid to rest at Plains Lebanon Cemetery, the Carter clan all gathered to pay their last respects and swap Billy stories. There was the one about the morning in 1976 when Carter was walking with Ohio senator John Glenn, a possible vice presidential choice, down Main Street in Plains. Billy pulled up next to the two in his pickup truck, introduced himself to Glenn, then cracked open a can of Budweiser for breakfast while his brother winced. Another time Billy, tired of being mocked in the press as a "weirdo," swung back: "My sister Ruth is a faith healer, my sister Gloria is a motorcycle rider, my mother joined the Peace Corps when she was seventy, and my only brother thinks he is going to be President. And you all think I—a gas station owner and farmer—am crazy?"[76]

A wave of relief hit Carter as Bush-Quayle clobbered Dukakis-Bentsen on November 4. Immediately he sent a message of congratulations to the new president-elect, one of condolence to Dukakis. It did not please Carter that Dukakis had lost, and he certainly wasn't a friend of Bush, but at last, after eight agonizing years, Ronald Reagan would be living where he belonged: Beverly Hills and Hollywood. "I was anxious to start fresh with a new president," Carter recalled.[77]

T hroughout 1988 Carter had worked closely with Gerald Ford in creating American Agenda, an unusual bipartisan group that formulated options papers on the most pressing issues that were expected to confront the next president. "For the first time in the nation's history," an ebullient Carter had commented in May, "we'll have a bipartisan effort to help heal the political divisions of our election process."[78] The Carter-Ford team had collaborated on three previous written endeavors—the education commission report that America was moving backward in achieving racial equality, the 1984 crusade for spending cuts and tax increases to balance the budget, and a joint article for *Reader's Digest* on the Middle East—but none reached such a large audience as *American Agenda: Report to the Forty-First President of the United States of America* (1988), which, published as a special supplement, became a Book-of-the-Month Club selection.[79]

The ex-presidents joined in the project—funded by a $500,000 grant by the Times-Mirror Company—at the request of two former senior White House aides, James Cannon and Stuart Eizenstat. The 282-page-long report recommended a deficit reduction plan based on taxing gasoline, tobacco, and alcohol, combined with a limit on military spending, to balance the federal budget by 1993. The ex-presidents, reinforced by their bipartisan team of twenty-five experts, claimed that balancing the budget was critical to everything else: national security, arms control, trade deficit, Third World debt. "Unfortunately," Ford later joked, "Bush praised our report, then never implemented any of our recommendations."[80]

Both Carter and Ford presented the in-depth report of American Agenda to Vice President Bush on November 21, at a White House ceremony. It was an important moment in Carter's postpresidential career—not because Bush ever took Gary Sick's Persian Gulf or Robert Pastor's Central America essays seriously, if he ever read them at all, but because of the cordial afternoon he spent at the White House with Bush and Ford. "Already the ugliness of the Reagan years was dissipating," Carter recalled, comfortable with moderate Republicans like Lamar Alexander and Donald Rumsfeld, who attended the reception.[81] He went back to Atlanta with high hopes that a new, less ideological era in U.S. foreign policy was fast approaching, one where positive changes in the Soviet Union and Middle East could lead to dramatic peace initiatives and nuclear stockpile reductions. And with Dukakis relegated to the dustbin of defeat, Jimmy Carter, in a strange, unanticipated way, found himself in the odd role of being the titular head of the Democratic party, the only ex-president they had.

That December 10 Carter announced that he was forming an organization aimed at mediating civil wars around the world, and recounted for journalists from the *New York Times* and *Atlanta Journal & Constitution* recent upbeat conversations he had with UN secretary general Javier Pérez de Cuéllar, leaders of the Organization of American States and the British Commonwealth. With the Carnegie Corporation of New York and Sweden providing the funding, Carter spoke of the over twenty-five civil wars his Conflict Resolution Program (CRP)—which had just created the International Negotiation Network (INN)—hoped to halt. "Almost all of these are internal in nature," Carter said. Although Carter didn't say it at the time, the Ethiopian-Eritrean civil war, which had been raging for thirty years, was going to be INN's first case study. He had visited Ethiopia that autumn, and was convinced that track-two diplomacy could end the bloodshed. Bursting with ambition, Carter believed that if that African conflict could be solved by track-two diplomacy, then so could at least a dozen thorny others. "They are domestic wars. The problem is that the United Nations doesn't have any authority or responsibility for internal disputes."[82]

Things were, for once, slowly improving in the Holy Land. With the *intifada* raging unabated and no signs of progress on the diplomatic front, PLO political aspirations had been unexpectedly aided in July 1988 when King Hussein, as Carter hoped, renounced Jordan's claim to the West Bank, effectively removing himself as the competitor to Arafat. At a November 1988 meeting of the quasiparliamentary Palestine National Council (PNC) in Algiers, the PLO took its first formal step toward recognizing Israel. "It was an extremely important occasion," Carter recalled. Simultaneously the PLO issued a declaration of independence for the West Bank and Gaza while explicitly accepting both UN General Assembly Resolution 181 of 1947, the so-called partition resolution, calling for a two-state solution to the conflict, and UN Security Council Resolution 242, which called for Israeli withdrawal from occupied land in exchange for peace. "Though derided at the time," Carter recalled, "the PNC's acceptance of Resolution 181 marked an unprecedented acknowledgement of the legitimacy of Israel in Palestine."[83]

As 1988 wound down, Carter stood up for Muslims in a strange, almost surreal way that caused some eyebrows to be raised in Jewish-American circles but transformed him into an overnight hero in Islamic countries. Just in time for the Christmas book season, Viking published Salman Rushdie's controversial novel *The Satanic Verses* (1988). Muslims around the world were infuriated, perceiving the work as insulting to their religion. The novel was banned in a dozen countries and caused riots in India, Pakistan, and South Africa. Claiming that *The Satanic Verses* was blasphemy, Iran's Ayatollah Khomeini announced that Rushdie and his publisher should be executed, and multimillion-dollar bounties were offered to anyone who could carry out this murderous decree.[84]

Immediately, free-expression groups like PEN and Amnesty International as well as hundreds of individual authors, publishers, and public figures around the world came to Rushdie's defense. In one of the strangest moments of his postpresidential life, Carter, infuriated that *The Satanic Verses* mocked the Qur'an, took to lambasting Rushdie. Martin Scorsese's recent film *The Last Temptation of Christ* had also angered Carter because "the sacrilegious scenes" were "distressing" to Christians who "share my faith." According to Carter, Rushdie went "much farther" than Scorsese in "vilifying the Holy Koran." But Carter also made it clear that he deplored the ayatollah's death sentence on Rushdie.[85]

Not content just to let his views bounce around the Carter Center, the former president, to the deep chagrin of Stein and Pastor, wrote an op-ed piece for the *New York Times* that cemented his reputation as a holy man in Arab circles. "While Rushdie's First Amendment freedoms are important, we have tended to promote him and his book with little acknowledgement that it is a direct insult to those millions of Moslems whose sacred beliefs have been violated and are suffering in restrained silence the added embarrassment of the Ayatollah's irresponsibility," Carter wrote. "Western leaders should make it clear that in protecting Rushdie's life and civil rights, there is no endorsement of an insult to the sacred beliefs of our Moslem friends."[86] While many of Carter's liberal friends like poet James Dickey were "shocked beyond comprehension," those who understood how deeply in tune the ex-president had become to the teachings of Mohammed (who Rushdie derisively called Mahound) saw the commentary as vintage Carter.[87] "It's not right to ridicule another person's religion," Carter noted.[88]

FOURTEEN

BUSINESS AS USUAL, CARTER STYLE

‿∞‿

E ven while the Carter Center programs were expanding at a rapid pace, Jimmy Carter continued his regular work with Habitat for Humanity. As Habitat grew globally, Carter became the organization's roving ambassador and diplomatic point man. When two Habitat workers were denied visas to India in February 1988 to build in Khamman, Carter promptly sent a handwritten letter to Prime Minister Rajiv Gandhi, asking him for intervention. Within forty-eight hours the Habitat volunteers got their visas.[1] When the Indonesian government tried to charge Habitat interest on some land that Millard Fuller purchased to build houses on, Carter got His Excellency Jenderal Soeharto to drop the demand.[2]

"Whenever necessary," Carter recalled, "I would make direct appeals to world leaders on Habitat's behalf."[3] As Carter brought his Global 2000 agricultural efficiency and health care programs to Africa, he waxed enthusiastically about Habitat to Kenneth Kaunda in Zambia and Julius Nyerere in Tanzania, anxious to get their nations to embrace the Americus-based organization even more fully. In January 1985 the Habitat dump truck was suddenly confiscated in Gulu, Uganda, by the Ugandan army. Fuller tried in vain working through the U.S. embassy to get it back. Finally, after a month without transportation to that project, Fuller turned to Carter for assistance. Another long handwritten letter was dispatched, this time directly to President Milton Obote asking his assistance in securing the truck's "immediate return" to the Habitat project.[4] "We got the truck back promptly—personally delivered by General Okello, who overthrew Obote six months later," Millard Fuller later noted.[5] And as Carter proudly stated later, showing no sense of Christian mercy: "The commander was transferred to a distant and undesirable post."[6]

But more than anything else, Carter wanted to build. Still inspired by his New York experience, Habitat for Humanity initiated in 1986 the first annual Jimmy Carter Work Project, a yearly house-building initiative held at a different location every summer. For five days (June 8 to 12, 1986) in Chicago's drug-infested West Garfield neighborhood as a part of the work of Westside Habitat for Humanity, Jimmy and Rosalynn attempted to completely build, from the foundation up, four townhouses.[7] "For that time in Habitat history," Fuller noted about the Chicago build, which drew 150 workers, "it was the largest number of volunteers ever gathered."[8]

Among those participating in the Chicago build was Chuck Colson, of Watergate disgrace and the founder of Prison Fellowship. Colson brought with him twelve inmates who had been granted permission to leave a federal penitentiary to build with the Carters that week. Carter had never met Colson, the felon who said he would "walk over his grandmother" to reelect Richard Nixon in 1972, before. "We were also somewhat cynical about his supposed religious 'conversion,' " Rosalynn Carter recalled.[9] Their doubts soon subsided.

The Carters were impressed by Colson's repentance for his past sins, his frankness about Watergate, and his robust sense of humor, which stayed with him through his prison ordeal. Interviewed on one of the Chicago talk shows about the Jimmy Carter Work Project, Colson said, "I don't know what's in store for me this week. The last time I worked for a president, I got three years!" Side by side, Jimmy Carter and Chuck Colson hammered away for Jesus; even a constant downpour of rain didn't stop the swinging.[10]

Carter was appalled to learn from Colson that the United States had the highest per capita incarceration rate in the world, with over 1 million fellow citizens behind bars. He was particularly concerned that more African-American young men were in prison than in college. Convinced that Habitat should extend a caring hand to prisoners, Carter promoted the creation of an outreach program similar to Colson's. Soon Habitat South director Luther Millsaps established a prison furlough program in the Mississippi Delta, working with county and state prisoners to build houses. "Several of the prisoners," Millsaps noted, "have professed Christ because of their experiences."[11]

Carter was extremely impressed with Colson's Prison Ministries, which rehabilitated inmates for adjusting to life after incarceration. In 1989 Carter even arranged the hiring of prisoners from Sumter County Correctional

Institute, located just outside of Americus, to work part-time for the National Park Service, replastering the old Plains High School that was being transformed into a visitor center–museum as well as doing yardwork. Occasionally Carter would stop by the school to talk with the prisoners, clad in baggy white prison uniform with blue stripes, who got a day of fresh air outside prison walls thanks to the former president. Word of the "easy" time in Plains spread throughout the prison community, and soon when new inmates reported to the warden, the would-be "cooks" now claimed credentials as "plasterers."[12] This was not the first time Carter had showed compassion for incarcerated criminals: his housekeeper since 1970, Mary Fitzpatrick, was a convicted murderess.

The story of Mary Fitzpatrick tells much about Jimmy Carter's brand of compassionate Christianity, where the Barabbases of the world can be saved through simple forgiveness. Mary was born on December 23, 1945, in Richland, Georgia, thirteen miles from Plains, where Miss Lillian was reared at the turn of the century. When Mary was seven, her family moved to Trenton, New Jersey, where she became enamored with the rhythm-and-blues music of Jackie Wilson and Sam Cooke, deciding as a teenager to make it as a lounge singer. Paying jobs were hard to come by on the R&B circuit, so Mary became a go-go dancer, wearing skimpy flapper-style dresses, shimmying to her distant Macon-born cousin Little Richard's "Tutti Frutti" and "Long Tall Sally," from the crackled speakers of the Celebrity Club on Sunrise Highway in Nassau County, Long Island. One special evening she got to sing backup for Wilson Pickett, whose hit single "In the Midnight Hour" pretty much summed up her all-night existence.[13]

The birth of an illegitimate child started to change Mary's good-time habits. No longer able to dance, she headed back to Georgia, where she had relatives, and started working days as a maid in the Thunderbird Motel in Columbus, sometimes moonlighting at a "live-girl" bar that catered to the crew-cut soldiers at Fort Benning. To her chagrin, instead of finding the stability she craved in Georgia, Mary's life was in a dreadful turmoil, which came to a head one night in Lumpkin, Georgia, not long after Martin Luther King Jr. was shot in Memphis. Mary tried to take a gun away from her cousin, who was waving it at the cousin's ex-boyfriend, when the gun went off. Neither Mary nor the cousin knew the bullet had hit an innocent bystander until a sheriff came to pick them up later. Unable to prove self-defense in court, Mary was sentenced to a long prison term. Her life had dead-ended.

Then fortune came her way. Jimmy Carter was elected governor of Georgia in 1970, and at his inauguration in January 1971, he shocked America by flatly stating that it was "time to end racial segregation in the South." Carter, an equal-opportunity governor, was determined to reform all state institutions in Georgia, with prisons topping his priority list. That January, as an act of goodwill, Mary Fitzpatrick was assigned to work as a housekeeper in the governor's mansion as part of a prison trustee program. By the year's end Mary had become an ad-hoc member of the Carter family, serving as Amy's nanny, Chip's guidance counselor, and everybody else's beloved friend.[14]

When Carter won the 1976 presidential election, it was a foregone conclusion that Mary would come with them to Washington, D.C.: within a matter of six years her residential address changed from a Georgia prison cell to 1600 Pennsylvania Avenue. Ostensibly Amy's nanny, Mary was in fact her best friend: on any given day the two could be seen roller-skating down White House corridors, baking chocolate chip cookies in the kitchen, or playing tag on the South Lawn. Many days Mary had come a long way from the dance halls of Long Island to the Oval Office, discussing family matters and the state of the nation with the most powerful man in the world. Carter arranged to have her pardoned; in 1981 Mary was a free woman.[15]

After Carter's 1980 presidential election loss, Mary moved back to Georgia with the former first family, staying on in Plains as their all-purpose personal assistant. A devoted Christian, Mary said prayers every day for Jimmy and Rosalynn, and special ones for "her girl" Amy. While shingling and drilling together in Chicago, Carter sang the praises of Mary Fitzpatrick to Chuck Colson, further establishing a symbiotic bond between these two high-profile Christian house builders, who believed that every sinner could be saved. Although, to the consternation of Millard Fuller, Morris Dees, Charles Colson, and others, Carter refused to denounce the death penalty for first-degree murder—which seemed quite incongruous with the ex-president's Christian faith.[16]

At the end of the Carter-Colson construction week in Chicago, they had completed a four-unit townhouse for four families. The experience sealed the deal: every summer Habitat would hold a Jimmy Carter Work Project at a different global location. The next year, in July 1987, 350 volunteers joined Jimmy and Rosalynn to blitz-build fourteen houses in the Optimist Park area of Charlotte, North Carolina.[17]

Pundits had written off Habitat as an ultraliberal, left-wing Christian organization, due not only to its association with Jimmy Carter but because many of the volunteers were young "hippies" enamored with the Grateful Dead, peace studies, and environmental activism. Some residents of Americus, Habitat's international headquarters, complained about what they considered "tumbleweed tramps," who arrived in southwest Georgia unwashed and unshaven, disgusted with capitalism and conventional religion, committed instead to a communal lifestyle anchored around smoking pot and building homes for the poor. To the city fathers' dismay, Fuller, seen by some as a cult leader, embraced these tie-dyed youngsters, believing that they were all what Jack Kerouac called "angels of pure future." Much of the Confederate-bred conservative ruling class in Americus, the very people who loathed Clarence Jordan, now likewise saw Fuller as a troublemaker, the kind of wacky rabble-rouser who thought blacks were equal to whites, that long hair was acceptable for men and short hair acceptable for women. Instead of try-ing to straighten out these "lost souls," Fuller, they complained, took them in with open arms.[18]

Meanwhile Carter was starting to get slightly piqued at Fuller for con-stantly demanding favors and using his name. Just because he tolerated be-ing "shown off" in New York did not entitle Fuller to make unauthorized cardboard counter-display collection boxes with a black-and-white picture of Rosalynn and himself together under the slogan "No More Shacks," to be dispersed in 7-Elevens and Piggly Wiggly supermarkets. The ex-president loved Millard and was proud of his association with Habitat, but the Carter Center facilities officially opened October 1, 1986, and he needed to put all of his fund-raising efforts into that mammoth enterprise.[19]

As it was, hundreds of well-meaning people interested in helping Jimmy Carter wrote checks by mistake to Habitat, thinking that the organization was his own. This was a double-edged sword: on the one hand, Carter's surge in public approval was due largely to his work with Habitat, the visual image of an ex-president building homes for the poor having struck a re-sponsive chord with millions. The downside was that the public paid little at-tention to his Carter Center program. Sitting around with policy experts discussing SALT II or the Mexican debt was not good television; shingling a roof with Jane Fonda or John Elway was. Whenever Carter flew commer-cially, which was often, he made it a habit to walk down the aisle of the plane saying hello to everybody before takeoff, a reflexive gesture from being a good populist politician for thirty years. Virtually everybody congratulated him on Habitat for Humanity; few commented on his efforts to bring the Green Revolution to Africa or peace to Central America. Somehow Jimmy and Rosalynn had to disentangle themselves from being so dramatically as-sociated with Habitat.[20]

The issue came to a head in mid-March 1987, when Fuller wrote the ex-president telling him he wanted to unleash yet another Jimmy Carter so-licitation letter, which he planned to direct-mail to 1.6 million people. "Habitat will have to phase out my fundraising letters," Carter wrote back on March 31, standing up to Millard for the first time, tired of being treated as the presidential goose conscripted to laying monthly golden eggs. "I must shift my attention to raising money for my Center, including direct mail."[21] Instead of feeling slightly embarrassed, the brazen Fuller wrote Carter back on April 14, insisting that the former president had promised "that he would allow another round of letters to go out under his signature." An irked Carter, unable to tell Fuller to buzz off, inked in the margin of his letter "reluctantly approved"—nothing more—and sent it back. Carter had at least let it be known that there were limits to his being exploited for a good cause.[22]

The pronounced Christian aspects of Habitat, such as morning devotions, Scripture reading, and holy blessings of homes, were also causing Carter some consternation. While Carter, the savvy politician, had long ago mastered the ability to tone down his born-againism when politically appropriate, Fuller, constantly on the inspirational speaking circuit, tended to flaunt it. As the high-profile carpenter of Habitat, Carter often heard the shrill complaints of atheists and Jews convinced that Habitat—regardless of what their pamphlets and solicitation letters said—exuded the attitude that Christians were superior beings.

A striking example occurred when Fuller spoke in rambling fashion to a group of California Habitat supporters in mid-April 1987, extolling the virtues of Christ. In attendance was Steven Raas, whose engineering firm, M. Jacobs & Associates, had recently donated $2,000 worth of free services toward the construction of three low-income single-family dwellings in Santa Cruz County, California. Attending Fuller's talk, Raas was outraged to hear that only Christians could rightfully serve humanity. According to Raas, Fuller made unhinged statements like "Jews should feel shame at the site of the cross" and "Even a pagan can build a house with money; it takes a Christian to build a house with little money." Offended by what he heard, Raas wrote Carter a blistering letter about Fuller's "glaring anti-Semitism and insensitivity."[23]

Carter was distressed by the note but not angry at Fuller: he understood only too well how difficult it was for a dedicated Christian to control the impulse to preach the Gospel. More to the point, he knew Fuller and was sure that there was not a drop of anti-Semitism in his blood. The American Jewish Society for Service, for example, had recently joined forces with Habitat to build homes in San Antonio, undisturbed by Fuller's overt Christianity. Fuller was not dogmatic about his Christianity; after all, it was he who had insisted that the Muslims at the Karachi, Pakistan, project be given a Koran instead of the traditional Bible when they moved into their Habitat home. Sympathetic to both Raas's anger and Fuller's zeal, Carter mediated the misunderstanding, suggesting that the simplest solution was for Millard to offer an apology. "I understand the remark about pagans," Carter wrote Fuller on May 11, "but always try to remember that Jesus and his disciples were Jews."[24]

Just as it was getting dicier for Fuller to operate in his own hometown, Bob Hope joined the Jimmy Carter Work Project in Charlotte, swinging a golf-club-shaped hammer given to him by a jovial Carter—clad in faded jeans, Nike sneakers, and a heavy leather tool belt—only to bend the first nail he hammered. Every nail Hope tried to hammer in the board, he bent. But Fuller got a lot of mileage out of those crooked nails. Bob Hope wasn't important to Habitat as a field worker, but his involvement with the organization was a public relations bonanza.[25]

Using the successful Carter-Hope Charlotte build to spur on local Habitat affiliates nationwide, House-Raising Week '87, as Fuller called it, saw an estimated 275 homes built or completed in a dozen different states. It marked the beginning of what Fuller dubbed "blitz-builds," where during a designated week "the sound of hammers flying echoes across the world." It also triggered Fuller's insatiable desire to attract other celebrities to future work projects. In future years such show biz notables as Gregory Hines, the Indigo Girls, Willie Nelson, Richie Havens, and Tom Brokaw were wearing Habitat T-shirts, blitz-building for the poor.[26] "The hardest celebrity builder of all is Ali McGraw," Carter has maintained. "She is just wonderful, working all day long, really getting into the spirit of the build without even the slightest complaint."[27] Country singer Reba McEntire joined forces with Habitat's "Women Only" house-building program—which was initiated in Charlotte by a group of female workers—hammering nails at a Nashville site because she didn't want her involvement to be just "Reba writes a check." Paul Newman, in particular, became a most generous partner, working on builds in Kentucky and contributing money from his own nonprofit Newman's Own, which markets his famous salad dressings and other products, to help Habitat out. Although his primary concern was building shelters in America, Newman has sponsored projects in Mexico, Honduras, and Guatemala. "I am determined to get down to one of your work weeks," Newman wrote Carter in early 1988. "I would do almost anything to get a job! It's a dry year for old actors."[28]

Following Hope's initiative, Gerald Ford also publicly embraced Habitat. Millard and Linda Fuller had arranged an appointment to meet with Ford at his home in Rancho Mirage, California. Millard—wasting not a second—directly asked Ford if he would serve on Habitat's board of advisers, explaining that he needed a notable Republican to complement Jimmy Carter, to prove to conservatives that his ministry was bipartisan. "Sure I'll serve on the advisory board," Ford told Fuller. "But I'm not a carpenter like Carter.

Don't expect me to go around building houses." Thrilled to have another U.S. president, a Republican to boot, on his Habitat letterhead, Fuller reassured Ford that by just endorsing his ecumenical organization he would be rendering an important service. "No problem then," Ford replied. "I endorse Habitat."[29]

Cleverly Fuller had brought a small group of local journalists with him to Ford's office, including a leading television crew and a national magazine writer, who were all waiting outside for a postmeeting press conference. Somewhat surprised, Ford agreed to go out and say a few words, telling the reporters that because he "fully supported Habitat's good work," he had just "enthusiastically" agreed to join their board of advisers. "That single Ford statement opened the doors for other Republicans and conservatives to enter," Fuller recalled.[30]

Following in the Republican footsteps of Gerald Ford and Bob Hope, soon-to-be president George Bush's secretary of housing and urban development, New York congressman Jack Kemp, thought Habitat was a brilliant way for conservatives to demonstrate their sincere commitment to the poor while sticking to their principled guns that private social reform initiatives were vastly superior to government handouts—the failed housing projects of the 1960s being a prime example. Kemp and Fuller shared a mutual contempt for these horrendous urban war zones, rife with gang violence, teenage pregnancy, and lethal drugs. When asked what should be done with such wayward projects as Cabrini-Green in Chicago, Fuller's quick response was "bulldoze them down," because "they'll never function properly."[31] Kindred spirit on that and other housing issues, Kemp began showing up at Habitat projects ready to pitch in, one of the few politicians besides Carter who did not use Habitat merely for a photo op. "Habitat does more than build homes," Kemp was later quoted as saying; "it builds families, neighborhoods, and communities by bringing people together in a spirit of friendship and teamwork." Fuller, and Carter for that matter, liked Kemp. They thought he was sincere in his interest in helping all Americans have a decent roof over their heads.[32]

When Kemp came to help out on the Super Bowl Blitz in Atlanta, he was given the job of putting up a banister on a porch, which was being screwed instead of nailed. Someone handed him a screw gun, and the cameras began to roll. To Kemp's embarrassment, he kept trying to drive in the screw, but the harder he pushed, the more the screw warbled and refused to go in. Perplexed, he handed the gun to Fuller, who immediately noticed what was wrong. Someone had flipped the switch, which made the screw gun rotate backward instead of forward. Without Kemp seeing him, Fuller corrected the problem in a second and quickly drove a screw right in, shrugging as if nothing was wrong at all. "Jack and everyone else looked amazed," Fuller recalled. "That's when I confessed, and even Jack laughed. He took the gun away from me and quickly screwed in a few more for the cameras."[33]

By 1988 blitz-builds had become Habitat's most effective way of erecting houses, for they made a community event out of construction labor, one where thousands of volunteers at affiliates worldwide would simultaneously be sawing wood, hammering nails, and shingling roofs with, and for, the poor. But Fuller was not a man to rest on his laurels; he decided that in 1988 he could combine the House-Raising idea and the Jimmy Carter Work Project with a marathon consciousness-raising walk. The idea was a 1,200-mile trek to celebrate twelve years of Habitat for Humanity—it would be a "traveling work camp." Starting in Portland, Maine, walkers and builders would cover 1,200 miles over a period of twelve weeks, raising $1.2 million. Along the way they would build or renovate 120 houses. Jimmy and Rosalynn would split their time between two work projects—one in north-central Philadelphia to renovate five apartments, and the other in Atlanta to erect twenty new houses. The House-Raising Walk '88 would conclude in Atlanta, where the twelfth anniversary celebration would be held. Once again—as in the previous walks to Indianapolis and Kansas City—the theme song would be "We're Marching to Zion," which they were doing in a sense because Atlanta had become Millard Fuller's Jerusalem. "Down the East coast we came, pounding pavement and nails in an unforgettable twelve-week drama," Fuller later enthused.[34]

Habitat had brought Carter to inner cities all over America—but also to work sites all over Latin America and Africa. He was willing to maintain an association because it was a fitting part of his global mission to provide food, health care, and housing to the poor. "In political retirement, Carter has beaten the biggest knock against his presidency: that he could not inspire people," Carter's former speechwriter Christopher Matthews wrote in the *San Francisco Examiner* after spending a couple of days with his old boss at a 1990 Tijuana house-build. "Jimmy and Rosalynn Carter have contributed to a spirit of unabashed voluntarism that is too rare, despite George Bush's thousand points of light rhetoric."[35] And in the autumn of 1988, while election fever swept the United States, Carter's humanitarian attention was diverted from Habitat as his center began to tackle another major epidemiological challenge: river blindness.

Onchocerciasis, or river blindness, is a debilitating condition caused by a parasitic worm prevalent in the tropics, primarily in Africa. The World Health Organization, calling river blindness a "scourge of humanity since recorded history," estimates that it threatens more than 120 million people.

In some areas of Central and East Africa as many as 60 percent of those over age fifty-five are blind. The parasite *Onchocerca volvulus* is transmitted to human beings through the bite of the tiny blackfly, which breeds in swiftly moving streams (hence the term "river blindness"). Because people in endemic areas return again and again to rivers to collect water, bathe, and fish, they are at great risk for infection. "Nearness to large rivers eats the eye," unfortunately, is a widespread saying in West Africa.[36]

The life cycle of *Onchocerca volvulus* is complex; the blackfly serves as a two-way vector, initially allowing the worm to reach its human hosts and then serving as an incubator for its later larval stages. Young worms, or microfilariae, of *Onchocerca volvulus* cannot develop into larvae while in the human body. When female blackflies bite people with the skin-dwelling microfilariae, they ingest a certain number, which then mature inside the fly. The larvae are then retransmitted to humans by another bite, growing into adults. The worms live in the human skin for as long as years and produce millions of additional microfilariae, thus completing the human-fly-human transmission cycle.[37]

In humans, the blackfly bite causes a permanent, unsightly rash like poison ivy. Other symptoms include excessive weight loss, leaving victims with a skeletal appearance, and an incessant debilitating itching. Later, skin splotches that resemble leprosy appear, and nodules—enlargements as large as golf balls—grow on the body. The worst consequences appear after twelve years, when microfilariae colonize the eyes, creating lesions that can result in total, permanent blindness.[38]

Until 1987 there was no relief for river blindness—then a medical miracle occurred. Research scientists at Merck & Co. of Rahway, New Jersey, embodying Louis Pasteur's famous observation that "chance favors the prepared mind," discovered that Mectizan (ivermectin), long used to prevent heartworm in dogs and other animals, was effective in humans. A single Mectizan tablet each year could prevent or arrest river blindness, even though the drug alone could not eradicate the parasitic worm. After vigorous debate within the company, Merck concluded it was their moral responsibility to give away Mectizan. On October 21, 1987, Merck, a Fortune 500 corporate giant, announced plans to donate Mectizan for as long as might be needed to control river blindness. The pharmaceutical company, according to a Merck spokesperson, was in a "unique position" because Mectizan was needed by "people who couldn't afford it." In 1995, WHO reported that 18 million people were infected with the parasite, more than 750,000 were suffering from serious sight impairment, and 270,000 were completely blind.[39]

The next problem was distribution. Merck chairman Dr. Roy Vagelos turned to William Foege—the Carter Center's senior health policy fellow and a veteran in the war to eradicate smallpox—for help. Vagelos had an offer: if the Carter Center would develop a system to deliver the Mectizan, Merck would donate $80 million worth of tablets to the afflicted areas—a rare, stunning gesture of corporate philanthropy for Africa.[40]

Carter's response was an immediate "Let's do it." He had been touched by photographs of infected villagers, particularly by one of a young boy walking, followed closely by an old man, tethered to the child by a wooden stick. The boy is sighted; his elder is blind. Without the tether and the boy, the old man cannot make his way through a once familiar world. Carter learned that river blindness caused adverse social and economic consequences, because entire communities would abandon the fertile riverside for less productive areas to escape blackfly infestation. The move led to food shortages and the disintegration of community life, additional burdens on already impoverished Africa. Carter concluded that combating river blindness, like eradicating guinea worm disease, was a necessary health step for achieving the mini–Green Revolution of Global 2000 in Africa.[41]

The war was to be fought on two fronts: pesticides to combat the blackfly, and a logistical initiative to get Mectizan to 6 million people by 1993. The first battle was already ongoing. Since 1974 the Onchocerciasis Control Program (OCP), funded by the World Bank, used helicopters to spray larvicides on breeding sites in eleven West and Central African countries. After careful review, the Mectizan Expert Committee concluded that OCP could also deliver the tablets. Distribution systems were set up in countries such as Benin, Burkina Faso, Côte d'Ivoire, and Togo. The Carter Center then began to solicit, review, and approve applications from governments and NGOs wanting to distribute Mectizan. To facilitate the daunting task of effective distribution, the Carter Center drew upon its most precious asset: Jimmy Carter's access to state leaders. "What we can do at the Carter Center is go directly to the president of a nation, the prime minister of a nation, the health minister, the finance minister, the education minister, and the agricultural minister and get all of them working together," Carter observed. "That's the only way to really reach every village with Mectizan."[42]

Carter's long-term vision included sustained, ongoing delivery of Mectizan as an important component of improved primary health care services for Africa's impoverished populations. The Carter Center's Mectizan Donation Program would help distribute 29 million tablets between 1988 and 1995, with the hope that the World Bank and host government would provide additional funding.[43]

Letters went out to the agricultural minister of Niger and Baptist missionaries in Senegal. Besides cutting through the bureaucratic underbrush, Carter found himself caught up in distribution-related matters such as

Guinea-Bissau's poor highway system. Telephone calls were placed to world leaders looking for help in combating both guinea worm disease and river blindness. A fund-raising campaign was launched for institutional support to help underwrite the massive distribution program. Carter attained financial support from Africare and Helen Keller International, Interchurch Medical Assistance, and the Lions Club, but the major angels were not institutions, but husband-and-wife philanthropists: John and Rebecca Moores of Houston, Texas.[44]

John Moores was forty-six years old when he first met Jimmy Carter. A modest self-styled "techno-nerd," Moores had devised a method to speed up information processing on mainframe computers. In the early 1980s Moores formed his own company, BMC Software of Sugar Land, Texas, on a shoe-string. In 1988 BMC Software went public, and Moores walked away with a $400 million fortune.

At first Moores and his wife, Becky, did what a lot of the newly wealthy do; they spent some of that vast sum on houses in Rancho Santa Fe, Carmel, Vail, and Houston, drove Ferraris and Corvettes, collected paintings by Peter Max and Georgia O'Keeffe, and buzzed around the world in their own corporate jet. Passionate about baseball as well as his adopted hometown of San Diego, Moores purchased the Padres in 1994 and also pledged $1.5 million to build the new San Diego Hall of Champions Sports Museum in Balboa Park.[45]

Moores's philanthropic attitude reflected his hard-nosed, no-nonsense business background: "Most Americans, most corporations want to do the right thing," Moores said. "What we're all deeply suspicious of is giving to a black hole, or trying to do something good and instead making the situation worse."[46] Moores first learned about river blindness in a *Houston Chronicle* profile of Dr. William Baldwin, dean of the College of Optometry at the University of Houston, who was trying to raise $35,000 to purchase a van, drive to Guatemala, and distribute free Mectizan to poor Indians at risk. Moores, intrigued by Baldwin's campaign, joined in with him and established the River Blindness Foundation to attack the disease in Latin America, East Africa, Uganda, and Tanzania. Moores had the opportunity to see the damage wrought by the parasite when he and Baldwin traveled to Ecuador to distribute Mectizan, often to nodule-covered children leading their permanently blind elders, beyond the help of the miracle drug.[47]

Out of his experience with Baldwin, Moores felt a moral obligation to increase Mectizan distribution in Africa. He learned of Jimmy Carter's similar interest in river blindness, as well as of his penny-pinching. Carter's micro-managing in the Oval Office may have been misguided, but his careful post-presidential husbandry of philanthropic dollars was widely respected by corporate America. "The word was 'Carter's tight with money,' " Moores noted. "He accounts for every nickel spent."[48] The philanthropist would not have to worry about a charitable black hole.

Moores had an opportunity to meet Carter at a Houston dinner in 1989 honoring South African bishop Desmond Tutu, and came away impressed. There the men broached the possibility of pooling resources to attack river blindness in Africa. This was followed by a Carter invitation to the Mooreses to spend a week with them in Guyana while the former president was on a democracy-building mission in that poor South American nation. Impressed with a close-up view of Carter in action in a Third World country, by the end of their week together in Guyana, Moores had pledged $25 million to the Carter Center, writing a $6 million check on the spot. "I was absolutely convinced that his guinea worm project and the river blindness project would both be successful, especially if Carter would step up to the plate and do all the heavy lifting," Moores recalled. The elegance and efficiency of the project was overwhelming: "Fighting river blindness with Carter was a chance to do something really clever on the cheap. I couldn't find anything that would have the return on investment as Mectizan distribution—it was staggering."[49]

With shared interests in baseball, the Bible, and computers, Moores and Carter got on well together. Becky and Rosalynn also became close friends. The two couples fished in Alaska, hiked Mt. Fuji, and monitored the 1994 Panamanian election. Carter and Moores also spearheaded a major drive to convince the World Bank—which had been involved with river blindness control since the early 1970s—to raise additional millions to set up sustainable community-based Mectizan distribution programs. Moores recalled that Carter didn't mince words in dealing with James D. Wolfensohn, president of the World Bank. "He just went in and said, 'We are passing out pills, we're doing this, we're doing that, now the World Bank must act.' " Wolfensohn was completely supportive of Carter's charge to him and, in conjunction with WHO, promised to raise $124 million for the cause.[50]

The Mooreses and the Carters became close despite their hugely different lifestyles and approaches to material possessions. To the austere Carter, luxuries and modern conveniences were largely unimportant. Americans in the twentieth century hardly knew what to make of a president who carried his own bags, never left on an unneeded light, bottled his own jams, pressed his own grapes into wine, and crafted much of the furniture in his house with his own hands. John Moores had a taste of the Carter mindset when he tried to give his presidential friend a special birthday gift—a custom-made British hunting rifle (price tag: $75,000). Carter politely declined, saying thanks but no thanks, that he already had a "hunt gun," a model that had belonged to his father. As Moores has observed of Carter, "I can't think of a single extravagance. For God's sake, he wears a nine-dollar rubber wristwatch!" Ironically, it was Jimmy Carter's unique ability to engage the world's problems while simultaneously rejecting its materialism that reassured John Moores that every penny donated to the Carter Center would be spent directly on the poor and in fighting river blindness.[51]

Besides river blindness and guinea worm disease, Carter was always on the watch for other global scourges to attack. In April 1990 the Carter Center's newly established International Task Force for Disease Eradication (ITFDE), under the direction of Donald Hopkins and William Foege, met at the Carter Center to inventory global maladies that could be eliminated. Setting the tone for the meeting, Carter used the occasion to announce that American Cyanamid had donated enough Abate larvicide—$2.6 million worth—to make guinea worm eradication possible within five years. Using the 1977 eradication of smallpox as its benchmark, the task force determined that yaws (which afflicted 2.5 million people yearly) and polio (which killed 25,000 people a year) could theoretically be eradicated in ten years. It would take an estimated $20 million to wipe both out, and Carter believed that "there was no reason for them to exist." The ITFDE also began targeting other potentially eradicable diseases including mumps, rubella, cysticercosis, and filariasis. Carter, whose mother nursed lepers in India, also embraced leprosy eradication, even though total eradication was not immediately feasible.[52]

Carter believed there were pragmatic reasons for the United States to combat such diseases, even if they didn't now afflict Americans; increased global travel meant there was always the chance that these scourges could someday invade our shores. He also believed that it was in our national interest to help Africa toward self-sufficiency because in the long run it would reduce the need for humanitarian aid.

In September 1994 Jimmy and Rosalynn, accompanied by Dr. Roy Vagelos, then CEO of Merck, visited Chad, one of the poorest countries in the world, with a population of 5.4 million people and a life expectancy of forty-seven years. Their purpose was to reach out to some of the 126,000 people inflicted with river blindness, as well as encourage greater action against guinea worm disease.[53]

A light breeze was blowing from the west as a small plane ferried the Carter delegation from N'Djamena, Chad, southwest toward the remote village of Nia. The thunderstorms that had threatened to cancel the trip moved east. Down below, the earth appeared benign, lush green bursting with new growth, streams and rivers flowing swiftly. On the ground it was a different story. They were about to land in a zone of hyperendemic river blindness in southern Chad. Nia, a sunbaked village of subsistence farmers, population 700, had no school, and the closest health clinic was a half day's walk down a pothole-ridden red clay road. Bitten as often as 12,000 times a day, most of the villagers were infected with river blindness. Nia's rate of blindness was as high as that reported anywhere in Africa. "When you see the lesions on their bodies and the blind stares from their eyes, it's an emotional experience," Vagelos noted about his experience in Chad.[54]

The most startling finding in Nia was just how young were some of those blinded by the disease. Carter met Christine, only twenty-four and blind; her son, Tiddum, was not, but was likely to be when he grew older. That afternoon Carter and Vagelos offered words of consolation to the tribal dignitaries and personally distributed Mectizan to villagers—one-half to two tablets, depending on body weight. Later they investigated a blackfly breeding ground along a muddy river. Carter pointed out a feeble peanut plant with ten tiny nuts, remarking to Vagelos that "in my fields this would have 100 peanuts." Once river blindness was controlled, he continued, the people could return to fertile land and increased yields. Carter's thoughts lay elsewhere; he was haunted by the image of beautiful unseeing Christine, a mother who would have been able to watch her son grow to maturity if only she had been given Mectizan two years earlier. "It may be too late for Christine, but it's not too late for her son Tiddum," Carter said out of the blue to Vagelos, who was somewhat startled by Carter's messianic gaze. Then, relaxing back into his everyday intensity, Carter related with a smile that Christine had told him that in her native tongue "Tiddum" meant "impossible dream." He was personally going to stay in touch with Tiddum to make sure he got an education and proper health care.[55]

In 1988, 255,000 Mectizan treatments had been administered worldwide. By 1996 the total—for that single year—exceeded 19 million, 3.8 million from the Carter Center program alone. As his fellow river blindness crusader Moores notes, "It's ongoing and incremental. But when you step back, it's sort of mind-boggling to see what's happened. Things like this change the world." Before Carter left Chad he held a press conference to announce that he had helped procure a $124 million World Bank grant, primarily to expand distribution of Mectizan in sixteen nations in a program known as the African Program for Onchocerciasis Control. "Someday river blindness won't exist in Chad," Carter said, then headed off to Ethiopia to begin inspecting Global 2000's agricultural sites, assess progress in his guinea worm eradication program, and, as always, talk human rights.[56]

FIFTEEN

SHOWDOWN WITH NORIEGA

ᔕ⌒ᔑ

If any one event moved Jimmy Carter back into Washington's inner circle, it was president-elect George Bush's selection of James A. Baker III as his first secretary of state. The wily millionaire son of a Texas attorney, the fifty-nine-year-old Baker had left his own Houston law practice to serve with distinction as Ronald Reagan's chief of staff from 1981 to 1985 and secretary of the treasury from then to 1988, when he became Bush's campaign manager. A nonideological political operator and close friend of Bush, Baker struck a power pose, striding through Washington in slicked-back hair, black pinstripe suits, and exquisitely knotted teal green ties, always shooting his cuffs in a way that somehow said he could get things done in the nation's capital. A few days after being tapped for the top job at State, Baker lived up to his reputation for making deals across partisan lines by traveling to Atlanta in December 1988 to pay a courtesy call on President Carter. "It was a very kind gesture," Carter said later. Baker "was a breath of fresh air."[1]

Over the years to come, an easy, natural friendship would develop between Carter and Baker based on mutual respect, a preference for southern living, a hearty appreciation of former DNC chairman Robert Strauss's Texas humor, and shared passions for quail hunting and fly fishing. Thus during the Reagan era, when Carter was out of the Washington loop, then–secretary of the treasury Baker helped the ex-president with getting a parkway built to his presidential library and answered his questions on Middle East policy. One Christmas he even arranged to get duties removed, at Carter's request, on the ex-president's favorite fishing flies from Asia. "Carter is really quite easy to deal with," Baker maintained. "He just wants to be useful. He never complains. But if you don't clearly spell out his assignment, and then ride herd over him, then he can get in your way."[2]

Just two weeks after the 1988 election, Democratic Speaker of the House Jim Wright—a cagey, smooth-talking Texan who had just won his eighteenth consecutive congressional term—met with Bush and Baker to discuss Nicaragua.[3] Out of that meeting Bush and Wright agreed to attempt to find a bipartisan effort to resolve the conflicts in Central America, where the Bush administration faced an incredible dilemma. Military aid to the Contras had been decisively defeated in the previous Congress, and the new Congress had even more anti-Contra House Democrats. At the same time humanitarian aid to the Contras was scheduled to expire on March 31, 1989— two months into the new administration. As Bush was preparing his inaugural address, the trial of Oliver North was about to begin; the shadow of the Iran-Contra scandal loomed dark over Washington. (Later that spring both North and his boss, Robert McFarlane, would be convicted on related felony charges.) Bush saw no sensible reason to keep Reagan's ideological crusade going in Central America. Instead, his administration would push for a bipartisan commitment to building democracy in the hemisphere.[4] As for Nicaragua, Bush would compromise with the Democrats: the United States would give the Contras $49.7 million in humanitarian aid while banning all military support until national elections were held the next year. "We want to wind this thing down," Baker told Wright on March 2.[5] After weeks of negotiation with Democrats and Republicans in Congress by Baker, the new administration prevailed. On March 24 Bush and Baker, surrounded by majority leader Wright and other congressional leaders, signed the Bipartisan Accord on Central America in the Rose Garden. As Baker put it in his memoirs, "A debilitating era of mutual antipathy was over."[6]

An architect of this new, bipartisan approach to hemispheric affairs was Baker's choice to be assistant secretary of state for inter-American affairs, forty-two-year-old Bernard Aronson—a former Harlan County labor organizer, Carter administration assistant, and DNC official. A well-respected moderate Democrat, Aronson had worked closely with Contra supporters in Congress like Bill Bradley and Sam Nunn on the Democratic side and John McCain and Henry Hyde on the Republican side to forge a bipartisan approach to Central America. What's more, Aronson was a close friend of Robert Pastor—and a consummate political broker whose bipartisan credentials contrasted with those of Elliott Abrams, his predecessor at Foggy Bottom, who was seen as a right-wing zealot. Thus began what became

known during the Bush years as "The Bob and Bernie Show"—an effective
bipartisan effort at hemispheric problem-solving. By appointing Aronson, a
Democrat trusted by Republicans, Baker made it clear he saw the hemisphere primarily as a domestic political matter: a low priority compared with
the unraveling of the Soviet Union, potentially "loose" nuclear weapons,
mounting tensions in the Persian Gulf, and an antidemocracy crackdown in
China. "Central America was a cutting-edge issue, but it was not the Soviet
Union," Baker recalled. "I hired Bernie Aronson to help solve our [hemi-
spheric] dilemmas. He did a first-rate job, but I constantly had to protect
him from the Republican Right."[7]

Baker made clear that the State Department would run Latin American
affairs, of course, but the Carter Center would be used from time to time for
track-two diplomacy, passing along "unofficial" messages and holding consultations. Baker and Carter would stay in touch occasionally by telephone,
working together to bring democracy through elections to such places as
Panama, Nicaragua, the Dominican Republic, and Guyana.[8] "Baker had no
desire to relive the decisive partisan battles on Central America that had
consumed so much of America's energy in previous years," Aronson recalled
later. "Pursuing a bipartisan policy was the right way to proceed."[9] In a reversal of Reagan policy, the Bush administration embraced the Arias (or Esquipulas) peace plan, which aimed to end armed conflicts between left- and
right-wing regimes and rebels.[10]

Just as the new Baker-Carter partnership was taking shape, a series of
events in Venezuela nearly threw the entire scheme off track. In late February 1989 Carter and Pastor flew to Caracas at the invitation of Carlos Andrés
Pérez to attend his inauguration. But the gala occasion also provided them
an unprecedented opportunity to hold private talks with Nicaragua's Daniel
Ortega and Cuba's Fidel Castro—the leaders of the only two governments
in the hemisphere the U.S. government refused to deal with. "Carter, and I
met with Ortega, Oscar Arias, Vinicio Cerezo, and Pérez to begin to set the
stage for focusing on the Nicaraguan electoral process," Pastor remembered. On their way to Caracas, Carter and Pastor stopped in Miami to meet
with Alfredo César, a Contra leader, and a wide range of Cuban-American
leaders, including Jorge Mas Canosa, the conservative head of the Cuban
American Foundation. Those meetings gave Carter the parameters within
which they talked with Ortega and Castro.[11] Ortega, who thought the GOP
had "shot its blot" in Nicaragua and lost, confidentially informed Carter
even before he told the Bush administration that he had agreed to move
democratic elections up by one year from February 1991 to February
1990—a gesture Bush had been urging. "The revolution stays and Reagan

leaves," Ortega had boasted just two months earlier, cocky that the gamble on democratic elections would resuscitate Nicaragua's failing economy— now sooner than later.[12]

Vice President Dan Quayle, who was representing the Bush administration at Pérez's inauguration, became indignant when he heard that Carter had met with Ortega. "When you have a former President meeting with heads of state we didn't meet with, it has a chance of complicating matters," Quayle told the press.[13] Once back in Washington, Quayle investigated whether it was legal for Carter to talk with Ortega and was disappointed to learn that the Logan Act of 1799 didn't apply (the law, still on the books after all these years, stipulates both fines and imprisonment for U.S. citizens who act independently and without federal authorization to correspond with a foreign government in order to influence the conduct of that government). As for Nicaraguan elections to be held in February 1990, Quayle called the entire idea a "sham" being foisted on the United States by Ortega.[14] "With Quayle so angry about Carter's meeting with Ortega, we thought it best to keep quiet about our meeting with Castro," Pastor admitted long after the fact.[15]

Carter's first face-to-face encounter with Castro had a humorous edge. Carter knew the Cuban *caudillo* was in town and was eager to size him up in person despite Pastor's advising against it.[16] The ex-president was in the middle of an hour-long interview with Flora Lewis of the *New York Times* in his hotel suite when a member of Castro's entourage knocked on the door and whispered to Pastor that the Cuban dictator was even then walking down from his suite three floors up en route to Carter's rooms. Pastor immediately sent somebody to detain Castro for the minute it would take to hustle Lewis out of the room; if the *New York Times* ran a story about Carter with Castro, on the heels of his meeting with Ortega, the ex-president's "new understanding" with the Bush administration would surely die aborning.

Pastor pulled Carter away from the interview as politely as possible to tell him about Castro's imminent arrival. Then, with Carter's consent, Pastor brought the interview to an abrupt end. "I almost picked her up and walked her to the elevator to get her out of there in time," Pastor recalled. "And ten seconds later Castro burst into the room."[17] For forty-five minutes Carter and Castro discussed a wide range of issues from Nicaragua to Mariel to the cost of transporting the corpses of relatives of Cuban Americans to Miami from Havana. "He surprised me with his intellect and humor," Carter said in retrospect. "Nothing much happened, but the meeting opened up a dialogue between us."[18]

But in truth, the former president's chats with Castro and Ortega were preludes to later adventures: Panama was the pressing issue. Panama was a likely nation for Carter to promote democracy in; his credibility there was sky-high in the wake of his tenacious effort to push the Panama Canal Treaties through a protracted Senate debate in the spring of 1978, where they passed by a single vote. While he was loathed by the Republican right for this accomplishment, it made Carter an éminence grise in Panama for the same reason. In Venezuela, therefore, Pastor talked to both Guillermo Endara, the main opposition candidate for the slated May 7 election, and with representatives of the Noriega regime about the Carter Center's possible involvement in the coming electoral showdown.

When Pastor returned to Atlanta from Venezuela he had a long conversation with Aronson. "I gave him a full briefing on all (but one) of our meetings in Caracas," Pastor informed Carter via a February 6 memorandum, "and told him that you had gone out of your way to tell the Latin leaders that you felt that the Bush administration will be a marked, positive departure of its predecessor. He told me that when he read Quayle's comments about you, he felt sick, as it represented a very different approach than the bipartisanship that Bush and Baker were emphasizing. He said he wanted to call you and apologize, but thought that might not be such a good idea at this time."[19]

Of course, for the Carter Center to assume this key role in Latin American policy Bernie Aronson would have to pass his confirmation hearings to succeed the hawkish Abrams. Some Democrats on the Senate Foreign Relations Committee had their doubts about Aronson—after all, he was pro-Contra and a confidant of conservative Illinois congressman Henry Hyde. Carter telephoned a number of key senators on the panel, including chairman Claiborne Pell, with a glowing endorsement of Aronson. Pastor recommended that the Democrats "press Bernie in hearings," not "draw blood," and in the end vote for him. It was important for the Republican right to think liberals disliked Aronson. In the end, Aronson was confirmed unanimously.[20]

As chairman of the Council of Freely Elected Heads of Government, Carter sent an informal delegation to Panama in mid-March to assess Panama's electoral system two months before the presidential, legislative, and municipal elections scheduled for May 7. The team was composed of representatives of Carter, Venezuelan president Carlos Andrés Pérez, and former Costa Rican president Daniel Oduber, and they met with Panamanian election officials, political party leaders, presidential and legislative candidates, Catholic Church leaders, journalists, and other participants in the nation's political process.[21] "The assessment will be conducted in accordance with recognized international standards," Carter announced in a press release. "The concern has been that the existing system of government, with total domination by the military, was unlikely to be relinquished or changed and that the election might be just a subterfuge unless it is monitored by respected and independent international groups."[22]

Panama's 2.2 million citizens had been ruled by two military strongmen—Omar Torrijos and Manuel Noriega—since 1968. Both Carter and the Panamanian people knew there were dramatic differences between the two dictators.[23] Torrijos, who was killed in a helicopter accident in 1981, had been much loved by his countrymen and widely celebrated for working with the Carter administration to craft the treaty that would transfer the control of the Panama Canal to its home country on December 31, 1999. Noriega, on the other hand, was considered ruthless to the bone, and became a pariah in the last years of the Reagan administration, when he was accused of drug trafficking.[24] Noriega had joined Libya's Muammar Qaddafi, Iraq's Saddam Hussein, and Cuba's Fidel Castro in the ranks of "dangerous thugs" whose reckless regimes were seen as threats to America's national security.

The U.S. government's opposition to Noriega arose from myriad reasons. Noriega had been on (and off during the Carter years) the CIA payroll for twenty-five years, and in the mid-1980s he had joined President Reagan in support of the Nicaraguan Contras fighting the Sandinista government.[25] On February 4, 1988, a U.S. attorney in Florida secured an indictment against Noriega for drug smuggling and racketeering.[26] As James Baker put it, Noriega was "up to his epaulets in drug trafficking"; what's more, the sort of intelligence information he used to sell to the CIA was no longer deemed worth the risk of dealing with him.[27]

"Both the President and Secretary Baker have stated repeatedly that the United States will make no accommodation with any regime dominated by Noriega," national security adviser Brent Scowcroft wrote Carter. "The elections, if conducted in good faith and fairness, offer Panamanians a way out of their long nightmare and a chance to normalize economic and political relations with [the] U.S. and other democratic countries. But Noriega's record and all of the information available to us indicates that he and his cronies will not allow truly free elections unless forced by circumstances to do it."[28]

Many pundits wondered whether Bush was not overreacting to Noriega, exaggerating the importance of holding democratic elections. "The press simply reported that Bush was going after Noriega," CIA director William Webster protested later. "That just wasn't the case. He had a broader vision to protect the Panama Canal, to maintain stability in the region."[29] Panama received an annual fee plus a percentage of the toll, amounting to about $75 million a year from canal revenues. Carter and Pastor agreed with the Bush administration that democratic elections in Panama would be the smartest legal way to end the illegal regime—but they also wanted an exit strategy, and they thought that lifting the severe economic sanctions at the right moment could facilitate it.[30]

Carter's delegation returned bearing notebooks brimming with horror stories about the Noriega camp's intimidation tactics. There were reports of ballots already stacked in favor of Noriega's relatives and cronies, particularly for presidential candidate Carlos Duque, a front man for certain military-owned enterprises. "Your prestige and reputation in Panama are such that the Noriega regime cannot but take notice of your views," Brent Scowcroft wrote Carter in late March. "I believe that your delegation's visit served a very useful purpose in impressing on Noriega and his people the seriousness with which the democratic world views events in Panama."[31] Carter remained anxious to work closely with the Bush administration in Panama despite his vehement opposition to its imposition of economic sanctions.[32]

"We knew in March, after the delegation reported back, that it was going to be real tough getting Noriega to allow election observers," Pastor recalled.[33] The Bush administration was encouraging broad international participation, hoping to flood Panama with election observers representing everything from the European Union to the United Nations to the Catholic Church. Carter had a personal stake in making sure that Noriega allowed an honest, fair, democratic election to take place in Panama. "Torrijos had promised me that democracy would take root in Panama," Carter averred.[34]

The ex-president was by no means alone in wanting to bring democracy to Central America; the notion had become popular due in large part to Congress's creation of the nonprofit National Endowment for Democracy (NED) in 1983. With communism being denounced as "evil" by the president, NED had a mandate to foster democracy abroad by bolstering institutions and processes that allowed democracy to work: legislatures that represented citizens and oversaw the executive; independent judiciaries that safeguarded the rule of law; political parties that were open and accountable; labor parties and business groups; and elections in which voters freely chose their representatives in government. From its origin, the organization suffered an eclectic range of detractors, including Democratic senator Dale Bumpers, his Republican colleague Hank Brown, the leftist *Nation* magazine, and the libertarian Cato Institute, not to mention liberal *Washington Post* columnist Mary McGrory, who denounced the endowment as a "Cold War relic" designed to waste taxpayers' money on pork-barrel international junkets. But the critics were wrong: the NED and the institutions it financed were in fact trailblazing groups that set the tone for promoting democracy in the post-cold-war era.[35]

Under a large umbrella, NED created institutes for both major political parties—the National Democratic Institute for International Affairs (NDI) and the International Republican Institute for International Affairs (IRIIA, or simply IRI)—to promote democratic processes and institutions in countries moving toward freedom. These branches of NED analyzed and observed elections, promoted civic education efforts, and helped build political programs in emerging democracies. NDI concentrated on creating programs open to a wide range of political parties; IRI usually pursued a similarly multipartisan approach but occasionally focused on helping one or more conservative parties. Supporters of NDI and IRI included Indiana Republican senator Richard Lugar, Connecticut Democratic senator Christopher Dodd, the *Wall Street Journal*, the conservative Heritage Foundation, the Progressive Policy Institute, and syndicated columnists David Broder and George F. Will. Writing in *Newsweek*, Charles Krauthammer praised NED as a "visionary" and "cost-effective" institution that was making important contributions to the growth of democracy worldwide. The genius of NED was that it brought liberals and conservatives together in an unprecedented effort to export free and fair elections to nations around the world.[36]

Election monitoring was not invented by NDI or IRI. The Organization of American States had sent observers to nineteen elections in fifteen countries from 1962 to 1982, and the U.S. government had sent observer delegations to numerous elections in Vietnam and El Salvador. But the fundamental purpose of these missions was to legitimize an election, not to monitor or assess its fairness. The UN and the OAS had an unusual problem when it came to election monitoring: they defended the principle of nonintervention in the internal affairs of their members, yet they were committed to universal rights that were often violated by the same members. Considering this inherent contradiction, it was little wonder that these organizations initially shied away from active election monitoring. NDI, IRI, and the Carter Center, unlike the UN and the OAS, were NGOs and didn't need to worry about nonintervention principles.

Jimmy Carter became attracted to NED's National Democratic Institute for International Affairs component in 1986 when Walter Mondale became its chairman. Although Carter did not join such fellow Democratic politicians as Bill Bradley, Mario Cuomo, and Charles Robb on the Senior Advisory Committee, he did see practical ways to get the Carter Center involved and thus satisfy his personal urge to participate in NED's push for free elections and democratic governments. Carter was impressed by the work of NDI and IRI in the Philippines, where the groups sponsored an international delegation to observe the historic February 1986 presidential election. The monitored vote prevented Ferdinand Marcos, who had tightened his authoritarian grip over twenty years, from manipulating the results, permitting genuine democrat Corazon Aquino, the widow of assassinated opposition leader Benigno Aquino, to take office.

In November 1987 Carter worked peripherally with NDI on elections in Haiti. "Your selfless and courageous efforts in support of human rights and democracy in places like Haiti are so impressive," NDI president Brian Atwood wrote Carter on November 4. "It was an honor to have served in your administration and an honor to be associated with you now."[37] NDI had invited a group of Panamanians to the 1987 legislative elections in the Philippines to study the efforts of the National Citizens Movement for Free Elections (NAMFREL), the 500,000-member poll-watching group whose "quick count" in 1986 showed an Aquino victory over Marcos. Upon their return two of the Panamanians began organizing a similar group, causing fear within the Noriega regime that NDI was exporting Philippine "people power" to Panama. Noriega, therefore, was expected to refuse an election-observing role for NDI.

Throughout the early months of 1989 the Carter Center, largely in the person of Robert Pastor, kept in daily touch with NDI concerning the upcoming Panamanian election. In fact, when then–NDI executive vice president Ken Wollack began coordinating an observer mission to Panama, he just assumed that Carter would lead the team. "We realized that it would be impossible for Noriega to say no to Jimmy Carter," Wollack noted later. He reasoned that if the media made a predictable fuss over Carter representing NDI and Gerald Ford representing IRI as cochairmen of an international election-monitoring team, then an honest, democratic election could perhaps be held in Panama—after all, the whole world would be watching. Baker and Aronson had the same idea.[38]

In policy speeches and other public gestures, Baker made it clear that the Bush administration's approach to hemispheric affairs would include multilateral consultations, respect for the democratic process, and the ultimate goal of ousting dictators: Baker and Carter both realized that in only five weeks Panama would explode into the administration's first genuine foreign policy crisis—and a litmus test for the new partnership. But as Baker later recalled, "We were confident that in open elections Noriega would lose badly."[39]

In a major address in Atlanta, the secretary of state—with Jimmy Carter, the president who had given the canal back to the Panamanians, perched symbolically at his side—signaled a significant departure from the Reagan administration's strident foreign policies. Baker called for an unprecedented collaboration between the United States and Latin America, one that would make democracy flourish, markets open, and drug cartels vanish: "I believe Latin America's democratic leaders are reaching out to the United States to offer a new partnership built on mutual respect and shared responsibility," he proclaimed.[40]

In the end, Carter was only too glad to accept Baker and Atwood's offer to head NDI's delegation to Panama, for which the group had received a USAID grant to cover election-monitoring expenses.[41] From the Bush administration's perspective, having Carter and Ford cochair the international monitoring effort made for a perfect symbol of the new, bipartisan approach to Central America. Almost at once, however, Carter became the key voice of reason in Panama's surreal politics of intrigue, paranoia, and corruption. Baker, well aware of the ex-president's incurable penchant for overstepping his mandate, preemptively warned him "not to do anything beyond observing the elections."[42]

Carter, disgusted by Noriega's well-documented character defalcations— drug running, sexual sadism, murdering the Reverend Hector Gallegos— feared that the dictator would make a mockery of democracy. It was also commonly believed in the Bush administration that Noriega was preparing to commit massive fraud to install his handpicked presidential candidate, Carlos Duque, into a five-year term; also at stake were the posts of 2 vice presidents, 67 national legislators, and 505 local representatives. "During the past week, the situation in Panama changed gradually from being somewhat hopeful to nearly hopeless," Pastor informed Carter in an April 23 memorandum. "The Panamanian government has moved in small steps to manipulate the vote, censor opposition radio programs, and restrict outside observation of the election."[43]

At Pastor's urging, Carter wrote the Panamanian strongman a stiff letter on April 24 in a last-ditch effort to set him straight before the May 7 election. "One month ago," he wrote, "the delegation representing the Council of Freely Elected Heads of Government, which I chair, received assurances from senior government officials and the Panamanian Defense Forces (PDF) that the elections would be conducted fairly, that the results would be respected regardless of the outcome, and that international observers would be welcome." He launched into a litany of reported Noriega's abuses, including manipulation of the voting register, restrictions on the press, last-minute changes to the electoral code, partisan activities, and coercion of public employees. "The refusal of the Electoral Tribunal to investigate these complaints vigorously further undermines confidence in the electoral process by many Panamanians and friends of Panama outside the country," Carter complained.

Then he got to the heart of the matter: Noriega's systematic effort to limit international visitors to Panama during the election. Carter let Noriega know in no uncertain terms that he intended "to be a leader of the delegation," then took the dictator to task for denying a visa to a Venezuelan diplomat, making it difficult for other designated observers to obtain visas. "Unless there is clear and concrete evidence that efforts are being made to restore confidence in the process and to ensure free and fair elections, I must assume that the commitment of your government as expressed to me will not have been fulfilled," Carter continued. "This will have very serious consequences for U.S.-Panamanian relations and for the legacy of goodwill established by Omar Torrijos and me when we lay the foundation for a new relationship between our two countries. I am now writing to you privately and in confidence. I have no wish to embarrass you or the Panamanian government, but as I have been critical of the U.S. government for some of its policies toward Panama, I too will feel compelled to protest an unfair election in Panama."[44]

On April 26 Carter dispatched Robert Pastor to Panama City to hand-deliver the letter to Noriega, and to try to convince him to accept international observers. Carter's missive dealt a devastating blow to Noriega's plans. If Carter, who was widely popular in Panama, and in fact across Latin America, denounced the election before it even took place, Noriega would be isolated and vulnerable to possible military intervention.

Pastor's ninety-minute meeting with the general got off to a rocky start. Suspicious that he was being boxed in by Carter and the Bush administration, Noriega made it clear at the outset that he could never trust the Yankee colossus. Then he started reading. "This is a letter of threats and lies," Noriega sputtered to Pastor. "This letter only listens to the opposition. Carter did not write this; he couldn't have. If you wrote it for him, my opinion of you has gone down a hundred percent." When Pastor raised the nuts and bolts of observing the upcoming election—the need for visas, freedom of the press, release of political prisoners, security, and the like—Noriega brushed him off: "How can a great statesman like Jimmy Carter speak of visas? But if he wants a visa, we will give him one eternally." When Pastor reiterated the need for free elections and visas for fifty election monitors, Noriega brought up the $10 million that the Reagan-Bush CIA had purportedly funneled to the Panamanian opposition. "How is democracy possible with that?" he asked Pastor.

Noriega was clearly feeling the heat. He couldn't understand, he said, why the United States was attacking Panama, the least populated country in Central or Latin America, while ignoring drug lords in Paraguay, Roberto

D'Aubuisson's death squads in El Salvador, and rigged elections in Bolivia. In alarming detail, he told Pastor how the Republicans had transformed him, a faithful friend, to a reviled enemy.

When Pastor broached the notion of a Carter-Ford election-monitoring team, Noriega balked, exclaiming, "We will not accept any intervention in our affairs, and you wouldn't either. Bush would not have accepted a Panamanian delegation to count Dukakis's votes." After some contentious haggling, Noriega reluctantly agreed to allow Carter and ten election observers into Panama, calling Carter's request excessive: "Fifty!" he shouted. "Carter couldn't control all fifty!" Pastor shot back: "Both Carter and Ford controlled a nation of 240 million; fifty delegates shouldn't pose a large problem for them."

Noriega wouldn't listen; Ferdinand Marcos's catastrophic experience in the Philippines had taught him all he needed to know about election-monitoring gambits. Nevertheless, he did grant Carter and Ford the privilege of traveling unrestricted through Panama to observe the voting and its tabulation. But when Pastor arranged a press conference with Panamanian television and announced that Carter and Ford would lead a delegation to observe the election, the Panamanian military thugs quickly scrambled the reporters' transmissions and escorted Pastor to the airport tarmac. An outraged Noriega had a letter faxed to Carter, arriving in Atlanta before Pastor did, declaring him persona non grata—not permitted to return to Panama.[45]

After hearing Pastor's account of his ordeal, a miffed Carter called Noriega to insist that Pastor be permitted to return. He followed with a handwritten note: "Here are the names of ten observers. This is not an adequate number to meet our needs and is not in accordance with assurances given to me. I hope that you will permit a total of twenty to come to Panama. President Ford and I will come as planned and hope that we can meet with the Electoral Tribunal during the evening of May 5th."[46] To avoid further bickering with Noriega over numbers, he sent along a list of the twenty observers, making clear that *all* had to be accepted. It did the trick: Noriega issued visas for all twenty representatives, including experts who had monitored elections in Chile, Pakistan, Paraguay, and the Philippines. Pleased at Carter's breakthrough with Noriega, NDI began training a prominent church laity group in Panama to conduct an independent vote count. The count, to be based on the actual results at a statistically significant number of polling sites, would be able to project the actual election results if Noriega tried to cheat during the tabulation of results at the regional or national level.[47]

Meanwhile, the Bush administration was growing slightly apprehensive about Carter. "They were worried that Carter had such a stake in the Canal treaties that he might condone fraud," Pastor explained. The concern intensified when U.S. intelligence produced a number of reports claiming that Carter was perceived by the Noriega regime as a patsy, a tool they would use to their advantage by only allowing him to eyewitness polling stations that were not fixed. "In view of your impending trip, I thought you would be interested in the attached [CIA] cable," Scowcroft wrote Carter on May 4. "This is just one of several we have received, all in the same vein, e.g. Noriega planning to use your presence to accomplish his objectives."[48]

The Bush foreign policy team, in no mood to play footsie with Noriega, kept a watchful eye on Carter to make sure he had not been taken in by vague promises from an untrustworthy dictator.

As May 7 approached, in addition to the Carter delegation's report, the CIA and State Department assembled mounds of other intelligence indicating that Noriega—who was not running for office himself—was nevertheless staging "a campaign of systematic fraud," including manipulation of voter registration lists, police intimidation of the opposition, and ballot stuffing on behalf of the general's handpicked candidates. "From all reports, Noriega has already rigged the results and will steal the election massively," Baker warned President Bush in a May 5 memorandum. The secretary of state then recommended that the United States send "a clear, decisive signal" to Noriega that it would not be "business as usual . . . once he steals the election." Every two weeks White House press secretary Marlin Fitzwater issued statements from the president warning the Noriega regime not to thwart the democratic process.

Tensions were clearly high on May 5 as Carter arrived at the Omar Torrijos Airport in Panama via a U.S. Air Force plane provided by President Bush. "Ten years ago, Omar Torrijos and I worked to build a new partnership between Panama and the United States based on mutual respect and new Canal Treaties," Carter said at a press conference right after he got off the plane. "Torrijos told me then that the fulfillment of Panama's aspiration for national sovereignty was a first step toward better relations between our two countries. The second step, he said, would be the fulfillment of Panama's aspiration for democracy. I have come with the hope of seeing Torrijos's second promise fulfilled." Carter then proceeded to go on local radio and television shows, speaking in Georgia-accented Spanish to entreat eligible voters to cast ballots: "Come out and vote. I want to see you. I will be at the polling places. We're going to be all over the country. We're going to be everywhere. And we want to see you. Please come out and vote."[49]

A cocksure Noriega had met with Jimmy and Rosalynn Carter shortly after they arrived in Panama two days before the election. Isolated in his military headquarters, insulated by his sycophantic advisers, brimming with braggadocio, and with 11,000 troops at his disposal, Noriega assumed that his chosen presidential candidate would either win or come close enough to require only a little fraud to gain the office. To the Carters' disappointment, Noriega simply would not promise to accept the outcome of the election. "[He] was obviously incapable of considering that his personal choices for high office might not win," Carter recalled.[50]

CIA intelligence reports predicted low voter turnout in the wake of Noriega's intimidation tactics, but Carter was confident, buoyed by Univision TV network polls showing that two-thirds of voters preferred opposition leader Guillermo Endara to Noriega's puppet Duque. (Of course, Carter knew from the same Univision poll that one-half of the Panamanians interviewed believed that Noriega would not honor the results and allow Endara to assume the presidency.)[51] Thus the former U.S. president was anxious to reassure the Panamanian public that participating in the democratic process was safe. Carter believed it was essential that the Panamanian people—not the U.S. government—be responsible for Noriega's dethroning.

To the surprise of the U.S. government, voter turnout was quite high. A record 800,000 Panamanians—three-quarters of those eligible—went to the polls (50.1 percent of eligible Americans voted in the 1988 presidential election). In addition, 50,000 volunteers fanned across the *mesas* (polling stations) to conduct the election and make sure the votes were tabulated legally, methodically, and accurately.

By sundown the democratic, if humid, air turned thick with imminent violence, as if a spark could ignite a wildfire. Carter's usually sanguine Secret Service detail genuinely feared for their charge's life: gunfire echoed through the lush countryside, and electricity was turned off for long stretches everywhere Carter went, as he spent virtually all that night visiting polling stations and talking with voters.

Lay members of the Catholic Church—which represented 85 percent of the Panamanian people—had organized a "quick count" of final tallies from a representative sampling of polling places to get an early glimpse of the likely outcome. By early morning, the church had enough results to make clear that the opposition had won. (At 3:00 P.M. the day after the election, the church announced that its representatives had counted the votes from 115 polling places, and that it looked like Noriega's candidate had lost by a margin of three to one. "There is no doubt that the opposition candidates won more than 70 percent of the total votes cast," Carter wrote in his travel diary.)[52]

As the import of the "quick count" dawned on Noriega in the early-morning hours, the dictator ordered his troops to try to squash it, and a priest was murdered. In fact, despite the voluminous intelligence reports describing his plan to steal the election, Noriega had no plan, so he began a sweeping campaign of electoral shutdown. "After the votes were counted and tabulated, Noriega acted to destroy the official records," Carter maintained. "In some locations his officials simply absconded with [them]. In other places armed gunmen took the actas at gunpoint. Few actas were delivered to the counting places in Panama."[53]

Kenneth Wollack remembered accompanying Carter early in the morning to a polling station the PDF had shut down. Carter demanded to be let in immediately. A group of guards began arguing among themselves as to the wisdom of disobeying official orders, until their leader proclaimed, "He has guts. Let him in." The image of Jimmy Carter as a sort of democracy-building Lone Ranger was taking root in Panama. "When the democratic process was subverted," Wollack recalled, "Carter spoke unequivocally and with force." The *Washington Times* later reported Carter's brazenness in a rare tribute to the "courageous" ex-president.[54]

Surprised by the rapidity of the quick count, Noriega was paralyzed. The Bush administration had granted Carter permission to negotiate Noriega's acceptance of free election results in exchange for the administration's willingness to let him seek exile in Spain, which had no extradition treaty with the U.S., but the general would not respond to a requested meeting. "I negotiated with Noriega through an intermediary all that day," Carter said later, "and I tried to convince him [that he] could be a hero, that all his problems would be over. I had the authority to tell Noriega, 'You can stay on as Commander in Chief until September [1989], when the new president takes over. You will not be extradited to the United States. You can stay in Panama if you wish, after you step down as Commander in Chief.' " Noriega never responded. Carter was later told that Noriega had considered the deal "very carefully."[55]

The new leadership in Panama met with Carter and urged him to arrange a peaceful transition with Noriega. The Republican members of the delegation felt otherwise; nervous about Carter in general, they continued pressing him hard to publicly denounce the election as fraudulent. "Some Republican delegation members were afraid that Carter was so concerned with defusing the situation that he was providing Noriega with credibility," Aronson noted.[56] But the former president was smarter than that: he understood that to denounce the election as a fraud without concrete evidence was to deny the results, which clearly favored the opposition.

With tensions thus sky-high, Carter telephoned with Baker and Scowcroft back in Washington to explain the chaotic situation. "We gave Carter a little extra time to sort things out," Baker recalled.[57] Some members of the IRI delegation were going "absolutely bat shit," Pastor recalls, wanting Carter to denounce the election as invalid at once.[58] With pandemonium reigning, Pastor spent hours on the telephone trying to convince the general's aides to persuade Noriega to meet with Carter. Meanwhile Carter went over to the National Counting Center and discovered with his own eyes that the tally sheets were being replaced with obviously crude fabrications, and tabulation was slowed to a crawl. "Little effort had been made to conceal their counterfeit nature," Carter recalled.[59]

Then, in one of the most dramatic moments of his life, a stern-faced Carter mounted the center's elevated platform and denounced the ballot stuffing in shouted high-school Spanish: "Estan ustedes honestos o ladrones?" (Are you honest or are you thieves?) As a murmur rippled through the crowd, Carter called for Pastor to meet him at the election commission office. They arrived with the ex-president's dander at an all-time high. "You've got to throw this out," he exclaimed, brandishing a bogus tally sheet. "This can't go by." The ensuing sea of shrugs from the assembled bureaucrats incensed Carter further, and he stormed out of the office, seething to Pastor, "That's it. I'm going to give a press conference."

It was the day after the election, but Pastor wanted to give Noriega one last chance to negotiate an exit. "Why don't we call Noriega and tell him that if he doesn't see us by 6:00 P.M., you'll give a press conference at 7:00 P.M.?" Pastor offered. Carter snapped back, "No. Tell him if he doesn't see us by five o'clock we're going to give a press conference at six."[60] As Aronson summed up later, "When Carter saw for himself that Noriega was stealing, he blew the whistle and the international community knew it was true."[61]

Noriega again refused to see Carter. Even worse, when Pastor tried to organize the press conference, members of the Panamanian Defense Forces shoved him away with bayonets and locked up the conference hall where the international news media were assembled. Carter fumed in his suite at the Marriott, watching CNN reports on the violence in the streets below, where government troops and civilian-clad vigilantes called "dignity battalions" held sway. Suddenly he barked at Pastor to throw together an impromptu press conference in the hotel lobby. "Carter was in a zone of total command," Wollack remembered. "He blasted Noriega in language much stronger than any of us anticipated."[62]

By all accounts Carter's press conference was well executed; he exuded deep sorrow, high-minded morality, and unflappable will. "There was pandemonium—a huge crowd of hundreds of people and all the press in a very tight space with deafening noise," Pastor recalled. "Carter walked to one corner, stood back—bodyguards on each side—and silenced the room instantaneously. Then, for forty-five minutes, he totally dominated the place. There was absolute quiet during his initial presentation, and then, despite the fears and anxieties, even the questions were polite and deferential."[63] Infuriated by Noriega's megalomania, Carter proclaimed that "the government is taking the election by fraud. It's robbing the people of their legitimate rights. . . . I hope there will be a worldwide outcry against a dictator who stole this election from his own people." Carter also made it clear that Noriega's candidate had lost in a three-to-one landslide.[64] "While the remarks of other observers alleging fraud and abuse in the electoral process were important," Senator Dennis DeConcini wrote Carter, expressing the sentiments of many, "it was your statements that were crucial in convincing the American people and the world that the elections had been stolen from the Panamanian people by the Noriega regime."[65]

Noriega's intelligence chief was standing next to Pastor, and as Carter hammered away at Noriega's abuses, he hissed, "Bob, we want your asses out of here at 5:00 A.M. tomorrow morning, or you're going to be in big trouble." Pastor replied, "Well, I think we're ready to go. This sort of does it."[66] It had been a bravado performance by the ex-president; as the *New Republic* noted, Carter's "icily passionate denunciation of the fraud" carried "concomitantly greater weight" than anyone else's could, because he had held back from criticizing the election process until he had concrete proof of its corruption.[67]

That night Noriega sent his tanks into the streets, declared a state of emergency, and nullified the election. Carter and twenty other monitors flew to Washington, D.C., to meet with President Bush and his foreign policy team to discuss the postelection crisis in Panama.[68] Carter urged Bush not to use military intervention to oust Noriega, instead advocating multinational pressure on the discredited general to accept asylum, most likely in Spain. (He even wrote to Spanish president Felipe Gonzalez to urge him to get involved).[69] Carter also thought that the drug indictments against Noriega should be lifted in exchange for the discredited dictator's departure. And most important of all, he deemed it crucial that Bush once again reassure the Panamanian people that the United States would honor its commitment to the Canal Treaties. "To do otherwise," Carter told Bush, "is to play into Noriega's hands and turn the Panamanian people, the military forces, and all Latin American leaders against us."[70]

As chairman of the Council of Freely Elected Heads of Government, Carter had already contacted many Latin American leaders and asked them to publicly denounce the Panamanian election, which most did gladly. Bush privately thanked Carter for spearheading this U.S. effort, and later praised President Carlos Andrés Pérez of Venezuela for speaking out against the fraud. The Bush administration and Venezuela convened an emergency meeting of foreign ministers at the OAS in Washington to respond to the crisis in Panama. Carter also exhorted the leaders of every country in the Organization of American States—which was handicapped by its charter's nonintervention clause—to take concerted action against Noriega, which they were unprepared to do. "Carter's word was believed by all the OAS leaders," Baker said, "but we had to work hard to convince them to denounce Noriega by name."[71] Carter appealed by fax to eighteen hemispheric leaders to denounce Noriega. "Your voice is a powerful factor in Panama and other nations," he wrote President Pérez. "I hope you will use your influence persistently to bring democracy to the Panamanian people."[72] A week later the OAS passed a resolution denouncing human rights abuses in Panama and designated its secretary general and the foreign ministers of Ecuador, Guatemala, and Trinidad and Tobago as special representatives to meet with leaders from all of Panama's political forces.[73]

Upon leaving Bush's White House on May 10, Carter held a press conference to state his opposition to the option of increasing the number of U.S. troops in Panama, then backed up his ideas privately in a detailed confidential memo. "Any sort of military involvement down there would immediately alienate the Panamanian people, who respect their nation's sovereignty as we do," Carter pronounced. "And obviously unilateral action is much weaker than actions in concert with other democratic countries. I think these are more fruitful."[74]

Later that same day he sent Scowcroft a "personal and confidential" memo outlining eleven points to consider regarding the Panama crisis, number one being "Do not make any statement threatening armed intervention in the country." The memo went on to urge Scowcroft to allow the Latin American leaders to remain in the forefront in public statements while working behind the scenes with Spain and the Catholic Church to get Noriega out of Panama. "Through their pulpits, the priests can be a powerful force," Carter wrote Scowcroft. "Father [Theodore] Hesburgh can provide good advice on this." Finally, Carter proposed the novel idea of having various Latin American leaders lobby Fidel Castro and Daniel Ortega to pressure Noriega to flee Panama. "This would be a devastating blow to him," Carter advised.[75]

On May 11, the day after Carter sent his memorandum to Scowcroft, President Bush declared that "the days of the dictators are over." Then he announced the evacuation from Panama of American dependents not living on military bases; the recall of U.S. ambassador Arthur Davis; the reduction of the American embassy's staff by two-thirds; the dispatch of an army brigade to bolster the 12,000 U.S. Southern Command troops permanently stationed in Panama; and, most important, the deployment of U.S. troops to training exercises in regions outside the Canal area. "It was psychological warfare," Baker wrote in *The Politics of Diplomacy*. "We wanted Noriega to believe we were coming if he didn't leave first." More to the point, the Bush administration wanted the Panamanian Defense Forces to understand that if they were incapable of toppling Noriega themselves, the U.S. military might complete the coup, whether by covert operations or direct force.[76]

It was a clear break with Carter's strategy. "President Carter's influence on Panama was over when he declared the election fraudulent," Aronson explained. Carter's strategy after the election was to take the issue to the OAS and get a tough mediator to use collective hemispheric pressure on Noriega to step down. He succeeded in the first step through letters to the presidents of all the OAS members. Carlos Andrés Pérez took the lead, and the OAS passed a resolution, but it sent a minimally competent team to negotiate. Carter offered his mediation services, but there was no interest from either the OAS or the Bush administration.[77]

But Carter was the election's media hero. Publications from the conservative *Wall Street Journal* to the leftist *Nation* praised Carter's gutsy reaction to the rigged election. Peter Jennings reported on ABC's *World News Tonight* that Carter's "strong commitment to peace and justice" was awe-inspiring. The *New York Times* ran a picture of Carter and Baker together next to an article headlined "Carter Begins to Shed Negative Public Image." And the *New Republic* gushed that "Carter's return to Panama was a masterpiece of guerrilla diplomacy."[78]

One unfortunate consequence of Carter's role in the Panamanian election was a minor rupture in his warm relationship with Gerald Ford. While Carter was denouncing Noriega, Ford had slipped out of Panama on election day to attend a celebrity golf match in California. The media made hay of the contrast, heaping accolades on Carter and lambasting Ford. "The Ford former presidency, complete with Secret Service entourage, is available for paid speeches, ribbon-cuttings, and the endorsement of real-estate developments," wrote Richard Cohen in the *Washington Post*. "Ford sits on corporate boards and is available as a golf partner for wealthy groupies."[79] An embarrassed Ford still liked Carter as a friend but felt his fellow ex-president was acting too big for his britches, constantly foisting his services on the Bush White House as though he were still in office.[80]

Carter continued to argue against military intervention in Panama, but turned his attention elsewhere: the ongoing civil war in Ethiopia, and the upcoming February 1990 Nicaraguan elections. One thing was certain: Carter was back as a major player on the world stage. A shingle was in essence hung in front of the One Copenhill headquarters: "We Monitor

Elections." Although virtually no one grasped what an acronym organizations like NDI, IRI, and NED could do to foster democracy, everyone understood that humanist Jimmy Carter was an honest observer for hire. Just days after the Panamanian presidential contest, Carter began getting requests from other Third World leaders to monitor elections in their countries; from that point on, poll watching became a Carter Center specialty.

A number of important elections intrigued Carter, but none as much as the one in Nicaragua. He dispatched Robert Pastor to Managua to wrangle invitations from the Sandinista government, the Nicaraguan Electoral Council, and the United Nicaraguan Opposition to monitor the February 1990 elections.[81] In the meantime, Carter turned his immediate attention to the three-decades-long civil war in Ethiopia.

Ever since the 1985 Geneva Conference on hunger, where Carter had formed a partnership with Ryoichi Sasakawa, he had been obsessed with the desperate plight of Ethiopia. A great fan of statistics, Carter was staggered by one: more than a half million people had died in Ethiopia since 1974 as a result of widespread famine and civil war. Even more startling was the fact that because the United Nations had designated the Ethiopian conflict a civil war, its charter prohibited the world organization from intervening. In other words, this was a perfect showplace for track-two diplomacy.[82]

His choice of the Ethiopian-Eritrean civil war, bewildering to such friends as Zbigniew Brzezinski and Edmund Muskie, was vintage Carter: it was the most intractable problem. Ethiopia, bordered on the west by Sudan, on the south by Kenya, and to the east by Somalia and Djibouti, was the world's poorest country, and thus least able to afford a civil war: per capita income was $120 a year, four out of five children did not attend school, and 94 percent of the population lacked clean drinking water. Hampered by a substantial trade deficit, largely attributable to its internal disorder, Ethiopia was incapable of exporting much of anything except refugees, misery, and animal skins. Thanks to a donation from the government of Norway to finance an Eritrean-Ethiopian summit, however, Jimmy Carter was ready to micromanage everything from breakfast menus to seating arrangements in order to bring peace to the Horn of Africa.[83]

On August 17, with great media fanfare, he announced that starting September 7, the Carter Center would mediate an unconditional peace summit in Atlanta, bringing representatives from the People's Democratic Republic of Ethiopia and the rebel Eritrean People's Liberation Front (EPLF). The Eritreans had been struggling for independence from Ethiopia since 1962, claiming that their region in the northern part of the country, which had been an independent nation before Italy colonized it in 1890, had been illegally federated with Ethiopia by a 1950 United Nations resolution. Now the time was right, Carter believed, to solve the conflict; the already overextended Soviet Union under Mikhail Gorbachev's progressive leadership was no longer interested in the region. "It's improper for a great nation like the United States to say that we aren't going to help those Ethiopian people because their leaders profess to be Marxist-Leninists," Carter maintained.[84]

He had arranged for the Eritrean-Ethiopian peace talks to take place in Atlanta after a series of three trips to Africa between April and July. During one visit on behalf of the United Nations and the International Committee of the Red Cross to investigate food distributors, Carter stayed in Haile Selassie's decrepit old palace, where he got acquainted with Ethiopia's Marxist president Mengistu Haile Mariam. A dictator and international pariah, Mengistu listened intently to Carter's ideas for resolving the conflict and soon agreed to make a real effort at peace talks with Eritrean rebel leader Isaias Afwerki. Both African leaders agreed to send four high-ranking officials to Atlanta to negotiate. As Eritrean Central Committee member Hagos Ghebrehiwat explained, Carter's initiative was embraced by the EPLF because "we were convinced of his concern for peace and human rights." As usual, Carter the human rights activist extracted a "personal favor" from Mengistu: the release of 200 Somalian prisoners of war who had been jailed for ten years.[85]

Carter was not the first outside party to try to quell the bloodletting in Ethiopia. In 1978, when he was president, a series of peace talks between the Ethiopian government and the EPLF had been held in East Germany, without success. Various other mediation attempts were made in Europe between 1982 and 1985, also to no avail. Carter blamed these failures on the fact that the talks began with preconditions and without third-party observers. This time Carter announced the talks with CNN cameras running, in an effort to publicly intimidate both sides into putting forth "their most attractive and responsible proposals and demonstrat[ing] a degree of good faith to prevent failure."[86]

The talks got off to a good start when Eritrean leader Isaias Afwerki hinted that his Eritrean rebels, who controlled much of the area bordering on the Red Sea, would be willing to negotiate access to the coast with the otherwise landlocked Ethiopians. Carter mediated the rest of the talks with great skill, getting the Ethiopian government and the EPLF to accept ten of the thirteen procedural items on the agenda. In addition, both sides agreed on matters such as the official language of the talks, procedural rules, and the agenda for further talks slated to be held in Kenya in November. "During the constant discussion, I used my laptop computer to record the points as we discussed them," Carter recalled. "The words in every sentence were debated, and I would print out a new version every time it seemed we reached an agreement."[87] Throughout the laborious sessions, Carter constantly urged both delegations to declare a cease-fire, exchange prisoners, and allow delivery of relief supplies to drought-ravaged areas. Despite fierce tensions, nobody walked out of the Atlanta talks. "There is no doubt they have negotiated in good faith," Carter said. "There has been an amazingly friendly mood."[88]

Rosalynn Carter remembered one lovely evening when the Carter Center hosted a patio dinner for the Eritrean and Ethiopian "enemies," the stars twinkling overhead and Atlanta's impressive skyline glittering in the distance. Everything was fine until an airplane flew overhead, disrupting the small talk and laughter. "Suddenly, one of the Eritrean men was under the table," Rosalynn Carter said. He quickly dusted himself, she added, and "said, 'Please excuse me, but in my country when an airplane flies over, it drops bombs.' It was shocking, and I realized how far away and impersonal war in Africa is to me, to us."[89]

When Thanksgiving rolled around, most Washington policy makers headed home to their families for the traditional feast; Jimmy and Rosalynn Carter brought the Eritrean-Ethiopian talks from Georgia to Kenya, serving turkey and gourd pie for the members of both delegations in Nairobi, all holding hands for Christian prayers, and teaching country gospel songs. (A few years later, while trying to solve the Rwanda-Burundi refugee problem, the Carters spent Thanksgiving in a tent deep in the back country of Uganda, cooking their meal over a can of Sterno.)

The sheer scope of Carter's quest for peace caused many in the Bush administration to scratch their heads, half in admiration but half in concern over the ex-president's zeal. On another afternoon Carter left the talks to fly to Managua to negotiate the return of 30,000 Nicaraguan Miskito Indians living in Honduras who had been fighting the Sandinista government since 1981. Carter worked out an agreement whereby the Miskito leader, Brooklyn Rivera, would be allowed to return to his Nicaraguan homeland if he agreed to halt his guerrillas' activities against the Sandinistas and promised to recognize the results of the upcoming February 1990 election.[90] To Carter's admirers he was a blue-blazered reincarnation of Mahatma Gandhi; to his detractors he was Jimmy Swaggart with an overstamped passport. In any case, one thing was certain: Carter, whose postpresidency had become a hymn to the Baptist missionary ethos, was revered wherever fields were fallow, disease rampant, and democracy stunted.[91]

All of Africa was impressed with Carter's Christian commitment and titanic personal stamina, which left Secret Service agents dropping from heat exhaustion on the streets of Nairobi when they tried to keep up with the sixty-six-year-old's daily five-mile runs. During his stay in Africa that November, Carter not only continued trying to end the Ethiopian civil war, over which tensions were so high that he often had to meet with each side separately, but also presided over talks between Sudan and the rebels of the Sudanese People's Liberation Front.[92] Carter was especially anxious to tackle the guinea worm problem in Sudan. John Lennon may have sung "Give Peace a Chance," but Jimmy Carter had upped the ante to make "Peace Now." As Zambian president Kenneth Kaunda noted, speaking for many, Carter was "not only a great person but a great servant of God and man."[93]

Ultimately, although Carter brokered temporary cease-fires in both Ethiopia and Sudan, he failed to achieve the lasting peace he sought in either nation. The war in Ethiopia ended in 1991, but on the battlefield instead of the peace table. "The conflicting goals, mutual distrust, and changing political and military situations in Ethiopia prevented a great ending to the talks we sponsored," Carter admitted in *Talking Peace*. "Yet we still helped to achieve a cease-fire in the country for over a year—and let the different groups begin to understand and acknowledge one another, a crucial step for the eventual democratization of the country." In Sudan his efforts continued into the late 1990s.[94]

Yet when it came to the main foreign policy issues of 1989, Carter was very much a sideline player. When on November 9 the Berlin Wall came down and East Germany opened its borders with West Germany, Carter was mediating the Eritrean-Ethiopian war. Meanwhile, a wave of democracy was sweeping the world: in a two-month span, the Communist party relinquished its stranglehold on East Germany and the Soviet Republic of Lithuania; Romania's Communist dictator, Nicolae Ceauşescu, was executed; playwright Vaclav Havel, leader of the anti-Communist underground, was elected president of Czechoslovakia; Poland's Communist party disbanded; and reformer Dimitur Popov took the helm from corrupt Communist leader Todor Zhivkov and became prime minister of Bulgaria. Democracy even held sway in Latin America, as Brazil held its first direct presidential election in thirty years and Chile drummed its military dictator, Augusto Pinochet, from power. Amid all this upheaval Carter was left only to comment, always praising Gorbachev ("the greatest leader in the world") and gently criticizing Bush ("he should be doing more" or "he doesn't match what Gorbachev is doing").[95]

The Bush administration, which Carter had criticized for inactive diplomacy when the Berlin Wall came crashing down (he favored something like a massive Marshall Plan loan program to Eastern Europe) had been just as roundly pilloried by the Republican right wing for missing an opportunity to help oust Noriega from power in a failed October coup attempt. Critics from the *Washington Post* to Republican House Intelligence Committee chairman Henry Hyde chastised the administration for its timidity and indecision. North Carolina Republican senator Jesse Helms lambasted Bush and his men for acting like "a bunch of Keystone Kops, bumping into each other."[96] Carter, on the other hand, praised Bush publicly for his "presidential restraint."[97]

Not surprisingly, having stared down the gringos and survived a coup attempt, Noriega had actually strengthened his grip on Panama and felt free to jail or torture anyone who had supported the aborted coup. He gladly took on the role of a modern Pancho Villa, defying the Yanquis at every turn. But with polls showing that 64 percent of the American public regarded drugs as the nation's number-one problem, Noriega didn't look to remain "Maximum Leader" for long.[98] His blatant anti-Americanism came into full view on December 15 in an inflammatory speech before Panama's puppet National Assembly, where Noriega bragged that "we will sit along the banks of the canal to watch the dead bodies of our enemies pass by." Spurred on by the general's jingoistic posturing, the assembly declared that a state of war existed with the United States.[99]

As could be expected, the day after Noriega's anti-American diatribe, the situation in Panama turned grimmer. All year long the PDF had been harassing U.S. soldiers in petty incidents ranging from theft to assault— occurrences that were routinely brushed aside. This time, however, with tensions running high, members of the PDF opened fire on a car carrying four American military officers after it failed to stop at a roadblock outside PDF headquarters in Chorrillo. A U.S. Marine lieutenant was killed, a second soldier injured, and a third, who had witnessed the incident, was detained and beaten, and his wife harassed by PDF troops.[100]

The murder of a U.S. soldier in Panama caused, as Pastor put it, "Bush to cross his Rubicon."[101] At an emergency White House meeting on December 17, Bush polled his foreign policy advisers one by one; all agreed that the United States had no choice but to invade Panama. Baker took the hardest line: "Let's take them up on their declaration of war. We shouldn't wait."[102] For the first time since Reagan's invasion of Grenada in 1983, the United States was going to war, and in the largest deployment of troops since Vietnam and the first unilateral military intervention in Latin America in over sixty years.

In the forty-eight hours between the emergency White House meeting and the launch of Operation Just Cause on December 20, 10,000 U.S.

troops backed by gunships and fighter-bombers flew into Panama to rendezvous with the 13,000 soldiers already stationed at the American bases around the canal. The U.S. Air Force dropped 422 bombs on Panama in thirteen hours, destroying the PDF by severing its principal lines of communication. The administration had not alerted Carter to Operation Just Cause, but Baker met with the ex-president the following day in Washington to discuss both Nicaragua and Panama. Carter's first reaction was to approve the invasion, but he soon turned strongly against it.[103]

A disoriented Noriega, with explosives everywhere, was left to dart about Panama City in a Hyundai, scampering to safety from a Dairy Queen to a schoolhouse to a hospital. "It was like a nightmare—like falling into a swimming pool and when you try to reach for the safety of a wall or touch bottom, you suddenly realize that walls and bottom had fallen away," Noriega wrote in his memoirs. "I couldn't grasp anything or stop my free fall. All I could see was an endless limitless ocean and thousands of weapons and men hoping to find me in their sights." Eventually Noriega escaped the U.S. manhunt by seeking refuge in the residence of Monsignor Sebastian Laboa, the papal nuncio to Panama.[104]

The Vatican was in a quandary. For the next two weeks American troops circled the papal nunciature, blaring Guns 'N Roses' "Eye of Destruction" and other noisy rock songs from giant speakers in a peculiar attempt to unnerve Noriega through questionable art. "It was a low moment in U.S. Army history," Scowcroft later admitted. "Blasting rock music was silly, childish, reproachable, undignified."[105] But in some strange, postmodern way, it worked. CNN broadcast the U.S. vs. Noriega showdown continuously as Panama's "Maximum Leader" was transformed into "Hunted Fugitive," a corrupt drug dealer who had thwarted the will of the Panamanian people and was now hiding in a papal basement. Hunkered down in a dirty T-shirt, baggy Bermuda shorts, and a baseball cap pulled low over his face while he was force-fed American rock and roll, Noriega had become an international joke overnight.

Although the OAS had passed a resolution on December 22 urging the withdrawal of U.S. troops, a CBS News poll taken in Panama in early January found that 92 percent of Panamanian adults approved of the American invasion. On January 3 Noriega, afraid of being lynched, walked out of the nunciature and surrendered to American forces. He was placed on a helicopter to Howard Air Force Base and delivered into the custody of the U.S. Drug Enforcement Agency. "We made sure Carter didn't interfere," Scowcroft put it.[106]

Carter, who now strongly opposed the use of military force, parted company with the Bush administration's bombing of Panama. "I basically don't approve of the military invasion of Panama and other countries just to depose a leader, no matter how disreputable a criminal that person is," Carter told the *Washington Post*. Like most Latin American leaders, the former U.S. president regarded the invasion as an unjustifiable violation of international law and Panamanian sovereignty. Elaborating on his opposition, particularly after reports came in of Panamanian citizens killed or wounded during the invasion, Carter bemoaned that the intervention was "damaging to our strongest supporters in Panama." He was on the side of the UN General Assembly, which called the invasion a "flagrant violation of international law," and of the OAS, which "deeply deplored" the intervention.[107] "There was very much I liked about Bush," Carter later noted, "but his belief that democracy comes through bombs instead of food and medicine and the ballot box was not one of them."[108]

In stark contrast, the American people largely approved of the Bush administration's invasion of Panama, with 74 percent of those polled calling it justified. In fact, the Panamanian invasion had liberated Bush from his predecessor's shadow and allowed him to shed his image as a "wimp" once and for all. Whether intervention in Panama was morally justified could be debated, but it worked for Bush: his overall approval rating skyrocketed to 76 percent. The success also gave Bush's foreign policy team a sense of cohesion and purpose—a post-cold-war military confidence that would surface again thirteen months later in the Persian Gulf War.

Three years later Panama did turn to the ballot box and Jimmy Carter once again. A bout of preelection fear in Panama City jarred the Tribunal Electoral and President Guillermo Endara to ask Carter on November 16, 1993, to quickly put together a team of high-profile election monitors to observe their May 8 election.[109] Carter accepted the job, contacting Jim Wright, the ex–House Speaker who had done so much to promote bipartisan cooperation in Central America but had been forced out of Congress on ethics charges, to join him. A public opinion poll published in *La Prensa* on April 15, 1994, captured the mood: 42.6 percent of the population believed there would be widespread violence during the election process. "Five years ago, we left Panama distressed that an opportunity for peaceful, democratic change was aborted," Carter, with Rosalynn at his side, stated in May as he arrived in Panama City. "Today we return confident that the Panamanian people will have the chance that was denied them by General Manuel Noriega—to fulfill the democratic right to choose their next leaders."[110]

As part of Carter's unfinished presidential agenda, he knew that to ensure the successful implementation of the Canal Treaties, the next Panamanian president, to be elected in two days, had to be the leader in office on December 31, 1999, when the U.S. relinquished control. Carter had a personal stake in making sure whoever won—either the forty-eight-year-old Ernesto Pérez Balladares, an American-educated banker who had overcome the stigma of being an associate of Noriega by associating with Torrijos; or Ruben Blades, the salsa singer and Hollywood star who had only recently returned to head the Papa Egoro (Mother Earth) party; or Mireya Moscoso of the ruling Arnulifista party, the widow of Arnulfo Arias de la Madrid, a popular president who was elected three times and thrown out all three times by coups—would uphold the democratic process in Panama. If democracy failed in 1994, Panama would be less able to fulfill its 1999 treaty obligations.

Carter, Wright, and Hollywood director Oliver Stone were just 3 of 1,200 international and Panamanian observers who declared the process fair. Pérez Balladares, nicknamed "Toro" ("Bull") for his beefy build, was the victor, with 33.2 percent of the vote. In addition, with heavy voter turnout 1.4 million Panamanians chose 2 vice presidents, 71 representatives, 67 mayors, 511 magistrates, and 24 local council members. "Aware that both the process and the result of voting in Panama can color the countdown to 2000, President Carter himself led an election observer mission," the *Washington Post* noted. "Despite widespread fears of disruption, the process was peaceful and fair."[111]

On the morning after the smooth election, Carter met with Pérez Balladares to congratulate him. Those close to Carter noticed that his adrenaline was down; since the election was fraud-free, his role was more that of a gentleman figurehead than a political mediator. As he prepared to fly home, mission accomplished, he paused for a moment, his eyes misty, and offered the press and dignitaries present a fitting departure statement: "Panama has a special place in my and Rosalynn's hearts, and we are confident that all Panamanians will continue to work to strengthen democracy in the future." Then, as he headed for the tarmac, a reporter shouted at him, "Will you come back to Panama?" Carter smiled his gentle smile and replied, "Yeah, in 1999."[112]

SIXTEEN

DEMOCRACY COMES TO NICARAGUA

◦○◦

A short eight weeks after the May 1989 election in Panama, Jimmy Carter received a written invitation from President Daniel Ortega of Nicaragua to attend the tenth anniversary of the Sandinista revolution. "I deeply regret that I cannot attend," Carter replied. But he added, "I remain deeply interested in developments in Nicaragua and am committed to trying to improve the relationship between our two countries,"[1] and sent Robert Pastor as his surrogate. The Carter Center wanted to get a head start on monitoring Nicaragua's February 25, 1990, elections, and this was an ideal opportunity to network with the Sandinista government who could facilitate it.[2] Ortega had already invited the OAS and the UN to monitor the upcoming election—the time had come to invite Jimmy Carter.[3] "Nicaragua had become the most domestically divisive American foreign policy issue since Vietnam," Carter maintained. "I wanted to end the killing, and a democratic election was the way."[4]

Pastor was well aware he could be jeopardizing his own diplomatic career just by being in Nicaragua for the Sandinistas' anniversary celebration. Treated as an honored guest on July 19, Pastor was seated in the VIP box behind the podium—along with such offbeat characters as Beach Boy Brian Wilson, whose legs had been run over by a train as he was protesting the Contras, an unshaven Iranian "student leader," and a member of Fidel Castro's cabinet—to listen to President Ortega deliver a rousing diatribe against the United States. "I worked overtime trying not to have my face shown on television," Pastor said later, worried about what the Republican right would say if they saw him consorting with a bunch of international pariahs and banana revolutionaries. "My goal was to try to elicit invitations to monitor the electoral process so that we would start early, avoid the mistakes made in Panama, and mediate the first election in Nicaragua's history that all the parties would accept."[5]

Determined not to repeat the mistakes he made with Noriega, Carter set out to strengthen his personal relationships with Daniel and Defense Minister Humberto Ortega during the six months remaining before the Nicaraguan election. One lesson from Panama was that it was a mistake for the Carter Center delegation to arrive on election eve. If Carter had gotten to know Noriega long enough in advance to establish a rapport of mutual trust with him, he might have persuaded the recalcitrant general to accept the devastating results of the Panamanian election.

Carter's experience with Noriega proved valuable in another way as well: it made him—along with the UN and OAS—a logical choice to monitor the Nicaraguan election. "Your defense of Noriega in the OAS is interpreted by Americans to mean that you want to commit the same kind of fraud that he did," Pastor remembered telling Ortega, the only leader in the hemisphere defending Noriega at the time. "The only way that you can prove to the world that you're sincerely interested in a free election is to invite the person who denounced the electoral fraud in Panama—Jimmy Carter."[6] It was a clever ploy, and it opened the door for Carter. In early August, less than two weeks after Pastor's return, the Carter Center received three separate invitations to monitor the upcoming election in Nicaragua: from Daniel Ortega for the Sandinista government, from Violeta Barrios de Chamorro of the United Nicaraguan Opposition (UNO), and from the Nicaraguan Electoral Council. "We encourage you to come to Nicaragua as many times as you can during the electoral process, to observe all aspects of the process, and to meet with the members of the Supreme Electoral Council, the political parties and the government," Ortega wrote Carter. "You will have unrestricted access to all aspects of the process."[7]

Carter accepted all three invitations. He would assemble a delegation of more than fifty "meticulously impartial" observers to monitor the election, and they would be encouraged to make at least one preelection visit to Nicaragua, which they all did. In addition, Carter said, the Council of Freely Elected Heads of Government would station three full-time staffers in Nicaragua to monitor the six-month campaign.[8] Carter had moved swiftly from the sidelines to center stage of the Nicaraguan civil war, an objective he had been working toward since he and the Ortegas had bounced around the unpaved back streets of Managua in a dusty jeep in early 1986. "Free and fair elections were Nicaragua's best hope for peace," Carter said later. "And I thought that Daniel Ortega probably had the best chance of winning."[9]

The joy at the Carter Center over being invited to monitor the Nicaraguan election was not shared by all Republicans. The far right regarded Carter's ridiculous romanticizing of Ortega as proof that he was hellbent on legitimizing the Sandinistas; the Bush administration worried that the ex-president was too anti-Contra to be fully trusted; and even Gerald Ford felt that his friend Jimmy Carter was "pushing himself" on Bush too much, and declined to serve as comediator of the highly sensitive election.[10] Sensitive to appearances, Carter wanted to assure his critics that he was not for the Sandinistas but for the democratic process. Thus, in dire need of a respected Republican to cohead the bipartisan delegation, Carter took Baker's advice and asked former Washington State governor and senator Dan Evans, a moderate internationalist, to participate in the historic election.[11]

On September 14 a team of experts from the Carter Center's Council of Freely Elected Heads of Government swept into Nicaragua to start negotiating the rules of the democratic game—to be acceptable to both parties. Democracy requires the art of compromise and accepting that the adversary is not an enemy but a proponent of a view that may just have some validity to it. This was more than one could reasonably expect in Nicaragua after a decade of civil war, but it was possible to get both sides to accept the basic elements of a democratic process. The majority Democratic Congress soon appropriated operational funds for the Carter Center to the tune of $500,000. The Bush administration accepted the earmarking. A Carter Center office was established in Managua.[12]

The center's job during the campaign would be to listen to both sides and mediate problems so that the election would be fair. Carter toured the country three times before the election; on his first trip on September 16, he and former Argentine president Raul Alfonsin visited Managua and Nicaragua's Atlantic coast to assess preparations for the election and facilitate the Miskito Indians' reentry into the political process.[13] Carter "operated like a political mechanic who by sheer will kept the government and the opposition parties—the entire Democratic process—on track," Alfonsin said of Carter's determination that the elections be fair and inclusive.[14] That autumn most outside polls indicated a sizable Sandinista lead, but Costa Rican polling, available to the administration, showed Chamorro as the frontrunner. Bush was taking the Sandinistas seriously, realizing they might very well become Nicaragua's legitimate government.[15]

Carter tried to foster better relations between the Bush administration

and the Sandinista leadership in hope that Washington would formally recognize their government before the election, contacting the State Department to laud Ortega's welcome release of all political prisoners in Nicaragua.
Bernie Aronson, who was convinced that UNO would win a fair and free
election, also believed that the Sandinistas would have an incentive to play
by the rules if the Bush administration made it clear that the United States
would fully recognize whoever won in the end. After all, this was the Sandinistas' one shot at legitimacy. On September 22 Carter wrote Ortega that
his conversation with Aronson had indicated that President Bush was ready
to begin "a step-by-step increase in embassy personnel"—a prelude to formal
recognition.[16]

Throughout October the Carter Center, in conjunction with the UN,
NDI, and OAS, spearheaded a mass voter registration drive in Nicaragua,
the likes of which hadn't been seen since the Freedom Summer of 1964 in
Mississippi. An astounding 1.75 million Nicaraguans registered—a full 89
percent of the nation's estimated voting-age population of 1.9 million. During the campaign former Democratic governors Bruce Babbitt of Arizona
and Mike O'Callaghan of Nevada joined the Carter Center team to monitor
firsthand fifty-nine voter registration sites in three regions of Nicaragua,
finding no irregularities. The governors did, however, express strong concerns about the Sandinistas' monopolized control over campaigning on television and radio.[17]

The Sandinistas realized that they had to win over American and world
opinion as well as that of the U.S. Congress in order to end the economically
devastating Contra war, lift the U.S. embargo, and unlock aid from Western
Europe. As a stunned Ortega watched communism collapse across Eastern
Europe, he went so far as to accept major revisions to his country's electoral
laws that the opposition had been demanding to eliminate some of the advantages of incumbency. Ortega was so desperate for the election to be seen
as legitimate that he permitted the Bush administration to provide generous
"overt" financial support to the UNO opposition. At the same time he promised to make a major campaign issue of any illegal covert aid funneled to
Nicaragua via the CIA, something the Bush administration had promised
Congress it would not do in the Bipartisan Accord.[18]

That September Carter garnered renewed commitments from the Bush
administration as well as the House and Senate intelligence committees that
there would continue to be no covert aid to the UNO, and a reassured Ortega, who would not believe Bush, took Carter's word for it. On October 21
President Bush signed into law House Resolution 3385, a bill to provide $9
million to the get-out-the-vote effort.[19] "I personally think that the $9 million

is excessive," Carter told Ortega. "I would like to have seen a smaller figure. But I can, I think, report to you accurately that the money will go into Nicaragua in a way that is compatible with Nicaraguan laws."[20]

UNO had been created on September 2, 1989, when fourteen disparate political groups in Nicaragua agreed, with urging from the Bush administration, to unify behind the candidacies of Violeta Barrios de Chamorro for president and Virgilio Godoy, leader of the Independent Liberal party, for vice president. Chamorro—by most standards a true democrat—was a symbolic choice for UNO: she was the widow of Pedro Joaquín Chamorro, the anti-Somoza newspaper publisher whose assassination in January 1978 had triggered the rebellion that led to the Sandinista revolution. She had served on the Sandinistas' first junta but had resigned as soon as the leadership took a Marxist-Leninist bent. "Mrs. Chamorro was a logical choice to be president because of her personal popularity, the symbolism and importance of the Chamorro family (four members had been president of Nicaragua), and, most importantly, because she did not belong to any party," Pastor wrote later.[21] Baker put it more succinctly: "We persuaded the fractured opposition to unite behind a single opposition candidate."[22]

That November, as the voter registration period ended, precampaign party rallies sprang up in earnest. Across the nation major issues were debated in plazas and town halls: access to the media, demobilization of the Contras, intimidation of opposition supporters, the dangers of abusive rhetoric, and a dozen other topics. On November 14 Carter held a day-long seminar on the Nicaraguan election in Atlanta, where the featured event was a debate between UNO candidate Alfredo César and Alejandro Bendana, secretary general of the Nicaraguan Foreign Ministry and a Harvard Ph.D. Fireworks erupted when Carter denounced the Sandinista government for trying to smear César—who had fought against Somoza and served in the Sandinista government as president of the Central Bank before breaking ranks in 1982—by accusing him of pro-Contra war crimes. "I've been quite concerned that *Barricada*, the official newspaper of the Sandinista government, has apparently published a totally fraudulent letter ostensibly written by Alfredo César," Carter said at the Atlanta symposium. "He informed the news media, including *Barricada*, that this was a false document. They have persisted in trying to besmirch his character and the UNO [by associating him] with the *contra* military activity in a completely illegitimate fashion."[23] After the *New York Times* reported Carter's outburst, Daniel Ortega quickly telephoned the Carter Center to assure the ex-president that "corrective action" was being taken to stop the assault on César's reputation in *Barricada*.[24]

In truth, the smear was just the Sandinistas' first salvo in a negative campaign aimed at associating UNO with both the Contras and Somoza's hated National Guard. Ortega believed his actions were justified: since Ronald Reagan's inauguration the United States had given the Contras more than $321 million in direct aid, at least $140 million of which had gone toward military equipment to kill other Nicaraguans. Ortega was not going to let UNO off the hook too easily, although Chamorro had publicly opposed military aid.[25] Ortega kept up his anti-CIA rhetoric but was diligent in his efforts to resolve any concerns Carter raised, so confident was he of winning. Even when Ortega learned that the United States and Honduras were openly violating the 1987 Esquipulas agreement by refusing to disarm the Contras and dismantle their bases, he shrugged it off in favor of gambling on the ballot box and Jimmy Carter's fairness to legitimize his Sandinistas' rule.[26]

Throughout the campaign Carter was plagued with UNO complaints that the Sandinistas were using dirty tricks to gain an electoral edge, including conscription of UNO activists into the military, detention of political prisoners, exclusion of Miskito Indian leaders, intimidation of UNO supporters trying to register, and state-sponsored violence at UNO rallies— complaints that took long hours to mediate. The principal Sandinista advantage—state control and use of public resources to campaign, from army trucks to state employees—continued until election day.[27] As the campaign wore on, some UNO members griped that Carter was hardly being impartial, constantly defending Ortega to the international press corps. On November 13, meanwhile, Ortega wrote Carter directly to complain about the lack of progress on the Contra demobilization plan. Carter, in an unusual move, responded publicly, asking UNO leaders to condemn the Contras. Chamorro, however, realized that thousands of campesinos and landowners in northern and central Nicaragua supported the Contras, and wisely refused. In fact, Chamorro understood what Carter did not: that one of the keys to making the Central American Bipartisan Accord work was that the United States kept the Contra army clothed and armed. One UNO official publicly chastised Carter, claiming that the ex-president must "share the guilt" for letting the Marxist-Leninist Sandinistas assume power while he was in the White House. That same official asked Carter to take up UNO's grievances with the Sandinistas, snidely remarking that "Ortega listens to you. He is a good friend of yours." Carter smiled and quickly shot back, "I am a friend of all Nicaraguans."[28]

Carter understood how essential it was to maintain the confidence and trust of all sides. Almost daily he would tell Ortega not to let his supporters intimidate UNO and Chamorro and to calm down about supposed Sandinista abuses and concentrate on "concrete proof, not rumors." The fragile campaign almost collapsed on December 10 after an innocent bystander was killed in a riot at a UNO rally in Masatepe. "We needed to figure out a way to keep political demonstrations from leading to violence," Carter recalled later of his thoughts when UNO subsequently threatened to quit the election. "After consulting with party leaders from both sides, we drafted an agreement that spelled out how schedules could be designed so that two rallies would never take place at the same time, what security inspections would be made ahead of time, and how close Sandinista police could come to the crowd." Carter put this proposal together on his computer and added another point: that outside election observers would be present at all major campaign rallies. It was the role Carter was best at, particularly where it involved going back and forth between polarized adversaries in search of common ground, and, eventually, national reconciliation. In a war-torn nation seething with mistrust, Jimmy Carter's was the voice of honest reason.[29]

After the trip to Nicaragua Carter sustained a jolt when he and President Carlos Andrés Pérez of Venezuela dropped in on Oscar Arias, Nobel laureate and president of Costa Rica, at his home in Rohrmoser for a four-hour discussion of the Nicaraguan election process. Carter greatly admired Arias's bold peace plan and saw him as a role model for global statesmanship. "I am proud of your good work," Carter had written his colleague on October 16, 1987, "and had predicted that you would win the Nobel Peace Prize for your initiative."[30] So it came as a shock to the former U.S. president when—after he had told the press that "all the evidence indicates that the procedure for the conduct of the elections is very good"—Arias broke ranks with him.

"We Costa Ricans, who have very elevated standards about free elections, are not satisfied with what is happening in Nicaragua," Arias stated bluntly. Worse still, he issued an official Costa Rican report on the Nicaraguan elections—written in part by former Supreme Elections Tribunal president Alfonso Guzman—that criticized the "Carter Group observers" in Managua for their patronizing attitude and attempts to prevent the Costa Ricans from conducting interviews with voters. When asked if he shared either Arias's opinion or that of the Costa Rican report, Carter answered, "No."[31]

By election day Nicaragua, a country the size of Iowa, teemed with 2,578 accredited foreign observers from 278 different organizations plus 1,500-odd foreign correspondents, making it the most directly monitored election in world history. The OAS alone fielded 435 observers to 3,064 voting sites (or 70 percent of the total), while the UN had 207 observers who monitored 2,155 sites. In addition to Carter, OAS secretary general Joao Baena Soares of Brazil and the UN secretary general's special representative, Elliot Richardson, a former U.S. attorney general and secretary of defense, made up an on-site troika Ortega dubbed "The Wise Men." Carter's Council of

Freely Elected Heads of Government delegation numbered sixty-two—forty more than went to Panama—and included seven former presidents, including Rafael Caldera of Venezuela, Raul Alfonsin of Argentina, and Daniel Oduber of Costa Rica.[32]

Ortega hoped the presence of Republican stalwarts Richardson and Dan Evans would strip America's extreme right-wing groups of their "arguments and weapons" against his government, and that "the confirmation of free elections in Nicaragua would eliminate pretexts that justify policies of isolation, especially policies of economic isolation."[33] As Richardson put it more succinctly, "Part of my job was to verify Jimmy Carter's verification of the election."[34]

Under pressure from members of Congress, Baker asked Carter to approach Ortega about accepting a bipartisan election monitoring group of twelve U.S. congressmen, a task the ex-president performed begrudgingly. Nevertheless, by asking Carter to serve as his envoy, Baker cleverly avoided ruffling the former president's feathers. Ortega was "paranoid" about the presidential commission, convinced that it was a crucial element in a Bush/Baker plan to eliminate the Sandinistas just as they had done to Noriega in Panama. After some extensive lobbying, Carter announced on January 28 that the U.S. congressmen would be welcome as observers only if they joined as delegates of the Carter Center, UN, or OAS. This arrangement was not acceptable to the U.S. government, so the bipartisan presidential commission did not go to Nicaragua, although eleven U.S. senators and congressmen of both parties joined the Carter Center delegation.[35]

As the presidential contest neared, UNO continued to protest that Carter was too sympathetic to Ortega and that he wasn't taking their complaints about the Sandinistas' intimidation tactics seriously enough.[36] The issue finally came to a head in early February when the *Washington Post* quoted Carter as saying that UNO's complaints were "highly exaggerated" and that the opposition was "laying down a marker, so if they lose they can say, 'Well, there were some irregularities.' " Carter and Richardson both saw that there were widespread discrepancies between UNO's charges of Sandinista intimidation and the concrete evidence, but only Carter publicly sided with the Sandinistas, over whom he said, he had "a great deal of leverage" precisely because they were "looking for a victory on the 25th" in an election they wanted "to be certified as being honest."[37]

Talking to reporters on February 7, Carter went so far as to predict a victory for Ortega, and to say that what concerned him most was demobilizing the Contras once the Sandinistas won. As one of Reagan's Latin America advisers, Robert Kagan, noted in his book *A Twilight Struggle*, Carter refused to worry about "the equally vexing problem of what might happen to the

Sandinista army after a UNO victory."[38] He did, however, engage both Ortega and Chamorro in a "confidential dialogue" on how to "promote national reconciliation" after the election.[39]

Carter had written Bush directly on January 19 to point out one by one the remaining obstacles to a fair election, which included alleged intimidation and harassment of opposition-party candidates and poll watchers; unequal access to the media; delays in the wiring of U.S. funds to UNO; and the Sandinistas' use of government facilities and vehicles for campaigning. The letter was designed in part to reassure Bush that Carter was impartial, that he was willing to pinpoint Sandinista abuses in writing, and that for all intents and purposes the election process was working in Nicaragua.[40]

Although Carter did send President Bush additional memoranda on January 21 and 29 listing a dozen thorny problems to be solved by election day, the tone was upbeat. "Our observer teams will receive two copies of the vote records and tabulations from each of the 4,394 voting places in the country," Carter reassured President Bush. "Furthermore, our observers will have unimpeded access to all voting sites, with the right to observe all voting procedures, handling of ballots, and tabulation and transmission of vote counts."[41]

Upon his return to the United States Carter flew to Washington to reassure President Bush, solidify his relationship with the OAS, and brief a wide range of congressmen in his most extensive lobbying effort since leaving office. The very notion of visiting Washington made Carter uncomfortable; to him the capital was an unpleasant beehive of lobbyists and influence peddlers. Nevertheless, the former president spent time, as James Baker put it, "touching base with philosophical soulmates," for example with the energetic Senator Dodd, discussing what might happen in a close race if UNO declared the election a fraud after the Sandinistas were pronounced the winners.[42] Cutting deals, back slapping, and cloakroom strategizing went against Carter's nature, but Nicaragua had become so highly politicized that Carter acknowledged the need to line up allies before the Sandinista victory which he anticipated.

Carter was not alone in predicting a Sandinista landslide. On February 20, just five days before the election, the Washington Post/ABC News poll showed Ortega trouncing Chamorro, 48 to 32 percent. Some in the Bush administration agreed: "The Sandinistas are going to win," NSC adviser Brent Scowcroft proclaimed. "The only question is how brazen they will be."[43] Baker even testified before Congress two days later, outlining certain guarantees the Sandinistas would have to make after winning the election if they wanted the Bush administration to normalize relations with Managua.[44]

(Nevertheless, the Latin hands at the State Department all believed UNO would win the election.) A day after that a group of distinguished former U.S. officials led by McGeorge Bundy and Sol Linowitz called for the administration to establish full diplomatic relations with the Sandinista government immediately following the election, including lifting the trade embargo and disarming the Contras.[45] Arizona governor Bruce Babbitt, a member of Carter's delegation, may have captured the expectations best when he said on election eve that the Sandinista leader had played the campaign like "a pinball machine, shaking and jiggling it to improve the score but never quite enough to light up the 'tilt' sign."[46]

All this supposed certainty made Ortega cocksure. He began talking about postelection negotiations with the Bush administration, promising to stop sending weapons to leftist guerrillas in El Salvador and even naming Spain's Felipe Gonzalez as his mediator in that dispute. Virtually every member of Ortega's inner circle smelled certain victory, and a massive post-election celebration was organized. As things turned out, Ortega should have heeded Fidel Castro's advice not to be taken in by Carter's guarantees of fairness—to realize that it's impossible to beat the gringos at their own democratic game. "If you get into the game," Castro had warned in 1989, "you should be prepared to lose." But Ortega had only smiled and crowed, "We will win, Commandante. If we do things right, we will win."[47]

On February 25, 1990, hundreds of thousands of voters lined up at polling places—an estimated 80 percent of registered voters. Nicaragua was the center of the world's attention, and Carter the man of the moment. The *New York Times* remarked that in contrast to the jubilation around Costa Rica's recent election, the mood in Nicaragua was one of "purpose and privacy"—as Carter noted early in the balloting, "It's very solemn, like a Mass." It was, in fact, a referendum on ten years of Sandinista rule. Asked how the midafternoon balloting was faring, Carter, himself solemn, simply answered, "So far, so good."[48]

What Carter didn't tell the press was that earlier in the day a brouhaha had erupted that could have canceled the election. As an electoral safeguard, voters had been required to dip a finger in indelible ink, a primitive but effective way for poll watchers to make sure that nobody voted twice. But "about noon, someone discovered that the ink could be washed off easily with Clorox," Carter recalled. "UNO accused the Sandinistas of trying to cheat, and that afternoon, while voting was still underway, both threatened to withdraw from the election." Carter immediately met with leaders from each side, urged them to reconcile, and convinced them to proceed—a job made easier because both were certain of victory. "The voting, in the end, was completely successful," Carter maintained.[49]

The Carter Center delegation split into fourteen teams that fanned across all nine of Nicaragua's electoral districts before the polls opened on February 25. At the end of the day, delegates were stationed at voting sites to observe the count and report the results independently to the UN and the OAS. "We concluded," Carter said later, "that although there were some irregularities, the number of violations were not significant enough to discredit the voting procedures."[50] Robert Pastor had worried all along about getting an accurate "quick count"; because the Carter Center's Council of Freely Elected Heads of Government lacked the manpower to produce one, the crucial task fell to the UN and the OAS. At ten o'clock on election night—four hours after the polls had closed—the UN's quick count came in. "The UN guys really did all the work but never got full credit," Richardson maintained. "Carter was following the UN lead."[51] Carter arrived at UN headquarters just as the 8 percent sample was tabulated and learned first-hand from Elliot Richardson that, against most predictions, Chamorro was ahead by the wide margin of 56 to 40 percent. "I knew, at that moment, that Ortega had lost," Carter said later. "The UN results made it very clear."[52]

As Richardson headed to the Official Counting Center, Carter repeatedly tried "frantically" to telephone Ortega to arrange a meeting to discuss the bad news and plan for the transition.[53] After many attempts he finally got through, and Ortega invited "the three wise men"—Carter, Richardson, and Baena Soares—to meet with the Sandinista leadership at Sandinista National Liberation Front (FSLN) headquarters. The troika arrived ten minutes before midnight to find the Sandinistas grim and in despair, a sharp contrast to the boisterous mood at the supposed victory celebration their supporters were even then throwing in the front plaza. "They were in shock," Pastor recalled, "absolutely in shock."[54]

From that point Carter, with Rosalynn at his side, took over. "You've lost," he told the Sandinista leadership, his eyes fixed on Daniel Ortega. But Ortega shook his head and said, "No, no, no. It's too early. We're going to win." Carter, in a soft, even-keeled voice, minced no words, declaring, "The quick count is definitive. You've lost." Ortega was stunned, unable to comprehend how the polls could have been so wrong. Pastor began explaining to the Sandinistas the difference between a poll, which is based on attitudes, and a quick count, which reports results, but Carter interrupted: "I've won an election, Daniel," he reassured. "I've lost an election. I can tell you from my own experience that losing is not the end of the world." To everyone's surprise, Rosalynn Carter interjected, "*I* thought it was the end of the world!" bringing instant laughter into the tension-filled room. Jimmy Carter shifted the mood again by telling Ortega, "Your greatest accomplishment as president will be if you lead a peaceful transition of power."[55]

Ortega swallowed the bitter pill and admitted defeat, promising to recognize UNO's victory provided that Violeta Chamorro not announce her victory before at least 15 percent of the results were publicized and he had a chance to talk to his supporters. Although not a precondition for accepting defeat, Ortega was also adamant that the Sandinista army be allowed to "protect citizens" from the armed Contras, who would be returning from Honduras; that the United States convince UNO leaders to disarm the Contras before allowing them to reenter Nicaragua; and that the Sandinistas be allowed to keep the property they had seized from the Somozas during the revolution. Carter told Ortega he considered those conditions reasonable, and that he would get President Bush to agree to them in principle.[56]

The Carters then left Sandinista headquarters and headed to Violeta de Chamorro's house to ask her to postpone declaring victory until the SEC began to publicize the initial results. The good news, Carter told her, was that Ortega was willing to concede defeat. Even so, UNO's leaders squabbled among themselves over whether Ortega's delaying was just another Sandinista trick. Carter persuaded Chamorro to withhold a "triumphalist" victory statement until the results were publicized and Ortega made a concession announcement.[57] Finally, at six-thirty the next morning, Ortega made a historic concession speech, proclaiming that "the president of Nicaragua and the government of Nicaragua are going to respect and obey the popular mandate coming out of the vote in these elections." A new wave of democracy had arrived in Central America.[58]

At four in the morning after election day, shortly before Ortega made his concession speech, Carter decided to telephone Baker in Washington with the stunning news of Chamorro's victory. "You'll wake him," Pastor warned Carter. "Trust me," Carter replied. "This is news he'll want to hear at once."[59] Within minutes Baker was on the other end, expressing happy disbelief. "I was glad to be woken with that kind of good news," Baker later enthused.[60] Carter updated the secretary of state on the situation, then blurted, "Get a piece of paper, I'll tell you what to say to the press and what official message should come from Bush to both Ortega and Chamorro." Baker took notes, and later wrote that "it was good that Carter was there to help convince Ortega to do the right thing."[61]

Carter met with the Sandinistas again shortly after Ortega made his concession speech to broker the difficult next phase: the transfer of power to UNO. Humberto Ortega had been appointed to head the transition, and he wasted no time in pitching Carter on the necessity of his staying on as minister of defense along with Tomas Borge as minister of the interior, responsible for intelligence and the police. Without hesitating Carter snapped, "That's completely unacceptable." Humberto Ortega backpedaled, sputtering, "Mr. President, it was just an idea—not a condition, just an idea." The pair then ironed out a plan whereby the Sandinistas would be permitted to review Chamorro's candidates for the defense and interior posts in the cabinet.[62]

Chamorro, however, bristled at this agreement: she distrusted Humberto Ortega and feared Sandinista control of the military. Others in UNO—especially her principal adviser, Antonio Lacayo—believed such an arrangement was necessary. For example, Lacayo considered it essential that a trusted man with "dark skin" such as Humberto Ortega head the military because virtually all of Nicaragua's soldiers also had dark skin. Carter arranged for Ortega and Lacayo to meet and form something akin to a transition committee. But Chamorro believed that true democracy meant she could appoint the cabinet of her choice; letting a Sandinista control the military was hardly what she had in mind. The critical question of who controlled the army was clouded in confusion. Meanwhile the Bush administration, which had been prepared to live with a Sandinista victory, assumed the posture that as long as the Sandinistas didn't overthrow President Chamorro they were fine.[63]

Despite her misgivings, Chamorro announced that Humberto Ortega would continue as chief of the army, though she became minister of defense. For many years right-wing Republicans like Jesse Helms claimed Carter and Pastor engineered Ortega's retention, and Helms's subsequent efforts to force the Bush administration to hold back economic aid were one consequence.[64] During the transition period 400 Nicaraguan enterprises were still being directed by the Sandinistas, including Humberto Ortega, who totally dominated the armed forces. "The Sandinistas used the days between their electoral defeat and Chamorro's inauguration to pass laws designed to give them privileges and powers after the change of government," syndicated columnist Jeane Kirkpatrick complained. "The result is that the government can control neither the troops nor the streets."[65] In truth, Carter never made such a deal. Frustrated that the Sandinistas still controlled Nicaragua's military, the Republican right chose to blame Carter and Pastor. They were furious that Pastor had brokered a deal whereby Humberto Ortega would stay as chief of the army for a transitionary six months—he ended up staying over four years. "I opposed Chamorro keeping Humberto at the time but in retrospect it worked for the best because Humberto was able to shrink the entire military from about 60,000 to about 15,000," Pastor would note. "That would have been very hard for anyone else to pull off."[66]

Carter and Pastor arrived at the State Department for lunch on February 28, 1990. Baker, Scowcroft, Aronson, and Deputy Secretary of State Lawrence Eagleburger were all there, listening intently as the former president recounted his jeep ride with Ortega to a Habitat for Humanity work site in 1986, the resolution he helped construct to the Miskito Indian problem, and the gloomy mood at Sandinista headquarters when Ortega finally admitted defeat. He told stories like a veteran just home from battle, and Baker remembered thinking how misunderstood Carter was among the Republican right. "At times he could debrief just brilliantly," Baker said. "This was one of those times."[67]

Although Carter was encouraged by the fairness of the Nicaraguan election, he understood that Chamorro faced the difficult tasks of restoring the economy, demobilizing the Contras, subordinating the military to civilian authority, and addressing her nation's pent-up social demands. "It is very important for the State Department to issue a statement declaring its support for an immediate demobilization of the Contras," Carter told the group; then he asked Baker to keep in mind that Daniel Ortega would remain president until April 25, and should therefore be dealt with even while consultations were held with president-elect Chamorro. "It is very important to get [the] FSLN to play the role of responsible opposition, as it will be the largest party and UNO is quite fragile," Carter cautioned.[68]

Most of the ninety-minute meeting at State dealt with the intertwined problems of disarming and resettling the Contras. Baker and company agreed that the Contras would have to be demobilized, as they promised to do in the Bipartisan Accord, but were not as eager as Carter to begin immediately. Carter pushed hard on this point, convinced that the Bush administration had to release a statement addressing the matter, so he forged a compromise: he drafted a statement pledging that the State Department would take immediate steps to "encourage" the Contras to demobilize. The vagueness in the verb "encourage" gave Baker room to maneuver with pro-Contra diehards in the U.S. Congress, but the Sandinistas thought the statement a disingenuous ploy to keep the guerrillas active.[69]

The meeting marked a triumph for the ex-president. Now he was advising Bush on foreign affairs and exchanging memoranda with Scowcroft, who had stated at the meeting that "Carter didn't just observe the election—he ran it."[70] In a detailed memorandum to Baker on how to deal with Nicaragua's remaining problems, Carter thanked the secretary of state for giving him such a meaningful role in the administration's foreign policy making, adding, "I had the feeling that we are looking at the present and prospective situation in Nicaragua with similar views."[71]

Carter was quickly inundated with letters of congratulation from all over the world, many from the unlikeliest of adversaries. "I hope you will allow me one completely abject compliment," wrote former Reagan administration deputy secretary of state John Whitehead. "I have never seen anywhere such a skillful diplomatic effort, or one that turned an utter failure into such a dramatic success. It was a masterful performance."[72] Only far right Republicans Jesse Helms, Pat Robertson, Dan Quayle, and Elliott Abrams remained bitter toward Carter for his closeness to Daniel Ortega, for his public pronouncement that the Contras be demobilized immediately.

As he had with Gerald Ford, Carter made quite an ally out of his new Republican election-monitoring partner, former Washington State governor and senator Dan Evans. Evans and Carter had also previously served together on the Trilateral Commission in the 1970s. "I feel privileged to have had the opportunity to co-chair the American delegation with President Carter," Evans wrote to Robert Pastor. "It was a deeply moving experience to watch people who care very much about their democratic opportunities. They proved conclusively that it does not necessarily take a sophisticated infrastructure to produce a free, fair, and truly democratic election."[73] Evans was so impressed with Carter's performance that he ended up becoming the former Democratic president's Capitol Hill apologist, tasked with defending Carter's intentions and integrity to the Republican right. "Several weeks ago I was in Miami," Evans wrote Elliott Abrams. "I had just come into my hotel room and turned on the television set while I was unpacking. There you were on CNN, speaking to the Conservative Political Action Committee convention. Elliott, it was one of the most ignorant, mindless speeches I have ever heard anyone give. You should know your subject better. But it was obvious that you were so intent on trashing President Carter that you had failed even to find out the facts. . . . I suspect your bitterness toward President Carter is the bitterness of one who continuously tried to sell a destitute policy to Congress and the people of the United States. . . . Fortunately, Elliott, you can only carp from the sidelines now."[74]

Abrams—whom in 1988 Carter had characterized as a "right-wing nut"[75]—was stunned to hear such criticism from a fellow Republican, particularly one like Evans, who was known for his graciousness. "Life is delightful, not the least for its constant surprises," Abrams wrote back. "After all, you have a reputation as a genuinely nice fellow, so the nasty, *ad hominem* last line of your letter brought me a chuckle." Abrams then launched into a lengthy defense of the Reagan administration's cold war policies in Latin America, challenging Evans to visit Nicaragua—alone—and ask Chamorro, who, between Carter and Reagan, had "contributed most to bringing on Sandinista rule and who contributed most to the successful struggle against it." What's more, Abrams opined, Carter had mismanaged his election-monitoring duties, constantly covering up the Sandinistas' indiscretions because he was either "ill-informed or biased."[76]

Carter had indeed formed a genuine friendship with Daniel Ortega during the Nicaraguan campaign—but it was precisely because the young revolutionary trusted Carter that his elder could convince him to relinquish power. On Chamorro's inauguration day Carter wrote Ortega a highly personal, paternal letter, expressing how proud he was of his friend's statesmanship. Speaking as a political mentor, Carter urged Ortega to help build Nicaraguan democracy by cooperating with President Chamorro. "I also want to congratulate you for joining a select club, which I also joined against my preference," Carter wrote. "Today, you become a former president. It is an honorable group. One of the most rewarding experiences for me in the last eight months was to become your friend. Now that you have more time, I hope you will remain good friends and come visit me in Atlanta. I would love to take you to a baseball game."[77]

A few days after Violeta Chamorro was sworn in as president of Nicaragua, Carter received a telephone call from former president of the Dominican Republic Juan Bosch, who asked if he would monitor the Caribbean nation's upcoming election. Carter replied that he would consider it, but only if the other political parties or the Dominican Republic's Electoral Board also extended an invitation.[78] On May 8—only eight days before the election—Carter received an invitation dated May 4 from the Electoral Board. Carter accepted with one condition: "total access to the electoral process, including to polling sites, and permission for our presence during the vote."[79]

Carter's delegation, which included former prime minister of Belize George Price, arrived just two days before the contest and was therefore unable to evaluate allegations of irregularities during the campaign, such as tampering with voter registration lists. Carter met with leaders from the four largest political parties, none of which presented documented evidence of preelection fraud. "The candidates all indicated that they would accept the results of a fair election," Carter stated later.[80]

Former president Bosch encouraged his American counterpart to observe the election because he considered the Electoral Board biased in favor of incumbent president Joaquín Balaguer. As in Panama and Nicaragua, Carter was trusted in the Dominican Republic for what he had done as U.S. president: in 1978, when the opposition Dominican Revolutionary party candidate Antonio Guzman was declared the winner, Carter had strongly protested the suspension of the vote count. On May 15, 1990, Bosch told

Carter that what he had done in 1978 "gives you moral authority in this election. Because you are here, there will be no fraud."[81]

More than 1,600 elective offices were at stake at the national and local levels in the May 16 election. Sixteen parties had met the legal requirements to participate; nine put forth presidential candidates. The two leading contenders were Social Christian Reform party candidate Joaquín Balaguer, who had occupied numerous government posts under the dictatorship of Rafael Trujillo from 1930 to 1961 and who had been elected president from 1966 to 1978 and then again in 1986, and Juan Bosch of the Dominican Liberation party, who had been elected president in 1962 and was overthrown eight months later by the military.

As it turned out, the May 1990 presidential election was one of the closest and most disputed in the history of the Dominican Republic. President Balaguer defeated former president Bosch by a mere 1.2 percent of the total vote. Bosch charged fraud and threatened to lead his angry supporters into the streets of Santo Domingo to prevent the Electoral Board from announcing his defeat. A political crisis of some magnitude was at hand.

Instead of allowing Balaguer to be declared the winner, Carter encouraged all parties to use legal channels and avoid violence in resolving the dispute; he also pledged that over the next eight weeks, an orderly investigation would be conducted into whether fraud had been committed. Based on its observations of the balloting, tabulation of the votes, and review of the irregularities alleged by various parties, the Carter delegation concluded that the accusations of fraud were not substantiated. "Your contribution has been fundamentally important in assuring the veracity of the electoral process in the Dominican Republic," the Electoral Board president wrote Carter on June 5.[82] A week later Carter wrote back, essentially declaring Balaguer the winner by stating, "I have not yet seen fraud, by which I mean a pattern of irregularities that favors a particular candidate or party."[83]

A s if monitoring three elections in one year was not enough, that July Carter went to Port-au-Prince at the request of Haiti's interim president, Ertha Pascal Trouillot, to discuss how a free and fair election might be held in that impoverished country—the second oldest in the hemisphere, but one that had never known real democracy.[84] François "Papa Doc" Duvalier and his son, Jean-Claude ("Baby Doc"), had ruled Haiti with iron fists for thirty years, beginning in 1957; in fact, the dictators Duvalier had their own private army, the Tontons Macoutes, who terrorized the Haitian people ruthlessly and regularly. But a popular uprising against the Duvaliers took place in 1986, causing Baby Doc to flee into exile. The following

year Carter went to Haiti to observe what was being touted as its first democratic election. The preparations went poorly, and on election day thirty-four
voters were shot or hacked to death by the Tontons Macoutes simply for lin-
ing up at a Port-au-Prince polling station. "The Haitian army leaders, who
may have been involved in the attack, seized the chance to call off the election, closing the polls just three hours after they opened," Carter recalled.
"Many people were understandably reluctant ever to go to the polls after
that incident."[85]

Then disaster struck. Just a few months before the election, one of Baby
Doc's foreign ministers, known murderer Roger Lafontant, returned to
Haiti and began to arouse the remaining Tontons Macoutes with inflammatory speeches and threats against the presidential candidates, particularly a
thirty-seven-year-old Roman Catholic slum priest named Jean-Bertrand
Aristide. Surrounded by a phalanx of goons and with the zealous support of
the Tontons Macoutes, Lafontant began issuing death threats to Aristide,
who had become a spokesman for Haiti's poor. "Because there were so many
candidates, it was unlikely that any one person would win a majority of
the votes," Carter remembered. "Yet when Father Aristide decided to run,
it was estimated that voter registration doubled in many regions of the
country."[86]

Meanwhile, the Haitian Electoral Commission ruled that Lafontant and
two other Tontons Macoutes candidates were not qualified to run for president. They responded to the snub by killing seven people and injuring fifty
others. "Haiti is now moving toward an election in December, but to succeed it needs the full support of the international community," Carter wrote
in the *New York Times* after the killings. "There can be successful elections
in Haiti if the UN, Organization of American States, the U.S. and other
nations will support a troubled but courageous people who hunger for freedom, justice, and a better life."[87]

On election day, with scores of international observers present, the voting went smoothly. The Carter Center, NDI, OAS, European Union, and
UN stationed observer teams all over Haiti to investigate reports of fraud;
they concluded that all procedures were legal. "After the polls closed and
while the ballots were being counted, I visited several voting places in the
poorest parts of Port-au-Prince," Carter remembered. "There was no electricity, and the election officials and observers were huddled around tables
to work by candlelight. Each ballot was passed around and examined before
being placed in the 'pro' stack to be counted."[88] A quick count showed that
Aristide had won with two-thirds of the vote. "It took 200 years to arrive at
our second independence," a jubilant Aristide proclaimed at his February 7
inauguration from the balcony of his gleaming white presidential palace. "At

our first independence we cried, 'Liberty or Death!' We now shout with all our strength, 'Democracy or Death!' "[89]

Although Carter generally disdained ceremonies, he returned to Port-au-Prince for Aristide's inauguration, having learned from the mistake in Nicaragua where his absence allowed the appointment of Humberto Ortega as chief of the army. "What has been achieved by the Haitian people is momentous in history and will send a signal of hope to the entire hemisphere," Carter said at the swearing-in.[90] As the former U.S. president surveyed the hundreds of thousands of people rejoicing in the streets on his way to a mass of thanksgiving, he was overcome with pride in his role in bringing about such a democratic change. "It was the most impressive demonstration of joy about democracy I have ever seen," Carter wrote in *Talking Peace*. "Little did we know during this wonderful occasion that the happy people amassed for the inaugural would soon face a tragic future."[91]

W hen it comes to elections," Archbishop Desmond Tutu of South Africa noted, "Carter's is the most listened-to voice in the world."[92] Even Republicans who had no use for Carter as president admired his post-presidential penchant for promoting free and fair elections. And to Carter elections took precedence over everything else. For example, while President Bush and his three Republican predecessors happily accepted the invitation to participate in the November 4, 1991, opening of the Ronald Reagan presidential library, perched high on a hill in Simi Valley, California, Carter declined. "He wrote saying that due to an upcoming election in Zambia he could not attend," Lodwrick Cook, the CEO of Arco and chairman of the Ronald Reagan Foundation, recalled. "Zambia. It was like a joke. All he would say is, 'I'm sorry, I'm needed in Zambia.' "[93]

Not satisfied with this excuse, Cook looked into the Zambian election slated for November 2—and found out that Carter really was the linchpin of the entire exercise. The only president Zambia had known, sixty-seven-year-old Kenneth D. Kaunda, who had guided the nation from independence from Britain in 1964 and led the international campaign to isolate South Africa, was in a close race with Frederick Chiluba, a former trade union leader.[94] Carter had been overseeing the entire preelectoral process for the past year, although scarcely a story appeared about it in the *Wall Street Journal*, *Washington Post*, or *New York Times*. "I quickly understood that it would be *impossible* for Carter not to be in Zambia," Cook noted. "The upcoming election was an important, defining moment in African democracy."[95]

Cook made a deal with Carter. He would provide the ex-president an

Arco corporate jet, leaving it with Carter in Lusaka so that when the election was over on November 3 he could be whisked back to Los Angeles in time for the library ceremony. "Carter made it clear that if fraud occurred he might have to stay longer," Cook said.[96]

As it turned out, the Zambian election was a false triumph for the ballot box. Zambians walked miles to voting stations across the countryside to exercise their right in the multiparty election for president. "Carter had an obsession with the notion of tamper-proof seals on the ballot boxes," remembered Eric Bjornlund, an NDI election observer, of the ex-president's last-minute frenzy to make sure everything went smoothly.[97] Unlike the close contests in Nicaragua and the Dominican Republic, in Zambia the forty-eight-year-old Chiluba defeated Kaunda in a landslide, triggering mass celebrations throughout the bankrupt country. Chiluba took 80 percent of the vote in an election Carter called "as orderly and prompt" as any he had ever witnessed.[98] As for Kaunda, a personal friend, Carter said he deserved a role as "respected senior statesman."[99]

Yet Carter learned a hard lesson in Zambia. The holding of a free and fair election did not necessarily mean good governance would follow suit. Carter naturally understood the risks of ballot-box democracy—after all, Adolf Hitler had been legitimately elected chancellor in January 1933—with tragic results. But nothing prepared him for the ruthlessness with which Chiluba seized control of Zambia in the coming years, jailing opponents, including Kaunda himself, and ignoring rampant corruption. The lesson Carter took away from Zambia's 1990 election, however, was not that democracy promotion in sub-Saharan Africa was wrong. Chiluba's ruthlessness only made Carter more adamant that the U.S. government promote democratic principles by refusing to do business with African autocrats. If the United States set economic aid levels to specific countries based in part on their democratic performance, then the Chilubas of Africa would eventually be ousted from power by voters. Regardless of what critic Robert Kaplan wrote in the *Atlantic Monthly* or Fareed Zakaria in *Foreign Affairs*, Carter saw liberal democracy as the appropriate way for Africa to proceed into the future.[100]

Bipartisan democracy promotion had been a hallmark of the Bush presidency, and was perhaps nowhere more evident than in the extraordinary collaboration that developed between James Baker and Jimmy Carter. With the help of the UN, NED, and the OAS, by 1992 these two statesmen had successfully contributed to bringing democracy to Panama, Haiti, the Dominican Republic, Guyana, Suriname, Zambia, and most important, Nicaragua. After Chamorro's victory, Carter returned to Nicaragua four times:

in 1991 to forge an agreement that brought inflation down from 36,000 percent to single digits; in 1994 when Chamorro asked for help in dealing with the thousands of disputes remaining from the Sandinistas' land grabs; in 1995 when the Carter Center and the United Nations Development Program cosponsored a conference on streamlining the diplomatic process in order to stimulate economic development; and in 1996 when Carter was invited to monitor the nation's second democratic election.[101]

The last visit brought matters full circle: Carter's election-monitoring cochairs were James Baker and Oscar Arias, both now "formers" themselves. Once again problems arose, this time in the form of administrative confusion over the vote count, which led to the disqualification of some 6 percent of the polling stations. In the end, as in 1990, it fell to Jimmy Carter to tell Ortega he had lost again—this time to Liberal Alliance party candidate Arnoldo Aleman, a conservative fifty-year-old lawyer and coffee farmer, by a margin of 48 to 38 percent.[102]

The morning after the October 2, 1996, election the *Washington Times* conducted a joint interview with Carter and Baker that showed the two agreeing on everything but the role of the Contras in forcing the Sandinistas to abide by the results of the 1990 election. But it was just a good-natured policy disagreement between two veterans who felt justifiably proud to witness the second democratic election in Nicaraguan history. "The important thing that happened in 1990 is that Democrats and Republicans in the United States got together and decided to take Central American foreign policy out of the domestic debate in the United States, and I think that is really important to continue," Baker noted. "I don't think that Ortega would have accepted the results in 1990 had President Carter not been down there to encourage that." Baker's praise was echoed by every leader in the hemisphere, including Fidel Castro, who recognized Carter's power as the Trojan horse of American-style democracy. Throughout the 1990s Carter tried desperately to convince Castro to hold democratic elections—but after watching what had happened in Panama and Nicaragua, the Cuban leader respectfully rebuffed his overtures.[103]

SEVENTEEN

DESERT STORM

❦

With Ronald Reagan out of the picture, it seemed to Jimmy Carter that it would be fruitful to try to orchestrate a Palestinian-Israeli peace settlement that would make Anwar al-Sadat proud. Although Carter had found recent consultations in Atlanta useful in understanding the intricacies of Arab-Israeli politics, he had grown weary of playing host to ambassadors, academics, and analysts who reveled in discussing problems rather than implementing solutions. It was time once more to travel and negotiate in the Middle East. And it was time to finally meet Yasir Arafat.

Carter had been stymied for a decade by the Reagan administration's wholehearted support of hawkish Likud governments in Israel. "They might pay lip service to Camp David (which they have never supported) so long as they are sure these two words will alienate the Jordanians and other Arabs," he had written Secretary of State George Shultz in December 1988. "In the long run, they will have to be run over, with maximum support from Jews and others around the world who are interested in a stable, secure and peaceful region."[1] Carter had regarded Arafat as "remarkably resilient" for managing to retain coherence among the disparate elements of the PLO both inside the Israeli-occupied territories and throughout the Palestinian diaspora since 1969.[2]

By March 1990 Carter was primed to take on Israel's Likud party and break the historic logjam that precluded peace. Carter saw the Bush administration policies on the Middle East as "comparable to those of Kennedy

and Johnson and Nixon and Ford and mine more than they were comparable with Reagan's policies."[3] Yet he also believed there was a huge deficit of
knowledge at Foggy Bottom about Palestinian society, institutions, movements within movements, and evolving leadership. Too often, Carter believed, State Department careerists were more concerned with protecting
themselves than with analyzing problems truthfully. The near unanimous assessment of every world leader Carter had spoken with since leaving the
White House—Mikhail Gorbachev, Deng Xiaoping, Nelson Mandela, Margaret Thatcher, Oscar Arias, Javier Pérez de Cuéllar, and, of course, all Arab
leaders—convinced him that it was impossible to bypass the PLO in dealing
with the Palestinian issue.

To Carter, that called for reshaping how Yasir Arafat was understood in
the United States, not as a terrorist but as a peacemaker. He knew that
Yitzhak Shamir and Menachem Begin had been members of Jewish underground terrorist organizations (and admitted so), and yet they had been re-
constituted as prime ministers, beloved by the U.S. Congress. There was no
reason, he believed, that Arafat couldn't be "made over" into a peacemaker.
Carter was ready to take on the task.[4]

Just before Carter was to depart for the Middle East, his only surviving
sibling, Gloria Carter Spann, died of pancreatic cancer. If Billy was seen as
the joker in the Carter family deck, Gloria was a different sort of wild card.
Arrested once for playing harmonica atop the Formica counter of an
all-night diner in Americus, she also publicly criticized many of her
brother's policies when he was president. She was a member of a motorcycle gang, and her many biker friends, dressed in full regalia, came by the
hundreds to pay their last respects. Gloria's coffin, escorted from the funeral home by thirty-eight Harleys, was laid to rest in the Lebanon Baptist
Cemetery in Plains, next to her siblings, Billy and Ruth, and the rest of the
Carter clan. Gloria's husband, Walter, and son, William, then in prison for
robbery, raised a tombstone for her that read, "SHE RIDES IN HARLEY
HEAVEN."[5]

Carter's grief was heightened by a sense that time was running out; he
was the last of his generation. It was not so much a fear of death, as Carter
told the *Baltimore Sun*. His family "approached the end of their lives with
great equanimity. We're a deeply Christian family and don't look upon death
as a terrible prospect." Carter's concern was to make good use of the time he
had left, and try to bring about Sadat's dream of Middle East peace.[6]

In his briefing with Bush, Baker, and Scowcroft, Carter told Secretary
Baker his plans to lobby Hafez al-Assad to gain the release of Terry Anderson, a correspondent for the Associated Press held in Lebanon, as well as to
pressure Israel about its human rights record. Baker wished him well, want-

ing to keep a safe distance from these particular kegs, but did ask Carter for
reasons of security not to visit terrorist-racked Lebanon or to meet clandestinely with President Elias Hrawi of Lebanon. Carter reluctantly agreed.[7]
"President Carter and I saw the Middle East from a similar perspective,"
Baker recalled in a later interview, although the secretary was not fully at-
tuned to the lengths Carter would go to bring about their shared objective of
Middle East peace. "But I had a full plate and didn't have time to closely
monitor what he was up to."[8] On Baker's plate: the impending collapse of
the Soviet Union, a scramble to dismantle nuclear weapons in Central Europe, and Germany's talk of reunification. If Carter wanted to put together
an international peace conference that included Palestinians while revolution was occurring in Europe, more power to him.

"Just as long as he reported to us, which he did, I had no problems with
him talking with Assad or Arafat," Baker recalled. "I frankly saw the Arab-
Israeli dispute as a pitfall to be avoided rather than an opportunity to be exploited."[9] With Iraqi dictator Saddam Hussein threatening to "burn half of
Israel" in retaliation for any Israeli attack in the Arab world, the danger of an
unintended war was greatly increased, and Baker was grateful for any policy
help he could get from the architect of the Camp David accords. At the very
least Carter's talks with Middle East leaders might be useful to Baker from
an intelligence-gathering perspective.

Baker had not been uninvolved in the Middle East since becoming secretary of state. The peace initiative he launched, known as the Baker plan, however, contributed to the collapse of the Israeli government in March 1990.
The Shamir government fell over differences within his ruling coalition over
a Baker plan provision that called for Israeli-Palestinian talks in Cairo to
pave the way for Palestinian elections in the Israeli-occupied territories.
Arafat had officially accepted the Baker plan, but the decision was now
stalled in Israel pending formation of a new government. Carter promised
Baker he would promote the existing policies and report his findings to the
secretary of state. "The policy approved by the president in early 1989 authorized me to search for a common basis on which Israel and the Palestinians could engage," Baker recalled. "We would continue the inherited
U.S.-PLO dialogue at a low level, but the Egyptians would be available to
talk directly with Arafat."[10]

It was Carter's first trip back to the Middle East since the *intifada*, and
he immediately detected a new optimism in the Arab leaders he met. The
intifada had changed the political dynamics of the region. In July 1988 King
Hussein announced a dramatic reduction in Jordan's administrative role in
the West Bank, encouraging local Palestinians to manage their own financial
and social affairs. At the same time, a new generation of Palestinian leaders

had emerged, professing loyalty to the PLO while internally pushing it toward negotiations with Israel and at the same time developing and extending its own more independent sphere of influence.

For Carter, the most heartening change grew out of the November 1988 Algiers meeting, at which the Palestine National Council (PNC), the legislative body of the PLO, overwhelmingly affirmed a proclamation establishing an independent Palestinian state while simultaneously endorsing UN Security Council resolutions 242 and 338, thereby recognizing Israel's right to exist. Arafat himself traveled to Geneva and Stockholm to publicly disavow terrorism as a means to achieve Palestinian goals. Encouraged by these pronouncements, the State Department lifted the conditional ban on U.S. dialogue with the PLO. Carter felt the new political dynamics provided many opportunities for a permanent peace, and it was up to the Americans to jump-start the process.[11]

Carter's four previous trips to Egypt from 1981 to 1987 were largely for fact-finding. This time Carter came away with a concrete accomplishment: a promise from Hosni Mubarak that the Egyptian president would hold bilateral talks with Syria's Assad in the next few months. In Cairo Carter was also briefed by PLO and Egyptian government officials on plans to hold an international peace conference soon.[12]

From Cairo, Carter flew to Damascus, where for seven hours he held conversations with Assad, hoping to help win freedom for hostages held in Lebanon. (Syria had roughly 40,000 troops in Lebanon and was the main power broker in the country.) "[Assad] seemed healthier, in better spirits, more relaxed and patient about the peace process than when we were there three years ago," he wrote Bush and Baker. "He has minimal confidence that the planned Israeli-Palestinian talks will amount to anything, but is willing to stand aloof, not interfere, and see what happens, waiting for an international peace conference to make a substantive difference."[13] Assad authorized Carter to tell Israeli leaders that he was willing to initiate peace talks on the future status of the Golan Heights, Syrian territory Israel had captured in the 1967 war and annexed in 1982. "His own proposal was that both sides withdraw from the international border, with a small force of neutral observers to monitor the neutral zone," Carter later noted. "When I asked him if each nation would have to fall back an equal distance, he replied that Syria might move its troops farther from the border because of the terrain."[14]

In Syria Carter also attempted to broker a deal allowing CNN to open an office in Damascus, working in tandem with Syria's public television network. Assad assented but CNN president Burt Reinhardt balked. CNN's only interest was a temporary office to cover the Terry Anderson story. Carter had misread his mandate. "I didn't understand that your purpose was

so narrowly defined," he wrote Reinhardt on his return. "I discussed with
the President and Foreign Minister a general long-range relationship expecting that this would build trust and mutual understanding, improving
CNN's chances at a hostage story."[15]

Following Syria, Carter went to Jerusalem. There he publicly declared
Assad's agreement to talk peace an important breakthrough. The Israeli government, in the midst of a domestic political struggle to form a new government, did not concur. Remembering only too well how Assad had used the
Golan to lob artillery shells into Galilee, Israel's agricultural heartland, before the 1967 war, Prime Minister Yitzhak Shamir immediately declared that
he had no intention of returning the territory. Disappointed, Carter went
on the offensive, publicly condemning Israel's settling of large numbers of
Soviet Jews in the occupied territories. As Carter saw it, in a letter he wrote
Baker from Jerusalem, it was essential for maximum political pressure to be
put on Israel to end this "illegal" settlement policy. Carter also had to report
that his scheduled meeting with Arafat, originally set for March 20 in Tunis,
had been postponed because the PLO chairman felt obliged to go to Wind-
hoek for the Namibian elections.[16]

A hornet's nest was stirred up by Carter's conversation with reporters following a meeting with Arab and Jewish human rights groups in Jerusalem.
Carter sharply criticized Israel for abusing Palestinian rights, shooting
demonstrators without cause, demolishing their houses, and jailing Arabs
without trial. Lashing out at the Israeli army for incarcerating 9,000 Palestinians without reason, and describing 1,000 of the captives as "prisoners of
conscience," Carter even supplied names of individual journalists and writers he regarded as wrongly incarcerated. "There have been about 650 Palestinians killed by excessive use of firearms by the military that are not under
life-threatening situations," Carter asserted, "and they are still demolishing
houses and still putting people in prison without charges." Later that day, to
Carter's horror, Israeli troops shot dead two seventeen-year-old Palestinian
teenagers—Osama Ashawish and Nael Zakkout—in the Gaza Strip.[17]

Speaking publicly to the press and privately with Prime Minister Shamir,
Carter also criticized Israel for deporting Palestinians and preventing the reunion of women and children from the West Bank and Gaza to Jordan if
they could not prove birth or legal residency in the area since occupation by
the Israeli military in 1967. Carter, carrying a fat folder with 251 documented cases of this administrative abuse, demanded that for the "sake of
common decency" the Israeli government cease its inhumane policy. "No
[Israelis] denied the accuracy of these reports," Carter later noted. Indeed,
Shmuel Goren, in charge of civilian administration in the occupied territories, promised Carter not only a policy change, but that the women and

children already deported would be allowed to return home and rejoin their families. At a press conference held at Tel Aviv airport, an elated Carter announced the change to CNN and then boarded a jet to Washington to personally brief President Bush on his Middle East tour.[18]

Because the Labor and Likud parties were struggling to form a new government at the time of Carter's stinging attack on Israeli human rights abuses, the ex-president was viewed as an intrusive outsider by the *Jerusalem Post*. Carter also found himself on the hot seat in the United States. *New York Times* columnist A. M. Rosenthal lambasted Carter for his pro-Palestinian bias. In a piece titled "Silence Is a Lie," Rosenthal correctly pointed out that when Carter was in Syria he never once publicly raised human rights abuses in a nation ruled by a despicable despot who stood accused of mass murder of his own citizens. Why didn't Carter publicly discuss the thousands of political prisoners packed in jail cells throughout Syria? Why didn't Carter criticize Assad for harboring the terrorists many experts believed bombed Pan Am 103, killing 270 people? Rosenthal accused Carter of a "growing double standard" that allowed him to routinely attack Israeli democracy while "remaining mute" about the Arab tyrannies of the Middle East. To Rosenthal the American linchpin of the Camp David accords and the Middle East peace process was behaving like a PLO functionary.[19]

Rosenthal wasn't the only U.S. citizen infuriated by Carter's attack on Israeli policies. Ken Stein, who had not accompanied Carter on this journey, questioned the former president's tactic in a candid letter to his boss on March 23: "If you continue on the course of only criticizing or minimizing Israel in your public presentations, you will be doing yourself a potentially devastating disservice, particularly if you want to be reengaged in any capacity in future Middle East diplomacy. The American and Israeli press have made you the bogey man."

Stein had good reason for concern. For the last eight years he had worked diligently to have the former president appointed an "official" U.S. mediator in the Middle East. Since Henry Kissinger was not trusted by Arabs, and Carter was, all Carter needed to cement the appointment was to convince Israel that he was not too pro-Palestinian. "I believe that not only is it wrong to set a double standard for Israel; but your willingness to be harsher on Israel in public does not help create confidence in your ability to be that sought-after mediator with all the experience you have achieved in Sudan, Ethiopia, and elsewhere," Stein warned Carter. "You will not become engaged if you continue to beat Israel over the head; what you are saying is neither totally accurate nor will it do any good if you want to get back into the negotiating saddle." Stein urged Carter to hold a press conference to apologize to Israeli and U.S. Jewish leaders, to reiterate his support for a secure Israel, and to remind everyone of his successful record as president in seeking freedom for Soviet Jews to emigrate.[20]

Carter was not accustomed to receiving such a scolding from a subordinate, especially not Stein. He did not dispute Stein's analysis but contended that he was in fact evenhanded, only varying his tactics according to political realities. In a democracy like Israel, the press was a means to focus attention on human rights issues and to ameliorate abuses, he claimed, citing his achievement with Shmuel Goren in undoing the unjustified administrative deportation of Palestinian women and children. In dealing with dictatorships like Assad's Syria, where there was no free press by which to sway public opinion, Carter saw direct personal appeals to the dictator as the more effective tactic. "I'm not comparing Israel with Syria as Rosenthal (and you?) prefer," a defensive Carter wrote Stein. "If U.S. Jewish leaders reacted to the mothers/children issue as they did to 'Who is a Jew?' we would be taking a big move toward peace—which requires acknowledging that Palestinians are equally human."[21]

Although Carter rejected Stein's advice to hold a press conference, he did agree to an interview on the Middle East with an Associated Press reporter. But Carter not only refused to backpedal, he stubbornly upped the ante: "I know that when any statement is made that is critical of Israel . . . it's going to be condemned," Carter stated. "I don't have any apology to make. I am concerned about genuine belief that I am biased, but a lot of the accusations about bias are deliberately designed to prevent further criticism of Israel's policies. And I don't choose to be intimidated."[22]

In a letter to the *New York Times*, published April 1, 1990, Carter disputed A. M. Rosenthal's claim that he was "a liar"; he also responded to William Safire's attack in a column on Baker foreign policy as anti-Israel. Carter's language was strong and unusually pointed. "What would your columnists' policy be if an Arab leader was taking Jewish mothers and children away from their homes and husbands, and forcibly deporting them to a foreign country?" Carter asked. "Palestinians are human also and their rights must be defended."[23]

What brought Carter jeers in some quarters brought him cheers from the Arab world. Having personally made sure that both Carter and Arafat were willing to embrace the other, Mary King quickly set up a meeting in Paris. "Mary and I arranged for the first meeting with Carter and President Arafat in Paris, which I attended," recalled forty-five-year-old Bassam Abu Sharif, who had been Arafat's spokesman since 1987. "It was a real big thing. The rest was easy. Once you break the ice, drinking the water is very easy."[24]

What was difficult for Stein and other Carter Center analysts to understand was that their boss had not really changed his objectives in the Middle East, merely his strategy. Rather than defer to Israeli sensitivities, he would instead work to interpret Arafat with the Bush administration, the world community via CNN, and the American public, and try to let the PLO leader be more realistically seen by Congress. If Arafat could be better understood in Western eyes, the peace process might be relaunched. In other words, Carter began coaching Arafat on how to not frighten democracies by using inflammatory rhetoric: it was a strategy that would eventually lead to the Oslo Agreements of September 1993.

Ken Stein agreed that Carter's proposed tête-à-tête with Yasir Arafat in Paris was the next logical next step to advancing peace. "From this meeting with Arafat you will have done more for the Palestinians, Arafat, and the PLO in American political life than any one else in history even if they disagree with you on the Camp David accords and the Egyptian Israeli peace treaty," Stein wrote Carter before his departure. "You should be sure that our Palestinian friends realize how important this meeting is to their dignity, honor, national pride, self-esteem, and goal to achieve self-determination."[25] Unfortunately for Stein, he stayed back in Atlanta while Mary King headed to Tunis to escort Arafat to Paris. Carter was beyond Stein's cautious influence; he was a man on a peace mission.

There was no world leader Jimmy Carter was more eager to know than Yasir Arafat, the master logistician and survivor of byzantine Middle Eastern politics. Arafat had survived Nasser and Sadat, danced around Assad, sparred with King Hussein, kept his radical left at bay, and assured James Baker of his commitment to abandon terrorism as a tool. Carter felt certain affinities with the Palestinian: a tendency toward hyperactivity and a workaholic disposition with unremitting sixteen-hour days, seven days a week, decade after decade. Both men were like modern Bedouins with airplanes instead of camels. Carter had three main objectives for the Paris meeting: to develop a personal rapport with Arafat, get the PLO leader to accept the Camp David accords, and replace the PLO National Charter, with its anti-Israel language, with the more recent Palestinian Declaration of Independence. Carter was also anxious to learn more about the *intifada*. In fact, he began mentoring Mubarak Awad and others at the Palestinian Center for the Study of Nonviolence, always stressing that, like Gandhi, they must pledge *total* nonviolence. Arafat, who had no direct dealings with Israeli leaders, was anxious to hear Carter's impressions of Shamir, Moshe Arens, Dan Meridor, Ehud Olmert, Yossi Beilin, and others.[26]

While Carter was always punctual for meetings, Arafat habitually ran late—often by days, weeks, and months. Arafat's tardiness led a Palestinian journalist, Dr. Afnan al-Qassen, to write a book called *Waiting Forty Days for the President*, a chronicle of forty unpleasant days on hold in Tunis. Every day a PLO representative promised that Arafat would meet with al-Qassen the next morning, but the interview never materialized. When the journalist's tart account of his experience arrived in East Jerusalem's bookshops, the Fatah organization simply bought the whole run.[27]

Determined not to wait forty days, let alone forty seconds, for Arafat, Carter dispatched Mary King from London to Tunis a day early to escort, if not shanghai, the PLO leader to Paris. "Make sure there is no embarrassment" was her mandate. She succeeded. Years later King recalled the flight with Arafat on the way to Paris, as they reminisced about their previous six years of conversations. "Arafat noticed that I was tired and insisted that I take his customary seat on his plane because it reclined in a certain way, so that I could sleep," King remembered. "I used my handbag as a pillow. After some time had passed, I noticed that a pillow was being ever so gently substituted for the handbag. Arafat himself was trying to place the pillow under my head without waking me. This reflected a caring side to his character which has rarely been evident to the international public as a whole."[28]

Arafat had with him a phalanx of his eight most influential supporters, including Mahmoud Darweesh, Hani al-Hassan, Hasib Sabbagh, Abdul Majid Shoman, and Bassam Abu Sharif. Carter's entourage consisted of only Rosalynn and Mary, both of whom took detailed notes. No reporters were present, and the conversation was not leaked. Before their private meeting on April 4, Carter and Arafat spent an informal half-hour with François Mitterrand at the Elysée Palace. Months earlier the French president had become the first major Western leader officially to receive Arafat. Mitterrand, who had revived France's Socialist party into a vibrant political force, praised Carter for his courage in meeting with the PLO leader and promised to make a "strong statement" urging Israel to make a "courageous move" toward peace.[29]

Carter began the two-hour private session at the Hotel de Crillon by reaffirming his "unalterable commitment to work to bring peace with justice in the Middle East." He then reiterated his standard disclaimer: he was a private citizen, a simple Emory University professor, who no longer spoke for the U.S. government. Arafat nodded his understanding and responded, "Yes, but you bring strong moral power."[30]

The conversation turned to personalities in the region. Carter, not unnaturally, commented that Israeli Labor party leader Shimon Peres was the most likely leader to push the peace process forward. Carter proudly recounted his recent showdown with Prime Minister Shamir over the Israeli policy of deporting women and children. He then asked the PLO leader to help him bring peace to war-torn Lebanon.

Shifting gears, Carter next inquired of Arafat's preferences for an international conference. Arafat responded that he preferred one organized by the five permanent members of the UN Security Council "because they are the powers who can give guarantees." Although sympathetic to Arafat's approach, Carter nevertheless pushed for a USSR-U.S. mediated conference (for which he had already obtained Assad's assent) because "Israel is in great fear of the UN." Arafat refused to commit to a Bush-Gorbachev-run conference on the grounds that it would be tantamount to an abandonment of UN friends such as China and France.

Talk then turned to Carter's concern over the PLO National Charter, which he felt was an impediment to the peace process. Arafat grew agitated as he pulled out two newly minted gold Israeli medallions and presented them to Carter. They featured a map of Israel that covered portions of Syria, Iraq as far as Baghdad, and a chunk of Saudi Arabia. He asked Carter to pass one on to President Bush, and then had an aide present Carter with another map that purported to show Zionist designs for the Middle East. "We have to speak about *their* charter too," was Arafat's point.

Carter nevertheless persisted with his concerns that sections of the PLO Charter—which required a two-thirds parliamentary vote to amend—contained provisions on the necessity of armed struggle, the elimination of Zionism, the illegality of Israel, and called upon all Arab states to declare Zionism illegal. "I'd like to ask you to consider amending the charter," Carter said. He asked Arafat, "What do you need to revoke this? It might make the ultimate change in my government, possibly even in Israel, to bring about a comprehensive peace and goals you want." Carter dangled some carrots, as instructed by Baker, which the United States might offer were the charter amended: PLO membership in the World Health Organization; lifting the ban on PLO members traveling in the United States; and perhaps the initiation of higher-level meetings between the PLO and the U.S. government. Carter suggested that the charter be replaced with the November 1988 Palestinian Declaration of Independence, which he termed "beautiful." Poet Mahmoud Darweesh, one of the authors of the declaration, who was present, beamed at the compliment, particularly when he was referred to as the Thomas Jefferson of Palestine.

Arafat argued that from his perspective the declaration had already "superseded" the charter, which was now merely a historical document, and then launched into an embittered litany of his Middle East woes. "Israel has 250 nuclear warheads and is assured of an absolute U.S. supply," Arafat pointed out. "The Palestinians have no homeland, no identity. This land was our land until 1948. Since 1969, we said we would accept a democratic Palestinian state. They refused. We are suffering in diaspora. The coin I gave you has all of Jordan, Lebanon, two-thirds of Iraq, a third of Saudi Arabia. We have one fear. Their Likud party slogan is 'The West Bank and the East Bank are ours!' In spite of all this, we accept the two-state solution."

Arafat rattled off a list of his betrayals at the hand of the Reagan administration, the secret agreements he had with former secretary of state George Shultz, through Philip Habib, which were never implemented. Rosalynn Carter, who had been silently taking notes, suddenly piped up, "You don't have to convince us," which elicited gales of laughter all round. Then she smiled. "I think my husband asked me to take notes so I can't take part in the conversation." Jimmy Carter bantered back, "Yes, but she tells me what to say before we come to the meeting."

The levity was short-lived, for Carter persisted in turning the conversation back to Arafat's intransigence on repealing the PLO Charter. "If your Parliament [the Palestinian National Council] declared the charter as superseded, that would be adequate," Carter told Arafat. "But I don't understand why you insist on maintaining a charter that is so terrifying to Israelis and of concern to me when [I hear] you say what you say. If this has not been made absolutely clear, it is the major impediment now." For the next thirty minutes Arafat tried to explain why the charter could not be scrapped. "I am facing fanatics—not Palestinian fanatics Arab fanatics," Arafat told Carter. "Fanatics in Syria, Libya, Iraq, Egypt, Algeria. Fanatical groups. Arab national fanatics. Islamic fundamentalists." Arafat said it would be political suicide for him to make an issue of the charter; it would diminish his credibility with his people and produce an outcry from the Arab extremists sprinkled liberally throughout the Middle East. The gesture was too risky for him simply to make Israel feel safe. Unyielding, Carter again reiterated that it would be very beneficial if Arafat could find an official way to demonstrate that the Declaration of Independence legally superseded the charter.

Arafat grew frustrated with Carter's insistence. Americans, it seemed, were always trying to exact a higher price from the Palestinians. He claimed that Philip Habib had lied to him about the UN protecting Palestinians in Lebanon; the cost was a "massacre" of his people. Carter agreed that the Reagan administration was not renowned as promise keepers, but assured Arafat that James Baker was a man of his word. If that were so, Arafat countered, why had the Bush administration downgraded PLO contacts to the ambassadorial level, and why was it trying an end run around the PLO by wanting "other Palestinians" at the much ballyhooed international peace conference as a precondition for U.S. participation? Arafat claimed that the United States was abandoning all provisions of the Camp David accords that dealt with the creation of a Palestinian homeland.

Carter seized on Arafat's concern over the accords to ask whether he could quote the chairman as endorsing them. There was great laughter in response. Arafat riposted with a jocular, "Yes, if you had invited me!" saying that he was still waiting for an invitation. An avuncular Carter patted Arafat on the knee. The chairman continued, "Yes! I accept the Camp David accords, and I fought bravely to recover Egypt; I fought alone for Egypt to return to the Arab fold." Carter again asked, "Can I quote you on this?" to which Arafat replied yes.

The exchange was heartening for Jimmy Carter. Over the last decade he had come to believe that Cyrus Vance's State Department had led him down the primrose path with its view of the PLO, even though Carter understood Begin never would have allowed Arafat to be present at Camp David. Carter felt responsible for this nonrepresentation, which "stalled peace." Now, in an atmosphere of cordiality, Arafat had accepted the accords and forgiven Carter for excluding him in 1978. Carter felt that a burden he had been carrying for years had been lifted. "I would like an easy relationship with you so that I might be able to help you because my heart is torn with anger and anguish and sorrow when I observe the suffering of the Palestinian people," Carter said. The room fell silent. "I have talked to farmers who are not allowed to plant their orange trees; I have seen trucks held up at the Allenby Bridge until the fruit rots; I have seen settlers whose wells were dug while the Palestinians were not allowed to dig theirs; I have met Palestinian students who finished high school but have never been allowed college. This is an obsession with me." The air thick with emotion, Carter spoke softly: "When I bring up the charter, you should not be concerned that I am biased. I am much more harsh with the Israelis. . . . I am satisfied with everything but the charter." Carter pointed out that all the evidence showed that the charter, which called for the elimination of Israel, was regarded as a legally binding document: therefore, an equally binding legal act was required stipulating that the declaration had replaced the charter as the PLO's official position.

Carter's open empathy with the disenfranchised Palestinian people had changed the meeting's tenor. Arafat now spoke at a more basic human level, addressing his Palestinian colleagues. "I cannot tell him [Carter] I can do something and three months later come back and say I could not do it." Arafat spoke of the crushing external and internal pressures on him as a leader. "If my father were still alive today, I would be considered a traitor," he went on quietly, reciting the history of compromises he had already made with Israel that the older generation and radical left viewed as capitulation to American demands.

Carter reemphasized his position. "I have a permanent, unassailable commitment to do what I can for the Palestinians . . . You can depend on me." The meeting ended with an exchange of gifts. When Arafat presented Rosalynn with a dress for daughter Amy, decorated with Palestinian embroidery, he mentioned that he had followed Amy's political activities with great interest, especially her anti-CIA stance in Nicaragua and antiapartheid activities in South Africa.

Mary King had arranged for Jimmy, Rosalynn, and Yasir to have a half-hour of private time after the meeting, in another room.[31] Arafat had never met a political couple like the Carters, and their working partnership intrigued him. In the course of conversation Rosalynn began describing her revulsion and dismay over a story about Israeli troops dumping garbage in front of a Palestinian orphanage during the Carters' trip to the West Bank. Innocent Palestinian children were being treated as trash. As she recalled the inexcusable humiliation of their treatment, her eyes filled with tears. And the men, too, began to sob. Carter grasped the hands of his companions, and the three briefly prayed together. Then they dried their tears, embraced, and said farewell.

Rosalynn Carter's clarity of compassion had qualitatively changed the nature of their relationship. The Carters left the elegant hotel drained by the emotional encounter, carrying with them a mother-of-pearl biblical scene made in Bethlehem and given to them by the PLO chairman.[32] Arafat returned to the main meeting room. His advisers saw that he was visibly shaken. Mary King had never seen him so wrought up. "His face was flushed," King recalled. "He was affected emotionally. He had been thrown off balance. I could tell Arafat had been moved."[33] The chairman regained his composure, briefly recounted what had been discussed, and then dismissed his entourage for a brief respite. For Arafat the meeting was a major turning point, and he now understood why Sadat had considered Jimmy Carter a brother. Carter was the highest, most respected senior American to have met with him. For the first time, he had met a statesman who could influence him and lead him to make the necessary decisions to open a dialogue with the United States.[34]

The next morning, King took Carter for breakfast with Rafiq Hariri, president of Lebanon and married to a Palestinian, at his Paris residence. At the end of meal and discussion, Hariri wrote out a check for $250,000 for the Carter Center.[35]

✂∽✎

T he Israeli press, never sympathetic to Carter, now pummeled him when
    he told reporters that the PLO chairman had "done everything he can, I
    think, in recent months to promote the peace process."[36] The Israeli
ambassador to the United States, Ovadia Sofer, publicly protested Carter's
meeting with Arafat. "The problem is that Arafat was in Baghdad two days
ago with Saddam Hussein at his side," Sofer complained, "and said he will
fight Israel with the Iraqi missile." Sofer's concern was not misplaced. Only
days before his meeting with Carter, Arafat was reported to have said while
in Baghdad that to achieve an independent state, Palestinians would fight
"with stones, with rifles, and with al-Abed," a missile the Iraqis had test-fired
in December and believed capable of striking Israeli targets. Arafat denied
making the statement, and Carter chose to believe him.[37]

Although Baker had quasi-endorsed the meeting with Arafat, President
Bush, for political reasons, maintained a distance. "Carter was not acting
with the blessing of, nor disapproval of, or anything else, of the administration," trying to cast him as a free agent. "Certainly, he as a former president
should be free to do his own thing, and that's exactly what he's doing."[38]
Bush's mild disclaimers did little to satisfy Richard Perle, Jeane Kirkpatrick,
William Safire, Joshua Muravchik, and other prominent Reaganites. They
accused the Bush administration of actually encouraging Carter to meet
with Arafat, whom they assailed as a terrorist. "The administration is
pushing the line that Arafat is a.) responsible, and b.) anti-terrorist, despite the fact that parts of the P.L.O. are still committing acts of terror,"
Elliott Abrams complained. "And Carter's meeting with Arafat helps again
to legitimize him and push the notion that he's a legitimate player, not a
terrorist."[39] But when a reporter inquired whether Carter hadn't become
the administration's most valued Middle East adviser, White House spokesman Marlin Fitzwater embraced the Carter initiatives: "President Bush is
delighted to have him."[40]

Following Paris, Carter and Arafat stayed in constant communication.
Letters and requests went back and forth, with Arafat telling Carter he
was willing to distance himself from Libya and from radical elements in
the PLO, even if it meant "sacrificing some material support for the Intifada." Carter had become not only Arafat's intermediary with the Bush administration but an Arafat speechwriter. On May 24 Carter drafted on his
home computer the strategy and wording for a generic speech Arafat was to
deliver soon for Western ears, one which the former president believed
might help to overcome the deficit of understanding over the Palestinian
plight:

The audience is not the Security Council, but the world community. The objective of the speech should be to secure maximum sympathy and support of other world leaders, especially including Americans and Israelis. The Likud leaders are now on the defensive, and must not be given any excuse for continuing their present abusive policies.

A good opening would be to outline the key points of the Save the Children report. This information did not come from Palestinians, but from an unbiased international organization. Then ask: "What would you do, if these were your children and grandchildren? As the Palestinian leader, I share the responsibility for them. Our response has been to urge peace talks, but the Israeli leaders have refused, and our children continue to suffer.

Our people, who face Israeli bullets, have no weapons: only a few stones remaining when our homes are destroyed by Israeli bulldozers. Our young men and women, like those in other nations, want to learn about the world of literature and science. They want to prepare for the future by attending university classes in an atmosphere of peace. Since January 1988, the Israelis have closed all the Palestinian universities. 93,000 of our young people are forced to spend their days on the streets, or huddled together with their families in darkened rooms under the interminable curfews. Then repeat: "What would you do, if these were your children and grandchildren? As the Palestinian leader, I share the responsibility for them. Our response has been to urge peace talks, but the Israeli leaders have refused, and our children continue to suffer."

This exact litany should be repeated with a few other personal examples: farmers not able to sell their oranges, villagers not permitted to dig a deeper well, 9,000 still imprisoned without legal counsel or family visits, mothers and children removed from their husbands and fathers at night and deported to Jordan, an entire people deprived of basic rights of self-determination.

The thrust of the speech should be to bring, not only the world's political leaders but every parent and grandparent, into a realization of the excessively patient suffering of the Palestinians.

In addition, it would be wise to align the Palestinian leaders with U.S. leaders. I can certify that there is a great deal of support now in Washington. They responded well to my personal call for international monitors, as suggested to me by Bassam Abu Sharif a few days ago.

A public endorsement of the Camp David principles (as has

already been done privately) would be a profoundly significant demonstration of flexibility and desire for peace, and would provide a legal core, officially endorsed by Prime Minister Begin and the government of Israel, around which peace talks can lead toward self-determination. This would short-circuit the peace process by several years, and put Shamir and his followers on the defensive better than anything else. Emphasize peace, not violence.

Remain strong and forceful, but design the comments to align Palestinians with legitimacy and the rest of the world and to isolate Israeli rejectionists.[41]

Carter sent a copy of this draft to his close friend and Carter Center founder, Hasib Sabbagh, who distributed it to his circle of independent Palestinian contacts. If a former U.S. president was now advising Yasir Arafat, the tide must have certainly turned in the PLO's favor. A flurry of exchanges soon followed between Carter and the PLO. During the next eighteen months a number of Palestinian intellectuals, professionals, and political activists visited with Carter in Atlanta: Sami Kilani, a physics professor from the West Bank city of Nablus who had been repeatedly detained by the Israelis; Zakariah Agha, head of the Arab Medical Association in Gaza; Raja Shehadeh, a lawyer who headed the esteemed human rights group al-Haq in Ramallah; and, of course, Mubarak Awad. As one visitor, Mayor Elias Freij of Bethlehem, phrased it, "To get information from President Carter is a perfect thing. No one knows it better." And Carter began spearheading the drive to create medical libraries for Palestinians in the West Bank and Gaza.[42]

On May 30 there was an attempted Palestinian terrorist raid on bathers at a Tel Aviv beach. Mohammed Abu'l Abbas, who sat on the PLO government's executive committee, claimed responsibility for the incident. On June 20 Washington suspended dialogue with Arafat over the attack. Carter urged Arafat to condemn the foiled operation, but he would only deny PLO involvement. By July Arafat was seeking Carter's clout to reopen the peace talks: "We are looking forward to your help and assistance to push the Peace Process forward and to resume the Palestinian dialogue," the chairman wrote. "Indeed we hope that your efforts will succeed to resume this dialogue on a higher level and with a deeper content that corresponds with the importance of the Middle East and the necessity to establish peace in our region." Arafat also hoped that Carter would convene an international peace conference, perhaps in Atlanta; Arafat said he was now prepared to participate. He reiterated his faith in the former president, saying that the

PLO fully trusted him. In an emotional four-page letter to Carter, Arafat detailed all the peace proposals he accused the Israeli government of rejecting, from 1967 to the present, reminding his friend that the PLO had embraced the Baker plan, while the "Israeli Government declared publicly its rejection to the formula proposed by the U.S.A. and the U.N."[43]

Carter's hope for an Israeli-Palestinian peace conference with Arafat was blown out of the water on August 1, 1990, when 10,000 Iraqi troops invaded Kuwait, igniting the first international crisis of the post-cold-war order. Within hours of the invasion, Iraqi dictator Saddam Hussein announced the formal annexation of Kuwait based on an assertion of historical rights to the territory, not to mention the opportunity to obtain port facilities on the Persian Gulf, and additional petroleum reserves, and to punish tiny Kuwait for exceeding its OPEC quota and thereby driving down the world price of oil. Hussein, after sustaining an eight-year war with Iran, had emerged full of hubris, his territory intact and a formidable war machine at his disposal. There was fear around the world that the next target of Hussein's aggression would be northern Saudi Arabia.

Bush condemned the invasion the following day and called upon world leaders to join him in action against Iraq. The next day Secretary Baker and Soviet foreign minister Eduard Shevardnadze issued a joint statement from Moscow calling for a worldwide embargo on arms for Iraq because of its "brutal and illegal invasion of Kuwait." The Arab League Council—to the surprise of many—immediately moved to condemn Iraq, with dissent only from Jordan, Yemen, Mauritania, Djibouti, and Sudan. On August 6 the UN Security Council adopted a comprehensive embargo against Iraq. President Bush began organizing a multi-national force to protect Saudi Arabia and the other Gulf countries from further Iraqi aggression, while steps were taken to compel Iraq to withdraw from Kuwait. Secretaries James Baker of state and Dick Cheney of defense flew to Saudi Arabia, where they convinced King Fahd that his country was threatened and persuaded him to agree to the deployment of large numbers of U.S. troops in his kingdom. On August 7 American paratroopers, an armored brigade, and fighter planes were on their way to Saudi Arabia to begin Operation Desert Shield. In a UN Security Council–supported operation, the Americans were quickly joined by token forces from Egypt, Morocco, and Syria.[44]

Carter initially urged caution. He generally saw the Bush administration as acting prudently but thought sending U.S. troops to Saudi Arabia was a potentially disastrous mistake. More troubling to him was the fact that Arafat voiced support for Saddam Hussein's belligerent acts. Carter realized that the Palestinian stance would forestall peace talks and lead the Gulf countries to cut funding to the PLO. Arafat would then be at his most vulnerable since his expulsion from Lebanon in 1982. "The Gulf War changed everything," Carter recalled. "It turned the Middle East peace process upside down."[45]

When the Iraqi invasion occurred, Mary King was "urgently" summoned by the PLO to fly to a private meeting with Arafat to discuss the brewing crisis. "We called Mary to Vienna in order to pass along a message," Bassam Abu Sharif recalled. "We got an OK from Saddam Hussein accepting [UN resolutions] 242 and 338 which means recognizing Israel. And that message was handed to Mary in order to carry to Carter and pass on to the [Bush] administration since we didn't have any contact with the administration."[46] After meeting with Arafat in Vienna, King immediately cabled Carter with this information, adding her opinion of Saddam Hussein, whom she had met once in Baghdad. "Saddam learned from the Israelis that might makes right—they took most of Palestine by force and 20 years later occupied the West Bank and Gaza," King wrote Carter on August 5. "In each case, international bluster was followed by acceptance." She told Carter that Hussein was "not crazy" but was "maniacal in his nationalistic ambitions." King had also learned from her PLO sources that Arafat had met with Hussein in Baghdad for two and a half hours after Iraq invaded Kuwait, and the two discussed using Jimmy Carter, the high priest of peace, as a card in resolving the Gulf crisis through mediation instead of full-fledged Middle East war.[47]

Throughout the Gulf crisis, Carter stayed in regular communication with Arafat. On August 13 the PLO leader informed Carter of his belief that the Israelis might carry out a provocative act disguised as Iraqis in order to trigger a military response. Arafat asked Carter to warn President Bush of the possibility, along with the message that "Baghdad does not want to attack the Saudis." Carter relayed the chairman's views to the Bush administration.[48]

On September 6, Mary King hand-delivered a letter to Arafat from Carter in Tunis. "I found him [Arafat] calm, collected, very well focused, forthcoming, and positive," King wrote Carter the following day. "All of his attention is concentrated on achieving a political solution to the Gulf crisis." Carter's letter urged Arafat to write Secretary Baker to the effect that even though the PLO had publicly embraced Saddam Hussein, in private they had deplored the invasion because it had disrupted the peace process.[49] Heeding Carter's advice, Arafat assigned one of his closest advisers, Bassam Abu Sharif, to write Baker, distancing the PLO from Saddam Hussein, saying their public support of the Iraqi dictator was a show of pan-Arab unity. "It is in the clear national interest of the Palestinians and their leadership to resolve the Gulf crisis in order to be able to focus on a just solution for the Palestinians," Sharif wrote Baker on September 8. "That is why the PLO remains in contact with the Saudi Arabians and the Iraqis and continues to search to find common ground for political solution."[50]

As Arafat's pro-Iraqi stance had left him politically isolated in world opinion, the somewhat chastened leader tried to justify himself to Jimmy and Rosalynn, explaining why he *had* to support the Iraqi invasion of Kuwait: "I am a popular leader of the people. I have always got to be with my people. Either inside or outside the Occupied Territories, they are with Saddam. I have given nothing. Everything I have done was lost by the Americans stopping the dialogue. I looked like a failure. Saddam is their only hope because he has linked oil for the first time with their cause. He has linked missiles to their cause. They feel stronger because of him. All the Arab nations feel stronger because of him including both nationalists and fundamentalists."[51]

Arafat's solution—Iraqi withdrawal from Kuwait hinged on Israeli withdrawal from West Bank–Gaza—was, of course, never a serious possibility. Yet that September Arafat was urging Carter to lobby President Bush to raise the linkage issue so that the United States would not miss an opportunity to counteract growing Arab antagonism toward Washington for its "hypocrisy."[52]

When in early October President Bush made a statement at the UN indirectly linking the Gulf crisis and the Israeli-Palestinian conflict, Arafat saw the hidden hand of Jimmy Carter at work. Mistaken as to Carter's actual influence with the Bush administration, Arafat then asked the ex-president on October 11 to act as conduit to the White House, sending a memo outlining various details of Arafat's position: Iraqi withdrawal from Kuwait in return for guaranteed linkage with the eventual Israeli withdrawal from the West Bank; a proposed timetable for how the linkage plan could be implemented; copies of the agreements George Shultz had made with Arafat in December 1988; and a memo to Bush from Arafat imploring him to "speak in warmer tones" toward Palestinians who, he pointed out, were stuck between two merciless hammers: Iraq and Israel.[53]

In his October 11 letter, Arafat also told Carter that thirty-two Palestinians had been killed by Israeli soldiers in Jerusalem on October 8, not the nineteen reported by CNN. "Our Moslem and Christian holy places are more valuable than oil," Arafat went on. "If the Americans are interested in oil, we are interested in our sacred places."[54] He also asked Carter to try to garner UN permission to send food for the Palestinians in both Iraq and Kuwait. Carter forwarded Arafat's materials to Bush, but the president was not interested. With Munich 1938 and Vietnam on his mind, not to mention the price of oil, Bush had drawn a "line in the sand," a January 15 deadline.

If Iraq did not leave Kuwait, the United States would declare war. With a cold shoulder from Bush, Carter now became the most high-profile American to urge peace talks with Saddam Hussein instead of war.

The irony of Carter's antiwar stance was that as president, in his State of the Union address before a joint session of Congress on January 23, 1980, he had warned that an "attempt by any outside force to gain control of the Persian Gulf region will be regarded as an assault on the vital interests of the United States of America, and such force will be repelled by any means necessary, including military force." President Carter had made the speech, which was dubbed the Carter Doctrine, as a warning to the Soviet Union, which had invaded Afghanistan a month earlier. Immediately, critics such as George F. Kennan and Edward M. Kennedy charged that President Carter had overreacted, abandoning diplomacy for war threats. Now, ten years later, Bush was evoking the Carter Doctrine, while the man who it was named after, in a reversal, assumed the stance of dove.[55]

That fall, using every resource at his disposal—including a two-hour Carter Center roundtable session with Admiral William Crowe, Senator James McClure, former defense secretary James Schlesinger, and Prince Bandar ibn-Sultan of Saudi Arabia that was televised by the Discovery Channel as "Crisis in the Gulf"—Carter relentlessly promoted negotiations.[56] He wrote articles for *Time* and *Newsweek*, both of which chastised Bush for refusing to engage in "negotiations or exploratory talks, which might imply weakness or a willingness to reverse adamant public statements." Carter seized upon a statement by General Norman Schwarzkopf, commander of the UN forces in Operation Desert Shield, that in the first three weeks of the crisis Iraq could have overrun Saudi Arabia without opposition, as evidence that Saddam Hussein had never intended to invade Saudi Arabia. Carter, pushing for the so-called linkage solution to the crisis, consistently touted King Hussein of Jordan, who had remained neutral, as the ideal mediator to "help bring about a peaceful settlement of the gulf crisis."[57]

Carter employed a dozen different arguments in a dozen different locations to attack the Bush administration's response to the Persian Gulf crisis. In Atlanta a worried Carter pointed to the likelihood of famine in Sudan; the United States had stopped sending food to Khartoum because of its support of Saddam Hussein.[58] In Wilmington, Delaware, he asked why Bush was ignoring the linkage solution being proposed by "prominent Arab leaders."[59] In Iowa he questioned the administration's true intentions. "There is no doubt in my mind that the level of the military that is currently being marshalled into Saudi Arabia is far beyond what is necessary to defend Saudi Arabia," Carter sniped in a speech at Buena Vista College on September 29.[60] In Arizona he stated that "no matter how you look at what's happening in Kuwait, no matter how you look at what's happening in Lebanon, the core issue is now, and will continue to be, Israel-Palestine."[61] Everywhere Carter traveled, he pounded Bush and Reagan for having abandoned the energy conservation policies his administration had set in place. Now with imported oil accounting for almost 50 percent of U.S. petroleum consumption, the Bush administration, Carter argued, felt compelled to protect Kuwaiti petroleum for economic reasons. From Carter's perspective, the world could get along quite well without either Iraqi or Kuwaiti oil. There was no justification whatsoever for Americans to die for the emir of Kuwait.[62]

Carter's dissent was part of a larger pattern of criticizing U.S. military intervention policy. He had been outraged at the Reagan administration for giving tacit approval to Israel's disastrous invasion of Lebanon in 1982, which was followed by the deaths of 241 U.S. Marines ill-advisedly deployed in Beirut. He saw the invasion and defeat of Grenada and the Bush administration's bombing and invasion of Panama as moral outrages. "In none of these cases," Carter contended, "did we first exhaust the opportunities for peaceful resolution of the dispute."[63]

Meanwhile Carter had enlisted Yasir Arafat for help with a personal crusade to free a fellow Georgian. His friend and longtime political supporter David Rabhan had been imprisoned in Iran since October 1984 for allegedly violating foreign currency regulations. Over the years Carter had used every channel at his disposal to accumulate information on Rabhan's health and location. "I wrote or talked with Ronald Reagan and Bush about him, as well as their Secretaries of State and National Security Advisors, and other government officials," Carter recalled in a sworn affidavit. "The paucity of information and contact was painfully frustrating, as we had sporadic information that Mr. Rabhan had been tortured, especially after we heard that his treatment by his Iranian captors had worsened after the Iranians learned of Mr. Rabhan's close friendship with me."[64] After leaving the presidency, Carter described Rabhan as a "hostage," but neither the Reagan or Bush administration considered him one, and his plight went largely unreported. "He was a hostage," Carter maintained. "He was never a spy. He never had any kind of connection with the CIA or with any sort of espionage or spying."[65]

After trying every conceivable avenue from the U.S. State Department to the Swiss embassy, Carter, swallowing his pride, wrote his archenemy the

Ayatollah Khomeini on October 30, 1988, asking for "assistance in freeing an American national."[66] The letter initiated the laborious process that ultimately led to Rabhan's freeing from his closetlike cell about five and a half feet deep and eight feet wide. "After Carter sent the letter my prison life improved," Rabhan later noted. "Khomeini sent word to find out 'Who the hell was Rabhan?' For a while it was played up in all the Iranian newspapers blasting Carter for interfering with their internal affairs."[67] Meanwhile Carter began peppering the new secretary of state, James A. Baker III, with requests for assistance in freeing his longtime friend David Rabhan.[68]

Whatever little information Carter learned, he shared with Rabhan's family—including three children—in Savannah. While in prison Rabhan was tied in gunnysacks and beaten, tortured, and kept in complete darkness for weeks at a time. He witnessed executions both random and planned, watched as guards amputated limbs from thieves and stoned to death adulterers buried to the ribs in sand. He twice lived through mock executions: tied to a post blindfolded, the firing squad leader shouted, "One, two . . . ," then the guns clicked.[69] A breakthrough occurred in December 1988, when Carter was granted a phone call to Rabhan at Evin Prison. "For once in your life go back to your cell and try to be nice," Carter cajoled his friend at the end of their brief conversation, insisting that somehow he would procure his release.[70]

But Rabhan's future brightened considerably in early September 1990, when Arafat, at Carter's direct request via a sealed letter carried by Mary King, promised to try and procure the American's release. "Achieving positive and quick results under such conditions, the Gulf Crisis, and the presence of foreign troops in the area will not be an easy matter," Arafat wrote Carter on September 6 from Tunis. "I will, however, continue making every possible effort in that regard and will soon dispatch my personal envoy to Iran to convey our point of view on the issue. We ask God for success." As promised, Arafat pressed former Iranian premier Mehdi Bazargan and former foreign minister Ibrahim Yazdi to free Rabhan as a personal favor to the PLO.[71] Carter also enlisted the Algerian government to help him procure Rabhan's release. The Algerian-Arafat appeal worked: on September 15 Rabhan was released after spending nine years, eight months, and twenty-four days in various Iranian prisons.

Carter's credibility throughout the Arab world surged. His U.S. stump speeches for a peaceful resolution of the Gulf crisis were widely covered throughout the Middle East and Europe, praised in *Le Monde* and the *Daily Mirror*. So convinced was Carter of the necessity of averting war that he took a step that, to put it mildly, tarnished his credibility with the Bush administration and branded him a peace outlaw with the Pentagon. On November 19 Carter wrote the heads of state of the other members of the UN Security Council—French president François Mitterrand, British prime minister Margaret Thatcher, Chinese premier Li Peng, and Russian president Mikhail Gorbachev—a direct appeal to hold "good faith" negotiations with Saddam Hussein before entering upon a war. Carter implied that mature nations should not act like lemmings, blindly following George Bush's inflammatory "line in the sand" rhetoric.[72]

The letter was also sent to a dozen other world leaders, presidents, and prime ministers Carter believed could exert influence in the UN General Assembly. "Recent statements from Washington and other national capitals make it increasingly clear that patience and persistence are being abandoned, and that great pressures are being exerted for approval of a military solution to the present Gulf Crisis," Carter wrote. "History has shown that momentum of this kind is extremely difficult to reverse. Since armed intervention by forces of the United States and other nations is predicated on prior approval of the United Nations Security Council, your own decision can be a deciding factor in making this momentous judgement."

In his letter Carter urged these influential world leaders to abandon U.S. leadership and instead give "unequivocal support to an Arab League effort, without any restraints on their agenda." If this were allowed to occur, Carter believed, an Arab solution would not only force Iraq to leave Kuwait but at long last also force Israel to withdraw from the occupied territories.[73]

Secretary of Defense Richard Cheney was the first Bush administration member to learn of the Carter letter. Prime Minister Brian Mulroney of Canada had telephoned Cheney at the Pentagon to read him Carter's astonishing call to world leaders to abandon the U.S. war effort. Cheney was stunned; at the time he felt the letter verged on treason, an act of treachery unfathomable from a former U.S. president. Years later Cheney's ire had not diminished: "Writing it was just plain wrong. For him to go behind our backs and ask world leaders to denounce our war policy was reprehensible, totally inappropriate for a former president." Carter's defense, that he had notified the Bush administration of his letter, is disputed by Cheney. "Later Carter tried to finagle what he did, pretending that he had warned us," Cheney commented. "He didn't. I don't care what Carter says, we did not know about his interference in advance."[74] Carter *had* sent President Bush a copy of the November 19 letter, dated on November 20 as an afterthought, as if it were written directly and only for him. But he never informed the Bush administration that he had blanketed world leaders with his protest letter. "I believe there is widespread support in the Congress and the public at large for our basic objectives," Bush wrote Carter on December 11, "just as there is equally strong understanding of what is at stake."[75]

President Bush was outraged. According to Bush's former CIA director, William Webster, from then on, whenever Carter's name came up the president would "just shake his head in dismay."[76] He simply could not fathom why Carter would work international back channels in the Arab world and at the UN to sabotage U.S. foreign policy on the eve of war. "I recognized his right to speak out," Bush wrote on July 27, 1995. "What I violently disagreed with was his writing to heads of foreign governments urging them to stand against what we were trying to do in the UN. I believe Jimmy Carter's approach was wrong, and I felt that we did all the diplomacy to 'give peace a chance,' then we had to use force. The bottom line is I would never have personally contacted and advocated to foreign leaders that they oppose a policy of a seated President."[77]

As the January 15 deadline approached, a vociferous debate ensued in the United States over whether saving Kuwait was worth American lives. Opponents of war like Carter argued that economic sanctions were working, an opinion shared by Bush's CIA director, William Webster. Testifying before the House Armed Services Committee, Webster asserted that if sanctions continued, within three months the Iraqi air force would lose its flying ability, and within nine months Iraq's ground forces would lose their combat readiness. Secretary Cheney disagreed with Webster, telling the Senate Armed Services Committee that "there is no guarantee that sanctions will force Hussein out of Kuwait" and warning that if military action were delayed, the multinational coalition might falter. Just how strongly Carter believed in linkage can be seen in his January 2, 1991, *New York Times* op-ed piece, in which he wrote, "Now is a propitious time for Israel to come forward with a genuine peace initiative, shifting the onus of the consequences of Saddam Hussein's invasion to Israel."[78] Meanwhile, Carter's dream for getting Iraq out of Kuwait by forcing Israel out of the West Bank and Gaza was dismissed in no uncertain terms by Baker on January 6.[79]

Carter's last hope to avert war was to convince Arab leaders aligned with the U.S. position to abandon the January 15 deadline and to call for additional time to find a peaceful solution to the crisis. (To the surprise of many, the U.S. coalition even included Assad. Baker had flown to Syria—branded a terrorist nation by the United States—and returned with Assad's support for Operation Desert Storm. The tradeoff Baker struck with Assad stipulated that for Syrian support of Desert Storm, the United States would allow Syria free rein in Lebanon.) In particular Carter hoped to personally convince King Fahd, Assad, and Hosni Mubarak to abandon the hawkish United

States stance for a negotiated Arab solution. Carter hoped to gain an eleventh-hour change of heart from the three Arab leaders. Again, working alone, on January 10 Carter wrote them an urgent plea. "I am distressed by the inability of either the international community or the Arab world to find a diplomatic solution to the Gulf crisis," his letter began. "The devastating consequences of this failure require maximum peace efforts from all of us. I have repeatedly urged President Bush and other American leaders to consider the long-term consequences of war. I have asked many in Congress to deliberate carefully before sanctioning military action. I urge you to call publicly for a delay in the use of force while Arab leaders seek a peaceful solution to the crisis. You may have to forego approval from the White House, but you will find the French, Soviets, and others fully supportive. Also, most Americans will welcome such a move."[80]

Carter's astonishing act may in part be explained by his commitment to the primacy of seeking nonviolent solutions to conflict, his elevating humanity over country, a principle of individual good conscience over realpolitik. Although many politicians claim that they adhere to the principle that one turns to war only when diplomacy fails, Carter fervently believed in this dictum. He was convinced that all diplomatic channels had not been exhausted. He disagreed not about the gravity of Saddam Hussein's crime but about how to reverse it. Carter was prepared to do just about anything to avoid a Middle East war, even if it meant working directly against his own government. "I hope you will act to postpone a war to dislodge Iraq and Kuwait," Carter wrote the three Arab leaders. "Western bombing attacks and a ground invasion of Iraq, with the resulting deaths of tens of thousands of Arab civilians, the violation of intense Muslim sensitivities, and apparent confrontation between Western and Arab forces, will have horrifying consequences for all Middle Eastern peoples. The economic, social and political aftermath of such a war will last for years, perhaps decades. The advances you have made in guiding your nation's progress might well be lost. This war may also postpone indefinitely any efforts to resolve the Palestinian issue."[81]

But King Fahd, with 550,000 war-ready UN troops stationed in Saudi Arabia, and poised to pledge $16.8 billion to the war effort, was not about to heed Carter's plea to break ranks with Washington. Likewise, Mubarak and Assad, who might agree with Carter in principle, realized that to change course at the last minute, to double-cross the Bush administration, would be unwise. Amazingly enough, word of Carter's letters to the Arab leaders never got back to the U.S. government. Seven years after the fact, Bush, Baker, Webster, Scowcroft, Powell, and Cheney still did not know the true extent of Carter's antiadministration maneuvering. If for years they had been incensed by Carter's November 19, 1990, letter to world leaders, one can only imagine how disturbed they would be to learn of the letter to the Arab leaders only five days before Operation Desert Storm commenced.[82]

Bush had not asked Congress for a declaration of war, but his request for a resolution supporting the use of force was its functional equivalent and unleashed an intense congressional debate with compelling arguments made for continuing sanctions as well as an immediate strike. The Senate doves— including Sam Nunn—feared a strike against Iraq could lead to war throughout the Middle East. The final vote, on January 12, was close. Fifty-two senators, mainly Republicans, voted for war, but forty-seven were opposed. In the House, where sentiments also split mainly along partisan lines, 250 voted for, 183 against. It was not a whopping mandate for Bush.

Carter, who had also written a strong antiwar letter to some fifteen senators, gasped in horror—for the first time in its history, the United States was preparing to spill Arab blood.[83] (When planning the Iranian hostage mission, then-president Carter's aversion to gratuitous force was so profound that he asked if the guards outside the embassy could be taken out with tranquilizer guns.)[84] Completely sidelined, Carter watched the Gulf War on CNN like everyone else, bemoaning the fact that 79 Americans and over 100,000 Iraquis died.

Once the Gulf invasion started, Carter kept a low profile, saying only that he supported American troops. The apocalypse he foretold never materialized. With no air force, a battered and helpless army, and the failure of Saddam's Scud missile attacks on Israel either to rally other Arab states to his side or to do any serious damage to the American military machine in the desert, Hussein was quickly forced to leave Kuwait. On February 26, retreating Iraqi troops torched Kuwait's oil wells, leading to an environmental disaster that Carter could only bemoan all the more. The next day Bush declared that "Iraq's army is defeated and Kuwait is liberated." He announced that the coalition would immediately cease hostilities.

Carter endorsed Bush's decision not to try to capture Baghdad or hunt down Saddam Hussein. Bush never intended to assume such risks or entanglements. American casualties in the one-hundred-hour war had been low: 79 killed, 213 wounded. But street fighting in Baghdad would likely inflict much higher casualty rates and the operations might take months to complete. Not only could Bush's astonishing popularity rating (90 percent, the highest ever for any president) not have survived a protracted war, but no UN resolution authorized the occupation of Iraq and the coalition's Arab partners would never have supported a move on Baghdad. In any case, Bush, and virtually everyone else, expected that either humiliated Iraqi army leaders would overthrow Saddam Hussein or the people would revolt against him. As it turned out, neither happened, and just a few years later Hussein was boasting that he was stronger than ever.[85]

Three years after the war, the *New York Times* reported on Carter's November 19, 1990, antiwar letter. Even former Carter foreign policy hands such as Zbigniew Brzezinski, Cyrus Vance, and Sol Linowitz regarded their old boss's attempt to circumvent the U.S. government as mistaken. Months later Carter finally began to own up that the tactics he used in his peace effort were "not appropriate perhaps." But he remained unrepentant.[86] *Washington Post* columnist Richard Cohen, in a piece largely supportive of Carter's postpresidential activities, best encapsulated his misguided antiwar lobbying: "It was breathtakingly brazen, not to mention in bad taste and confusing to other governments. Former presidents, of all people, do not have their own foreign policies."[87] Carter never apologized to the Bush administration.

Desert Storm had produced profound strategic and geopolitical changes in the region. The defeat of Israel's most powerful enemy by a coalition that included both the United States and the Soviet Union and every major Arab state (with the exception of Jordan, which had remained neutral) temporarily enhanced Israel's sense of security, although the Iraqi Scud missiles convinced them that no amount of fortress-building could bring security. Never before had Egypt, Syria, and Saudi Arabia joined forces with the Persian Gulf sheikdoms to combat a former ally. No one was more aware of the shift in the regional balance of power than Yitzhak Rabin. He told an audience at Tel Aviv University that "I am convinced our deterrent capability has increased as a result of the crisis in the Gulf." He cited "the fact that this time the United States stood firm and was ready to become involved against an aggression in the Middle East" as the principal reason for Israel's heightened sense of security.[88]

If Israel felt more secure, the PLO felt languid and more defenseless as a result of Saddam Hussein's defeat. Saudi Arabia and Kuwait expelled 300,000 Palestinian workers who were now no longer desired in their kingdoms. Not only did the PLO lose an estimated $133 million, or two-thirds of its annual budget gleaned from the taxes on these expatriate workers, but without employment the Palestinians also no longer sent remittances (estimated at $400 million annually) to their families in the West Bank and Gaza, depriving the PLO of additional income. As a result, the PLO had to close hospitals, health clinics, social welfare centers, and newspapers. There was scant money to pay the monthly stipends to an estimated 90,000 widows of men who had died for Palestinian liberation.[89]

Carter realized that the PLO was hemorrhaging. For the first time the

Arab radicals were in retreat: Libya had been marginalized, the PLO was shaken, and Syria had lost its principal benefactor, the Soviet Union. With this temporary realignment of Arab states, Baker felt—after making a series of visits to the West Bank in which he met Palestinians from the occupied territories like Hanan Mikhail Ashrawi, Faisel Husseini, and Sari Nusseibeh— that he could persuade the moderate Arab leaders to sit down with the Israelis at the negotiating table. The result was the Madrid Peace Conference in October 1991. The hard-line government of Yitzhak Shamir agreed to attend only if the PLO was not present. The Palestinians would participate, but only as part of the Jordanian delegation, composed of Palestinian residents of East Jerusalem from outside the West Bank and Gaza, "diaspora" Palestinians whose credentials would be vetoed by the Israeli government.[90]

Unhappy over his exclusion from Madrid, Arafat had little choice but to accept the conditions. Carter helped convince Arafat and others in the PLO of the necessity to join the U.S.-Soviet-sponsored Madrid talks, reassuring him that the control of Fatah still lay in his hands, and that he would be able to pull strings from Tunis. Carter's assessment was correct. Throughout the Madrid conference, the Palestinian delegation kept in constant touch with Arafat in Tunis by cellular phone. Arafat, in turn, stayed in touch with Carter in Plains; together they strategized on how to recover the PLO's standing in the United States, so badly tarnished by Arafat's unilateral siding with Saddam Hussein in the Gulf War.[91]

A turning point in the Carter-Arafat relationship occurred on April 7, 1992, when the PLO leader's Russian-built turboprop plane crashed in the remote Libyan Sahara due to a blinding sandstorm. When news of the crash hit PLO headquarters in Tunis, Bassam Abu Sharif immediately telephoned Mary King in Washington, D.C., asking that she contact Carter to see if the U.S. government would help search for the missing plane.[92] When she called Carter at his mountain cabin to tell him of Arafat's crash, he telephoned the White House Situation Room, urging the Bush administration to launch an all-out satellite effort to find the PLO chairman. Before Bush could respond to Carter's request, Arafat's plane was located, nine hours after the crash landing.[93]

Although the three crewmen were killed and the plane destroyed, Arafat had somehow survived, emerging from the wreck with only a few bruises. He was rushed to a hospital in Misrath, on the Mediterranean coast 125 miles east of Tripoli, and embraced by Libyan leader Muammar Qaddafi. "We have treated him fully and comprehensively," a Libyan doctor told the Associated Press. "His health is excellent." News that Arafat had survived set off wild celebrations in Palestinian communities throughout the world, adding to his legendary status as the ultimate survivor.[94] "On behalf of president Yasir Arafat, the Palestinian people and the P.L.O. leadership, I would like to express our deepest thanks to your efforts," Sharif cabled Carter shortly after Arafat was found. "It is always true that on a dark night only those who are great can help."[95]

Then, back in Tunis on April 17, Arafat himself wrote Carter a heartfelt appreciation laden with references to "God Almighty" and "His Mercy." By all accounts Arafat was touched that Carter had gone to such lengths to locate him. "This bears witness to your support for the just cause of our Palestinian People, their right to exercise self-determination and to end the Israeli occupation to their homeland, as well as the need to alleviate their plight, which stems from the continuation of this occupation," Arafat wrote Carter. "[T]his bears witness to your commitment to the establishment of a just peace, in the land of peace, the blessed land of Palestine. We consider your support to our people's right to a free and decent life as an embodiment of your stance in support of human rights and the exercise of the right to self-determination and to life." The letter ended with Arafat suggesting that they forge a "permanent and continuous" friendship based on their "common best interest."[96] As with Sadat, Carter had developed a fondness for Arafat that transcended politics, based on their emotional connection and the shared belief that they were both ordained to be peacemakers by God. "They are both like priests," observed Bassam Abu Sharif.[97]

But while Carter's reputation skyrocketed with Arafat, it floundered with Bush, who saw no role for a freelance mediator like Carter in his "new world order." The administration had used the former president with great success in Central America, but he was a loose cannon in the Middle East. The name Jimmy Carter was now anathema in the White House, although Bernard Aronson continued his dialogue with the Carter Center on Latin American affairs. Carter's monitoring of upcoming elections in Guyana and Zambia, which barely registered on the Bush administration's radar screen, received support, but there would be no more collaboration. "We saw Carter as incredibly self-centered, stubborn and dangerously naive," Scowcroft later commented.[98] It was considered impossible to trust a man who was defiantly marching to the beat of his own drum.

Only James Baker kept in occasional contact with the former president, ever curious about Arafat and Assad and always marveling at Carter's boundless gumption. "Carter would still call and say, 'Can I have a plane to go here or there?'" Baker recalled. "I [now] said no."[99] As long as Carter worked with Habitat for Humanity or Global 2000 or the National Democratic

Institute for International Affairs, the administration didn't mind, but they cringed at the very notion of his parachuting for peace. "Carter did a lot of positive humanitarian things," Scowcroft recalled. "But his political judgment was just awful."[100] After a run of bipartisan accomplishment, Carter's last, best hope was that a Democrat would be elected president in 1992.

EIGHTEEN

DEMOCRATIC PROSPECT

❧

I f 1990 had been Jimmy Carter's year for significant accomplishments—
Nicaragua, Haiti, and the Dominican Republic; the Golan Heights compromise; Arafat diplomacy; Habitat's "Miracle on the Border" Tijuana
blitz-build—1991 was a year of setbacks. Carter found himself off the Bush
"team," criticizing the administration for the Gulf War, its civil rights and
welfare policies, its anti-poor and pro-gun posturings, and Dan Quayle.
Even some of his international accomplishments were falling apart: almost
from the start Aristide's government in Haiti proved unable to consolidate
power, while Arafat's PLO was banned from the international peace talks in
Madrid as punishment for supporting Saddam Hussein's invasion of Kuwait.
Reporters who covered Carter in early 1991 also recalled how livid the ex-
president became over a slew of unflattering stories in *Ramparts*, *Time*, the
Atlanta Journal & Constitution, and other periodicals about his close friendship with BCCI's ailing Agha Hasan Abedi, on whose behalf Carter convinced a heart specialist from Stanford University to fly to London. "Carter
snapped a lot during this period," Elizabeth Kurylo of the *Atlanta Journal &
Constitution* recalled.[1]

By 1991, at least Habitat for Humanity appeared to be on a roll, with observers around the globe offering humanitarian awards to Millard Fuller and
accolades to Jimmy Carter. With Athens, Georgia, becoming an alternative-
music mecca thanks to nationally known local rock bands like R.E.M. and
the B-52s, the Peach State's First Family somehow became "cool"—as Joey

Ramone of the garage-punk band the Ramones gushed, "God I'd love to build a house with Jimmy Carter."[2]

Millard Fuller and Habitat's Gary Cook seized the moment, establishing campus affiliates at universities and colleges across the nation. By 1995 Habitat had 350 campus chapters and more than 900 associated groups in the United States, plus 7 chapters in other countries.[3] In addition to the youngsters, even Republicans—spurred on by Bob Hope, Jack Kemp, and Gerald Ford—started joining Habitat in droves.

Yet all was not well at the organization. Five female Habitat employees, all based in Americus, publicly accused Fuller of sexual harassment at different intervals in 1990; at issue was his practice of greeting people with affectionate hugs. Applied equally to both genders, these embraces were considered by Fuller mere expressions of Christian warmth, but the five women claimed they were lewd, overt sexual gestures. Rumors began circulating to the effect that he had overstepped his bounds to the point that this group of women was preparing to take legal action.

Determined to save his friend, on March 26, 1990, Carter wrote a heartfelt letter to Habitat's board of directors, asking them to resolve the crisis before it became national news. "The reputation and future of Habitat are now at stake, depending on how this emergency is handled," Carter wrote. "Any enterprising news reporter could make a national scandal out of it, á là [Jim] Bakker and [Jimmy] Swaggart. The draft press statement that I have seen would be a disaster. The question is what might be done now to protect the interests of everyone, and in particular Habitat for Humanity."[4]

Carter's letter enraged the five women who had filed sexual harassment charges against Fuller. One of them even wrote the former president to say she was "sad and disappointed" that he would use "the power of [his] pen in this way."[5] The case was brought before a meeting of the International Habitat Board of Directors in Washington, D.C., that March. The board rejected Carter's appeal and voted unanimously to dismiss the touchy-feely Fuller from his responsibilities as head of the organization, setting off a fierce yearlong debate. Habitat had grown since its mom-and-pop days at Koinonia Farms; in place of the occasional $50 contribution check, millions were now being deposited into the organization's bank account. House-building projects were now underway in thirty-one countries and five hundred American cities, and many in Habitat thought it time to take the hyperactive Fuller down a peg. Both Millard and Linda Fuller were stripped of their leadership roles and barred from Habitat's daily operations, although they were permitted to continue raising funds from the Atlanta office, where they could be kept out of sight and out of mind.[6]

Knowing full well Fuller's penchant for hugging almost everybody he encountered, the Carters firmly believed in his innocence. Furious at the board for treating "the true heroes of Habitat" so harshly, Carter flat-out quit the organization, only offering to stay on for the blitz-build in Miami that June because he had already committed his time to the local affiliate. "As you know, I have not been kept informed or involved in the management of Habitat's offices and do not want to be now or in the future," Carter complained in a letter to Habitat's Jeff Snider on May 10, 1991. "When I have attempted to address the ongoing confrontation between the Fullers and some of the key Board members in recent months, my influence has been minimal at best. The fact is that this altercation has been handled in a tragic fashion and has brought permanent damage to the organization." Carter then took Habitat to task for subjecting the Fullers to "an inquisition," adding that he hoped the board had "judgment enough to anticipate that there would be a severe drop in enthusiasm, confidence, spirit, and funding and felt that dealing harshly with Millard and Linda was worth the enormous cost." He therefore suggested reinstating the Fullers immediately, before the imbroglio became an "uncontrollable catastrophe" for Habitat's funding. "I agree with those who say that Habitat is bigger than the Fullers, the Carters," and other prominent members, Carter went on. "However, it is smaller without any of these families or without any of the thousands of those less famous or influential. But our key people and the general public have been alienated. No personal appeal or mail solicitation can fully overcome these events unless the damage is known to have been repaired."[7]

Within a matter of weeks, Habitat started to rapidly unravel. Funds began drying up, enthusiasm waned, and nobody stepped forward with the sustained drive and far-reaching vision to push the ecumenical group ahead. In fact, Carter's intent to resign caused Atlanta First Bank to withdraw Habitat's line of credit, foreseeing a cash-flow problem. Even some Habitat board members began to worry that negative fallout from the Fuller flap would handcuff the nonprofit organization by putting it under a cloud of public suspicion. In response, that May the International Board discharged forty-three Habitat employees, including top managers and chaplains, most of whom were outspoken Fuller supporters. The situation was getting ugly, and Carter was in despair. In a last-ditch attempt to resolve matters, he wrote to former Ohio governor Richard Celeste, a Habitat board member: "We intend to complete our present obligations, including the work camps in Miami and Washington, D.C., but will otherwise phase out our involvement, including mass mailings and future annual work projects, unless it is clear that the Board is willing to go a second mile in reinstating Millard in a way that will be gratifying and honorable for him." The former president gladly embraced the mediation, telling Celeste, "I deeply appreciate your ability and willingness to help overcome this continuing and unnecessary crisis. If anyone can bring an end to it, you can."[8]

Soon, however, providence shone on both Carter and Fuller. Realizing the probable impact of losing Carter's support, on June 15 a committee from Habitat's International Board of Directors, including Richard Celeste, met in Miami for a blitz-build and voted unanimously for Fuller to stay on. "I am tremendously elated over the decision," Fuller told the *Americus Times Recorder*, "and will work harder than ever so that my life's goal of helping more low-income persons throughout the world have a house instead of a shack will continue."[9]

When told of the committee's decision, Jimmy and Rosalynn Carter issued a public statement that with Millard and Linda Fuller back in charge they would not abandon Habitat but would help it prosper. Sixty-six-year-old Jimmy and fifty-six-year-old Millard would lead Habitat into a new, even more productive era. As they pounded nails together under the sharp-edged Miami sun, the Christian dreamers discussed in earnest their next carpentry feat.[10]

The beauty of Habitat was the concrete results. By 1992 the organization had built over 7,000 sturdy homes without a single foreclosure. When Hurricane Andrew struck South Florida that August, all twenty-seven of the Habitat houses the Carter Work Camp had built the previous year in Miami—most of which were in the direct path of the storm—survived. A *Miami Herald* headline read, "Tally: Habitat 27, Andrew 0."[11] The very organization that the American right had eyed suspiciously in the early 1980s as a socialist cabal coddling the likes of Jimmy Carter—the man who gave away the Panama Canal—was now being championed by all parties as a model of social reform efforts without federal government intervention.

By the fall of 1991 Democratic presidential hopefuls who earlier had wanted nothing to do with the legacy of Jimmy Carter began having their staffers arrange house-building appearances with the former president. Ever anxious to sell Habitat on Capitol Hill, Fuller cleverly scheduled the 1992 Jimmy Carter Work Project for June 14 to 20 in Baltimore and Washington, D.C., just a month before the National Democratic Convention in New York.[12] Billed as "The Carters' Return," the Habitat build got a couple hours' work out of any number of politicians and recognizable civil servants eager to get office-worthy photographs of themselves in dungarees and tool belts with a former president at their sides. "House building separates the genuine humanitarians from the phonies in search of a photo op," Carter maintained.[13]

Conspicuous by their absence were any representatives of five-time Arkansas governor Bill Clinton's team. Clinton's campaign manager, James Carville, a shrewd Louisiana operator, wisely did everything he could during the 1992 campaign to put some distance between his client and Jimmy Carter. Carter may have been regarded as America's best ex-president, but that did not mean a majority of the voting public looked kindly on his years in the White House. The Democratic Party had not recaptured the White House since 1980 in part because of the ghost of Jimmy Carter and the chains of double-digit inflation he wore. Republican operatives were already trying to paint Clinton as Carter reborn, a liberal Baptist southern governor— a hamhock-happy hillbilly who, like his Democratic predecessor, would not be able to function effectively in the major leagues of Washington, D.C. The Bush campaign had a habit of suggesting guilt by association, so Carville deemed it an unnecessary risk to let his candidate appear on television with the ex-president. By the same token, however, Georgia's thirteen electoral votes made it an important state, and Carter's active endorsement there, while not essential, was worth something. "We didn't embrace Jimmy Carter during the campaign," Carville admitted. "But he helped us in Georgia. House building with him gave us a golden opportunity to do something popular with Carter."[14]

While keeping his pledge not to embrace any candidate officially before the Georgia primary on March 3, Carter did declare that the two key politicians of the campaign should be against a tax cut for the middle class, and advocate telling American voters the truth—both qualities he attributed to former Massachusetts senator Paul Tsongas. According to *Washington Post* reporter David Maraniss, the Clinton camp felt his warm comments were meant as a criticism of the Arkansas governor's morals and ethics.[15] At the annual Jefferson-Jackson Day Dinner in Atlanta in early February, Carter advised Tsongas to make the maximum effort in every state and to use his Massachusetts friends to campaign "person to person," just as Carter's own Peanut Brigade of Georgians had done for him in 1976. Carter also invited Tsongas to come spend some time with him in Plains, an offer Clinton's last serious rival seized at once.[16]

On February 22 Tsongas spent a rainy afternoon in Plains with the thirty-ninth president and an entourage of reporters trailing the pair as they toured the Jimmy Carter National Historic Site. Tsongas endeared himself to Carter by saying that his visit to the little hamlet constituted "one of the 'mecca steps' along the way to the White House." The point was clear: if Bill

Clinton did not want to be associated with Jimmy Carter, Paul Tsongas certainly did. After a private two-hour conversation, wives included, Carter and Tsongas held a joint news conference. "I think the South is quite receptive to the kind of message that Senator Tsongas brought to New Hampshire," Carter said, a comment Carville and company saw as just a shade away from an endorsement.[17]

Taking direct aim at Clinton, Carter then went on to say that, as in 1976 in the immediate wakes of Watergate and Vietnam, Americans wanted someone in the White House who never, ever lied. "The beginnings are very similar," Carter claimed of himself and Tsongas. "Nobody thought we had a chance. Then, people were looking for somebody to tell the truth. I think there is a kind of similar desire on the part of the American people now to just have a candidate tell them the truth and be honest and acknowledge maybe some unpopular decisions." Carter then quipped that although the Georgia Democratic establishment supported Clinton, the only support that really counted was that of the voters. "People are looking for somebody who is honest and tells the truth," Carter repeated as Tsongas beamed at his side.[18] "I was grateful that President Carter embraced me and showed me around Plains," Tsongas recalled later. "He is such an honest man—like Truman. Clinton is like Reagan, just tell the people what they want to hear to get elected."[19]

None of this boded well for a future relationship between Clinton and Carter. But this awkward Plains moment aside, Carter made it clear that he would enthusiastically endorse Clinton—or any other Democrat, for that matter—if he received his party's nomination. By May 20, with Texas billionaire Ross Perot's probable independent candidacy grabbing the national headlines while Clinton was being lambasted for adultery, draft dodging, and failing to inhale, Carville had decided that an afternoon with the squeaky-clean former president would have a beneficial, cleansing effect. The New York Times even reported a Clinton aide as saying that the Arkansas governor believed Carter had "won high marks in honesty and public service," and would help boost voters' trust in the candidate. Carter did his bit for the party: at an Atlanta press conference with Clinton at his side, he praised the Arkansas governor as having the "knowledge and integrity to be President."[20]

Because both Clinton and Carter were moderate southern governors—supposed "Washington outsiders" trying to capture the White House at a time of widespread disgust with the nation's politics—comparisons were often drawn between them. Closer scrutiny, however, made it clear that Jimmy Carter and Bill Clinton had about as much in common as, well, a peanut farmer from the Deep South and a Yale-and-Oxford-educated lawyer from Arkansas, a state that is as much western and midwestern as it is southern. Carter's American roots dated back to the early 1800s, when his ancestors acquired some of the very land he farmed in the 1950s and '60s. What's more, Earl and Lillian Carter presided over a tight-knit family that imbued their four children with the importance of hard work, education, and Christian faith.[21]

Clinton, by contrast, had no more real roots than the outpost state he was raised in, where settlers often just loaded up on supplies before heading out to Texas or the Western frontier. "Arkansas is a state where everything loose in the nation tumbled into," former Arkansas senator William Fulbright once noted. "Carter had deep roots; Clinton had none."[22] Bill Clinton was the product of a broken marriage, his father killed in an automobile accident three months before his son was born. The infant was cared for by his grandparents in Hope while his mother went to New Orleans to train for a nursing career she pursued the rest of her life. The bright and personable boy continued to be reared by his grandparents and other relatives until 1950, when his mother married Roger Clinton, a used-car salesman. Young William Jefferson Blythe changed his name to Clinton when his younger half-brother, Roger Clinton Jr., started school so that they would both have the same last name. Unlike Carter in his Bible Belt home of Plains, Clinton grew up in Hot Springs, a resort town that prided itself on offering gambling and other forbidden fruits.[23]

Carter, the only president to graduate from the U.S. Naval Academy, had the longest military career of any twentieth-century chief executive except Dwight D. Eisenhower. Clinton, like so many of his generation, viewed the Vietnam War as immoral and avoided military service altogether. Carter married his high school sweetheart at age twenty-two and never had an extramarital affair. Clinton, by most accounts, did not place marital fidelity high as a life priority. While Clinton's Democratic political heroes were John F. Kennedy and the ever-pragmatic Franklin D. Roosevelt, Carter preferred Woodrow Wilson and Harry Truman for their "inbred honesty" and "moral integrity."[24] Where lying was anathema to Carter, for Clinton it was synonymous with being a good politician; while Carter scorned compromise to his political detriment, to Clinton deal making was what politics was all about. The engineer in Carter always wanted to know the right answer; the lawyer in Clinton believed that right answers are usually unattainable, so the key to political success must be improvisation. Although a so-called liberal in many of his political views, Carter felt more comfortable with southern conservatives than Clinton, who, given his druthers, would take the eastern seaboard or southern California over any inch of old-time Dixie. The real comparison between Carter and Clinton proved only how vastly different they were in everything from personal temperament to leadership style.

Thus it made sense that there was no easy camaraderie between the two Democrats. In fact, now that he was well used to being seen as a political liability, Carter found it amusing that Clinton was going to such exaggerated lengths to disassociate himself from his predecessor. "Jimmy Carter and I are as different as daylight and dark," Clinton noted in a campaign interview. "I say that as someone who really admires him. I'm much less sort of mechanical and more intuitive in dealing with politics than he is. And I'm much more experienced not only at being Governor, but in dealing with Congress in national political issues just because I've been around so much longer than he had [been] when he ran for President."[25] Indeed: Carter was fifty-two when he ran in 1976, a Navy veteran, father of four, successful agribusinessman, homeowner, and former state senator as well as governor of Georgia. In 1992 Clinton was forty-six and had one child and no residence, much less any business. Carter took Clinton's cavalier remark in stride, with a simple shrug and a smile.

But the greatest strain on their relationship stemmed from an incident twelve years earlier. In the summer of 1980 President Carter had allowed 100,000 Cuban refugees to land on the beaches of Florida in what was known as the Mariel boatlift. Governor Clinton, who was then up for reelection, had to that point been staunchly loyal to the beleaguered Carter, defending his record in the press and refusing to support Senator Edward Kennedy's primary challenge to the president. Clinton stuck by him through double-digit inflation and the Iran hostage crisis, but the Mariel boatlift was one Carter action that candidate Clinton could not ignore—in mid-May, 18,000 of the Cuban refugees were sent to Fort Chafee in northwest Arkansas, many with criminal records or documented mental illness.

That fall Clinton faced a tough challenge for the governorship. His opponent, Frank White, a well-connected Republican savings and loan executive, attacked the governor for his close ties to the Carter administration as well as for presiding over a poor state economy—a hard enough rap to overcome without citizens around Fort Chafee incensed at the Carter administration's hellbroth of Cuban refugees invading their neighborhood. The situation turned into a statewide crisis on June 1, when several hundred of the refugees broke out of the resettlement camp at Fort Chafee and began rioting in the streets, forcing Governor Clinton to call in a few dozen National Guard troops. White House aide Eugene Eidenberg was tasked with trying to calm down the livid governor, who had been forced to order his state police to stop the Cubans, who were marching down a highway chanting, "Libertad! Libertad!" A confrontation ensued in which sixty-seven people were injured, including a few policemen but mostly Cubans, some of whom had their heads cracked open with billy clubs. Not missing a beat, Frank White began airing negative TV ads depicting Cuban chaos in the streets of Arkansas, chanting anti-American slogans, all a direct result of the Clinton-Carter resettlement policy.[26]

Throughout the crisis Clinton played the good soldier, taking instructions from Eidenberg, the White House official in charge of the refugee situation— mostly because Carter promised no more refugees would be sent to Arkansas. Then, on August 1, the Carter administration betrayed him again. Without consultation, the White House announced that all the Cuban refugees still in Pennsylvania, Wisconsin, and Florida would be gathered together and sent to Fort Chafee. Clinton aide Randy White, who was in the room at the Governor's Mansion in Little Rock when Clinton got the news, remembered his boss pounding the desk and spouting obscenities. "You're fucking me!" White heard Clinton shout into the phone at a White House official. "How could you do this to me? I busted my ass for Carter. You guys are gonna get me beat. This is ridiculous. Carter's too chickenshit about it to tell me directly!" Clinton spent the rest of the weekend trying to convince the Carter administration to change its mind—to no avail. One Clinton friend urged him to "kick and fuss and holler and just tell Jimmy Carter no," but the governor ruled out that option. Clinton had been a loyal Carterite and a mainstream Democrat all along, and he deemed it politically unwise to break ranks over the refugee crisis—although after the election he told friends that Jimmy Carter's idiotic policies had cost him thousands of votes. And for years to come he seethed in private anger at Carter's betrayal.[27]

On election night 1980 Clinton watched the grim returns on television at the Governor's Mansion; Ronald Reagan won by a landslide, and his own Republican challenger Frank White defeated him handily. "The guy screwed me and never tried to make amends," Clinton said of Carter later to Rick Stearns, a political friend from Oxford University and George McGovern's 1972 campaign. When *Washington Post* political reporter David Broder visited Clinton in Little Rock, all the defeated governor could do was gripe about the refugee fiasco, Carter's duplicity, and the fact that he had lost the first election of his promising career because of a peanut farmer unfit for high office.[28]

Clinton would win the governorship back in 1982, but he never forgave Carter. Throughout the 1980s he would attend Democratic fund-raisers at Pamela Harriman's Georgetown house and talk with great passion about the "disastrous Carter years." He even forged a friendship with Senator Edward Kennedy in which mutual disdain for Carter became a favorite topic. Thus it was that Clinton made a priority of keeping Carter away from his 1992 presidential campaign; he would be the anti-Carter, a southern governor but a normal guy, not some born-again political blunderer like his predecessor from Plains.[29]

But all grievances were put on hold when the Democratic National Committee asked Carter to address the convention at Madison Square Garden in New York City on July 14. Unlike at the 1984 San Francisco conference, party strategists now decided to showcase Carter before a prime-time television audience. Carter spoke about the need for imaginative urban-renewal programs. "With federal funding slashed to the bone," Carter explained, "there are now ten times as many homeless people in Atlanta, Georgia, as there were when I left the White House. Violent crimes among juveniles have increased 300 percent in just the last five years. Their lack of hope for a better life seems to be equaled among America's leaders."[30] With his soft, gentle voice hard to hear over the mayhem on the floor, Carter's speech was not a highlight. The ex-president did, however, offer strong praise about the Clinton-Gore ticket that was greatly appreciated. "The best you could say about Carter's convention talk," quipped a longtime Democratic strategist Ted Van Dyk, "is that he didn't do any real damage."[31]

Carter was still an outsider in his own party. With no political constituency of his own, Carter—still smarting from the Ted Kennedy challenge—commented in 1990 that "liberal is not a good word in Georgia" and that during his presidency the Democratic party was "a burden instead of an asset."[32] Instead of following the Democratic party platform on urban policy issues, Carter burst out on his own with the Atlanta Project. On October 25, 1991, at a news conference at the Carter Center, the sixty-seven-year-old former president announced a new program to help Atlanta's underclass: hence his reason for discussing urban renewal at the Democratic National Convention. Though vague as to the program's scope and financing, he brimmed with a reformer's zeal not seen since Dorothy Day and used the occasion to rally Georgians to make their capital city a research laboratory for curing urban ills. "Atlanta has a major affliction of self-delusion," Carter pronounced. "We're proud of getting the Olympics, we're proud of the Braves, Atlanta's skyline and that sort of thing. But underneath, Atlanta's rotten in many ways and this needs to be addressed frankly."[33]

Thus began the Atlanta Project, a grassroots program designed to help alleviate poverty, reduce homelessness, curb crime, and provide health care to all city residents. Carter pointedly disavowed depending on taxpayers' money—the funding would come from private foundations and the business community. "The idea was essentially to give people the resources to solve their own problems, neighborhood by neighborhood," Carter explained.[34] TAP was immediately declared by the national media to be the most ambitious urban renewal project in America; as the *Wall Street Journal* noted, "The Atlanta Project is being scrutinized nationwide. If it works other cities are sure to hold it up as a model."[35]

After years of mediating disputes overseas and building houses, Carter was now was turning his attention to his own backyard. The ex-president's Christian conscience had gnawed at him all the five years he sat in his plush Carter Center office, no more than a hundred yards away from vacant city-owned lots overgrown with weeds and dotted with tarpaper shacks where urban squatters lived in penniless squalor and groped through garbage cans for their lunch. It was a personal embarrassment to Carter that such stark poverty existed right outside the perimeter of his sparkling center, to which he was chauffeured right past the shacks. Something had to be done. One afternoon Carter simply walked out of his comfortable office to talk to the homeless folks and find out firsthand about their problems. After two hours of questioning them, Carter found that these impoverished people were neither lazy nor mentally ill; in fact many of them had marketable skills.[36]

Around the same time, Jimmy and Rosalynn Carter also visited Atlanta's Grady Memorial Hospital, where a doctor brought them to see "Baby Pumpkin," a cocaine-addicted newborn whose mother was a chronic substance abuser. After taking turns holding the baby, both Carters broke down crying when a doctor told them her chances of survival were slight (she died two years later). It was then that the Carters determined they would no longer pretend that preventable suffering did not hold sway over much of Atlanta, and that they would work to marshal the resources of the rich to attack the problems of the poor. "My experiences with Habitat had taught me that there was a tremendous latent readiness for community volunteerism," Carter said later.[37]

As president, Carter had supported public service job programs, housing construction grants, youth employment initiatives, and a national health care program for children. A decade after his White House years, the Task Force for Child Survival—housed at the Carter Center—was immunizing children all over the globe. Now, infused with his unusual blend of fiscal conservatism and social liberalism, Carter considered how to get Atlanta's Fortune 500 corporations to bankroll TAP. "Jimmy has always had a knack for public-private partnership efforts," explained his former domestic affairs adviser, Stuart Eizenstat.[38] If he had not done enough in his previous political incarnations as state senator, governor, and president to help the down-trodden achieve racial and economic equality, he was going to compensate tenfold as ex-president with the Atlanta Project.

Carter believed the liberal "Santa Claus" approach to urban reform would never work efficiently. "Even the accepted practice of providing a stream of new, improved services to needy families will, at best, give only transient benefits," he noted. "Soup kitchens, homeless shelters, food stamps, housing assistance, schools in juvenile detention centers, and emergency health care are all valuable but give little promise of permanent change in living conditions." The Atlanta Project would be different: it would focus on partnerships and collaborative efforts with other organizations, both public and private, bringing the entire community together to wage war on poverty.[39]

The idea for TAP came from Emory University president James Laney. Using the fund-raising and motivating techniques he had learned from working with Millard Fuller at Habitat, Carter searched for sponsors to help him raise $32 million TAP needed. Most of Atlanta's church groups immediately embraced the program, as did Mayor Maynard Jackson, Andrew Young, Coretta Scott King, and Governor Zell Miller. The business community, however, was initially skeptical. They knew only too well Carter's famed penchant for overcommitment, although they also knew he somehow usually managed to deliver on his bold promises.[40]

Carter challenged the skeptics with a sermon about the obligation of the rich to help the poor. Addressing 1,500 of Atlanta's leading business and civic leaders in November 1991, he preached movingly about his "neighbors" who had no homes. "I was told one of them was recently arrested for urinating in the kudzu," Carter told the tony crowd. "We don't even provide portable toilets, and then we arrest them. It bothers me that we aren't doing anything about it. We ought to be helping, but not with a supercilious, 'I'm better than you' attitude. In a way that will make us a truly great city." *Fortune* magazine had named Atlanta the best place in America to do business, Carter noted, but it was a horrible place to be poor. "I think that somewhere in this nation—somewhere in the world—there needs to be an all-out effort made to see if we can have some success overcoming poverty, drugs, crime, and, above all, the alienation of one group of people from another."[41]

An inspired Carter apparently touched all the right buttons at that power breakfast, for the business community quickly came forward with resources and commitments. If Carter was willing to put his prestige on the line for TAP, then Coca-Cola, Delta Airlines, NationsBank, Turner Broadcasting Systems, Georgia Power, and the Home Depot—all Atlanta based—were willing to risk theirs too. And he didn't stop there: when Carter found himself in Manhattan in December 1991 with a couple of hours to kill, he picked up the phone and called United Parcel Service (UPS) chairman of the board Kent "Oz" Nelson, whose company was preparing to relocate from Greenwich, Connecticut, to Atlanta within months. "I'm coming to visit you this afternoon," Carter told a flabbergasted Nelson, who clearly was unaccustomed to former U.S. presidents dropping in on him unexpectedly. Carter directed his limousine over the Triborough Bridge to Greenwich, walked into Nelson's office, welcomed UPS to Georgia, and asked for $3 million for the Atlanta Project. Without much hesitation Nelson saw to it that the UPS Foundation gave TAP $1.5 million and that the Annie E. Casey Foundation, a nonprofit UPS affiliate, matched the amount to get Carter the sum he wanted. Excited by TAP, Nelson soon became a member of the Carter Center's board of trustees and executive committee.[42]

The UPS contribution was just one of Carter's many fund-raising coups. "You know," he confessed, "as President I underestimated just how generous corporations can be."[43] Under TAP, local corporations could "adopt" public schools by supplying them with volunteer tutors, mentors, and a variety of other educational services and materials. In addition, in May 1993 a capital campaign was launched to begin raising money for TAP's infrastructure; less than two months later more than $11 million in cash and pledges had come in, and more than $10 million had been received in in-kind donations. A five-year Phase I operating budget of $32 million was put together to address the entire spectrum of urban woes—and they were many. Progressive Atlanta, with its famed civic pride and glass towers on Peachtree Street, ranked ninth in the nation in the number of families with incomes below 50 percent of the poverty level—while Georgia ranked forty-ninth in infant mortality, forty-fifth in the number of underweight babies born, forty-eighth in high school dropout rates, and forty-seventh in maintaining the overall well-being of children. Carter had also learned from Millard Fuller that an estimated 12,000 to 15,000 homeless people lived in the Atlanta area, yet nearly 12 percent of the units owned by the Atlanta Housing Authority lay vacant. Crime statistics were harrowing: in the early 1990s drug cases in Fulton County Juvenile Court increased by 170 percent, weapons charges by 73 percent, robbery by 240 percent, and all violent crime by nearly 300 percent.[44] Reversing this spiral of wretchedness was not going to be easy, but Carter's attitude was that "the real failure, for Atlanta and cities like it, would be not to try."[45] Upon catching wind of the Atlanta Project, Lyndon Johnson's former national security adviser Walt Rostow sent Carter his own urban revitalization plan for Austin, Texas, which was mobilizing the entire town to wipe out poverty there. If successful, the pilot projects in Atlanta and Austin would prove to America that when it came to urban problems, prevention was more cost-effective than damage control. The general premise of both projects—not to mention Habitat—was "If you're the one who plants the grass you won't walk on it," Rostow said. "It's important to make the kids realize they're not losers."[46]

Not all of Atlanta's poor and their advocates were excited by TAP. In fact, many in the city's African-American community suspected that this so-called urban renewal program was just a clever way for the federal government to slash funds for the poor. When Carter met with some of Atlanta's black clergy-men, he was surprised to encounter bitterness and skepticism. "Reassure me that this is not an extension of the institutionalization and privatization of public service," Bishop John Hurst Adams of the African Methodist Episco-pal Church demanded. "Is this not another effort to dump some more re-sponsibility on churches and community agencies that the government was created to perform?" Such comments showed that there was not only an economic gap between rich and poor, but also a definite racial divide that would be difficult to bridge. TAP program director Dan Sweat, a white cor-porate executive with superb business contacts, was unfairly charged with being racially insensitive by some black community organizations. African-American educator James Young went so far as to resign from TAP's secre-tariat, citing "racial arrogance" within the program.[47]

Sensing this tension, Amy Carter pleaded with her parents to get the rap group Arrested Development to write a song promoting the Atlanta Project, a sure-fire way to reach African-American youth. Instead, the theme song for TAP came from a local country rock band that oozed the sort of white-bread music that inner-city teenagers could only mock.[48] However, in May 1993 Carter did arrange for "King of Pop" Michael Jackson to appear at the Omni before 12,500 people—mainly youngsters who had partici-pated in the Atlanta Project's massive immunization program for child-ren. Other black celebrities, including Oprah Winfrey and Gladys Knight, immediately became involved with TAP, giving it money and meeting with youngsters.[49]

The Atlanta Project's original mission was to help twenty of the city's blighted neighborhoods, an area encompassing 500,000 people—more than 15 percent of Atlanta's population. These neighborhoods—or "clusters"—were selected using statistics showing the high incidence of teenage pregnancies and single-parent families. Fewer than one-third of the cluster families were headed by married couples, and a large portion were on welfare, lived in substandard housing, and suffered chronic unemployment. TAP aimed to end this vicious cycle at the beginning by offering pre-natal care, day-care centers, and inoculations for children. "If you don't be-gin at the beginning," as Congresswoman Barbara Jordan of Texas had warned, "you'll never get the right results."[50]

TAP's success would depend on three elements: private funding, volun-teer workers, and the ability to untangle enough red tape to get neglected neighborhoods the assistance they needed. The Carter Center, in Dan Sweat's words, would act as "traffic cops" for TAP. With the start-up money in hand and a roster of nearly 100,000 at least occasional volunteers pitching in, Carter went at the red tape and won.

Several months before the Atlanta Project was launched, Carter had met with more than a hundred federal agency leaders and issued them a chal-lenge. "Isn't there a less cumbersome way," he inquired, "for poor people to apply for public assistance? Since a candidate for housing assistance fre-quently qualifies for food stamps and Medicaid as well, couldn't the govern-ment distill the pages and pages of separate program applications into one common, easy-to-complete form—a one-page call for help?" Carter set about to answer his own question, working his way through the state bureau-cracy in search of a way to streamline services for the poor. In time, no fewer than ten major state agencies managed to get together and boil down sixty-four sheets of bureaucratic imperatives into a single, user-friendly eight-page application for seven Georgia programs: Aid to Families with Dependent Children (AFDC); Supplemental Security Income (SSI); Women, Infants and Children Program (WIC); Medicaid for the Aged, Blind or Disabled; AFDC Medicaid; Food Stamps; and Housing. Known as the Georgian Com-mon Access Application (GCAA) when it became available to the public in March 1994, the unboondoggling initiative drew praise from Republicans such as George Bush and Newt Gingrich for reducing government waste. "This has been like a miracle," Carter himself noted. "When I was President I tried very hard to simplify the paperwork, but it's almost impossible to get federal agencies to cooperate with each other."[51]

Although the results were decidedly mixed, TAP tried an endless variety of creative community solutions in Phase I. Whether it was setting up com-puter labs in public housing, offering high-tech vocational courses in public schools, distributing a million donated books to school libraries, cosponsor-ing a Motown music night at Frederick Douglass High School, or instituting free shuttle bus service to a neighboring YMCA, the Atlanta Project carried on full of moxie and determination to win this new war on poverty. Others took note; more than two hundred delegates from cities around the country journeyed to Atlanta to study TAP's techniques and early results. In 1993 even the *Atlanta Journal & Constitution* got into the civic spirit by launching a new weekly section called "City Life," which devoted two full pages of each issue to TAP.

The grassroots side of TAP drew the most attention. "TAP Into Peace"— a heavily promoted antiviolence campaign—had Jimmy Carter and 5,000 others go door to door canvassing their fellow citizens on how best to curb violence in their neighborhoods. Almost without exception residents pointed to gun control, more police, and more activities for teenagers as potential solutions. "To hear this constant litany of concern about firearms, most of which are automatic weapons, from 9mm pistols up to submachine guns, makes it seem absolutely ridiculous and stupid for members of the legislature not to pass restraints on the sale of these weapons to young people," Carter exploded to the press trailing him as he went door to door. Carter made the same argument on national television shows such as CNN's *Larry King Live* and the syndicated *Regis and Kathie Lee,* and Washington politicians began paying attention. In December 1994 President Clinton designated Atlanta one of six U.S. cities to receive an Empowerment Zone award—which meant four Atlanta Project clusters (Grady, Carver, Southside, and Washington) were given $100 million in cash and $150 million in tax incentives to stimulate economic development.[52]

The Carters themselves created the highest publicity event of all, the "President and Mrs. Jimmy Carter's Crested Butte Winter Weekend" they hosted every February. Twenty lucky Atlanta Project kids—mostly low-income African Americans who had demonstrated "leadership qualities" in TAP's youth leadership development program known as Future Force—got to frolic in the snowy Rocky Mountains for an extended five-day weekend, many seeing the vast open spaces of the American West for the first time. Treated as "honored guests," these Future Force youths got to mingle with CEOs and civic leaders; even better, they got to ski, exhorted by a former president of the United States, who said, "I want to see every one of you at the top of the mountain before the week is over."[53]

The Crested Butte event had been started by Jimmy and Rosalynn in 1992 as a fund-raising scheme. The Carter Center offered 150 guests paying $2,500 each the chance to ski, hike, and talk about world affairs or community concerns with the former First Family. The highlight every year was the auction on Saturday when Carter—sometimes imitating Johnny Carson's Carnac the Magnificent, right down to the turban—raffled off such items as his handwritten poems and handcrafted furniture, Amy Carter's sketches and paintings, and other celebrity collectibles from the likes of Jane Fonda, Ted Turner, and Hank Aaron—netting an average of $400,000 a year for TAP.[54]

Yet for all the good press and energy lavished on the Atlanta Project, the program was not a success. The clusters were essentially leaderless, and once the novelty wore off the volunteer base began to shrink. The corporations did their part, but concrete, positive results were few and far between; by trying to solve all the problems at once, TAP was spread too thin to solve any. With no clear game plan and no way to judge its incremental success, Phase I disappointed many in Atlanta, which began to see TAP as more talk than action. "We were flying the plane as we built it," Sweat admitted.[55] Some in the clusters criticized Carter for always showing up for photo opportunities but not rolling up his sleeves and digging into the daily work. These complaints hit home hardest when Emory University political science professor Michael W. Giles—under a $350,000 grant from the Atlantic Richfield Company (ARCO) and the Rockefeller Foundation—issued an internal report based on more than 2,150 interviews with TAP volunteers and community organizers. The Giles Report, made public in February 1995, criticized the Atlanta Project for having a cloudy vision, putting too little emphasis on coordinating services, and making poor use of volunteers. "Neighborhood leaders have made little or no effort to identify and work with other organizations in their areas that are working on issues related to poverty," the report concluded. Giles summed up that "the progress to date toward TAP's goals appears modest relative to the amount of effort and money expended."[56]

Carter, who had received the Giles Report in October 1994, took it in stride. In fact, it helped him realize that he had failed to take into account how volunteers' initial excitement would wane as the labor persisted, but had little to show for it. "The Giles Report should not necessarily be interpreted as a sign of trouble or failure," the *Atlanta Journal & Constitution* editorialized on February 20, 1995. "It merely identifies problems that need to be fixed, and project officials seem eager to respond. After all, the only true failure is surrender, and it's reassuring that neither Carter nor The Atlanta Project seem close to surrendering."[57] Taking the Giles Report findings to heart, a new director, Jane E. Smith, wisely began trying to reorganize TAP, under a realistic plan based more on resource availability than overweening ambition.[58]

Its chronic shortcomings aside, at least TAP was forcing Atlantans to grapple with their economic and racial divisions. The city was justifiably elated over hosting the 1996 Olympics, but TAP forced residents to recognize that real urban problems could not be glossed over with boosterism. Jimmy Carter—the most respected man in the state—was setting an example of what genuine civic responsibility was all about. Although he had operated more on enthusiasm than wisdom in Phase I, Carter also had gained respect for raising social concerns that are too often ignored.

W hile Bill Clinton had been politically wise to avoid being too closely identified with Carter during the primary season, he now wanted to make amends. James Carville had arranged for Bill and Hillary Clinton to work on a Habitat house in Atlanta in early August, an event the Carters looked forward to with great anticipation. No matter how much Clinton's character left to be desired, Carter had to admit that he had done an excellent job as governor of Arkansas and would certainly do more than George Bush to help the have-nots of America. More important, Carter genuinely liked Al and Tipper Gore. The Tennessee senator's new book, *Earth in the Balance: Ecology and the Human Spirit*, struck the ex-president as a well-written update of his own *Global 2000 Report*'s warnings about environmental degradation. Senator Gore had further endeared himself by attending several Carter Center policy forums, always arriving well prepared to discuss whatever issue was at hand. Moreover, both Jimmy and Rosalynn Carter supported Tipper Gore's crusade to put warning labels on rock and roll albums that contained offensive lyrics. All things considered, to Carter, Clinton-Gore was not such a bad ticket—and unlike Mondale-Ferraro or Dukakis-Bentsen, the southern duo seemed quite capable of winning.[59]

On August 19, Millard Fuller, clad in beachwear, greeted a meticulously groomed Clinton at Atlanta's Hartsfield Airport. "What are you doing here?" Clinton laughed when he saw Fuller, who had said he would not make the build. "What do you think? Building a house with you," Fuller responded, and together they headed over to Manuel's Tavern just a couple of blocks from the Carter Center for a press opportunity and dinner. This was not the first meeting between Clinton and Fuller: they shared a friend in Phil Lader, founder of the Renaissance Weekends, and had spent some "chat time" together at his secluded Hilton Head resort. Jimmy and Rosalynn Carter, along with other leading Georgia Democrats, were already packed into Manuel's and ready to wish Bill Clinton a happy forty-sixth birthday.[60]

The Fullers, Carters, Clintons, and Gores all ate together in a private room, trading campaign trail stories, laughing about the oddities of Ross Perot, and chatting happily about how they would build a house together the following morning. Gore presented a copy of *Earth in the Balance* to Fuller, who read it immediately and was inspired to create an environment department that would make sure all Habitat houses were ecologically sound. In the end, the four couples (and thirteen-year-old Chelsea Clinton) did build for an entire day in Atlanta. "By day's end, we had built a house," Fuller boasted. "Clinton and Gore were great."[61]

Carter had more than carpentry on his mind as he used the Habitat opportunity to tout Warren Christopher for secretary of state. "My hope was that some of my best people—like Christopher or Eizenstat or Bob Pastor—would be awarded top positions in a Clinton administration," Carter said later.[62]

Nobody championed Warren Christopher for the big job at State more aggressively than Jimmy Carter. While the media had always portrayed Christopher as distant and aloof, Carter knew better—that he was a warm gentleman infused with the kind of old-fashioned integrity and humility one would expect from a low-key North Dakota native. Unlike Carter, he actually enjoyed the deskbound life, but like Carter he was more of a diplomatic technician than a conceptual thinker, the perfect number-two man who now wanted to climb the last rung at Foggy Bottom. Since Christopher had delivered the keynote speech at the Carter Center on October 1, 1986, he had increased his public profile by serving as chairman of the commission that examined the Los Angeles Police Department for five months and concluded that Chief of Police Daryl Gates should step aside. Christopher had continued to maintain a strong hand in his 550-lawyer Los Angeles firm, the prestigious O'Melveny and Myers, which he had first joined in 1950. Meanwhile he also continued to serve as Carter's trusted counsel, which put him in an unusual position during the 1992 presidential campaign: adviser to both Bill Clinton and Jimmy Carter.[63]

By the spring of 1992 the cautious Christopher had emerged as perhaps Clinton's leading foreign policy strategist. While Anthony Lake, Sandy Berger, and others instructed the nominee on how to score points against Bush, Christopher offered sound policy advice beyond the politics of the moment. He advised Clinton on Middle East terrorism, NATO expansionism, loose nuclear weapons in the former Soviet Union, and the ghastly situation in Somalia. At the same time Christopher wrote at Carter's request "A Plan for the Continuity of the Carter Center," which he submitted to his client on October 5.[64] "In 1992, when I got ready to do an analysis of what the Carter Center should do in the future, I asked Chris to head up a small committee to look into it," Carter recalled.[65] Christopher's report recommended that the center build up an endowment of $100 million while reestablishing a new, more closely integrated relationship with Emory University. "The summary is deliberately skeletal in form," Christopher wrote Carter. "No effort was made to address the legal complexities that may be involved, though I would think that they are manageable."[66] Christopher felt that the Carter Center should do just one or two things well, while the ex-president liked to do many things at once.

When election day rolled around, Carter pulled the lever for Clinton-Gore and hoped that Christopher would soon head the State Department. In a three-way race Clinton was elected president with only 44 percent of the vote against 37 percent for George Bush and 19 percent for Texas billionaire Ross Perot. After Clinton's victory, Washington, D.C., teemed with speculation as to who would be rewarded with the top cabinet posts. First, however, Clinton appointed Warren Christopher and Vernon Jordan, to lead the president-elect's transition team.

While Washington gossiped that Clinton planned to hire a number of former Carter administration officials, the scuttlebutt held that it was best to claim to have shaken off ties with the former president. *New York Times* columnist Leslie Gelb captured the mood perfectly, offering instructions to potential cabinet appointees: "Deny you worked in the Carter administration, even if you did. If they say they have proof, respond that it happened so long ago that you forgot. If pressed, assert that you spent all your time there fighting for democracy in China and doing anonymous volunteer work for the Children's Defense Fund. (Jimmy Carter faces a somewhat trickier problem in denying that he worked for the Carter administration.)"[67]

Although Gelb had tongue firmly in cheek, he captured the essence of Warren Christopher's dilemma. In fact, when he finally tapped him for secretary of state, Clinton made it clear to Christopher that the Californian had to sever all ties with Jimmy Carter and serve only one president—Bill Clinton. Carter himself understood the strategy: "I can just imagine Clinton and Gore sitting around in the headquarters after the election saying, 'You know, this has to be our administration. We don't want this to be perceived as a Carter administration.' "[68]

Two days before Christmas, Christopher accepted the post, and Carter called to congratulate him. The secretary of state designate followed his new boss's orders and took days to return the call, the first link in a chain of miscommunication between the two men. For Congress's sake, Christopher started trying to remake his Carter-era reputation for conciliation into an image of a man who Republicans could believe would be "discreet and careful" in using force to maintain the United States as a world power. At his confirmation hearings before the Senate Foreign Relations Committee, Christopher reiterated his full backing for the Bush administration's tough policy toward Iraq, and left behind his own reputation as Jimmy Carter's human rights workhorse.[69]

Unbeknownst to Carter, who was anxious to work closely with the new administration, Clinton was determined to keep the ex-president at arm's length. Four years earlier, when James Baker had been tapped as Bush's sec-retary of state, he had paid a courtesy call on Carter in Atlanta; just a few months later he visited the Carter Center again to deliver a major policy ad-dress. During his entire four years as Clinton's secretary of state, Warren Christopher never visited the Carter Center. When asked why, he re-sponded, "I was never asked."[70]

NINETEEN

CARTER VS. CLINTON

꒰ᴏ꒱

Jimmy Carter and Bill Clinton got off to a bad start. The diligent Carter telephoned the president-elect a number of times in November and December to discuss what he regarded as pressing foreign policy issues—the political deterioration of Haiti and the importance of NAFTA. Preoccupied with the White House transition, Clinton asked the former president to deal directly with secretary of state designate Warren Christopher. Carter was not discouraged by the referral, for Christopher had been an old friend. But when his phone call to Christopher was not returned, Carter was perplexed. He phoned again; this time his call was returned by a low-level staffer. Not accustomed to being ignored, particularly by his former lawyer, Carter put the best face possible on his treatment. He would press the Carter Center's agenda with Christopher at the inauguration.[1]

1993 had started calmly and auspiciously for Carter. His latest book, *Turning Point: A Candidate, A State and a Nation Come of Age*—a riveting memoir of his first political campaign for Georgia State Senate in 1962—was well received by reviewers and the public alike and spent a dozen weeks on the *New York Times* best-seller list.[2] On January 12 hundreds of admirers queued patiently in a downpour outside a Barnes & Noble bookstore on Fifth Avenue to have their copies signed by Carter—the kind of turnout generally accorded celebrity authors of more recent vintage, such as Madonna and Stephen King. In less than two hours Carter signed 700 books, breaking the former store record held by General Norman Schwarzkopf. "Mr. Carter sat at a desk in blue blazer and gray flannel slacks, quietly scribbling his name on books at an ever-increasing clip," Alessandra Stanley of the *New York Times* reported. "At some moments, he looked perilously like Lucille Ball feverishly working the candy factory assembly line." One woman even came up to Carter and said, "If you still lust in your heart, Mr. President, I'm available"—a comment the former president enjoyed so much that he later repeated it on both *The Tonight Show with Jay Leno* and *The Late Show with David Letterman*. Carter was clearly in vogue.[3]

Stanley met Carter for lunch the next day at the Peacock Alley restaurant in the Waldorf Astoria for an interview, where the discussion turned sharply away from *Turning Point* and directly to president-elect Bill Clinton, whose inauguration was only seven days away. Stanley bent Carter's inclination to the confessional mode, which was usually a strength, into weakness. His reminiscence about not being chosen a Rhodes Scholar came out—at least in print—as Clinton envy. Carter had been a finalist in 1946, but he lost out to an Elizabethan scholar from Mississippi ignorant of foreign affairs. As the story was written, Carter came off as a priggish know-it-all who haunts every classroom. "They couldn't ask me any question in *Newsweek* or *Time* that I couldn't answer, but they chose him," he told Stanley. He was trying to be jovial in the interview, but Stanley did not record the conversation as such.

A surprising moment in the interview occurred when Carter talked of Clinton's 1980 gubernatorial loss and dismissed the notion that Cuban refugees housed at Fort Chafee had anything to do with it: the "ignominious defeat" occurred because the Arkansas electorate wanted to bring Clinton "down a notch." Asked how Clinton fared at the August 1992 Habitat for Humanity house building in Atlanta, Carter again came across as petty and snide. "I wouldn't want to comment on his prowess," he said with a smile, "but he was obviously not an experienced carpenter."

Stanley finally got the headline she was looking for when Carter hit an exposed nerve with both the American electorate and the Clintons: their decision, announced some days earlier, to send daughter Chelsea to a private school rather than a District of Columbia public school during their residence in Washington. Critics had immediately leaped on them as classic limousine liberals, paying lip service during the campaign to the centrality of public education and then turning around and enrolling their own child in a school for the elite where the only minority students represented were the offspring of Arab princes or South American plutocrats.

Stanley asked Carter what he thought of the Clintons' schooling decision, and he replied that he was "very disappointed." After all, he and Rosalynn had faced the same decision for their ten-year-old Amy in 1976, and they had opted for a public elementary school. "Amy really enjoyed going to a very low income school with students whose parents were the servants of foreign ambassadors," Carter went on, his self-righteous button having been pushed. The implication was clear: unlike the Clintons, the Carters were un- afraid of Washington's public school system; indeed, they had actually used their choice as a potent symbol that the First Family ought to remain ordinary citizens.[4]

Carter's offhand criticism of the Clintons' school choice became the lead in Stanley's January 14 *New York Times* story, and that evening Carter's commentary reverberated across all of the nightly network news broadcasts. The Clintons were beside themselves. Jimmy Carter was the one person whose voice carried any real weight on the school issue. Clinton's Republican enemies used Carter's ill-considered assessment as fodder against Clinton, the begrudging tag line being that at least Jimmy Carter practiced what he preached. By all accounts Clinton took Carter's invidious comparison with Amy as an implied criticism of Chelsea. If Harry Truman was once ready to punch out a music critic who wrote ungenerously about his daughter's singing, Clinton felt a tinge of similar outrage at Carter for interfering with his family.[5]

The Clinton camp talked of blackballing the Carters from the inaugural events. Since protocol prohibited such a draconian response, they did the next best thing: cold-shouldering the Carters throughout the festivities. A good snubbing might teach the self-righteous Georgians a badly needed lesson. And more importantly, it would publicly make the point that even though the new administration had recruited many former Carter administration officials, they were in no way beholden to the former president himself. When it came time for the Clinton "New Democrats" to honor predecessors, they mentioned the legacies of every Democratic president since FDR—Harry Truman, John Kennedy, and even to a lesser degree, Lyndon Johnson—but the name of Jimmy Carter, the president with whom they had the most in common, never crossed their lips. In coming months Clinton would even praise the accomplishments of Richard Nixon, Ronald Reagan, and Gerald Ford.[6]

The Carters arrived in Washington unaware of just how unwelcome they had become. At virtually every opportunity Bill and Hillary Clinton treated Jimmy and Rosalynn Carter as if they were invisible. Clinton would thank a bevy of celebrities for coming to his inauguration, from Barbra Streisand to Kenny G, without so much as a nod the Carters' way. Whether the snub was done out of long-delayed revenge for Carter's Cuban refugee double-cross in 1980 or for his apparent embrace of Tsongas in 1992 or for the flap over Chelsea is unclear. But it happened. "It was rude beyond belief," is the way

Rosalynn saw the icy reception they received during the inauguration. "Not even Reagan would have done a thing like that."[7]

But Jimmy Carter took it in stride. At the inauguration Carter did manage to have a word or two with Christopher at a State Department reception in his honor about the need for a meeting again, but received a courteous brush-off. Still, Carter was hopeful; the coming weeks would bring a parade of former Carterites to pass congressional muster, including Madeleine Albright as ambassador to the UN and Richard Holbrooke as ambassador to Germany. Anthony Lake, who had been head of policy planning at the State Department during the Carter administration, was appointed to be the NSC director for Clinton. Carter reasoned it would be foolish to let a protocol glitch affect the prospect of a fruitful working relationship with the incoming Clinton foreign policy team.

In early March a junior-level State Department staffer finally contacted Carter about setting up a meeting at Foggy Bottom. When asked for his proposed agenda, Carter testily fired back a list of twenty-five items covering nearly all his center's ongoing programs, from attacking guinea worm in Sudan to growing maize in Ethiopia. "Carter was getting real mad at being ignored," Robert Pastor recalled. "But at last a date was set."[8]

Six weeks after the inauguration Carter, accompanied by the new executive director of the Carter Center, John Hardman, a psychiatrist by training, whose grandfather had been governor of Georgia in the 1930s, and Robert Pastor, headed north to Washington to discuss their role in the new administration. The day before the meeting Carter had sent Christopher a letter requesting State Department documents pertaining to his recently released Iranian hostage friend, David Rabhan, offering the following handwritten salutation: "Signed by me, Jimmy Carter."[9] Carter and company first met with Warren Christopher at the State Department on March 4. They made an earnest pitch to be officially involved in Liberia, Haiti, Ethiopia, Somalia, Cuba, and the Middle East.[10] "I outlined for Chris [Christopher] my standard premise," Carter recalled. "That these are difficult issues, quite often with one or more parties to a dispute, many involving political pariahs. You can't talk to Arafat. You can't talk to so-and-so. We can talk to them. And I don't want to ever get any publicity, you know, I just would like to be briefed and included."[11]

"Well," Christopher said, "I appreciate your offer, Mr. President, but as you know in most cases we're going to have to take the lead." Carter did not disagree: "I want you to take the lead. But when there's a closed door to you, let us help. I have no reticence about meeting with Arafat and the PLO, and you can even disavow my involvement, separate yourself from it."[12]

Christopher was well acquainted with the scope of Carter's agenda, but didn't believe such high-priority national security concerns as Cuba and the Arab-Israeli conflict should be farmed out to a private citizen. He also wanted no part of what was referred to as his former boss's "ready-fire-aim" approach to international affairs, particularly the way he would cultivate rogues and embrace leaders the State Department had branded as outside the pale.[13]

Since leaving the White House, Carter had turned the establishment of personal rapport with political outlaws into a diplomatic art form. If Warren Christopher was dubious about such an approach, Jimmy Carter was not. Carter reminded Christopher that his work with the Carter Center was the proof of his success. Again and again he had witnessed the eagerness of people in war-torn nations to alleviate their suffering by simply ending the factional fighting—by what Carter called "the peaceful interposition of American power." Instead of simply getting the job done, Carter thought Washington dichotomized foreign conflicts: "We select a favorite side in a dispute, and that side becomes angelic and the other side becomes satanic." In Carter's experience, "this all-white or all-black orientation is usually not true." He thought Washington's primary objective ought to be the prevention of present and future suffering, not the blame game of which side in a civil war is more guilty of past atrocities.[14]

In the inevitable tensions between justice and stability, Carter sought a way to establish both. Justice, he argued, can only prevail once order has been established. "The Nuremberg trials could not have taken place while the Second World War was raging," he pointed out. Carter was more interested in healing and forgiveness than retribution and continuing bloodshed. But in his first official meeting with the Clinton administration these arguments fell on deaf ears.[15]

Carter then met with George E. Moose, assistant secretary of state for African affairs, to discuss Sudan, and with Edward P. Djerejian, assistant secretary of state for Near Eastern affairs, to discuss the Arab-Israeli conflict. The attitude was one of placation, with everyone careful not to insult the ex-president. "We gave them a thumbnail sketch of everything," Hardman recalled. "We explained to them how an NGO can work with the government."[16] To Clinton's wary new State Department team, Jimmy Carter apparently came across as a warmed-over Woodrow Wilson without the authority of office. No matter how successful a Carter initiative might have been, it was denigrated on the grounds of power principles and governmental sovereignty. Although the State Department officials were unfailingly courteous to Carter during the meeting and diligently took notes, unlike

James Baker they apparently saw little value in the former president playing the role of diplomat without portfolio. "Christopher promised to follow up on the points I brought up," Carter later complained. "It never happened."[17]

But whatever Washington thought, Jimmy Carter was a global reality. His track-two diplomacy methods were already operating in a half-dozen countries. He had already become perhaps the most admired living American worldwide and possessed stature and authority that allowed him influence unrelated to transient office; Clinton's State Department made a strategic mistake not officially taking advantage of that. There were, after all, precedents for official assignments. Truman and Eisenhower had used Herbert Hoover to great effect on a number of official assignments. Carter was obsessed with being useful, and would have tackled virtually anything from mediating a Central American border dispute to drafting a report on African refugees. If you didn't, as Baker put it, ride herd over Carter, he would end up in policy areas where he was unwelcome. But Christopher, for whatever reasons, decided to keep Carter out of all Foggy Bottom activities.

The breach between Carter and the State Department was not total. Peter Tarnoff, undersecretary for political affairs and a former president of the Council of Foreign Relations, flew to Atlanta to see Carter. However, the meeting was mainly pro forma; no assignments were handed out, although Pastor could point to one achievement on an important policy matter. The U.S. government had been holding up foreign aid to Nicaragua because of various property-related issues, causing great discomfort to the Chamorro government; under Carter's prodding, the State Department agreed to turn on the spigot. Meanwhile the Carter Center continued its close involvement with North Korea, Haiti, and the Middle East, the State Department paying little heed to what they were up to. If Carter was now completely out of the State Department loop, that didn't mean he wasn't keeping tabs on what the Clinton administration was up to, especially in the Middle East. His main source for tracking peace negotiations, ironically enough, was Yasir Arafat.[18]

Early on the Clinton State Department had marked Carter as too proArab to mediate in the Middle East in any official capacity. "They made a deliberate decision not to use Carter in the Middle East," Assistant Secretary of State Edward P. Djerejian recalled. "It was very badly handled."[19] Foggy Bottom was not keeping Carter briefed about the Clinton administration's overtures—Arafat and Assad were. The PLO trusted Jimmy Carter. When passing along a message to Carter through Mary King, Arafat would often say, "When I say the President, I mean *Our* President—

President Carter."[20] It was Carter who had demonstrated to Arafat and other Palestinians that American interests in Middle East peace could also be coupled with concern for the correction of past injustices to the Palestinian people. It was Carter who gained Arafat's trust by treating the PLO with dignity and as a surrogate for self-governance, helping the Palestinians frame their case to appeal to the American public. Most important, it was Carter who by example provided the evidence that political and moral struggle could be more potent than violence and shopworn anti-Zionist threats of "armed struggle."

Even without an assignment from the Clinton administration, Carter spent late spring 1993 in a frenzy of activity. Besides monitoring the Middle East situation, he launched his children's immunization campaign in Atlanta; led an NDI delegation in Paraguay to monitor that country's first free and fair election since independence from Spain in 1811; faced down hecklers at a human rights conference in Vienna; mediated a civil war in Sudan; attended a conference in Kenya to encourage increased UN relief operations in Somalia; and published *Talking Peace: A Vision for the Next Generation*, a primer for young people emphasizing human rights.[21] Despite all the activity and global achievement, Carter still felt sidelined by Clinton. In the one theater that meant the most to Carter—the Middle East—the administration had rung down the curtain on him.

Without Carter's explicit help, prospects for a Palestinian homeland were growing increasingly brighter. In late 1992 Israel's newly elected Labor government embarked on a bold new peace initiative. While official peace talks took place in Washington, with apparently little success, secret meetings were also underway between Israelis and PLO representatives in Norway. Under the auspices of Norwegian foreign minister Johan Jørgen Holst, who had assumed his government position on April 2, the secret talks intensified, particularly after the April 7 summit in Cairo between Rabin and Mubarak proved fruitful. A deal was being hammered out whereby in return for recognition of Israeli sovereignty, the Palestinians would be granted self-rule in portions of the West Bank and Gaza. These first steps would serve as the basis for further negotiations to an ultimate resolution of the "final status" of Gaza and the West Bank, including East Jerusalem. Nothing would be excluded from the final status talks, and no particular outcome was preordained. That August, Rabin and Arafat began exchanging letters. A major breakthrough occurred on August 19, with Peres's pledge to write a letter preserving the status of existing Palestinian institutions in East Jerusalem. The biggest breakthrough in the Middle East since Camp David was at hand.[22]

∽∘∾

T he Carters, who had visited Sudan, Kenya, and Ethiopia in early August, had planned a trip to Togo, Eritrea, Albania, and Yemen from August 21 until September 3, a schedule that coincided with the culmination of the Oslo talks. Their first stop was Togo, a narrow sliver of a country on the Gulf of Guinea, sandwiched between Ghana and Benin in West Africa. Togo, a one-party republic ruled by a president who also served as the chairman of the only political party permitted, was about to hold its first multiparty democratic elections. As head of NDI's election-monitoring team, Carter had looked forward to ushering in an era of multiparty rule for the nearly 4 million inhabitants. His hopes were dashed when it became clear that voting fraud was rampant. For the first time in his postpresidential career as a monitor, Carter denounced the forthcoming elections as corrupt before a vote was cast, departing Lomé precipitously in disgust at the dishonesty of the authoritarian Togolese government.[23]

His next visit, drought-ridden Eritrea, began more auspiciously. Carter's arrival was marked by a thunderstorm, the first in months, and Asmara's newspaper celebrated the welcome showers as "The Carter Rains." Carter spent time discussing with government officials Global 2000's hopes of increasing agricultural productivity in the region. Mary King had flown in from London on Hasib Sabbagh's private plane, and the next day the Carters and Mary flew to Yemen. Carter's agenda in Yemen was threefold: visit the Masila oil fields, under development by Sabbagh; spread the Carter Center gospel among the Yemeni; and explore ancient archaeological sites in the region. En route Carter proudly announced that, counting Yemen, the Carters had visited an even one hundred nations since leaving the White House. "Carter had been diligently keeping a score card," King laughingly recalled.[24]

Yemen, tucked away on the southwestern corner of the Arabian Peninsula, was formed on May 22, 1990, when North Yemen and South Yemen voted to unite. Carter believed the Yemeni had not been properly credited for having held the most democratic elections ever in the Arab world.[25] What brought Carter to Yemen, besides its new democratic bona fides, was the chance to visit Hasib Sabbagh, longtime Palestinian friend and Carter Center founder. Now they were flying to the remote town of Hodaydah to see for themselves what Jimmy later called "the miracle in the desert." Sabbagh's company, Consolidated Contractors Company (CCC) had become the Middle East's largest engineering firm. The company built railways, harbors, roads and bridges, oil refineries and desalination plants, apartments and mosques throughout the Arab world and in points beyond. Development of Yemen's Masila oil field was one of Sabbagh's newest ventures, and the Carters were eager to tour the massive engineering project. They had lunch at his desert camp, where Hasib had flown in separately to meet them, and then set out to explore. They were awestruck at what they found. "Over some of the most difficult terrain I have ever encountered, we watched his teams landing planes, driving trucks, pumping water, servicing oil wells, purifying oil, and pumping it to ships through a new pipeline they had built to the seaport at Makulla," Carter later wrote. "As an engineer by training myself, I could discern how this accomplishment of developing a major oil field in only one year was almost incredible."[26]

It is difficult to overestimate the Carters' affection for Sabbagh, known throughout the Arab world as an unpretentious philanthropist who has also given generously to such American institutions as the Council on Foreign Relations and Harvard University. Carter later wrote of his friend, "I have found that Hasib Sabbagh lacks two human traits—meanness and pettiness. Treating bigotry and resentment as impostors, he instead welcomes affirmation and magnanimity. He has turned adversity, loss, hurt, and anger into a commitment to reconciliation and peace. From being a man without a country, he has become an example of what it means to be a great citizen of the world."[27]

A Palestinian homeland was the one construction that had eluded this Palestinian builder. Sabbagh's daughter Sana tells a story of the depths of his yearning revealed when her father met several U.S. senators on Capitol Hill to talk about the Middle East peace process. As her father stated his views unflinchingly, one senator, a Sabbagh admirer, asked, "What can we do for you personally, sir?" Sabbagh quickly replied: "An identity, I need an identity. I have fulfilled all my dreams and ambitions except one. I do not have an identity if I die. As a Palestinian, I want to be buried in Safad, in Galilee."[28]

The morning of August 31 was spent meeting with Yemen's president, prime minister, and other government officials, the afternoon to spreading the Carter gospel at the University of Sanaa in a speech on human rights and democracy. Carter's broad-ranging talk was enthusiastically received by the audience of the entire university including faculty, students, members of parliament, and other government officials. Carter's confess-and-repent, Baptist missionary style won him an important convert: Yemen's minister of health, Najweeb Ghanem. He later confessed to Carter that because he had had his hands full trying to combat amoebic dysentery, he had been less than forthcoming with the WHO, telling them that Yemen had no known cases of guinea worm since the disease also carried with it the stigma of Third World poverty. Carter's commentary on the crippling disease prodded Ghanem into acknowledging the presence of guinea worm and garnered a commitment that he would now take part in the global eradication effort.[29]

〜〜

I n Yemen Carter also received an urgent hand-delivered message from
Yasir Arafat, saying he was flying in and wanted to meet with Carter at
once. Quickly Mary King arranged for the two to meet secretly at the Taj
Sheba Hotel in Sanaa late that afternoon.[30] Arafat had personally journeyed
to Sanaa especially to bring his old friend into the loop by telling him that
even though the Washington talks appeared to have bogged down, secret
Oslo talks were proving epochal. "The [Washington] negotiations were not
going well," Arafat told Carter at the outset. "We had reached an impasse.
We started special channels between us and Israel directly—sometimes
through Egypt and the Norwegian foreign minister—including direct contacts with some Israeli ministers of government."[31] Carter, who had been
told of the secret talks by Peres that June in Austria, was startled that they
had advanced so quickly—that a major step toward creating a Palestinian
homeland had occurred only days ago.[32]

Assuring Carter that both Peres and Rabin were "supportive" of Oslo,
Arafat went on to describe how the Declaration of Principles, including an
interim self-governing authority in the West Bank and Gaza, was cobbled together. "In the Gaza Area and the Jericho Area, there is to be direct and immediate military withdrawal," an elated Arafat reported. Although issues
remained to be ironed out, Arafat made it clear that he and Rabin would
sign letters of mutual recognition between Israel and the PLO on September 9 in Paris.

An astonished Carter expressed disbelief. "The Israelis have agreed to
this?" Carter queried. "Yes," Arafat responded. "Rabin is in favor of total
withdrawal from the Gaza Area and Jericho Area. An interim period is to
run for five years in the rest of the Occupied Territories with eventual rede-
velopment and withdrawal of the military." Carter thought that "this sounds
like Camp David," to which Arafat readily agreed. "Definitely," he replied.
"We discussed my acceptance of Camp David in Paris. Some of the Camp
David terms have been used in the agreement, for example, 'deportees' and
'displaced persons.'"

Arafat told Carter that the PLO was in the process of informing the U.S.
government about the Oslo breakthrough, but wanted to personally let him
know first. The only others in the room were Rosalynn and Mary. Certain
that Warren Christopher would be supportive of Oslo, Arafat was concerned
that others in the State Department—Dennis Ross, Martin Indyk, or
Samuel Lewis—might try to derail the agreements secretly hammered out
in Oslo. The PLO leader asked Carter for help in making sure that these
Clinton administration figures did not erect obstacles. Carter assured Arafat

that he would "both write and telephone Bill Clinton about this when I get home."

The meeting ended with Arafat asking Carter to help him fund-raise in Saudi Arabia and elsewhere. While money would be appropriated for assuming the functions of the interim self-governing authority—i.e., health, welfare, education, housing, and social affairs—Arafat needed an additional $2 billion or so for infrastructure. The PLO would need money for agriculture, water authority, irrigation, harbors, airports, and general security or police—and those concerns were only the tip of the iceberg. Arafat, after having spent over twenty years in exile, was returning to Jericho as the recognized leader of the Palestinian people, but massive financial help was desperately needed. Exhilarated by the Oslo breakthrough, Carter immediately decided to fly to Jeddah to meet privately with King Fahd, who had ceased Saudi funding of PLO activities after the Palestinians sided with Iraq in the Gulf War. Carter was essentially on a fund-raising mission for the PLO, and a mediator for Yemen hoping to get King Fahd to forget the Gulf War and focus on the future.[33]

In Jeddah, Carter briefed King Fahd on his extraordinary news from Arafat and asked directly whether Saudi Arabia would assist the PLO financially while they set up a governing body, the Palestine Authority, in the West Bank. "I have kept informed of the final stages of the recent Middle East peace talks, including those in Norway," the king replied. "[I] have always kept good relations with the Palestinians," he went on. "They should continue to listen to Hosni Mubarak. *They will get assistance from us,* but mustn't ask for everything at once. It is best to postpone the discussion of Jerusalem. We will give help to President Clinton and others *at every step, but our financial contribution will not be public.*" By obtaining King Fahd's pledge of support, Carter had rendered the PLO an invaluable service, one which Arafat would not soon forget. In a handwritten note on PLO letterhead Carter conveyed his conversation to Sabbagh, reporting that King Fahd was already calling the PLO chairman "President Arafat."[34]

B y the time Carter arrived home—after a brief stop in Albania to promote religious freedom—the world was abuzz with news of the Oslo agreements. The signing of the Israeli-Palestinian agreement was to take place on September 13 on the South Lawn of the White House, where Egypt and Israel had made peace more than a decade earlier. Foreign and American dignitaries, including all of the former presidents, were invited to witness the historic event. "When Clinton asked me to the ceremony," former secretary of state James Baker recalled, "I accepted and told him that

Jimmy Carter should have a front-row seat."[35] Naturally the Carters were delighted to participate. They were also elated when Akram Hanieh—a respected journalist who had been expelled from the West Bank by Israel and would be named editor of *al-Ayyam*, an independent PLO-supporting newspaper in Ramallah—telephoned Mary King from Tunis with word from Yasir Arafat: "The chairman wants to see Jimmy Carter before going to the White House."[36]

Arafat arrived at Andrews Air Force Base outside Washington on Sunday afternoon, September 12, one day before the historic signing ceremony that would usher in Palestinian self-rule in the Israeli-occupied territories. The last time Arafat had set foot on U.S. soil was in 1974, when he appeared at the United Nations, a pistol strapped on his hip, and announced that he came "with an olive branch in one hand and a freedom fighter's gun in the other." This time Arafat disembarked from a Moroccan government Boeing 700, on loan from the king, with no weapon in evidence. In an olive military dress uniform and his trademark black-and-white kaffiyeh, Arafat was arriving not as a freedom fighter but as leader of the Palestinian people. There was no red carpet or military band awaiting Arafat, but he was met by Assistant Secretary of State for Near Eastern Affairs Edward P. Djerejian, who shook hands and extended a formal greeting: "I welcome you to the United States on this historic occasion, which we hope will lead to peace throughout the Middle East."[37] Arafat spoke briefly to reporters, then headed to his temporary headquarters at the ANA Westin Hotel at 2401 M Street for a 6:00 P.M. appointment with Jimmy Carter, the first person he wanted to consult upon arriving in America. Carter's standing in the eyes of the chairman was not lost upon the former president. "He insisted on seeing me before Clinton or Christopher," he proudly recalled.[38]

Arafat received Carter with hugs of solidarity and genuine affection. The talk quickly turned serious. Since their last meeting in Yemen, Arafat said he had gone to see Mubarak in Egypt, and then on to Syria, Tunis, and Oman. Carter inquired what Hafez al-Assad thought of the Declaration of Principles. "My meeting [with him] was warm, fruitful," Arafat reported. "He is not against this." When Arafat spoke of his plan to move to Jericho or Gaza within two months, Carter reveled in the historic moment: "We all owe you a debt of gratitude," he said. "You have been so patient and so wise." Carter also praised the Clinton administration for their willingness to talk directly with the PLO. Carter had now held three private meetings with Arafat, while Warren Christopher still had none, a statistic Carter did not forget.[39]

Arafat, who had just finished last-minute talks with Peres in Paris, seemed much more relaxed than Carter as he mentioned that Camp David terminology was being used in the new agreement. Carter, aware that the next phase of the Palestinian struggle—governance—was just beginning, was uninterested in the rhetoric of the agreement. He wanted to learn about the nuts and bolts of how Palestine would be created. "What sort of mechanism do you plan to use in Gaza?" Carter queried. "You can't run this out of your hip pocket. You can't be a dictator. You need structures. You need institutions. People in Gaza and the West Bank are depending on you." Arafat reassured his friend that the PLO would be able to consolidate control both in and out of the West Bank.

Carter was bearing good tidings for Arafat. That morning, at a Farragut Square brownstone, Carter had met with Sabbagh, who was not planning to be among 3,000 guests at the signing ceremony the next day, fearing that if he were seen on CNN it might damage business relationships in Lebanon or Syria. But Sabbagh asked Carter to pass a message on to Arafat: Once the PLO established themselves in Gaza, the Palestinian billionaire planned on moving CCC's extensive operations from Athens to the West Bank. Carter was pleased: "That is extremely important because it means engineers, doctors, scientists, etc. will eventually be moving to Gaza." Moreover, "I think two-thirds of his staff are Palestinian. In some ways, the movement of jobs can be more important than help from Abu Dhabi or the Japanese." Carter also relayed King Fahd's pledge for financial assistance, with its proviso that the PLO not ask for "everything all at once."

Carter's good news lifted everyone's spirits, and the conversation turned to banter about Arafat's upcoming appearances on *Larry King Live* and *CBS News with Dan Rather*. Abruptly Carter brought the discussion back to an issue of central concern to him: religion. Carter said he had taught Sunday school that morning at Maranatha Baptist in Plains and had prayed for peace in the Middle East. "I chose as my text the part of the Bible where it is said that in Christ, there are no distinctions between master and slave, women or men, Jew or Gentile," Carter told Arafat. "I thought it was an auspicious match for what will happen tomorrow." Arafat nodded and assured Carter that the PLO was developing "institutions in Jerusalem to protect the Christian and Muslim holy places," emphasizing that he always put the word "Christian" first. Rosalynn, now Distinguished Professor of Women's Studies at Emory University, invited Arafat's wife, Suha, to give a lecture during her course. Arafat promised to deliver the message.

As the meeting drew to a close, Carter went into mentor mode: "Be patient," Carter instructed Arafat. "Try to restrain your public statements. Be generous. Don't make demands and don't frighten the Israeli public. Statements made by leaders can cause violence and fear. The Palestinians and the Israelis have to live side by side for hundreds of years in the future." Hanan Ashrawi, the Palestinian spokeswoman at the Washington negotiations, tried

to address his concern by explaining the various liaison committees for cooperation and arbitration that had been established. Arafat then pointed out
the necessity of letting Hamas (Islamic Resistance Movement), an offshoot
of the Muslim Brotherhood founded in Egypt in 1928, participate in the
new Palestinian Authority. No one accused Carter of exaggerating when he
summed up the tangle of loose ends that devolved upon Yasir Arafat as an
"immense responsibility."[40]

At the White House the next morning, Carter's quest to transform Arafat
from terrorist to peacemaker was realized by a handshake and the stroke of a
pen. Three thousand white plastic folding chairs were arranged on the South
Lawn of the White House, where the 535 members of Congress, cabinet
members, foreign ministers, and other notables gathered to bear witness to
the 11:00 A.M. signing. George Bush was as elated as Carter, for it was the
Bush administration that had created a successful framework for the peace
talks begun in Madrid twenty-two months earlier. With Rosalynn between
them, the two former presidents sat front and center for the ceremony.

Last-minute bickering between the PLO and Israeli delegations delayed
the ceremony for nearly forty-five minutes. But at last, Foreign Minister
Shimon Peres of Israel and Mahmoud Abbas of the PLO signed a declaration of Palestinian self-government in Israeli-occupied Gaza and the West
Bank. "It was a beautiful moment," Carter later recalled, although the most
memorable moment occurred when President Clinton coaxed a handshake
out of Arafat and Yitzhak Rabin.[41] The PLO chairman was the first to extend
his hand. Hesitating for just a second, Rabin then followed suit, and the audience was jubilant. "Two hands that had written the battle orders for so
many young men, two fists that had been raised in anger at one another so
many times in the past, locked together for a fleeting moment of reconciliation," was how Thomas L. Friedman captured the historic moment for the
New York Times.[42] Dr. Abdul-Karim Iryani, foreign minister of Yemen, later
noted: "We saw the tear. We were all watching CNN and saw the tear roll
down Carter's cheek when the signing was completed. The whole world saw
the tear."[43]

The progression from Camp David to the historic signing of that morning is a monument to Jimmy Carter's tenacity. During this fourteen-year period Carter pressed harder and more consistently for a political solution to
the Arab-Israeli impasse than any other American diplomat on the world
stage. Even when he had no official role, Carter never let up, expending
enormous sums of his political, personal, and moral capital in the pursuit of
a peaceful Middle East solution. Other players may have momentarily held
center stage, dispatched by the UN or the United States or the European
powers to investigate, mediate, and conciliate, but they would all eventually

move on. Jimmy Carter was different—inner directed, heedless of institutional constraints, guided by his reading of history, inspired by his faith to do what was right, and relying on his own instincts as to whether leaders denominated outlaws by the U.S. government might be brought to talk peace. Carter had been ruthless in the pursuit of peace, and his payoff came on September 13, 1993, when the Declaration of Principles was signed on the same table on which the peace treaty between Egypt and Israel was signed in 1979. Driven to honor the memory of Anwar al-Sadat, a genuine martyr for peace and normalization in the Middle East, Carter was the Saint Paul of conflict resolution, preaching the alternatives to the terrorist gun wherever he went.

After the ceremony Carter wandered about the White House lawn, chatting with friends and leaders and accepting the congratulations of virtually everyone for starting the peace process with the Camp David accords. Carter praised Bill Clinton for the way he had conducted himself, not to mention the biblical references in the president's speech. Clinton had invited all his predecessors to spend the night at the White House, a gesture that both Carter and Bush accepted while Gerald Ford chose to bed down at the nearby Willard Hotel.[44]

Clinton seized the chance to press another item on his agenda. He asked the former presidents to lend their support for the North American Free Trade Agreement (NAFTA) by participating in a photo op at the White House the next day. Seldom if ever in American history had a trade pact created such a national debate as NAFTA had done in 1993. In the post-cold-war era, went the mantra of the Clinton administration, good trade policy was the sine qua non of a sound foreign policy; a world full of robust, market-based democracies would make the world a safer, richer place. If the villain of the cold war had been communism, in the post-cold-war era it was protectionism.[45]

NAFTA passage had been hotly opposed by many Democrats, but not Jimmy Carter, a NAFTA true believer who had spent much of the year buttonholing anyone who would listen on the merits of the agreement. Not only would NAFTA save jobs, he argued, but it would also open new markets for U.S. products by combining 250 million Americans, 90 million Mexicans, and 27 million Canadians into one giant no-tariff trading bloc with a combined GNP of some $7 trillion a year. During the Clinton transition, Carter even lobbied the president-elect, who was then undecided, to embrace NAFTA. Eventually the Clinton administration signed on to NAFTA, but the pro-NAFTA forces faced considerable opposition from those worried that passage would undermine America's labor base. Carter was also concerned about the political fallout from failure to pass NAFTA, coming to agree with Robert Pastor's contention that NAFTA's defeat in the United States would bring an abrupt halt to the movement to bring full democracy to Mexico.[46]

The trade agreement, which allowed U.S. businesses to form production partnership with Mexican and Canadian firms, was vociferously opposed by many, especially Texas billionaire Ross Perot, the AFL-CIO, consumer activist Ralph Nader, and all who saw NAFTA as an assault on American labor. Opponents predicted an increase in U.S. companies sending more work overseas, where wages were lower and work rules less stringent. Not only would the United States lose jobs, it would lose tax dollars as well. In Perot's immortal sound bite, "The sucking sound you hear is all the jobs heading south of the border." Clinton needed to muster all the allies he could get for passage.[47]

That evening at the White House, the adrenaline still flowing from the Rabin-Arafat handshake, an ebullient Bill Clinton and Jimmy Carter talked policy until the early morning hours. Bush had retired early, leaving the two Democrats alone. Carter retold his Camp David stories and filled Clinton in on his past meetings with Arafat. Clinton used the opportunity to pump Carter up for the next day's pro-NAFTA photo op. Carter brought up Warren Christopher's behavior toward him, the unreturned phone calls and unanswered letters. Clinton expressed shock and reassured Carter that he was an integral auxiliary of his administration, a cherished national resource whose service to his country was far from over. Clinton, for the time being, had won Carter over. "From that point onwards I saw the State Department as the problem," Carter recalled. "So whenever a problem arose, I went directly to Clinton for assistance, bypassing Christopher and those other State Department guys."[48]

Later that morning, at a White House ceremony, Clinton spoke eloquently about creating a common market in North America by gradually removing trade barriers among the United States, Mexico, and Canada as Carter, Bush, and Ford looked on. "These men," said Clinton, referring to his predecessors, as he prepared to sign three parallel agreements to NAFTA, "differing in party and outlook, join us today because we all recognize the important stakes for our nation in the issue." The three ex-presidents then offered their testimony in support of NAFTA. Carter stole the show with a frontal assault on Ross Perot. "Unfortunately in our country now," Carter said, "we have a demagogue who has unlimited financial resources and who is extremely careless with the truth, who is preying on the fears and uncertainties of the American public."[49]

That evening Carter's disparaging of Ross Perot as a demagogue was the lead news story, seriously wounding the bantam Texas billionaire. The next morning Perot went on the *Today* show to rebut Carter. "He cannot have read NAFTA," Perot fumed. "He cannot be aware of how the Mexican workers working in the U.S. companies live." Carter had clearly drawn blood from NAFTA's most careful opponent, setting the stage for Vice President Gore to debate the mogul on CNN's *Larry King Live*. Meanwhile, the *New York Times* editorial page defended Carter in his acrimonious exchange with Perot: "We have not quizzed Mr. Carter on his reading habits. We do know that he speaks Spanish, has traveled widely in the hemisphere and is intimately informed on housing and health issues. And not even his harshest critics have ever accused him of being anything but microscopically knowledgeable on treaties and international law. Only in the surreal mind that has produced the running television feature called Ross's Rant-O-Rama could Mr. Carter be accused of being underinformed. Mr. Carter has read one thing with absolute accuracy—the mind and heart of the Texas fulminator."[50]

Over the next nine weeks Carter did everything he could to cheerlead for NAFTA. Perhaps his greatest contribution came on November 2, when he delivered to President Clinton a statement from the Council of Freely Elected Heads of Government based at the Carter Center. In it, the council said it viewed NAFTA as the "first important step toward a hemisphere wide, free-trade area that could lift our people's standard of living higher than ever before and bring Simon Bolivar's dream of a united hemisphere closer to reality."[51] On November 17, 1993, the House passed NAFTA by a 234 to 200 vote, and an appreciative Clinton wrote to thank Carter for his help.[52]

With the NAFTA battle won, Carter could concentrate once more on the Middle East, for he had growing concerns that the "spirit of Oslo" was already dissipating, supplanted by what he regarded as an Israeli obsession with security concerns. To nurture the Oslo spirit both concretely and symbolically, Carter announced in December that a special Carter–de Menil Human Rights Foundation Prize, which carried a $100,000 honorarium, would be awarded to Norway's Institute of Applied Sciences (FAFO) for spearheading the secret peace talks between the PLO and Israel that led to the Declaration of Principles.[53] Carter planned on presenting the prize in Norway on May 8, 1994. "It would mean a great deal to me if you could join us in Oslo," Carter wrote Arafat. "I am also inviting Shimon Peres and Yitzhak Rabin. Not only would this allow us to honor our Norwegian friends, but you and I might also meet to discuss the future."[54] Mary King convinced Arafat to rearrange his schedule to be present.

∽◦∾

As stipulated in the Declaration of Principles (DOP), a five-year interim period began on May 4, 1994, with the signing of the Cairo accords, which marked the beginning of Palestinian self-rule in Gaza and Jericho and set the deadline for the conclusion of the final status talks for May 1999. The agreement formally established the Palestinian Authority (PA), whose jurisdiction covered an area around the West Bank town of Jericho and the entire Gaza Strip, excluding the substantial Jewish settlements in the Gaza Strip, the main roads leading to those settlements, and Israeli military installations. The agreement also stipulated that Israeli troops would complete their withdrawal within three weeks of signing the agreement, after which a Palestinian police force would provide security in the autonomous areas. Immigration procedures were to be jointly administered, while both sides pledged to take all measures necessary to prevent terrorism, crime, and other hostile acts directed against one another. Using his considerable influence with Shimon Peres and international human rights organizations, Carter was able to help convince Israel to release or turn over to the PA within five weeks of the Cairo agreement approximately 5,000 Palestinian prisoners or detainees. And as Carter had hoped, the agreement allowed the PA to print postage stamps, establish radio and television transmissions, and issue travel documents for Palestinian residents.[55]

The next round of Carter-Arafat talks occurred on May 18 in Oslo, with Norwegian foreign minister Bjorn Tore Godal also in attendance. Unlike at their Washington meeting, this time Arafat was the one filled with anxiety over the responsibilities of governance, nearly panic-stricken about where the PA would receive urgently needed funding. "We have big obstacles," Arafat told Carter. "I need your help. We've received many promises, but we're approaching the economic fields now and have received nothing from the donors and the World Bank." Carter calmly asked who at the World Bank was refusing to transmit the funds. Arafat answered the vice president of the Middle East and North Africa International Bank for Reconstruction and Development. "I will telephone the president of the World Bank and deputy in charge of the fund," Carter reassured Arafat. "I will give you a report. I might also be able to go public with an opinion piece once I have the information."[56]

At the top of Carter's agenda was arranging for an NDI–Carter Center delegation to monitor the first Palestinian election, which was to be held in January 1996, but Arafat deflected Carter's initial probe, returning to his search for capital. "It's a disaster if I go back empty-handed," Arafat pleaded. "There's starvation. We need food, hospitals." Arafat inventoried the perks Israel had gotten for signing the DOP—computer systems, F-15s, $65 million for redeployment from Gaza, massive grants—fuming that "I got nothing."

Carter and Godal sympathized with Arafat's plight, especially when he reported that Kuwait had blocked $100 million of PLO remittances, while Dubai had done the same with $56 million. "I even asked for a loan," Arafat shouted. "A loan! There was no response. From Italy. From Spain. There was no response." A discouraged Arafat asserted that the World Bank was still treating him as a pariah instead of a peacemaker. "It would be better for me not to go into Jericho than to put myself in a critical position."

Carter shifted the focus to Hamas, particularly the organization's radical leader Sheikh Ahmed Yassin, who had refused to disavow violence against the Rabin government. Carter conveyed to Arafat concerns Peres had recently raised with him about Yassin, and implored the PLO leader to censor the Hamas figurehead. "He is a Bedouin from the Neghev Desert," Arafat chuckled. "Yes, he is ready. I can get a statement from Fahred Yassin." Arafat also reiterated his position that all factions—including Hamas— would be allowed to participate in the January 1996 election. "I would like to help you with the election—both the local election and the legislative," Carter interjected once again. Finally, Arafat acceded: "Yes. Definitely. We are counting on it!" An agreement was struck: the Carter Center would dispatch an envoy to Tunis to work closely with Arafat on the journey to a democracy for the homeland.[57]

While the Carter-Arafat-Godal meeting was taking place, the Israeli Defense Force completed its partial withdrawal from the Gaza Strip, only to reemerge to protect the roughly 5,000 Israeli settlers who resided in the Gaza Strip. As promised, Carter contacted the World Bank on Arafat's behalf, but he held back from going public on the money issue on the advice of Hasib Sabbagh, who suggested that Carter not expend any of his "moral and political credibility" just yet, because Sabbagh believed the World Bank was properly holding up money to Arafat until the PLO leader had established an institutional framework to account for the monies. "Without institutions, the donors will not do much," Sabbagh had told Carter.[58]

That summer Carter wrote a warm introduction to a book on Hasib Sabbagh's life while the Palestinian businessman sent the former president a 22-karat gold-sheathed sword encrusted on both sides with rubies and emeralds for his seventieth birthday, as well as a slightly more practical gift. "We have two planes now, so whenever the elections take place, President and Mrs. Carter can have one of the planes, no matter when it is," Sabbagh told Mary King. "I will give them whatever it is they need to make their participation possible."[59]

On July 1 Carter and Sabbagh together watched as their friend Yasir Arafat, having dodged a minefield of political and financial woes, returned to the Gaza Strip via Egypt, the first time in more than two decades that he had set foot on Palestinian land. Waving the green, black, and red Palestinian flag of liberation, Arafat, with help from Carter and many others, had returned to Palestine, still beset by an array of administrative difficulties and opposed by those who negated the peace process, particularly a broad variety of Israeli forces and the Islamic rejectionist groups. Arafat had only limited autonomous authority over a small area of the West Bank, and ran the PA as he had in Tunis: one-man rule, nocturnal hours, haphazard decision making, and policy based on his celebrityhood—which was sky-high, even his enemies treating him as if he were a Hollywood star. In fact, he tried running the PA from his hip pocket, as Carter had warned him not to do. Meanwhile, the World Bank hesitated on providing Arafat with funds because he refused to follow their standard procedures, causing him to snap bitterly, "Who needs their money in any case? I have enough rich Palestinians who will bring billions to the country."[60]

In truth, Arafat's first months in Gaza brought with them stark economic woes as Palestinians complained about the collapse of the road system, electrical blackouts, sewer backups, telephone glitches, and a whole host of problems. The long-term residents in the West Bank and Gaza were suspicious of Arafat, who suddenly appeared in their communities, sometimes behaving dictatorially. They did not want to see their schools and mosques overrun with penniless Palestinian refugees taking advantage of their hard-earned social services. Despite the serious dilemmas, Carter still saw his friend's return as triumphant. "I'm so very proud of you," Carter would later tell Arafat.[61]

TWENTY

MISSION TO NORTH KOREA

‿‿◦‿‿

The division of the Korean peninsula, for thirty-five years a Japanese colony, on September 3, 1945, just weeks after Emperor Hirohito's surrender ended World War II, once satisfied the war-weary victors, but by the late 1970s it seemed outdated, irrational, and arbitrary to many—including Jimmy Carter. The unstable arrangement devised by the Americans and Soviets had gone haywire almost immediately. In 1948 North Korean Communists established the Democratic People's Republic of Korea, with Kim Il Sung as dictator; in the South, the United States installed the ostensibly pliable Syngman Rhee. When Carter first went to the region in 1949 as a naval officer aboard the submarine USS *Pomfret,* patrolling the Pacific and the Sea of Japan for the Communist enemy from the north, the cold war had dominated American foreign policy. A year later Communist battalions from the north poured across the 38th parallel.[1]

In 1953, after three years of dreadful war, which cost more than 50,000 American lives, an accord was signed by the combatants' generals. A demilitarized zone, supervised by UN forces, separated the belligerents but did not end the hostility. As the cold war smoldered on, both Koreas steadily increased their military preparedness, the North by building an army of 1.1 million men, the South by outfitting 600,000 men trained with U.S. assistance. Animosity between the two Koreas was pervasive. No spot on earth, except Berlin, was a more dangerous cold war flashpoint than the intensely militarized Korean peninsula.[2]

As a candidate for U.S. president in 1975, Jimmy Carter, a one-term Georgia governor with little experience in foreign affairs, campaigned to withdraw American troops from the Korean peninsula. The Vietnam War was finally winding down to its inglorious conclusion, and many Americans were receptive to calls for Washington to reduce its military commitments abroad. It was in this political climate that candidate Carter advocated bringing home American troops from South Korea, the only remaining U.S. military deployment on the Asian mainland after withdrawal from South Vietnam. Only the U.S. Air Force would stay active in South Korea, Carter declared on the campaign trail, also eager to remove nuclear weapons from the region: "We've got 700 atomic weapons in Korea. I see no reason for a single one." When Carter won, he was in a position to turn these campaign promises into policy.[3]

For two and a half years an obdurate President Carter fought doggedly for the withdrawal of all U.S. ground troops from Korea despite strong opposition from both Seoul and Tokyo. A primary rationale for Carter's position, regarded as reckless by most U.S. military analysts, was his bedrock conviction that the Pentagon had too many troops stationed overseas. Carter had no interest whatsoever in the projection of U.S. military might around the globe: "Contrary to the opinion of many U.S. leaders, then and now, it was not a goal of mine to deploy as many of our forces around the globe as host countries would accommodate," was the way Carter would put it in 1994.[4] Most of the leading foreign policy experts of Carter's administration— Harold Brown, Cyrus Vance, Warren Christopher, and Richard Holbrooke, among others—eventually opposed their boss's withdrawal policy. They feared that without the deterrent of 40,000 U.S. ground troops, a million-plus North Korean soldiers could sweep across the border again, just as they had done in 1950, virtually unimpeded. The experts also had serious strategic concerns that withdrawal would destabilize Asia in the wake of Vietnam.[5] "Carter felt he was up against the establishment," Brown noted about the withdrawal issue, "whereas we felt we were trying to save him from doing things that would cause big trouble with allies."[6]

Not surprisingly, Carter's withdrawal policy was eagerly embraced by Kim Il Sung, known in his closed society as the Great Leader, whose autocratic regime had long blamed the United States for keeping the peninsula divided. For Kim, Carter's campaign pledge came as a gift from heaven. Throughout the cold war Kim had repeatedly stated that a central goal of his government was the removal of all American troops from the Korean peninsula. In November 1976, immediately following Carter's electoral victory, Kim wrote directly to the president-elect in Plains, asking to establish immediate contact between Pyongyang and Washington, D.C. On the eve of Carter's inauguration Kim, eager to bond with Carter, noticeably softened his normally fierce anti-American rhetoric, hoping to initiate a rapprochement.

Once in office Carter accepted communiqués from Kim, lifted the U.S. ban on travel to North Korea, and for the first time invited Pyongyang's UN representative to an official U.S. reception. Before long Kim was sending intimate letters to Carter through President Omar Bongo of Gabon, President Josip Broz Tito of Yugoslavia, and President Nicolae Ceauşescu of Romania. Kim's missives were intended to drive home two points: it was time for the American president to honor his campaign pledge of troop withdrawal, and Korean unification was possible provided South Korean president Park Chung Hee was excluded from negotiations. Carter of course refused the latter, but tried to make good on the former. Meanwhile, Kim publicly referred to Carter as "a man of justice."[7]

Virtually everyone in his administration wanted Carter to abandon the scheme, often maneuvering behind his back so as not to cross swords with the commander in chief: only Brzezinski stood by him, worried about his boss flip-flopping on too many foreign policy issues. The strategy of the administration's "withdrawal opponents" was to do everything possible to delay, modify, or water down their boss's desire to pull up U.S. stakes in South Korea. Since Carter had promised $1.9 billion in military aid to Seoul, "in advance of or parallel to the withdrawals," congressional approval was mandatory.[8] Holbrooke vividly recalls senators Charles Percy and Jacob Javits visiting him in the State Department and pounding on his glass table, saying, "We'll never let you get away with it."[9]

It is difficult to explain why Carter clung so tenaciously to his withdrawal policy in the face of adamant opposition from all of his top advisers. Character accounts, in part: a stubborn streak, an inability to admit he was wrong, and his post-Watergate-fueled insistence that he not renege on a campaign promise. Fiscal conservatism also played a role. Carter believed that with the South Korean economy now booming, due largely to a massive infusion of yen, the South should defend itself. Bucking conventional wisdom and geopolitical realities, Carter also believed that Kim Il Sung was not an Adolf Hitler or Joseph Stalin but far less ruthless, and that North Korea might very well be ready to enter the family of nations. And finally, after the killing fields of Vietnam and the secret bombings of Laos and Cambodia, he believed there was no moral reason for the United States to remain armed to the teeth in Asia. His ultimate objective was a nuclear-free Korean peninsula, with North and South eventually unified.[10]

By January 1, 1979—when full U.S. diplomatic relations with China were established—Carter's policy of troop withdrawal from South Korea was in disarray, with virtually no support from any corner. The Camp David accords suggested a new strategy. If Carter was thwarted in achieving the disengagement of U.S. troops from the Korean peninsula, why not at least invite President Park and Kim Il Sung to meet him in the demilitarized zone to initiate peace talks? Bringing the two arch-antagonists together, Carter believed, might be the first step toward permanent peace, reunification, and demilitarization on the Korean peninsula. Word of the president's proposal for a Korean peace summit produced a panic attack at the State Department's Asia desk. Did Carter really believe he could trust Kim Il Sung? Did he really think it wise to treat Communist North Korea as though it was a civilized nation? Did he understand that South Korea would never agree to such a plan?

Desperate to get Carter to immediately abandon the dovish scheme before it was leaked to the world press, an incredulous U.S. foreign policy establishment implored Brzezinski, who had Carter's ear, to dissuade the commander in chief from even fantasizing about such a potentially catastrophic, high-risk gambit. In June President Carter journeyed to South Korea as a face-saving gesture for his doomed withdrawal policy and to discuss, among other topics, the future of U.S. troops on the peninsula. It was a difficult summit. The careful choreography of the State Department almost fell victim to the president's stubbornness. Carter did not care for President Park, who took power as a military dictator in a 1961 coup, considering him arrogant and immoral, a "democratic" president who ignored human rights.[11] Holbrooke later characterized the contentious bilateral Carter-Park meeting as "the worst imaginable exchange between two treaty allies."[12]

Carter's withdrawal policy did serve as an effective bargaining chip in Seoul. Eventually a deal was struck between Carter and Park. Carter would scrap his disengagement policy if Park promised to increase South Korean military expenditures and release eighty-seven dissenters from jails as sign of Seoul's commitment to improve on its dismal human rights record. Park agreed, and Carter agreed to put off retraction to the beginning of a second term that never happened.[13]

If Carter regarded Park Chung Hee as an immoral military dictator, that was no reason to bypass an opportunity to do some soul-saving. Once they had struck their deal, Carter inquired into the nature of Park's religious beliefs. A startled Park replied that he had none. "I would like you to know about Christ," Carter said, offering to send the American-educated Baptist evangelist Chang Hwan (Billy) Kim to Seoul "to explain our faith." Park agreed to receive the television preacher, but no doubt was left to ponder Carter's unorthodox style of mixing church and state, his relying on the healing power of love to meliorate the estrangement between Washington and Seoul now that the acrimony had subsided. Only four months after Carter's Christian conversion overture, and just days after learning about Jesus Christ from Billy Kim, Park was assassinated by the chief of his own intelligence agency.[14]

If Carter lost the battle on troop deployment, he won some skirmishes on the nuclear front. After all the brouhaha stirred up by the president, his administration reduced the total U.S. military strength in Korea by only 3,000 troops, leaving 37,000 in place. But he did succeed in reducing the number of U.S. nuclear weapons from nearly 700 to around 250, and consolidating those remaining from haphazard deployment about the countryside to a single-site air base. But overall, as former *Washington Post* journalist Don Oberdorfer would later write, a major lesson was learned: "Even a determined president proved unable to decouple the United States from the high-stakes military stand-off on the Korean peninsula. The major impact of Carter's unsuccessful effort was to intensify the concern among his Asian allies that had been generated by the American withdrawal from Vietnam."[15]

Carter was so embarrassed by his failed attempt to withdraw U.S. troops from Korea that he omitted any mention of it from his presidential memoir, *Keeping Faith*. During the Reagan years the number of U.S. troops in South Korea actually increased, and North Korea drifted into further isolation. In 1987 a South Korean aircraft disappeared over Burma, and an investigation by Seoul concluded the plane had been destroyed by a bomb. Later, a North Korean woman responsible for the plane's destruction claimed she was acting on instructions from Kim Jong Il, Kim Il Sung's son, and heir apparent. Tensions between the U.S. and North Korea—always stressful—were at their nadir, but the collapse of the Soviet Union soon changed the dynamic.[16]

The end of the cold war heralded the possibility of a new era of peaceful coexistence between the two Koreas. In December 1991 an accord was reached between Seoul and Pyongyang, replacing the 1953 armistice, and calling for a Korean peninsula free of nuclear weapons and the opening of roads, rail links, and regular family exchanges between North and South.[17] The eighty-year-old Kim Il Sung, still in power in North Korea, invited Carter, now out of office, to Pyongyang that year, hoping to establish a personal rapport with the only high-profile American leader who had ever supported the U.S. troops' withdrawal from South Korea. Carter declined at the request of the State Department.[18]

Encouraged by the Carnegie Endowment for International Peace and the Rockefeller Foundation to establish direct contact with North Korea— an important vacuum to fill, since Washington had no official diplomatic relations with the nation—in January 1992 Carter held an International Negotiating Network (INN) consultation at the center to discuss the future of the Korean peninsula with representatives from thirty-six countries and six continents. With luminaries like Oscar Arias, Eduard Shevardnadze, and Bishop Desmond Tutu, the INN consultation was widely covered by the international media. After two days of discussion INN participants concluded that for the Korean peace process to move forward, three things had to happen: international disarmament expertise should be shared; the U.S. government should normalize relations with North Korea and support North-South negotiations; and open telecommunications should be established between North and South, who since birth had acted like scorpions in a bottle. The Carter Center also announced an INN Council trip to North Korea, to include Jimmy Carter.[19]

Carter was eager to establish a personal rapport with Kim, as he had done with other outlaws du jour as Daniel Ortega, Hafez al-Assad, Mohammed Farah Aidid, Mengistu Haile Mariam, and Yasir Arafat; dialogue with the ostracized was the Carter Center's modus operandi. But Secretary of State Baker nixed a Carter visit to North Korea under the auspices of INN on the grounds that his trip would only complicate ongoing official negotiations. The South Korean government also sent word that they were opposed to a Carter visit because of his past advocacy of withdrawing U.S. troops from their country. Carter reluctantly agreed to stay home, and declined a second visit later that year. The Bush administration wanted no part of Carter's conflict resolution theories tested on the Korean peninsula. That the headstrong Carter twice agreed not to fly to North Korea is great testimony as to just how much Carter respected Baker, but he continued to keep an eye on the divided nation and the U.S. investment in troops there. He saw little rationale for stationing U.S. troops there en masse now that the cold war was over, believing that perhaps $30 billion per year could be saved if the United States simply brought the ground troops home.[20]

In early 1992 it momentarily appeared that U.S.–North Korean relations were improving. In bilateral talks Kim seemed eager to forge a better relationship with Washington, since his alliance with Moscow had collapsed and his relationship with Beijing was strained. In this new spirit of accommodation, North Korea permitted inspectors from the International Atomic Energy Agency (IAEA), a semi-independent UN technical agency created in 1957 to stop the spread of nuclear weapons, to inspect its facility at Yongbyon.[21]

On an early fact-finding mission, the IAEA inspectors concluded that North Korea had produced plutonium at Yongbyon, although it was unclear whether they had manufactured the eight to sixteen pounds needed for an atomic weapon. The CIA asserted that the North Koreans had diverted enough plutonium for one or two bombs, while Kim claimed they produced only a small quantity. The world community shuddered to think that North Korea must have become a nuclear power and lied about the purpose of their Yongbyon facility. Reiterating that North Korea had no intention of making a bomb and that the Yongbyon facility had been only for the peaceful development of nuclear energy, Kim, angered by accusations that he was dishonest, banned all further inspections. "In the last half of 1992 and the early months of 1993, the euphoria that had resulted from opening North Korea's nuclear program to international inspection gave way to suspicion, antagonism, and eventually crisis," Oberdorfer later wrote. "The rewards Pyongyang had expected from agreeing to nuclear inspections had not developed; instead, the presence of the inspectors provided the focal point for accusations of cheating and new international pressures."[22]

While the Bush administration grappled with the fact that North Korea could produce plutonium, in disregard of the nuclear nonproliferation treaty both Koreas had signed, Carter focused on an old unfinished presidential agenda item: getting the presidents of North and South Korea to hold a summit. "There was no reason why North and South Korea weren't holding direct talks," Carter maintained. "It was foolish." Carter was also concerned about the enormous economic disparity on the divided peninsula, with the South's GNP fifteen times greater than the North's. He examined the likely social and economic consequences should the two Koreas reunify, as Germany had done, and how to deal with the anticipated flood of refugees from the North that would pour into the South.[23]

By the time Clinton entered the White House, Carter had become well versed on the issues of the North Korean plutonium controversy. As an Annapolis-trained nuclear engineer, Carter was in a much better position than the average citizen to understand and evaluate some of the complex technical issues. North Korea had signed the Nuclear Nonproliferation Treaty in December 1985, but their old-style reactors used natural uranium for fuel and graphite rods to moderate the pace of nuclear reactions instead of water. This nuclear reactor, capable of power generation, was also spawning substantial amounts of plutonium waste, which was capable of being reprocessed into bomb material. America's security interests were potentially at stake.[24]

One possible option, as Carter saw it, was for North Korea to scrap its old

A quiet moment with Israeli prime minister Shimon Peres. *(Anthony Allison, courtesy of the Carter Center)*

President Clinton signing the North American Free Trade Agreement, September 14, 1993. Joining him are, from the left, former president Gerald Ford, House Speaker Thomas Foley of Washington, Senate majority leader George Mitchell of Maine, former president Carter, Senate minority leader Bob Dole of Kansas, former president George Bush, House minority leader Bob Michel of Illinois, and Vice President Al Gore. *(AP/Wide World Photos)*

Monitoring elections in Panama, May 6–9, 1994. *(Miguel Valencia, courtesy of the Carter Center)*

With his close Middle East adviser and friend, Mary King. *(Courtesy of Mary King)*

Carter and North Korean president Kim Il Sung toasting during Carter's visit to North Korea, June 17, 1994. *(Courtesy of the Carter Center)*

Senator Sam Nunn of Georgia, President Carter, and General Colin Powell arriving at the Port-au-Prince airport in Haiti, September 17, 1994, on their mission to avert an American invasion. *(AP/Wide World Photos)*

President Carter and Bosnian Serb leader Radovan Karadzic in Pale, Bosnia, December 20, 1994, after both sides in the conflict agree to a four-month nation-wide cease-fire. *(AP Photo/Michael Butler)*

A memorial service at the site of a mass slaughter in Rwanda, November 1995. *(Courtesy of the Carter Center)*

Carter, James Baker, and former Costa Rican president Oscar Arias election-monitoring in Nicaragua, October 1996. *(Courtesy of the Carter Center)*

Jimmy and Rosalynn Carter at the Carter Center—with their wedding picture in the background. *(Rick Diamond, courtesy of the Carter Center)*

Jimmy Carter is named an honorary chief in a Nigerian village where he fought guinea worm disease, March 1995. *(Courtesy of the Carter Center)*

President Carter, Yasir Arafat, and Arafat's baby daughter, January 19, 1996, in Gaza City, the day before the Palestinian election. *(Billy Howard, courtesy of the Carter Center)*

President Carter, Robert Pastor (right), and George Price, prime minister of Belize (left) in one of many trips to Haiti to mediate the electoral process. This one was in 1990. *(Courtesy of the Carter Center)*

Being greeted by his grandchildren moments before entering his surprise birthday tribute, September 30, 1994. *(Rick Diamond, courtesy of the Carter Center)*

President Carter and Ellen Mickiewicz, director of the Carter Center, October 20, 1996. *(Courtesy of the Carter Center)*

A contemplative moment at the Carter Center. *(Courtesy of the Carter Center)*

reactors, and with U.S. technical and financial assistance build newer light-water reactors, which were less usable for making atomic weapons in disregard of international inspections. Was "less plutonium" still too much plutonium in North Korea's hands? If IAEA was concerned about nuclear reactors in North Korea, so was he—particularly when on March 12, 1993, Pyongyang announced its intention to withdraw from the nonproliferation treaty. The Clinton administration debated how to respond. Pentagon officials argued that it was more important to limit the North Korean program in the future than to resolve the mystery of the past diversion, a position shared by Carter. Meanwhile, the Rockefeller Foundation—anxious for track-two diplomatic effort with Kim—wrote Carter in April letting him know they would pay all his expenses if he ever decided to visit North Korea.[25]

In late 1993, as the crisis escalated, Kim Il Sung invited Carter to Pyongyang for a third time. Secretary of State Warren Christopher asked Carter not to accept, and the former president reluctantly complied. The Clinton administration had one policy: North Korea must not develop nuclear weapons. Dialogue with North Korea would be impossible until Kim froze plutonium production and allowed the IAEA inspectors unhampered access to Yongbyon to determine whether and how much plutonium had been diverted when the reactor was shut down in 1989.[26]

With tensions mounting, President Clinton dispatched the Reverend Billy Graham to North Korea in January 1994, his King James Bible and a resolute note from Clinton in hand. The essence of the American message: cooperate on the nuclear issue immediately or face dire consequences. Kim was visibly angered and insulted by the note. "Pressure and threats cannot work on us," Kim scolded Graham, reiterating that if North Korea was not treated with dignity by Clinton, there would be no nuclear dialogue.[27]

When Graham arrived back in the United States he wrote Carter, urging him to sojourn to North Korea to defuse the nuclear crisis with track-two diplomacy.[28] By May, Kim, his nation in dire economic straits, decided to use his nuclear program as a bargaining chip to extract economic and military assistance from the Clinton administration. North Korea started removing fuel rods from the Yongbyon reactor. The plan backfired. Instead of increasing exports Kim got a highly visible reinforcement of American–South Korean "Team Spirit" forces in the Korean peninsula—70,000 South Korean troops and 50,000 American troops—engaged in war maneuvers. The Pentagon also deployed Patriot missiles, the antimissile weapons used by U.S. forces in the Gulf War. A face-off loomed large. The IAEA, impatient with being manipulated by Kim Il Sung's regime, established a deadline of February 21 for continuing its inspections of the Yongbyon nuclear facilities. If not met, the UN regulatory agency would turn this serious matter over to the UN Security Council.[29]

Meanwhile Carter's close friend James Laney—a former president of Emory University and now U.S. ambassador to South Korea—entered the picture in a dramatic fashion. Laney, who had once been a missionary in Korea and was fluent in the language, had been telephoning to keep him apprised on the escalating war tensions on the peninsula.[30] Desperate to avoid war, Laney flew to Washington in mid-February to alert Clinton to the potential risks of his brinkmanship and the growing possibility of "accidental war." Laney warned the president of the terrifying prospect of U.S. military and civilian casualties in a new Korean war: that "you could have 50,000 body bags coming home." Laney's graphic description led Clinton to appoint Robert L. Gallucci, assistant secretary of state for political-military affairs, as overall coordinator of U.S. policies toward North Korea for the duration of the crisis.[31]

Ambassador Laney also met with Carter in Atlanta that February, to discuss the possibility that Carter might have to make an emergency visit to Pyongyang, promising to continue to inform the ex-president about what was *really* happening on the Korean peninsula so he wouldn't have to rely on position papers filtered by the State Department. Laney felt that the Clinton administration had made a grievous error in painting Kim Il Sung into a corner, deploying Patriot missiles to the region, and putting the South Korean military on red alert. Panic was sweeping the Asian Pacific, particularly in South Korea. Laney, one of the individuals most involved in the Carter Center, was the only Clinton administration official who knew in February that Carter was making real plans.[32]

For a fleeting moment that March it looked as if the crisis had been resolved; inspections were allowed at six maintenance sites at Yongbyon, but the IAEA inspectors were banned from making sophisticated measurements at the plutonium reprocessing plant. Thwarted in carrying out their work, the international inspectors left, unable to verify North Korea's bomb-making capacity. The Clinton administration immediately began consulting Seoul about rescheduling "Team Spirit" military exercises, canceled all future talks with Pyongyang, and began preparing to seek UN sanctions against North Korea. The war atmosphere was best expressed by North Korean negotiator Park Young, who ominously told his South Korean counterpart, "Seoul is not far from here. If war breaks out, it will be a sea of fire."[33]

As the United States and its allies pushed for UN Security Council sanctions against North Korea, Kim Il Sung threatened that "sanctions are a declaration of war." Although the Clinton administration wanted to avoid a military engagement, it had to take seriously the CIA's estimate that North Korea had enough plutonium for two Hiroshima-sized bombs. The unloading of the irradiated fuel rods from the 5-megawatt reactor at Yongbyon in the way it was done, to prevent IAEA inspectors from making precise measurements, was a serious matter. Moreover, the material that was unloaded could, according to Secretary of Defense William Perry, potentially be converted to enough plutonium for four or five nuclear weapons. Pyongyang was doing everything possible to make sure the inspectors had no accurate reading of whether additional bomb material had already been extracted that could make North Korea a nuclear power. Removing irradiated fuel rods was construed by the United States as a deliberate act designed to destroy the reactor's verifiable operating history.

By early June IAEA had sent the UN Security Council a letter calling for immediate international action against North Korea, by way of UN sanctions. The call drove Kim Il Sung to the brink of war. Kim had his own domino theory, as illustrated by the analogy he used with his friend, Norodom Sihanouk, the Cambodian chief of state: "They want us to take off our shirt, our coat and now our trousers, and after that we will be nude, absolutely naked. What they want us to be is a man without defense secrets, just a naked man. We cannot accept that. We would rather accept a war. If they decide to make war, we accept the war, the challenge we are prepared for." For Kim, inspections were tantamount to losing national sovereignty. This sentiment was formalized on June 5, when North Korea announced to the UN that "sanctions mean war, and there is no mercy in war."[34]

Mercy, however, was Jimmy Carter's specialty. As tensions mounted, Carter, who adamantly opposed UN sanctions, wanted to find a graceful exit for Kim Il Sung. Interestingly, Clinton had the same instincts, and in late May, at Secretary Perry's and Ambassador Laney's urging, he proposed sending Senators Sam Nunn (Democrat of Georgia) and Richard Lugar (Republican of Indiana) to North Korea to meet the Great Leader in hopes of defusing the crisis. Kim Il Sung refused to accept their visit; he was too busy and not interested in negotiating with parliamentarians.[35] Not long after that Carter telephoned Clinton, who was about to leave for Europe to participate in the fiftieth anniversary of D-day ceremonies, to express his deep concerns over the impending North Korean crisis. Clinton responded: on June 5 Assistant Secretary Gallucci was dispatched to Plains to give Carter a "definitive briefing" at his home.[36] "I was amazed at how well-versed

President Carter was on the technical aspects of the crisis," Gallucci re-called. "His nuclear background allowed him to understand the intricacies of the nuclear reactor."[37]

While Carter liked Gallucci personally, he was aghast by what he was told: there was no U.S. contingency plan for further dialogue with Kim. Carter informed Gallucci that his patience was wearing thin. The next day after the North Koreans reaffirmed Carter's standing invitation to visit Pyongyang, Carter telephoned Vice President Al Gore, advising him of his "strong inclination to accept." Gore told Carter to put his "request" in writing and he would present it to President Clinton with his adamant recommendation. On June 7 Gore telephoned Carter with President Clinton's approval.[38]

The prospect of Jimmy Carter running loose in North Korea made the State Department nervous. The general consensus was that this was no time to experiment with Carter's Christian freelancer approach to diplomacy. Gore, Carter's most consistently vocal supporter in the administration, argued that this was precisely the kind of crisis situation where Carter's mediation skills should be tried. Clinton sided with Gore, provided Carter made it crystal clear that he was a private citizen. Like the Reverend Billy Graham that past January, Carter was not to imply, even remotely, that he was an official U.S. envoy.

With Clinton's green light, Marion Creekmore, a former U.S. ambassador to Sri Lanka and now program director of the Carter Center, made arrangements for his boss to arrive in Seoul on June 13, spend a day with Ambassador Laney and South Korean officials, and then cross the DMZ to meet with Kim Il Sung.[39] For Carter's mission to be successful—i.e., to derail the move toward UN sanctions—North Korea would have to permit monitoring of the spent fuel they had recently removed from Yongbyon, refrain from processing new plutonium, and agree not to refuel the reactor. Carter received various briefings before his journey, including one by a Georgia Tech nuclear engineer and from a CNN crew that had recently visited the country. The Rockefeller Foundation continued to brief Carter throughout the crisis, as did the Reverend Billy Graham.[40]

On June 10, only days before Carter's scheduled departure, Emperor Akihito of Japan, the son of Hirohito, arrived in Atlanta to lunch with Carter and discuss how to deal with North Korea's defiance of nuclear inspections. Carter was widely respected in Japan, and a museum in Konu had been built to honor his peacemaking career. From his discussions with the Emperor, Carter was even more convinced that the UN sanctions were a dreadful mistake. The emperor, not allowed to officially speak for Japan, told Carter that his country believed that sanctions of any kind would cause Tokyo severe economic problems. Japan had a substantial Korean minority split between citizens from the North and South, and a crisis of this magnitude would trigger all kinds of domestic havoc.[41] Later that afternoon Carter and Creekmore flew to Washington for additional Defense and State Department briefings. NSC adviser Anthony Lake made it clear to Carter that he no authority to speak for the U.S. "We were to find some of the assessments of our North Korea experts sharply different from our later observations," Carter would later record in his travel diary.[42]

Selig Harrison of the Carnegie Endowment for International Peace returned from a three-day trip to North Korea, where he floated the notion of a "nuclear freeze" to a receptive Kim Il Sung. By the time he left Pyongyang on June 11, only a few days before Carter's arrival, Harrison had procured from Kim a verbal agreement to freeze the North Korean nuclear program in return for light-water reactor components from the United States. "We want nuclear power for electricity," Kim told Harrison, insisting he did not have nuclear weapons, "and we have shown this by our offer to convert to light-water reactors."[43] Interestingly enough, the State Department never bothered to inform Carter of Harrison's meeting with Kim. "There was no need to tell Carter about Harrison," Gallucci recalled. "We had our own policy we were mobilizing behind. And remember, many in the administration thought it disastrous for Carter to go."[44]

Jimmy and Rosalynn arrived in Seoul on June 13, to find the city of over 10 million in near panic. The stock market had plummeted by 25 percent in two days, bomb shelters were being constructed, grocery stores were overrun with customers desperate to stockpile rice and noodles, and families were filling jugs of water in preparation for war. South Korean president Kim Young Sam called Carter's visit "ill timed" and worried publicly that the ex-president would be duped by Kim's "stalling tactics." Meanwhile, General Garry E. Luck, the United States Commander in Korea, had just informed Congress that he would need 400,000 troops to supplement the 37,000 in South Korea should there be a second Korean war, and that it would take approximately sixty days to deploy them. "General Luck, Commander of all military forces in South Korea, was deeply concerned about the consequences of a Korean war," Carter wrote in his travel diary. "He estimated that the costs would far exceed those of the later 1950s."[45] Back home, there was only tenuous political support, even for air strikes. A Time/CBS News poll reported that 51 percent of Americans favored military action to destroy the Yongbyon facility to ensure that North Korea could never manufacture nuclear weapons.[46]

Ambassador Laney, the Carters' host in Seoul, had war jitters. Never had he imagined that the Carter Center's conflict resolution program, which he helped create in 1982, would be deeply involved in a diplomatic tête-à-tête of such grim magnitude. At the time of Carter's arrival Laney was preparing to evacuate American civilians, including his own family, from South Korea. "I thought Jimmy had an outside chance to deescalate the crisis," Laney recalled. "But I wouldn't have put money on it."[47] Meanwhile, Laney's boss, Warren Christopher, had telephoned Carter to convey Clinton's alarm that North Korea was preparing to eject two IAEA inspectors. According to the *Washington Post*, Christopher told Carter, "The outcome of the whole crisis could depend on what happened to the inspectors."[48]

Before leaving Seoul, Carter met with South Korean president Kim Young Sam, a clever politician, who gave Carter permission to raise the possibility of a North-South summit with Kim Il Sung, an objective of Seoul since Eisenhower was president. Carter had never given up his hope of brokering an accord between the two Koreas, even as he was trying to deescalate the nuclear inspection crisis.[49] All of Carter's spiritual beliefs and training in conflict resolution were being put to the test—a point that disturbed the *Wall Street Journal*, which thought that Clinton should have sent Norman Schwarzkopf "with a few sample photos of high-tech warfare in the Gulf."[50]

On June 15 a historic event occurred: the Carter delegation was permitted to cross the DMZ on its way to Pyongyang, which had rarely been allowed since the 1953 armistice. Carter, along with his wife, Creekmore, and Dick Christenson, the Korean-speaking deputy director of the State Department's Korea desk, crossed the heavily policed DMZ at Panmunjom.[51] Accompanying them was CNN correspondent Eason Jordan with a film crew, who as always played an important role in the negotiation strategy. The Clinton administration had been unaware that CNN would be on hand.[52] The delegation was handed off like human batons by the South Korean military to the North Korean military at the DMZ. Carter described it as "a bizarre and disturbing experience, evidence of an incredible lack of communication and understanding."[53] For more than forty years, Koreans and Americans had stared across the DMZ with suspicion, hatred, and fear.

Korea was the most high-stakes undertaking of Carter's postpresidency. Election monitoring grabbed headlines in the name of democracy, and his exchanges with Arafat were dramatic, but North Korea, with war talk on everybody's lips, was track-two diplomacy at its nerve-racking zenith. "The chances of success were probably minimal," Carter recalled thinking, "because so much momentum had built up on both sides of the sanctions issue. Certainly I realized that my reputation was on the line. But Kim Il Sung's invitation to talk was something I couldn't turn down; it was perhaps the only hope left before war commenced."[54] For example, that very day—June 15—former NSC director Brent Scowcroft and former under-secretary of state Arnold Kantor published an op-ed piece in the *Washington Post* advocating a U.S. military strike to destroy the Yongbyon facility. "The time for temporizing is over," Scowcroft and Kantor wrote.[55]

The Carter delegation had been turned over to Vice Foreign Minister Song Ho Kong, who had accompanied them on the drive to Pyongyang by armored truck. "We had a pleasant two-hour drive over an almost empty four-lane highway," Carter recalled. "He explained to us that they did not produce luxury cars but only buses, trains, subways, and trucks." Evidence of Kim's cult of personality was clear in the capital city of Pyongyang; portraits of the Great Leader decorated building walls and tanks around every bend.[56]

The first official appointment was with Foreign Minister Kim Yong Nam, who Carter later described as a hard-line belligerent, adamant that his country would go to war if the UN imposed sanctions. "It was obvious that the threat of sanctions had no effect on them whatsoever, except as a pending insult, branding North Korea as an outlaw nation and their revered leader as a liar and criminal," Carter wrote in his travel diary. "This was something they could not accept." Economic sanctions, it seemed, meant little to the North Koreans, since their basic philosophy, which verged on a religion, was "Ju-che," which meant self-reliance. The Gulf War had also taught North Korea a major lesson: if you plan to go to war with the United States, strike before they have built up their forces—although the consequences of Pearl Harbor ought to have been a part of the curriculum too.[57]

That first morning Carter awoke early, facing the specter of war. He sat down at 3:00 A.M. and wrote President Clinton a note beseeching him to start high-level talks with North Korea before it was too late. He woke Marion Creekmore and dispatched him to drive to Panmunjom to arrange to pass the message on to the White House only if Creekmore got word that Carter's mediation with Kim failed. "It was nerve-racking," Creekmore recalled.[58]

Later that day at the Presidential Palace, when the Great Leader and the Man from Plains first laid eyes on each other, it was all smiles, as if they had known each other for years. There was a warmth and humanity to Kim that Carter had long intuited but which the CIA had dismissed. "We found him to be vigorous, alert, intelligent, and remarkably familiar with the issues," Carter wrote in his diary. "He consulted frequently with his advisers, each of whom bounced up and stood erect while speaking to the Great Leader." Carter immediately made his standard disclaimer: he was a private citizen, although with Dick Christenson of the State Department serving as interpreter, the distinction between official and unofficial had certainly been blurred.[59]

By all accounts, a good-natured, respectful rapport was struck between the two men. Carter spoke of the need for the United States and North Korea to develop relations, regardless of their stark societal differences, for the sake of future generations. Kim quickly agreed: "Creating trust is the main task." As expected, Kim reiterated his dismay at being called a liar by the Clinton administration and at their refusal to take his word that his government neither had nor desired to manufacture any nuclear weapons. If America helped to supply light-water reactors, North Korea would dismantle its gas-graphite reactors and rejoin the nonproliferation treaty. Kim, clearly more distrustful of South Korea than of the United States, expressed concern that Seoul would find ways to sabotage peace talks, that any progress they made on nuclear inspections would be undermined by Kim Young Sam.[60]

Before Carter had left Atlanta, Gallucci had agreed he could explore two issues with Kim without entering into official negotiations: whether he would agree to a temporary nuclear freeze, and whether he would permit the last two IAEA inspectors to remain at Yongbyon and not expel them to Beijing within the next twenty-four hours, as threatened. This last point had great symbolic significance: the UN Security Council would interpret expulsion as a sure sign that North Korea was marching forward with its own nuclear program. Carter broached both topics, signaling their gravity with a solemn demeanor.[61]

Carter got a rare glimpse of the legendary Kim, a man who had been in power since Harry Truman was president, in action. Kim immediately claimed ignorance about the plight of the remaining inspectors. He turned to his deputy foreign minister and chief negotiator Kang Sok Ju, and for perhaps five minutes Kim and Kang conversed earnestly in Korean, while Jimmy and Rosalynn, who had been taking notes, waited for an answer. At last Kim turned to Carter, nodding his agreement on both points. "I breathed a great sigh of relief," Carter recalled. "It was the deciding moment. I sent word immediately for Marion not to send the 3:00 A.M. letter I had written on to Clinton."[62]

Carter remembered suddenly feeling "unburdened" and reassured Kim that he would recommend that the U.S. government support light-water reactors, and that a third round of negotiations between Washington and Pyongyang be scheduled. Voicing his personal distaste at the thought of UN sanctions, Carter also personally reassured Kim that no U.S. nuclear weapons were stationed in South Korea nor were there any U.S. nuclear submarines patrolling the waters around the peninsula. Whatever the truth of these assurances, when they were voiced by the only American president who ever pushed for U.S. troops to leave the peninsula, Kim apparently took Jimmy Carter at his word.[63]

The meeting ended with a warm embrace, as if peace had just been made, as if there was cause to celebrate. But Carter was not quite ready to break out the champagne. "Although at the time I had no way to confirm his sincerity," Carter recalled, "I knew that all these commitments would soon be put to the test through Kim's own actions and official U.S.–North Korean negotiations."[64] After lunch he scheduled a meeting with First Vice Minister Kang, Kim's chief negotiator on nuclear questions, to solidify the agreement and to verify that he had not misinterpreted the Great Leader. Kang told Carter that part of the reason the North Koreans were so incensed by sanctions was the abusive and inflammatory language used by UN ambassador Madeleine Albright: if UN sanctions were imposed, he reiterated, North Korea would feel obliged to strike militarily against South Korea. "If the sanctions pass," Kang told Carter, "all the work you have done here will go down the drain."[65] If the crisis was not totally defused, at least for the moment Kang confirmed to Carter that the Great Leader had indeed agreed to a temporary nuclear freeze.

On June 16, once Carter finished clarifying points with Kang, he telephoned the White House. Clinton's senior foreign policy team had assembled that morning to decide their next steps in the North Korean crisis. They were discussing dispatching an additional 10,000 troops to the region when Gallucci left the room at 10:30 A.M. to pick up the receiver. If Gallucci was astonished to hear Carter say the crisis was over, that Kim Il Sung had agreed to a nuclear freeze and would allow the two IAEA inspectors to stay, then he was stunned to learn that Carter himself would momentarily be appearing live on CNN International to share the good news of a diplomatic breakthrough with the world community.[66]

By going live on CNN, Carter was not only seizing the limelight from the president of the United States; he was also making a preemptive strike to limit the Clinton administration's policy options. "I took notes on President Carter's main points," Gallucci recalled. "And when he mentioned CNN I failed to discourage him from talking, like I probably should have."[67] His announcement would make it much more difficult for Washington to maneuver; at one stroke, a military response would not be credible, and

Russian and Chinese resistance to UN sanctions against North Korea would be reinforced.

Carter had become the past master of the art of "telediplomacy," the conduct of foreign policy in near real time through the use of CNN and similar media. Over the years Carter forged a unique relationship with the twenty-four-hour-a-day global news company. If Carter wanted a television crew to follow him on a human rights foray, Ted Turner, a fellow Georgian and now fly-fishing buddy, would provide one. In return, Carter gave CNN rights of first refusal before offering his story to the network news stations, and as now, before checking in with his own government.

During the course of Carter's travels, he had also discovered that since everyone from the PLO to the Sudanese People's Liberation Front watched CNN regularly, he could use CNN as a vehicle of direct communication with them. For example, when U.S. peacekeeping troops were bogged down in a bloody campaign to capture Somali warlord Mohammed Farah Aidid, Carter deliberately used an interview with CNN's Judy Woodruff to try to defuse the situation by sending a signal to Aidid, for Carter knew Aidid was a CNN watcher.[68] Now Carter was ending the North Korean crisis, but doing it his way: by telling the world through CNN International that Kim Il Sung was a reasonable man who had accepted a nuclear freeze.

Not since the presidency of Lyndon Johnson had so many barnyard expletives echoed off the Cabinet Room walls as when Gallucci returned fifteen minutes later to tell Clinton the good news and who was about to announce it globally. "You told him not to go on CNN, right?" NSC adviser Anthony Lake asked: "Well, no, I didn't," Gallucci admitted.[69] At that moment pens were thrown down in disgust, ready for the worst. "We didn't realize he was bringing a CNN crew with him," Lake later lamented. "We were never told."[70] White House officials found themselves bystanders, gathered around the television like everyone else as Carter spoke by satellite to CNN White House correspondent Wolf Blitzer, only a few yards away on the White House lawn. Their emotions ran the gamut from outrage to amusement to relief to admiration.[71]

Carter recounted on CNN his fruitful meeting with the eighty-two-year-old Great Leader and claimed that "very important" and "very positive" steps had been taken to end the crisis. "Nothing should be done to exacerbate the situation now," Carter told CNN, in a veiled reference to UN sanctions. "The reason I came over here was to prevent an irreconcilable mistake."[72] While properly stating the obvious—that the Clinton administration would have to take the next step—he urged the resumption of talks between the U.S. and North Korea. Carter had purposefully gone on CNN to repudiate the UN sanctions strategy. "He knew some countries were wavering and I think he figured that if he went on CNN and said we have the makings of a deal . . . it would cause any nation that was wavering to stand back and say, wait a minute, let's not rush to sanctions," a diplomat directly involved later recalled.[73] The press saw that a private citizen, albeit a former president, was doing all the talking. "It looked as if we were contracting out our foreign policy," as one Clinton aide lamented.[74]

Dumbstruck by Carter's improvised CNN performance, Clinton and his foreign policy team reconvened in the Cabinet Room to weigh their options. Carter's telediplomacy had altered the entire dynamic of the situation. Suddenly the administration found itself on the defensive, forced to address what Carter had described as a "new breakthrough," even though from the administration's viewpoint Kim was simply stalling. Clinton had seen Carter's mission as an attempt to gain a clearer picture of North Korea's position and had not expected to get swept into negotiations being played out on cable television. The fear now was that Carter had been bamboozled by Kim Il Sung, that the North Koreans had effectively forestalled UN sanctions. Carter's anti–Gulf War letter was recalled by one cabinet member, who called their uncontrollable envoy a "treasonous prick." Gore, defending Carter, called for an end to the name-calling, and asked that they start preparing a substantive followup response. "Can we make lemonade out of this lemon?" Gore asked.[75]

Christopher advised ignoring Carter and continuing to push for sanctions. National Security Council aide Stanley Roth offered a smart counter to what Carter had described on CNN: ratify the freeze, but only on U.S. terms, while dropping the precondition, which the Pentagon had never deemed essential, of tracing past plutonium diversions. For the next five hours everybody brainstormed, rethinking the entire equation. Gallucci drafted the new U.S. requirements for a North Korean freeze, read the page aloud to the group, incorporated changes, and directed an aide to get Carter on the telephone, which took quite some time. NSC adviser Anthony Lake, always cool in a tense situation, was chosen to convey the administration's terms for a freeze to Carter: North Korea would have to agree specifically not to put in place new fuel rods for those that had been removed. The president wanted a detailed agreement, Lake told Carter, based on specifics, not a handshake agreement with Kim Il Sung secured only by Carter's personal belief in Kim's earnestness.[76]

Carter was irate. Forcing the Great Leader to be so specific with conditions would be seen in North Korea as an insult. In a heated exchange, the normally soft-spoken Lake raised his voice, insisting that Carter follow the instructions of his government. "It was an awkward moment," Lake recalled. "A difficult exchange."[77] Carter eventually agreed to write a note to Kim Il

Sung, outlining the Clinton specifics. Lake was not about to take any chances with his unmanageable envoy; he had the U.S. terms immediately sent to the North Korean Mission in New York, with instructions that it be sent to Kang at once.[78] "If today's developments mean that North Korea is genuinely and verifiably prepared to freeze its nuclear program while talks go on, and we hope that this is the case, then we would be willing to resume high-level talks," Clinton announced. "In the meantime we will pursue our consultations on sanctions."[79] The foundations of a deal had been put in place; an international crisis had been averted.

Later that morning the Carters received a letter from Kim Il Sung not only agreeing to the Clinton conditions but inviting the couple for a scenic cruise on the Taedong River aboard his presidential yacht. It would be a memorable occasion for the Carters. Because Rosalynn had been invited for the cruise, Kim was accompanied by his wife, Kim Song Ae, who was rarely seen in public. Painted as a paranoid dictator in the West, Kim was a quick study of politics, CNN style, using television to present himself as a courteous, civil family man, a kindly grandfather brimming with the milk of human kindness. Kim even allowed the CNN crew to film their "peace celebration" aboard his yacht, where North Korean noodle dishes, fresh fish, and sparkling wines were served.[80] As David E. Sanger noted in the New York Times, Kim, like Carter, was "a brilliant manipulator of television-age politics."[81]

Both men also had agendas beyond the merely social. As the yacht sailed past peasants plowing their fields with oxen, rice paddies, and a bird refuge, Kim clearly wanted to show off the "barricade," a remarkable five-mile-wide dam built by North Korean soldiers that separated the river from the sea. As talk turned to the Korean War, Carter raised a project that had been on his mind: the possibility of their two countries forging a joint effort to search for the remains of U.S. servicemen killed in the so-called Forgotten War. A U.S. colonel in Seoul had raised the issue with Carter, saying that army intelligence knew where 3,000 bodies were buried. Kim equivocated, suggesting that they postpone the subject to another time. Carter, whose penchant for not taking no as a final answer is well documented, pressed Kim further, arguing that such an announcement would greatly improve relations between Washington and Pyongyang. Kim's wife, a Rosalynn Carter in her own right, put in her two cents, saying she thought it was a terrific idea, and Kim eventually agreed: "Okay, we'll do it."[82]

They toasted the decision. Carter turned the discussion to their deal on the nuclear freeze, and then did an astonishing thing. With CNN recording,

Carter told Kim that the Clinton administration had "stopped the sanction activity in the United Nations"—a patent falsehood. Within the hour the Clinton administration was on the airwaves, denying Carter's assertion and reaffirming that sanctions were still very much an option. The next day Carter issued a clarification; his statement had been misunderstood. What he meant to say was that sanctions would be held in abeyance only if North Korea agreed to open their nuclear program for full inspection. Clinton was forced to respond to Carter's claim: "The position is just exactly what it was yesterday. We are pursuing our sanctions discussion in the U.N."[83]

Some media commentators chose to regard Carter's original statement as inadvertent, the by-product of exhaustion. But President Clinton and his administration saw it as a provocative misrepresentation of U.S. policy verging on treason, just one more example of the diplo-evangelist's hubris. Carter was lampooned in the U.S. press for his misstatement to Kim, disparaged by Clinton, and scolded in Seoul. Suspicions were sky-high in Washington that Carter had tried to tie their hands by deceit. The next day both Russia and China took the Carter position and publicly opposed sanctions.[84]

Observers were struck by just how well Kim and Carter got along. Just as he had done with South Korean president Park Chung Hee in 1979, Carter steered the conversation to Christianity. "One of the things he pointed out to me was that he was very grateful to Christians, because when he was a young man in China, when the Japanese occupied all of Korea and China, he was in prison, and a Christian pastor was the one who saved his life," Carter reported after returning to Plains. "So he's been very deeply interested in Christianity. There are Christian churches in Pyongyang, and recently he invited Billy Graham to come over there and have the beginning of a crusade." Carter felt affirmed in his belief that there are no unalterably evil people, only forces of evil that will dissipate when the world embraces Jesus Christ. From Carter's born-again perspective, Kim was not by nature evil.[85]

At a more mundane level, the two men also bonded over a shared passion for hunting and fishing. The octogenarian told Carter that he had recently killed two bears and two hundred boar—a feat unlikely to win over converts for agape among members of the animal rights movement. His devotion to rainbow trout was, Kim said, a prime reason why he was trying to stock North Korean streams from two nurseries. "We agreed," Carter wrote in his travel diary, "that I would send in some biologists and fly fishermen to analyze North Korea's fishing opportunities."[86] Carter also told Kim an exaggerated story about how, when Dean Rusk was a young colonel after World War II, he divided Korea in half. "Truman put his OK on it and that was it." Kim Il Sung responded, "Well, a Georgian divided our country, maybe a Georgian can help us unite our country."[87]

If this faintly surreal vision of diplomacy on the Taedong River bore a certain resemblance to a Fellini film, Carter was still operating in the world of realpolitik, managing to pull off a major diplomatic coup of substance: he got Kim Il Sung to agree to a peace summit with South Korean president Kim Young Sam. Carter had sought such a summit since 1979, despite the opposition of his foreign policy advisers; now, fifteen years later, he procured a commitment from Kim Il Sung. For the first time since the Korean peninsula had been divided five decades ago, the rulers of North and South would actually sit across a table and talk peace.[88]

The next day, when the Carters arrived at the DMZ, they held a press conference, taking questions from CNN, the North Korean news media, and crews from China and Russia. South Korea's president immediately met with Carter at Blue House, the presidential mansion in Seoul, and almost immediately accepted Kim's offer to hold a North-South summit. "In a sudden and entirely unexpected reversal of fortune, the immense tension and great danger in the Korean peninsula gave way to the greatest hope in years for a historic rapprochement between the leaders of North and South," Oberdorfer wrote.[89] Kim Young Sam laughed, however, at Carter's description of Kim Il Sung as in good health. "Carter is a smart man," the South Korean president joked, "but he doesn't know much about old people."[90]

If a euphoric Carter publicly declared his entire mission a "miracle," the Clinton administration saw it as a three-day migraine headache, played out on CNN.[91] Ambassador Laney had to inform Carter that he was once again persona non grata at the White House. "We were amazed to discover that our actions in North Korea had been met by criticism and partial rejection in Washington," Carter recorded in his travel diary. "I discussed this on a secure telephone line with V.P. Gore, and told him I would like to go by Washington before going home to explain the result of my trip in more detail. I considered all my actions to have been in accord with the policies of the administration."[92] His diary did not comport with his subsequent behavior. At a news conference outside Laney's house, Carter stated his view in no uncertain terms that economic sanctions were absurd and doomed to fail. "The declaration of sanctions by the UN would be regarded as an insult by them, branding it as an outlaw country," Carter maintained. "This is something in my opinion which would be impossible for them to accept."[93] Anthony Lake thought it was inappropriate for Carter to "trash sanctions" while still in North Korea.[94]

Instead of coming home a national peace hero, Carter was met with mixed reviews at best. "I wouldn't want to call him naive or gullible," a senior Clinton official said as Carter arrived in Washington, D.C., on June 19. "But let's just say that we're a lot more skeptical than he is about whether

the North Koreans mean what they say."[95] A furious President Clinton refused to meet with Carter, staying at Camp David when the ex-president arrived in Washington, designating Anthony Lake and Robert Gallucci to take
the debriefing, although Clinton and Carter talked by telephone for thirty
minutes in an exchange described as "tense." As Gallucci later characterized
the Carter-Lake meeting, "To put it mildly, it was not a pleasant exchange."[96]
"I found out they had made arrangements for me to come back to Plains and
not go to Washington to give them a briefing, but I decided to go to Washington anyway." Carter complained about the snubbing he encountered:
"When I got there, the president wasn't there. The vice president wasn't
there. No cabinet officers were there. Nobody met me out in front of the
White House, but I went in and gave them a briefing, and I believe what we
did actually prevented war."[97]

Republicans, relishing the spectacle of Clinton farming out his foreign
policy, started lambasting Carter's peace mission, portraying him as an ap-
peaser, a placator of dictators, a born-again Neville Chamberlain. On the
ABC news program *This Week*, George Will, the conservative columnist,
called Carter's performance "very injurious" and "a reminder of how important and good the 1980 election was."[98] In his *Washington Post* column
headed "Peace in Our Time," Charles Krauthammer compared Carter to
Neville Chamberlain, lampooning diplomats "convinced that all that stands
between war and peace is their dining with a dictator."[99] William Safire's
blistering *New York Times* column—"Jimmy Clinton"—tongue-lashed both
Democratic presidents for cowering to authoritarians and failing to stop
"rogue states from becoming nuclear powers."[100] A wave of former Bush administration foreign policy hands—including Robert Gates, Brent Scowcroft, Arnold Kantor, Richard Haas, and Philip Zelikow—all denounced
Carter's diplomacy. A furious former secretary of state Lawrence Eagleburger was "horrified" to hear Carter "taking the word of this murderer who
runs North Korea."[101]

At his first Sunday school class after returning to Plains, Deacon Carter
tried to smite his recent critics—Henry Kissinger, Rush Limbaugh, Jerry
Falwell, and Bill Clinton—by telling the congregation that Christ was also
lampooned for preaching peace, and he quoted from Matthew 22, in which
Jesus says, "Give to the emperor what is the emperor's. Give to God what is
God's." As later reported in the press, Carter had taken to describing Kim Il
Sung from the North Korean perspective "as almost a deity, as a George
Washington, as a Patrick Henry, as a worshipful leader all rolled into one."[102]
What struck Washington officialdom as bizarre and unacceptable was that
Carter had kinder words for the North Korean dictator than for the U.S.
president. From the White House perspective, Carter seemed confused

about who his emperor was, so to speak. No one was sure whether Carter, as *Newsweek* queried, was "A Stooge or a Savior."[103]

Like it or not, Clinton's North Korean policy was linked to Jimmy Carter, and in the days ahead the administration wisely decided to bite the bullet and embrace the ex-president's diplomacy. Carter, the administration men claimed, had provided Kim Il Sung with a credible way to back down without losing too much international face. But they negated the ex-president's exaggerated boast that he had averted war. When asked to respond to GOP criticism about his deal with Kim Il Sung, Carter reiterated that he didn't feel "duped" but admitted that the "proof was in the pudding."[104] Within a day the push for UN sanctions was dropped, the plan to reinforce U.S. troops in the region filed away, and the written confirmation from North Korea of its agreement of the U.S.-devised freeze on its nuclear program embraced. Carter's freelance diplomacy had worked. "Granted, it was not a masterpiece of clarity and coordination," a *New York Times* editorial noted on June 21. "But former President Jimmy Carter and the Clinton administration, which approved his trip, appeared to have moved the crisis over the North Korean nuclear program back toward the negotiating table."[105] Based on the Carter breakthrough, that October 21 Pyongyang signed the Agreed Framework with the United States, halting its nuclear program in exchange for safer light-water nuclear reactors, a supply of fuel oil security guarantees, lifting of the American economic embargo, and gradual diplomatic normalization. As of early 1998 North Korea had lived up to its agreements.[106]

Even though Carter had stolen the Clinton administration's thunder, as weeks went by the bad blood dissipated, leaving behind a shared legacy of successful, if unorthodox, crisis management. Two important books were published detailing Carter's diplomatic efforts and giving him credit for averting war—Don Oberdorfer's *The Two Koreas* (1997) and Leon V. Sigal's *Disarming Strangers* (1998). Anthony Lake—defending the NSC—lamented that these studies exaggerated Carter's role in stopping a war that was never going to occur.[107] But almost everybody agreed on one point: what had transpired with North Korea would never become a model case study taught at Tufts' Fletcher School of Diplomacy or at Georgetown—except perhaps as a cautionary tale of telediplomacy—but it had worked. Whether or not analysts eventually chalk it up to plain dumb luck—as Dean Acheson had said of Kennedy's handling of the Cuban missile crisis—the Korean peninsula for the time being was an indisputably safer place because of the Carter-Kim dialogue. Global arbitrator Jimmy Carter's track-two diplomacy had worked.

That July 7, less than three weeks after he hugged Carter good-bye, Kim Il Sung died of a massive heart attack, after a day spent preparing for the

North-South summit Carter had engineered.[108] As a consequence, an official three-year mourning period would take place in North Korea before his son Kim Jong Il was allowed to assume formal leadership. The sixty-nine-year-old Carter received the news in Japan, where he had just climbed to the top of Mount Fuji's 12,388-foot summit, with security escorts in tow. Carter offered his condolences to the people of North Korea on the death of their Great Leader, telling CNN International, and by extension the world, that talking peace, even with international outlaws like Kim, was nearly always the right thing to do.[109] If the joke around the State Department was that Kim had died laughing from negotiating with Carter, that evening in Tokyo there were no snickers heard about Carter's daring diplomacy, only accolades. With the first change in North Korea's leadership since 1945, everybody in Japan was glad it had occurred with the nuclear crisis deescalated. Camp David redux or old-fashioned luck, Jimmy Carter's peace mission had been miraculously vindicated. And in the coming months he would successfully negotiate North Korea's participation in Atlanta's 1996 Summer Olympics.[110]

TWENTY-ONE

HAITIAN CRISIS

༺ం༻

O f all the countries Jimmy Carter focused on after 1980, tiny, tragic Haiti was the most frustrating. He had visited the Caribbean nation seven times since 1987, studied its history and fragile political system, and monitored an election, all in hopes of bringing democracy to a land ruled by tyrants since its independence from France in 1804. When Jean-Bertrand Aristide—a diminutive thirty-seven-year-old Roman Catholic priest who rose from a small parish to crusade against the Duvalier family dictatorship— was elected president by two-thirds of the vote on December 16, 1990, Carter thought that at long last strife-ridden Haiti had seen its final despot.[1] The slight, shy-looking Aristide led the Lavalas ("flashflood" or "avalanche" in Creole) movement, representing the impoverished. To shantytown beggars and rural peasants, Aristide was the only man in Haiti with the courage to speak the truth. At Aristide's February 7, 1991, inauguration, Carter, an honored guest, stood onstage in Port-au-Prince, marveling at the sea of joyous Haitian faces celebrating democracy. "It was a moving experience for all of us," Carter later wrote Aristide about the inauguration. "We were impressed by your speech and your emphasis on national reconciliation."[2] The euphoria was short-lived. Seven months later, on September 30, 1991, the military toppled the government, and only the intervention of the U.S. government saved Aristide's life. Aristide left for exile in Venezuela and later in America.

A coup d'état was hardly news in Latin America or the Caribbean, but the disapprobation expressed by Haiti's neighbors was unprecedented. Within days, at the urging of the United States, the foreign ministers of the Organization of American States (OAS) held an emergency session, condemned the overthrow, demanded Aristide's immediate restoration, and sent a delegation to negotiate with the junta's chief, Lieutenant General Raoul Cédras, demanding that he step down. The OAS, unable to convince the Haitian military to restore Aristide to power, adopted unanimously their first-ever trade embargo against a hemispheric coup d'etat. On October 29 President Bush likewise banned all U.S. commercial trade with Haiti to punish the repugnant military junta.[3]

For the next three years the exiled Aristide traveled the world to rally support for his constitutional cause, while attempting to negotiate the terms for his restoration to power in Haiti with the OAS, the UN, and the U.S. State Department. His temporary home was a modest Georgetown apartment, which also doubled as an office. There, between his forays, he spent long hours alone finishing his doctoral thesis in psychology, playing guitar, writing poetry, and waiting, always waiting, to return.[4]

One obvious stop on Aristide's itinerary was Atlanta. Carter had chaired the Carter Center/NDI delegation that had monitored his 1990 election victory, and now commiserated with Aristide's plight. In November he invited Aristide to become a member of the Council of Freely Elected Heads of Government. Aristide was only too pleased to accept. By early 1992, just a few months after the coup, the Carter Center had become one of Aristide's bases of operation, where he could network with other hemispheric leaders to put pressure on the Bush administration to engineer his return to power. Throughout his exile, Aristide used the council's prestige to bolster his rightful claim as the first freely elected president in Haiti's 190-year history.[5]

Despite their shared belief in democracy, Carter and Aristide were not easy comrades. Carter was more interested in promoting the process of democracy in Haiti; he did not champion Aristide or any other single candidate. He was suspicious of Aristide's reputation as an altruist and found the Haitian priest aloof and erratic, a demagogue imbued with populist mysticism. If Carter disbelieved CIA reports that Aristide was a violent psychopath, he was concerned over Amnesty International reports that the unpredictable Aristide had condoned "necklacing"—putting a tire around a victim's neck and setting it on fire—claiming that machetes and tires were part of the "people's arsenal."[6]

Aristide soon grew disenchanted with both Bush's Haitian embargo policy and Carter's lack of clout. Nineteen ninety-two was an election year in the United States, and most politicians tried to distance themselves from the troubled Caribbean nation, particularly since thousands of Haitian refugees were fleeing the island in unseaworthy boats, heading for the Florida Keys or Guantanamo Bay, hoping to begin a new life in the United States. A grim, morally problematic refugee crisis was at hand. The Bush administration, after a serious policy review, adopted a hard-line position and ordered the U.S. Coast Guard to send the boat people back. In just one month, February 1992, 381 Haitian refugees were forcibly repatriated, despite their claims that they would be severely punished on their return. Haitians, President Bush decided, were not automatically eligible for political asylum in the United States, because most were seeking better economic conditions, not trying to escape political repression. It was a distinction Carter refused to swallow.[7]

Carter called the Bush policy an insensitive affront to U.S. law, UN international refugee protocol, and the New Testament. With 90 percent deforestation, a 60 percent unemployment rate, a severe shortage of cultivable land, an AIDS epidemic of unmanageable proportions, an ineffective police force, a growing number of poor and homeless, horrendous sanitation conditions, and a skyrocketing population density, Haiti was in dire straits. Carter thought it criminal for a robust United States to turn its back on such a despairing neighbor, and saw the refugee problem as one of the Bush administration's own making. Carter told Emory students that they should "in effect adopt Haiti" spiritually and financially because it was a "basket case" of poverty that needed "love" from Americans. Carter also told the students that President Bush should have provided Aristide with massive economic aid after the December 1990 election to jump-start Haiti on the new road to prosperity.[8]

Carter grew increasingly irritated that the president was "content" to let the OAS negotiate for Aristide's return instead of directing the State Department to play a more prominent role. "Bush acted as if the Haitians weren't people," Carter lamented, "that their free and fair election was insignificant." Carter insisted that the United States had a moral responsibility to help the 6,600 Haitian castaways. When Bush announced in December 1991 that Haitian boat people would not automatically be allowed to stay in the United States, Carter, echoing the outraged Congressional Black Caucus, denounced the policy as "racist." As Carter saw it, Bush was discriminating against black-skinned people. If the refugees had been English or German or Canadian, Carter argued, the administration would have likely embraced them.[9]

Carter's pointed criticisms aside, the Bush administration was merely following U.S. law, which stated that an individual must prove that he or she faces a well-founded fear of political persecution in order to qualify for asylum. And Bush's support for Aristide was very real. The United States was the first government to recognize Aristide's election, eventually providing the parish priest with more economic aid than all the nations in the world combined. Bush's ambassador, Alvin Adams, had even saved Aristide's life at the risk of his own the night of the September 1991 coup.[10]

Hoping to change the refugee policy and create a Democratic alternative to Bush's Haitian policy, Robert Pastor began consulting with Bill Clinton's foreign policy adviser, Anthony Lake, in December 1991, offering an array of policy options designed to address the Caribbean crisis. In a series of campaign stump speeches Clinton began berating Bush for allegedly violating international law by sending the Haitian refugees back, without a hearing, to their brutal oppressors. But as election day drew near, Pastor began to fear that Clinton's speeches might be misconstrued in Port-au-Prince as an open-door invitation for Haitians to immigrate permanently to America. The concern was not misplaced. The day after Clinton's victory, reports of Haitians building rafts to journey to America reached ABC News. With a more flexible new leader coming into power, Haitians, it seemed, now expected to be welcomed in Miami.[11]

From the beginning, Carter believed the key to solving the refugee crisis was the restoration of Aristide. Shortly after Clinton's election, Pastor went to Kingston to meet with former Jamaican prime minister Michael Manley, the OAS's envoy with Haiti. In Jamaica, Pastor discussed ideas for a new, invigorated strategy toward Haiti and invited Manley to Atlanta in early December, while Carter did the same with UN secretary general Boutros Boutros-Ghali. Carter's objective was to facilitate a UN-OAS-mediated solution to the Haitian problem. The first step, in his view, was to arrange for Boutros Boutros-Ghali to appoint him as UN mediator and to ask Brazil's Baena Soares to have Manley work with him on a common approach. The Carter-Manley efforts would then be fortified by the potential threat of UN force leading to Aristide's reinstatement, and the end of the refugee crisis. The Atlanta meetings took place, and Carter spoke with Clinton several times after those meetings, but the incoming Clinton team did not pick up the ideas.[12]

"Clinton embarrassed both Carter and I [sic]," Manley recalled. "Even though the UN and OAS had wanted us to mediate, Clinton squashed us before we could get started."[13] Boutros Boutros-Ghali now asked former foreign minister of Argentina Dante Caputo to serve as UN envoy. Caputo was a smart, savvy statesman, but he had virtually no political clout to produce an agreement acceptable to an intransigent bully like Cédras. Carter, who had worked diligently since 1987 to bring democracy to Haiti, was now sidelined.

The waters were soon muddied even more. Shortly before his inauguration Clinton announced that he would continue the Bush administration's policies of economic embargo against Haiti and the return of refugees—a complete reversal of his campaign rhetoric. Carter was duly perturbed. "I think that Clinton was intimidated by the Bush people," Carter later recalled. "He did not want his administration to begin with a massive flood of refugees."[14] For the duration of 1993 Carter had virtually no direct role to play in Haiti, although in June, before the Governor's Island (New York) negotiations, both Aristide and Cédras sought advice from the Carter Center. When the U.S.-sponsored Governor's Island negotiations broke down—with Aristide signing only a promise to grant amnesty upon his return to individuals who had committed political crimes—Clinton's Haitian policy took a turn for the worse. On October 11, 1993, two hundred lightly armed U.S. and Canadian peacekeepers under a UN mandate were dispatched to Port-au-Prince on the USS *Harlan County*, only to be ordered back when the ship was met by an angry mob of Haitians waving machetes and shouting anti-American slogans. A humiliated Clinton's Haitian policy was in shambles, and his administration looked weak and ineffectual.[15]

In the wake of the *Harlan County* embarrassment, President Clinton became more amenable to soliciting Carter's recommendations on Haiti. "All blame for a lack of progress should be laid on the military and not on Aristide," Carter wrote Clinton on October 22, "but his degree of flexibility on bringing in opposition cabinet members, etc., should be explored privately. Something will have to be devised to let Cédras, et al. save face." Carter also recommended that the U.S.-Canada naval blockade be tightly maintained and that the Congressional Black Caucus be encouraged to take the lead in condemning Cédras's drug trafficking. Once again Carter offered himself up as a mediator. "I am somewhat reluctant to make this suggestion, because a similar offer earlier this year was not accepted, even though both Cédras and Aristide were requesting that this be done," Carter wrote Clinton. "Let me assure you that this is only a very tentative suggestion and not a request." Clinton did not want the Carter Center directly involved in Haiti, so he ignored the ex-president's "very tentative suggestion."[16]

By spring 1994 Clinton's economic and diplomatic U.S. embargo was going nowhere. Once again Clinton turned to Carter for suggestions on how to restore U.S. credibility with Aristide and his supporters, Haiti's military and civilian power structures, and the American public. Carter responded to Clinton's request on May 11, urging that the United States not engage in a unilateral military intervention but making clear that without a "genuine threat of force" it was unlikely that Cédras would accommodate Aristide's return. Carter also mentioned that he was troubled by a *Los Angeles Times* report that the United States was considering dispatching six hundred armed soldiers to Haiti. Treating the newspaper story as fact, Carter warned Clinton that "too small of a force" would accomplish nothing except "resistance by the [Haitian] military."[17] Only a larger collective intervention would work.

While Carter reiterated his view that the solution to the Haitian crisis remained "forceful mediation to reinstate Aristide," at the same time he reminded the president that Aristide, although "highly intelligent," was also "politically naive, sees himself as the anointed savior of the downtrodden, and finds it difficult to compromise on basic issues." Therefore Carter advised the White House to get tough with the mesmerizing Aristide, to secure guarantees from him to form a consensus government under Haiti's parliamentary system, to guarantee the rights and safety of all Haitians, to accept a real negotiation deadline, and to support military action should internationally respected compromises be rejected. "As the recognized President, his approval is important to give legitimacy to such drastic action as the use of military force," Carter wrote Clinton.

Carter also suggested that the United States forge a new "democratic compact" with leaders of the Haitian establishment not aligned with Cédras, including political moderates who still controlled the news media and international trade. And, once again, Carter, like a broken record, asked Clinton to involve his center's Council of Freely Elected Heads of Government to lead the high-level negotiation effort, since Dante Caputo was getting nowhere. Once again, Clinton ignored the request.[18]

There was another Caribbean crisis besides Haiti on Carter's mind: the Cuban refugee dilemma. In the summer of 1994, Cuban rafters had once more begun paddling to the United States seeking political asylum from Fidel Castro. Carter feared that another Mariel disaster was brewing. Capitalizing on the relationship he had struck up with Castro in February of 1989 in Venezuela, Carter began a series of lengthy telephone talks with the Cuban dictator on how to resolve the quandary.[19] When President Clinton learned of Carter's calls to Castro he issued an order to the NSC and the State Department: keep Jimmy Carter out of Cuban policy. Pastor found himself in an extremely awkward position. Having been passed over to be assistant secretary of state for Latin American affairs, despite or perhaps because of Carter's recommendation to Warren Christopher, Pastor was left in limbo until the end of 1993 when the president decided to appoint him ambassador to Panama. A sloppy and often incompetent nomination process combined with effective delaying tactics by Republican senator Jesse Helms resulted in his nomination being stalled in the Senate Foreign Relations Committee in August when the Cuban rafters problem began. Pastor advised Carter on his conversations with Castro, but realized that his boss was stepping beyond the bounds of the president's policy. Pastor wanted to avoid a clash with the administration on such a politically charged issue, but unlike the Clinton team, he knew his boss well. So he implemented the James Baker principle: never close a door on Carter unless you find another one to open. Pastor decided to steer his boss away from Cuba and back to Haiti. The Haiti crisis was heating up because of the hawkish efforts of Clinton's ambassador to the UN, Madeleine Albright. "I had been watching Haiti very closely," Pastor recalled. "Carter had a good relationship with both Cédras and Aristide so I thought we could play a significant role."[20]

That July, Albright succeeded in persuading the UN Security Council for the first time in its history to pass a resolution allowing individual member states to use force to restore a constitutional government. It was a watershed event in international affairs: unilateral intervention was now sanctioned under a UN Security Council resolution. Immediately following this new UN mandate, Clinton ordered a U.S. aircraft carrier off the shores of Florida and began lobbing threats at the Haitian military dictatorship.[21]

General Cédras began reaching out to Jimmy Carter, signaling that he wanted the former president to come to Port-au-Prince to talk peace, hoping to turn the tables on Clinton. The murderous Cédras realized that the odds of a U.S. invasion had increased with the UN resolution, which explained why he and Emile Jonassaint, the military-installed president, used various intermediaries to request a visitation by Carter. In August, however, the Senate passed a resolution asserting that the use of military force in Haiti required congressional approval, raising the murky issue of presidential power to declare war without Capitol Hill's blessing. Congress, many believed, would have denied its approval had the president asked. Clinton was prepared, like his predecessors, to proceed without Congress. After procuring UN authorization and stationing naval forces off Haiti, not to mention the lingering humiliation of the *Harlan County* incident, to have remained idle would have been degrading to Clinton personally and weakened the integrity of the United States abroad.[22]

Republicans and conservatives in America opposed as absurd the thought of an invasion to restore Aristide—a radical populist and practitioner of liberation theology. Senator Helms even branded Aristide a Communist, pronouncing his overthrow "good riddance." When columnist Robert Novak

HAITIAN CRISIS419

and *Washington Times* correspondent Dan James caught wind of Cédras's overtures to Carter, they supported a Carter visit to Port-au-Prince. The far right believed that Carter's mediating efforts would slow the momentum for invasion and undermine the administration's strategy, and thus thwart Aristide's undesired return. They knew that Carter had met Cédras during the 1990 elections, when the then-colonel was in charge of security, and had stayed in touch with him ever since. On August 6, Cédras even told CNN that Carter—a man he "trusted"—might be able to resolve the crisis. For once the GOP right actually *wanted* Carter to undertake a diplomatic foray.[23]

To the Clinton administration, especially Deputy Secretary of State Strobe Talbott, who had been pressing for military intervention, the notion of a Carter sally to Haiti to negotiate with Cédras was ludicrous. A renegade Carter mission, they feared, would only strengthen Cédras's dictatorial hand. They had barely tolerated Carter's North Korean intervention; now they wanted him out of Haiti, even though if they allowed him to negotiate with Cédras and he failed, he probably would have supported U.S. military intervention.[24] Pastor had been secretly told in early September by Michael Barnes, a former U.S. congressman and legal adviser to Aristide, that despite earlier comments to the contrary, "there was *not* another channel to negotiate with Cédras and the White House doesn't want one."[25]

The White House had in fact used its own back channel to Cédras, but only to deliver an ultimatum, not to enter into direct talks. The administration saw only one issue: when and how the brutally stubborn Cédras would depart. The Pentagon now believed that this would happen only if U.S. armed forces took him out. The *New York Times* reported in August that Clinton had approved a plan to "set the clock ticking." Unless Cédras resigned within three weeks, the United States would be prepared to invade Haiti as of September 19. Clinton, like Bush during the Gulf crisis, had drawn his own line in the sand.[26]

Carter viewed this as a tragedy. The flaw of Christopher and Talbott, he believed, was their inability to learn a fundamental foreign policy premise: the more internationally unpopular the dictator, the more he craved respect and was willing to make concessions. Why couldn't the State Department engineer a face-saving departure for Cédras? Pastor had a different explanation. "The problem is that I don't think Cédras is yet convinced that an invasion is coming," Pastor wrote Carter in a memo entitled "The Ticking Clock" on September 13, "and therefore, the administration is correct that he is not yet serious about negotiating his exit. It is important, therefore, to try to convince him that his end is approaching."[27] That same day Joseph H. Blatchford wrote the lead editorial in the *Los Angeles Times*, urging Carter to take on another "11th Hour Job." A copy of the editorial was passed around the Carter Center and faxed to friendly congressmen.[28]

Throughout mid-September Carter talked regularly with Cédras by telephone. His detailed notes from the talks were being communicated directly to the White House. Since the U.S. embassy in Haiti had been instructed not to interfere with the military dictatorship, the only American directly speaking with Cédras was Carter. The prior Bush-Clinton envoys to Cédras, as well as those from the OAS and the UN, had gotten nowhere with the stubborn strongman, in part because they lacked credibility. But a former U.S. president was bathed in a different aura.

After hours of discussions with Cédras, on September 14, Carter finally decided it was time to go to Haiti. Pastor thought such a trip should occur only if Carter procured the "blessing of the Clinton administration." Pastor recommended that his boss first talk with Senator Sam Nunn of Georgia. Like Carter, Nunn had always felt that U.S. military intervention in Haiti made little sense. The end result would be dead U.S. servicemen and ghastly chaos in Haiti. Carter telephoned Nunn in Washington, D.C., to strategize about how to stop the invasion, suggesting that perhaps Senator Richard Lugar could join them on a three-person mission to Haiti. Nunn thought it would be more useful to bring retired general Colin L. Powell into the picture, in part because the former chairman of the Joint Chiefs of Staff was Caribbean American.[29]

Soon Clinton was having private deliberations with Carter, Powell, and Nunn on Haiti. Publicly, however, the president painted a different picture. In a strongly worded televised speech from the Oval office on Thursday September 15, the president implied that all diplomatic options had been exhausted and urged Cédras and his generals to cede power immediately. "Your time is up," Clinton warned.[30] Thirty thousand U.S. troops were poised for deployment to Haiti. In truth, the tough language had been carefully worded to leave open the possibility of a last-minute peace mission.

Clinton had promised to telephone Carter after the speech with a verdict on whether the former president could go to Port-au-Prince as an official envoy. "About two hours after the speech, I received a phone call from Carter saying that Clinton had not called," Pastor recalled. "Carter was very upset, saying we should go down anyway."[31] About an hour later, nearing midnight, Clinton telephoned his painstaking decision: Carter would be allowed to lead the three-man mission. It was a policy swerve most of Clinton's foreign policy advisers—with the notable exceptions of Anthony Lake, Leon Panetta, George Stephanopoulos, and Al Gore—viewed as a foolish gamble. Christopher feared that Carter's intervention would complicate the situation when clarity was needed.[32]

The high-profile emissaries were authorized by Clinton to discuss what arrangements the United States was willing to consider for peaceful departure of Haiti's ruling junta, not to engage in negotiations, a distinction that left the envoys a certain amount of latitude. Immediately Carter phoned Cédras and his brother, Alex, who served as interpreter. The news elicited enthusiastic approval of the three-man diplomatic mission from the dictator. At 5:00 P.M. on Friday, September 16, the White House announced that Carter, Nunn, and Powell would leave the next morning at 7:00 A.M. (Carter obtained special permission from Clinton to allow Pastor to join them.) "We all have to hope this succeeds," former secretary of state Lawrence F. Eagleburger exclaimed, "because the insanity of an invasion is something we should not even have to contemplate."[33]

Only five hours before flight time, Larry Rossin, director of inter-American affairs of the NSC, telephoned Pastor with ostensibly bad news. The U.S. station chief in Haiti had sent a top-secret cable claiming that Cédras knew nothing about the Carter-Powell-Nunn mission, that the junta was opposed to it, and that if the high-profile Americans landed in Port-au-Prince their lives would be in grave danger. The cable claimed that the airport runway would be blocked and the U.S. plane would not be allowed to land. The NSC was considering scrubbing the mission. The Clinton administration was apparently unaware of the long talks Carter had with Cédras just a few hours earlier. Refusing to wake Carter, who had gotten little sleep during the past week, Pastor told Rossin that regardless of the report, the mission was on. "I've been working for Carter for twenty years," Pastor told him, "and I think I can predict his reaction to this report. He is going."[34]

Throughout the night and morning the three special envoys were repeatedly warned by the NSC that the airfield in Port-au-Prince had barrels on it, making landing impossible. Pastor telephoned the de facto foreign minister in Haiti and learned that barrels *were* on the runway, but the barricades would be lifted as the Carter plane approached. "We never considered turning back," Powell would recall.[35]

While en route to Haiti, via Puerto Rico, Major General Jared Bates of the Joint Chiefs of Staff, Larry Rossin and Tom Ross of the NSC, and Michael Kozak of the State Department briefed Carter, Nunn, and Powell but were soon dismissed. "They had old information," Carter recalled. Since 1987 Carter had been studying Haiti, and with eight visits under his belt, he was not about to follow the stale instructions of young government desk officers. Carter understood that his job was to convince Haiti's leaders that even in the face of strong opposition from Congress and the public, President Clinton stood prepared to make good on his threats. No matter what, 250,000 U.S. soldiers were about to land in Haiti: the question was whether it would be peaceful or bloody. En route aboard the U.S. Air Force jet, Carter began discussing talking points to use with Cédras and other junta leaders like Chief of Staff Brigadier General Philippe Biamby.[36]

The three American envoys arrived in Port-au-Prince at noon on Saturday, September 17, for a diplomatic initiative that Carter described on the tarmac as "the most important and urgent visit I have ever made." The first consultations began with a handful of trusted Haitian leaders, including former general Hérard Abraham, whom Carter had gotten to know when he monitored Haiti's 1990 democratic elections, and de facto foreign minister Charles David. At the time, although neither the Carter team nor the Haitians knew it, the U.S. invasion of Haiti was set for one minute past midnight on Monday, September 19—less than thirty-six hours away. And the clock had started ticking.[37]

From the outset, the U.S. government officials accompanying the three envoys were concerned because the trio was not following their White House script. "The only thing Carter was authorized to discuss on behalf of Clinton," a senior official recalled, "was the modalities of departure." This comment was vague enough to leave open to interpretation. The White House, according to Carter, had only instructed him to arrange for "Cédras to leave," which he took to mean leave power, not physically depart Haiti. Carter had told Clinton that he would need mediation "flexibility," and the president agreed. A nonstop blitz to cut a deal was on, under circumstances that might have been orchestrated by the Keystone Kops.[38]

The U.S. negotiators arrived at 1:30 P.M. at the National Military Headquarters—a ramshackle white building surrounded by 2,000 of Cédras's attachés (or neighborhood enforcers), shouting and waving machetes—and were led up to a second-floor office to meet General Raoul Cédras. The mayhem outside the building created an almost unbearable level of disquiet. Cédras, a muscular, serious man, was visibly distraught as the American envoys, augmented by Robert Pastor, entered. "I noticed an M-16 assault rifle loaded with a banana clip, leaning against the wall," Powell recalled. "The tension in the air made me decide never to be too far away from that M-16."[39]

As a mediator's tactic, Carter started by dangling carrots, including amnesty, and suggesting that the officers might not be banned from returning to Haiti in the future. Cédras shot back, "Our constitution does not allow exile." An emphatic Carter insisted that Clinton was not bluffing. While telling the junta he was personally opposed to an invasion, Carter stressed that "it was going to happen" if Cédras did not relinquish power. Clinton had given his envoys twenty-four hours to convince Cédras to step down; if their diplomatic mission failed, thousands of U.S. troops would invade the island nation.[40]

Nunn spoke next, pointing out that just the day before he had been on the Senate floor criticizing the prospect of an invasion of Haiti. "But I want you to know," Nunn told Cédras, "that if an invasion of Haiti occurs, I will support it and so will the whole Senate. There will be no disagreement in our country on this."[41] It was Colin Powell, however, who made the biggest impression on the Haitians. Powell described, in cinematic detail, how the invasion dubbed Operation Restore Democracy would occur, as he dramatically described the wave of firepower that would envelop Haiti if Cédras did not resign. Powell painted a picture of the naval, air, and ground troops, an unstoppable fighting force, with high-tech equipment and weaponry, reminiscent in a much smaller setting of his briefings during Desert Storm. When Powell had finished, a stunned Cédras leaned back in his chair and stared directly at the former chairman of the JCS. "Well," Cédras finally said, "after all that arrives, we will no longer be a militarily weak nation."[42]

Everyone laughed, easing the tension somewhat. The American negotiators had clearly driven home the point that Cédras was not facing another *Harlan County*; this time around, President Clinton meant business. From that point on the discussions focused solely on negotiating the specific points of a departure agreement. Carter, in particular, turned his attention to the concerns of the Haitian generals. The Clinton administration wrongly thought that the junta's main concern would be how to guarantee their foreign assets or move them out of Port-au-Prince, but they never mentioned that issue. Instead, they feared for the "country"—or rather the elite they represented if Aristide returned triumphant. The Haitian officers thought Aristide was a twisted socialist, a rabble-rouser of the masses, a Marat who would unleash mob rule and foment a bloody civil war. An edgy Cédras even believed that one of Aristide's followers would assassinate him if he tried to leave. "I would rather take an American bullet in the chest," he told Carter, "than a Haitian bullet in the back." The talks broke up inconclusively at 4:00 P.M.[43]

That evening at a small dinner with leaders of Haiti's private sector, Marc Bazin, a former World Bank official in Port-au-Prince and the second-place finisher in the December 1990 elections, advised Carter and Powell that if they wanted to convince Cédras to step down, it was essential to persuade his willful wife. It was a piece of offbeat advice Carter took seriously, for he seldom made a momentous decision without Rosalynn, his partner in peace. War, Carter understood, was a family matter, even to dictators. After dinner the Americans returned to negotiation with the increasingly somber Cédras.

For hours the parties debated the provisions of Carter's agreement draft. "We reached deadlock on several key issues," Carter recalled. "Cédras was willing to resign voluntarily the following year, but not immediately or under pressure." These negotiations adjourned at 3:00 A.M. on Sunday, September 18, with only modest progress. As Carter was leaving the National Military Headquarters, he engaged Cédras in a "more relaxed conversation," saying he would like to meet his family, and the general agreed. Later that evening Rosalynn, in a telephone conversation from Plains, also stressed to Jimmy the importance of cultivating Cédras's wife, reminding him how pivotal their meeting Mrs. Kim Il Sung proved to be in North Korea.[44]

As the Carter delegation began taking their leave, a Colonel Dorelien, the personnel chief of the Haitian forces, started to extend his right hand to Carter, then abruptly pulled back. "Have you shaken hands with Aristide recently?" the colonel inquired. "No," Carter said. "Why?" To which Dorelien responded, "His spirit would still be on you, and I would not like to be touched by it." For Carter, it was a vivid reminder that voodoo superstition was still a potent force in nominally Christian Haiti, where Aristide was deemed by some to be a manipulative sorcerer.[45]

At 5:00 A.M. that Sunday Carter asked Pastor to arrange a 7:00 breakfast with the Cédras family.[46] That morning at Cédras's Mediterranean-style villa in Petionville, the ruling-class suburb of Port-au-Prince, the American envoys met Yannick Cédras, the general's petite but strong-willed wife. Nunn described her as "very attractive, very smart, and very tough," and Powell sketched her as a "striking woman with glossy black hair and a café au lait complexion."[47] She dominated the conversation by telling the delegation that just a few hours earlier she had rounded up her three children—a seventeen-year-old son, a fourteen-year-old daughter, and a ten-year-old son—to join their parents in bed, because it would be their last night on earth. She calmly told the Carter delegation her belief that she and her children had been targeted by a U.S. special forces team, who had "surreptitiously been surveying their house," and they had made a family pact to die together.[48] "There was no theatrics," Carter recalled. "There was no question that what she was telling us occurred."[49]

The room was permeated by a bizarre air of politeness mixed with sad, sullen resignation. When the Cédrases' younger son wandered in, Carter sat him on his knee and gave him a blue pocketknife with a Carter Center insignia. Cookies were passed around, and Cédras's daughter asked Carter to autograph a picture of himself. "We will die before we leave Haiti," Mrs. Cédras continued, "and my husband will do the same." She spoke proudly of how Haiti was the oldest black republic, founded in 1804 by slaves who defeated the French army, and of her own family's heroic military heritage.

She insisted that proud Haitians would never accept the insult of a U.S. invasion. "When she finished," Carter recalled, "we sat in silence. We thought our mission had failed."[50]

At that moment a U.S. aide informed the Carter team that President Clinton was on a secure telephone wanting to speak with Powell. "General Cédras immediately looked like he had been stricken" when Powell left the room, Nunn recalled. "It became very apparent to me then that he was relying on Colin Powell to convince his wife that it was not the day for the general and his family to die."[51] Powell apparently also sensed the subliminal message, for when he returned, he made great headway. Treating Raoul and Yannick Cédras with respect, Powell spoke to them about military honor. He told them that when a mission became impossible, the duty of the commander was to protect the soldiers serving under him, not allow them to be slaughtered for a hopeless cause. Powell struck a responsive chord; Cédras seemed to be on the verge of agreeing to step down and allow unopposed entry of U.S. troops. Powell was willing at this point to fudge on the administration's demand for a specific timetable. "We didn't absolutely need the exact date that Aristide would return," Powell recalled. "That was preferable but not essential. Once our troops landed peacefully, the rest would be sorted out."[52]

From the Cédras home the negotiators returned to the National Military Headquarters. Working frantically to sew up an agreement by noon, the hour the Carter team had been ordered to evacuate, Cédras agreed in principle to allow the undisturbed entry of U.S. troops but was vague as to when or how. He also tried to negotiate the number of U.S. troops and tanks allowed into Haiti—a condition Carter rejected outright. Carter had a secure speaker phone set up in a private room, and along with Nunn and Powell, they telephoned the president to brief him and seek an extension of their deadline. "It's noon," Clinton told them. "We set a timetable. You're finished. There is no agreement. You've got to leave." Carter said, "No, Mr. President, you don't understand. We've got an agreement." Nunn then jumped in. "Mr. President, this agreement is not going to stand the test of an international lawyer, but it's good enough. It's going to keep our people from getting shot, from dying." Powell then added his voice: "Look, Mr. President, we've got an agreement to bring in our troops. We will control this situation." Clinton gave them a little more time to negotiate several points, including Cédras's resignation by a fixed time period.[53]

After the call, the president held a 1:00 P.M. White House meeting of his top foreign policy advisers. At that meeting General John Shalikashvili, chairman of the JCS, told Clinton that if the Eighty-second Airborne was to parachute into Haiti that evening, they had to start loading their gear on the planes. "Pack 'em," Clinton said, in no uncertain terms. By sticking to the invasion schedule, Clinton had painted himself into a potentially serious foreign policy crisis and his American envoys into a perilous position.[54]

An hour later the Carter team faxed the White House a revised agreement. "That precipitated a big confusion," Pastor recalled. Based on subsequent talks, "I think the White House thought this was our initial proposal, but it was the Cédras regime's response to our proposal in their words."[55] An astonished Talbott, worried that Carter had been hoodwinked, drafted a modified agreement, inserting a junta departure date of October 15. The White House didn't want an agreement that did not stipulate the precise date of Cédras's departure and Aristide's arrival. After discussing the language of the agreement for a few more minutes, Clinton finally said, "This isn't going to work. You've got to get out." Cédras had agreed to give up power, and had accepted the peaceful arrival of U.S. troops. An additional element in the agreement repeated the point made in the Governor's Island accord, granting amnesty for the military. Aristide had accepted that then. Cédras was emphatic on another point: he would not accept exile. "There was never any question in my mind, never any discussion at all about whether the generals would have to leave Haiti," Carter recalled. "This never came up [in] my instructions from the White House. It was just that they would have to leave their offices." The White House also insisted that Cédras's stepping down could not be conditional on amnesty. The junta had to step down by October 15, whether the Haitian parliament granted amnesty or not.[56]

Aristide, just a few blocks away from the White House, was extremely bitter over what he regarded as Carter's eleventh-hour antics. The deposed leader insisted to presidential aides that the Carter-Powell-Nunn agreement was unacceptable; he wanted the entire military junta stripped of all vestiges of authority. How could he return to Haiti if Cédras's menacing thugs were still roaming free, burning churches and murdering Lavalas supporters? While Aristide sulked, a perturbed Carter was insisting that it was unreasonable for the White House to suddenly demand that Cédras not simply resign but leave Haiti.[57]

W hat the Carter team did not know at the time of this frantic back-and-forth was that the invasion was already in progress. Just offshore of Haiti, on the USS *Enterprise*, Lieutenant General Harry H. Shelton was pacing as he watched CNN, unable to believe that a former American president was still in a country that the United States was about to invade. A dumbfounded Shelton was bombarding the White House by telephone, pleading, "Goddamnit, get them out of there!" The great fear was that Haiti's military dictatorship would take the Carter team hostage. The Pentagon had even activated a Delta Force team with orders to shoot any Haitian who interfered with rescuing the three Americans, but the prospect of having to rely on derring-do to save such high-profile envoys must have caused a few sweaty palms inside the beltway.[58]

Just before 4:00 P.M., the negotiations were taking a turn for the better, and Powell telephoned the White House to urge President Clinton to take the compromise deal without a specific deadline date. Once U.S. troops had landed peacefully, Powell argued, General Shelton would be "King of the Island."[59] Clinton refused. Shortly thereafter Brigadier General Philippe Biamby—the number-two man after Cédras—burst into the negotiating room in a vicious rage, waving a submachine gun at Carter, Powell, and Nunn. "General Cédras, my commander in chief, we have to leave here right now," Biamby shouted. "The negotiations are over. We have been betrayed. We have intelligence information that the Eighty-second Airborne are getting their parachutes and loading on the planes at Fort Bragg and heading here." An astonished Carter immediately stood up and turned to Cédras, his face beet red. "You must accept this agreement right now, or your children will be killed," Carter shouted. "Your country will be burned."[60] Powell was amazed to watch the president dubbed the "malaise man" by his former boss Ronald Reagan act so resolute. "There was such power in his presentation," Powell recalled. "He was tougher and more dogged than I had thought."[61]

With war imminent, Carter went into overdrive. Desperate to save the day, he floated a wild-card scheme. The Carter delegation would take Cédras from the National Military Headquarters to the Presidential Palace and get provisional president Emile Jonassaint—the eighty-one-year-old former Supreme Court Justice who had been installed by the junta in May—to sign the deadline agreement. "Bob," Carter instructed Pastor, "you finish up the agreement and bring it to us there." Then, instead of waiting for Pastor, the two delegations, at Carter's suggestion, went out the back door and drove over to the Presidential Palace. Carter and Nunn rode in one vehicle while Powell accompanied Cédras in his personal car, with loose grenades rolling on the floor and a Haitian soldier clutching an assault rifle in the backseat.[62]

Pastor was left in a room full of angry Haitian military officers, led by General Biamby, pumping themselves up for war. Nervously, he typed up a revised agreement on his laptop, carefully wording the final language—a frightening and surreal experience. "I was trying to get my printer to work," Pastor recalled, "and these guys were cleaning their guns for war. I had two thoughts: one was to ask them to keep the noise down as I was trying to finish the agreement, but instead, I just smiled and kept the thought to myself. It also occurred to me that they might shoot me." Pastor finally printed out the copies, packed his papers, said good-bye, and raced down the stairs, "head-first into the mob of attachés, swinging their machetes." Where was his boss? The impatient Carter had not waited. The mob, however, was more interested in trying to reach Jimmy Carter's armored vehicle, which was zigzagging around an enormous square heading to the Presidential Palace, than in hassling Pastor.

Pastor sprinted for the palace, which he reached in about ten minutes, drenched in sweat and out of breath. At first, guards would not let him in, but a Haitian intelligence officer recognized him and escorted him inside. Pastor rushed up the stairs, his heart pounding. When he finally arrived in Jonassaint's office, he found the Carter team already engaged in stressful negotiations. "What took you so long?" Carter snapped. "Well, you left me," Pastor replied. "I have always told you, you have to keep up," Carter said, "or you get left behind. Where's the agreement?" It was Pastor's turn to rib his boss: "Oh, I must have left it over there." Then he produced the amended document, which included the Clinton-requested October 15 deadline for the junta to step down.[63]

Carter unceremoniously presented the one-page agreement to Jonassaint, who was calm and collected, a distinguished-looking elder who exuded the moral authority great age sometimes confers. If signed, the agreement would allow American soldiers to enter Haiti as friendly occupiers rather than hostile invaders. Jonassaint went around the room, consulting the cabinet. Point-blank he asked General Cédras, "Can you defend our country from an attack by the United States? Can you?" Cédras dropped his head like a scolded schoolboy. "I cannot defend it against U.S. armed forces," was his reluctant reply. Jonassaint, without hesitation, concluded, "Well, we have no choice but to sign this agreement. Does anybody disagree?" A dissenting minister of defense responded, "You cannot sign the agreement; it's a betrayal of our sovereignty." After a few minutes of arguing, President Jonassaint matter-of-factly fired the dissenting minister on the spot. "General Cédras has told me that he has no other alternative," Jonassaint said. "He cannot defend our country so we must accept this agreement. We'll have peace, not war." The Haitians insisted that the accord be translated into French before it could be signed.[64]

It was just after 6:00 P.M. The planes from Fort Bragg were in the air.

Everything was in motion; U.S. commanders had loaded sixty-one plane-loads of troops from three American bases. Nunn recalled walking out on a balcony to look at the raucous crowds outside the Presidential Palace. As he turned back into the room, he saw a television monitor CNN's live broadcast from outside the palace and watched the back of his own head—"the bald spot on the top of my head was very apparent"—disappearing into the room. "I mean, it was all weird," the usually phlegmatic Nunn recalled.[65] "We were in one heck of a fix because President Clinton had told us that we could not get the signature of President Jonassaint, whom we didn't recognize. Cédras said it was a court-martial offense for Jonassaint to sign for the government because he wasn't the government." A worried Nunn told Carter, "We can't do this unless we call Clinton."[66] Carter got the president on an ordinary, un-secured telephone and informed him that Jonassaint was prepared to sign the agreement. Carter reassured the president that the deal was "almost there." Clinton gave the go-ahead for him to sign it with Jonassaint, but told Carter: "I'm going to have to order you out of there in thirty more minutes. You've got to get out."[67]

Now, with Clinton's blessing, Jonassaint and Carter signed the French and English versions, Carter on behalf of the president of the United States. The agreement stipulated that "certain military officers," identified in the UN resolutions, in Haiti's junta would have to resign by October 15. The original parliament would grant amnesty to a number of unspecified military officers, and economic sanctions imposed by the United States, the UN, and the OAS would be lifted. Thereafter a new parliament would be elected "in a free and democratic manner." Most crucial of all, 250,000 U.S. troops would work with the Haitian military to assure the peaceful transition to an Aristide administration.[68] Powell then asked Cédras outright whether he would implement the agreement. Cédras, who had been chain-smoking, stood up, clicked his heels, and said he would "obey the orders of my presi-dent." Jonassaint told the Americans, "You have our assurance."[69]

At 6:00 P.M. Carter telephoned the White House and reported to Presi-dent Clinton that "we had an agreement," as Carter later told *Time*, "and he turned the planes around"—if not the USS *Enterprise*.[70] Bloodshed had been averted. Even though the Clinton administration had dismissed Jonas-saint as an illegitimate president, they were backed into a corner and forced to take his signature rather than that of Cédras. "Our proposals were ap-proved by President Clinton and the Haitian leaders late Sunday afternoon," Carter wrote in his travel diary, "almost six hours beyond the earlier deadline for our departure and 75 minutes after the first wave of paratroopers had left the U.S. mainland to invade Haiti."[71]

∽०∾

greement in hand, the Carter team headed immediately to the airport,
obeying the presidential order to leave. On the way, Carter asked Pastor
to stay. "The four of us," Carter said, "are the only ones who know what
was negotiated. You'll need to brief the Ambassador and General Bates and
arrange a meeting tomorrow with General Cédras." Pastor agreed but asked
Carter to get the president's permission, which Carter did. "You're in control
now, Bob," Carter said, as they reached the plane. "In control of what?" Pastor responded. "There is no Emory campus in Port-au-Prince. I have no authority, and I don't even have a car." As the trio boarded Air Force One,
Carter's last decision was to request a car from the ambassador for Pastor,
and to smile, saying he was "leaving Haiti in your [Pastor's] hands."[72]

Back in Washington, the White House went into overdrive. First, in a
televised press conference, Vice President Gore announced that General
Cédras would soon depart Haiti and Aristide would be reinstated on October 15. This would be news to Cédras, who had never agreed to leave his
homeland. Aristide was upset when he learned that the Carter agreement
meant that the Haitian military wouldn't be destroyed. Confusion reigned.
The NSC urged Aristide, who worried he had been double-crossed by Clinton, not to speak with the press until events were sorted out. The president
himself was planning to go on nationwide television that evening to announce the agreement. He had several political hot potatoes to juggle just
weeks before the 1994 elections: how to reverse course and paint Jonassaint
as a legitimate signatory, and how to avoid accusations of appeasing Cédras,
a man he had publicly called a murderous dictator.[73] "Cédras was just horrible," Lake recalled. "He would cut people up, slash their faces."[74]

In Port-au-Prince, Pastor drove to the U.S. embassy with Ambassador
William Swing and began to brief him on the thirty hours of negotiations.
Around 10:00 P.M. Sunday, Pastor learned, for the first time, that the U.S.
invasion had only been postponed, not canceled. Lieutenant General Shelton, commander of the Eighteenth Airborne Corps, would be landing 140
helicopters and 1,800 special forces the next day at 10:00 A.M. Operation
Restore Democracy—a sort of Peace Corps with guns—would soon com-
mence. At 10:30 P.M. Pastor listened to Clinton's television announcement
from the Oval Office that a last-minute deal had been struck. Immediately
Pastor requested help from the embassy to locate Cédras to make sure the
transfer of power went smoothly. Embassy officials promised to use all their
contacts to locate Cédras.[75]

That evening Pastor called Carter on his air force plane, but the former
president was fast asleep after his grueling marathon. Pastor finally woke

him before the plane landed to let him know about the invasion and that there might not be enough time to reach Cédras as agreed to by both sides before the U.S. Army arrived. He also relayed that some of the officials in the de facto government had found parts of President Clinton's speech incompatible with the agreement. To add to the confusion, Pastor's telephone conversation was picked up by a ham radio operator and given to CNN, which broadcast it in the early morning. It was not long after that Ambassador Swing relayed an order from Secretary of State Christopher: Pastor was to leave Haiti immediately.

"Are there any flights leaving Haiti?" Pastor inquired. Swing said no. "Let me know when there are. In the meantime, I'm going to try to contact Cédras to set up a meeting with you, General Bates, and me, as is called for under the agreement reached last night."

Embassy officials told Pastor they could not locate Cédras, and they suspected the reason was either he was in hiding, or he was about to welch on the agreement, just as he had done with *Harlan County*. With one and a half hours before touchdown by the U.S. Army, the resourceful Pastor then decided to call Yannick Cédras, through a Creole interpreter, and pretend he was Carter. It worked. She finally answered the phone. "Mrs. Cédras, this is not Jimmy Carter. It's Bob Pastor. We met at breakfast yesterday, though it seemed a week ago. We were all impressed by your strength. I have a simple message for you, and I want you to take it down and repeat it to me: At 10 A.M., U.S. helicopter gunships and special forces will be landing at Port-au-Prince airport. For no one to be hurt, it is essential that your husband meet with me and some U.S. government officials in twenty minutes at the National Military Command Headquarters."

She understood, and five minutes later she called back to tell Pastor that the meeting was set. Pastor asked Ambassador Swing and General Bates to join him in a wild ride to the military headquarters. As they drove through downtown Port-au-Prince, Bates commented at how he had expected half of the buildings to have been destroyed and hundreds of people to be dead in the streets this morning. Instead, they saw young children going to school.

The meeting with Cédras and his command went well. Bates asked Cédras to accompany them to the airport to meet the U.S. commanding officers who would be landing on the first wave. Cédras said he wouldn't and asked them to bring the officers to him. Bates had his orders, but Cédras would not move. Pastor suggested that one of Cédras's general staff accompany him to the airport, and Cédras accepted that. In separate cars, Pastor went with the Haitian general, and Bates rode out with the ambassador. They all reached the airport at the moment that the American troops were coming in.[76]

ᘉᘐᘚᗄᘚ

The Carter team had landed at Andrews Air Force Base at 3:30 A.M. Monday and were ferried to the White House to grab whatever was left of a night's sleep. The envoys were scheduled to meet with Clinton for breakfast to recount the hectic last days and then hold a joint press conference in order to display a united front. To everyone's astonishment, Carter awoke at 6:00 A.M., telephoned CNN president Tom Johnson to arrange a live interview, and ordered the Secret Service to drive him to the news network's nearby studio. Carter was once again about to go solo, giving the nation his version of the Haiti saga on CNN before debriefing President Clinton. Just before Carter went on the air, Pastor reached him from Port-au-Prince to inform him of Secretary Christopher's order that he leave Haiti. "You are to stay exactly where you are," Carter commanded. "I will work this thing out with Christopher and the President."[77]

On CNN, Carter defended Cédras, saying it was "a serious violation of inherent human rights for a citizen to be forced into exile." According to Carter, whether or when "Cédras and his generals would leave Haiti was up to them."[78] Carter praised Cédras—somehow forgiving his past atrocities—for his willingness to cooperate with the U.S. commanders and preserve order in the country. (Cédras eventually reevaluated the wisdom of remaining in Haiti.) "Subsequently, I helped to arrange for the Cédras family to move to Panama before President Aristide was scheduled to return," Carter noted. "We also ensured that proper compensation was made for the property that the Cédras family agreed to abandon."[79]

Carter had used his positive relationship with Panamanian president Ernesto Pérez Balladares to broker the deal whereby the Cédras family could move to Panama City. Carter vouched for the Cédrases, saying that he was "confident" that they would "fully respect" their Panamanian residency terms. "Your decision many not be immediately popular," Carter wrote Pérez Balladares on October 14, "but like the Panama Canal Treaties have been in the United States, your decision will be seen as far-sighted and wise."[80]

After Aristide heard Carter's CNN remarks defending Cédras's human rights, he told Representative Joseph P. Kennedy II that "crimes against humanity" were being "amnestied" away. But all Aristide could do was sulk in his Washington apartment and listen to Anthony Lake try to explain that he had not been tricked by Bill Clinton.[81]

From the CNN studio Carter returned to the White House, joined Powell and Nunn, and met President Clinton in the Oval Office. Clinton was furious, and Carter himself was not exactly in a pacific mood. Exploding in anger, Carter berated Clinton for ordering an invasion while they were still in Haiti and for not being candid with his designated emissaries, putting their lives at risk. One is hard pressed to recall another occasion in U.S. history when two presidents head-butted one another in the White House with such hostility.

Eventually Nunn managed to settle down both men, and a serious policy discussion took place. Nunn kept stressing the importance of a united front. "They both had performed brilliantly," Nunn recalled. "It was important not to forget they were a team."[82] At the broadcast news conference, held in the chandelier-studded East Room, Carter stood behind Clinton, deferential and respectful. When Clinton finished speaking it was Carter's turn. He mentioned that five minutes ago he had spoken with Bob Pastor, who was with Cédras, and that "everything was going perfectly." The reference to Pastor surprised some senators, including Jesse Helms, who communicated their views to the State Department. In the late afternoon Pastor spoke with Strobe Talbott, who told him that his ambassadorial nomination was in "serious jeopardy" and suggested that he return at once.[83]

Carter left Washington dejected. Instead of praise from Clinton for his effective diplomacy, all he got was flack from the White House about his "unconscionable" glory-hogging on CNN and his ill-considered defense of Cédras's human rights. "I need to know frankly what it is about the Carter Center that displeases people," Carter told Newsweek, deflecting criticism of his actions to the center. "Because it's certainly not to our advantage to have come back from a crisis like this one or the one in North Korea where war was imminent and find to my amazement that what we've done is considered by some people inappropriate."[84] In Haiti particularly, Carter had righteousness on his side. While he was struggling under potentially life-threatening circumstances to avoid bloodshed in Haiti, Warren Christopher and his deputy, Strobe Talbott, were off in a State Department limousine to view a late afternoon showing of the Robert Redford film Quiz Show. The joke making the rounds of Washington was that if Warren Christopher were alive, Clinton wouldn't need Jimmy Carter.[85]

Rather than stoically walk away from the State Department's complaints about his diplomacy, Carter upped the ante. In what some regard as a high-water mark of individualism run amok in American diplomacy, Carter nearly immolated himself in a September 20 interview with Maureen Dowd of the New York Times in Atlanta. Carter spoke of being "ashamed" of the Clinton administration policy imposing tough sanctions on Haiti. The only people adversely affected by the embargo, Carter lamented, were the poor, who could no longer feed or clothe their babies. The embassy in Port-au-Prince, Carter claimed, had been "unhelpful," the State Department a bunch of do-nothings. Carter praised Cédras for the dictator's courage and invited him to Plains to attend his Sunday school class. All week long Carter was on the phone with Cédras; by Thursday Cédras was opining to CBS's Dan Rather that it would be unconstitutional for him to be forced to leave Haiti.

The Dowd interview made the front page of the *New York Times* and caused Carter endless but self-inflicted grief. Carter's answers betrayed a preachy flakiness that perplexed his admirers and angered his detractors. Asked by Dowd whether it was awkward to praise Cédras after Clinton had demonized the dictator, Carter responded by having his secretary retrieve his poem "With Words We Learn to Hate," from what would soon become Carter's best-selling volume of sentimental verse, *Always a Reckoning*. The poem was a condemnation of those with a jingoistic penchant for war over peace. Clinton's Haiti policy was not Carter's only target. Carter also used the interview to explain how he had also worked against George Bush in the Gulf War, writing letters to UN Security Council members in hope of derailing Desert Storm.[86]

It was a sad, self-defeating way for Carter to behave on the heels of such an important diplomatic triumph. Even his lawyer, Terrence Adamson, e-mailed Carter, telling him to refrain from interviews; he was talking away his accomplishment. Had Carter not gone solo on CNN or talked candidly with the press, he may not have received the credit he deserved nor perhaps made the October 3 covers of both *Time* and *Newsweek*. But Carter didn't know when to stop. The White House considered the Maureen Dowd interview outside the pale.[87]

The Clinton administration now saw Carter as a serious political problem that had to be contained. Midterm elections were nearing, and Carter's loose-lipped denunciations of the White House and State Department at the very moment Clinton was trying to muster public approval for his Haiti policy had to be quelled. Since most of Carter's arrows were aimed at the State Department, Warren Christopher was dispatched to Plains on September 24 to mend fences with his old boss. "Perhaps I should have gone sooner," Christopher later admitted.[88]

The journey to Plains was a grudging one for Christopher. His relationship with Carter had become so strained that even polite conversation had become difficult. Carter cordially refrained from publicly criticizing the Clinton administration any further, but the two men were unable to repair their bad feelings.[89] Cartoonist Garry Trudeau spoofed the Christopher sojourn in a poem entitled "Chris," published on the *New York Times* op-ed page and ostensibly written by Carter: "The finest public servant/This private man has known/Conceals his pain/Hops on a plane/ Too proud to use the phone./Chris, this stage is big enough/ To walk in brotherhood/ Let's call in sick/And catch a flick/I hear 'Quiz Show' is good/Oh, you've already seen it?"[90]

Conservative critics of the Carter-brokered Haitian agreement popped up everywhere in late September. Predictably *New York Times* columnist William Safire wrote "Jimmy Clinton II" about Carter's unsated lust for a Nobel Peace Prize.[91] General Norman Schwarzkopf bemoaned the "Carter Factor" in U.S. foreign policy to an Alabama audience, by which he meant the appeasing of dictators.[92] Journalist David Brock in the *American Spectator* compared Carter's CNN appearance to Alexander Haig's "I am in control here" speech.[93] Great sport was made of an imagined Carter flirtation with Yannick Cédras, and his inviting her husband to read the Book of Job at Maranatha Baptist Church in Plains. The word "naive" peppered the dozen or so stories about Carter. Gag rumors circulated that Clinton was now going to let Carter divide Jerusalem and negotiate with Castro. According to *Newsweek,* the egotistical Carter was "preachy and subtly vain—nearly obsessive in the pursuit of what he sees as the one true path in international politics, and plainly concerned for his place in history."[94]

Carter was rightfully proud of avoiding needless bloodshed in Haiti. He saw his role there simply as a typical, if more highly publicized, example of his conflict resolution theory in operation—the raison d'être of the center he created in 1982. Like Carter's June intervention in North Korea, the United States faced confrontation with a government whom the Clinton administration could not communicate with officially because it withheld diplomatic recognition. As a nongovernmental organization, the Carter Center was able to seek out a peaceful solution to a hemispheric crisis that could have led to armed conflict. The Carter Center was filling an institutional vacuum.

After the acrimony died down, even the Clinton administration felt begrudgingly grateful to Carter. After all, thousands of U.S. troops landed on September 19 without resistance, fanning out across the island by ship and helicopter as part of a goodwill mission. The Haitian population gave the Eighty-second Airborne a stupendous welcome, treating the U.S. soldiers as liberators, not invaders. It was, as essayist Bob Shacochis claimed in *Harper's*, an "immaculate invasion," albeit an unwieldy one. Operation Restore Democracy had formally become Operation Uphold Democracy.

The seven-point accord signed by Carter and Jonassaint may have been vague, but the Clinton administration had little problem interpreting it to its taste. Carter's faith that Cédras was a man of his word proved correct. But in reality it was the Eighty-second Airborne—not Cédras's better angels—that convinced the military dictator to step down. The deposed Haitian dictator implemented his part of the agreement after U.S. troops arrived; in return, the U.S. government rented his home at a modest price, permitting him to

relocate to Panama. Because the landing did not involve combat and because no American soldiers died from hostile action, President Clinton was
spared an ugly confrontation with Congress—one that he might have lost.
And Aristide returned on October 15 virtually unopposed.[95]

Bob Pastor visited Haiti in December on Carter's behalf with Michael
Manley and came back with an upbeat assessment of the U.S. troops' peacekeeping. As the media repainted his September mission as a success—
including accolades from the *Atlanta Journal & Constitution,* the *Wall
Street Journal, USA Today,* and the *New York Times*—Carter began to think
better of Bill Clinton.[96] "President Clinton faced vociferous objection to our
going and the way we performed," Carter wrote his friends John and Betty
Pope. "And that's why I think he made one of the most politically courageous decisions that any president has ever made. He didn't have popular
support of the country, he didn't have support in the Congress, he didn't
even have support among some of his key advisors in the White House and
the State Department. And he took a chance on us. Three guys that had
disapproved of some facets of his Haitian policy."[97]

Even critics who had opposed sending U.S. forces admitted that Clinton-
Carter diplomacy in Haiti proved better than expected—at least temporarily. Unfortunately for the administration, these successes did not help
Democrats in the November congressional elections. But it did encourage
Carter to weigh in on another pressing international crisis: Bosnia. "President Kim and leaders in Haiti and Bosnia wanted to have someone who
would listen to them and talk to them," Carter said. "I'm not excusing the
crimes that might have been committed by these men. But we had to open
the avenue of communication. These are the kinds of things the Carter Center will continue to do."[98] It was the prospect of a December Jimmy Carter
diplomatic foray to Bosnia that put Clinton's State Department on red alert
only weeks after the immaculate invasion was launched.

TWENTY-TWO

ALWAYS A RECKONING

A t the Carter Center's surprise party on October 1, 1994, to celebrate Jimmy's seventieth birthday, speculation was rampant that Carter, nominated yet a fifth time for the Nobel Peace Prize, would finally be honored that year for his significant role in North Korea and Haiti.[1] Senator Daniel Patrick Moynihan of New York, endorsing Carter's candidacy, exclaimed that he had deserved "five Nobel Prizes" for Haiti alone. But the 1994 honor went to Yasır Arafat, Shimon Peres, and Yitzhak Rabin for their efforts to create peace in the Middle East, while the following year the award went to the Pugwash Conferences on Science and World Affairs and their British president, Joseph Rotblat, for their efforts to eliminate nuclear weapons.[2]

Carter generally shrugged off or dismissed any suggestion that he was disappointed by Oslo's failure to recognize his work, but that December, when James Wooten, a senior correspondent for ABC News, dared to broach this sensitive issue, he elicited a more candid response. Of course Carter would accept the Nobel Prize if it was awarded to him, but winning it was not the motivating force of his humanitarian endeavors. "My goodness, what if it were?" Carter asked rhetorically, and then proceeded to answer his own question in a way that suggested this wasn't the first time he had contemplated the question. "What if the Nobel were really the be-all and end-all of my existence? And what if it never happened? Which it probably won't. There are so many hundreds of people working for the same things, just as hard as I am and some of them probably much harder. But, what if that's what really mattered most and it never came about? Well, what sort of dried up, shriveled up, disappointed, frustrated old prune of a man would I be then? Poor Ol' Jimmy Carter. He never got his prize."[3]

Why the Nobel Peace Prize Committee had consistently bypassed Carter is a topic of endless conjecture. Some theorized that since Henry Kissinger's 1973 award for his work in negotiating the Vietnam War cease-fire agreement, given before disclosure of his covert role in the bombing of Cambodia and Laos, the Oslo octogenarians had shied away from U.S. government officials, past or present. Others contend that Global 2000's agricultural work in Africa was simply an extension of earlier work by Nobel laureate Norman Borlaug. Guilt-by-association theorists pointed to the center's massive funding from Ryoichi Sasakawa, a tainted Japanese billionaire who spent the last years of his life trying to buy the prize. Other speculators attributed spread-the-wealth motives to the Nobel Committee, saying it now lionized only global causes in desperate need of international credibility, like the East Timor independence movement (1996) or the International Campaign to Ban Landmines (1997), ignoring Carter since he was more than adept at grabbing headlines and funding on his own.[4] None of these hypotheses were any solace to fervent Carter admirers such as Andrew Young; at a conference in Miami the former UN ambassador scolded Claus Nobel himself for apparently blackballing Jimmy Carter.[5] In any case, optimists close to Carter believed 1998 would be the year Carter got his Nobel due, for it marked the fiftieth anniversary of Eleanor Roosevelt's UN Declaration of Human Rights; after all, they argued quite persuasively, no single individual had done more in the past half century to promote the concept of human rights than Jimmy Carter. But Carter wasn't holding his breath.

But Carter did get one noteworthy honor on his seventieth birthday: the J. William Fulbright Prize for International Understanding. "Jimmy Carter has done more for public service in general and for promotion of mutual understanding among nations in particular than any American chief executive since John Quincy Adams," awards committee chairman Stanley Katz of the American Council of Learned Societies noted.[6] What Gore Vidal wrote of John Quincy Adams in 1997 was an apt description of Carter: "Ineffectual President became impassioned tribune of the people."[7] Adams, who left the White House in 1824, returned to Washington as a member of the House of Representatives. In Congress he fought eloquently against slavery as well as helping to draft the charter of the Smithsonian Institution. Another former president, Theodore Roosevelt, actually formed his own progressive party—the Bull Moose party—to challenge William Howard Taft in the 1912 presidential election. But Carter, by contrast, reinvented the postpresidency without benefit of party platform or political office. His working capital was the so-called bully pulpit of a former U.S. president who must persuade and exhort.[8]

Comparing Carter to Adams was commonplace that Christmas season, as Times Books released *Always a Reckoning*, Carter's first volume of verse.[9] Besides Carter, only John Quincy Adams and Abraham Lincoln were in communion with the poetic muse. "That is good company for our most useful and perhaps most versatile former President," the *New York Times* opined.[10] The fifty-one poems of *Always a Reckoning*, an amalgam of Carl Sandburg at his worst and Rod McKuen at his best, ranged widely: from boss politics, possum hunting, and barefoot fishing to the plight of the homeless and familial relationships. The slender volume, illustrated by Carter's granddaughter Sarah Elizabeth Chuldenko, became a *New York Times* best-seller, to the surprise of literary critics. Carter the versifier was in instant demand—for a Dylan Thomas poetry tribute and Maya Angelou fund-raiser, the PBS documentary *Spokenword*, and a gathering of Nobel laureates in literature. His poems found their way into literary journals such as the *New England Review*, *Common Sense*, and the *New Orleans Review*. If no one acclaimed Carter as a great poet, Joseph Brodsky was willing to credit him with "professional competence," while Seamus Heaney compared his "coyless style" to that of Theodore Roethke.[11]

Carter's poetry teacher, Miller Williams of Arkansas, named Bill Clinton's second inaugural poet in January 1997, saw Carter's gift as a poet in his ability to make "the memorable out of the ordinary."[12] There was an authenticity to Carter's poems; and readers were also taken with their candor, as Carter touched on his tough times with Rosalynn and his bouts of despair. Carter, ever respectful of professional poets, considered himself a "hard-working amateur" and had fun on the tour circuit. After a reading at Emory University he signed five hundred copies of *Always a Reckoning* in two hours. Asked whether he was getting writer's cramp, Carter quipped, "Naw, this is how I make a living. It beats picking cotton."[13]

While Carter spent the shank end of 1994 winning awards and reading poetry, Bill Clinton was in political doldrums. Clinton Democrats took a pasting in the November 4 congressional elections as Republicans picked up eight Senate seats, fifty-two House seats, and eleven governorships. A new wave of GOP conservatives was about to swamp the 104th Congress in what the media declared a "revolution." Most pundits saw the Republican landslide as a reaction against big, "intrusive" government, the coda to Ronald Reagan's repudiation of FDR's New Deal and LBJ's Great

Society. The insurgents' leader was Newt Gingrich, a fifty-one-year-old Georgia congressman whom Jimmy Carter knew well.[14]

Gingrich, a Yankee by birth, made his first professional foray into Georgia politics in 1970—as the Republican party campus coordinator and energetic opponent of Jimmy Carter's campaign for governor. Carter's Republican rival, television anchor Hal Suit, "had no base beyond the reach of his television channel," as Gingrich noted. Gingrich saw Carter as assiduous in building a broad constituency: "Carter, on the other hand, was a wonderful professional politician who had worked for four solid years crisscrossing the state, visiting every Baptist church, and talking to everybody."[15] After Carter's victory, Gingrich sniped away at Governor Carter in the pages of the *Atlanta Journal & Constitution*, attacks that Carter dismissed as the flaky rantings of a John Bircher using a pseudonym.[16]

Gingrich, who understood and respected Dixie-style politics, was himself elected to the House of Representatives in 1978 and soon became one of the GOP's leading strategists. As Ronald Reagan prepped for his debate with Carter during the 1980 presidential campaign, Gingrich advised Reagan and his coach, James Baker III, on how to avoid being snared in rhetorical traps laid by Carter. "Carter will always state the case in such a way that if you accept any of the propositions of the statement and then try to knock it down, you are in his arena," Gingrich later noted. "Jimmy—like Eugene and Herman Talmadge—was brilliant at this; it was a style which allowed him to say astonishing things. And everybody knew it wasn't true, but they knew what it meant, which was the thing that was true. 'Why do you want to abolish Social Security and Medicare?' 'Why have you always been a racist?' By the time you say, 'I am not a racist,' people are saying, 'Ah ha!' What you have to do is literally reframe his debate." Gingrich's shrewd political advice helped Reagan disarm President Carter in the 1980 debates with such jibes as his notorious "There you go again."[17]

Since the 1980s Gingrich and Carter have waltzed around each other gingerly. "Newt is bright and crazed with ambition. But who am I to talk? I ran for president," Carter has commented wryly. Their relationship was bound to be adversarial on most political issues, ranging from affirmative action and abortion to the United Nations and taxation. And yet, unlike the nation at large, Carter did not dislike the abrasive Cobb County rightwinger; he found Gingrich sincere in his "erroneous ideas." He stood up for what he believed in, unlike Clinton, who rarely tackled issues head-on.[18]

Gingrich, while contemptuous of Carter's diplomatic dealings with dictators like Hafez al-Assad or Kim Il Sung, had a more nuanced view of the totality of the Carter enterprise. "I think Jimmy means well, but he doesn't understand the world," was Gingrich's explanation. "He has an enormous willingness to put himself on the line and a good work ethic. Those are his strengths. And he is technically smart. His weaknesses are that the world is organic, it is not mechanical. The good intentions are the beginning, they are not the result. Carter's worldview is clearly an amalgam of a very small town and an atlas."[19]

Gingrich, unlike other Georgia Republicans, did not eschew Carter projects he deemed worthwhile. For instance, he joined the Plains Historic Trust, whose mission was to preserve the former president's hometown legacy. Gingrich was also strongly supportive of Carter's domestic initiatives like the Atlanta Project and his work with Habitat for Humanity. Gingrich, unafraid of a Carter association, actually began touting the Atlanta Project as exemplary of community-corporate partnerships in which citizens are urged to take control of their future without direct federal intervention or interference. And, as Gingrich learned more and more about Habitat for Humanity from Carter, he grandfathered the ecumenical organization into his conservative canon. When he was sworn in as Speaker of the House in January 1995, he wore a Habitat for Humanity lapel pin with its distinctive logo designed by Carter's friend Lisa Swisher, of Americus, Georgia. Cynics argued that the pin symbolically inoculated Gingrich against Democratic charges that he, like other Republicans, was heartless, and indifferent to the poor. Carter, however, defended Gingrich's bona fides: "Contrary to the anti-Gingrich accusations, Newt's commitment to Habitat is genuine."[20]

Soon after Gingrich assumed the speakership, he invited Millard Fuller, founder of Habitat for Humanity, to pay a courtesy call at his Capitol Hill office. At their meeting, the Speaker asked how he could best help out Habitat. Fuller refrained from giving Gingrich the full fifteen-point treatment he gave Carter in 1984, pruning his agenda to three requests: keep wearing the lapel pin; attest to his beliefs by raising money for, and helping build, a house in Cobb County; and support a $25 million congressional bill for Habitat to buy public land and build houses on. "Newt immediately agreed to all three requests," Fuller maintained.[21] Though Carter vehemently disagreed with the Speaker's "naive premise" that government-financed public housing was unnecessary—that the private sector alone could and would supply housing for poor people—Carter found common ground and a growing respect for Gingrich. "We became friends," Carter said, and few doubted his words. In fact, National Security Council director Anthony Lake soon found himself in the peculiar position of asking Jimmy Carter on several occasions to lobby Gingrich on behalf of the Clinton administration's foreign policies.[22]

‿⚬‿

W hile the Clinton administration was focused on the impact of the Republican ascendancy, Carter was about to embark on perhaps his most brazen postpresidential derring-do yet. In mid-December he accepted an invitation from Bosnian Serb warlord Radovan Karadzic to visit him in an effort to broker a cease-fire. If Carter was successful—and the prospects were quite dim—he would have contributed to ending Europe's bloodiest conflict in the last half century. During Josip Broz Tito's thirty-five-year rule following World War II, the multiethnic Yugoslavia managed to submerge its ethnic and religious divisions, but the power struggle following Tito's death unleashed pent-up animosities, which politicians channeled into virulent militaristic nationalism. Hostilities broke out in early 1992 as the former Yugoslavia fissured into ethnic battle zones over which three warring factions—Eastern Orthodox Serbians, inheritors of most of Tito's armaments; Catholic Croatians; and Bosnian Muslims—laid claim. The world was shocked by ghastly reports of "ethnic cleansing," mass rapes, and genocidal acts—primarily by Serb troops, perpetrated against Muslim civilians—and of atrocities by Serbian forces against Bosnians held in detention camps. The Bosnian capital, Sarajevo, a once cosmopolitan city that had hosted the 1984 Winter Olympics, was now a killing field.[23]

The Balkan horrors had become a repellent staple of television news coverage around the country and the world, and Bosnia was quickly becoming a domestic policy crisis for the administration. Congressional Republicans strongly favored providing arms to the Bosnian Muslims so they could better defend themselves against the heavily armed Serbs. Clinton steadfastly resisted unilateral action by the United States, supporting the multinational approach at the time exemplified by the largely ineffectual efforts of UN peacekeepers. The UN had made some strides—sporadically halting the sustained artillery shelling of Sarajevo's civilian population and establishing a war crimes tribunal in the Hague—but the killing continued unabated.

On February 5, 1994, when sixty-eight civilians in Sarajevo died in a mortar attack, public outrage forced the administration to take a more aggressive tack. Clinton called on NATO to protect Bosnian Muslim "safe havens," and by April NATO jets were hitting ground targets in Gorazde. Then, with U.S. prodding, a Bosnian-Croatian peace agreement was signed, ending the "war within a war" and suspending the second front. However, a genuine and lasting cease-fire proved elusive despite the efforts of the UN, the United States, the European Union, and NATO. The administration was torn between maintaining NATO and UN credibility and its unwillingness to commit U.S. troops. Enter Jimmy Carter.[24]

Carter had systematically avoided getting involved in Bosnia, saving himself to play a "neutral" track-two role if the proper opportunity presented itself. When former State Department official Patricia Derian tried to get a joint letter signed by former presidents and secretaries of state in late 1992, Carter refused. Even after Richard Nixon and Gerald Ford signed onto the letter, Carter balked—lending his name might preclude him from a future mediation role. Like Cyrus Vance, who was trying to mediate with the Bosnian Serbs, Carter believed peace negotiation was preferable to NATO bombings or UN threats. Instead of blaming the Bosnian Serbs, Carter adopted the "ancient enmities" line.[25]

The Carter Center had held consultations on the former Yugoslav federation in late 1993, but Carter had not been regularly and systematically kept apprised of the situation.[26] He could see no obvious role for himself in the Balkans, where for centuries the European and Ottoman powers had played out their power struggles against a backdrop of ethnic and racial enmity. Any Bosnian assignment for Carter appeared tantamount to being a permanent negotiator, a job title he had little interest in assuming. Generally, Carter accepted the so-called Contact Group plan as a sound basis for a comprehensive cease-fire in Bosnia-Herzegovina. The plan offered 49 percent of Bosnia to the Serbs and 51 percent to the Muslim-Croat federation. The plan, while agreed to by the United States, Great Britain, France, Germany, and Russia, was rejected in July 1994 by the Bosnian Serbs, who by military conquest held a preponderance of Bosnia's territory. The Contact Group of countries had not been able to find a diplomatic settlement; its efforts were moribund. Still, Carter accepted the Contact Group's proposal without question even though it made no sense within the region. It had been embraced by the Bosnian government only because the Bosnians had no choice; furthermore, they accepted it in the certain knowledge that the Serbs would reject it.[27] Meanwhile the Clinton administration had not spoken with the Bosnian Serbs since August. "My view was that there wasn't much of a peace process anyway," Carter told journalist James Wooten. "You can't be a Contact Group if you're only dealing with one side—and since no other progress was being made, I decided it was worth at least some effort on my part."[28]

Carter's first direct involvement in the 32-month-old conflict, which had already left 200,000 people missing or dead in Bosnia-Herzegovina, came via a letter. In early December a letter of entreaty arrived from Daniel Boudin, a pro-Serbian French contractor and friend of Karadzic. Boudin wrote that he thought the indefatigable Carter, who had been successful in North Korea and Haiti, might be able to broker a temporary cease-fire, despite the failures of the UN and European Union. If Carter had any concerns that he might be a pawn in a game whose rules were devised by the Bosnian Serb strongman, he set them aside—he was intrigued. On

December 9 he traded messages with Boudin. The upshot: Radovan Karadzic, the militant Serb nationalist and virulent anti-Muslim, regarded as a war criminal by most close observers of the Bosnian war, wrote Carter through an intermediary—Los Angeles attorney Tom Hanley—proposing that the ex-president come to Pale to discuss a cease-fire and resumption of negotiations. A pro–Bosnian Serb delegation was sent to Plains to talk peace with a former president of the United States. Naturally, before committing to such a tarriance, Carter telephoned President Clinton for approval. "Please see them, and find me no matter where I am to let me know what they say," Clinton said. The president was clearly willing to grasp at any straw that might bring an end to the intractable Bosnian war, while concluding that the fallout from trying to block a Carter mission would be much worse than green-lighting it. The State Department, to no one's surprise, was aghast, and prepared for a diplomatic fiasco.[29]

A week later, the small delegation of Bosnian Serb lobbyists, led by physician Borko Djordjevic, a plastic surgeon from Santa Barbara with close ties to Karadzic, arrived in Plains. Their talks went well, so Carter agreed to speak directly with Karadzic by telephone. Karadzic, anxious to improve the image of Bosnian Serbs in the United States, promised Carter he would open the closed Sarajevo airport to humanitarian flights, allow freedom of movement to UN peacekeeping convoys, and release all Muslim prisoners, under nineteen years of age. The kicker, however, was that he would declare a unilateral four-month cease-fire, provided Carter would visit him in Pale, his mountaintop headquarters twenty miles southeast of Sarajevo. Carter was elated. It was the first time the Bosnian Serbs had ever been willing to even consider the plan. But he was also skeptical: "After I talked with Karadzic, I called CNN and told Tom Johnson what was happening," Carter recollected. "He said, 'I will have Judy Woodruff confirm all this for the international media,' which to me is much more binding a confirmation than an indirect conversation with Clinton. So Judy Woodruff interviewed Karadzic for thirty minutes, and he confirmed all the promises that he had made to me. That's why I went over."[30]

Clinton loosely approved the mission, hoping Carter could jump-start negotiations. The Carter Center was immediately inundated with representatives of the NSC, CIA, and State Department. "They told us we were walking into a minefield of hatred and an ancient history of distrust and violence," Rosalynn Carter recalled.[31] The NSC's top Bosnian specialist, Alexander R. Vershbow, warned Carter against allowing Karadzic to use him for his own propaganda reasons. The administration was also concerned about perceptions: "We thought it was particularly important that he see the leaders of the Bosnian government first, since they are the legitimate government," a senior Clinton spokesman allowed. "So far, President Carter and his people [had] met only with the Serbian insurgents."[32] The administration provided transport by U.S. military plane from Germany to Croatia and then by UN plane to Sarajevo, but the White House was careful to keep its distance. Press Secretary Dee Dee Myers made it clear that Carter was traveling as a representative of the Carter Center and was not on an official mission.[33]

News of Carter's Bosnia mission was met with instant derision. NATO secretary general Willy Claes dismissed Karadzic's promises as no more than a provisional cease-fire. "I do not see why it is necessary to ask the former President of the United States to come in order to obtain simply a cease-fire."[34] While Yasushi Akashi, UN special representative of the secretary general for Yugoslavia, said he was "grateful and hopeful" about Carter's mission, the U.S. ambassador to Croatia, Peter Galbraith, couldn't even dredge up diplomatic niceties, saying he was "negative."[35]

Privately, Warren Christopher discounted the Carter mission; why would Karadzic even consider a solution that would require him to give up turf he had captured by force? Wouldn't Carter be moonstruck by Karadzic, a psychiatrist by training, who might ruthlessly exploit his professional skills to manipulate a well-intentioned but naive man? White House chief of staff Leon Panetta went on CNN's *Evans and Novak* to dampen expectations that Carter would accomplish anything, in light of the Bosnian Serbs' dreary history of promise breaking. "If he can find a way to solve some of these problems, fine," said Panetta. "But we're skeptical."[36]

On December 17 the Carter team left Atlanta for Frankfurt, using the flight time to practice proper pronunciation of Bosnian Serb and Muslim names. While changing planes in Frankfurt for Zagreb on December 18, Jimmy and Rosalynn were thrilled to learn from Croatian president Franjo Tudjman that Karadzic had partially fulfilled two of his preliminary promises: two UN planes had been allowed to land at Sarajevo airport, which had been closed since November 21, and the movement of seventeen out of twenty UN humanitarian convoys had been approved. Lest hopes be raised too high, Tudjman also reported that nearly 2,000 rounds of small arms gunfire, coming from scattered sources, had been recorded in the Sarajevo area that day.[37] In Zagreb, the Carters once again changed planes. The only flights permitted by the Bosnian Serbs into besieged Sarajevo were UN planes of Russian manufacture. This prospect did not especially unnerve the intrepid couple, but when they were handed flak jackets and blue helmets as they prepared to board, Rosalynn's anxiety was manifest. A high-ranking UN representative sought to reassure her, saying that the occasional sniping usually came from drunken soldiers firing small weapons skyward, and that only one UN pilot had ever been hit. (As it turned out, Rosalynn's concerns were well founded. On the return trip to Zagreb and safely past the Sarajevo airport, they learned the full story: 260 incidents of bullet-damaged aircraft had been reported.)[38]

The flight into Sarajevo was disheartening, to say the least. The once resplendent Bosnian capital stood in ruins—Ottoman bridges flattened, mosques, churches, and monasteries razed, high-rises demolished, and rubble everywhere. Edifices that had survived the shelling lacked heat and electricity. The Carters were whisked into an armored vehicle and driven to the headquarters of UNPROFOR (United Nations Protective Forces), an old mansion now housing UN offices, dining facilities for staff, and the living quarters of Lieutenant General Sir Michael Rose, British head of UN forces but then on leave. The Carters were domiciled in Rose's quarters—two small rooms with army cots and a large bathroom—for their two-night stay in the war zone. "The furnishings were spartan but comfortable, and we felt very fortunate," Rosalynn recalled. "The temperature outside was 20 degrees, very cold. We had an electric heater and hot water. We were cozy; most people in Sarajevo were not."[39]

After a briefing by UN officials, the Carters met with President Alija Izetbegovic, head of Bosnia's Muslim-dominated government, and his cabinet. The president expressed his astonishment that the Carters of all people would come to Sarajevo at the behest of Radovan Karadzic, a man he and many others regarded as a war criminal of Hitlerian proportions, not simply a military opponent. Lacking the weapons to turn the tide, and smarting from military losses, the Bosnian government was eager to adhere as closely as possible to the 49 percent Serb, 51 percent Muslim-Croat division that had been proposed by the Contact Group international mediation in 1994. Izetbegovic, fearing that the Bosnian Serb delegation to Plains had already recruited Carter to their cause, didn't mince words: "What is the purpose of your arrival? What can we expect?" Sensing Izetbegovic's suspicions, Carter made explicit the basis of his planned negotiations: "My complete commitment is to support, not in any way to subvert, the Contact Group plan."

Izetbegovic was relieved by Carter's words but nonetheless skeptical: "Your statements eliminated one fear. There was some kind of presumption you were here with another plan. Journalists messed me up."[40] He loosened up somewhat and began recounting a lengthy litany of "ancient enmities" Bosnian Muslims had against Serbians. The good news, from Carter's viewpoint, was his assent to a four-month cease-fire, provided certain terms were met. Carter promised to return the next day after his meeting with Karadzic to debrief the Muslim leader. "Our assurances helped to alter their concerns," Carter recorded in his diary.[41]

It was bitterly cold when Jimmy Carter awoke at dawn the next day. He donned a white turtleneck sweater for extra warmth and drafted a laptop proposal to present to Karadzic. Then he and Rosalynn set out for Pale in an armored vehicle with a UN escort. Accompanying the Carters was Tony Banbury, a young UN civil affairs officer well versed in every painful aspect of the Bosnian war. Banbury first gave the Carters a "windshield tour" of Sarajevo, refusing to let them stop for fear of assassination. Rosalynn Carter recorded the horror of Sarajevo in her diary: "Graves, graves, graves . . . everywhere . . . thousands and thousands of them, all over the city, in any available space and filling what at one time were beautiful parks. There are no trees. All have been cut down for fuel. The Olympic stadium is totally demolished. Town Hall, destroyed. Remains of summer vegetable plots along the streets; garbage everywhere."[42]

The Carters passed a toppled statue of Tito. Unlike the gripping images of Lenin's statue being torn down, which were at least freighted with the possibility of new beginnings, the headless statue bespoke only Yugoslavia's disintegration. They entered Sniper Alley, but not a single gunshot was heard. Sarajevo, a once cosmopolitan outpost where a confluence of religions and cultures had managed to live in peace, was now, in the words of Bosnian-born writer Ivo Andric, a "muffled land" of "silence and uncertainty."[43] At last the armored caravan reached the outskirts, passing through three checkpoints before entering Serb territory. The contrast between city and countryside was startling. Just beyond the hell of beseiged Sarajevo, the Carters found the countryside peaceful. Sheep grazed on pastures; firewood was neatly stacked in yards; the soldiers along the way were well dressed and amply equipped. This was the staging area of the 1984 Winter Olympics, and the remains of ski slopes were jutting out of the snow.

At Bosnian Serb headquarters in Pale, the Carters were met by Radovan Karadzic and his wife, Liliana, along with Serb army commander Ratko Mladic. To Carter's surprise, Borko Djordjevic and the other members of his Serbian delegation to Plains were also present. The Carters met with the Karadzic retinue for ninety minutes, listening to the dictator's litany of Bosnian Muslim atrocities against his people as he displayed Serbian war maps delineating his military conquests. The two couples then retired to a private room for further discussions.[44]

Karadzic was clearly au courant on Carter's recent missions to North Korea and Haiti, in which the wives of Kim Il Sung and Raoul Cédras had played unexpectedly important roles. He was at great pains to portray himself as a family man of good conscience. His wife, he related, was also a psychiatrist, and president of the Red Cross. Together the Karadzics spun yarns to illustrate their compassion for suffering humanity. In a reprise of Haiti the couple paraded daughter Sonya before visitors; she spoke of high-minded aspirations to be a physician and save lives.

Carter produced the cease-fire agreement he had drafted that morning and read it aloud. Karadzic then whipped out his own proposal, which demanded the lifting of economic sanctions against the Serbs as a precondition to a cease-fire and peace negotiations. The Carter Center's Harry Barnes explained to Djordjevic and Hanley that unless Karadzic withdrew his demands on sanctions, Carter would be unable to continue his mission.[45] "It took a while, a lot of persuasion, and some tense moments before Karadzic finally withdrew the demand," Rosalynn recalled. Karadzic had relented and agreed to Carter's draft. Toasts followed by a feast of trout, lamb chops, potatoes, and sour cabbage sealed the agreement.[46]

While the couples dined, the UN's Tony Banbury reviewed the Carter draft. He learned that the wording would be unacceptable to the Bosnian government. Carter's draft stipulated negotiations "based on the Contact Group Plan," the precise wording requested by the Clinton administration and the Contact Group. Banbury explained that the Bosnian government would demand that Karadzic agree to "accept the Contact Group Plan as the basis for negotiations." Without the word *accept*, Izetbegovic would refuse to sign on. Carter replied that he saw the semantic difference as minimal, but on Banbury's recommendation he attempted to convince Karadzic to add *accept* to their agreement; the psychiatrist stoutly refused. After haggling unsuccessfully, Carter backed off, agreeing to the original language. He would have to persuade Izetbegovic to accept the document as it stood.

After a late lunch, in front of a blazing Yuletide fire, Karadzic entertained the Carters with Serbian folk songs, accompanying himself on a one-stringed *gusla* instrument. Outside, a freezing press corps waited for word on how the afternoon went. Carter was fortunate that they were kept at bay; they would have had a field day ridiculing the cozy scene inside, a Perry Como Christmas special orchestrated by the Butcher of Pale. But public ridicule had never stopped Jimmy Carter; the Karadzic case was no different, as far as he was concerned, exemplifying his core belief in international conflict resolution: Let war crime trials begin once the violence has ended. He put the finishing touches on the agreement and then telephoned the White House to say that Karadzic had agreed to a four-month cease-fire and negotiations based on the Contact Group plan. "The text was acceptable from the Washington standpoint," Barnes recalled. It was 8:00 P.M. by the time the agreement was signed and the requisite press conference held.

"We couldn't wait to get back to Sarajevo and go to bed," Rosalynn Carter recorded. "It was not to be."[47]

Once back at UNPROFOR headquarters in Sarajevo, the Carters learned that the U.S. State Department was "condemning" their mission, according to statements broadcast on CNN International and BBC Radio. While toasts were being exchanged in Pale and Karadzic was strumming, the Bosnian Serbs were shelling Bihac, a UN-designated safe zone in the northwest corner of Bosnia—an inauspicious sign of Serb bona fides. The Bosnian government—through Ejup Ganic, vice president of the Muslim-Croat Federation—was calling the Carter-Karadzic agreement a farce.[48] Carter immediately tried to telephone Karadzic and sent word for Ganic to meet him in Sarajevo. Izetbegovic refused to meet with Carter, claiming he had "other engagements"; Ganic would represent him. Apparently Ganic, a tall, imposing man, had vociferously denounced a statement made on TV by one of Karadzic's associates after the Carters had left Pale. At their UN quarters, they found an angry Ganic; he was rude to Carter, mocking his naïveté. When Ganic learned that *accept* was not in the signed agreement, his fury and abusiveness redoubled. "Jimmy was better than I have ever seen him," Rosalynn recalled. "He didn't give an inch, becoming just as harsh with Ganic as Ganic was with him." Carter was finally able to convince Ganic that the signed cease-fire was the best he could broker. "I'll think about it overnight," Ganic said as he left.

At that very moment a message came in that Karadzic was calling by shortwave radio. Carter went outside to the radio control post, a tiny room now crowded with UN personnel, all wanting to hear the conversation Shouting over the transmitter to be heard, Carter informed Karadzic about the shelling in Bihac and demanded that it be stopped immediately. "Small sacrifice to make in the cause of peace," Karadzic replied, saying he would consult with his field commanders and get back to Carter.

At sunrise the next morning, December 20, Carter met with Izetbegovic and other Muslim officials. As Carter briefed them on the previous day's talks in Pale, a fax arrived from Karadzic; he refused to halt the shelling of Bihac. A crestfallen Carter pleaded with Izetbegovic to sign the agreement Karadzic had signed yesterday. Carter would then return to Pale and try to procure the cease-fire. Following consultations with his entourage, Izetbegovic refused to begin negotiations without the word *accept*. However, he did agree to a cease-fire. The leader inked in a few changes to the document and handed his revision to Carter. The ball was now in Karadzic's court.

The Carters immediately left for Pale. No fanfare greeted their arrival this time. The dozen or so Bosnian Serb leaders present, including General

Mladic, said they felt Carter had betrayed them by making such a big deal out of occasional shelling in the hinterlands of Bihac. Biljana Plavsic, the only woman official present, depicted Carter's concerns over Bihac as unworthy of him, insisting, "Talking of peace in Bihac is below your level . . . yesterday's discussion was something you can or should talk about. But talks of one little region is not in your domain . . . or rather it is below you." Her primitive attempt to manipulate Carter while giving short shrift to any ordinary meaning of "cease-fire" or "safe haven" only inflamed tensions.[49]

The tension having become unbearable, Carter finally called for a time-out. As he handed out Carter Center pocket knives as mementoes, a strange souvenir to hand out in a war zone, Carter suggested they break for lunch, except for himself, Karadzic, and Banbury. What transpired in that meeting is unclear, but Carter emerged two hours later with a new signed agreement. This provided for a nationwide cease-fire, to be implemented within seventy-two hours, and a pledge to resume peace talks under the auspices of the Contact Group. Although he was never able to resolve the *accept* dilemma, Carter had brokered a cease-fire. Additional provisions were agreed upon, including unrestricted movement of UN relief convoys for the delivery of humanitarian services during the cease-fire. Karadzic also handed Carter a five-point "Memorandum of Understanding" that, if implemented, would have radically redrawn the map for Bosnia. It was meant to replace the Contact Group map by a new fifty-fifty territory split.[50] What was so important in the Carter text, starting with the initial version early that first morning in Sarajevo, was the fact that he included several human rights–related provisions, such as access by the Red Cross to prisoners and the return of refugees to their homes, in addition to the airport opening and the resumed freedom of movement of convoys.[51] "It was a time for rejoicing," Rosalynn wrote in her diary, "and we were on our way back to Sarajevo."[52]

Carter's final task was to make sure that Izetbegovic didn't pull an about-face. Carter telephoned him from the Sarajevo airport, and went over the main points of the new agreement. The Bosnian Muslim leader agreed that a nationwide cease-fire would begin on December 23. But he had signed an agreement with a separate text from the one that Karadzic had because of the semantic dispute over *accept*. After two days of shuttle diplomacy, Carter had brought the Muslim-led Bosnian government and the Bosnian Serbs closer to the negotiating table than they had been for six months.[53] In an impromptu press conference Carter flashed a cheery thumbs-up to Rosalynn and the press, answered a few questions, and then departed for Belgrade, the capital of Serbia and the truncated Yugoslavian federation.

∽○∾

ALWAYS A RECKONING
451

The Carters may have been proud about the Bosnian cease-fire, but critics took immediate aim at their mission. They equated Jimmy's white turtleneck to a white flag of surrender, laughed at his mispronunciation of Slavic names and his mangling of ethnic groups (he called the Bosnian Serbs "the Serb-Croats"), his cozying up to a war criminal, and his supposed overstating the importance of the cease-fire he had brokered.[54] It was difficult for many to fathom how Carter, a champion of human rights, could stand to break bread with Karadzic. After all, the critics pointed out, this was the thirtieth cease-fire announced since the war broke out in 1992, and despite the periodic halting of hostilities, none of the deep differences between Muslims and Serbs that led to the war had been resolved. When CNN asked Ganic whether the cease-fire constituted a breakthrough, the vice president of the Muslim-Croat Federation answered, "Unfortunately not ... I still worry, because President Carter signed some papers with Karadzic, and we don't know what is in those papers. So we have to wait and see."[55]

Carter was accustomed to this type of reproof, it was part of his job description. But he was disappointed, even hurt, that the Clinton administration had nothing positive to say about his peacemaking accomplishment. The *New York Times* of December 21 quoted a senior White House official as saying, "I don't think Carter has pulled anything out of his hat. What has he accomplished that hasn't been accomplished in Bosnia ten times before and then disintegrated in a few hours or days? We've been down this path before."[56]

The White House tended to be shortsighted in judging Carter's diplomatic efforts. By focusing on the superficial—the mispronounced names, violating a diplomatic dress code—and by reducing the moral issues to sound bites, the Clinton administration overlooked the helpfulness of Carter's willingness to deal with the world's top candidate for trial for war crimes. The administration was also not likely to bestow public credit on Carter for doing Clinton's dirty work, for fear of once again being attacked as outsourcing foreign policy. But no administration officials wanted to pose for a photo op with Karadzic, spend the week before Christmas in a war zone, or put their lives on the line for a peace initiative with daunting odds of success; Carter didn't mind.

Journalist John Pomfret made a more upbeat assessment of the historical dimensions of Carter's work in a *Washington Post* article: "Carter waded into the Balkan morass and emerged without getting any visible mud on his spanking white turtleneck—or on his reputation as the Houdini of American foreign policy. And what he obtained was significant—a commitment to silence Bosnia's guns by tomorrow and the first negotiation between Serbs and Muslims since a breakdown in talks this summer led to a nasty autumn of intensified warfare."[57]

Not that Carter naysayers were wrong in their policy assessment; the cease-fire was short-lived and marred by sporadic fighting on both sides, and it lapsed without any direct talks between the combatants. But it gave everyone some breathing space. When in late January 1995 the United States reported that Bosnian Serb forces were shelling the Muslim safe haven of Bihac, Carter faxed Serb leader Slobodan Milosevic, via the U.S. embassy in Belgrade, trying to halt the violence. Meanwhile the White House also asked Carter to intervene with Karadzic in an effort to make the wobbly cease-fire stick and relaunch negotiations on the future of Bosnia. Due to the bombing of Bihac, Carter could not claim to have brokered a full-fledged four-month cease-fire.[58]

When the cease-fire expired, in April, Serb forces took several hundred UN peacekeepers hostage and shot down American pilots flying a NATO mission in the region. The resurgence of violence prompted many in Congress to renew their calls for a unilateral end to the UN arms embargo. Carter, concerned about the escalating violence, testified before the Senate Armed Services Committee on June 14, 1995, jointly with General John Galvin, former supreme allied commander in Europe and America's first representative in Bosnia after it declared its independence. The hearing marked Carter's first testimony before a congressional committee and also made him the first former president since Harry Truman to testify on the Hill. "The United Nations is facing an almost impossible dilemma," Carter said, "serving as peace enforcers where there is no peace, . . . With almost no prospect for ending the crisis through military means, it is time to reassess the possibilities for a mediated settlement." Carter refused to grasp the nature of the problem: NATO had to use force to cut the Bosnian Serbs down to size before a settlement could be possible.[59]

Shortly after Carter testified, in July 1995, the so-called Bosnian Muslim safe havens of Srebrenica and Zepa fell. Thousands of Muslim civilians were killed. Washington's promise of protection was shown to be hollow, and NATO's credibility was called into question by the Serbian capture of these towns. Soon after, following a Bosnian Serb attack on Sarajevo, NATO, with Bosnian government support, launched a lightning offensive to recapture Krajina and free Bihac. NATO, in September, after another shelling of a market in Sarajevo, staged two weeks of air strikes against Bosnian Serb military targets. At the height of the NATO bombing, Carter served as a channel from the U.S. government to Karadzic to try to convince him to withdraw heavy artillery from near Sarajevo. Karadzic promised to do so, but then failed to execute his promise. This exertion of NATO military might brought the rivals to the negotiation table. On October 5, a new Bosnian cease-fire was announced.[60]

Relying heavily on special envoy and assistant secretary of state Richard C. Holbrooke, Clinton immediately called for a peace summit to be held at Wright-Patterson Air Force Base in Dayton, Ohio, far from war-ravaged Bosnia. While preparing for the Dayton summit, Holbrooke consulted with Carter on the "psychology of Camp David"—how to mediate between bitter adversaries; how to create a climate of accommodation. "Carter was helpful," Holbrooke recalled. "He told me if the negotiators got too heated to take a break, to give them time to cool off."[61]

Although Holbrooke's Dayton discussions with Carter were largely a courtesy, the former president appreciated the consideration. With Slobodan Milosevic representing the Bosnian Serbs, Alija Izetbegovic the Bosnian government, and Franjo Tudjman the Bosnian Croatians, Holbrooke, as tenacious a mediator as Carter, brokered a peaceful settlement. The Dayton peace agreement had resolved territorial differences and constitutional questions, while forcing the combatants to lay down their arms. Carter believed that one day Dayton, like Camp David, would become diplomatic shorthand for successful conflict resolution. "Holbrooke did a very good job," Carter noted. "It reminded me a lot of what we did at Camp David."[62]

The tenets of the Dayton agreement of November 21 were officially memorialized in the Paris Peace Accord signed December 14 by the presidents of Bosnia, Serbia, and Croatia. That same month Clinton, in the face of staunch opposition, committed American troops to Bosnia as part of a NATO-led multinational force, in an effort to prevent further bloodshed and support the new Dayton peace agreement. Sending in U.S. troops, Clinton told the nation in a televised address, would signal to other countries that America was not shirking its responsibilities as the world's most powerful nation. Twenty thousand U.S. troops joined 40,000 troops from other NATO and Partnership for Peace countries. The U.S. Congress never officially supported the president's decision, but neither did it attempt to block it.[63] Carter was proud of the Clinton administration, and Holbrooke in particular, for stopping the bloodshed in the Balkans. The NATO Implementation Force (IFOR), Carter believed, would do an exceptional job of maintaining the cease-fire, stopping the widespread killing of civilians, and restoring security to Sarajevo, where people could once again walk the streets in safety. And he remained proud of his December 1994 journey to Bosnia to talk peace with undesirables. "I'm sure the cease-fire saved lives," Carter would maintain, and few Bosnian experts would now disagree.[64]

∽○∾

For the balance of Bill Clinton's first term, the president followed consultant Dick Morris's advice and maintained a ten-foot-pole's distance from Carter. It didn't require the wisdom of a Morris to motivate Warren Christopher and Strobe Talbott to steer clear of Carter at all costs. The State Department, apparently as payback for Robert Pastor's role in Haiti and Cuba, let his nomination as ambassador to Panama languish without a fight. Although the Senate Foreign Relations Committee had voted for Pastor's nomination 16–3, Jesse Helms succeeded in preventing the full Senate from voting before the recess. When the November 1994 election brought Helms back as chairman, Christopher thought a "tactical sacrifice" of Pastor's nomination might actually endear him to Helms. When Pastor learned that Helms would not permit a vote on him, and Clinton didn't want to expend any political capital on his behalf, Pastor eventually withdrew his name. *New York Times* columnist Anthony Lewis called Pastor the "only fatality" of the Haiti invasion.[65]

Whatever influence Carter might have had on the Clinton administration had fallen to nonexistent. Throughout the spring of 1995 Carter lobbied on behalf of the Carter Center's William Foege, the man who eradicated smallpox, as director of UNICEF. Carter wrote letters urging both Clinton and Gore to push for Foege's appointment, but nobody in the White House was listening.[66] Publicly the Carter Center tried to paper over the deteriorated relationship, concerned that a public show of friction might hurt fundraising efforts with various Democratic constituencies. Nobody was fooled for a second. The rift had become so serious that when Hillary Clinton visited Atlanta for a fund-raiser with leading Democratic women in Georgia at Mary Macs Tea Room, barely two miles from the Carter Center, Rosalynn was not on the guest list. "It was very hurtful," was all Rosalynn would say.[67]

Clinton's ultimate Carter snub occurred on April 12, 1995, on the fiftieth anniversary of FDR's death, when Carter was to be honored with the FDR Four Freedoms Award in a ceremony at the Little White House in Warm Springs, Georgia. Even though Carter was widely considered America's "consensus best ex-President,"[68] as *Time* magazine put it, his nomination evoked lively debate among the directors of the Franklin and Eleanor Roosevelt Institute (FERI) in New York, which administered the award. Carter's spartan discipline, obsessive attention to detail, and solemn earnestness made him the polar opposite of the breezy, visionary, and freewheeling Roosevelt. Carter was a Democratic hybrid who defied traditional party typology, but in the end, the man from Plains was the choice.[69]

Three days before the ceremony, Clinton decided to attend as a sign that he and Hillary were the authentic heirs of Franklin and Eleanor. Advance teams on both sides made careful arrangements for the two presidential motorcades to arrive at the Little White House at exactly the same time. But Carter's back hairs were raised by Clinton's eleventh-hour decision; as he told the friend accompanying him, "Knowing Clinton, he'll probably still be rude and keep us waiting."[70] Clinton was punctual; but that was the extent of the courtesy he showed to Carter. The presidents greeted one another frostily, then went their separate ways to greet some of the 3,000 guests.

Clinton spoke first, his felicitous half-hour summing up of FDR's achievements delivered without notes. Then it was Carter's turn. He began with a recounting of his reaction, as a twenty-one-year-old cadet at the U.S. Naval Academy, to the news of Franklin Roosevelt's death, his eyes growing misty in reverie. He related how he broke down sobbing, fearful for America's future, now that it was bereft of the only president he had ever known. He spoke of life in rural Georgia during the Great Depression, and of how hard times were for small farmers before the New Deal came to their rescue; and he celebrated the bold civil and human rights achievements of Eleanor Roosevelt, and what he saw as FDR's most lasting achievement—the United Nations.[71]

When the applause died down, Andrew Young, followed by many others, rushed to embrace the ex-president. Clinton, however, stood aloof. At a subsequent meeting with Clinton at the White House, FERI president William vanden Heuvel asked the president why he had cold-shouldered Jimmy Carter in Warm Springs. Clinton, who had been animated until then, suddenly fell mute. The topic was changed.[72]

The Clinton administration's snubbing of Jimmy Carter in 1995 was deliberate. The word came down from the Oval Office: the days of Carter's telediplomacy were over. The reasons were manifold. The State Department felt bruised by Carter's parachuting for peace into North Korea, Haiti, and Bosnia. Carter wasn't a team player; not only did he upstage his president by running to CNN to claim credit for interventions, but at the same time he bad-mouthed the State Department. Grandstanding might have been tolerated had Carter not publicly belittled the administration's policies.

There was also widespread concern that Carter's religious fervor was no longer in check. Carter's first loyalty, he said, was serving Christ, not the State Department, on his global missions. "Jesus went to his death and Paul spent his final years in prison rather than conform to religious and secular laws which they could not accept," Carter would write in *Living Faith* (1996). "We are not required to submit to the domination of authority without assessing whether it was contrary to our faith or beliefs."[73] The 1960s mantra "Question Authority," couched in the words of religiosity, lay at the core of Carter's track-two diplomacy; and it frightened just about every pragmatist at Foggy Bottom and the White House.

A story was making the rounds of the Clinton White House about the time Jimmy met Pope John Paul II in 1979. After the meeting, journalist Richard Burt of the *New York Times* asked Zbigniew Brzezinski his impression of how the exchange went. "My impression," Brzezinski told Burt, "was that the Pope would have made a wonderful politician and Jimmy Carter would have made a wonderful Pope."[74] Carter's intense faith, fortified by daily prayer, allowed him to play fearlessly on the world stage. But that same fearlessness was frightening to the practical run of men and women. Because Carter saw himself as doing's God's will, he in effect made himself the final arbiter of God's will. His belief that he was beyond reproach, as if he were the last Christian in the Colosseum of modernity, made him too unreliable and unpredictable to be an ally to the administration.

The first quarter of Carter's 1995 calendar typified most of his days. In touring six countries and a dozen major American cities, Carter negotiated a cease-fire in the Sudanese civil war; oversaw the final eradication of guinea worm disease in Pakistan; led a fund-raising drive for the Atlanta Project in Crested Butte, Colorado; cut a deal to write a monthly syndicated column in the *New York Times*; promoted Habitat for Humanity in the underdeveloped world; returned to Haiti with Senator Sam Nunn and General Colin Powell to inspect the American troops stationed there; read poems from his best-selling collection, *Always a Reckoning*, on community stages and national television; held conflict resolution meetings with leaders of various other nongovernmental organizations; taught Sunday Bible classes at Maranatha Baptist Church; and worked on his eleventh book, a children's story entitled *The Little Baby Snoogle-Fleejer* (the tale of a sea monster who befriends a crippled boy), illustrated by his daughter, Amy. "Nobody can keep up with Jimmy Carter," media magnate Ted Turner said of his fly-fishing companion. "He does more hard work in a single day than most humans do in a lifetime." Turner does not exaggerate.[75]

Carter was earnest in every sense of the word: attentive, resolute, solemn, and tireless. He enjoyed what most people merely endure: long-winded presentations at technical conferences, being the focal point of all eyes at international meetings, listening on a headset to stilted translations, being badgered to sign autographs by the hundreds at coffee breaks. Carter never dozed off at such meetings, and he seldom left early. Public policy planners, human rights activists, agriculturalists, and health care specialists had grown to respect Carter for his high moral purpose, power of concentration, and meticulous attention to detail. "Sometimes, I even have fun doing my duty," Carter told James Wooten. "Imagine that."[76]

With the demise of Robert Pastor's ambassadorial nomination, the Carter Center was freed up to launch an unprecedented process of confidential consultations with Cuba. Between April and August 1995 Carter held a lengthy telephone conversation with Fidel Castro and consulted with Jorge Mas Canosa, leader of the Cuban American Foundation.[77] Carter invited both Cuban officials and Cuban exiles to convene in Atlanta to begin negotiating how to bring democracy to the island nation. Pastor flew to Cuba for a seven-hour conversation in July 1995, and found that Castro was candid and respectful of Carter but that he was not much interested in dialogue or real change.[78]

Nevertheless, under Carter's prodding, Castro said he was considering dispatching a high-level Cuban delegation to Atlanta in March 1996. At that time, the U.S. Congress was debating the Helms-Burton Bill, which would tighten the thirty-three year U.S. economic embargo against Cuba. Carter scorned the measure for several reasons. It would, he claimed, restrict U.S. officials from talking to the Cuban government until after full democracy had been established and damage U.S. foreign policy in general by penalizing foreign governments, companies, and individuals who did business with Cuba by excluding them and their products from the United States. "It seems to be an absolutely ridiculous piece of legislation, which is very likely to pass the Republican Congress," Carter declared about Helms-Burton on September 19, 1995. "And my hope is that President Clinton will veto this bill."[79]

President Clinton always exploded in rage when he heard Carter was meddling in Cuban policy. To make sure Carter got the message, in August 1994 he appointed Al Gore to keep a watchful eye on Carter. In a heated, decidedly unfriendly exchange, Gore, usually considered the only Carter champion in the administration, admonished Carter to lay off Cuba; he was interfering with America's national security. Because Castro feared falling into a Carter trap, and because Clinton insisted that Carter stay away from Cuba, the negotiations broke off. Carter may have been thwarted for the time being, but he was not about to give up his hope for Cuba.[80] "The most sensitive political issue in our country is Cuba," Carter told two thousand students at Emory University in September 1995. "When we talk to the leaders in Congress who always make an issue of animosity toward Cuba, they tell us privately, 'We hope you will do something about that, but don't tell anybody that I told you that.'" When Clinton did not veto Helms-Burton, Carter viewed it as a politically expedient move to gain Florida's twenty-five electoral votes for his reelection bid in 1996. If Carter's attempt

458 THE UNFINISHED PRESIDENCY

to derail Helms-Burton had failed, at least Fidel Castro knew there was at least one American down in Atlanta perpetually open to talk democracy.[81]

On March 19–28, 1995, the Carters visited Nigeria, Sudan, Kenya, and Ghana. They meant primarily to discuss health issues; but they soon found themselves embroiled in an array of vexing political tangles. The Carters' visit to Sudan was crucial to their goal of eradicating guinea worm. Because the Carter Center had been denied access to the endemic southern region of the country owing to civil war, the disease flourished unchecked there. Cases of guinea worm, imported by Sudanese refugees, had been reported in Kenya and Ethiopia. Carter had come to Khartoum to get head of state Al Bashir to agree to a cease-fire. To accomplish his mission the former president was going to dangle bait: he had brought along CNN reporter Gary Strieker. "This presented an attractive reason for Al Bashir to agree to a cease-fire," Rosalynn wrote in her diary. "We could announce it to the world."[82]

Carter shuttled around Khartoum trying to broker a "two month cease-fire for health reasons." If the Sudanese government and leaders of the Sudanese People's Liberation Front and South Sudan Independence Movement would temporarily lay down arms, Carter would oversee a blitzkrieg effort focusing on guinea worm disease, river blindness, and immunization. "The dove is the usual symbol of peace," Cairo's English-language weekly *al-Ahram* noted. "But in Sudan, it's the worm."[83] Carter was not above a little moral blackmail for the sake of a worthy cause. At a conference with Al Bashir and representatives from other African countries, Carter put the Khartoum government on the spot. "There is no guinea worm in Guinea, and we have decided to name the worm after the country that is the last to finish eradicating the disease," Carter said. "We don't want to have to call it 'Sudan Worm.' "[84]

Carter offered the possibility of reopening a Global 2000 office in Khartoum, as well as in Nairobi, and indicated his willingness to have the cease-fire monitored by humanitarian organizations. "Jimmy told Al Bashir that he would even send our son, who could be in direct contact with us about any violations that occurred or any problems that arose," Rosalynn Carter wrote. "It was at this point, when he mentioned sending Chip, that [the Sudanese government's] attitude changed noticeably."[85] On March 28 the government of Sudan declared a cease-fire before CNN cameras, and forty-five-year-old Chip unexpectedly found himself saying good-bye to his family in Georgia and flying to Khartoum. Carter's willingness to put a family member on the line had moved Al Bashir to give peace a chance, at least temporarily.[86]

A short-lived Sudanese cease-fire was Carter's primary accomplishment on this African tour, but it was his days in Nigeria that attracted the most attention. The West African country, more than three times the size of California, was populated with 100 million people from 250 ethnic groups speaking hundreds of dialects. Former Nigerian president Olusegun Obasanjo, a fifty-eight-year-old Carter friend who had turned the military government over to democratic rule while in office in the 1970s, had been detained on his return from Denmark along with forty others a week earlier for purportedly staging a coup attempt against the current head of state, General Sani Abacha. Obasanjo was considered by African standards a "democrat," although when he was president, thirty-nine people were executed after a failed coup. "We are deeply concerned about General Obasanjo and other political detainees," Carter said. "This is a flagrant violation of their human rights. General Obasanjo serves as a member of the Carter Center International Negotiation Network, and I have the utmost respect for him. We will continue to push for his release."[87]

The fifty-two-year-old General Abacha, an uncompromising figure whose trademark dark sunglasses gave him an air of inscrutability, had seized power in a military coup in November 1993 with a bogus promise to restore democracy. The pledge not only proved empty but masked a ruthless and bloody tyrant. Instead of setting an election date, Abacha began systematically imprisoning, murdering, intimidating, or otherwise silencing one perceived rival after another. If he paused in his ruthless campaign of repression, Abacha risked appearing weak, perhaps inviting his own overthrow. Carter was hoping to convince him to pause. But with Western oil companies anxious to keep Nigeria's petroleum fields gushing, General Abacha was betting that beyond the withdrawal of ambassadors or expulsion from the Commonwealth, few in the West would want to risk further destabilizing Africa's most populous, oil-rich country.[88]

Although Carter was ostensibly in Nigeria to secure a guarantee from Abacha not to delay or levy tariffs on 40 tons of Du Pont Precision Fabrics woven cloth filters needed to eradicate guinea worm, he was also on a human rights mission to free Obasanjo. "I emphasized that the detention of Obasanjo was seriously damaging Nigeria throughout the world," Carter wrote in his diary, "and urged him to permit Obasanjo to return to his farm while allegations of coup plotting charges are being investigated."[89] In talks with Carter, Abacha would only promise to give the proposal to free Obasanjo "serious consideration."

The next day the Carters visited the endemic guinea worm village of Enugu, about fifty miles from Amorie, with Mrs. Maryam Abacha as their guest. When they arrived, the entourage was greeted by throngs of

Nigerians, some perched in trees to get a glimpse of the fifty-three-car motorcade. "We were welcomed royally," Rosalynn wrote in her travel diary. "Children sang and danced for us, waving signs of welcome. One read, 'Guinea worm you better go away. President Carter is coming!' "[90]

In a formal ceremony the chiefs gave Jimmy a parcel of land on which to build a palace, and both Carters were crowned and robed as honorary chiefs. Rosalynn was named "Chief Ozoha I of Ishielu," savior of the community, and Jimmy was named "Chief Ochendo I of Ishielu," the protector or the shield/umbrella of the community. Villagers presented them with walking sticks, horsetail whisks, and leather fans. For the Carters, the most vivid memory of the day was meeting victims of the unsightly disease. "All had worms emerging from their bodies," Rosalynn recorded in her diary. "It is hard just to look at them, sick and suffering so much. And they look at us with their hollow eyes, but also, with a look of expectation that we might be able to help them. I will never forget the eyes of one little boy with two worms coming out between his knuckles. His hand was swollen as though it would burst, and he kept lifting it to me, as though I could make the hurting go away." Touring the guinea-worm-infested villages of Nigeria only fortified Carter's determination to eradicate the scourge.[91]

The Carter Center had already made great progress toward total eradication. Due largely to the efforts of Carter, and his health care associates Donald Hopkins and William Foege, guinea worm cases officially reported worldwide had dropped from nearly 900,000 in 1989 to about 125,000 cases in 1994—an 86 percent decrease in four years. Carter's efforts received a further boost when the U.S. Agency for International Development awarded the Carter Center a $3.5 million grant to support its global effort to eradicate the guinea worm, and the World Health Organization had also set a target date of 1995 for the global elimination. If the global army missed WHO's ambitious target, it was able to celebrate 97 percent eradication by December 1995.[92]

On the guinea worm front, the Carters secured a pledge from Mrs. Abacha to have a water tank installed in Enugu within the month so the people "won't have to drink dirty water and be sick anymore." Meanwhile as a gift to Carter, General Abacha permitted Obasanjo to return to his farm in Otta under house arrest while charges that he plotted a coup were investigated. Foreign Minister Tom Ikimi requested that Carter announce Abacha's temporary clemency for Obasanjo to the worldwide media, and the former president gladly acquiesced.

Carter's use of the house arrest of one person by the murderous Abacha as evidence that Nigeria was making progress on the human rights front, however, finally found him reaping the whirlwind.[93] When the Carters returned from Africa, a public outcry was launched against them by such pro-African democracy groups as the Congressional Black Caucus and Trans-Africa Forum, a research organization headed by Randall Robinson. An increasing number of prominent African Americans, once reluctant to rebuke sub-Saharan countries for abusing their citizens, had begun calling for the same type of pressures—diplomatic isolation and economic sanctions—on the military government of Abacha as had been applied against South Africa. "Nigeria is saddled with a military dictatorship that has looted its treasury and victimized its people," Robinson maintained. While the Carters were in Africa, a group of prominent African Americans, including Bryant Gumbel of the NBC News program *Today*, civil rights activist Jesse Jackson, actor Danny Glover, and retired federal judge A. Leon Higginbotham Jr., called on the Clinton administration to ban the import of Nigerian oil.[94]

In April 1995, at a talk at the University of Georgia, Nigerian novelist Wole Soyinka, a Nobel laureate, denounced Carter for "extremely harmful naïveté" in painting General Abacha as even a gradual reformer. "What Carter did in Nigeria," Soyinka maintained, "was truly reprehensible." On April 24 Soyinka met privately with Carter in Atlanta. "He admitted that he was wrong and we patched things up," Soyinka noted. "But the damage had been done."[95] The Nigerian government, under the auspices of the Patriotic Youth Movement of Nigeria, ran a full-page ad in the *New York Times* denouncing Robinson and the TransAfrica Forum and praising Carter. "We ask you to heed President Jimmy Carter's advice and visit Nigeria," the open letter cajoled. "Study the situation on the ground. Talk to policy-makers and market women. Talk to people with differing shades of opinion. You will see that what you are clamoring for is already underway." Carter found himself embroiled in the middle of a heated moral debate over Nigeria's future.[96]

Carter was indeed terribly misguided in believing that Abacha could be transformed. In November 1995 the Nigerian despot hanged opposition playwright Ken Saro-Wiwa and eight associates, to outrage around the world, as a demonstration of the embattled regime's resolve.[97] If history had clearly placed Carter on the wrong side of human rights in Nigeria, he was at least able to admit the enormity of his error: "I made a mistake with General Abacha."[98]

Carter's contribution to the well-being of millions of Africans is not nearly as well known to the American public as his diplomatic exploits in the world's hot spots. If Nigeria was a fiasco, he could point with pride at solid achievements elsewhere in Africa in 1995. The Carter Center worked to enhance the visibility of their river blindness program. During their five trips to Africa in 1995, wherever the Carters traveled, they worked to get Mectizan distributed into rural endemic areas. Carter had gotten Merck, the U.S. pharmaceutical giant, to donate Mectizan, which cures the disease, so he turned to canvassing for financial backers to support its distribution. By December 1995, due to Jimmy's persistent lobbying, the Carter Center was able to forge a partnership with the World Bank and others to jointly sponsor a twelve-year, $120 million project to fight river blindness in sub-Saharan Africa. Millions of Africans would no longer risk blindness, in large part because of Jimmy Carter's efforts.[99]

On the agricultural front, the Carter Center's most successful program was proving to be Global 2000, founded in 1987 to end hunger by teaching small farmers new means to achieve subsistence. The Carters felt especially exhilarated by teaching farmers new planting techniques, introducing them to new seeds, and helping them solve grain shortage issues. Besides successful pilot programs in Ghana, Tanzania, Zambia, and Sudan, Carter, with Nobel laureate Norman Borlaug at his side, had also brought their Global 2000 initiative to Ethiopia in 1993 as part of the national extension service of the Ministry of Agriculture. Carter may have made headlines over North Korea, Haiti, and Bosnia in 1995, but one of his greatest humanitarian accomplishments that year went relatively unnoticed.

In both 1994 and 1995 Jimmy and Rosalynn journeyed to Ethiopia, an agriculturally-oriented nation of 58 million people, where farms are typically only a few acres. The civil war between Ethiopia and Eritrea they had worked so hard to end was over. On one visit they invited Prime Minister Meles Zenawi to accompany them on an inspection tour of small farms experimenting with the new program. They were met with "gleeful enthusiasm" from farmers who were seeing 300–400 percent increases in their grain yield. "We talked to local farmers who had no idea who we were," Carter wrote. "We were astonished at the dramatic increases in their farms' food production, and we realized how close this poor nation was to achieving a dream—an end to hunger." With Meles's support, less than three years later, in January 1997, Ethiopia, having increased total grain production from 5.4 million tons in 1994 to 11.7 million tons in 1996, was actually helping to feed other nations, shipping maize to Kenya, which had developed a drought emergency.[100]

In October 1995 Carter joined President Julius Nyerere of Tanzania, Archbishop Desmond Tutu of South Africa, and former president of Mali Amadou Toumani Toure to try to solve the crisis of Rwanda, where over 800,000 Tutsis had been murdered, and 1.7 million Rwandan refugees had been driven out to camp in neighboring countries. For most of 1996 Carter worked with UN officials and African leaders to create a stable environment in Rwanda that would encourage the refugees to go home. Almost single-handedly Carter arranged for a Cairo summit of the heads of state of the Great Lakes region and toured villages in Rwanda where the genocide took place, seeing for himself rivers that had been dammed with human bodies and church altars stacked high with human skulls.[101]

By 1997 the Carter Center had initiated humanitarian programs in twelve African countries and opened offices throughout the continent. If almost everybody else had given up on Africa, Carter, with missionary zeal, put his direct action philosophy to work, saving lives and encouraging human rights. In the process he achieved a legendary status on the continent never before achieved by any American. "Not everyone can play in the NBA, win a Nobel Prize, or make millions in the stock market," Carter exhorted his Bible class at Maranatha Baptist Church. "But everyone can be successful according to the standards of God. Each of us can honor God through our life's commitment, in our activities, and through giving and sharing our time and talents with others."[102] No one—not the Clinton administration, not Gingrich Republicans, and not the Congressional Black Caucus—could question the tenacity of his humanitarian commitment to honor God in Africa. The former president made it clear that he would go to the grave trying to help Africa make the difficult leap to hope and prosperity.

TWENTY-THREE

THE PALESTINIAN ELECTION

✑᷒᷒᷒᷒᷒᷒᷒᷒᷒᷒᷒᷒᷒᷒᷒᷒᷒᷒᷒

It was snowing in Jerusalem when Jimmy and Rosalynn Carter arrived on January 18, 1996, in the midst of a fluke winter squall that threatened to depress voter turnout in Palestinians' first-ever democratic election, two days hence. In front of the Helen Keller School, excited children built snowmen while taxis unaccustomed to the slippery conditions skidded toward stoplights. This was Carter's seventh trip to Israel (he first went in 1972, as Georgia governor); this level of interest and the Camp David accords had put his name in the index of every important modern book on Middle East history—sometimes as a peacemaker, other times as a meddler, but always as a player in the Holy Land. Carter had last visited just two months earlier for the funeral of Prime Minister Yitzhak Rabin of Israel, who had been assassinated on November 4, 1995, by Yigal Amir, an extremist Jewish radical, proving that opposition to Palestinian statehood could take as murderous a turn as Egyptian terrorists had toward Anwar al-Sadat's peace efforts.[1]

This time, however, the former president was in Jerusalem for a happier reason: to cochair a forty-person election-monitoring team from the Carter Center and the National Democratic Institute for International Affairs (NDI).[2] Seven hundred candidates had entered their names for the new eighty-eight-seat Parliament Council in this first national election for Palestine, but only two—sixty-five-year-old PLO chief Yasir Arafat and seventy-year-old Samiha Khalil, the female leader of a respected West Bank charity—had registered for the presidency. Over one million Palestinians were registered to vote. No one doubted that Arafat would win in a land-slide.[3] "I genuinely hope there will be strong opposition in the elected coun-cil because this will strengthen Palestinian democracy," Arafat had told the newspaper *al-Ayyam* a few weeks earlier anyway.[4]

Ever since the 1993 Oslo accords, Arafat had insisted that Jimmy and Rosalynn Carter lead a delegation to watch the first Palestinian polls. To pre-pare, representatives from the Carter Center and the NDI had begun work-ing in the West Bank and Gaza Strip in 1994, holding voter-education workshops and galvanizing women to participate in the burgeoning demo-cratic process. The work was not new to them: over the past decade the two organizations together and apart had sponsored international monitoring teams to observe more than fifty elections around the world. Democracy had replaced dictators in such countries as Argentina, Brazil, Chile, the Do-minican Republic, Nicaragua, Panama, Guyana, Paraguay, and the Philip-pines.[5] "On behalf of my delegation, I appreciate the invitations we received to observe these elections," Carter noted upon arrival in Jerusalem. "Be-cause this historic moment was envisaged in the Camp David Agreement, and because it represents a critical milestone for the peace process and for the Palestinian people, I feel honored to be here at this time."[6]

NDI had asked Carter to select ten of the forty American delegates in tribute to his high-profile efforts to make election monitoring an accepted international function. He immediately filled the billets with the Middle East experts he had come to rely on: William Quandt, Harold Saunders, Ken Stein, and of course Mary King, as well as William Chace, the new president of Emory University, and former AFL-CIO head Thomas Donahue. In a move that would inspire the *New Republic* to sneer that the entire Palestine election-monitoring effort had been a "Carter family outing," the former president also appointed Rosalynn, his twenty-eight-year-old daughter Amy, and his oldest grandson, Jason—a twenty-year-old political science major at Duke University.[7] Carter felt he had all the right people, with one glaring ex-ception: Henry Kissinger. In fact, as he scoured the Palestinian polling sta-tions for chicanery, Carter repeatedly expressed regret at the absence of Kissinger, whom he credited with initiating the entire Middle East peace process via his shuttle diplomacy for Nixon in 1973 and '74. But Kissinger was a busy man, and where election commissions usually have at least six months to prepare, the organizers could offer only six weeks' notice.[8]

The afternoon before the election, during lunch with Shimon Peres at the Israeli prime minister's office in Tel Aviv, Carter said, "I'm very proud of this election step and am glad it wasn't postponed." Carter also expressed his concerns about Jewish settlers in Hebron becoming disruptive and about the possibility that too many Israeli police patrolling in East Jerusalem could intimidate Palestinian voters. He added that he was troubled by posters in East Jerusalem purportedly hung by Likud members and proclaiming that Palestinians who voted would have their taxes raised and their travel permits revoked. "Do you object if I quote you disavowing these posters?" Carter asked Peres. "No problem," the prime minister responded. "Nobody will be punished for voting." Much of the rest of their conversation centered on Syria's President Hafez al-Assad and the need to create a new dialogue with him about the Golan Heights. Peres noted that Syria's attitude had been just open enough to keep the talks alive, but progress had been slow; he and Carter agreed that an Israeli-Syrian agreement would be the most straight-forward route to regional harmony. "When the time is right with Assad, an agreement can come quickly," Peres said, adding, "Assad is very good on the past, and very bad on the future." As they parted, Peres asked the ex-president not to go to Hebron for security reasons, and Carter agreed.[9]

Carter then journeyed back to Jerusalem to hear grievances from human rights advocates. As if to prove his credibility, he began by detailing his friendship with the PLO leader, declaring, "I'll be having supper tonight with Chairman Arafat. . . . When nobody would talk to Arafat, I did." Khalil Shaklil, director of the Center for Palestine Research and Studies, pleaded with Carter to procure a statement of human rights from Arafat. Carter said he would, adding on his way out, "I would like Palestine to become an example to the world."[10]

That evening Jimmy and Rosalynn headed to Gaza City to have dinner with Arafat and his American-born wife, Suha. The evening turned into a near-surreal lovefest: as Arafat's pink-jumpsuited baby daughter bounced on Jimmy's knee, the two statesmen reminisced about Carter's days in the White House and about their first meeting in Paris in 1990. To Carter, the Palestinian election was the capstone on his postpresidential efforts to fulfill the promise of the Camp David accords; for his part, Arafat kept repeating how his return to Gaza City would not have been possible without Carter's "persistent efforts toward our cause." The former president presented the PLO chieftain copies of *Always a Reckoning* and *The Little Baby Snoogle-Fleejer*; Arafat recalled sending Rosalynn a traditional Palestinian embroidered jacket one Christmas when she was First Lady. They joked about Mary King's successful clandestine diplomacy over the years. The good humor persisted: in addition to the election Arafat expressed great interest in constructing a major international airport in Gaza City so Palestinians would not have to fly out of Tel Aviv, and inquired whether Carter would ask Peres for a public statement denouncing torture. "Recently somebody died resulting from shaking," he lamented. "We want Peres to restore his commitment to human rights and democracy. He needs to denounce authoritarianism."

More serious talk followed on the difficult task Arafat faced in controlling the Palestinians' limited self-rule and stabilizing Hamas reactionaries. As the evening wound down, the Arafats promised Jimmy and Rosalynn that they would visit them in Plains. "I want to see the land that gave birth to Jimmy Carter," Arafat said. When the Carters returned to the American Colony Hotel, they were still abuzz over the Arafats' gracious hospitality.[11]

Despite an Islamic militant boycott, the first Palestinian general election on January 20 attracted a huge voter turnout: over 80 percent in both the Gaza Strip and most of the West Bank, but a poor showing in East Jerusalem and Hebron—two areas under Israeli control. "This is the first legislative election for Palestinians, and this is a foundation for a Palestinian state," Arafat said after he voted at a high school in Gaza City.[12] Meanwhile his friends the Carters began the day at 7:00 A.M. in Bethlehem, the purported birthplace of Christ, observing the opening of one of 1,697 polling stations. Carter stayed in campaign mode all day until the polls closed at 7:00 P.M., inspecting ballot boxes at the Islamic Scientific College in Abu Dis and observing the vote count at Al-Sarra's theater in Ramallah. He held quick meetings with human rights spokesperson Hanan Ashrawi, whom he invited to an Atlanta Braves baseball game, and with Carol Lidbom, head of a 650-member team of observers from the European Union, Canada, China, and Russia. Flitting from poll to poll, the Carters saw red, white, black, and green Palestinian flags fluttering in central squares throughout the West Bank and Gaza. A festive holiday mood prevailed at the stations, where each voter dropped his two ballots, red for the president and white for the council, in wooden boxes. At a polling place in Jericho, Carter asked that one of the boxes be sent to him so he could place it in his Plains High School museum.[13]

As the election wore on, Carter's primary concern was with a problem he had predicted: too many Israeli police surrounded the polling stations in East Jerusalem, as a dreary Palestinian turnout of only 25 percent there proved. As he entered a main post office in East Jerusalem, Carter had run directly into policemen in full riot gear filming voters with video cameras while others watched from rooftops with binoculars. "There's no doubt they're doing everything they can to intimidate Palestinians," Carter told the press who followed his motorcade all that day.[14] When interrogated, one officer said, "We are not filming everybody, only when we have a problem." Carter shot back, "Well, why are you filming me? Am I a problem? We don't want you to photograph these people; that intimidates voters."[15] The police refused to back off and stop filming, so Carter telephoned Prime Minister Peres, threatening to declare fraud if the East Jerusalem security forces didn't ease up. Peres agreed to order a halt to the videotaping and to keep the polling stations open until 10:00 P.M. to encourage more Palestinians to vote. "Peres couldn't have been more cooperative," Carter noted later. "It was the lower-level officials who were trying to intimidate voters."[16]

In the end Arafat won 88.1 percent of the vote, while his Fatah party took 75 percent of the council seats. Despite its predictability, when the predictable outcome was announced on Sunday evening, wild jubilation erupted throughout the West Bank and Gaza, with guns fired in the air and cars honking until dawn. "I look upon yesterday as one of the historic turning points in the history of Palestine and the Middle East," Carter announced.[17]

Earlier Sunday morning his top priority had been directing his motorcade from Jerusalem to Gaza City for a congratulatory session with Arafat. It was a special, personal moment when Carter extended his hand and legitimately called Arafat "President" instead of "Chairman" for the first time, with the international media there to record the occasion. Arafat, still wearing his military tunic and checkered kaffiyeh on his head, told reporters that the election would not have been possible without the help of his friend Jimmy Carter, the architect of Camp David. In truth, the election was a referendum on Arafat's legitimacy: the PLO icon had passed with flying colors as the Palestinians celebrated what they called an "Intifada of Democracy." "This is a new era," Arafat proclaimed. "This is the foundation of our Palestinian state."[18]

Carter—interviewed by Daniel Zwerdling on National Public Radio shortly after the Palestinian election—apparently agreed, twice referring to Arafat as the "president of Palestine." When Zwerdling questioned his choice of words, Carter replied that "Palestine" was exactly what he meant to say, as in his mind it was now a nation.[19] In fact, from January 20 onward, whenever Carter spoke about the Middle East, he referred to Palestine as a country distinct from Israel. But while these statements afforded a morale boost to the Palestinians, Carter was lampooned in the Jerusalem Post and elsewhere for greatly exaggerating the significance of the election. Far from being the flowering of democracy in the West Bank and the Gaza Strip, critics charged, the election proved the autocratic nature of Arafat's regime—a fact Carter refrained from discussing. The 88.1 percent that elected the PLO leader was the kind of fixed vote dictators usually garnered in mock elections; what's more, Arafat had encouraged an obscure seventy-two-year-old woman to run against him for the Palestinian presidency while suppressing any challenges from opponents with real followings. As for the Palestinian Council elections, voters had a choice between candidates endorsed vigorously by Arafat and those he merely approved. "Carter is hardly unique in his beaming approval of yesterday's exercise," a Jerusalem Post editorial noted. "The 700 international election observers will give the election a stamp of legitimacy. Even the observers who spent some time in the country before the balloting and who witnessed the Palestinian Authority's pre-campaign manipulation and suppression of the media, the arrest, intimidation, and bribery of unwanted candidates and their staff, and the hate-filled campaign rhetoric calling for Israel's destruction will undoubtedly not allow facts to get in the way of the fairy tale the world wants to hear."[20]

The newspaper had a point: by March much of the election euphoria had vanished, and the Israelis' gamble that Arafat would establish internal discipline by taking full charge of security within a de facto Palestinian state had proved a pipe dream. Hamas terrorists had killed fifty-seven civilians in four suicide bombings in Israel in just nine days, leaving angry Israelis screaming "Death to Arabs" in the streets of Tel Aviv, while some Palestinian youths treated the Arab suicide bombers as heroes of the liberation. Although Arafat expressed his sincere condolences and denounced terrorism in general, he lost much of his international credibility when the bombs went off.[21]

A groundswell of rage against the peace process contributed to the May 1996 election of hard-line Likud leader Binyamin Netanyahu as Israel's prime minister, who brought with him a Likud-led government hostile to the very concept of the land-for-peace deal on which the Oslo accords rested. Suddenly Carter's main postpresidential priority—a Palestinian state with membership in the United Nations—was put on hold. Nonetheless, in the coming months he continued to speak of "the Palestinian nation" and to praise "President Arafat" as a visionary.

Carter's close personal relationship with Arafat may have kept him from seeing the duplicitous side of the Palestinian president. In July 1996, for example, Arafat was quoted in the Israeli newspaper *Ma'ariv* as saying that Yihye Ayyasgh, the Hamas bomb maker who had murdered at least sixty Israelis, was a "holy Palestinian"; a few months later, at an Arab rally in Dehaishe, Arafat declared, "We know only one word: *Jihad, Jihad, Jihad!*"[22] In each instance Arafat claimed he had been misquoted. Although it was true that the PLO leader had come a long way since his days as an admitted terrorist, Carter was perhaps misguided to view him as a man of peace: Arafat was, in fact, a shrewd Palestinian nationalist maintaining autocratic control over his people.

Arafat knew how to keep the right promises, however; true to his word, as Anwar al-Sadat had in 1981, he made the pilgrimage to Plains to pay his respects to Jimmy Carter in March 1996. Unfortunately, flight controllers misdirected Arafat's jet to DeKalb-Peachtree Airport in suburban

Atlanta instead: "This doesn't look like Plains to me," Arafat quipped upon landing. Because of the snafu Carter had to wait two hours for the Palestinian leader to take a sixteen-car motorcade to Plains, along the way getting his first glimpse of America's rural South and its Baptist churches, Winn Dixie grocery stores, Waffle Houses, and cotton fields. Arafat's only other U.S. trips had been to New York and Washington, and he relished this peek at the southwest Georgia countryside.[23]

When the motorcade finally arrived, Rosalynn served Arafat and her husband coffee and cookies as the two statesmen sat on a sofa discussing Middle East politics. After that brief conversation the pair drove down Main Street in Plains, past the train depot where sixteen years earlier Carter had spoken to the rain-soaked neighbors who welcomed him back after his loss to Ronald Reagan. They arrived at Plains High School, now the visitor center for the Jimmy Carter National Historic Site, to a crowd of hundreds who gave the Palestinian leader a standing ovation. Carter used the occasion to criticize Prime Minister Netanyahu of Israel, saying the peace process had "moved backward since he was elected" and predicting that Jewish settlements would "create the possibility of violence" in East Jerusalem. Then, in the same words he had used to describe Sadat on his visit to Plains, Carter declared Arafat "a man of great courage and a deep commitment to peace." To his mind, the most pressing task on his unfinished presidential agenda— the creation of a Palestinian homeland as stipulated in the Camp David accords—had been accomplished.[24]

AFTERWORD

TYRANT FOR PEACE

〜◦◦〜

A mericans have always treasured iron-fisted warriors like George S. Patton and Douglas MacArthur as national heroes, but few knew how to respond to a tryant for peace. Jimmy Carter was no Eleanor Roosevelt leading goodwill missions, A. J. Muste holding peace seminars, James Lawson teaching civil disobedience, or Cyrus Eaton talking global harmony: he was more a Richard the Lion-Heart crusading against war. He proved consistently willing to buck conventional wisdom and gamble that even brutal dictators such as North Korea's Kim Il Sung and Bosnia's Serbian leader Radovan Karadzic had consciences and were thus capable of redemption.[1] This tenacious temperament made for a certain quirkiness to Carter's modus operandi, but when it succeeded, the world's diplomats sat up and took notice. There was no question that Carter relished going against the grain in Foggy Bottom; even as president he had complained that the State Department "had not produced a new idea in twenty years." State was hampered, Carter maintained, by a careerist mentality that made foreign service officers overly protective of their own areas of expertise and overly afraid of making mistakes.[2] It also perturbed him that at America's bastion of foreign policy the word "peacekeeping" was usually followed by "forces," that unlike our Canadian "neighbors," Mexicans were referred to as "foreigners," and that the State Department shunned the word "love" in diplomatic speeches.[3]

While not a pacifist in the Quaker or Mennonite sense, as a practicing Christian Carter took the ideas of redemption and reconciliation seriously.

(Twice the American Friends Service Committee, an organization that puts into practice the beliefs of the Religious Society of Friends—Quakers— nominated Carter for the Nobel Peace Prize.) Although he believed that if America's national security was directly threatened, a military response might be justifiable, it could be so only as a last resort—for all practical purposes, the former president had become a true believer in Quaker nonviolence. Thus it was not surprising that Carter disapproved of every U.S. military intervention since he had left the White House, including those in Libya, Grenada, Lebanon, Panama, and the Persian Gulf, not to mention the covert military operations Reagan and Bush had conducted in Central America. Carter's extraordinary letters of December 1990 and January 1991 promoting peace to the UN Security Council and Arab leaders, which some critics saw as tantamount to treason, exemplified just how loose a cannon Carter would let himself look if it meant preventing armed conflict.[4]

After all, to a good Christian, there were things far worse than treason. As Carter wrote in *Living Faith*, "Civil disobedience is in order when human laws are contrary to God's commands to us. Jesus went to his death and Paul spent his final years in prison rather than conform to religious and secular laws which they could not accept."[5] These religious underpinnings informed Carter's approach to his projects, especially the dogged determination to resolve civil wars and border disputes that made his years after the White House so brazenly unique.

Carter's mania for peace could seem just that; what's more, the specter of Neville Chamberlain still raises the question of when the search for peace at any price becomes appeasement. Given Carter's single-mindedness, it was little wonder that the former president gave Clinton's State Department fits by announcing, for example, that he was going to try to resolve complex international conflicts from Sudan to Bosnia-Herzegovina. Washington officialdom saw Carter as a bull in the china shop of diplomacy; fellow Baptists thought he was continuing a time-honored missionary tradition. But Carter paid neither his critics nor his champions much mind, marching to the beat of his unfailing belief in Jesus Christ as his personal savior, with grace notes from Norman Vincent Peale's *Power of Positive Thinking*. "Developments since September 18 have underscored both the strengths and weaknesses of Carter's approach," Daniel Schorr wrote in the *New Leader* after the former president's intervention in Haiti. "His strategy obviously is to identify himself with the person he is seeking to influence, flatter him, say nice things about his country and his wife, and even side with him against Washington to forge a personal relationship."[6] In other words, this righteous—some would say self-righteous—soldier for peace marching to "Onward, Christian Soldiers" would do whatever it took—passing secret messages, flattering wives, hugging dictators, embracing war criminals, pleading with murderers—to save lives, make peace, and feed the poor.

To his admirers Carter had become America's global conscience; to his detractors he was a failed ex-president who gave overachieving a bad name. If one adhered to Dwight D. Eisenhower's dictum never to question a person's motives, only his actions, Carter's postpresidential activities would earn high marks—but when Carter claimed he was only doing his Christian and civic duty, his detractors saw calculated attempts to rehabilitate a mediocre White House record while simultaneously guaranteeing its owner a spot in heaven.

But everybody could agree on one character trait: Carter's unwavering confidence that he could succeed where others had failed, be it at ending a religious dispute in Albania or a tomato pickers' hunger strike in Florida. "We'll never know whether something new and wonderful is possible unless we try," Carter told his Bible class in Plains. "Let's scratch our heads, stretch our minds, be adventurous! Serve God with boldness, and who knows what wonders the Lord may work?"[7] Disease eradication thus became a Carter speciality: he didn't aim merely to raise funds for cancer research but to wipe out ancient plagues. Often he would intervene to help destitute individuals with ailments get proper medical treatment or poor children get vaccinated against disease. A compassionate hubris allowed him to believe that if a Georgia peanut farmer could become president, why shouldn't that same farmer solve a Central American border dispute or end an Ethiopian civil war or get a prison sentence reduced for a teenage murderer? This last example occurred in August 1988 when a stranger Carol Johnson of Lithonia, Georgia—wrote Carter a heartbreaking letter asking him to interface with the judge who had sentenced her fifteen-year-old nephew to prison on first degree murder charges. Without knowledge of the case, Carter wrote the Virginia judge, hoping to get the teenager's prison sentence reduced. "The young man is truly penitent," Carter wrote, "and can have a good life."[8] The judge did not respond favorably. That the world didn't always cooperate and often thwarted his ambitions is what caused Carter the greatest anguish. Yet he soldiered on, engraving his determination in stone in 1997 when the Atlanta Project floundered. Recognizing his missteps, Carter adopted a motto for his center derived from Ecclesiastes 11:4: "The worst thing that you can do is not try."[9]

Since leaving the White House, Carter had grown to respect international bodies such as the United Nations, the World Bank, the Organization of American States, and the Organization of African Unity as the most promising venues for tackling global issues. In fact, Auschwitz survivor and Nobel laureate Elie Wiesel had pushed for Carter's nomination as secretary general of the United Nations—once Boutros Boutros-Ghali stepped down in 1996—"because he has the prestige, commitment, and vision." Carter admitted shortly thereafter that it was "flattering for Elie to promote me in such a way," but concluded he was "too old to take on that burdensome job. If it had been offered me five years ago I would have taken it."[10] Many admirers believed that Carter would have made a sterling successor to such previous UN secretary generals as Trygve Lie of Norway, Dag Hammarskjold of Sweden, and U Thant of Burma. That said, Carter thought that Boutros's successor, Ghana's Kofi Annan, would be an ideal choice to emphasize a new role for the UN beyond its traditional focus on diplomacy, peacekeeping, and social programs. Disarmament and the wars against drugs and terrorism were areas in which Carter believed the UN under Annan's leadership could make a profound difference.[11]

Despite his lack of personal wealth, Carter contributed to a landmark moment in philanthropic history: September 18, 1997, when fifty-nine-year-old media magnate Ted Turner pledged $1 billion to help the United Nations fight disease and hunger, find homes for refugees, and clean up land mines around the globe. A week before Turner decided to funnel $100 million a year for ten years into the UN, he had conferred with Carter in his owner's box at an Atlanta Braves baseball game. The former president assured Turner that the UN was the right recipient for such a generous gift. "We had a long discussion about whether he should help the UN and how," Carter noted. "He didn't want to show off but set an example for other wealthy people to follow." Carter advised Turner to create his own foundation rather than get entangled with the UN's bureaucracy, and Turner continued to consult with Carter regularly about establishing such a foundation. Carter also suggested that the new United Nations Foundation launch an intensified campaign to vaccinate children against such diseases as polio. With the ex-president's encouragement, Turner pointed his pledge at those members of Congress who had voted for America's shameful refusal to pay more than $1 billion in back dues to the UN in an effort to force the organization to streamline its operations.[12]

An old aphorism holds that we grow more conservative with age—but the opposite happened with Jimmy Carter. As the Democratic party edged to the right throughout the 1980s and '90s, Carter shifted decidedly left, in part as a consequence of his experiences trying to complete his unfinished presidential agenda. By the early 1990s his liberal convictions put him philosophically closer to former senator George McGovern than to President Bill Clinton. Again and again Carter lashed out at his own government's insensitivity to the poor at home and abroad. Carter had taken the most liberal and successful policies of his presidency—human rights, peacemaking, and concern for the poor—and made them the vortex of his own political resurrection. "He's a pure Calvinist," former UN ambassador Andrew Young maintained, "the kind of man who's got to wake up every morning with a full schedule. . . . He makes me feel guilty for serving on corporate boards because he's shunned all that." On the domestic front he lobbied for better education, public health, homeless shelters, AIDS research, and environmental policies; he turned against developers and tobacco conglomerates, the "haves" so heedless of the health and welfare of the "have-nots."[13]

Until he intervened in North Korea, Haiti, and Bosnia, the American public had little idea of the magnitude of Jimmy Carter's postpresidential activities. Some of his humanitarian efforts—such as the annual Habitat for Humanity house buildings for the poor, which were aimed at whipping up publicity to goad others into volunteering—got a great deal of press. But scant fanfare attended most of the Carter Center's achievements, no matter how remarkable: who knew that as of 1998 the center had monitored elections in seventeen countries, distributed medications for preventing river blindness to over 11 million people in Africa and Latin America, and nearly eradicated some diseases from the planet? Or that Carter's personal appeals to world leaders had freed thousands of political prisoners, or that the Carter Center's Global 2000 program was feeding the hungry in Ethiopia, Sudan, Ghana, and Zimbabwe?[14]

Africa also provided the conduit for Carter's rapprochement with the Clinton administration. After his reelection, Clinton made direct overtures to patch up his differences with Carter, especially in early 1997 when Madeleine Albright replaced Warren Christopher as secretary of state. Unlike Carter's own former aide, Albright made a concerted effort to keep the ex-president personally and regularly apprised of foreign developments. "I don't think there's any doubt that both the White House and particularly Madeleine Albright have just gone out of their way to share some ideas with us," Carter noted before heaping superlatives on the new secretary. After only a few weeks in office, Albright had consulted with Carter on Sudan and asked him to urge one African leader to stay out of the civil war in Zaire (Congo). "One of the first things Secretary Albright wanted to do was to see how we could enlist as aggressively as possible the considerable talents of former president Carter," explained Timothy E. Wirth, Clinton's undersecretary of state for global affairs, who quit government to head Ted Turner's new United Nations Foundation.[15]

President Clinton extended olive branches to Carter in a number of other ways as well, telling the press he liked Carter's new religious book,

Living Faith, so much he read it twice and that the Carter Center was a marvelous institution, even consulting with the former president before a 1997 tour of Latin America. "If you look at President Carter's achievement, by establishing the Carter Center and having not just a library, but an active, vibrant place where he could promote agricultural development and fight disease and advance democracy and human rights and monitor elections and all of the things he's done, I mean, there's really almost no parallel for it in the history of the country," Clinton noted in February 1997. "He is a great resource that ought to be used to the benefit of the country wherever possible." Although the two Democrats still disagreed on a number of issues and policies—such as whether the United States should sell arms to Latin American countries, which Carter opposed—for the most part the more left-leaning Carter had come not only to respect Clinton's extraordinary skills as a campaigner but to consider him a clearly better president than any of the Republican alternatives.[16]

For all his fund-raising acumen, amassing personal wealth never occurred to Jimmy Carter. His government pension, which stood at $107,300 a year in 1997—along with the six-figure advances he had received from publishers for his ten postpresidential books—provided more than enough for him to live comfortably in his modest home in Plains. He made it a point of honor not to accept consulting fees, which he considered a sham. "Carter deserves great credit for being the first president to decline serving on international corporate boards," consumer activist Ralph Nader said. "As post-president he became a real folk hero."[17] It was true that no ex-president had ever done more charity work or more to champion the disenfranchised than Jimmy Carter. As Andrew Young noted, "Carter is a throwback to the Rooseveltian idealism of believing that the U.S. has to be a moral leader for ideas/values, not just money/power."[18] But he knew how to raise money for the Carter Center. At Hamilton Jordan's recommendation, the Carter Center launched a $150 million endowment initiative in 1997. At a board of directors' meeting shortly thereafter, Houston–San Diego businessman John Moores, who had already pledged $25 million to the center, announced an astonishing additional gift of $50 million to defray operational costs and continue the battle against river blindness.[19]

The greatest strength of the Carter Center as an institution has been the activist American president at its heart—which may also be the center's greatest weakness. Not that planning ahead has been ignored: Carter even penned a humorous poem entitled "A Committee of Scholars Describe the Future without Me" to address the dilemma of deciding the Carter Center's future in the absence of its founder.[20] In a more serious vein, in 1997 the center began a restructuring process based on a strategic plan created by

Jordan and established an executive directorship supported by three division heads responsible for health, conflict resolution, and operations. Jordan's plan also called for the center to assemble a cadre of former ambassadors to head ongoing task forces and form a network of knowledgeable supporters. That there was a plan for the future sent rumors circulating throughout the center that Sam Nunn and Andrew Young were the likeliest candidates to take the helm when the time came.

As Jimmy Carter entered his mid-seventies, he began to show signs of slowing down, preferring to spend time in Plains writing a novel about the Revolutionary War in Georgia rather than commute to Atlanta to operate his center or teach at Emory University. Of course the Carter Center would continue its Global 2000 program and election-monitoring work, but the prospects for undertaking diplomatic initiatives of the magnitude of those in Haiti and North Korea grew even slimmer. The Carter Center had matured as a public policy institution, but when the ex-president wasn't around, the telephone inevitably rang far less frequently. Without the activist former president the Carter Center would become something very different: a more conventional public policy institute run by Emory University.

Carter's good works were not confined to Carter Center programs such as Global 2000, the International Task Force for Disease Eradication, and the Council of Freely Elected Heads of Government; the Jimmy Carter Work Projects for Habitat also continued apace. The genius of Jimmy and Rosalynn's work with Habitat for Humanity lay in their extraordinary ability to inspire others to embrace the theology of the hammer. Yet at times Carter became exasperated with Habitat's constant calls on him to serve as its front man. In the Watts neighborhood of south Los Angeles, for example, a Jimmy Carter Work Project scheduled for June 1995 was almost canceled because some people in the neighborhood feared their real estate values would go down if Habitat built simple, modest homes nearby. Dragged into mediating the silly dispute, an exasperated Carter asked Fuller, "Millard, how long do you expect me to keep doing all this work for Habitat?" Fuller didn't miss a beat before replying, "Until you're eighty-five, and then we'll talk about it." Carter's mood changed instantly. He put his head down and gently laughed, "All right."[21]

Jimmy Carter was equally proud of his White House and postpresidential accomplishments; he considered them completely intertwined. Cynics who claimed Carter's postpresidential flurry of activities was designed to redeem his White House tenure overlooked a crucial factor: he did not believe his presidency needed redemption. This was obvious when for the entire weekend of October 17–19, 1997, Jimmy and Rosalynn played host to 750 of their former campaign workers and administration officials along with current employees of the Carter Center to celebrate the twenty years in the limelight of the Man from Plains. The event highlighted the continuity between Carter's presidency and his extraordinary accomplishments since 1980: as a huge banner hanging behind the stage at downtown Atlanta's Regency Hotel summed up, it was the "Carter-Mondale Reunion and the Carter Center 1977–1997."

"What we're doing at the Carter Center is an extension of what we were doing in the White House," Carter told the assembly, who agreed that the center was carrying out the work of an unfinished presidency, particularly in the area of human rights.[22] Carter told the crowd how, as he traveled the world, people constantly came up to him and said they owed their lives to his human rights policy. It was of course his greatest legacy: all of Carter's public accomplishments, from the Panama Canal Treaties to monitoring the 1989 Panamanian election, from the Camp David accords to his back-channel diplomacy with Yasir Arafat, from the Alaska Lands Act to his campaign for public health, fell under the catchphrase, and Carter agreed, saying, "Peace is a human right, environmental quality is a human right, democracy and freedom are human rights."[23]

That evening it would have been impossible to watch Jimmy and Rosalynn Carter slow-dancing to Ray Charles rhythm and blues standards without thinking of how different they were from Bill and Hillary Rodham Clinton in every respect but southern roots and party affiliation. The difficult relationship between Carter and Clinton had continued to seesaw, in part because of their opposite styles: where Clinton was a political sailor who understood the international seas' unpredictability and that good captains learned to tack with the wind and change direction with the weather, Carter was a nuclear submariner who always powered straight through the currents from Port A to Port B. The threat of this direct approach—as acted out in North Korea, Haiti, and Bosnia—was among the reasons Carter had not been invited to the August 1996 Democratic National Convention in Chicago until just a few weeks before it took place, and then halfheartedly. An embarrassed Carter had declined the eleventh-hour offer; while the Democratic delegates danced the macarena and renominated Clinton, the Carters went fly-fishing in Montana with Ted Turner and Jane Fonda.[24]

As it turned out, the Carter-Mondale reunion ended on an unusual note, if one typical for Jimmy Carter. After most of his former associates had gone home after brunch on Sunday, Carter appeared on CNN's *Late Edition* and levied a direct attack on Bill Clinton's ethics. Siding with the president's foes, Carter opined that accusations of improper fund-raising gave the "not always erroneous" impression that to get help from Washington, "you've got to contribute money and a so-called legal bribe." A livid DNC chairman Dan Fowler loudly objected to Carter's use of the word "bribe." And that wasn't all: Carter became the first leading Democrat to recommend that an independent counsel could "defuse this big issue . . . and get it out of the front pages and get out of these everyday new, minor revelations that are having such a devastating effect on Vice President Gore's reputation and presidential hopes."[25]

The next morning, Monday, October 20, as the last of the participants in the Carter-Mondale reunion flew home, no story about their joyous convocation appeared in USA Today, only one under the bold headline CARTER BACKS INDEPENDENT COUNSEL CALL.[26] To the former president's admirers, it was vintage Carter, speaking with Trumanesque candor. To those still within the realm of Democratic politics, it was an aggressive attack on Clinton that would once again create a fissure in the president's relationship with his Democratic predecessor. Republican James A. Baker III, reading the story while waiting to board a fogged-in plane at San Francisco airport, could only chuckle, imagining the expletives Clinton must have unleashed when he opened his morning newspapers in the Oval Office and read about Carter's independent counsel clarion call.[27]

A few months later Clinton was mired in an ugly sex scandal known as Zippergate—regarding a liaison between himself and a twenty-one-year-old White House intern named Monica Lewinsky. Carter visited the Oval Office in January 1998, a few days after the story broke. The president was deeply concerned as he spoke privately with Carter for ninety minutes about the right-wing conspiracy out to get him. As Carter prepared to leave the Oval Office, Clinton asked the former president to pray for him in his hour of darkness. It was the most intimate moment the two men ever shared.

Throughout 1998 Carter was pained to see the White House in crisis, as President Clinton was forced to admit he had lied to the American people about his relationship with Lewinsky. Occasionally the media drew Carter out about the scandalous affair: on September 22 at an Emory University town-hall meeting he offered his widely publicized opinion that Clinton had "not been truthful in the deposition given in the Paula Jones case or in the interrogation by the grand jury." But for the most part, however, Carter went about administering his Center's various programs: most noteworthy were his journey to Central America to survey the damage caused by Hurricane Mitch; his tour to promote his fourteenth book, The Virtues of Aging, a short polemic about turning one's senior citizen years into a joyous and productive time; and his attendance at ceremonies inaugurating the U.S.S. Jimmy Carter, a nuclear submarine named in his honor. He also drew international accolades for monitoring the December 6 Venezuelan elections amidst widespread rumors of death threats and ballot box tampering. [28]

It was not until Clinton was impeached by the House of Representatives on December 19 that Carter directly entered the political fray. Joining forces with Gerald Ford, the two ex-presidents co-authored an op-ed piece titled "A Time to Heal Our Nation," and submitted it via fax to *The New York Times*. Published in the newspaper's December 21 edition, the former presidents pleaded for a "bipartisan resolution of censure by the Senate." The Carter/Ford censure resolution recommended that President Clinton acknowledge that he "did not tell the truth under oath" in regard to his grand jury testimony and that this acknowledgement could not "be used in any future criminal trial to which he may be subject." They concluded that this censure resolution "will go a long way toward healing our divided nation." Throughout the Christmas season, the Carter/Ford censure resolution was the talk of Washington, D.C.; it died on the vine, however, when President Clinton made it clear he would *never* admit that he lied before the grand jury.[29]

But many Americans, even Republicans, took to praising Carter's public morality and bedrock honesty. An NBC/*Wall Street Journal* poll would rank Carter as having the highest moral character of any president, with 67 percent of those surveyed giving him "very high" marks; Clinton hovered near the bottom with Nixon. Jimmy Carter, the ultimate antipolitician, was still as outspoken and honest as ever, characteristics the American people had grown to respect about their ex-president. Two lines from his favorite poet, Dylan Thomas, perfectly illuminated his postpresidential moralistic disposition and unyielding rectitude: "Do not go gentle into that good night. / Old age should burn and rave at the close of day."[30]

ACKNOWLEDGMENTS

In writing *The Unfinished Presidency*, I incurred numerous debts. My thanks to Jimmy and Rosalynn Carter for allowing me to participate in their lives, sharing their thoughts, stories, and archives, and for tolerating my many probing questions. They are among the most decent and honest people I know. Robert Pastor, Millard Fuller, Hendrik Hertzberg, Terrence Adamson, David Rabhan, Mary King, Norman Borlaug, William Foege, and others allowed me special access to their personal papers. Without these archival records I would have been unable to document many important themes. A special thanks is due to John and Betty Pope of Americus, Georgia, for their gracious southern hospitality while I was researching in Sumter County.

The staff at the Jimmy Carter Presidential Library were always helpful and courteous. Particular thanks go to Director Donald Shewe and John Easterly. Additional assistance was rendered by Robert Bohanan, David Stanhope, Keith Shuler, Jim Herring, Ceri Ecsodi, Bert Nason, Betty Nason, Betty Egwenike, Chuck Stokely, and James Yancey. At the Carter Center the former president's staff, particularly Faye Dill, Nancy Koiningsmark, and Carrie Harmon, were understanding from the start and tolerant of my endless requests for information.

My staff at the Eisenhower Center of the University of New Orleans—especially Assistant Director Annie Wedekind and Project Coordinator Kevin Willey—always managed my myriad administrative duties when the demands of the book called me away. They also helped me transcribe interviews for the Jimmy Carter Oral History Project. At the University of New Orleans, Dean Robert Dupont, researcher Beryl Gauthier, Professor Nick Mueller, and Chancellor Greg O'Brien deserve special mention for their consistent support of my Carter project. Two history students at the University of New Orleans, Melissa Smith and Michael Edwards, proved invaluable during the fact-checking phase of *The Unfinished Presidency*.

William Quigley, a former student of mine from Hofstra University, helped me locate important *New York Times* articles. Elizabeth Kurylo of the *Atlanta Journal & Constitution*, who has logged nearly one hundred stories on Carter's postpresidency, was a source of constant wisdom. Nobody knows more about the Carter Center than Elizabeth. At the Jimmy Carter National Historic Site in Plains/Archery, Superintendent Fred Boyles and his assistant Bonnie Blaford were superb guides and helped me better understand our thirty-ninth president's rise to prominence.

Over the past three years I've written a number of essays on Carter's postpresidency. I would like to thank James Chace and Stephen Schlesinger at *World Policy Journal*; John Kennedy Jr. and Elizabeth Mitchell at *George*; James Hoge and Fareed Zakaria at *Foreign Affairs*; Hendrik Hertzberg at the *New Yorker*; Michael J. Hogan at *Diplomatic History*; Ralph Adamo at *New Orleans Review*; and Charles Maynes at *Foreign Policy* for publishing portions of *The Unfinished Presidency*. They are all friends who work hard to make sense of the modern international condition.

Historians Stephen E. Ambrose and Arthur Schlesinger Jr., both of whom had worked with former presidents and understood the potential pitfalls of my arrangement with President Carter, provided expert guidance and sage counsel on writing contemporary history. They constantly reminded me that it was irrelevant whether or not President Carter embraced *The Unfinished Presidency*. Perhaps out of his deep well of experience, Ambrose told me, "No matter what book you write, Carter won't like it. What is important is that you're being truthful to the reader." I could not have asked for better guiding lights.

Over the years I've collaborated on two books with Townsend Hoopes, who critiqued a number of the foreign policy chapters, and our friendship remains stronger than ever. Ambassador William vanden Heuvel, president of the Franklin and Eleanor Roosevelt Institute, talked with me weekly about Carter; his insights and humor, as well as his deep friendship, were always appreciated. After weeks researching in Atlanta and New Orleans, it was always a tonic to return to New York to listen to friends' tales of Carter over lunch at the Century Club or coffee at the Council on Foreign Relations.

A number of individuals critiqued draft chapters of *The Unfinished Presidency*, including James A. Baker III, Bernard Aronson, Harry Barnes, Robert Pastor, Zbigniew Brzezinski, Sol Linowitz, Stephen Ambrose, Gary Sick, Roy Gutman, Carrie Harmon, Anthony Lake, Don Oberdorfer, Terry Adamson, Robert Gallucci, Millard Fuller, Kenneth Wollack, Mary King, Hamilton Jordan, Peter Bourne, Jack Watson, Jane Smith, Peter Grose, Walter Isaacson, and Hendrik Hertzberg. Their comments were always helpful, and they prevented a number of errors from being enshrined in print. Historian Steve Hochman at the Carter Center did a superb job of fact-checking, raising nary an eyebrow when I found his boss wanting. It goes without saying that any errors or omissions are the author's sole responsibility.

Shelby Sadler, a brilliant essayist, was my editorial guru. Without her efforts, *The Unfinished Presidency* would be a much lesser book. Likewise, my old friend Helaine Randerson helped me realign a number of chapters, offering wise counsel, as always, along the way. Greg Smith, with whom I produce my regular *Weekend Edition* commentary on National Public Radio, taught me a number of writing lessons for which I'm eternally grateful.

My publisher, Viking, is first-rate. My dear friends Cathy Hemming and Barbara Grossman, whom I treasure greatly, offered constant counsel and good advice. Susan Petersen, Viking Penguin's "commander in chief," has demonstrated great faith in me as a historian. Her enthusiasm for this book was a tremendous motivator. A special thanks is due Senior Editor Wendy Wolf, not only for the nuts-and-bolts editing of *The Unfinished Presidency* but for having the gall to ask me to cut the manuscript by a third. It was a painful chore, but one that was necessary and made the book more accessible to a wider range of readers. She was magnificent to work with. Wendy's assistant editor, the exuberant Nelly Bly, did a hundred important tasks to help bring this project from rambling manuscript to tightly edited book. Production Editor Kate Griggs deserves a special mention for her meticulous work with the manuscript and galleys and for her pleasant disposition. Viking's Paul Slovak and Ivan Held did a fantastic job of promoting *The Unfinished Presidency* to booksellers and the media. My agent, Lisa Bankoff of ICM, not only shares a December birthday with me but is one of my most cherished friends. The book would not have been possible without her steadfast counsel.

Life is meaningless without interesting friends, and a number of them deserve special attention for diverting me from work: H. S. Thompson, Deborah Fuller, Oliver Treibeck, Juan and Jennifer Thompson, Gerry Goldstein, Stacey Haddash, Heidi Opheim, Julie Oppenheimer, Ramblin' Jack Elliot, Tommy Cimalore, Terry Henke, Emma House, Andrei Codrescu, Lindy Boggs, Jim Wentzel, Tom Piazza, Coco Griffin, Moira Ambrose, Hugh

Ambrose, Brian Lamb, David Amram, George Tobia, Mark Bilnitzer, Steve Land, Glenda Cooper, Judy Edelhoff, Elizabeth Gilbert, Jimmy Dale Gilmore, Mike Snider, Jeff Nancarvis, Kees van Minnen, Ann Hoopes, Glenda Cooper, Ethelbert Miller, Chris Felver, Joe Lee, Lee Levert, John Allen Gable, Julia Moffet, and Woody Widmer. Jessica Wopat, of my local coffeehouse, allowed me to work there without paying rent, always cheerfully refilling my cup. The folks at the Firedog Saloon in Bay St. Louis, Mississippi, likewise provided me with a late-night haven to write. On a very special note, Amy Hanavan has provided endless moral support and tireless encouragement throughout the three years it took to research and write the book—great thanks is owed her for her rare fellowship. My parents, Edward and Anne Brinkley, though Reagan Republicans, nevertheless rooted for me in writing about Jimmy Carter. My political discussions with them were always fruitful.

Finally, and most importantly, my fiancée, Tammy Cimalore, did more than anyone to make this book a reality. Suffice it to say that I love her dearly.

NOTES

ABBREVIATIONS

JCPL	Jimmy Carter Presidential Library
JCPPP	Jimmy Carter Post-Presidential Papers
JCPP	Jimmy Carter Presidential Papers
NYT	*New York Times*
MBCT	Maranatha Baptist Church Tapes

PREFACE: CITIZEN CARTER

1. Evan Thomas, "Under the Gun," *Newsweek*, October 3, 1994; and Bruce W. Nelan, "Road to Haiti," *Time*, October 3, 1994.

2. Jimmy Carter, interviews: October 29, 1993; December 13, 1993; March 1, 1994; and June 4, 1994.

3. The intrepid traveler theme was fully developed in the 1976 campaign biography by James Wooten, *Dasher: The Roots and Rising of Jimmy Carter* (New York: Summit Books, 1978).

4. Francis Hertzog, interview, December 1993, Long Beach, Calif.

5. William Crowe, interview, January 1994, Washington, D.C.

6. *New Republic*, November 6, 1994.

7. Rush Limbaugh, "If I Were President," *George*, December 1995–January 1996, 208.

8. William Safire, "Jimmy Clinton II," *NYT*, September 22, 1994.

9. Douglas Brinkley, "Jimmy Carter's Modest Quest for Global Peace," *Foreign Affairs* 74, no. 6 (November–December 1995): 90–100.

10. Ibid.

11. Gaddis Smith, *Morality, Reason and Power: American Diplomacy in the*

Carter Years (New York: Hill and Wang, 1986), 8. For useful insider accounts of Carter's presidential foreign policy accomplishments, see Jimmy Carter, *Keeping Faith: Memoirs of a President* (New York: Bantam Books, 1982), particularly good on the Panama Canal Treaties, Camp David accords, and recognition of the People's Republic of China; Zbigniew Brzezinski, *Power and Principle: Memoirs of the National Security Adviser, 1977–1981* (New York: Farrar, Straus & Giroux, 1983); Cyrus Vance, *Hard Choices: Critical Years in America's Foreign Policy* (New York: Simon & Schuster, 1983); Robert Pastor, *Condemned to Repetition: The United States and Nicaragua* (Princeton, N.J.: Princeton University Press, 1987); Stansfield Turner, *Secrecy and Democracy: The CIA in Transition* (Boston: Houghton Mifflin, 1985); Gary Sick, *All Fall Down: America's Tragic Encounter with Iran* (New York: Random House, 1985); William Sullivan, *Mission to Iran* (New York: Morton, 1981); and Rosalynn Carter, *First Lady from Plains* (Boston: Houghton Mifflin, 1984). Also of interest in this regard is Kenneth W. Thompson, ed., *The Carter Presidency: Fourteen Intimate Perspectives of Jimmy Carter* (Lanham, Md.: University Press of America, 1990).

12. Haynes Johnson, *In the Absence of Power: Governing America* (New York: Viking Press, 1980), 280–300; and Henry Kissinger, interview, March 1994, New York.

13. Curtis Wilkie, "Blessed Is the Peacemaker," *Boston Globe Magazine*, April 12, 1990.

14. Richard Norton Smith and Timothy Walch, eds., *Farewell to the Chief: Former Presidents in American Public Life* (Worland, Wyo.: High Plains Publishing, 1990).

15. Joseph P. Lash, *Eleanor: The Years Alone* (New York: W. W. Norton, 1972).

16. Carter, *Keeping Faith*, 575.

17. Godfrey Sperling, "Jimmy Carter Rediscovered," *Christian Science Monitor*, November 14, 1989; "A Diminished

Ron, a Refurbished Jimmy," *Newsweek*, April 2, 1990; Richard Cohen, "The Carter Distinction," *Washington Post*, May 11, 1989; and Stanley W. Cloud, "Hail to the Ex-Chief," *Time*, September 11, 1989. Also see Mark J. Rozell, "Carter Rehabilitated: What Caused the 39th President's Press Transformation," *Presidential Studies Quarterly* 23, no. 2 (spring 1993): 317–30.

18. "1997 Carter Center Election Monitoring Report," Robert Pastor Personal Papers, Atlanta.

19. Jimmy Carter to Douglas Brinkley, February 1, 1995.

20. This was the theme of my Bernath Lecture, delivered at the April 1995 Organization of American Historians Meeting in Chicago and published as Douglas Brinkley, "The Rising Stock of Jimmy Carter," *Diplomatic History* 20, no. 4 (fall 1996): 505–29.

ONE: ELECTION DAY 1980

1. Terence Smith, "Carter Saying Defeat 'Hurt,' Pledges Fullest Cooperation," *NYT*, November 5, 1980; Hedrick Smith, "President Concedes," *NYT*, November 5, 1980; and Jack W. Germond and Jules Witcover, *Blue Smoke and Mirrors: How Reagan Won and Why Jimmy Carter Lost the Election of 1980* (New York: Viking Press, 1981), 310–21.

2. Jody Powell, interview, July 1995, Washington, D.C.

3. Tip O'Neill with William Novak, *Man of the House: The Life and Political Memoirs of Speaker Tip O'Neill* (New York: Random House, 1987), 328–29; and Frank Moore, interview, July 1995, Washington, D.C.

4. Thomas Foley, interview, April 1995, Hempstead, N.Y.

5. Germond and Witcover, *Blue Smoke and Mirrors*; Peter G. Bourne, *Jimmy Carter: A Comprehensive Biography from Plains to Postpresidency* (New York: Scribner's, 1997); and Jody Powell, *The Other Side of the Story* (New York: Morrow, 1993).

6. Stuart Eizenstat, interview, September 1995, Brussels, Belgium.

7. Robert Lipshutz, interview, January 1997, Atlanta.

8. Hamilton Jordan, interview, August 1994, Atlanta.

9. Steven R. Weisman, "Carter, in Texas, Outlines His Priorities in Second Term," *NYT*, November 2, 1980.

10. Germond and Witcover, *Blue Smoke and Mirrors*, 243–306; see also William Leuchtenburg, *In the Shadow of FDR: From Harry Truman to Ronald Reagan* (Ithaca, N.Y.: Cornell University Press, 1989).

11. Powell, interview.

12. Hedrick Smith, "A Turning Point Seen," *NYT*, November 6, 1980; and Paul F. Boller Jr., *Presidential Campaigns* (New York: Oxford University Press, 1996), 362.

13. Jimmy Carter, *Why Not the Best?* (Nashville, Tenn.: Broadman Press, 1975), 9–10; and Jules Witcover, *Marathon: The Pursuit of the Presidency, 1972–1976* (New York: Viking Press, 1977), 106–8.

14. Jimmy Carter, transcript of campaign speech, Town Hall Meeting, September 2, 1980, Truman High School, Independence, Mo., JCPL.

15. Jimmy Carter, interview, October 1995, Plains, Ga.

16. Leuchtenburg, *In the Shadow of FDR*, 199–208.

17. Hamilton Jordan, *Crisis: The Last Year of the Carter Presidency* (New York: G. P. Putnam's Sons, 1982), 369.

18. Rosalynn Carter, interview, October 1995, Plains, Ga.

19. Jimmy Carter to Walter Mondale, May 9, 1985, JCPPP, Box 9, JCPL.

20. Jimmy Carter, White House diary, January 19, 1978.

21. Douglas Brinkley, "Jimmy Carter: The Final Days," *George*, February 1997.

22. O'Neill, *Man of the House*, 297–329.

23. John Brademas, interview, September 1997, New York.

24. Mark Hatfield, interview, April 1997, Washington, D.C.

25. Bethine Church, interview, April 1995, Warm Springs, Ga.

26. Peter Goldman, "Hail the Conquering Hero," *Newsweek*, December 1, 1980, 30–32.

27. Hendrik Hertzberg, "Jimmy Carter, 1977–1981," in Robert A. Wilson, ed., *Character above All* (New York: Simon & Schuster, 1995), 180.

28. Kenneth Kline letters, vertical files, "Biography: Carter Assessment of 1981–1983," JCPL.

29. Jesse Helms to Kenneth Kline, October 28, 1981, vertical files, "Biography," JCPL.

30. Theodore M. Hesburgh to Kenneth Kline, December 10, 1981, vertical files, "Biography," JCPL.

31. David Brinkley to Kenneth Kline, May 6, 1981, vertical files, "Biography," JCPL.

32. Joseph Kraft, "The Post-Imperial Presidency," *NYT Magazine*, November 2, 1980.

33. Jimmy Carter, interview, October 1995.

34. Brinkley, "Jimmy Carter."

35. John F. Stacks, *Watershed: The Campaign for the Presidency, 1980* (New York: Times Books, 1981), 232–45; Jeff Greenfield, *The Real Campaign: How the Media Missed the Story of the 1980 Campaign* (New York: Summit Books, 1982); and Elizabeth Drew, *Portrait of an Election: The 1980 Presidential Campaign* (New York: Simon & Schuster, 1981), 262–68.

36. Burton I. Kaufman, *The Presidency of James Earl Carter* (Lawrence: University Press of Kansas, 1993), 199.

37. Hertzberg, "Jimmy Carter, 1977–1981," 172–201.

38. E. L. Doctorow, *Jack London, Hemingway, and the Constitution* (New York: Random House, 1993), 95.

39. Allen Ginsberg, interview, September 1994, Lowell, Mass.

40. John Kenneth Galbraith, interview, May 1997, Cambridge, Mass.

41. Arthur Schlesinger Jr. to Douglas Brinkley, April 14, 1997; and Arthur

Schlesinger Jr., interview, May 1995, New York.

42. Susan M. Hartmann, "Feminism, Public Policy and the Carter Administration," in Gary M. Fink and Hugh Davis Graham, eds., *The Carter Presidency: Policy Choices in the Post New Deal Era* (Lawrence: University Press of Kansas, 1998).

43. The best accounts of the hostage crisis are James A. Bill, *The Edge and the Lion: The Tragedy of American-Iranian Relations* (New Haven: Yale University Press, 1988); Gary Sick, *All Fall Down: America's Tragic Encounter with Iran* (New York: Random House, 1985); Warren Christopher et al., *American Hostages in Iran: The Conduct of a Crisis* (New Haven: Yale University Press, 1985); and Jordan, *Crisis*.

44. Gerald Rafshoon, interview, July 1995, Washington, D.C.

45. Jordan, *Crisis*, 270–90; Hertzberg, "Jimmy Carter, 1977–1981," 172–201; and David Martin, "Inside the Rescue Mission," *Newsweek*, July 12, 1982. For a good critique of the media's role in the Iranian revolution, see Barry Rubin, *Paved with Good Intentions* (New York: Penguin, 1981), 337–64.

46. Paul Nitze, interview, September 1994, Washington, D.C.

47. Stephen E. Ambrose and Douglas G. Brinkley, *Rise to Globalism: American Foreign Policy since 1938*, 8th ed. (New York: Viking Penguin, 1997), 293–314.

48. "What Jimmy Carter Has Learned," *NYT*, November 2, 1980.

49. Jimmy Carter, interview, October 1995.

50. See various press clippings mentioning this same quip, Carter Center.

51. Lou Cannon, *Reagan* (New York: Putnam, 1982), 272–90; and Drew, *Portrait of an Election*, 262–68.

52. John Updike, *Rabbit Is Rich* (New York: Knopf, 1981).

53. Adam Clymer, "The Campaign's Final Week: Basic Themes Stressed," *NYT*, November 2, 1980.

54. Steven Rattner, "The Economy of

the Ballot," *NYT*, November 2, 1980; Adam Clymer, "Reagan and Carter Stand Nearly Even in the Polls," *NYT*, November 3, 1980; and William E. Leuchtenburg, "Jimmy Carter and the Post–New Deal Presidency," in Fink and Graham, *Carter Presidency*.

55. Russell Baker, "Not to Worry, Jimmy," *NYT*, January 10, 1981.

56. Hertzberg, "Jimmy Carter, 1977–1981," 188–89.

57. Terence Smith, "Experts See '76 Victory as Carter's Big Achievement," *NYT*, January 8, 1981.

58. Ibid.

59. *Time*, October 1982.

60. "Excerpts from President Carter's Conversation with Reporters in Oval Office," *NYT*, November 6, 1980; and Carl M. Brauer, *Presidential Transitions: Eisenhower through Reagan* (New York: Oxford University Press, 1986), 170–255.

61. Frederick C. Mosher, W. David Clinton, and Daniel G. Lang, *Presidential Transitions and Foreign Affairs* (Baton Rouge, La.: Louisiana State University Press, 1987), 223–49; and Carter, *Keeping Faith*, 542–62.

62. Laurence I. Barrett, *Gambling with History: Reagan in the White House* (Garden City, N.Y.: Doubleday, 1983), 25; and "The Candidates' Stands on the Economy, Defense and Other Issues," *NYT*, November 3, 1980.

63. Robert Strong, *Working in the World: Jimmy Carter and the Making of a Foreign Policy* (manuscript draft); and William Stueck, "Placing Jimmy Carter's Foreign Policy," in Fink and Graham, *Carter Presidency*.

64. Douglas Brinkley, "The Rising Stock of Jimmy Carter," *Diplomatic History* 20, no. 4 (fall 1996): 514–15.

65. Hendrik Hertzberg, "The Child Monarch," *New Republic*, September 9, 1991, reprinted in Dorothy Wickenden, *The New Republic Reader: Eighty Years of Opinion and Debate* (New York: Basic Books, 1994), 336–55.

66. Carter, *Keeping Faith*, 577–80.

67. Ibid., 579–80. Also Richard V.

Allen, interview, September 1995, Washington, D.C.

68. Edward Meese, interview, October 1995, Washington, D.C.

69. Richard Darman, interview, April 1997, Hempstead, N.Y.

70. Carter, *Keeping Faith*, 577–89; Barrett, *Gambling with History*, 85–87; and Alexander Haig Jr., *Caveat: Realism, Reagan and Foreign Policy* (New York: Macmillan, 1984), 174–77. Also see Henry Scott Stokes, "Outlook Darkens for South Korean Dissident Leader," *NYT*, November 10, 1980.

71. "Reagan's Son Has a Few Choice Words for Carter," *NYT*, December 15, 1980.

72. Jimmy Carter speech, January 20, 1977, *Public Papers of the Presidents of the United States: Jimmy Carter, 1977* (Washington, D.C.: Government Printing Office, 1978), vol. 1, 2F; and "Mrs. Reagan Said to Drop a Gentle Hint," *NYT*, December 13, 1980.

73. Jimmy Carter speech, December 6, 1978, *Department of State Bulletin* 79 (January 1979).

74. Carter, *Keeping Faith*, 143.

75. Jimmy Carter speech, May 22, 1977, *Department of State Bulletin* 76 (June 1977).

76. Patricia Derian, interview, September 1, 1995, Washington, D.C. For a more detailed and wide-ranging discussion of Carter's presidential human rights record, both pro and con, see Joshua Muravchik, *The Uncertain Crusade: Jimmy Carter and the Dilemmas of Human Rights* (New York: Hamilton Press, 1986); Sandy Vogelgesang, *American Dream, Global Nightmare: The Dilemma of U.S. Human Rights Policy* (New York: W. W. Norton, 1980); Lars Schoultz, *Human Rights and U.S. Policy towards Latin America* (Princeton, N.J.: Princeton University Press, 1981); Kenneth W. Thompson, *Morality and Foreign Policy* (Baton Rouge: Louisiana State University Press, 1980); and Jerel A. Rosati, *The Carter Administration's Quest for Global Community and*

Beliefs and Their Impact on Behavior (Columbia: University of South Carolina Press, 1987).

77. Tony Smith, *America's Mission: The United States and the Worldwide Struggle for Democracy in the Twentieth Century* (Princeton, N.J.: Princeton University Press, 1994), 239–65.

78. Ibid., 260.

79. Jimmy Carter, interview with Viki Quade, "Jimmy Carter Works the World," *Human Rights* (American Bar Association), spring 1990.

80. Gaddis Smith, *Morality, Reason and Power: American Diplomacy in the Carter Years* (New York: Hill and Wang, 1986), 246–47; Richard E. Neustadt and Ernest R. May, *Thinking in Time: The Uses of History for Decisionmakers* (New York: Free Press, 1986), 187–90; and "Schmidt and Mrs. Thatcher See Close Ties to Reagan," *NYT*, November 18, 1980.

81. Jeane Kirkpatrick, "Dictatorships and Double Standards," *Commentary* (November 1979): 34–35; and Smith, *America's Mission*, 264.

82. Jimmy Carter, interview, March 1994, Plains, Ga.

83. Robert M. Gates, *From the Shadows: The Ultimate Insider's Story of Five Presidents and How They Won the Cold War* (New York: Simon & Schuster, 1996), 176–79.

84. Martin Walker, "What's Important to Remember About Jimmy Carter," *Washington Post*, national weekly edition, June 27–July 3, 1994; and Martin Walker, *The Cold War: A History* (New York: Crown, 1994), 244–68.

85. Jimmy Carter to Andrei Sakharov, February 5, 1997, JCPL. Also Robert Strong, manuscript, "Working in the World," chapter 3, "A Tale of Two Letters: Human Rights, Sakharov and Somoza."

86. Gates, *From the Shadows*, 177.

87. Ibid. For Carter's get-tough approach with Poland after losing the 1980 election, see Jimmy Carter, "Text of U.S. Statement on Poland," *NYT*, December 4, 1980; Bernard Gwertzman, "Poland's

Crisis Puzzle for U.S.," *NYT*, October 12, 1980; David Binder, "U.S. Cautioning on Intervention in Polish Crisis," *NYT*, December 3, 1980; Bernard Gwertzman, "Russians Are Ready for Possible Move on Poland, U.S. Says," *NYT*, December 8, 1980; and Bernard Gwertzman, "Leaders in Poland Make Urgent Plea for End to Unrest," *NYT*, December 4, 1980. For an extraordinary inside look at the December 1980 Polish crisis, see Zbigniew Brzezinski, White House diary, October 4 to December 12, 1980, Brzezinski Personal Papers, Washington, D.C.

88. Walker, "What's Important to Remember about Jimmy Carter," *Washington Post*, national weekly edition, June 27–July 3, 1994.

TWO: PASSING THE TORCH

1. Garry Wills, *Lead Time: A Journalist's Education* (Garden City, N.Y.: Doubleday, 1983), 256.

2. Jimmy Carter, *Keeping Faith: Memoirs of a President* (New York: Bantam, 1982), 125–37.

3. Jimmy Carter, interview, April 1995, Atlanta.

4. John C. Barrow, "An Age of Limits: Jimmy Carter and the Quest for a National Energy Policy," in Gary M. Fink and Hugh Davis Graham, eds., *The Carter Presidency: Policy Choices in the Post New Deal Era* (Lawrence: University Press of Kansas, 1997); Charles O. Jones, *The Trusteeship Presidency: Jimmy Carter and the United States Congress* (Baton Rouge: Louisiana State University Press, 1988); and Richard H. K. Victor, *Energy Policy in America since 1945: A Study of Business-Government Relations* (Cambridge: Cambridge University Press, 1984).

5. Carter, *Keeping Faith*, 576–82; Jeffrey K. Stine, "Environmental Policy during the Carter Presidency," in Fink and Graham, *Carter Presidency*; "Carter Signs Law that Establishes Fund for Chemical Waste Cleanup," *NYT*, December 12, 1980; and Roderick Nash, *Wilderness and the American Mind*, 3d ed. (New Haven: Yale University Press, 1982).

6. Seth S. King, "Carter Signs Bill to Protect 104 Million Acres in Alaska," *NYT*, December 3, 1980; and Walter Hickel, interview, May 1994, Anchorage, Alaska.

7. Ibid. Also Jimmy Carter, interview, April 1995, Plains, Ga.

8. Nash, *Wilderness*, 272–315; and "Carter Sends the Senate a Treaty on Protecting Antarctic Wildlife," *NYT*, December 3, 1980.

9. Steven V. Roberts, "Senate Votes to Bar Justice Department Suits," *NYT*, November 18, 1980; George Goodman Jr., "Rush Is On for U.S. Funds in Final Days of Carter Era," *NYT*, December 21, 1980; Martin Tolchin, "Senators Approve Revenue Sharing; Bill Goes to Carter," *NYT*, December 13, 1980; Ben A. Franklin, "Landmark Designates Are Upheld by New Law," *NYT*, December 14, 1980; "Carter Signs Methane Bill," *NYT*, December 15, 1980; Terence Smith, "Carter's Veto: A Last Hurrah," *NYT*, December 6, 1980; and "Northeast Power Law Signed," *NYT*, December 7, 1980.

10. Jimmy Carter, interview, March 1994, Plains, Ga.; and Carter, *Keeping Faith*, 575–76. Carter continued to fight for keeping Alaska pristine throughout his postpresidency. See Jimmy Carter, "A Tundra Industrial Complex? NO!" *Los Angeles Times*, December 1, 1990.

11. Jimmy Carter, statement on the death of President Anwar al-Sadat, October 6, 1981, Plains Ga., JCPPP, Box 1, JCPL.

12. Mohammed Anwar al-Sadat to Nobel Peace Prize Committee members, April 11, 1981, JCPPP, Box 1. Also Ashraf A. Ghorbal to Jimmy Carter, April 14, 1981, JCPPP, Box 1.

13. Carter, interview, March 1994. Also James Wall, "Jimmy Carter: Doing Work That Speaks for Itself," *Christian Century*, May 16–23, 1990.

14. Henry Kissinger, interview, March 1994, New York.

15. Rosalynn Carter, *First Lady from Plains* (Boston: Houghton Mifflin, 1984), 344.

16. Terence Smith, "Carter and Begin

Reflect upon Mideast," *NYT*, November 14, 1980.

17. "Sadat in Note to Carter Stresses Peace Process," *NYT*; and Carter, interview, March 1994.

18. Bernard Gwertzman, "Reagan Tells Egypt and Israel He Backs Camp David Process," *NYT*, December 7, 1980.

19. Juan de Onis, "Senate and House Conferees Approve More Aid for Egypt and Israel," *NYT*, November 21, 1980.

20. "Carter Meets with Cabinet, Probably for Last Time," *NYT*, December 4, 1980; Carter, *Keeping Faith*, 583–84; Carter, interview, March 1994; and Michael Putzel, "Legacy of Jimmy Carter," *Atlanta Journal & Constitution*, July 3, 1983.

21. Douglas Brinkley, "Jimmy Carter: The Final Days," *George*, February 1997.

22. For an interesting psychobiographical interpretation of Carter, see Bruce Mazlish and Edwin Diamond, *Jimmy Carter: An Interpretive Biography* (New York: Simon & Schuster, 1979); and Betty Glad, *Jimmy Carter: In Search of the Great White House* (New York: W. W. Norton, 1980).

23. Carter, *Why Not the Best?* 69–70.

24. Bourne, *Jimmy Carter*, 378–79; Zbigniew Brzezinski, interview, July 1995, Washington, D.C.; Rosalynn Carter, *First Lady from Plains*, 143–352; and Charlotte Curtis, "Mrs. Carter Speaks Out," *NYT*, June 14, 1983.

25. Hamilton Jordan, interview, September 1994, Atlanta.

26. Rosalynn Carter, interview, March 1994, Plains, Ga.

27. "Carter, Reunion Over, Plans a Long Georgia Weekend," *NYT*, January 3, 1981.

28. Jimmy and Rosalynn Carter, *Everything to Gain: Making the Most of the Rest of Your Life* (New York: Ballantine, 1987), 10–11; Charles Kirbo, interview, August 1993, Atlanta.

29. "Carter Says a Farewell at Sunday Bible Class," *NYT*, January 4, 1981.

30. Edward Cowan, "Carter Urges Rises in Military Outlay, Cuts in Other Areas," *NYT*, January 16, 1995.

31. Bernard Weinraub, "White House Staffs Slide by Each Other," *NYT*, January 21, 1981.

32. Stephen Glass, "Peddling Poppy," *New Republic*, June 9, 1997.

33. Curtis Wilkie, "Carter's Memoirs, the Other Version: A Handful of Reporters Get the Private Rundown from the President 10 Days before He Left Office," *Boston Globe*, October 17, 1982.

34. Rosalynn Carter, *First Lady from Plains*, 342–44.

35. Achsah P. Nesmith, Miller Center Interviews, Carter Presidency Project, vol. 3, December 3–4, 1981, JCPL. Also John H. Patton, "Jimmy Carter and Citizenship: The Communication of Humane Values," unpublished paper presented at the Carter Library 10th Anniversary Conference, February 22, 1997.

36. Hendrik Hertzberg, White House diary, March 11, 1977, and June 8, 1980, Hendrik Hertzberg Personal Papers, New York.

37. Carter, interview, March 1994.

38. Christopher Matthews, interview, October 1996, Washington, D.C.

39. Jimmy Carter, Farewell Address to the Nation, January 14, 1981, *Public Papers of the Presidents: Jimmy Carter, 1980–81* (Washington, D.C.: Government Printing Office, 1982), 2889–93. Also "Transcript of President's Farewell Remarks on Major Issues," *NYT*, January 15, 1981; and Terence Smith, "Carter in Farewell Speech, Cites Peril of Arms Buildup," *NYT*, January 15, 1981.

40. Ibid. Also Hendrik Hertzberg, interview, September 1995, New York.

41. William Safire, "Farewell," *NYT Magazine*, February 1, 1981.

42. William E. Leuchtenburg, "Jimmy Carter and the Post–New Deal Presidency," in Fink and Graham, *Carter Presidency*; and Eugene McCarthy, interview, June 1995, Kent, Ohio.

43. Jimmy Carter to Hendrik Hertzberg, January 1981 (signed picture), Hertzberg Personal Papers.

44. Carter, interview, March 1994.

45. Jordan, *Crisis*, 390–406; and Carter, *Keeping Faith*, 581–96.

46. Warren Christopher et al., *American Hostages in Iran: The Conduct of a Crisis* (New Haven, Conn.: Yale University Press, 1985).

47. Ibid.

48. Jordan, *Crisis*, 399.

49. Terence Smith, "Putting the Hostages' Lives First," *NYT Magazine*, May 17, 1981.

50. For Reagan's reaction to the hostages' release, see Ronald Reagan, *An American Life* (New York: Simon & Schuster, 1990), 227; Wilber Edel, *The Reagan Presidency* (New York: Hippocrene Books, 1992), 308–9; Stephen E. Ambrose and Douglas G. Brinkley, *Rise to Globalism: American Foreign Policy since 1938*, 8th ed. (New York: Viking Penguin, 1997): 281–302; and Bernard Gwertzman, " 'Alive, Well and Free'; Captives Taken to Algiers and Then Germany—Final Pact Complex," *NYT*, January 21, 1981.

51. Jordan, *Crisis*, 395–406.

52. "Return to Plains," *NYT*, January 20, 1981; and Terence Smith, "A Weary Carter Returns to Plains," *NYT*, January 21, 1981.

53. Jimmy Carter, *Turning Point: A Candidate, a State, and a Nation Coming of Age* (New York: Times Books, 1992); Robert C. McMath Jr., "Old South, New Politics: Jimmy Carter's First Campaign," *Georgia Historical Quarterly* 77, no. 3 (fall 1993): 547–59; and Tom Baxter, "A 'Turning Point' for Carter," *Atlanta Journal & Constitution*, December 13, 1992.

54. The most interesting book review was James Fallows, "Plains Talks," *Washington Monthly*, November 1992.

55. Jimmy Carter, *Living Faith* (New York: Times Books, 1996), 104.

THREE: EVERYTHING TO GAIN

1. Jimmy and Rosalynn Carter, *Everything to Gain: Making the Most of the Rest of Your Life* (New York: Ballantine Books, 1987), 20–21; and Terence Smith, "A Weary Carter Returns to Plains," *NYT*, January 21, 1981.

2. John Pope, interview, January 1995, Americus, Ga.; Betty Pope, interview, January 1995, Americus, Ga.; and Jimmy Carter, interview, October 1993, Plains, Ga.

3. Betty Pope, interview.

4. Carter, interview, October 1993.

5. Reginald Stuart, "Competitors for Carter Library Site Wait for Cue," *NYT*, February 13, 1981.

6. Harry J. Middleton, "A President and His Library: My Recollections of Working with Lyndon B. Johnson," in Richard Norton Smith and Timothy Walch, eds., *Farewell to the Chief: Former Presidents in American Public Life* (Worland, Wyo.: High Plains Publishing, 1990), 113.

7. "Georgia Board Approves Plan on Carter Presidential Library," *NYT*, July 15, 1982; Robert Lipshutz, interview, April 1995, Atlanta; and "Carter Picks Library Site," *NYT*, July 24, 1981. For the story of how Plains became a National Historic Site, see Howard Pousner, "The Future of Plains," *Atlanta Journal & Constitution*, March 12, 1995.

8. Terence Smith, "A Weary Carter Returns to Plains," *NYT*, January 21, 1981.

9. Terence Smith, "Hometown Plans to Give Carter a 'Festive Welcome,' " *NYT*, January 11, 1981. Also Miller Williams, "Some Words on the Lives and Lines of Jimmy Carter," *New Orleans Review* 20, nos. 1–2 (spring–summer 1994): 9–12.

10. Alexander M. Haig Jr., *Caveat: Realism, Reagan, and Foreign Policy* (New York: Macmillan, 1984), 77.

11. Jordan, *Crisis*, 407.

12. Terence Smith, "Carter Charges Iran Subjected Hostages to 'Acts of Barbarism'; for 52 Haircuts, and Calls Home," *NYT*, January 22, 1981; and "U.S. Says Abuse of Captives Exceeded Fears of Officials," *NYT*, January 23, 1981.

13. Jordan, *Crisis*, 406–19.

14. Bruce Laingen, interview, July 1995, Washington, D.C.

15. Ibid.

16. Barry Rosen, "The Hostage Crisis," in Herbert D. Rosenbaum and Alexej Ugrinsky, eds., *Jimmy Carter: Foreign Policy and Post-Presidential Years* (Westport, Conn.: Greenwood Press, 1994).

17. Smith, "Carter Charges Iran"; "U.S. Says Abuse of Captives Exceeded Fears of Officials," *NYT*, January 23, 1981; and Jordan, *Crisis*, 395–419.

18. Carter, *Keeping Faith*, 518; and Carter, interview, April 1995, Atlanta.

19. Laingen, interview; and Carter, interview, April 1995, Atlanta.

20. Jordan, *Crisis*, 419.

21. Haig, *Caveat*, 78.

22. Bernard Gwertzman, "New Administration Says It Will Honor Accord on Hostages," *NYT*, January 23, 1981; Howell Raines, "Reagan Rejects Revenge on Iran as Unworthy of U.S.," *NYT*, January 29, 1981; and Haig, *Caveat*, 78.

23. William Safire, "History on Its Head," *NYT*, April 9, 1981.

24. Gary Sick, "The October Surprise: Hear the Case," *NYT*, November 19, 1991. For an early refutation from a Carter administration insider, see Lloyd Cutler, "The October Surprise Made Unsurprising," *NYT*, May 15, 1991.

25. Gary Sick, interview, August 1995, New York.

26. Gary Sick, *October Surprise. America's Hostages in Iran and the Election of Ronald Reagan* (New York: Random House, 1991); "Bush Invites Inquiry on Iran Hostage Release," *NYT*, June 16, 1991; and Neil A. Lewis, "A Book Asserts Reagan Solved Hostage Release," *NYT*, November 8, 1991.

27. Carter, interview, April 1995, Atlanta.

28. Richard L. Berke, "Inquiry Is Ordered on 1980 Campaign," *NYT*, August 6, 1991; Bourne, *Jimmy Carter*, 469–73; Neil A. Lewis, "House Inquiry Finds No Evidence of Deal on Hostages in 1980," *NYT*, January 13, 1993; and Gary Sick, "Last Word on the October Surprise," *NYT*, January 24, 1993.

29. Sick, interview.

30. "October Surprise: Not Guilty,"

NYT, January 16, 1993; and Neil A. Lewis, "House Inquiry Finds No Evidence of Deal on Hostages in 1980," *NYT*, January 13, 1993.

31. Jimmy and Rosalynn Carter, *Everything to Gain*, 2; and Don Oldenburg, "For the Carters, Another New Beginning," *Washington Post*, May 23, 1987.

32. Lewis L. Gould, "'Big Bill' and Silent Cal: William Howard Taft and Calvin Coolidge as Former Presidents," in Smith and Walch, *Farewell to the Chief*, 10–20.

33. Phil Wise, interview, February 1995, Atlanta; and Jody Powell, interview, July 1996, Washington, D.C.

34. Jimmy Carter, interview, September 1993, Plains, Ga.

35. Jimmy and Rosalynn Carter, *Everything to Gain*, 13.

36. "Lillian Carter Mends," *NYT*, February 14, 1981; Phil Wise, interview, February 1995, Atlanta; and Steve Hochman, interview, February 1995, Atlanta.

37. Wise, interview.

38. Dan Lee, interview, October 1995, Atlanta; and Robert Lipshutz, interview, April 1995, Atlanta.

39. "President Will Receive a Pension of $69,630," *NYT*, November 6, 1980.

40. Jimmy and Rosalynn Carter, *Everything to Gain*, 9; "Carter and Staff to Use U.S. Building in Atlanta," *NYT*, January 18, 1981.

41. Charles Kirbo, interview, August 1993, Atlanta; "Intervention with Charlie Kirbo," *U.S. News and World Report*, December 20, 1976; and "Charles Kirbo Oral History," January 5, 1983, Carter Presidency Project, Miller Center, University of Virginia, Charlottesville.

42. "Old Warehouse Notes—Old Deeds," Sale of Carter's Warehouse File, JCPP, Box 21, JCPL. Also "It's Dwayne's World," *NYT*, January 16, 1996; and Don Oldenburg, "For the Carters, Another New Beginning," *Washington Post*, May 23, 1987.

43. Jimmy Carter, interview, March 1994, Plains, Ga.

44. Wooten, *Dasher*, 10–40; Bourne,

Jimmy Carter, 9–191; and Douglas Brinkley, "Jimmy Carter: Poet from Plains," *New Orleans Review* 20, nos. 1–2 (spring–summer 1994); Norman Mailer, "The Search for Carter," *NYT Magazine*, September 26, 1972, 19–21; and Richard Hyatt, "Just Plains Folks," *Columbus Ledger-Enquirer*, March 19, 1995.

45. David Brock, "Jimmy Carter's Return," *American Spectator*, December 1994.

46. Edwin McDowell, "Carter Hires Josephson as Literary Agent," *NYT*, January 27, 1981.

47. Edwin McDowell, "Carter Sells Memoirs to Bantam Books," *NYT*, March 14, 1981.

48. Rosalynn Carter, interview, October 1995, Plains, Ga.; Jimmy and Rosalynn Carter, *Everything to Gain*, 28; Elizabeth Mehren, "The Couple that Writes Together . . . Fights Together," *Austin American-Statesman*, May 26, 1987; and Sam Hopkins and Greg McDonald, "Memoirs from Mrs. Carter, Also?" *Atlanta Journal & Constitution*, January 25, 1981.

49. Arthur Link, interview, January 1995, Atlanta; and "Carter Seeks Privacy during Princeton Visit," *NYT*, March 18, 1981.

50. Steven H. Hochman, "With Jimmy Carter in Georgia: A Memoir of His Post-Presidential Years," in Smith and Walch, eds., *Farewell to the Chief*, 128.

51. Douglas Brinkley, "Introduction," in Jimmy Carter, *Why Not the Best?* paperback reissue (Fayetteville: University of Arkansas Press, 1996), xi–xxi; and Jimmy Carter, "From Politics to Poetics," *Washington Post Book World*, July 2, 1995.

52. "Carter Imposes Restrictions on His Staff's Use of Presidential Papers," *NYT*, December 18, 1980; and Edwin McDowell, "Carter, Brzezinski, Writing Books," *NYT*, January 15, 1981.

53. James Reston, "Jimmy Carter at 57," *NYT*, September 30, 1981; also James Reston, "Lost but Not Defeated," *NYT*, November 7, 1980.

54. Jimmy Carter, interview, March 1994. Also June Preston, "Carter Tells of His 6,000-page Diary Detailing Four Years in White House," *Atlanta Journal & Constitution*, December 2, 1984.

55. Hochman, "With Jimmy Carter in Georgia: A Memoir of His Post-Presidential Years," in Smith and Walch, eds., *Farewell to the Chief*, 123–34; Edwin McDowell, "Publishing: The President's Researcher," *NYT*, July 17, 1981; and Steven Hochman, interview, September 1995, Atlanta.

56. Richard Barnett, "An Outsider in Washington," *New Yorker*, January 17, 1983.

57. Robert G. Kaiser, "Wasn't Carter the President Who Said He'd Never Lie to Us?" *Washington Post*, November 7, 1982.

58. Christopher Lehmann-Haupt, "Book of the Times," *NYT*, November 3, 1982; and *Time*, November 1, 1982.

59. Gerald Rafshoon, interview, September 1995, Washington, D.C.

60. Adam Clymer, "Carter Says Reagan Has Failed to Accept His Responsibility," *NYT*, October 1, 1982.

61. Bruce Cook, "Carter Takes His Memoirs on the Road," *USA Today*, October 12, 1982; also Greg McDonald, "Memoirs Given Blockbuster Hope," *Atlanta Journal & Constitution*, October 7, 1982.

62. Bill Lotz, interview, April 1995, Atlanta.

63. David T. Morgan, *The New Crusades, the New Holy Land* (Tuscaloosa: University of Alabama Press, 1996), 1–12.

64. Gayle White, "Reading Up and Out," *Atlanta Journal & Constitution*, June 18, 1995.

65. Hugh Carter, interview, October 1993, Plains, Ga.; and "Church Formed by Split Welcomes Carter Family," *NYT*, January 26, 1981.

66. "Carters Attend Church," *NYT*, January 26, 1981.

67. Richard Hyatt, "Still Keeping the Faith," *Columbus Ledger-Enquirer*, March 19, 1995.

68. Daniel Ariail, interview, January 1995, Plains, Ga.

69. Jimmy Carter, *Living Faith* (New York: Times Books, 1996), 20–38; Carter, *Why Not the Best?* 53–58.

70. Francis Hertzog, interview, December 1993, Long Beach, Calif.

71. Betty Glad, *Jimmy Carter: In Search of the Great White House* (New York: W. W. Norton, 1980), 112–119; and Ruth Carter Stapleton, *The Gift of Inner Healing* (Waco, Tex.: World Books, 1976).

72. For books on Carter's religious beliefs, see David Kucharsky, *The Man from Plains: The Mind and Spirit of Jimmy Carter* (New York: Harper & Row, 1976); Niels C. Nielson, *The Religion of President Carter* (Nashville, Tenn.: Thomas Nelson, 1977); Wesley G. Pippert, *Jimmy Carter: In His Own Words* (New York: Macmillan, 1978); and Howard Norton and Bob Slosser, *The Miracle of Jimmy Carter* (Plainfield, N.J.: Logos International, 1976).

73. William Martin, *A Prophet with Honor: The Billy Graham Story* (New York: William Morrow Company, 1991), 462–64.

74. Ariail, interview.

75. Ibid. Also Dan Ariail and Cheryl Heckler-Feltz, *The Carpenter's Apprentice: The Spiritual Biography of Jimmy Carter* (Grand Rapids, Mich.: Zondervan Publishing House, 1996).

76. Carter, *Living Faith*, 38. A selection of Carter's Sunday school lessons have been published; see Jimmy Carter, *Sources of Strength* (New York: Times Books, 1997).

77. Jimmy Carter, interview, June 1994.

78. Wayne King, "Carter Redux," *NYT Magazine*, December 10, 1989.

FOUR: INTERREGNUM

1. "Carter Plans Low-Key Party Role," *NYT*, December 10, 1981; and Terence Smith, "Carter Foreseeing Only Limited Role in Rebuilding Party," *NYT*, November ber 13, 1980.

2. Mark Rosenberg, "Carter for Congress," *NYT*, March 13, 1981.

3. Laurence I. Barrett, *Gambling with History: Reagan in the White House* (Garden City, N.Y.: Doubleday, 1983), 146.

4. "Georgians Vote for Top State Offices," *NYT*, August 11, 1982; "Jordan Says He Is Now Well and Will Run for U.S. Senate," *NYT*, December 3, 1985.

5. Bernard Weinraub, "Mondale's Tightrope Act on the Carter Problem," *NYT*, October 24, 1983; and Steve M. Gillon, *The Democrats' Dilemma: Walter F. Mondale and the Liberal Legacy* (New York: Columbia University Press, 1992), 333–402.

6. Jimmy Carter, interview, June 1994, Plains, Ga.

7. Ibid.

8. Seth S. King, "U.S. Help to States for Parks May End," *NYT*, February 20, 1981; Steven R. Weisman, "President Proposes 83 Major Program Cuts; Tells U.S. Congress Faces 'Day of Reckoning,'" *NYT*, February 19, 1981; Harold S. Schonberg, "Cultural Leaders Disturbed by Slashes Planned for Arts Agencies," *NYT*, February 20, 1981; Juan de Onis, "U.S. Lifts Carter's Ban on Trade Assistance for Chile," *NYT*, February 21, 1981; Irvin Molotsky, "Ex-Nuclear Chairman Whom Carter Ousted Is Named Acting Head," *NYT*, March 3, 1981; "Senator Hatch Says Labor Panel Will Study CETA Program Grants," *NYT*, March 4, 1981; Richard Halloran, "Reagan to Request $38 Billion Increase in Military Outlays," *NYT*, February 10, 1981; Edward Cowan, "Reagan Delivers His Budget to Congress with a Warning to Remember 'Our Mandate,'" *NYT*, March 11, 1981; "Walt Says He'll Expedite Alaskan Oil-Gas Search," *NYT*, March 13, 1981; "Less Reticent White House Acts on Military Aid," *NYT*, March 29, 1981; Bernard Gwertzman, "President Is Expected to Act Today to End Curb on Grain Sale to Soviet," *NYT*, April 24, 1981; Seth E. King, "Environment

Policy Still Being Planned: Reagan Administration Is Hoping to Spur Private Development of Government Property," *NYT*, May 31, 1981; and Clyde H. Farnsworth, "Phosphate Ban Is Ended," *NYT*, April 25, 1981. For the State Department purging of Carterites, see "Shoving Them Out," *NYT*, March 13, 1981. Also John Dumbrell, *American Foreign Policy: Carter to Clinton* (London: Macmillan, 1997), 53–78.

9. Timothy J. McNulty, "Born Again: Why Jimmy Carter May Be Our Most Successful Ex-President," *Chicago Tribune*, July 8, 1990.

10. Starting in 1993, Maranatha Baptist Church started taping Carter's Sunday school lessons. The church would sell cassettes to tourists and mail order customers. Before each lesson Carter would offer a candid preamble about global affairs. These cassettes offer Carter's most unvarnished assessments of world events and leaders. Reagan does not come off well. The cassettes can be ordered from Ray Rockwell, Tape Coordinator, P.O. Box 165, Plains, GA 31780.

11. Stephen E. Ambrose, *Nixon: Ruin and Recovery, 1973–1990* (New York: Simon & Schuster, 1991), 534.

12. Carter, interview, June 1994.

13. Monica Crowley, *Nixon off the Record* (New York: Random House, 1996), 23. Also see Adam Clymer, "3 Ex-Presidents Tentatively Favor Sunday Voting Plan," *NYT*, May 8, 1981.

14. "Reagan Has Not Asked Him for Any Advice, Carter Says," *NYT*, January 26, 1984.

15. Richard V. Allen, interview, August 1995, Washington, D.C.

16. Ibid.

17. Carter, interview, June 1994.

18. Allen, interview.

19. Joseph B. Treaster, "Carter Warns against Withholding Censure of Human Rights Breaches," *NYT*, May 18, 1981.

20. Howell Raines, "Carter Forsaking a 'Moratorium' Denounces Policies of Successor," *NYT*, July 9, 1981. Also see "Excerpts from Carter Letter to Aides," *NYT*, July 9, 1981; "Mr. Carter's View

about That Other Fellow's Policies," *NYT*, July 12, 1981; and "Timerman Criticizes Reagan on Human Rights Policy," *NYT*, June 15, 1981.

21. Jody Powell, interview, July 1995, Washington, D.C.; and "Mr. Carter's View."

22. Jimmy Carter, welcoming remarks to President Anwar al-Sadat, August 9, 1981, Plains, Ga., JCPPP, Box 16, JCPL. Also Jimmy Carter, notes of meeting with Anwar al-Sadat, August 9, 1981, JCPP, Box 16, JCPL; and "Carter Criticizes Reagan on Middle East," *NYT*, August, 10, 1981.

23. John Pope, interview, January 1995, Americus, Ga.; Steve Hochman, interview, September 1995, Atlanta; and Phil Wise, interview, February 1995, Atlanta.

24. "Marian Uldine 'Deen' Day Smith," *Atlanta Business Chronicle*, July 29–August 4, 1994; Cynthia Mitchell, "Deen Day Smith Believes in Giving Back to Society," *Atlanta Journal & Constitution*, January 13, 1993; "God Gives You Resources . . . Use Them," *Atlanta Journal & Constitution*, February 21, 1991; and Kevin Helliker, "How a Motel Chain Lost Its Moorings," *Wall Street Journal*, May 26, 1992.

25. Tasheen Basheer, interview, April 1995, Atlanta.

26. "Carter Going to China," *NYT*, June 27, 1981.

27. Jimmy Carter, White House diary, January 29, 1979, in Carter, *Keeping Faith*, 202.

28. James P. Sterba, "Carter Finds Chinese Reassured by Reagan on Ties," *NYT*, August 29, 1981.

29. Carter, *Living Faith* (New York: Times Books, 1996), 92–96; and Carter, *Why Not the Best?* 37–51.

30. Jimmy Carter, interview, March 1994, Plains, Ga.

31. Carter, *Keeping Faith*, 48.

32. Ibid., 198–211. See also Leonard Woodcok, interview, February 1995, Washington, D.C.; Smith, *Morality, Reason and Power*, 91–95; and Kaufman, *Presidency of James Earl Carter*, 129–31.

NOTES   497

33. James P. Sterba, "Carter and
Chinese Premier Urge Strong Ties,"
NYT, August 28, 1981; "Carter Warmly
Greeted on Arriving in Peking," *NYT*, Au-
gust 25, 1981; "Carter's Chinese Catch,"
NYT, August 31, 1981; and Sterba,
"Carter Finds Chinese Reassured by Rea-
gan on Ties," *NYT*, August 29, 1981.

34. Carter, interview, March 1994. See
also James P. Sterba, "Carter Leaves
Them Puffing at Great Wall," *NYT*, August 27, 1981.

35. James P. Sterba, "Carter Ending
China Trip, Stresses Taiwan Issue," *NYT*,
September 4, 1981.

36. Powell, interview.

37. Sterba, "Carter Ending China Trip."

38. Henry Scott Stokes, "Carter, in
Japan, Warns of Another Oil Crisis and
Assails Khomeini," *NYT*, September 5,
1981.

39. "Carter Meets Japanese Leader,"
NYT, September 8, 1981.

40. Kenzaburo Oe, interview, April
1995, Atlanta.

41. Bourne, *Jimmy Carter*, 267.

42. George Busbee, comments about
YKK and Tadao Yoshida, March 31,
1995, YKK Archive, Macon, Ga.

43. Jimmy Carter, remarks on death of
Tadao Yoshida, July 29, 1993, YKK
Archive.

44. Ibid. Also Carter, interview, June
1994.

45. Seizaburo Sato, Keninchi Koyama,
and Shunpei Kumon, *Postwar Politician:
The Life of Former Prime Minister
Masayoshi Ohira* (New York: Kodansha
International, 1990).

46. Jimmy Carter, remarks on death of
Yoshida. Also James Brasher III, interview, June 1994, Atlanta.

47. Wolfgang Saxon, "Talk with Haig
Ends Begin's U.S. Visit," *NYT*, September 16, 1981.

48. Carter, interview, June 1994.

49. Anwar al-Sadat, *In Search of Identity: An Autobiography* (New York:
Harper & Row), 1978.

50. Carter, interview, June 1994.

51. Jimmy Carter, statement on death
of Anwar al-Sadat, October 6, 1981,

JCPPP, Box 16, JCPL.

52. Howell Raines, "3 Ex-Presidents in
Delegation to Funeral but Reagan Is
Not," *NYT*, October 8, 1981.

53. Carter, interview, June 1994.

54. Howell Raines, "Sadat's Successor
Invited by Reagan to Visit U.S. in 1982,"
NYT, October 9, 1981.

55. Ambrose, *Nixon: Ruin and Recovery*, 544–45.

56. Gerald Ford, interview, April 1995,
Beaver Creek, Colo.

57. Howell Raines, "Sadat's Successor
Invited by Reagan to Visit U.S. in 1982,"
NYT, October 9, 1981.

58. Carter, interview, June 1994.

59. Raines, "Sadat's Successor Invited."

60. Ford, interview; and Ambrose,
Nixon: Ruin and Recovery, 544–45.

61. Carter, interview, June 1994.

62. William E. Farrell, "3 Ex-Presidents
Call on Mubarak and Mrs. Sadat," *NYT*,
October 10, 1981; and Ann Crittenden,
"Egyptian City Is Quiet after Clashes,"
NYT, October 10, 1981.

63. Jimmy Carter and Gerald Ford,
interview by Steve Bell (ABC), Jim Anderson (UPI), and Haynes Johnson
(*Washington Post*) during return trip
from Cairo, October 10, 1981, JCPPP,
Box 16, JCPL.

64. Carter, interview, June 1994.

65. Gerald Ford, *A Time to Heal: The
Autobiography* (New York: Harper &
Row, 1979), 441. Also "Ford's Advice to
Carter," *NYT*, January 27, 1981.

66. Carter, interview, June 1994.

67. Ford, interview. Also "Excerpts
from an Interview with Ford and Carter
on the Future of Egypt," *NYT*, October 12, 1981.

68. "Carter and Ford Say U.S. and
PLO Will Have to Talk," *NYT*, October 12, 1981.

69. "Reagan Reaffirms U.S. Policy,"
NYT, October 13, 1981.

70. Bernard D. Nossiter, "PLO Observer at UN Praises Carter-Ford Stand,"
NYT, October 13, 1981.

71. "Carter to Lobby Senate on
AWACS," *NYT*, October 13, 1981;
Charles Mohr, "Reagan to Send Con-

gress a Note on Awacs Sale," *NYT*, October 14, 1981; and Phil Gailey, "Carter Is Critical of Reagan Policies," *NYT*, October 14, 1981.

72. Lynn Rosellini, "A Reunion for Carter and Colleagues," *NYT*, October 14, 1981.

73. Carter, interview, June 1994.

74. Anthony Lewis, "One Little Tattler," *NYT*, October 19, 1981.

75. Robert Akerman, "Carter Suit and T.R.," *Atlanta Journal & Constitution*, October 25, 1981.

76. Diana McClellan, "The Ear," *Washington Post*, October 5, 1981.

77. "Washington Post Faces Suit," *Salisbury (N.C.) Post*, October 12, 1981.

78. Phil Gailey, "Carter Intent on Suing *Washington Post* on Rumor," *NYT*, October 15, 1981.

79. "Gossip Item Has Carter in Mood to Sue," *Miami Herald*, October 6, 1981.

80. Thomas Griffith, "Going Eyeball to Eyeball—and Blinking," *Newsweek*, November 2, 1981; and David Halberstam, *The Powers That Be* (New York: Knopf, 1979).

81. Jonathan Friendly, "The Bugging Rumor: Carter Raises a Press Issue," *NYT*, October 16, 1981; *"Post's* Antics Reflect on Press Everywhere," *Columbus (Ga.) Ledger*, October 21, 1981; "Post on Its 'Ear,' " *New Orleans Times-Picayune*, October 18, 1981; and "All the News That Fits," *Charleston (S.C.) News & Courier*, October 27, 1981.

82. *National Review*, October 30, 1981; and Phil Gailey, "Carter Threatens to Sue for Libel," *NYT*, October 9, 1981.

83. Terrence Adamson, interview, September 1995, Washington, D.C.; Lyle Denniston, "The Libel Landmark That Wasn't," *Washington Journalism Review* (January 1982); and CNN transcript, October 9, 1981, CNN Archive, Atlanta.

84. Terrence Adamson to Katharine Graham, October 8, 1981, Terrence Adamson Personal Papers, Washington, D.C.

85. "Rumor about Carter Unbelievable," *NYT*, October 14, 1981.

86. Lloyd Cutler, interview, April 1995, Atlanta.

87. Ben Bradlee, interview, September 1994, Washington, D.C.

88. Meg Greenfield, "FYI," *Washington Post*, October 14, 1981.

89. Cutler, interview.

90. Phil Gailey, "Carter Intent on Suing *Washington Post* on Rumor," *NYT*, October 15, 1981.

91. Mary Madison, "Meg Greenfield Is Bugged about Her *Post* Editorial," *Palo Alto–Redwood City (Calif.) Peninsula Times Tribune*, October 27, 1981.

92. Phil Gailey, "Carter May Drop Plans to Sue Paper for Libel," *NYT*, October 24, 1981.

93. "Bernstein Says, 'Ear' Item Can Hurt Post's Credibility," *Frederick (Md.) News*, October 15, 1981.

94. Agronsky & Company television transcript, October 18, 1981, 6:30 P.M., with guests James Kilpatrick, Hugh Sidey, Carl Rowan, and George Will, Adamson Personal Papers.

95. Ben Bradlee, press statement, October 15, 1981, Adamson Personal Papers.

96. Bradlee, interview.

97. Ibid. Also David Shaw, "Writer Identified Source of Confirmation for the *Post's* Ear Item about Carters," *Washington Post*, November 12, 1981.

98. Paul Taylor, "Post Apologizes to Carter for Gossip Column Item," *Washington Post*, October 23, 1981.

99. Paul Taylor, "Carter Drops Plans for Suit against Post," *Washington Post*, October 25, 1981. Also "Publisher's Letter to Carter," *NYT*, October 24, 1981; Bryce Nelson, "Carter Accepts Apology, Won't Sue *Post* for Libel," *Los Angeles Times*, October 25, 1981; and "Text of Carter Statement on Paper's Apology," *NYT*, October 25, 1981.

100. Terrence Adamson to Meg Greenfield, November 13, 1981, Adamson Personal Papers.

101. Phil Gailey, "Carter Is Critical of Reagan Policies," *NYT*, October 14, 1981.

102. Ibid. Carter also attacked Reagan at a Council on Foreign Relations event in New York; see Bernard D. Nossiter,

"Carter Denounces Policy on Soviet," *NYT*, December 18, 1981.

FIVE: BUILDING FOR PEACE

1. Jimmy and Rosalynn Carter, *Everything to Gain: Making the Most of the Rest of Your Life* (New York: Times Books, 1987), 30–31.
2. Charles Kirbo, interview, August 1993, Atlanta.
3. Warren Christopher, interview, August 1995, Washington, D.C.
4. "The Carter Center, 1982–1988," published by the Carter Center, Carter Center Archives, Atlanta; Elizabeth Kurylo, "Peacemaker Is Redefining the Ex-Presidency," *Atlanta Journal & Constitution*, November 11, 1990; and Jimmy Carter, *Talking Peace: A Vision for the Next Generation* (New York: Dutton, 1993), 21–33.
5. Jimmy Carter, interview, October 1995, Plains, Ga.
6. James Brasher III, interview, September 1994, Atlanta; Carter Center Fund Raising Clipping File, Carter Center Archive, Atlanta; and Dudley Clendinen, "Carter Library Rises Despite Problems with Money and Road," *NYT*, October 10, 1985.
7. Brasher, interview.
8. Hamilton Jordan, interview, September 1994, Atlanta.
9. Brasher, interview.
10. Ibid. Also David Hamburg, interview, May 1994, New York.
11. Carter Center Fund Raising Clipping File, Carter Center Archive, Atlanta.
12. "Jimmy Carter Speaks Out in an Exclusive Interview," *Emory Spoke*, December 7, 1997, 10.
13. Rita Reif, "Auctions: Jimmy Carter and His Chairs," *NYT*, September 20, 1983; Phil Gailey, "To Build a Library, Some Chairs Go Up for Bids," *NYT*, September 23, 1983; Enid Nemy, "Carters Attend Gala Preview of Sotheby Auction," *NYT*, October 5, 1983; and Leslie Bennetts, "Carter Auction Brings $320,000 for New Center," *NYT*, October 8, 1983.

14. Hamilton Jordan, memorandum to Jimmy Carter, February 25, 1982, JCPPP, Box 14, JCPL.
15. Rosalynn Carter, interview, January 1995, Plains, Ga. Also Green Folder, Parkway Info, King & Spalding, JCPPP, Box 25, JCPL; and Lynn Burnett McGill, "Thoughts of Home: The Carter Presidential Living Quarters," *Southern Homes*, July/August 1988, 73–82.
16. William E. Schmidt, "Work Halted on Road to Carter Library in Atlanta," *NYT*, February 23, 1985; "Atlanta Council Urges Halt to Carter Parkway," *NYT*, February 27, 1985.
17. James A. Baker III, interview, September 1995, Houston, Tex.; William Clark, interview, September 1995, Santa Barbara, Calif.; and Andrew Young, "The Presidential Parkway Would Strengthen Neighborhoods in Which It's Built," *Atlanta Journal & Constitution*, February 27, 1988. Also Parkway Papers, JCPPP, Box 25, JCPL; and "Judge Orders Halt to Work on Carter Library Road," *NYT*, September 5, 1985.
18. "Memorandum of Understanding between Emory University and Carter Center," November 15, 1980; "The Emory-Carter Center Future," January 6, 1994; and Terrence Adamson to Charles Kirbo, May 6, 1994, Terrence Adamson Personal Papers, Washington, D.C. Also Robert Lipshutz to Jimmy Carter, January 7, 1994; minutes of Carter Presidential Center Administrative Board meeting, February 19, 1987; and Robert Lipshutz to Jimmy Carter, March 21, 1994, Robert Lipshutz Personal Papers, Atlanta; and Robert Lipshutz to Douglas Brinkley, April 10, 1995. For Carter's relationship with his presidential library, see Jimmy Carter to Gerald P. Carmen, July 20, 1983, Lipshutz Personal Papers.
19. Jimmy Carter, interview, April 1995, Atlanta.
20. Jimmy and Rosalynn Carter, *Everything to Gain*, 30.
21. Andy Zipser, "Down on His Luck," *Barron's*, June 1995; and Tyler Bridges,

"Rover City Stakes Are High for Hemmeter," *New Orleans Times-Picayune*, March 29, 1995.

22. Jimmy and Rosalynn Carter, *Everything to Gain*, 30–31; Christopher Hemmeter, interview, June 1995, Denver, Colo.; and Jimmy Carter, interview, April 1995, Atlanta.

23. Hemmeter, interview.

24. Edward Fox, "Monument to the Man from Plains," *Travel and Leisure*, February 1988.

25. Ibid. Also "Library Offers Unique View of History," *Carter Center News*, spring 1990, 16.

26. Jerry Schwartz, "Peacemaker without Portfolio: Jimmy Carter Goes Where Presidents Fear to Tread," *Atlanta Magazine*, December 1989.

27. Hemmeter, interview.

28. Stephanie Anderson Forest, "Big Trouble in the Big Easy," *Business Week*, October 16, 1995; and Mike Hughlett, "Hemmeter's Financial Hole Grows Deeper," *New Orleans Times-Picayune*, September 3, 1995.

29. Jimmy Carter, interview, October 1993, Plains, Ga.

30. Lillian Carter and Gloria Carter Spann, *Away from Home: Letters to My Family* (New York: Simon & Schuster, 1977), 9–16.

31. Ibid.

32. John Pennington, "Grandmother with a Mission," *Atlanta Journal & Constitution*, January 19, 1969.

33. Lillian Carter to Gloria Carter Spann, October 30, 1967, in Carter and Spann, *Away from Home*, 108.

34. Quoted in "Lillian Carter," *Current Biographer* 39, no. 1 (January 1978).

35. Lillian Carter to Gloria Carter Spann, August 15, 1968 in Carter and Spann, *Away from Home*, 153.

36. "The President's Mother Goes to Africa," *Ebony*, October 1978; and Henry Mitchell, "To Far Away Places," *Washington Post*, September 29, 1976.

37. Beth Dawkins Bassett, "Once upon a Time in Newton County," *Emory Magazine* 63, no. 1 (March 1987).

38. "Jimmy Carter to Teach at Emory," *NYT*, April 22, 1982; and James T. Laney, interview, February 1994, Atlanta.

39. Laney, interview.

40. Hamilton Jordan, memorandum to Jimmy Carter, February 25, 1982, JCPPP, Box 14, JCPL.

41. Andrew W. M. Bierle, "Vision of James T. Laney," *Emory Magazine*, winter 1994.

42. *Emory Wheel* newspaper clippings, Jimmy Carter File, Emory University, Atlanta.

43. Rob Townes, interview, April 1995, Atlanta.

44. Laney, interview.

45. Jimmy Carter, interview, June 1994.

46. Laney, interview.

47. Laney, interview, June 1994, Atlanta; and Zbigniew Brzezinski, interview, August 1995, Washington, D.C.

48. Jimmy Carter, interview, October 1993, Plains, Ga.

49. "Carter Visits Plains Station," *Paper* (University of Georgia College of Agricultural Experiment Stations), November 1976; and Early Jimmy Carter Files, Southwest Georgia Branch Experiment Station, Plains, Ga.

50. Jimmy Carter, *Why Not the Best?* (Nashville: Broadman Press, 1975), 59–70.

51. Ibid.

52. "Carter Visits Plains Station," *Paper*, November 1976.

53. "Carter Praises Peanut Research," *Paper*, November 1976.

54. Ibid. See also Fred B. Saunders, Robert B. Moss, and W. Jerome Ethredge, "Costs and Returns for Selected Enterprises at the Southwest Georgia Branch Experiment Station" (written from 1966–1968), Southwest Georgia Branch Experiment Station, Plains, Ga.

55. "Jimmy Carter Interview," *Atlanta Journal & Constitution*, April 7, 1982.

56. "Sapelo Island Acknowledgments," JCPPP, Box 13; JCPL.

57. Kenneth Stein, interview, June 1995, Atlanta.

58. Ibid.

59. Sol Linowitz, interview, September 1995, Washington, D.C.; Laney, interview; and Zbigniew Brzezinski, interview, June 1994, Washington, D.C.

60. William D. Davidson and Joseph V. Montville, "Foreign Policy According to Freud," *Foreign Policy*, no. 45 (winter 1981–82): 145–55.

61. Laney, interview. Also Wayne King, "Carter Redux," *NYT Magazine*, December 10, 1989.

62. Dean Rusk, interview, January 1990, Athens, Ga.

63. *Atlanta Magazine* is quoted in "The Carter Center, 1982–1988," published by the Carter Center, Carter Center Archives, Atlanta.

64. Laney, interview.

65. Linowitz, interview.

66. Stein, interview.

67. For Vance's view of the Iranian hostage crisis, see Cyrus Vance, *Hard choices* (New York: Simon & Schuster, 1983).

68. Jimmy Carter, interview, October 1993, Plains, Ga.

69. George Ball, interview, September 1995, Princeton, N.J.

70. Lawrence X. Clifford, "An Examination of the Carter Administration's Selecting of Secretary of State and National Security Adviser," in Herbert D. Rosenbaum and Alexej Ugrinsky, *Jimmy Carter: Foreign Policy and Postpresidential Years* (Westport, Conn.: Greenwood Press, 1994), 5–17.

71. Richard Burt, "Brzezinski Calls Democrats Soft toward Moscow," *NYT*, November 30, 1980.

72. Zbigniew Brzezinski, *Power and Principle: Memoirs of the National Security Adviser, 1977–1981* (New York: Farrar, Straus & Giroux, 1983).

73. James Reston, interview, May 1992, Washington, D.C.

74. Jimmy Carter, interview, April 1995, Atlanta.

75. Stein, interview. Also see Bernard Gwertzman, "Vance and Brzezinski Feuding Chapter by Chapter," *NYT*, May 26,

1983; and Bernard Gwertzman, "Vance Looking Back Lauds Pact on Arms and Retorts to Brzezinski," *NYT*, December 3, 1980.

76. Carter, interview, April 1995, Atlanta.

77. Ellen Mickiewicz, interview, October 1995, Durham, N.C. Also profile in "The Carter Center, 1982–1988," Carter Center Archives, Atlanta.

78. John Pope, interview, October 1993, Americus, Ga.

79. Enid Nemy, "A Small Blue Ridge Pine Cabin Is the Carters' Rustic Treat," *NYT*, July 14, 1983.

80. Jimmy Carter, *An Outdoor Journal: Adventures and Reflections* (New York: Bantam Books, 1988). Also Nelson Bryant, "Outdoors: No Dilettante Angler," *NYT*, September 24, 1984; Mark Haley, "Carter Writes of Fishing in Spruce Creek," *Altoona Mirror*, August 14, 1988; and Charles Mohr, "On Fly Fishing: By Jimmy Carter," *NYT*, January 7, 1982.

81. Carter, interview, April 1985, Atlanta.

82. Ted Turner, interview, June 1995, Atlanta.

83. Quoted in Steve Eng, review of *Citizen Turner: The Wild Rise of an American Tycoon*, by Robert Goldberg and Gerald Jay Goldberg, *Creative Loafing*, July 1995.

84. Goldberg and Goldberg, *Citizen Turner*, 1–321; and Porter Bibb, *It Ain't as Easy as It Looks: Ted Turner's Amazing Story* (New York: Crown Publishers, 1993), 182–83.

85. Turner, interview.

86. Goldberg and Goldberg, *Citizen Turner*, 191; and Turner, interview.

87. Jimmy Carter to Ted Turner, February 17, 1987, JCPPP, Box 13, JCPL.

88. Jimmy Carter, interview, April 1995, Plains, Ga.

89. Goldberg and Goldberg, *Citizen Turner*, 324–29.

90. Turner, interview.

91. Ibid.

92. Warren P. Strobel, *Late-Breaking Foreign Policy. The News Media's Influ-*

ence on Peace Operations (Washington, D.C.: United States Institute for Peace Press, 1997), 85, 111, 179, 188. Also Judy Woodruff, interview, December 1997.

SIX: SEARCHING FOR MIDDLE EAST PEACE

1. Jimmy Carter, *Keeping Faith: Memoirs of a President* (New York: Bantam Books, 1982), 267–429; and Jimmy Carter, *The Blood of Abraham: Insights into the Middle East* (Boston: Houghton Mifflin, 1993), 1–20. Also Aaron S. Klieman, *Foundation of British Policy in the Arab World: The Cairo Conference of 1921* (Baltimore: Johns Hopkins University Press, 1970).

2. Kenneth Stein, interview, July 1995, Atlanta.

3. For an insider's account of Camp David, see William B. Quandt, *Camp David: Peacemaking and Politics* (Washington, D.C.: Brookings Institute, 1986).

4. Ilan Pappé, *The Making of the Arab-Israeli Conflict, 1947–51* (London: I. B. Tauris, 1994); and Benny Morris, *The Birth of the Palestinian Refugee Problem, 1947–1949* (Cambridge, England: Cambridge University Press, 1987).

5. Avi Shlaim, *War and Peace in the Middle East* (New York: Penguin Books, 1994), 51.

6. Ronald Reagan, "A New Opportunity for Peace in the Middle East," *Current Policy* (U.S. State Department, Bureau of Public Affairs), no. 417 (September 1, 1982). Also Steven L. Spiegel, *The Other Arab Israeli Conflict: Making America's Middle East Policy, from Truman to Reagan* (Chicago: University of Chicago Press, 1985), 418–29.

7. David K. Shipler, "Israel Rejects Reagan Plan for Palestinians' Self Rule, Terms It 'A Serious Danger,' " *NYT*, September 3, 1982.

8. "Carter Rebuts Israelis on Reagan Proposals," *NYT*, September 3, 1982.

9. Carter, *Blood of Abraham*, 1.

10. Morris, *Palestine Refugee Problem*, 297–98.

11. Stein, interview, July 1995.

12. Carter, *Blood of Abraham*, 5.

13. Jimmy Carter, interview, January 1996, Jerusalem.

14. William Quandt, "Prospects for Peace in the Middle East," memorandum, January 1, 1983, JCPPP, Box 2, JCPL.

15. Zbigniew Brzezinski to Jimmy Carter, January 3, 1983, JCPPP, Box 2, JCPL.

16. Carter, *Blood of Abraham*, 103–23.

17. Charlotte Curtis, "Nixon Says U.S. Can Use Carter's Help on Mideast," *NYT*, November 14, 1982.

18. "Carter and Ford Criticize Israelis," *NYT*, January 18, 1983.

19. Iver Peterson, "Ford and Carter Tell of Difficult Communication in Government," *NYT*, February 11, 1983.

20. Transcript of Ford-Carter forum, February 9–10, 1983, Gerald R. Ford Presidential Library, University of Michigan, Ann Arbor; and "The Carter-Ford Act," *NYT*, January 15, 1983.

21. "Reunion of Presidents," *NYT*, February 10, 1983; and Gerald Ford, interview, July 1995, Beaver Creek, Colo.

22. Jimmy Carter, interview, April 1995, Atlanta; and Peterson, "Ford and Carter Tell of Difficult Communication in Government," *NYT*, February 11, 1983.

23. "Tribute to Rickover," *NYT*, February 12, 1983; and "3 Ex-Presidents Join in Dinner Honoring Rickover," *NYT*, March 1, 1983. For Bob Dole story, see Frank Rich, "Springtime for Nixon," *NYT*, December 16, 1995.

24. "Jimmy Carter's Frankest Interview," *Penthouse*, March 1983.

25. "Carter, in Middle East Trip, Hopes to Meet with Arafat," *NYT*, March 1, 1988.

26. "Carter, on a Middle East Trip, Rules Out an Arafat Meeting," *NYT*, March 2, 1983.

27. "Carter in Egypt; Sees Habib and Mubarak," *NYT*, March 3, 1983; William E. Farrell, "Carter Meets PLO Officials in Egypt," *NYT*, March 9, 1983; and Carter, *Blood of Abraham*, 143–64.

28. Carter, interview, April 1995, Atlanta.

29. Elizabeth Kurylo, "Egyptian Cler-

gyman Pays Visit to Carter," *Atlanta Journal & Constitution*, October 14, 1989.

30. Jimmy Carter, "Human Rights Agenda, Amnesty and Letters of Concern 1982–86," JCPPP, Box 4, JCPL.

31. Christopher Hemmeter, interview, June 1995, Denver, Colo.

32. Ibid. Also Carter, *Blood of Abraham*, 143–64.

33. Carter, interview, May 1995, Atlanta.

34. William E. Farrell, "Carter Meets PLO Officials in Egypt," *NYT*, March 9, 1983.

35. Carter, interview, May 1995, Atlanta.

36. Farrell, "Carter Meets PLO Officials"; and Carter, *Blood of Abraham*, 143–64.

37. Zbigniew Brzezinski, *Power and Principle: Memoirs of the National Security Adviser, 1977–1981* (New York: Farrar, Straus & Giroux, 1983), 234–88. For the rupture in the Carter-Begin relationship, see Harry Z. Hurwitz, *Begin: A Portrait* (Washington, D.C.: B'nai B'rith Books, 1994), 168–69.

38. Carter, *Blood of Abraham*, 50.

39. Jimmy Carter, *Why Not the Best?* (Nashville, Tenn.: Broadman Press, 1975).

40. David K. Shipler, "Carter Meets with Begin," *NYT*, March 9, 1983; and Carter, interview, May 1995, Atlanta.

41. David K. Shipler, "West Bank Arabs Protest Carter's Visit," *NYT*, March 10, 1983; and Hemmeter, interview.

42. Shipler, "West Bank Arabs Protest"; and "3 Soldiers Hurt in Attack," *NYT*, March 11, 1983.

43. Hemmeter, interview.

44. David K. Shipler, "Carter in Israel, Says Arabs Move toward Peace," *NYT*, March 13, 1983.

45. "Carter Sees Hussein in Jordan," *NYT*, March 14, 1983.

46. Carter, *Blood of Abraham*, 129.

47. "West Bank Settlements Are Illegal, Carter Says," *NYT*, March 15, 1983.

48. Carter, *Blood of Abraham*, 124–42.

49. Ibid.

50. Ibid. Also "Carter Sees King Fahd," *NYT*, March 16, 1983.

51. Carter, *Blood of Abraham*, 124–42.

52. Stein, interview, July 1995.

53. Carter, *Blood of Abraham*, 168–78.

54. James Brasher III, interview, July 1995, Atlanta.

55. Carter, *Blood of Abraham*, 60–82; "Carter Visits Syria," *NYT*, March 17, 1983; and Brzezinski, *Power and Principle*, 527. Also Kenneth Stein to Jimmy Carter, January 25, 1983, JCPPP, Box 2; and Zbigniew Brzezinski, memorandum for the record, January 3, 1983, Middle East File, JCPPP, Box 2.

56. Stein, interview, July 1995. Also see Kenneth W. Stein, "Syria Now Key Player in Middle East Drama," *Atlanta Journal & Constitution*, July 3, 1989.

57. Douglas Brinkley, "Jimmy Carter's Modest Quest for Global Peace," *Foreign Affairs* 74, no. 6 (November–December 1995): 90–100.

58. Carter, *Blood of Abraham*, 60–82; and Patrick Seale, *Assad: The Struggle for the Middle East* (Berkeley: University of California Press, 1990), 290–304.

59. Kenneth Stein, memorandum to Jimmy Carter, February 1983, JCPPP, Box 2.

60. Carter, *Blood of Abraham*, 60–82.

61. Stein, interview, July 1995.

62. Carter, *Blood of Abraham*, 62–78.

63. Hemmeter, interview.

64. Carter, interview, May 1995, Atlanta; and Ken Stein to Patsy and Christopher Hemmeter, March 20, 1983, JCPPP, Box 2.

65. Rosalynn Carter, interview, December 1995, Plains, Ga.

66. Carter, interview, May 1995, Atlanta.

67. Carter, *Blood of Abraham*, 83.

68. Ibid., 83–102.

69. Ibid.

70. Ibid.

71. Stein to Patsy and Christopher Hemmeter.

72. Kenneth Stein, interview, August 1995, Atlanta.

73. Joseph Verner Reed (U.S. ambassador to Morocco) to Jimmy Carter, March 28, 1983, JCPPP, Box 2.

74. Jimmy Carter, "Middle East Peace," talk at the Council on Foreign Relations, New York, March 24, 1983, JCPPP, Box 2.

75. Kenneth Stein to Jimmy Carter, April 14, 1983, JCPPP, Box 2.

76. Stein to Carter, August 5, 1983, JCPPP, Box 2.

77. "Carter Assails Demand on Tokyo," NYT, July 21, 1983; and Hemmeter, interview.

78. "Carter Meets Japanese Leader," NYT, July 22, 1983; and "Advice from the Top," NYT, August 20, 1983.

79. Jimmy Carter to Faye Dill, October 10, 1983, JCPPP, Box 2.

80. "Eulogist Hails Good Works at Mrs. Carter's Burial," NYT, November 2, 1983; and Wolfgang Saxon, "Ruth Carter Stapelton Dies; Evangelist and Faith Healer," NYT, September 27, 1983.

81. Kenneth Stein to Jimmy Carter, June 5, 1983; and Carter to Stein, June 5, 1983, JCPPP, Box 2.

82. Jimmy Carter, notes of meeting with Sol Linowitz, September 30, 1983, Carter Center, Atlanta, Kenneth Stein Notes, JCPPP, Box 2; and Sol Linowitz, interview, September 1995, Washington, D.C.

83. Kenneth Stein, Middle East Conference Papers (November 1983), JCPPP, Box 1. Also "Catching Up on the Middle East," Time, November 2, 1983.

84. William Quandt, interview, September 1996, Charlottesville, Va.

85. "Israel to Shun Conference," NYT, October 26, 1983; Ma'ariv (Israel), November 18, 1983; and Meir Rosenne to Kenneth Stein, July 5, 1983, JCPPP, Box 2.

86. William E. Schmidt, "Mideast Conference in Atlanta Draws Arab and U.S. Officials," NYT, November 9, 1983.

87. Greg McDonald, "Leaders Hear Carter, Ford on Mideast Meeting," Atlanta Journal & Constitution, November 18, 1983.

88. Carter, interview, May 1995, Atlanta.

89. William E. Schmidt, "Mideast Conference in Atlanta Draws Arab and U.S. Officials," NYT, November 9, 1983; and Greg McDonald, "Leaders Hear Carter, Ford on Mideast Meeting," Atlanta Journal & Constitution, November 18, 1983.

90. Ibid. Also William E. Schmidt, "Carter and Ford Oppose U.S. Strike," NYT, November 7, 1983.

91. Atlanta Journal & Constitution, November 11, 1983. On November 17 Carter and Ford went to Washington to brief Senator Howard Baker, Tip O'Neill, and George Shultz on the consultation.

92. Kenneth Stein to Jimmy Carter, October 2, 1983, JCPPP, Box 2.

93. Crown Prince Hassan of Jordan to Jimmy Carter, March 9, 1984, JCPPP, Box 3. Also Hassan to Carter, May 14, 1983, JCPPP, Box 3.

94. Jimmy Carter to Crown Prince Hassan, March 23, 1983, JCPPP, Box 3.

95. Jimmy Carter to Lee Hamilton, June 6, 1984, JCPPP, Box 3.

96. George Shultz to Charles Percy, March 14, 1984, JCPPP, Box 3.

97. Mary King, interview, January 1996, Jerusalem.

98. Ted Kolleck to Jimmy Carter, May 25, 1984, JCPPP, Box 3.

99. Jimmy Carter to Ted Kolleck, June 13, 1984, JCPPP, Box 3.

100. Jimmy Carter, transcript of interview with Mike Wallace, 60 Minutes, March 24, 1985, JCPPP, Box 3. For interesting reviews of The Blood of Abraham (1985), see Bernard Gwertzman, "Book of the Times," NYT, April 18, 1985; and Bernard Lewis, "The Search for Symmetry," NYT, April 28, 1985.

101. Ronald Reagan to Jimmy Carter, December 31, 1985, JCPPP, Box 3.

102. Kenneth Stein to Jimmy Carter, March 10, 1986, JCPPP, Box 3.

SEVEN: THE POLITICS OF RENEWAL

1. "Impact on Hunger," statement, January 2, 1984, JCPPP, Box 2, JCPL. Ex-president Ford also signed the statement. Also see NYT, January 3, 1984.

2. "Carter and San Francisco," NYT, May 24, 1984.

3. Ken Stein, interview, May 1995, Atlanta.

4. Jimmy Carter–Ellen Mickiewicz correspondence, 1985, JCPPP, Box 1; and "Dr.

Ellen Mickiewicz Soviet-Space/U.S.S.R. TV Project," JCPPP, Box 32.

5. Raymond L. Garthoff, *The Great Transition: American-Soviet Relations and the End of the Cold War* (Washington, D.C.: Brookings Institute, 1994), 68–191; and Michael Beschloss and Strobe Talbott, *At the Highest Levels: The Inside Story of the End of the Cold War* (Boston: Little, Brown, 1993), 6–7.

6. Ronald Reagan, *An American Life* (New York: Simon & Schuster, 1990), 545–48; and D. R. Baucom, *The Origins of SDI, 1944–1983* (Lawrence: University of Kansas Press, 1992).

7. Phil Gailey, "Carter Is Critical of Reagan Policies," *NYT*, October 14, 1981.

8. Jimmy Carter, interview, June 1994, Plains, Ga.; Norman Podhoretz, "The Reagan Road to Detente," *Foreign Affairs* 63, no. 3 (winter 1984–1985); "Reagan, Man of Peace," *NYT*, June 13, 1984; and Norman Podhoretz, interview, September 1995, New York.

9. Jimmy Carter, interview, April 1995, Plains, Ga. For a listing of President Reagan's military initiatives, see Jimmy Carter, *Talking Peace: A Vision for the Next Generation* (New York: Dutton, 1993), 43–45.

10. Martin Walker, "What's Important to Remember about Jimmy Carter," *Washington Post*, national woolly edition, June 27–July 3, 1994.

11. Ellen Mickiewicz, interview, June 1995, Durham, N.C.; and Carter, interview, April 1995, Plains.

12. Transcript of the Carter Center of Emory University consultation on arms control negotiations, May 31, 1984, JCPPP, Ellen Mickiewicz (Nuclear Arms Consultation) Files, Box 1. For an edited version of the discussions, see Roman Kolkowicz and Ellen Propper Mickiewicz, eds., *The Soviet Calculus of Nuclear War* (Lexington, Mass.: Lexington Books, 1986). 143–68.

13. Carter, interview, April 1995, Plains; and Art Harris, "Citizen Carter," *Washington Post*, February 22, 1990. Also see "U.S. Group Starts Drive Opposing Star Wars," *NYT*, June 20, 1984.

14. "Weinberger Defends Reagan's Missile Plan," *NYT*, June 21, 1984.

15. Jimmy Carter to George Wallace, January 31, 1984, JCPPP, Campaign 1984 File, Box 16.

16. "Carter Backs Mondale Effort but Bars Primary Campaign," *NYT*, October 18, 1983; and "Carter on Mondale's Stance," *NYT*, February 13, 1984. Also Steve M. Gillon, *The Democratic Dilemma: Walter F. Mondale and the Liberal Legacy* (New York: Columbia University Press, 1992), 365–402.

17. Chip Carter, interview, April 1995, Decatur, Ga.

18. Ibid.

19. Jimmy Carter's speech at the San Francisco Democratic National Convention was published in *NYT* on July 17, 1984; also Hendrik Hertzberg, interview, June 1995, New York.

20. Gerald Rafshoon, interview, July 1995, Washington, D.C.

21. News release from Proposition One, University of Vermont, Governor Richard Snelling Papers, Burlington, Vt.

22. Reagan quoted in *NYT*, September 24, 1984.

23. Maureen Dowd, "Ferraro Sharpens Criticism of Reagan's Foreign Policy," *NYT*, September 30, 1984; for Hart, see Bernard Weinraub, "Hart Risking Party Split, Attacks Carter-Mondale Team as Inept," *NYT*, May 1, 1984. For a wonderful analysis of Hart's condemnation of the Carter years, see James Reston, "Hart's Fatal Blunder," *NYT*, May 2, 1984.

24. Jimmy Carter, interview, May 1995, Atlanta.

25. Robert Pastor, interview, May 1995, Atlanta. Also Roy Pattishall, "The Trouble in Nicaragua," *Emory Magazine* 64, no. 2 (1987): 22–29.

26. Sol Linowitz, *The Making of a Public Man: A Memoir* (Boston: Little, Brown, 1985), 22–29.

17. Carter, interview, May 1995, Atlanta.

28. Pastor, interview.

29. Ibid.; and Rosalynn Carter, interview, May 1995, Atlanta.

30. Alan Riding, "Brazil Welcomes

Jimmy Carter on Latin Tour," *NYT*, October 9, 1984; and *NYT*, October 14, 1984.

31. Ibid.

32. Ibid.

33. Martin Andersen, "Argentines Thank Carter for Human Rights Efforts," *Washington Post*, October 11, 1984; and "For Mr. Carter, Honor Deserved," *Washington Post*, October 13, 1984.

34. "Thank You, Jimmy," *Buenos Aires Herald*, October 10, 1984.

35. Carter, interview, May 1995, Atlanta.

36. Martin Andersen, "Argentines Thank Carter for Human Rights Efforts," *Washington Post*, October 11, 1984. Also see Jacobo Timerman, *Prisoner without a Name, Cell without a Number* (New York: Knopf, 1981).

37. Martin Andersen, interview, August 1995, Washington, D.C.

38. Joanne Omang, "Ardito Barletta Installed as Panama's President," *Washington Post*, October 12, 1984.

39. Pastor, interview, August 1995.

40. Walter Mondale to Jimmy Carter, January 25, 1985, JCPPP, Campaign 1984 File, Box 16.

41. Gerald Ford, interview, April 1995, Beaver Creek, Colo.; Jimmy Carter, interview, April 1995, Plains, Ga.; and William Hyland, interview, October 1995, Washington, D.C.

42. Douglas Brinkley, *Dean Acheson: The Cold War Years, 1953–1971* (New Haven, Conn.: Yale University Press, 1993), 2.

43. Transcript of the taped Nuclear Arms Consultation Meeting (Washington, D.C.), October 27, 1983, JCPPP, Ellen Mickiewicz (Nuclear Arms Consultation) Files, Box 1.

44. Jimmy Carter, notes on meeting with Anatoly Dobrynin, February 29, 1983, JCPPP, Mickiewicz Files.

45. By far the best account of American impressions of the new Soviet premier is in Garthoff, *The Great Transition*, 197–251.

46. Ellen Mickiewicz, interview, August 1995, Maine.

47. Ellen Propper Mickiewicz and Roman Kolkowicz, eds., *International Security and Arms Control* (New York: Praeger, 1986), x. This book contains all the important transcribed exchanges that took place during the consultation. The second quote is from Henry Kissinger, interview, October 1993, New York.

48. Mickiewicz, interview, June 1995.

49. For a good overview of the Reagan administration's anti-Soviet defense strategies following the Korean airline shooting and INF walkout, see Robert C. McFarlane and Zofia Smardz, *Special Trust* (New York: Cadell & Davies, 1994), 275–322.

50. Wayne Biddle, "Soviet and U.S. Aides in Atlanta, Trade Accusations on Arms Control," *NYT*, April 14, 1985. Also see Mickiewicz and Kolkowicz, *International Security*, 33–35 and 44–52.

51. Jimmy Carter, "Overview: Options and Recommendations," in Mickiewicz and Kolkowicz, *International Security*, 113–17; and Jimmy and Rosalynn Carter, *Everything to Gain*, 140–41. Also General David Jones, interview, August 1995, Arlington, Va.

52. For Shultz, see Biddle, "Soviet and U.S. Aides." Nunn is quoted in Mickiewicz and Kolkowicz, *International Security*, 77.

53. See April–May letters to President Carter, JCPPP, Misc. Files, Box 1. Carter is quoted in Mickiewicz and Kolkowicz, *International Security*, 127–28. Also Mickiewicz, interview, June 1995.

54. "Carter Denounced Star Wars," *NYT*, September 29, 1985.

55. Paul Nitze, interview, September 1994, Washington, D.C.

56. Leslie Gelb, "Three Past Presidents May Brief Reagan," *NYT*, November 5, 1985. For a detailed discussion of the 1985 summit, see Garthoff, *The Great Transition*, 197–251.

57. For a collection of Carter's views on Reagan, see the "Reagan Administration 1981–88" file, JCPPP, Box 10.

EIGHT: THEOLOGY OF THE HAMMER

1. Millard Fuller, interview, January 1995, Americus, Ga.

2. Jimmy and Rosalynn Carter, *Everything to Gain*; and Millard Fuller with Diane Scott, *No More Shacks!* (Waco, Tex.: Word Publishers, 1986).

3. Jimmy Carter, interview, December 1993, Plains, Ga.

4. Ibid.

5. Fuller, interview, January 1995.

6. Carter, interview, December 1993.

7. Millard Fuller and Diane Scott, *Love in the Mortar Joints* (Clinton, N.J.: New Win Publishing, 1980), 39–53; Morris Dees, interview, September 1995, Montgomery, Ala.; and Donald Dale Jackson, "Millard Fuller's Blueprint for Success," *Reader's Digest*, June 1988, 155–59.

8. Fuller and Scott, *Love in the Mortar Joints*, 39–53.

9. Dees, interview.

10. Millard Fuller, *Bokotola* (Piscataway, N.J.: New Century Publishers, 1977).

11. Fuller, interview, August 1995.

12. Fuller, *Bokotola*, 7–8.

13. Fuller, interview, August 1995; and Fuller and Scott, *Love in the Mortar Joints*, 55–62.

14. Fuller and Scott, *Love in the Mortar Joints*, 55–62; and Fuller, *Bokotola*, 16–25.

15. Dallas Lee, *The Cotton Patch Evidence: The Story of Clarence Jordan and the Koinonia Farm Experiment, 1942–1970* (Americus, Ga.: Koinonia Partners, 1971). Clarence Jordan wrote a series of Cotton Patch books, including *Practical Religion of the Sermon on the Mount* and *The Epistle of James in the Koinonia 'Cotton Patch' Version* (Americus, Ga.: Koinonia Farm, 1964); *The Cotton Patch Version of Luke and Acts, Jesus' Doing and Happenings* (New York: Association Press, 1968); *The Cotton Patch Version of Paul's Epistles* (New York: Association Press, 1968); *Letters from Partners, Rock Jack and Joe,*

Koinonia 'Cotton Patch' Version (Americus, Ga.: Koinonia Farm, 1969); and many others. Also see Clarence Jordan and Bill Lane Doulos, *Cotton Patch Parables of Liberation* (Kitchener, Ontario: Herald Press, 1976).

16. Lee, *Cotton Patch Evidence*, 121–42; and Millard Fuller, interview, March 1995, Americus, Ga.

17. Ibid. Also Millard Fuller, *A Simple, Decent Place to Live: The Building Realization of Habitat for Humanity* (Dallas, Tex.: Word Publishing, 1995), 21.

18. Fuller, *Bokotola*, 32–60.

19. Fuller, *No More Shacks!* 30.

20. Fuller and Scott, *Love in the Mortar Joints*, 85–99.

21. Fuller, *A Simple, Decent Place to Live*, 22–24.

22. Ibid., 26. Also Fuller, *Bokotola*, 61–173.

23. Fuller, interview, August 1995. Also Fuller, *Bokotola*, 61–133.

24. Ibid.

25. John R. Alexander, ed., *How to Start a Habitat for Humanity Affiliate* (Americus, Ga.: Habitat for Humanity International, 1989); Millard Fuller, *The Theology of The Hammer* (Macon, Ga.: Smyth & Helwys Publishing, 1994), 7–18.

26. Jimmy Carter, address to First Presbyterian Church, October 16, 1982, Habitat for Humanity Archive, Americus, Ga.

27. Fuller, *No More Shacks!* 75–76.

28. Ibid, 76–78.

29. Millard Fuller to President and Mrs. Jimmy Carter, February 8, 1984, Habitat for Humanity Archive.

30. Fuller, *No More Shacks!* 81.

31. "Down Home with Carter," *NYT*, March 28, 1984.

32. William R. Greer, "Carter Visits Housing Site for the Poor," *NYT*, April 2, 1984.

33. Ibid. Also Fuller, *No More Shacks!* 84–85.

34. Jimmy and Rosalynn Carter, *Everything to Gain*, 94.

35. Carter, interview, December 1993.

36. Esther Fein, "Carpenter Named Carter Comes to New York," *NYT*, September 3, 1984.

37. Jimmy Carter, remarks at memorial service for Florence Sheffield, February 12, 1996, First Methodist Church, Americus, Ga.

38. Betty Pope, interview, January 1995, Americus, Ga.; and Carter and Carter, *Everything to Gain*, 95.

39. Fuller, *No More Shacks!* 86–87.

40. Betty Pope, interview, January 1995.

41. Carter and Carter, *Everything to Gain*, 95–96.

42. Fuller, interview, August 1995.

43. Phyllis Wheeler, interview, September 1995, Americus, Ga.

44. Fuller, *No More Shacks!* 89.

45. Carter and Carter, *Everything to Gain*, 108.

46. "A Day of Cameras and Hammers for Ex-President," *NYT*, September 4, 1984; and Fuller, *No More Shacks!* 90–93.

47. Fuller, interview, August 1995.

48. Fuller, *No More Shacks!* 92; and "A Day of Cameras and Hammers for Ex-President," *NYT*, September 4, 1984.

49. Betty Pope, interview, January 1995.

50. William G. Blair, "Carter's Volunteer Group Plans Nicaragua Project," *NYT*, September 9, 1984.

51. "Birthdays," *NYT*, October 2, 1984.

52. Carter and Carter, *Everything to Gain*, 104.

53. Stephen Kinzer, "Nicaragua Appeals to U.S. on Pact," *NYT*, September 28, 1984; and Habitat for Humanity File, JCPPP, Box 5, JCPL.

54. Jimmy Carter–Millard Fuller correspondence, Habitat for Humanity Archive.

55. Fuller, *No More Shacks!* 93–94.

56. Ibid.

57. John Pope, interview, January 1995, Americus, Ga.

58. Fuller, *No More Shacks!* 96–97.

59. Kathleeen Casey, "Carter's Surprise Visit Thrills Edison Church," *(Newark) Star-Ledger*, July 30, 1985.

60. Fuller, *No More Shacks!* 97–98.

61. Fuller, interview, August 1995.

62. E. Walter Cleckley Jr., interview, February 1996, Lancaster, Penn. Also Jimmy Carter to the Reverend and Mrs. E. Walter Cleckley Jr., August 5, 1985, E. Walter Cleckley Jr. Personal Papers, Lancaster, Penn.

63. Carter and Carter, *Everything to Gain*, 106.

64. Fuller, interview, August 1995.

65. Larry Rohter, "For Carter, an Old Job in Housing," *NYT*, July 29, 1985; "The Subject Was Hammers and Nails," *NYT*, August 1, 1985.

66. Fuller, interview, August 1995.

67. "Carter at Housing Dedication," *NYT*, October 13, 1985.

NINE: THE WORLD'S HEALTH

1. Kenneth Stein, "Semi-annual Report of the Carter Center," July 15, 1984, JCPPP, Ken Stein (Middle East) 1983–1986 File, Box 2, JCPL.

2. Ibid.

3. Jimmy Carter to Ken Stein, July 23, 1984, JCPPP, Ken Stein (Middle East) 1983–1986 File.

4. Jody Powell, interview, July 1995, Washington, D.C. Also Dan Lee, interview, May 1995, Atlanta; and Dudley Clendinen, "Carter Library Rises Despite Problems with Money and Road," *NYT*, October 10, 1985.

5. William Foege, interview, July 1995, Atlanta; Kevin Sottak, "Healing Mission," *Harvard Public Health Review*, fall 1994.

6. Ibid. Also see Albert Schweitzer, *Out of My Life and Thought* (London: Allen and Unwin, 1933).

7. Sottak, "Healing Mission," 23. Also see Thomas Weller, "Medical Research as Measured against the Needs of All," *New England Journal of Medicine* (Massachusetts Medical Society) 283, no. 10 (September 3, 1970): 537–39.

8. Foege, interview, July 1995.

9. Horace G. Ogden, *CDC and the Smallpox Crusade* (Washington, D.C.: U.S. Department of Health & Human Services, 1987), 48–55; and Sottak, "Healing Mission." For Foege's own account, see William H. Foege, "Should

the Smallpox Virus Be Allowed to Survive?" *New England Journal of Medicine* 300 (1979): 670–71.

10. Elizabeth W. Etheridge, *Sentinel for Health: A History of the Centers for Disease Control* (Berkeley: University of California Press, 1992), 1–7.

11. Ogden, *CDC and the Smallpox Crusade*, 9.

12. Etheridge, *Sentinel for Health*, 188–210.

13. Cheryl Heckler-Feltz, "Knockout Doc," *Lutheran*, March 1995, 15; and William Foege, interview, August 1995, Atlanta.

14. Joseph Califano, interview, September 1995, New York.

15. William Foege to Assistant Secretary for Health, April 23, 1980, Record Group 90, 87-0077, Box 2, CDC Records, Atlanta Federal Records Center, East Point, Ga. This collection includes thousands of boxes from the CDC.

16. Quoted in Griffen, "Calling the Shots," *Columns*, June 1994, 19.

17. Jimmy Carter, interview, October 1995, Plains, Ga.; and Art Harris, "Citizen Carter," *Washington Post*, February 22, 1990. Also see Randy Shilts, *And the Band Played On: Politics, People, and the AIDS Epidemic* (New York: St. Martin's Press, 1987); and *Sentinel for Health*, 321–40. For Carter's AIDS concerns, see William Foege Papers, Global 2000 Archive, Charles Kirbo Building, Atlanta. A fantastic history of combating viruses is Laurie Garrett, *The Coming Plague: Newly Emerging Diseases in a World Out of Balance* (New York: Penguin, 1994).

18. Rosalynn Carter, *First Lady from Plains* (Boston: Houghton Mifflin, 1984), 298–300; and Rosalynn Carter, interview, May 1995, Atlanta.

19. Foege, interview, August 1995.

20. Ibid. Also Jimmy Carter, interview, May 1995, Atlanta.

21. For documentary information pertaining to the conference, see letters, memos, etc., JCPPP, Dr. Foege File,

1985–1987, Box 4, JCPL. Also "Carter Opens Forum on Early Death," *NYT*, November 27, 1984.

22. Jimmy and Rosalynn Carter, *Everything to Gain: Making the Most of the Rest of Your Life* (New York: Ballantine, 1987), 40–60; and Jimmy Carter, interview, March 1994, Plains, Ga.

23. Young quote is from transcript of *MacNeil/Lehrer NewsHour*, March 22, 1995, Show 5189.

24. Jimmy Carter, interview, March 1994, Plains, Ga.; Chip Carter, interview, August 1995, Decatur, Ga.

25. Jimmy Carter to Yohei Sasakawa, July 5, 1990; and 1990 Notebook, Foege Papers.

26. Steve Hochman, interview, April 1995, Atlanta.

27. Jimmy Carter, "In Perspective," *Carter Center News*, spring 1993, 2, 12; Jimmy and Rosalynn Carter, *Everything to Gain*, 45–50.

28. Jimmy Carter, "Proposed Tobacco Tax Would Raise Money and Save Lives," *NYT*, February 16, 1993.

29. Robert W. Amler and H. Bruce Dull, *Closing the Gap: The Burden of Unnecessary Illness* (New York: Oxford University Press, 1985), 188–90.

30. Jimmy and Rosalynn Carter, *Everything to Gain*, 50–54. See also Paul Clancy, "Billy Carter's Coverage: 'I Thought I Was Cured,'" *USA Today*, March 25–27, 1986.

31. Oxford University Press published this consultation's findings as Amler and Dull, *Closing the Gap*. Also see Jimmy and Rosalynn Carter, *Everything to Gain*, 34–67; and "Health Risk Appraisal," JCPPP, Box 4. The health questionnaire is included in Jimmy Carter, *Talking Peace: A Vision for the Next Generation* (New York: Dutton, 1993), 84–85.

32. Hamilton Jordan, *Cancer: The Second Time Around* (printed privately, 1996).

33. Jimmy and Rosalynn Carter, *Everything to Gain*, 34–66.

34. Jimmy Carter to President Ibrahim Babangida, August 29, 1990, Foege Papers, Charles Kirbo Building.

35. See Jimmy and Rosalynn Carter, *Everything to Gain*, Book Reviews, vertical files, JCPL. In particular, see reviews by Christopher Lehmann-Haupt, *NYT*, May 28, 1987; Elizabeth Mehren, *Los Angeles Times*, May 26, 1987; and James D. Fairbanks, *Houston Chronicle*, May 24, 1987.

36. Rosalynn Carter, interview, November 1995, Plains, Ga.

37. Rosalynn Carter Symposia Papers, Mental Health Program, Carter Center, Atlanta; and John Gates, interview, May 1995, Atlanta.

38. Rosalynn Carter (with Susan K. Golant), *Helping Yourself Help Others* (New York: Times Books, 1994); and the Rosalynn Carter Institute for Human Development Clipping Files, Georgia Southwestern University, Americus, Ga.

39. Joe Goodman interview of Rosalynn Carter, "From a Woman Who's Been There, Help for Caregivers," *Barnes & Noble Magazine*, December 1994.

40. Amy Carter, interview, August 1995, New Orleans; and Chip Carter, interview, August 1995, Decatur, Ga. Also Sandra L. Quinn-Musgrove and Sandford Kanter, eds., *American Royalty: All the Presidents' Children* (Westport, Conn.: Greenwood Press, 1995), 221–26.

41. See local newspaper clippings at the Jimmy Carter National Historic Site, Papers Collection, Post–White House File, Plains, Ga.; and Carter Family Files, Lake Blackshear Regional Library, Americus, Ga.

42. Faye Dill to Jimmy Carter, April 11, 1985 (Carter wrote his opinion of Willie Nelson on a piece of paper attached to her letter), JCPPP, Misc. Files, Box 2.

43. David Beasley, "Billy's Back," *Atlanta Journal & Constitution*, June 5, 1986.

44. William E. Schmidt, "With Tourists Gone and Traffic Slow, Plains, Ga., Celebrates Its Centennial," *NYT*, May 18, 1985. Also the Plains Centennial (1885–1985) Program Book, JCPPP, Misc. Files.

45. Phil Gailey, "Memories and Catching Up in Plains," *NYT*, September 2, 1985; and Maxine Reese, interview, October 1994, Plains, Ga.

46. Dan O'Briant, "Jimmy Carter Stalks the Great Outdoors in His Latest Memoir," *Atlanta Journal & Constitution*, May 22, 1988.

47. Chip Carter, interview.

48. Jimmy Carter, interview, February 1995, Atlanta; and Chip Carter, interview. For Carter's boyhood hunting escapades, see Jimmy Carter, *Why Not the Best?* (Nashville, Tenn.: Broadman Press, 1975), 13–22; and Jimmy Carter, *An Outdoor Journal: Adventures and Reflections* (New York: Bantam Books, 1988), 36–50.

49. Jimmy Carter to Harryette Hodges, December 3, 1986, JCPPP, President Carter's Misc. Files 1986–87, Box 5. On that particular Arkansas hunt Carter shot a mallard drake (December 1) with a band number around its foot. He reported it to the Game Management Division.

50. Jimmy Carter to Peter Bourne, July 30, 1986, JCPPP, Trip Letters File 1986–87, Box 10.

51. William Foege, interview, November 1995, Atlanta.

52. Jimmy and Rosalynn Carter, *Everything to Gain*, 91–92.

53. Rosalynn Carter, interview, October 1995, Plains, Ga.

54. William Foege, interview, November 1995, Atlanta.

55. Jimmy Carter, interview, August 1990, Foege Papers, Charles Kirbo Building.

56. Jeffrey Clark to Jimmy Carter, January 22, 1990; Jimmy Carter to Jeffrey Clark, January 30, 1990, Foege Papers, Charles Kirbo Building. Also Peter Bourne, interview, January 1997, Washington, D.C.

57. For the creation of the Task Force for Child Survival and Development (TFCSD), see "An Overview of the Task Force" (compiled in 1994), Foege Papers, Carter Center, Atlanta; "Task Force Celebrates Fiftieth Anniversary," *Carter Center News*, fall 1989, 13; and Jimmy Carter, *Talking Peace*, 81–83.

58. Foege, interview, August 1995.

59. Sottak, "Healing Mission," 25; "An Overview of the Task Force," Foege Papers, Carter Center; and Jimmy Carter, *Talking Peace*, 81–83. Ortiz is quoted in the *Carter Center News*, spring 1992, 3.

60. Carter, interview, May 1995, Atlanta.

61. Sottak, "Healing Mission," 22; and Ogden, *CDC and the Smallpox Crusade*, 4.

62. Foege, interview, August 1995; Carter, interview, May 1995, Atlanta. Also Betancur File ("Closing the Gap"), JCPPP, Box 12.

63. Jimmy and Rosalynn Carter, *Everything to Gain*, 163–68. Also Robert H. Dix, *The Politics of Columbia* (New York: Praeger, 1987).

64. Jimmy Carter to William Foege, November 21, 1985; and William Foege to Jimmy Carter, December 4, 1985, JCPPP, Dr. William Foege File, Box 4.

65. Foege, interview, August 1995.

TEN: AFRICA'S GREEN REVOLUTION

1. For President Carter's Nigerian visit and the impact of his postpresidency, see Russ Rymer, "The Mission," *In Health* 4, no. 2 (March–April 1990): 1–2.

2. Andrew Young, interview, October 1005, Atlanta. For his glowing assessment of the Carter administration's African policy, see Andrew Young, "The United States and Africa: Victory for Diplomacy," *Foreign Affairs: America and the World* 59, no. 3 (1980): 648–66.

3. Peter G. Bourne, *Jimmy Carter, a Comprehensive Biography from Plains to Postpresidency* (New York: Scribner's, 1997), 491.

4. Walter E. Fauntroy to Jimmy Carter, September 20, 1985, JCPPP, Personal Favors File, Box 11, JCPL.

5. Jimmy Carter to President Pieter W. Botha, September 30, 1985, JCPPP, Personal Favors File.

6. The Sasakawa Africa Association publishes a monograph series about its work in Africa, while Global 2000 publishes its workshop proceedings and reports. Those consulted in this chapter include "Agricultural Projects in Sudan: Final Report" (1986–1993); "Feeding the Future: Agricultural Strategies for Africa" (1989); and "The SG 2000 Agricultural Project in Ghana," 1990.

7. Gregg Easterbrook, "Forgotten Benefactor of Humanity," *Atlantic Monthly*, January 1997, 82.

8. Richard Critchfield, "Grain Man," *World Monitor*, October 1990, 1–4.

9. Critchfield, "Grain Man," 13–19; and Norman Borlaug, interview, September 1995, College Station, Tex. Other information about Borlaug's life and career is taken from this interview. Also see "Living History Interview with Dr. Norman E. Borlaug," *Transitional Law and Contemporary Problems* (University of Iowa College of Law), fall 1991, 539–54; and Borlaug, "World Food Security and the Legacy of Canadian Wheat Scientist R. Glen Anderson," *Canadian Journal of Plant Pathology* 14 (1992): 253–66.

10. Paul Raeburn, *The Last Harvest: The Genetic Gamble That Threatens to Destroy American Agriculture* (New York: Simon & Schuster, 1995), 91–93; and Betty Fussell, *The Story of Corn* (New York: Knopf, 1992), 93.

11. Norman Borlaug to Jimmy Carter, October 3, 1986, JCPPP, World Food Prize File, Box 11.

12. "Sowing a Green Revolution," *Time*, November 2, 1970.

13. Garrison Wilkes, interview, March 1995, Boston.

14. Norman Borlaug to Jimmy Carter, October 3, 1986, JCPPP, World Food Prize File.

15. Gregg Easterbrook, "Forgotten Benefactor of Humanity," *Atlantic Monthly*, January 1997, 80.

16. Elizabeth Kurylo, "Sasakawa, Philanthropist Who Aided Carter, King Centers, Dies in Japan," *Atlanta Journal & Constitution*, July 21, 1995.

17. Anne Lowrey Bailey, "The Controversial Charity of Ryoichi Sasakawa," *Chronicle of Philanthropy*, June 2, 1992.

18. Jimmy and Rosalynn Carter,

Everything to Gain: Making the Most of the Rest of Your Life (New York: Ballantine Books, 1988), 156.

19. Jim Brasher III, interview, May 1995, Atlanta; and Bailey, "Controversial Charity," 10.

20. Jimmy and Rosalynn Carter, *Everything to Gain*, 156–57.

21. Borlaug, interview, September 1995.

22. Reverend Theodore Hesburgh, interview, September 1995, South Bend, Ind.

23. Norman Borlaug to Jimmy Carter, October 3, 1986, JCPPP, World Food Prize File. Also Borlaug, interview, September 1995; and Jimmy Carter, *Talking Peace: A Vision for the Next Generation* (New York: Dutton, 1993), 70–76.

24. Jimmy Carter, interview, May 1995, Atlanta.

25. Borlaug, interview, September 1995.

26. James Brooke, "Man with a Plan," *NYT*, October 16, 1987.

27. Global 2000 Annual Reports, William Foege Papers, Charles Kirbo Building, Atlanta.

28. Mike Toner, "Carter Food Projects Yield Hope in Africa," *Atlanta Journal & Constitution*, March 20, 1988.

29. Tape transcription of Jimmy Carter's Sunday school class at Maranatha Baptist Church (September 1994), Maranatha Baptist Church Tape Archive, Plains, Ga.

31. Jerry Rawlings to Jimmy Carter, May 23, 1988, JCPPP, Africa File, Box 12; and Jimmy Carter to Rawlings, June 17, 1988, JCPPP, Africa File.

32. "Rawlings Hails 'Big 3,'" *Feeding the Future* (SG2000 newsletter printed in London), fall 1989, 4.

33. *Carter Center News*, fall 1992, 10. Also see Robert M. Press, "Program Plants Seeds of Change," *Christian Science Monitor*, October 16, 1990.

34. Jimmy Carter to Jerry Rawlings, January 27, 1986; and Carter to Rawlings, July 3, 1986, JCPPP, Trip Letters 1986–1987 File, Box 10. For more on the Carter-Rawlings relationship, see the transcript of their joint *CNN Worldview* interview, July 12, 1995.

35. Jimmy Carter to Jerry Rawlings, June 17, 1988, JCPPP, Africa File.

36. See "Global 2000 Overview Report (1994)," Carter Center, Atlanta (courtesy of Andrew Agle, director of operations, Global 2000); "Global 2000 Agricultural Project in Sudan: Final Report (1986–1992)"; and Norman Borlaug, interview, August 1995, College Station, Tex.

37. Carter, interview, May 1995, Atlanta; and "Global 2000 Overview Report."

38. Bernard Gwertzman, "Aid to Zimbabwe Suspended by U.S.," *NYT*, July 10, 1986.

39. Edward Lanpher, interview, October 1995, Washington, D.C.

40. "Carter Leads Walkout at Party in Zimbabwe," *NYT*, July 5, 1986.

41. Jimmy Carter to Prime Minister Robert Mugabe, July 5, 1986; and Mugabe to Carter, July 7, 1986, JCPPP, Trip Letters 1986–87 File.

42. See Bernard Gwertzman, "U.S. Is Cutting Off Aid to Zimbabwe," *NYT*, September 3, 1986; and the editorial "Cutting Off Noses in Zimbabwe," *NYT*, September 5, 1986.

43. Jimmy Carter, interview, November 1995, Plains, Ga.

44. "Carter Faults Reagan Zimbabwe Aid Cut," *NYT*, September 12, 1986. A friendly anti-Reagan correspondence developed between W. P. M. Mangwende and Carter, JCPPP, Personal Requests File, Box 11, JCPL.

45. Lanpher, interview.

46. Jimmy and Rosalynn Carter, transcript of open meeting at the Carter Center, October 1995. (The event was taped by C-SPAN.)

47. Andrew Agle, interview, February 1996, Atlanta.

48. Carter, interview, May 1995, Atlanta.

49. Russ Rymer, "The Mission," *In Health* 4, no. 2 (March–April 1990).

ELEVEN:
CENTRAL AMERICA AND THE
POLICY OF PROTEST

1. For a good review of U.S.-Nicaraguan relations in the twentieth century, see Robert Pastor, *Condemned to Repetition: The United States and Nicaragua* (Princeton, N.J.: Princeton University Press, 1987), chaps. 1–3; and Thomas W. Walker, *Nicaragua: The Land of Sandino* (Boulder, Colo.: Westview Press, 1991).

2. Jeane Kirkpatrick, "U.S. Security and Latin America," *Commentary*, January 1981; and Kirkpatrick, "Dictatorships and Double Standards," *Commentary*, November 1974. Also William LeoGrande, "The Revolution in Nicaragua: Another Cuba?" *Foreign Affairs*, fall 1979.

3. Roy Gutman, *Banana Diplomacy: The Making of American Policy in Nicaragua* (New York: Simon & Schuster, 1989).

4. Jimmy Carter, *Talking Peace: A Vision for the Next Generation* (New York: Dutton, 1993), 133–37.

5. Robert Kagan, *A Twilight Struggle: American Power and Nicaragua, 1977–1990* (New York: Free Press, 1996), 51–189.

6. Rose Cunningham, "A Day at the Farm with Governor Carter and President Figueres," *Atlanta Journal & Constitution Sunday Magazine*, June 11, 1972; and Robert Pastor, interview, October 1995, Atlanta.

7. Eric Bord, interview, October 1995, Washington, D.C.

8. Jimmy Carter, transcript of press conference in Managua, Nicaragua, February 7, 1986, JCPPP, Central American Files 1985–86, Box 1, JCPL.

9. Jose Altamirano to Jimmy Carter, February 23, 1988, JCPPP, Human Rights File, Box 12.

10. Art Harris, "Citizen Carter," *Washington Post*, February 22, 1990.

11. Jimmy Carter to Bosco Vivas, February 9, 1986, JCPPP, Trip File 1986–87, Box 10.

12. Bord, interview. For the Nicaraguan house-building, see Millard Fuller, *A Simple, Decent Place to Live* (Dallas, Tex.: Word Publishing, 1995), 168.

13. James M. Wall, "Jimmy Carter: Finding a Commonality of Concern," *Christian Century*, May 30–June 6, 1990.

14. Jimmy Carter, interview, *Washington Times*, October 29, 1996.

15. Bord, interview.

16. Jimmy Carter to President Daniel Ortega Saavedra, February 8, 1986, JCPPP, Trip File 1986–87.

17. Elliott Abrams, interview, August 1997, Washington, D.C.

18. Central American Trip Itinerary February 3–13, JCPPP, Central American Files 1985–86. Also "Carter in Nicaragua, Meets with Officials and Opposition," *NYT*, February 8, 1986.

19. "Salvadorans Call a Strike to Protest Carter Visit," *NYT*, February 11, 1986. Also see Jimmy Carter, interview, May 1995, Atlanta.

20. Jimmy Carter to José Napoleon Duarte, February 11, 1986, JCPPP, Trip File 1986–87.

21. Jimmy Carter, transcript of press conference in Mexico City, Mexico, February 21, 1986, JCPPP, Central American Files 1985–86.

22. Pastor, interview.

23. Octavio Paz, interview, May 1995, Atlanta.

25. Bord, interview; and Pastor, interview.

26. Robert Pastor to Douglas Brinkley, September 18, 1997.

27. Bord, interview.

28. Hank and Sue Struck to Jimmy Carter, February 10, 1986; and Reverend Grant Gallup to Jimmy Carter, February 10, 1986, JCPPP, Central American Letters File, Box 1.

29. "Amy Carter in Brown Protest," *NYT*, March 8, 1986. For a more detailed discussion of public dissent toward Reagan's Central American policies, see Christian Smith, *Resisting Reagan: The U.S. Central American Peace Movement* (Chicago: University of Chicago Press, 1996).

30. Amy Carter, interview, August 1995, New Orleans; "Amy Carter Arrested in Apartheid Protest," *NYT*, March 20, 1986; and "Amy Carter's Big Day," *NYT*, May 14, 1986.

31. Amy Carter, quoted in Matthew L. Wald, "Amy Carter Today: Causes and Arrests," *NYT*, December 5, 1986. Also see Amy Carter, interview.

32. Quoted in Matthew L. Wald, "Amy Carter Tells Court She Sat in Road to Alter CIA Policy," *NYT*, April 14, 1987. Also see "Trial Opens for Amy Carter and 14 over a Protest," *NYT*, April 10, 1987.

33. Ramsey Clark, interview, October 1995, New York.

34. Quoted in Matthew L. Wald, "Amy Carter Is Acquitted over Protest," *NYT*, April 16, 1987.

35. For Carter on Hoffman and on CIA, ibid. (also note Jimmy Carter's endorsement of Abbie Hoffman's collected essays); and Jimmy Carter, quoted in Wald, "Amy Carter Is Acquitted."

TWELVE: THE CARTER CENTER OPENS

1. Conflict Resolution/Dayle Powell Papers, JCPPP, Box 12, JCPL.

2. Catherine Rudder, interview, September 1995, Washington, D.C.

3. Quoted in Tony Smith, *America's Mission: The United States and the Worldwide Struggle for Democracy in the Twentieth Century* (Princeton, N.J.: Princeton University Press, 1994), 239.

4. Warren Christopher to Jimmy Carter, December 20, 1984, JCPPP, Carter Center File, Box 12.

5. Patricia Derian, interview, June 1995, Washington, D.C.

6. Jimmy Carter to Leah Leatherbee, July 5, 1988, JCPPP, Human Rights File, Box 12. For an account of the number of political prisoners Carter got released from 1982–1986, see Amnesty and Letters of Concern, JCPPP, Box 4.

7. Jimmy Carter to Prem Tinsulanonda, October 14, 1987, JCPPP, Amnesty International File, Box 11.

8. For John Healy–Jimmy Carter correspondence see JCPPP, Amnesty International File, particularly Healy's letters of September 2, 4, 5, and 23, 1987.

9. Jimmy Carter to His Majesty King Bhumibol Adulyadej, October 14, 1987, JCPPP, Box. 11.

10. Healy-Carter correspondence, JCPPP, Amnesty International File.

11. Jimmy Carter to Minister Yitzhak Rabin, May 28, 1987, JCPPP, Personal Favors File, Box 11.

12. Yitzhak Rabin to Jimmy Carter, July 2, 1987, JCPPP, Amnesty International File.

13. Jimmy Carter to Secretary General Mikhail Gorbachev, February 17, 1988, JCPPP, Human Rights File.

14. For information on the Carter-Menil Foundation, see clipping files at the Carter Center Office of Public Information. Ms. de Menil is quoted in the *Carter Center News*, spring 1988, 11. Jimmy Carter to Dominique de Menil, October 14, 1985, JCPPP, De Menil Prize File, Box 12.

15. Dominique de Menil to Douglas Brinkley, August 12, 1995.

16. Kai Bird, "The Very Model of an Ex-President," *Nation*, November 12, 1990, 1.

17. *Fortune*, May 1989.

18. Jimmy Carter, "Acceptance Address of the William J. Fulbright Prize for International Understanding," *Fulbright Association Newsletter* 17, no. 2 (1994). For the Carter-Coke connection, see Mark Pendergrast's *For God, Country, and Coca-Cola* (New York: Scribner's, 1993), 347–64.

19. Betty Pope, interview, January 1995, Americus, Ga.

20. "Democrats Calling on Carter," *NYT*, September 12, 1986; and "Southerner Is Needed in '88, Carter Asserts," *NYT*, September 24, 1986.

21. Karen Heller, "Jimmy Carter: Building a Solid Reputation," *Philadelphia Enquirer*, March 19, 1990.

22. Jimmy Carter to Nicolae Ceauçescu, December 4, 1987, JCPPP, Box 11.

23. This complaint comes from interviews with over ten Carter Center associates.

24. Stuart Eizenstat, interview, October 1995, Brussels; and *NYT*, December 28, 1980.

25. Howard Baker Jr. to Kenneth Kline, March 23, 1981; and Claude Pepper to Kenneth Kline, November 2, 1981, Jimmy Carter vertical files, 1981–1985, JCPL.

26. John Lucas, *American Heritage*, September 1994.

27. Barry Goldwater quoted in *Parade*, April 1995; Benjamin Hooks to Kenneth Kline, January 21, 1982, vertical files, 1981–1985; and Anthony Lewis, interview, October 1995, London.

28. "Carter Center Dedicated," *Carter Center News*, summer 1987, 1–3; *Atlanta Journal & Constitution*, October 2, 1986.

29. For Carter's glowing opinion of Christopher's service in his administration, see Jimmy Carter, *Keeping Faith: Memoirs of a President*, 521.

30. Warren Christopher, interview, August 1995, Washington, D.C.

31. *Arizona Republic* quoted in "Carter Center Dedicated," *Carter Center News*, summer 1987, 2.

32. William E. Schmidt, "Joy over Carter Library Fails to Stop Fight over Parkway to It," *NYT*, October 2, 1986.

33. William E. Schmidt, "President Praises Carter at Library," *NYT*, October 2, 1986. Also *NYT*, *Washington Post*, and *Atlanta Journal & Constitution* published Reagan's remarks in full.

34. Ibid.

35. Christopher, interview.

36. Warren Christopher, "Remarks at the Opening of the Carter Center," transcript, October 1, 1986, given to author by Terrence Adamson, Terrence Adamson Personal Papers, Washington, D.C.

37. Timothy J. McNulty, "Born Again: Jimmy Carter May Be Our Most Successful Ex-President," *Chicago Tribune Magazine*, July 8, 1990.

38. Jimmy Carter, interview, April 1995, Atlanta.

39. Bernard Weinraub, "President Turns Fire on Carter in Southern Drive," *NYT*, October 25, 1986.

40. Morris H. Morley, *Washington, Somoza, and the Sandinistas: State and Regime in U.S. Policy toward Nicaragua, 1969–1981* (Cambridge: Cambridge University Press, 1994).

41. Maureen Dowd, ". . . And Carter Urges Reagan to Talk," *NYT*, December 10, 1986.

42. Carter, interview, April 1995, Atlanta.

43. Ronald Reagan to Jimmy Carter, December 15, 1986, JCPPP, Box 10.

44. Global 2000 Clipping Files, Charles Kirbo Building, Atlanta.

45. Donald R. Hopkins et al., "Dracunculiasis Eradication: Beginning of the End," *American Journal of Tropical Medical Hygiene* 49, no. 3 (1993): 281–89.

46. Peter Bourne, interview, September 1997, Washington, D.C.

47. Susan K. Reed and Giovanna Breau, "The Terminator: Dr. Donald Hopkins Wears Victory in His 15-year Battle to Eradicate a Clipping Parasite, Guinea Worm," *People*, October 30, 1995, 119–21.

48. Donald Hopkins, interview, November 1995, Chicago. Also Donald Hopkins, *Princes and Peasants: Smallpox in History* (Chicago: University of Chicago Press, 1983).

49. Hopkins et al., "Dracunculiasis Eradication," 281–89; Hopkins crippled girl quote from Beth Dawkins Bassett, "Let Not the Sinuous Worm Strike Me . . . ," *Carter Center News*, fall 1995, 4.

50. Donald R. Hopkins and E. Ruiz-Tiben, "Strategies for Dracunculiasis Eradication," *Bulletin of the World Health Organization* 69, no. 5 (1991): 533–40; and Hopkins, interview.

51. Jimmy Carter, interview, October 1995, Plains, Ga.

52. Timothy J. McNulty, "Born Again: Why Jimmy Carter May Be Our Most Successful Ex-President," *Chicago Tribune Magazine*, July 8, 1990, 1–6.

53. Terrence Adamson to Douglas Brinkley, February 16, 1998.

54. Russ Rymer, "The Mission," *In*

Health 4, no. 2 (March–April 1990): 66–76.

55. Jimmy Carter to Agha Hasan Abedi, July 20, 1985, JCPPP, Box 10.

56. Larry Gurwin, "Who Really Owns First American Bank?" *Regardie's* 10, no. 9 (May 1990): 66–88.

57. "Global 2000 Inaugurates Bangladesh Development Program" and "Global 2000 Inaugurates Pakistan Development Program," Carter Center press releases, November 1–2, 1986, JCPPP, Bangladesh-Pakistan File, October 26–November 6, 1986, Box 6.

58. Carter, interview, October 1995.

59. Donald Hopkins et al., "Eradication of Dracunculiasis from Pakistan," *Lancet* 346 (September 2, 1995): 621–24.

60. Jimmy Carter to Agha Hasan Abedi, July 20, 1985, JCPPP, Box 10.

61. Douglas Brinkley, "Jimmy Carter's Modest Quest for Global Peace," *Foreign Affairs*, November–December 1995. Also Steve Sternberg, "Pesticide Gifts Goal: Cut Illness by Killing Guinea Worm," *Atlanta Journal & Constitution*, March 28, 1990.

62. "A Conversation with Sam Nunn," *Georgia Tech Alumni Magazine*, spring 1990, 16.

63. The conference proceedings were published as Robert Pastor, ed., *Democracy in the Americas: Stopping the Pendulum* (New York: Holmes & Meier, 1989).

64. Robert Pastor, "The Latin American and Caribbean Program: The Carter Center of Emory University: A Three Year Plan, 1986–89," December 1, 1985, Robert Pastor Personal Papers, Atlanta.

65. Robert Pastor, "Nurturing Democracy in the Americas," memorandum, October 22, 1986, Pastor Personal Papers.

66. Jimmy Carter to Robert Pastor, comments in the margins of Pastor's October 22, 1986, memorandum, Pastor Personal Papers.

67. Robert Pastor, interview, October 1995, Atlanta.

68. Cerezo quoted in Carter Center summary notes, "Reinforcing Democracy in the Americas," Latin American and Caribbean Studies Files, Carter Center, Atlanta.

69. Pastor, interview.

70. Robert Pastor, "How to Reinforce Democracy in the Americas: Seven Proposals," in Robert Pastor, ed., *Democracy in the Americas*, 139–55. The twelve leaders that decided to create the council included Jimmy Carter, Gerald Ford, Raul Alfonsin, Errol Barrow, Vinicio Cerezo, Nicolas Ardito Barletta, Fernando Belaunde, Rafael Caldera, Osvaldo Hurtado, Daniel Oduber, George Price, and Pierre Elliot Trudeau.

71. George Price, interview, February 1995, Port-au-Prince, Haiti.

72. "Latin American Council Created in Atlanta," *Christian Science Monitor*, November 18, 1986.

73. Michael Manley, interview, November 1995, Kingston, Jamaica.

74. Jimmy Carter, trip report (Haiti, October 1987), Pastor Personal Papers; and Carter Haiti trip itinerary, October 21–23, JCPPP, Box 9.

75. "Hope for Haiti," *Miami Herald*, October 23, 1987.

76. Elliott Abrams to Jimmy Carter, October 26, 1987, JCPPP, Haiti File 1987, Box 11.

THIRTEEN: TRAVELS WITH CARTER

1. Jimmy Carter, interview, May 1995, Atlanta.

2. Elaine Sciolino, "U.S. Officials Urge Carter to Cancel a Damascus Trip," *NYT*, March 3, 1987.

3. Jimmy Carter to Ken Stein, December 16, 1986, JCPPP, Middle East Trip Files, Box 6, JCPL.

4. Ken Stein to President and Mrs. Carter, December 1, 1986, JCPPP, Middle East Trip Files.

5. Faye Dill, interview, May 1995, Atlanta. Also Middle East trip schedule and newspaper clippings, March 15–31, 1987 (Egypt), JCPPP, Middle East Trip Files.

6. "Carter Says Assad Ready to Talk," *Jerusalem Post*, March 27, 1987; and *NYT*, March 20, 1987.

7. "Reagan Is Faulted on Middle East," *NYT*, March 20, 1987.

8. *Jerusalem Post*, March 27, 1987.

9. Randall Ashley, interview, July 1995, Atlanta.

10. Carter, interview, May 1995, Atlanta.

11. John G. Healy to Jimmy Carter, March 6, 1987, JCPPP, Middle East Trip Files. Healy, head of Amnesty International, alerted Carter to a number of human rights abuses in Syria: "Amnesty International is concerned with the wellbeing of some 33 Lebanese nationals arrested in their homes by Syrian security forces and transferred to incommunicado detention in Syrian prisons. We had recruited consistent reports that Syrian detainees are tortured by officials in the state security system."

12. Carter, interview, May 1995, Atlanta.

13. "Former President Carter's March 25 Press Conference in Amman," official State Department transcript, Intercontinental Hotel, Amman, Jordan, JCPPP, Middle East Trip Files; and *Jerusalem Post*, March 27, 1987.

14. Shimon Peres, interview, February 1996, Tel Aviv.

15. *Egyptian Gazette* (story carried globally by Reuters and UPI), March 20, 1997. For the Carter Center's attempt to arrange a meeting with Begin, see JCPPP, Middle East Trip Files.

16. Abraham H. Foxman, "A Double Standard," *Jerusalem Post*, July 27, 1985.

17. Randall Ashley, interview, July 1995, Atlanta.

18. Jimmy Carter–George Shultz meeting, April 3, Middle East Trip Files. Shultz had a government plane pick Carter up in Americus at 6:45 A.M. so he could arrive in time for breakfast.

19. Mary Elizabeth King, "Palestinian Nonviolent Resistance and the *Intifada*," unpublished manuscript, Mary King Personal Papers, Carter Center, Atlanta. For King's experiences with SNCC, see Mary King, *Freedom Song* (New York: Morrow, 1987); Mary King Collection, Wisconsin State Historical Society; and Clayborne Carson, *In Struggle: SNCC and the Black Awakening of the 1960s*

(Cambridge, Mass.: Harvard University Press, 1981).

20. Ibid.

21. Mary King, interview, December 1995, Washington, D.C.

22. For Bourne's extraordinarily close relationship with Carter, see Peter G. Bourne, *Jimmy Carter: A Comprehensive Biography from Plains to Postpresidency* (New York: Scribner's, 1997). Also Peter Bourne, interview, October 1993, Atlanta.

23. King, interview, December 1995.

24. Julian Bond, interview, April 1994, Birmingham, Ala.

25. King, "Palestinian Nonviolent Resistance."

26. Mary King, interview, July 1997, Washington, D.C. Also King, "Palestinian Nonviolent Resistance."

27. Douglas Brinkley notes of Carter-Arafat meeting, Friday, January 19, 1996, Gaza City, Israel. I took notes at a three-hour-long dinner with Arafat and Carter.

28. Odeh Aburdene, interview, January 1998, Washington, D.C.

29. King, interview, December 1995.

30. Jimmy Carter, report on Mary King to the John Simon Guggenheim Memorial Foundation, November 26, 1985, King Personal Papers.

31. King, interview, December 1995; and Jimmy Carter, "The Middle East Consultation: A Look at the Future," *Middle East Journal* 42, no. 2 (spring 1988): 191.

32. Ibid.

33. Shawn Tully, "The Big Moneymen of Palestine, Inc.," *Fortune*, July 31, 1989, 108–13.

34. Mary King to Jimmy Carter, October 22, 1987, JCPPP, Box 8.

35. Jimmy Carter to Faye Dill, October 22, 1987, JCPPP, Box 28. Also King, interview, December 1995.

36. King, interview, December 1995.

37. Mubarak Awad, interview, January 1996, Jerusalem; King, interview, December 1995; and Jimmy Carter, interview, January 1996, Jerusalem. Gene Sharp's three-volume work *The Politics of Nonviolent Action* (Boston: Porter Sargent, 1973) was widely distributed in the

occupied territories in the years prior to the Palestinian *intifada*. In his later books he categorizes nonviolent action as a civilian-based defense—a classification that, he insists, should have parity with military strategy.

38. Hanan Ashrawi, interview, January 1996, Jerusalem.

39. Awad, interview.

40. King, interview, December 1995.

41. Carter wrote two policy essays with the assistance of Ken Stein following his Middle East journey: *Time*, April 20, 1987; and *Washington Quarterly*, summer 1987. Besides briefing the Reagan administration, Carter gave talks on the Middle East to the Council on Foreign Relations, CSIS, and the American Jewish Congress.

42. Bill Kovach, "Life after the White House," *Atlanta Journal & Constitution*, July 12, 1987.

43. Margaret Thatcher, *The Downing Street Years* (New York: Harper Collins, 1993), 68–69.

44. Quoted in Kovach, "Life after the White House."

45. Jimmy Carter to Deng Xiaoping, June 17, 1987, JCPPP, Trip File (China), Box 7. Also Kovach, "Life after the White House."

46. Kovach, "Life after the White House."

47. Ibid.

48. Jimmy Carter, interview, March 1994, Plains, Ga.

49. Jimmy Carter, *Talking Peace*, 106–7.

50. Kovach, "Life after the White House."

51. Ibid.

52. Jimmy Carter to Anatoly Dobrynin, July 2, 1987, JCPPP, Trip File (USSR), Box 7.

53. For the outcome of the consultation, see "Searching for Peace in the Middle East," *Carter Center News*, spring 1988.

54. Carter, *Talking Peace*, 104.

55. Quoted in Kovach, "Life after the White House."

56. *Financial Times*, London, November 26, 1987.

57. William Quandt, interview, July 1997, Charlottesville, Va.

58. Robert O. Freedman, ed., *The Intifada: Its Impact on Israel, the Arab World and the Superpowers* (Gainesville, Fla.: University Press of Florida, 1991); and David Makovsky, *Making Peace with the PLO: The Rabin Government's Road to the Oslo Accord* (Boulder, Colo.: Westview Press, 1996).

59. Carter, interview, May 1995, Atlanta.

60. Jimmy Carter, "The U.S. Needs to Lead in Israel," *NYT*, February 14, 1988.

61. Ibid.

62. Quandt, interview.

63. Bernard Weinraub, "For Bush, Issues of Early 80s Lie," *NYT*, May 1, 1988.

64. Ibid. Also see vice presidential papers of George Bush (May–July 1988), Bush Library, Texas A & M, College Station, Tex.

65. E. J. Dionne Jr., "Dukakis Says Bush Has Blank Record," *NYT*, May 2, 1988. Also Michael Dukakis, interview, August 1997, Boston. After losing, Dukakis never blamed Carter—"I'm a huge fan of Carter's, in no way did his legacy cause me to lose."

66. The Commission on Minority Participation in Education and American Life (Washington, D.C.: U.S. Government Printing Office, May 1988).

67. Marshall Frady, *Jesse: The Life and Pilgrimage of Jesse Jackson* (New York: Random House, 1986), 402–17. Also Jimmy Carter, interview, February 1995, Port-au-Prince, Haiti.

68. Robin Tower, "Dukakis Restates Position on Israel," *NYT*, June 11, 1988.

69. Maureen Dowd, "Man-About Banks Proves Belle of Ball," *NYT*, July 15, 1988; and Ronald Smothers, "Carter Sidesteps Mediating Dispute," *NYT*, July 16, 1988.

70. Paul Kirk, interview, July 1997, Boston.

71. Curtis Wilkie, "Carter's Image

Seen Regaining Luster," *Boston Globe*, July 19, 1988; and Maureen Dowd, "Star Twinkle amid Glitches in a Show of Unified Strength," *NYT*, July 19, 1988.

72. Jimmy Carter to Senator Edward Kennedy, July 25, 1988; Senator Edward Kennedy to Jimmy Carter, July 25, 1988, JCPPP, 1988 Democratic Convention, Box 31.

73. Kirk, interview.

74. Mondale quoted in Dowd, "Star Twinkle"; and Kirk quoted in Wilkie, "Carter's Image."

75. *NYT*, September 18, 1988; and *NYT*, September 21, 1988.

76. For Billy Beer statistics, see *NYT*, May 2, 1988. Other Billy Carter stories emanate from Billy and Sybil Carter (with Ken Estes), *Billy* (Newport, R.I.: Edgehill Press, 1989); and Hugh Carter, *Cousin Beedie & Cousin Hot: My Life with the Carter Family of Plains, Georgia* (Englewood Cliffs, N.J.: Prentice-Hall, 1978).

77. Carter, interview, May 1995, Atlanta.

78. Martin Tolchin, "From Carter and Ford, an American Agenda," *NYT*, May 24, 1988.

79. Jimmy Carter and Gerald Ford, eds., *American Agenda: Report to the Forty-First President of the United States* (Camp Hill, Penn.: Book-of-the-Month Club, 1989). Also R. W. Apple, "2 Ex-Presidents Advise Bush: Forget Vow and Raise Taxes," *NYT*, November 22, 1988.

80. Gerald Ford, interview, July 1995, Beaver Creek, Colo.

81. Carter, interview, May 1995, Atlanta.

82. Quoted in "Carter Calls for Mediation Unit," *NYT*, December 11, 1988.

83. Makovsky, *Making Peace with the PLO*, 8–9; and Carter, interview, May 1995, Atlanta.

84. Salman Rushdie, *The Satanic Verses* (New York: Viking, 1988).

85. Jimmy Carter, 'Rushdie's Book Is an Insult," *NYT*, March 5, 1989.

86. Ibid.

87. James Dickey, interview, March 1993, Columbia, S.C.

88. Carter, interview, May 1995, Atlanta.

FOURTEEN: BUSINESS AS USUAL, CARTER STYLE

1. Jimmy Carter to Rajiv Gandhi, February 11, 1988, Habitat File, JCPPP, Box 10, JCPL.

2. Jimmy Carter to His Excellency Jenderal Soeharto, February 10, 1988, Habitat File.

3. Jimmy Carter, interview, December 1993, Plains, Ga.

4. Jimmy Carter to His Excellency Milton Obote, February 27, 1985, Habitat File.

5. Millard Fuller, interview, August 1995, Americus, Ga.

6. Jimmy and Rosalynn Carter, *Everything to Gain: Making the Most of the Rest of Your Life* (New York: Ballantine Books, 1987), 106.

7. Jimmy Carter Work Projects, "Historic Summary," Habitat for Humanity International Chicago (June 1986), Habitat for Humanity Archive, Americus, Ga.

8. Fuller, interview, August 1995.

9. Jimmy and Rosalynn Carter, *Everything to Gain*, 116–17.

10. Ibid. Also "Prisoners Find Freedom in Service," *Habitat World* 1, no. 1 (March 1984).

11. Millard Fuller with Diane Scott, *No More Shacks!* (Waco, Tex.: Word Publishers, 1986), 196.

12. Fred Boyles, interview, August 1995, Plains, Ga.

13. Mary Fitzpatrick (Prince), interview, January 1996, Americus, Ga.

14. Amy Carter, interview, April 1996, New Orleans.

15. Fitzpatrick, interview.

16. Millard Fuller, interview, December 1997, Americus, Ga.

17. Jimmy Carter Work Projects, "Historic Summary," Habitat for Humanity International, Charlotte, N.C. (July 1987), Habitat for Humanity Archive.

18. Rudy Hayes (*Americus Ledger-*

Journal), interview, January 1996, Americus, Ga.; Betty Pope, interview, January 1996, Americus, Ga.; and Jim Galloway, "Habitat's Founder Hits Road for Housing Funds," *Atlanta Journal & Constitution*, August 4, 1983.

19. Millard Fuller, correspondence to 7-11s and Piggly Wiggly, JCPPP, Habitat for Humanity File, Box 5 out of 6.

20. "Jimmy Carter and Habitat for Humanity," February 10, 1995, Carter quote sheet used for promotional purposes, Habitat for Humanity Archive.

21. Jimmy Carter to Millard Fuller, March 31, 1987, JCPPP, Habitat for Humanity File.

22. Millard Fuller to Jimmy Carter, April 14, 1987, JCPPP, Habitat for Humanity File.

23. Steven Raas to Jimmy Carter, April 27, 1987, JCPPP, Habitat for Humanity File.

24. Jimmy Carter to Millard Fuller, May 11, 1987, JCPPP, Habitat for Humanity File.

25. Millard Fuller, *A Simple, Decent Place to Live: The Building Realization of Habitat for Humanity* (Dallas, Tex.: Word Publishing, 1995).

26. Ibid., 76–77.

27. Carter, interview, April 1995, Atlanta.

28. Jimmy Carter to Paul Newman, January 26, 1988; Newman to Carter, February 7, 1988, JCPPP, Box 10. Also Carter to Newman, November 1, 1985, JCPPP, Habitat for Humanity File; Millard Fuller and Linda Fuller, *The Excitement Is Building: How Habitat for Humanity Is Putting Roofs over Heads and Hope in Hearts* (Dallas, Tex.: Word Publishing, 1990), 16–19; and Fuller, *A Simple, Decent Place to Live*, 141.

29. Gerald Ford, interview, July 1995, Beaver Creek, Colo.

30. Fuller, interview, August 1995.

31. Fuller, interview, January 1996, Americus, Ga.

32. "What People Are Saying about Habitat for Humanity," March 1996, Habitat for Humanity Archive.

33. Fuller, *A Simple, Decent Place to Live*, 77.

34. Fuller and Fuller, *The Excitement Is Building*, 21–23.

35. Christopher Matthews, "Jimmy Carter Finds His Place in the Sun," *San Francisco Examiner*, August 19, 1990.

36. David Wigg, *And Then They Forgot to Tell Us Why: A Look at the Campaign against River Blindness in West Africa* (Washington, D.C.: World Bank, 1993).

37. Ibid. Also, D. H. Molyneux, "Onchocerciasis Control in West Africa: Current Status and Future of the Onchocerciasis Control Programme," *Parasitology Today* 11, no. 11 (November 1995): 399–402.

38. Erik Eckholm, "River Blindness: Conquering an Ancient Scourge," *NYT Magazine*, January 8, 1989; and Carter, *Living Faith* (New York: Times Books, 1996), 176–77.

39. "The Decision to Donate Mectizan: Historical Background," Merck & Co., Inc., Archives, Rahway, New Jersey; and Mectizan Expert Committee, Organization Meeting, February 23–24, 1988, JCPPP, Box 32.

40. Ibid.

41. Transcript of Jimmy Carter Sunday school class, November 1994, Maranatha Baptist Church, Plains, Ga.; and "Carter Center and Merck Step Up Efforts to Fight River Blindness in Africa," *Carter Center News*, winter 1995.

42. "Why the Carters Came," *African Journal*, Merck & Co. Archive.

43. Jimmy Carter, transcript of speech, Joint Programme Committee (JPC) Onchocerciasis Control Programme (OCP), December 6–8, 1995, World Bank Headquarters, Washington, D.C.

44. "Jimmy Carter River Blindness Initiative, Summary Report 1996," Merck & Co. Archive, Rahway, N.J.

45. Ross Newman, "The $400-Million Fan," *Los Angeles Times*, May 26, 1996.

46. John Moores, interview, October 1997, San Diego, Calif.

47. Ibid.

48. Ibid.

49. Ibid.

50. Moores, interview, February 1996, Atlanta.

51. Donald Hopkins, interview, June 1995, Chicago; and William Foege, interview, April 1995, Atlanta. Also Richard W. Stevenson, "The Chief Banker for the Nations at the Bottom of the Heap," *NYT*, September 14, 1997.

52. "World Can Ease Guinea Worm, Polio, U. S. Health Officials Say," *Houston Post*, April 8, 1990; Hopkins, interview; and Carter, *Living Faith*, 173–74.

53. "Seven Years of Sight-Saving," *African Journal*, Merck & Co. Archive.

54. William Foege, notes from September 1994 journey to Chad, Mectizan Program Notes, William Foege Papers, Charles Kirbo Building, Atlanta.

55. Ibid.

56. "Seven Years of Sight-Saving." Also William Foege to Douglas Brinkley, January 30, 1998; "Carter Center Steps Up to Control River Blindness," *Carter Center News*, summer 1996; and Warren E. Leary, "With One Disease Nearly Erased, Assault Is Planned on Another," *NYT*, December 6, 1995.

FIFTEEN: SHOWDOWN WITH NORIEGA

1. Jimmy Carter interview, May 1995, Atlanta.

2. James A. Baker III, interview, September 1995, Houston, Tex.

3. Jim Wright, *Worth It All* (McLean, Va.: Brassey's, 1993), 218–19.

4. Robert Kagan, *A Twilight Struggle: American Power and Nicaragua, 1977–1990* (New York: Free Press, 1996), 620–29.

5. Wright, *Worth It All*, 223.

6. James A. Baker III, *The Politics of Diplomacy: Revolution, War and Peace* (New York: Putnam, 1995), 58.

7. Baker, interview.

8. Bernard Aronson, "Preliminary Thoughts on Latin America," February 7, 1989, Bernard Aronson Personal Papers, Washington, D.C.

9. Bernard Aronson, interview, August 1997, Washington, D.C.

10. Robert Kagan, *A Twilight Struggle*, 497–515.

11. Robert Pastor, interview, April 1995, Atlanta. Costa Rican president Oscar Arias had helped broker a five-nation Central American peace plan in 1987. Reagan had opposed the plan, claiming that its prohibition outside of nonmilitary intervention would undermine the Contras in Nicaragua.

12. Ortega quoted in Kagan, *A Twilight Struggle*, 620.

13. "Quayle Chides Carter for Talk with Ortega," *NYT*, February, 3, 1989.

14. Robert Pear, "Quayle Calls Managua Vote Plan a Sham," *NYT*, June 13, 1989.

15. Pastor, interview.

16. Jimmy Carter, interview, August 1994, Americus, Ga.

17. Pastor, interview.

18. Carter, interview, August 1994.

19. Robert Pastor, memorandum to Jimmy Carter, February 6, 1989, re conversation with Bernie Aronson, Robert Pastor Personal Papers, Atlanta.

20. Pastor, interview.

21. Robert Pastor, memorandum to Council of Freely Elected Heads of State, March 2, 1989, Pastor Personal Papers. Also "The May 7 Panamanian Elections: A Pre-Election Report," April 24, 1989, prepared by the NDI/IRI International Delegation.

22. Quoted in Carter Center press release, March 12, 1989, Carter Center Collection Files, Carrie Harmon Office, Atlanta.

23. Sergio Benedixen, analysis to Robert Pastor, May 3, 1989, Pastor Personal Papers. USIA sponsored a survey in Panama in April 1994 that found that 70 percent of Panamanians viewed Torrijos favorably, as compared to only 5 percent viewing Noriega favorably. Conversely, 22 percent viewed Torrijos unfavorably, as compared to 89 percent who viewed Noriega unfavorably.

24. Colin Powell with Joseph E. Persico, *My American Journey* (New York: Random House, 1995), 412–13.

25. For a discussion of Noriega's relationship with the CIA, see Manuel Noriega and Peter Eisner, *American Prisoner: The Memoirs of Manuel Noriega* (New York: Random House, 1997), 58–66.

Noriega believes that the December 20, 1989, invasion of Panama would never have taken place if Reagan's CIA director, William Casey, had lived. "Casey had the power and the inclination to defend me against the conspiracy that was developing against me, spurred on by Panamanian opponents and their friends in Washington," Noriega wrote. "Casey knew what was going on in Panama. The drug trial would not have worked it he were alive because I would have had him as a living testament and defender; he knew the truth about all the charges against me."

26. Ibid., 195–217. Not everyone concurred. Perhaps the most credible witness, who claims the drug trafficking charges against Noriega were trumped up is General Fred Woerner, the southern command chief until the fall of 1989, when he was replaced by General Colin Powell. "Overall, I never saw any credible evidence of drug trafficking involving General Noriega," Woerner said. "My analysis was that the U.S. policy of isolating Panama and its military was counterproductive to U.S. interests." Yet it must be remembered that Woerner was removed by Bush because he was reluctant to provide options for intervening in Panama.

27. Baker, *The Politics of Diplomacy*, 180.

28. Brent Scowcroft to Jimmy Carter, March 28, 1989, Pastor Personal Papers.

29. William Webster, interview, April 1997, Hempstead, N.Y.

30. Pastor, interview.

31. Scowcroft to Carter, March 28, 1989.

32. Carter, interview, May 1994, Atlanta.

33. Pastor, interview.

34. Jimmy Carter, interview, May 1995, Atlanta.

35. Thomas Carothers, "The NED at 10," *Foreign Policy*, spring 1993, 123–38. Also National Democratic Institute Annual Report, NDI Archives, Washington, D.C.

36. Ibid.

37. Brian Atwood to Jimmy Carter,

November 4, 1987, JCPPP, Haiti File 1997, Box 11. Also Kenneth Wollack, interview, August 1997, Washington, D.C.

38. Brian Atwood, interview, December 1995, Washington, D.C.; and Wollack, interview.

39. Baker, interview. Also "The Hemispheric Agenda Conference" (final report), March 29–30, 1989, JCPPP, New Hemispheric Agenda File, Box 31.

40. Address by Hon. James A Baker III to the Carter Center of Emory University's Consultation on a New Hemispheric Agenda, Atlanta, March 30, 1989, U.S. Department of State Press Release no. 56.

41. Brian Atwood to Jimmy Carter, April 24, 1989, Pastor Personal Papers.

42. Robert Pastor, memorandum to Jimmy Carter, April 5, 1989, Pastor Personal Papers.

43. Robert Pastor, memorandum to Jimmy Carter, April 23, 1989, Pastor Personal Papers.

44. Jimmy Carter to Manuel Antonio Noriega, April 24, 1989, Pastor Personal Papers.

45. Robert Pastor, memorandum to Jimmy Carter re conversation with Noriega, April 30, 1989, Pastor Personal Papers. Pastor's conversation with Noriega took place in Room 230 of the Marriott Hotel in Panama City from 7:00 to 8:40 P.M. on April 26, 1989. For Pastor's being declared persona non grata, see General Manuel Noriega to Jimmy Carter, April 27, 1989, JCPPP, Panama File, Box 31.

46. Jimmy Carter to General Manuel Noriega, April 28, 1989, Pastor Personal Papers.

47. Wollack, interview.

48. Brent Scowcroft to Jimmy Carter, May 4, 1989, JCPPP, Panama File, Box 30.

49. Jimmy Carter, statement upon arrival in Panama, May 5, 1989 (plus working drafts), Pastor Personal Papers. Also Pastor, interview.

50. Jimmy Carter, *Talking Peace*, 130–31.

51. Sergio Benedixen to Robert Pastor

(Analysis and Poll Results in Panama), May 5, 1989, Pastor Personal Papers.

52. Jimmy Carter travel diary, May 9, 1989, Carter Center, Atlanta.

53. Ibid. Also see "The May 7, 1989 Panamanian Elections," International Delegation Report (NDI/IRI), 43–48. Carter and Ford wrote a joint foreword to the report.

54. Wollack, interview.

55. "Carter: I Negotiated with Noriega to No Avail," *Atlanta Journal & Constitution*, February 18, 1990.

56. Carter, interview, May 1995, Atlanta; and Aronson, interview, August 1997.

57. Baker, interview.

58. Pastor, interview.

59. Jimmy Carter, "In Perspective: Panama in Crisis," *Carter Center News*, spring 1989, 2.

60. Pastor, interview.

61. Aronson, interview, August 1997.

62. Wollack, interview.

63. Pastor, interview.

64. Lindsey Gruson, "Noriega Stealing Election, Carter Says," *NYT*, May 9, 1989. Also see Frederick Kempe, "Noriega Slows Vote Tally to Crawl in Panama," *Wall Street Journal*, May 9, 1989.

65. Senator Dennis DeConcini to Jimmy Carter, May 11, 1989, JCPPP, Panama File, Box 31.

66. Pastor, interview.

67. Hendrik Hertzberg, "Actions Restore Carter's Posture as a President," *New Republic*, May 1989.

68. Bernard Weinraub, "Bush Urges Effort to Press Moriega to Quit as Leader," *NYT*, May 10, 1989.

69. Jimmy Carter to President Marquez Felipe Gonzales, May 10, 1989, Pastor Personal Papers.

70. Jimmy Carter, White House meeting notes, May 9, 1989, Pastor Personal Papers.

71. Baker, interview. Also see Jimmy Carter's "Statement on Panama to the Consultation of the Foreign Ministers of the OAS," May 17, 1989, JCPPP, Panama File, Box 31.

72. Jimmy Carter to President Carlos Andrés Perez, May 10, 1987, Pastor Personal Papers.

73. Carter, "In Perspective: Panama in Crisis," *Carter Center News*, spring 1989, 2.

74. Weinraub, "Bush Urges Effort to Press Noriega to Quit as Leader," *NYT*, May 10, 1989.

75. Jimmy Carter to Brent Scowcroft, May 10, 1989, Pastor Personal Papers.

76. Baker, *The Politics of Diplomacy*, 184.

77. Aronson, interview, October 1997.

78. E. J. Dionne Jr., "Carter Begins to Shed Negative Public Image," *NYT*, May 18, 1989; and *New Republic*, May 1989.

79. Richard Cohen, "The Lost Dignity in Public Service," *Washington Post*, May 14, 1989.

80. Gerald Ford, interview, July 1995, Beaver Creek, Colo.

81. "Role Likely for Carter in Nicaragua Elections," *NYT*, August 8, 1989. Also Pastor, interview.

82. "Carter to Bring Together Ethiopian Foes," *NYT*, August 18, 1989.

83. Ibid.

84. Interview transcript, November 1989, JCPPP, Ethiopia-Eritrean Peace Talks File, Box 42.

85. Stanley Cloud, "Hail to the Ex-Chief," *Time*, September 11, 1080, 51–54. In 1985 Carter had started writing Mengistu asking for the release of Jabril Obssie from prison. See Jimmy Carter to Chairman Mengistu Haile Mariam, August 21, 1985, JCPPP, Personal Favors File, Box 11.

86. "Carter to Bring Together Ethiopian Foes," *NYT*, August 18, 1989. Also see "2nd Rebel Group Joins Carter's Ethiopia Talks," *NYT*, August 25, 1989; R. W. Apple Jr., "Carter the Peacemaker Now Turns to Ethiopia," *NYT*, September 8, 1989; and Wayne King, "Carter Redux," *NYT Magazine*, December 10, 1989.

87. Carter, *Talking Peace*, 119–24.

88. "Ethiopia Talks Make Progress," *NYT*, September 16, 1989.

89. Rosalynn Carter story is included in Carter, *Talking Peace*, 122.

90. Jerry Schwartz, "Carter Reports Progress in Ethiopia Peace Talks," *NYT*, September 21, 1989.

91. *NYT*, November 21, 1989; *NYT*, November 24, 1989; and William Foege, interview, April 1995, Atlanta.

92. "Sudanese Agree on Food Flights, Carter Says," *NYT*, December 3, 1989.

93. Kaunda quoted in Cloud, "Hail to the Ex-Chief," *Time*, September 11, 1989, 51–54.

94. Carter, *Talking Peace*, 124.

95. "Carter Lashes Bush's Response to Eastern Europe," *Houston Post*, November 7, 1989.

96. Noriega and Eisner, *American Prisoner*, 165–67; and Baker, *The Politics of Diplomacy*, 185–88.

97. Carter, interview, May 1995, Atlanta.

98. Bruce Bagley, "U.S. Foreign Policy and the War on Drugs: Analysis of a Policy Failure," *Journal of Inter-American Studies and World Affairs* 31 (summer/fall 1989).

99. Baker, *The Politics of Diplomacy*, 108.

100. Ibid.

101. Robert Pastor, *Whirlpool: U.S. Foreign Policy toward Latin America and the Caribbean* (Princeton, N.J.: Princeton University Press, 1993), 92.

102. Baker, *The Politics of Diplomacy*, 188–94. Also, for a history of U.S. intervention in Panama, see Walter LeFeber, *The Panama Canal: The Crisis in Historical Perspective* (New York: Oxford University Press, 1978).

103. Robert Pastor to Douglas Brinkley, November 23, 1997.

104. Noriega and Eisner, *American Prisoner*, 10–11.

105. Brent Scowcroft, interview, April 1997, Hempstead, N.Y.

106. Ibid. Also, Stephen E. Ambrose and Douglas G. Brinkley, *Rise to Globalism: American Foreign Policy since 1938*, 8th ed. (New York: Viking, 1997), 372.

107. Art Harris, "Citizen Carter," *Washington Post*, February 22, 1990.

108. Carter, interview, May 1995, Atlanta.

109. Eduardo Valdes (president of Panama's Tribunal Electoral) to Jimmy Carter, November 16, 1993; "1994 Panama Election Report," Carter Center, Atlanta. Carter accepted the offer on April 25, 1994.

110. Jimmy Carter, arrival statement, May 6, 1994, Panama City, Panama, "1994 Election Report."

111. *Washington Post* (editorial), May 10, 1994. For Wright's role in the election, see Tracey Wilkinson, "Noriega's Party Wins Panamanian Election," *Fort Worth Star Telegram*, May 9, 1994.

112. Jimmy Carter departure statement, May 9, 1994, Panama City, "1994 Election Report."

SIXTEEN: DEMOCRACY COMES TO NICARAGUA

1. Jimmy Carter to Daniel Ortega Saavedra, June 30, 1989, Nicaragua Files, Carter Center, Atlanta.

2. Robert Pastor, interview, August 1997, Atlanta.

3. Javier Pérez de Cuéllar, *Pilgrimage for Peace* (New York: St. Martin's Press, 1997), 414–16.

4. Jimmy Carter, interview, May 1995, Atlanta.

5. Pastor, interview.

6. Ibid.

7. Daniel Ortega Saavedra, June 30, 1989, Nicaragua Files. Also Mariano Fiallos Oyanguren (president of Nicaraguan Supreme Electoral Council) to Jimmy Carter, August 4, 1989; and Dr. Gustavo Tablada Zelaya (National Opposition Union of Nicaragua) to Jimmy Carter, August 4, 1989, Nicaragua Files.

8. Jimmy Carter to President Daniel Ortega Saavedra, August 8, 1989, Nicaragua Files.

9. Carter, interview, May 1995, Atlanta.

10. Gerald Ford, interview, July 1995, Beaver Creek, Colo.

11. James A. Baker III, interview, September 1995, Houston, Tex.

12. "Summary Report on Pre-Election

Trip to Nicaragua," September 16–18, 1989, Observer Delegation, Council of Freely Elected Heads of Government, Carter Center. Also Pastor, interview.

13. Jimmy Carter to President Daniel Ortega Saavedra and Brooklyn Rivera and the Indian Leaders of Nicaragua, September 22, 1989, Nicaragua File.

14. Raul Alfonsin, interview, February 1995, New York.

15. Pérez de Cuéllar, *Pilgrimage for Peace*, 414–16.

16. Jimmy Carter to President Daniel Ortega Saavedra, September 22, 1989, Robert Pastor Personal Papers, Atlanta.

17. "Summary Report of Second Pre-Election Visit to Nicaragua," October 20–23, 1989, Council of Freely Elected Heads of Government, Carter Center.

18. Robert Kagan, *A Twilight Struggle* (New York: Free Press, 1996), 691–718.

19. White House press release, statement by the press secretary, October 21, 1989, Nicaragua File.

20. Jimmy Carter to President Daniel Ortega Saavedra, October 22, 1989, Pastor Personal Papers.

21. Robert Pastor, "The Making of a Free Election," *Journal of Democracy*, summer 1990, 13–25.

22. James Baker, *The Politics of Diplomacy: Revolution, War and Peace, 1989–1992* (New York: Putnam, 1995).

23. "The Nicaragua Elections: A Turning Point?" transcript of Carter Center symposium, November 14, 1989, Carter Center.

24. "Carter Says Sandinistas Are Trying to Smear Foes," *NYT*, November 15, 1989.

25. "Observing Nicaragua's Election, 1989–1990," Carter Center Special Report 1, 9–40.

26. Ibid.

27. Jimmy Carter, *Talking Peace*, 133–37.

28. Kagan, *Twilight Struggle*, 706.

29. Carter, interview, May 1995, Atlanta. Also Carter, *Talking Peace*; and Kagan, *Twilight Struggle*, 698.

30. Jimmy Carter to Oscar Arias Sanchez, October 16, 1987, Central American Files, JCPPP, Box 11, JCPL.

31. Emma Daly, "Carter, Arias Disagree on Nicaragua Prospects," *Tico Times*, December 22, 1989.

32. Pastor, "The Making of a Free Election," *Journal of Democracy*, summer 1990, 13–25.

33. Kagan, *Twilight Struggle*, 670.

34. Elliot Richardson, interview, October 1997, Washington, D.C.

35. Pérez de Cuéllar, *Pilgrimage for Peace*, 414–15; and Robert Pastor to Douglas Brinkley, December 31, 1997.

36. Pastor, interview; and Carter, interview, May 1995, Atlanta.

37. Helen Dewar and Don Podesta, "U.S. Observer Tram Disbands before Nicaraguan Elections," *Washington Post*, February 8, 1990.

38. Kagan, *Twilight Struggle*, 706.

39. Jimmy Carter to Violeta Barrios de Chamorro, November 22, 1989; and Jimmy Carter to President Daniel Saavedra Ortega, November 22, 1989, Nicaragua File.

40. Jimmy Carter to President George Bush, January 19, 1990, Pastor Personal Papers.

41. Jimmy Carter to President George Bush, January 21, 1990; and Jimmy Carter to President Bush, January 29, 1990, JCPPP, Nicaragua Election File, Box 39.

42. James A. Baker III, interview, October 1997, San Francisco, Calif.

43. Kagan, *A Twilight Struggle*, 707.

44. John M. Goshko, "Baker Sets Conditions on Nicaragua Relations," *Washington Post*, February 23, 1990.

45. John M. Goshko, "Renewed U.S.-Nicaragua Ties Eyed," *Washington Post*, February 24, 1990.

46. Bruce Babbitt, "Poll Position," *New Republic*, March 19, 1990.

47. Andres Oppenheimer, *Castro's Final Hour: The Secret Story behind the Coming Downfall of Communist Cuba* (New York: Simon & Schuster, 1992), 206–8. Also Kagan, *A Twilight Struggle*, 693.

48. "Big Day in Nicaragua," *NYT*, February 24, 1990.

49. Carter, *Talking Peace*, 136.

50. Carter, interview, May 1995, Atlanta.

51. Richardson, interview. Also Elliot Richardson's February 16, 1990, letter to the *NYT*.

52. Carter, interview, May 1995, Atlanta.

53. "Jimmy Carter's Second Chance," *U.S. News & World Report*, March 12, 1990, 35. Also Larry Garber and Glenn Cowan, "The Virtues of Parallel Vote Tabulations," *Journal of Democracy* 4 (April 1993): 95–107.

54. Pastor, "The Making of a Free Election," *Journal of Democracy*, summer 1990, 13–25. Also Pastor, interview.

55. Peter G. Bourne, *Jimmy Carter: A Comprehensive Biography from Plains to Postpresidency* (New York: Scribner's, 1997), 494; Rosalynn Carter meeting notes, February 25, 1990, Pastor Personal Papers; Richardson, interview; and Carter, interview, May 1995, Atlanta. Also Jimmy Carter, transcript of interview, *MacNeil/Lehrer NewsHour*, February 26, 1990.

56. Jimmy Carter, transcript of press roundtable, February 26, 1990, Pastor Personal Papers. Questions asked by Mark Ihlig of the *NYT*.

57. Pastor, interview.

58. "Excerpts from Address by Ortega," *NYT*, February 27, 1990.

59. Pastor, interview. Also Robert Pastor, memorandum to Jimmy Carter, February 23, 1990, Pastor Personal Papers.

60. Baker, interview, September 1995.

61. Ibid. Also Pastor, interview.

62. Pastor, interview.

63. Robert Kagan, unpublished chapter for *A Twilight Struggle*, Robert Kagan Personal Papers, Washington, D.C.

64. Pastor, interview; and Jimmy Carter, interview, September 1997, Atlanta. Also memorandum of conversation, Department of State, February 28, 1990, 12:35–1:40 P.M. (Participants: Secretary of State Baker, NSC Adviser Scowcroft, Deputy Secretary Eagleburger, Assistant Secretary of State Aronson, Carter, and Robert Pastor); and Bernard Aronson, interview, September 1997, Washington, D.C.

65. Jeane Kirkpatrick, "Sandinistas Have Stacked the Deck to Retain Power," *Miami Herald*, October 7, 1990.

66. Robert Pastor to Douglas Brinkley, December 31, 1997.

67. Baker, interview, September 1995.

68. Memorandum of conversation, Department of State, February 28, 1990, Pastor Personal Papers.

69. Jimmy Carter to Secretary of State James Baker, March 1, 1990, Pastor Personal Papers.

70. Memorandum of conversation, Department of State, February 28, 1990, Pastor Personal Papers.

71. Jimmy Carter to Secretary of State James Baker, March 1, 1990, Pastor Personal Papers. Also see Jimmy Carter, transcript of departure remarks, Department of State, Washington, D.C., February 28, 1990, Pastor Personal Papers,.

72. John C. Whitehead to Jimmy Carter, February 28, 1990, Pastor Personal Papers.

73. Daniel J. Evans to Robert Pastor, March 27, 1990, JCPPP, Box 52.

74. Daniel J. Evans to Elliott Abrams, March 27, 1990, JCPPP, Box 52.

75. Jimmy Carter to Faye Dill, March 21, 1988, JCPPP, Box 9.

76. Elliott Abrams to Daniel J. Evans, April 2, 1990, JCPPP, Box 52.

77. Jimmy Carter to Daniel Ortega, April 25, 1990, Nicaragua Files. Also see "Carter Council . . . Monitor Nicaraguan Elections," *Carter Center News*, spring 1990, 1.

78. *1990 Elections in the Dominican Republic: Report of an Observer Delegation*, cosponsored by the Council of Freely Elected Heads of Government and the National Democratic Institute for International Affairs, fall 1990, 7, Carter Center.

79. Dr. Froilan J. R. Tavares to Jimmy Carter, May 8, 1990; and Jimmy Carter to Froilan J. R. Tavares May 9, 1990, Dominican Republic Files, Carter Center.

80. Carter, interview, May 1995, Atlanta.

81. *1990 Elections in the Dominican*

Republic, 8. Also "Election Tally Is Suspended in the Dominican Republic," *NYT*, May 21, 1990.

82. Dr. Froilan J. R. Tavares to Jimmy Carter, June 5, 1990, Dominican Republic Files.

83. Carter to Tavares, June 13, 1990, Dominican Republic Files.

84. *1990 Election in Haiti: Report of an Observer Delegation*, cosponsored by the Council of Freely Elected Heads of Government and the National Democratic Institute for International Affairs, spring 1991, Carter Center.

85. Carter, *Talking Peace*, 140–41.

86. Ibid.

87. Jimmy Carter, "Haiti's Election Needs Help," *NYT*, October 1, 1990. Also see Robert A. Pastor, "A Short History of Haiti," *Foreign Service Journal*, November 1995, 20–21.

88. Carter, *Talking Peace*, 139.

89. Howard W. French, "Haiti Installs Democratic Chief, Its First," *NYT*, February 8, 1991.

90. Ibid.

91. Carter, *Talking Peace*, 140–41.

92. Bishop Desmond Tutu, interview, May 1995, Atlanta.

93. Lodwrick Cook, interview, March 1995, Houston, Tex.

94. Karl Maier, "Kaunda Swept from Office in Lopsided Zambian Vote," *Washington Post*, November 2, 1991.

95. Lodwrick Cook, interview, October 1991, Los Angeles.

96. Ibid.

97. Eric Bjornlund, interview, August 1997, Washington, D.C.

98. Jimmy Carter/Brian Atwood Statement from International Z-Vote Delegation on Zambian Elections, November 2, 1991, JCPPP.

99. Jane Perlez, "With Pride and Economic Pain Ahead, Zambia Swears in New Leader," *NYT*, November 5, 1991.

100. Howard W. French, "In Africa's Harsh Climate, Fruits of Democracy," *NYT*, January 4, 1998; Robert Kaplan, "Was Democracy Just a Moment?" *Atlantic Monthly*, December 1997, 55–72; and Fareed Zakaria, "The Rise of Ill-

Liberal Democracy" *Foreign Affairs*, 76, no. 6 (November–December 1997): 22–43.

101. "Nicaragua Property Disputes," report prepared by the UN Development Program of the Carter Center, April 1995, Nicaragua Files.

102. "Democracy Prevails in Nicaragua's 1996 Presidential Election," *Carter Center News*, winter 1997, 1; Douglas Farah, "Nicaragua's Presumptive President, Aleman, Promises to End Sandinista Legacy," *Washington Post*, October 23, 1996; and Larry Rohter, "Scourge, and Sometimes Victim, of the Sandinistas," *NYT*, October 23, 1996.

103. "Carter, Baker Stress Nicaraguan Reconciliation," *Washington Times*, October 29, 1996. Also "Jimmy Carter, Report on Trip to Nicaragua," October 18–22, 1996, Nicaragua Files.

SEVENTEEN: DESERT STORM

1. Jimmy Carter to Secretary of State George Shultz, March 22, 1988, JCPPP, Middle East Private File, Box 11, JCPL.

2. Mary King, interview, December 1995, Washington, D.C.; and Bassam Abu Sharif, interview, October 1997, Washington, D.C.

3. Carter quoted in "Carter Riding New Wave of Popularity," *Albany Sunday Herald*, April 24, 1990.

4. King, interview, December 1995; and Sharif, interview.

5. Gloria Carter Spann Clipping File, Lake Blackshear Regional Library, Americus, Ga.

6. Paul West, "Years Out of Office, Carter Solidifies Spot on World Stage," *Baltimore Sun*, April 8, 1990.

7. Ibid.

8. James A. Baker III, interview, September 1995, Houston, Tex.

9. Ibid. Also James A Baker III, *The Politics of Diplomacy: Revolution, War and Peace, 1989–1992* (New York: Putnam, 1995), 115–19.

10. For a discussion of the Baker Plan, see Baker, *Politics of Diplomacy*, 118.

11. Jimmy Carter–Ken Stein, Middle East Program File (1989–91), JCPPP, Box 50.

12. Jimmy Carter to Congressman Robert Michel, March 26, 1990, JCPPP, Middle East Trip File, Box 38.

13. Jimmy Carter to President George Bush and Secretary of State James Baker, March 20, 1990, JCPPP, Middle East File, Box 38.

14. Jimmy Carter, *The Blood of Abraham: Insights into the Middle East* (Boston: Houghton Mifflin, 1985), 201–2. Carter constantly updates the book by adding new afterwords. Also see Ihsan A. Hijazi, "Carter Says Syria Aids on Hostages," *NYT*, March 17, 1990.

15. Jimmy Carter to Burt Reinhardt, March 22, 1990, JCPPP, CNN File, Box 51; and Joel Brinkley, "Syria Is Willing to Talk to Israel, Carter Says," *NYT*, March 19, 1990.

16. Jimmy Carter to President Bush and Secretary Baker, March 20, 1990, JCPPP, Middle East File.

17. "Carter Criticizes Israelis on Palestinian Rights," *NYT*, March 20, 1990.

18. Jimmy Carter, letter to the editor, *NYT*, April 1, 1990.

19. A. M. Rosenthal, "Silence Is a Lie," *NYT*, March 22, 1990.

20. Ken Stein to Jimmy Carter, March 23, 1990, JCPPP, Middle East File.

21. Jimmy Carter to Ken Stein, March 23, 1990, JCPPP, Middle East File. Carter inked the line on the top margin of Stein's letter.

22. "Carter Riding New Wave of Popularity," *Albany Sunday Herald*, April 24, 1990.

23. Jimmy Carter, letter to the editor.

24. Sharif, interview.

25. Ken Stein to Jimmy Carter, March 30, 1990, JCPPP, Middle East File.

26. For an excellent biography of the PLO leader, see Janet Wallach and John Wallach, *Arafat: In the Eyes of the Beholder* (Secaucus, N.J.: Birch Lane Press, 1997).

27. Danny Rubenstein, *The Mystery of Arafat* (South Royalton, Vt.: Steerforth Press, 1995), 101–2.

28. Mary King to Marjorie Miller (Jerusalem Bureau Chief, *Los Angeles Times*), August 31, 1995, Mary King Personal Papers, Carter Center, Atlanta.

29. John Phillips, "Meeting Regis at Elysee Palace," transcript of UPI wire story, King Personal Papers.

30. Mary King, "Meeting of President Jimmy Carter and Rosalynn Carter with Chairman Yasir Arafat, April 4, 1990," transcript, King Personal Papers. After the meeting both Jimmy and Rosalynn Carter proofed the transcript, inking in only a few cosmetic changes for clarity's sake. King also sent the Paris meeting transcript to Hasib Sabbagh.

31. Ibid. Also King, interview, September 1997, Washington, D.C.; and Jimmy Carter, interview, Mary 1995, Atlanta.

32. Jimmy Carter to Yasir Arafat, April 6, 1990, JCPPP, Middle East Files; and Mary King to Yasir Arafat, October 14, 1993, King Personal Papers.

33. King, interview, December 1997.

34. Wallach and Wallach, *Arafat*, 455–56.

35. Mary King to Douglas Brinkley, January 8, 1998.

36. "Carter Meets Arafat in Paris, Praises Him as Peacemaker," *NYT*, April 5, 1990.

37. Sharon Waxman, "Carter, Arafat Meet on Middle East Peace Plan," *Washington Post*, April 5, 1990.

38. Jonas Bernstein, "Carter Earns Mixed Ratings for His Role as a Peace Broker," *Insight*, April 30, 1990.

39. Ibid.

40. Paul West, "Years Out of Office, Carter Solidifies Spot on World Stage," *Baltimore Sun*, April 8, 1990.

41. Jimmy Carter, draft speech for Yasir Arafat, May 24, 1990, King Personal Papers.

42. Elizabeth Kurylo, "Carter Counsels Arabs," *Atlanta Journal & Constitution*, December 7, 1991.

43. Yasir Arafat to Jimmy Carter, July 7, 1990, King Personal Papers.

44. Stephen E. Ambrose and Douglas G. Brinkley, *Rise to Globalism: American Foreign Policy since 1938*, 8th ed. (New York: Viking, 1997), 381–97.

45. Jimmy Carter, interview, May 1995, Atlanta.

46. Sharif, interview.

47. Mary King to Jimmy Carter, August 5, 1990, King Personal Papers. Also Mary King, memorandum to Jimmy Carter, August 27, 1990, King Personal Papers.

48. Yasir Arafat, message to Jimmy Carter, August 13, 1990, and Jimmy Carter to Yasir Arafat, August 31, 1990, King Personal Papers; Mary King, memorandum to Jimmy Carter, August 27, 1990, King Personal Papers.

49. Jimmy Carter to Yasir Arafat, September 6, 1990, and Mary King to Jimmy Carter, September 7, 1990, King Personal Papers.

50. Bassam Abu Sharif to James Baker, September 8, 1990, King Personal Papers.

51. Yasir Arafat, message to Jimmy Carter attached to Mary King's letter of September 13, 1990, King Personal Papers. Also see Edward Cody, "PLO Sees Possibility of Linking Issues," *Washington Post*, October 3, 1990.

52. Mary King to Jimmy Carter, September 29, 1990, with message from Arafat, King Personal Papers.

53. Mary King, memorandum to Jimmy Carter, October 11, 1990, "Messages from PLO Chairman Yasir Arafat," King Personal Papers.

54. Ibid.

55. For a good discussion of the Carter Doctrine, see Gaddis Smith, *Morality, Reason and Power: American Diplomacy in the Carter Years* (New York: Hill and Wang, 1986).

56. "Carter Forum Explores Future of Persian Gulf," *Carter Center News*, fall 1990, 1; and Elizabeth Kurylo, "Carter Culling Mideast Experts for TV Special," *Atlanta Journal & Constitution*, September 11, 1990.

57. Jimmy Carter, "The Need to Negotiate," *Time*, October 22, 1990; and Jimmy Carter, "First Step toward Peace," *Newsweek*, December 17, 1990.

58. "Famine in Sudan" *USA Today*, October 8, 1990; and "Sudan's Pro-Iraq Stance Shouldn't Stop Aid," *Reuters News Report*, October 7, 1990.

59. B. J. Phillips, "Carter: Odds Better Than 50–50 for War in Persian Gulf," *Philadelphia Inquirer*, October 22, 1990.

60. Paul Smith, "Carter Praises Iowa Quality of Life," *Carroll (Iowa) Today*, September 29, 1990; Chuck Offenburger, "A Fine Evening with Jimmy Carter at Buena Vista College," *Des Moines Register*, September 27, 1990; and Larry Fruhling, "'Major War' in Mideast Is Likely, Carter Tells Storm Lake Audience," *Des Moines Register*, September 26, 1990.

61. William H. Carllie, "Carter Urges Resolution of Arab-Israeli Conflict," *Arizona Republic*, October 9, 1990.

62. "Carter Says Gulf Crisis Teaching U.S. a Lesson," *Fairfield (Iowa) Daily Ledger*, September 26, 1990; and "Carter Says Crisis Will Revive Energy Policy," *Waycross Journal Herald*, September 29, 1990.

63. Jimmy Carter, *Living Faith* (New York: Times Books, 1996), 138.

64. Affidavit of Jimmy Carter on behalf of David Rabhan, August 23, 1993, Terrence Adamson Papers, Washington, D.C.

65. "Carter's Ex-Pilot Freed from Iranian Prison," *St. Paul Pioneer Press*, September 15, 1990.

66. Jimmy Carter to the Ayatollah Khomeini, October 30, 1988, Adamson Papers.

67. David Rabhan, interview, January 1997, Swainsboro, Ga.

68. Jimmy Carter to James Baker, May 4, 1990, Terrence Adamson Personal Papers, Washington, D.C.

69. Bill Shipp, "Georgia's Forgotten Hostage," *Georgia Trend*, September 1992, 30.

70. David Rabhan, interview, January 1997, Swainsboro, Ga.

71. Yasir Arafat to Jimmy Carter, September 6, 1990, King Personal Papers.

72. Jimmy Carter to François Mitter-rand, Margaret Thatcher, Mikhail Gorbachev, et al., November 19, 1990, JCPPP, Gulf War Crisis (1990–91) File, Box 46.

73. Ibid.

74. Richard Cheney, interview, April 1997, Hempstead, N.Y.

75. George Bush to Jimmy Carter, December 11, 1990, JCPPP, Gulf War Crisis (1990–91) File.

76. William Webster, interview, April 1997, Hempstead, N.Y.

77. George Bush to Douglas Brinkley, July 27, 1995.

78. Jimmy Carter, "Needed: Middle East Peace Talks," NYT, January 2, 1991.

79. Ambrose and Brinkley, Rise to Globalism, 387–97.

80. Jimmy Carter to King Fahd, President Mubarak, and President Assad, January 10, 1991, JCPPP, Gulf War Crisis (1990–91) File.

81. Ibid.

82. George Bush to Douglas Brinkley, July 27, 1995; Colin Powell, interview, February 1995, Port-au-Prince, Haiti; Brent Scowcroft, interview, April 1997, Hempstead, N.Y.; Cheney, interview; Webster, interview.

83. Jimmy Carter, letter to twenty U.S. senators, January 5, 1991, JCPPP, Gulf War Crisis (1990–91) File.

84. Eleanor Clift, "A Man with a Mission," Newsweek, October 3, 1994.

85. Ambrose and Brinkley, Rise to Globalism, 395–97.

86. Douglas Brinkley, "Jimmy Carter's Modest Quest for Global Peace," Foreign Affairs 74, no. 6 (November–December 1995): 95–96.

87. Richard Cohen, "In Defense of the Carter Post Presidency," Washington Post, December 27, 1994.

88. Wallach and Wallach, Arafat, 433.

89. Ibid., 432–33. Also Helen Cobban, "The Palestinians and the Iraqi Invasion of Kuwait," in Robert O. Freedman, ed., The Middle East after Iraq's Invasion of Kuwait (Gainesville: University of Florida Press, 1993), 253–74.

90. David Makovsky, Making Peace with the PLO: The Rabin Government's Road to the Oslo Accord (Boulder, Colo.: Westview Press, 1996), 11; Shimon Peres, Battling for Peace: A Memoir (New York: Random House, 1995), 274–84; King, interview, September 1995; and Wallach and Wallach, Arafat, 434. For Baker's visits to the West Bank, see Hanan Ashrawi, This Side of Peace (New York: Simon & Schuster, 1996), 81–94.

91. Mary King to Douglas Brinkley, November 1, 1997.

92. Douglas Brinkley, meeting notes, Jimmy Carter–Yasir Arafat, January 19, 1996, Gaza City.

93. Jonathan C. Randal, "Arafat Survives Crash Landing," Washington Post, April 9, 1992.

94. Ibid.

95. Bassam Abu Sharif to Jimmy Carter, April 4, 1992, King Personal Papers.

96. Yasir Arafat to Jimmy Carter, April 17, 1992, King Personal Papers.

97. Sharif, interview.

98. Scowcroft, interview.

99. Baker, interview.

100. Brent Scowcroft, interview, April 1997, Hempstead, N.Y.

EIGHTEEN: DEMOCRATIC PROSPECT

1. Elizabeth Kurylo, interview, October 1997, Atlanta. The article that particularly upset Carter was Jonathan Beaty and S. C. Gwinne, "Masters of Deceit," Time, April 1, 1991, 54–58.

2. Joey Ramone, interview, June 1994, New York.

3. "Habitat for Humanity 1994 Report" (1995), Habitat for Humanity Archives, Americus, Ga. Also see Millard Fuller, The Theology of the Hammer (Macon, Ga.: Smyth & Helwys Publishing, 1994); and Fuller, A Simple, Decent Place to Live (Dallas, Tex.: Word Publishing, 1995).

4. Jimmy Carter to Habitat for Humanity Board of Directors, March 26, 1990, JCPPP, Habitat for Humanity File, Box 51, JCPL.

5. Private correspondence provided to author.

6. Report of Millard Fuller's activities, Habitat for Humanity Board of Directors, JCPPP, Habitat for Humanity File.

7. Jimmy Carter to Jeff Snider, May 10, 1991, JCPPP, Habitat for Humanity File.

8. Jimmy Carter to Richard Celeste, May 7, 1991, JCPPP, Habitat for Humanity File.

9. *Americus Times-Recorder*, June 16, 1991.

10. Jimmy and Rosalynn Carter, statement on Millard Fuller's return to Habitat, June 15, 1991, JCPPP, Habitat for Humanity File.

11. Fuller, *The Theology of the Hammer*, 110–12.

12. Jimmy Carter Work Project, Baltimore–Washington, D.C., June 14–20, 1992, Habitat for Humanity Archives.

13. Jimmy Carter, interview, May 1995, Atlanta.

14. James Carville, interview, August 1995, Washington, D.C.

15. David Maraniss, interview, October 1997, Silver Spring, Md.

16. *NYT*, February 20, 1992.

17. Karen DeWitt, "Carter Welcomes Tsongas to Plains," *NYT*, February 23, 1992. Also Carville, interview.

18. DeWitt, "Carter Welcomes Tsongas."

19. Paul Tsongas, interview, May 1994, Boston.

20. Gwen Ifill, "Carter, with Clinton at His Side, Praises the Candidate's Qualities," *NYT*, May 21, 1992.

21. For Carter's ancestral roots, see Betty Glad, *Jimmy Carter: In Search of the White House* (New York: W. W. Norton, 1980), 23–43; James Wooten, *Dasher: The Roots and Rising of Jimmy Carter* (New York: Summit Books, 1978), 63–95; and Peter G. Bourne, *Jimmy Carter. A Comprehensive Biography from Plains to Postpresidency* (New York: Scribner's, 1997), 9–82.

22. J. William Fulbright, interview, October 1993, Washington, D.C.

23. David Maraniss, *First in His Class: A Biography of Bill Clinton* (New York: Simon & Schuster, 1995), 21–148.

24. Jimmy Carter, interview, October 1993, Plains, Ga.

25. Douglas Brinkley, "Clintons and Carters Don't Mix," *NYT*, August 29, 1996; and James Bennet, "A Presidential Cold War Begins to Thaw," *NYT*, May 21, 1997.

26. Maraniss, *First in His Class*, 375–90.

27. Ibid.

28. Ibid. Also David Maraniss, "Cuban Refugee Uprising Offers View of Clinton's Reaction of Crisis," *Washington Post*, October 22, 1990.

29. Pamela Harriman, interview, December 1991, New York.

30. "Excerpts from Remarks Delivered by Carter at the Convention," *NYT*, July 15, 1992.

31. Ted Van Dyk, interview, June 1994, Washington, D.C.

32. Kai Bird, "The Very Model of an Ex-President," *Nation*, November 12, 1990; and Timothy J. McNulty, "Born Again," *Chicago Tribune Magazine*, July 8, 1990.

33. Jerry Schwartz, "Carter Plan Seeks to Help Atlanta's Poor," *NYT*, October 26, 1991.

34. Carter, interview, April 1995, Atlanta.

35. *Wall Street Journal*, January 20, 1992.

36. Carter, *Talking Peace*, 151–61.

37. Jane Smith, interview, April 1995, Atlanta. Also Carter, interview, May 1995, Atlanta.

38. Stuart Eizenstat, interview, September 1995, Brussels.

39. Jimmy Carter, "The Atlanta Project," *Rotarian*, January 1994, 28. For his most eloquent explanation of the Atlanta Project, see Jimmy Carter, *Turning Point: A Candidate, a State, and a Nation Coming of Age* (New York: Times Books, 1992), 205–11.

40. James Laney, interview, May 1995, Atlanta; and Carter, *Talking Peace*, 149.

41. Jimmy Carter, TAP Speeches, Chronological Series of Events, TAP, JCPPP, Box 58.

42. Nicholas D. Snider (UPS community service manager), interview, February 1996, Atlanta.

43. Jimmy Carter, roundtable discussion, Hay-Adams Hotel, December 12, 1995, Washington, D.C.

44. "Because There Is Hope: Gearing Up to Renew Urban America," *The Atlanta Project Report 1995*, Carter Center.

45. Ibid.

46. Walt W. Rostow, interview, February 1996, Austin, Tex. Also W. W. Rostow and Elspeth D. Rostow, *The Austin Project* (printed privately, 1992). The report was provided by Mr. Rostow.

47. Seth Coleman and Don Melvin, "Carter to Launch National Version of Atlanta Project," December 14, 1994; and "The Atlanta Project: Carter's Challenge," *Atlanta Journal & Constitution*, April 19, 1992.

48. Amy Carter, interview, January 1995, Jerusalem.

49. "Pop Star Enthralls Atlanta Project Gathering," *Atlanta Journal & Constitution*, May 6, 1993. Celebrities working with the Atlanta Project are discussed in Douglas Brinkley, *The Majic Bus: An American Odyssey* (New York: Harcourt Brace, 1993), 101–10.

50. Rostow, interview; and "Carter Announced Vaccination Plan," *NYT*, March 13, 1997.

51. "An Experiment in Easing Paperwork: 64 Pages Reduced to 8," *NYT*, April 19, 1994; and Peter Scott, "Aid for Poor Finally Made '1-Step' Away," *Atlanta Journal & Constitution*, April 19, 1994.

52. For "TAP Into Peace," see Peter Scott, "Target 50,000 Households for Peace," *Atlanta Journal & Constitution*, April 28, 1994; and Peter Scott, "Ex-President Carter Pushes Gun Control in Atlanta Project Visit," *Atlanta Journal & Constitution*, April 30, 1994.

53. *Time*, March 14, 1988.

54. Shepard Barbash, "Learning from Corporate Partnerships," The Atlanta Project, publication 1995 (pamphlet).

55. Anne Lowrey Bailey, "Critical Report Leads Jimmy Carter's Atlanta Anti-Poverty Drive to Make Changes," *Chronicle of Philanthropy*, March 9, 1995.

57. "Project's Growing Pains," *Atlanta Journal & Constitution*, February 20, 1995.

58. Smith, interview.

59. Albert Gore, *Earth in the Balance: Ecology and the Human Spirit* (Boston: Houghton Mifflin, 1992); and Jimmy Carter, interview, December 1993, Plains, Ga.

60. Phil Lader, interview, June 1997, Napa Valley, Calif.; Millard Fuller, interview, August 1994, Americus, Ga.; and Fuller, *A Simple, Decent Place to Live*, 81–82.

61. Fuller, interview, August 1994; and Fuller, *A Simple, Decent Place to Live*, 81–82.

62. Carter, interview, May 1995, Atlanta.

63. Robert Reinhold, "Warren Minor Christopher," *NYT*, December 23, 1992.

64. Warren Christopher, "A Plan for the Continuity of the Carter Center," October 5, 1992, Terrence Adamson Personal Papers, Washington, D.C.

65. Carter, interview, May 1995, Atlanta.

66. Warren Christopher to Jimmy Carter, October 5, 1992, Adamson Personal Papers.

67. Leslie Gelb, "Jobs, Jobs, Jobs," *NYT*, November 22, 1992.

68. Carter, interview, May 1995, Atlanta.

69. Elaine Sciolino, "Christopher Sees a Place for Force," *NYT*, January 14, 1993.

70. Warren Christopher, interview, May 1995, Washington, D.C.

NINETEEN:
CARTER VS. CLINTON

1. Jimmy Carter, interview, May 1995, Atlanta; and Warren Christopher, interview, May 1995, Washington, D.C.

2. Jimmy Carter, *Turning Point: A Candidate, a State, and a Nation Coming of Age* (New York: Times Books, 1992).

3. Alessandra Stanley, "Words of Advice, Bittersweet," *NYT*, January 14, 1993.

4. Ibid.

5. Interviews with two White House advisers to President Bill Clinton. (The sources asked not to be identified until after Clinton leaves the White House.)

6. Ibid.

7. Rosalynn Carter, interview, May 1995, Atlanta. Also CNN videotapes of inaugural events, CNN Archive, Atlanta.

8. Robert Pastor, interview, August 1997, Atlanta.

9. Jimmy Carter to Warren Christopher, March 3, 1993, Terrence Adamson Personal Papers, Washington, D.C.

10. Memorandum of meeting with Warren Christopher, March 4, 1993, JCPPP, Christopher File, Box 54, JCPL.

11. Carter, interview, May 1995, Atlanta.

12. Ibid.

13. Richard Holbrooke, interview, January 1995, New York.

14. Jimmy Carter, Living Faith (New York: Times Books, 1996), 138–39.

15. Douglas Brinkley, "Jimmy Carter's Modest Quest for Global Peace," Foreign Affairs 74, no. 6 (November–December 1995): 96–106.

16. John Hardman, interview, November 1997, Atlanta. Also see Thomas L. Friedman, "Clinton Rounds Out State Department Team," NYT, January 20, 1993.

17. Carter, interview, May 1995, Atlanta.

18. Pastor, interview, August 1997.

19. Edward P. Djerejian, interview, February 1998, Houston.

20. Mary King, "Meeting with Chairman Arafat in Tunis," special report to President Jimmy Carter, February 3, 1992, Mary King Personal Papers, Carter Center, Atlanta.

21. Jimmy Carter, Talking Peace; James Brooke, "First Free Elections To Be Held Today in Paraguay," NYT, March 19, 1993; "Hecklers Stop Carter Speech at Vienna Rights Discussion," NYT, June 13, 1993; and Carter Center News, fall 1993.

22. David Makovsky, Making Peace with the PLO: The Rabin Government's Road to the Oslo Accord (Boulder, Colo.: Westview Press, 1996); and "The January 20, 1996 Palestinian Elections," special report published by the National Democratic Institute for International Affairs and the Carter Center.

23. "Togo Election Report," August 1993, African Files, Carter Center, Atlanta.

24. Mary King, interview, October 1997, Washington, D.C.

25. Jimmy Carter, "Human Rights and Democracy" speech, August 31, 1993, Sanaa, Yemen (tape), King Personal Papers.

26. Jimmy Carter, introduction to Mary-Jane Deeb and Mary King, eds., Hasib Sabbagh: From Palestinian Refugee to Citizen of the World (Lanham, Md.: University Press of America, 1996), vii and viii.

27. Ibid.

28. Sana Sabbagh, "Honor All," in Deeb and King, Hasib Sabbagh, 15–18.

29. Carter, "Human Rights and Democracy"; King, interview, October 1997; and Jimmy Carter, memorandum, August 31, 1993, JCPPP, Yemen File.

30. Mary King, interview, May 1997, Washington, D.C.

31. Jimmy Carter–Yasir Arafat meeting, transcript, August 31, 1993, Sanaa, Yemen, King Personal Papers.

32. Carter, interview, May 1995, Atlanta.

33. Carter-Arafat meeting, August 31, 1993.

34. Jimmy Carter to Hasib Sabbagh, September 2, 1993 (author's possession).

35. James A. Baker III, interview, September 1995, Houston, Tex.

36. Mary King, interview, December 1997, Washington, D.C.

37. Elaine Sciolino, "Arafat Arrives in U.S. to 'Make Peace,'" NYT, September 13, 1993.

38. Ibid. Also Carter, interview, May 1995, Atlanta.

39. Jimmy Carter–Yasir Arafat meeting, transcript, September 12, 1993, Washington, D.C., King Personal Papers.

40. Ibid.

41. Carter, interview, May 1995, Atlanta.

42. Thomas L. Friedman, "Rabin and

Arafat Seal Their Accord as Clinton Applauds 'Brave Gamble,'" *NYT*, September 14, 1993.

43. Dr. Abdul-Karim Iryani, interview, January 1998, Sanaa, Yemen.

44. David E. Rosenbaum, "Splintered on Trade," *NYT*, September 15, 1993.

45. Douglas Brinkley, "Democratic Enlargement: The Clinton Doctrine," *Foreign Policy*, spring 1997, 111–27; and William A. Orme Jr., *Understanding NAFTA* (Austin: University of Texas Press, 1996).

46. "NAFTA: An Unprecedented Bipartisan Effort," *Carter Central News*, fall 1993; Robert Pastor, interview, September 1997, Atlanta; and Barbara Sinclair, "Trying to Govern Positively in a Negative Era: Clinton and the 103rd Congress," in Colin Campbell and Bert A. Rockman, eds., *The Clinton Presidency: First Appraisals* (Chatham, N.J.: Chatham Publishing House, 1996), 100–111.

47. Stephen E. Ambrose and Douglas G. Brinkley, *Rise to Globalism: American Foreign Policy since 1938*, 8th ed. (New York: Viking Penguin, 1997), 410.

48. Carter, interview, May 1995, Atlanta; and David E. Rosenbaum, "A White House Slumber Party," *NYT*, September 15, 1993.

49. Gwen Ifill, "Clinton Recruits 3 Presidents to Promote Trade Pact," *NYT*, September 15, 1993.

50. "Well Spoken, Mr. Carter," *NYT*, September 18, 1993.

51. "NAFTA: An Unprecedented Bipartisan Effort," *Carter Center News*, fall 1993.

52. Bill Clinton to Jimmy Carter, November 17, 1993, JCPPP, NAFTA File, Box 63.

53. Dominique de Menil to Douglas Brinkley, August 12, 1995 (author's possession).

54. Jimmy Carter to Yasir Arafat, April 12, 1994, King Personal Papers.

55. "January 20, 1996, Palestinian Elections"; Bassam Abu Sharif, interview, October 1997, Washington, D.C.;

and Hanan Ashrawi, interview, January 1996, Jerusalem.

56. President Carter–Yasir Arafat meeting, transcript, May 18, 1994, Oslo, Norway, King Personal Papers.

57. Ibid. For a profile of Sheikh Ahmad Yassin, see *Jerusalem Post*, May 26, 1989.

58. Mary King, memorandum to President Carter, May 26, 1994, Mary King Personal Papers, Washington, D.C.

59. Mary King to Jimmy Carter, October 10, 1994, Mary King Personal Papers, Washington, D.C.

60. Carter-Arafat meeting, September 12, 1993.

61. Douglas Brinkley, notes of Jimmy Carter–Yasir Arafat meeting, January 19, 1996, Gaza City. Also see Sara Roy, "Civil Society in the Gaza Strip: Obstacles to Reconstruction," in Augustus Richard Norton, ed., *Civil Society in the Middle East* (Leiden: E. J. Brill, 1996), 221–27.

TWENTY: MISSION TO NORTH KOREA

1. Carter, *Living Faith* (New York: Times Books, 1996), 93–97.

2. For a brilliant history of the Korean War, see Bruce Cumings, *The Origins of the Korean War*, 2 vols. (Princeton, N.J.: Princeton University Press, 1981–90).

3. Don Oberdorfer, *The Two Koreas: A Contemporary History* (New York: Addison Wesley, 1997), 89.

4. Ibid., 86–87.

5. Richard Holbrooke, interview, December 1997, New York.

6. Oberdorfer, *Two Koreas*, 94.

7. Ibid., 94–101. Also Jae Kyu Park, "North Korean Policy toward the United States," *Asian Perspectives* 5 (fall–winter 1981): 144.

8. Ibid.

9. Holbrooke, interview.

10. Jimmy Carter Sunday school class, transcript, June 26, 1994, Maranatha Baptist Church Tape Collection, Plains, Ga.

11. Oberdorfer, *Two Koreas*, 101–7.

12. Holbrooke, interview.

13. Oberdorfer, *Two Koreas*, 101–7.

14. "Private Meeting with President Park, Seoul, Korea," handwritten notes by Carter, July 1, 1979, JCPL.

15. Oberdorfer, *Two Koreas*, 101–8.

16. Ibid., 109–248. Also Murray Sayle, "Closing the File on Flight 007," *New Yorker*, December 12, 1993; Dae-Sook Suh, *Kim Il Sung* (New York: Columbia University Press, 1988); and Nicholas Eberstadt, Marc Rubin, and Albina Tretyakova, "The Collapse of Soviet and Russian Trade with the DPRK, 1989–1993," *Korean Journal of National Unification* 4 (1995).

17. Kim Hak Joon, *Unification Policies of North and South Korea, 1945–1991* (Seoul: Seoul National University Press, 1992).

18. Jimmy Carter, interview, May 1995, Atlanta.

19. *Carter Center News*, spring 1992.

20. Carter, interview, May 1995, Atlanta.

21. Leon V. Sigal, *Disarming Strangers: Nuclear Diplomacy with North Korea* (Princeton, N.J.: Princeton University Press, 1998), 17–51.

22. Oberdorfer, *Two Koreas*, 271.

23. Carter, interview, May 1995, Atlanta.

24. Oberdorfer, *Two Koreas*, 271–304.

25. Sigal, *Disarming Strangers*, 144.

26. INN Consultation, JCPPP, Box 67, JCPL.

27. Oberdorfer, *Two Koreas*, 299.

28. Carter Sunday school class, October 1994.

29. Sigal, *Disarming Strangers*, 87–127.

30. James T. Laney, interview, June 1995, Atlanta.

31. Oberdorfer, *Two Koreas*, 302.

32. Laney, interview.

33. Oberdorfer, *Two Koreas*, 304.

34. Ibid., 306–11.

35. Ibid., 317.

36. Jimmy Carter, "Report of Our Trip to Korea," June 1994, Jimmy Carter Personal Papers, Carter Center, Atlanta.

37. Robert L. Gallucci, interview, December 1997, Washington, D.C.

38. Sigal, *Disarming Strangers*, 152.

39. Marion Creekmore, interview, May 1995, Atlanta.

40. Jimmy Carter, "Report of Our Trip to Korea."

41. Catherine S. Manegold, "Japan's Emperor Unflappable in Atlanta," *NYT*, June 11, 1994.

42. Carter, "Report of Our Trip to Korea."

43. Oberdorfer, *Two Koreas*, 321–23.

44. Gallucci, interview.

45. Jimmy Carter, "Report of Our Trip to Korea"; and Sigal, *Disarming Strangers*, 153.

46. Oberdorfer, *Two Koreas*, 323.

47. Laney, interview.

48. R. Jeffrey Smith and Ann Devroy, "One Small Concession Looms Large," *Washington Post*, June 26, 1994.

49. Carter, "Report of Our Trip to Korea."

50. Karen Elliott House, "Korea: Raise Another Desert Shield," *Wall Street Journal*, June 15, 1994.

51. Carter, "Report of Our Trip to Korea."

52. Anthony Lake, interview, December 1997, Annapolis.

53. Carter, "Report of Our Trip to Korea."

54. Jimmy Carter, interview, May 1995, Atlanta.

55. Brent Scowcroft and Arnold Kantor, "Korea: Time for Action," *Washington Post*, June 15, 1994.

56. Carter, "Report of Our Trip to Korea."

57. Ibid.

58. Creekmore, interview.

59. Jimmy Carter, "Report of Our Trip to Korea."

60. Oberdorfer, *Two Koreas*, 326–30.

61. Ibid.

62. Carter, interview, May 1995, Atlanta; and Jimmy Carter, "Report of Our Trip to Korea."

63. Ibid.

64. Carter, interview, May 1995, Atlanta.

65. Oberdorfer, *Two Koreas*, 329.

66. Sigal, *Disarming Strangers*, 157.

67. Gallucci, interview.

68. Warren Strobel, *Late-Breaking Foreign Policy: The News Media's Influence on Peace Operations* (Washington, D.C.: United States Peace Institute, 1997), 84–85; and "CNN Diplomacy?" *Washington Post*, January 31, 1995.

69. Sigal, *Disarming Strangers*, 157; and Gallucci, interview.

70. Anthony Lake, interview, December 1997, Annapolis, Md.

71. Oberdorfer, *Two Koreas*, 331.

72. Jimmy Carter, interview with CNN's Wolf Blitzer, tape transcript, June 16, 1994.

73. Sigal, *Disarming Strangers*, 158.

74. R. Jeffrey Smith and Ann Devroy, "One Small Concession Looms Large," *Washington Post*, June 26, 1994.

75. Sigal, *Disarming Strangers*, 159; and Gallucci, interview.

76. Oberdorfer, *Two Koreas*, 332; and Sigal, *Disarming Strangers*, 159–60.

77. Lake, interview, December 1997.

78. Oberdorfer, *Two Koreas*, 332.

79. Michael R. Gordon, "Clinton May Add G.I.'s in Korea While Remaining Open to Talks," *NYT*, June 17, 1994.

80. Carter, "Report of Our Trip to Korea."

81. David E. Sanger, "Surprise! Kim Il Sung Smiles for the Camera," *NYT*, June 19, 1994.

82. Cheryl Heckler-Feltz, "It Was the Most Unusual Postcard from Abroad," *Richmond Times-Dispatch*, July 2, 1994; and Carter, "Report of Our Trip to Korea."

83. David E. Sanger, "Carter Visit to North Korea: Whose Trip Was It Really?" *NYT*, June 18, 1994.

84. Douglas Jehl, "Carter, His Own Emissary, Outpaces White House," *NYT*, June 20, 1994.

85. Carter Sunday school class, June 26, 1994.

86. Carter, "Report of Our Trip to Korea."

87. Carter Sunday school class, June 26, 1994.

88. Michael R. Gordon, "Clinton Offers North Korea a Chance to Resume Talks," *NYT*, June 22, 1994; and David E. Sanger, "Two Koreas Plan Summit Talks on Nuclear Issue," *NYT*, June 19, 1994.

89. Oberdorfer, *Two Koreas*, 334.

90. Ibid.

91. Elizabeth Kurylo, "Revisiting a Mission to Korea," *Atlanta Journal & Constitution*, July 3, 1994.

92. Carter, "Report of Our Trip to Korea."

93. David E. Sanger, "Two Koreas Plan Summit Talks on Nuclear Issues," *NYT*, June 19, 1994.

94. Lake, interview, December 1997.

95. Jehl, "Carter, His Own Emissary."

96. Gallucci, interview. Also, "U.S. Official to Meet Carter," *NYT*, June 19, 1994.

97. Cheryl Heckler-Feltz, "It Was the Most Unusual Postcard."

98. Jehl, "Carter, His Own Emissary."

99. Charles Krauthammer, "Peace in Our Time," *Washington Post*, June 24, 1994.

100. William Safire, "Jimmy Clinton," *NYT*, June 27, 1994.

101. Sigal, *Disarming Strangers*, 162–64.

102. Carter Sunday school class, June 26, 1994.

103. "A Stooge or a Savior," *Newsweek*, June 27, 1994.

104. Jehl, "Carter, His Own Emissary."

105. "The Carter Opening," *NYT*, June 21, 1994. Also see Douglas Jehl, "Clinton Is Hopeful Yet Cautious About Carter's North Korea Trip," *NYT*, June 21, 1994; and Godfrey Hodgson, "Jimmy Carter's Comeback," *London Independent on Sunday*, June 19, 1994.

106. Sigal, *Disarming Strangers*, 229–54; and Oberdorfer, *Two Koreas*, 337–441.

107. Anthony Lake, interview, January 1998, Annapolis, Md.

108. Andrew Pollack, "Mourning Over, North Korea Has No Coronation," *NYT*, July 9, 1997; and Oberdorfer, *Two Koreas*, 336–68.

109. "Jimmy Carter Makes a Molehill

Out of a Mountain in Japan," *NYT*, July 6, 1994; Jimmy Carter, interview, CNN International transcript, July 7, 1994, Japan.

110. Jimmy Carter, on NBC News, "Meet the Press," transcript, July 21, 1996.

TWENTY-ONE:
HAITIAN CRISIS

1. For Carter's role in monitoring both the 1987 and 1990 Haitian elections, see Jimmy Carter, *Talking Peace: A Vision for the Next Generation* (New York: Dutton, 1993), 137–41; and Robert A. Pastor, "A Short History of Haiti," *Foreign Service Journal*, November 1995, 20–25.

2. Jimmy Carter to Jean-Bertrand Aristide, October 12, 1994, Haiti File, Carter Center, Atlanta.

3. Colin Powell (with Joseph E. Persico), *My American Journey* (New York: Random House, 1995), 544–46; and James Baker, *The Politics of Diplomacy: Revolution, War and Peace* (New York: Putnam, 1995), 601–2.

4. Amy Wilentz, "Blood and Guts," *Vibe*, February 1995, 52–56.

5. Jimmy Carter–Bertrand Aristide correspondence (1992), JCPPP, Haiti File, Box 87, JCPL.

6. Jimmy Carter, interview, February 1995, Port-au-Prince, Haiti.

7. Pamela Constable, "Haiti: A Nation in Despair, a Policy Adrift," *Current History*, March 1994, 108–9.

8. "Carter Urges Students to Help Haiti," *Associated Press*, February 21, 1991; and Jimmy Carter, interview, May 1995, Atlanta.

9. Quoted in *Atlanta Journal & Constitution*, JCPPP, Haiti Clipping File, Box 70. Also Carter, interview, February 1995.

10. Bernard Aronson to Douglas Brinkley, January 9, 1998.

11. Robert Pastor, interview, September 1997, Atlanta.

12. Robert A. Pastor, "With Carter in Haiti," *World View* 8, no. 2 (spring 1995): 5–7.

13. Michael Manley, interview, February 1995, Kingston, Jamaica.

14. Carter, interview, February 1995.

15. Martin Walker, *The President We Deserve: Bill Clinton, His Falls and Comebacks* (New York: Crown, 1996), 317.

16. Jimmy Carter to Bill Clinton, October 22, 1993, Robert Pastor Personal Papers, Atlanta.

17. Jimmy Carter to Bill Clinton, May 10, 1994, Pastor Personal Papers.

18. Ibid.

19. Jimmy Carter, interview, August 1994, Americus, Ga.

20. Pastor, interview.

21. Thomas Blood, *Madame Secretary* (New York: St. Martin's Press, 1997); and Martin Walker, *The President We Deserve*, 189–263.

22. Gaddis Smith, "Haiti: From Intervention to Intervasion," *Current History* 94, no. 589 (February 1995): 57–58.

23. Jimmy Carter, Haiti Clippings, JCPPP, Haiti File; and Carter, *Living Faith* (New York: Times Books, 1996), 147–53.

24. Elaine Sciolino, "On the Brink of War, a Tense Battle of Wills," *NYT*, September 20, 1994.

25. Robert Pastor, memorandum to Jimmy Carter, "The Ticking Clock," September 13, 1994, Pastor Personal Papers.

26. Sciolino, "On the Brink of War."

27. Pastor, "The Ticking Clock."

28. Joseph H. Blatchford, "Another 11th Hour Job for Jimmy Carter," *Los Angeles Times*, September 13, 1994.

29. Sam Nunn, interview, February 1995, Port-au-Prince, Haiti.

30. R. W. Apple Jr., "Changing Tack on Haiti," *NYT*, September 17, 1994.

31. Pastor, interview.

32. Sciolino, "On the Brink of War."

33. Apple, "Changing Tack on Haiti."

34. Pastor, interview.

35. Colin Powell, interview, February 1995, Port-au-Prince, Haiti.

36. Carter, interview, May 1995, Atlanta.

37. Larry Rohter, "Clinton May Be

Easing Terms with Junta," *NYT*, September 18, 1994.

38. Evan Thomas, "Under the Gun," *Newsweek*, October 3, 1994, 29; and Bruce W. Nelan, "Road to Haiti," *Time*, October 3, 1994, 35.

39. Powell, *My American Journal*, 598.

40. Carter, interview, May 1995, Atlanta.

41. Pastor, interview.

42. Nelan, "Road to Haiti," *Time*, October 3, 1994, 35.

43. Ibid. Also Pastor, interview.

44. Carter, *Living Faith*, 147–48.

45. Powell, *My American Journey*, 599.

46. Pastor, interview.

47. For Nunn's description, see Nelan, "Road to Haiti," 36; and for Powell's, see Powell, *My American Journey*, 600.

48. Carter, *Living Faith*, 150.

49. Carter, interview, February 1995.

50. Ibid. Also Carter, *Living Faith*, 150; Powell, *My American Journey*, 600–601; and Nelan, "Road to Haiti," 36.

51. Nunn, interview.

52. Powell, interview.

53. Robert Pastor, "Haiti Notes," September 18, 1994, Pastor Personal Papers.

54. Thomas, "Under the Gun," *Newsweek*, October 3, 1994, 30.

55. Pastor, interview.

56. Thomas, "Under the Gun," 31. Also Carter, interview, May 1995, Atlanta.

57. Sciolino, "On the Brink of War"; and Anthony Lake, interview, January 1998, Annapolis, Md.

58. Ibid. Also Pastor, interview; and Anthony Lake, interview, December 1997, Annapolis, Md.

59. Thomas, "Under the Gun," 31.

60. Robert Pastor, "Haiti Notes"; Carter, interview, May 1995, Atlanta; and Carter, *Living Faith*, 151–52.

61. Powell, interview.

62. Pastor, interview; and Powell, *My American Journey*, 601–3.

63. Pastor, interview.

64. Thomas, "Under the Gun," 31; Robert Pastor, "Meeting Notes, Haiti," September 18, 1994, Pastor Personal Papers; Pastor, interview; and Jimmy Carter, "Report of Trip to Haiti," September 1994, Carter Center, Atlanta.

65. Helen Dewar, "Nunn's Surprise," *Washington Post*, October 2, 1994.

66. Nelan, "Road to Haiti," 37.

67. Sciolino, "On the Brink of War."

68. "An Agreement Reached in Port au Prince, Haiti," September 18, 1994, signed by Jimmy Carter and Emile Jonassaint, Haiti File, Carter Center.

69. Powell, *My American Journey*, 601.

70. Nelan, "Road to Haiti," 37.

71. Jimmy Carter, travel diary, September 18, 1994, Carter Center.

72. Pastor, interview.

73. Michael Wines, "As President Claims Victory, Doubts Remain," *NYT*, September 20, 1994.

74. Lake, interview, January 1998.

75. Pastor, interview.

76. Ibid. Also William L. Swing, interview, February 1995, Port-au-Prince, Haiti; and "President Tells Nation," *NYT*, September 18, 1994.

77. Jimmy Carter, CNN interview, September 19, 1994, CNN Archive, Atlanta; Judy Woodruff, interview, November 1997, Atlanta.

78. Ibid. Also Wines, "As President Claims Victory."

79. Carter, *Living Faith*, 153.

80. Jimmy Carter to Ernesto Pérez-Balladares, October 14, 1994, Pastor Personal Papers.

81. Wines, "As President Claims Victory."

82. Nunn, interview.

83. "Words of Clinton and His Envoys: A Chance to Restore Democracy," *NYT*, September 19, 1994. Also Pastor, interview.

84. Ann McDaniel and Vern E. Smith, interview of Jimmy Carter, September 20, 1994, excerpts published in *Newsweek*, October 3, 1994, 37.

85. Maureen Dowd, "Despite Role as Negotiator, Carter Feels Unappreciated," *NYT*, September 21, 1994.

86. Ibid.

87. Terrence Adamson, interview, July 1996, Washington, D.C.

88. Warren Christopher, interview, June 1995, Washington, D.C.

89. Elaine Sciolino, "Carter and Christopher to Meet in Georgia to Discuss," *NYT*, September 24, 1994; and "Christopher, Carter in Friendly Talks," *NYT*, September 25, 1994.

90. Garry Trudeau, "The Fireside Carter," *NYT*, October 2, 1994.

91. William Safire, "Jimmy Clinton II," *NYT*, September 22, 1994.

92. "Schwarzkopf on Hussein: Calculating 'Carter Facts,'" *NYT*, October 13, 1994.

93. David Brock, "Jimmy Carter's Return," *American Spectator*, December 1994.

94. Thomas, "Road to Haiti," 38.

95. Bob Shacochis, "The Immaculate Invasion," *Harper's*, February 1995; Gaddis Smith, "Haiti: From Intervention to Intervasion," *Current History*, February 1995, 58; and "Assessment Mission to Haiti—December 11–14, 1994," Carter Center report, January 5, 1995.

96. *Wall Street Journal*, September 21, 1994; *Atlanta Journal & Constitution*, September 26, 1994; *NYT*, September 18, 1994; and *USA Today*, September 21, 1994.

97. Jimmy Carter to Betty and John Pope, October 5, 1994, Pope Personal Papers, Americus, Ga.

98. "NGO's Can Play Vital Role in Crisis Negotiations," *Carter Center News*, winter 1995, 5. Also "Assessment Mission to Haiti."

TWENTY-TWO: ALWAYS A RECKONING

1. Juan J. Walte, "Carter's Coup Could Pay Off with Peace Prize," *USA Today*, September 20, 1994.

2. Irwin Abrams, "Nobel Peace Prize," in Bruce W. Jentleson and Thomas G. Patterson, *Encyclopedia of U.S. Foreign Relations* (New York: Oxford University Press, 1997), vol. 3, 253–57.

3. James Wooten, "Meddler, Moralist, or Peacemaker?" *NYT Magazine*, January 29, 1995. The article ran under the subhead "The Conciliator."

4. Anthony Spaeth, "The Split Peace Prize Pair," *Time*, October 21, 1996; and Gina Bellafonte, "Kudos for a Crusader," *Time*, October 29, 1997.

5. Andrew Young, interview, October 1997, Atlanta.

6. "Former President Carter Wins 1994 J. William Fulbright Prize for International Understanding," *Fulbright Association Newsletter* 1, no. 2 (fall 1994).

7. Gore Vidal, "Reel History," *New Yorker*, November 10, 1997, 112–20.

8. H. W. Brands, *TR* (New York: Basic Books, 1997); and Paul C. Nagel, *John Quincy Adams: A Public Life, a Private Life* (New York: Knopf, 1997).

9. Jimmy Carter, *Always a Reckoning* (New York: Times Books, 1997).

10. "Jimmy Carter's Contribution," *NYT*, September 18, 1994.

11. Seamus Heaney, interview, April 1995, Atlanta; and Joseph Brodsky, interview, April 1995, Atlanta.

12. Miller Williams, "Some Words on the Lives and Lines of Jimmy Carter," *New Orleans Review* 20, nos. 1–2 (spring–summer 1994): 9–12.

13. "Poetry for Peanuts," *New Orleans Times-Picayune*, December 30, 1994.

14. Elizabeth Drew, *Showdown: The Struggle between the Gingrich Congress and the Clinton White House* (New York: Simon & Schuster, 1996), 23–47.

15. Newt Gingrich, interview, August 1993, Jonesboro, Ga.

16. Jimmy Carter, interview, April 1995, Atlanta.

17. Gingrich, interview.

18. Carter, interview, April 1995, Atlanta.

19. Gingrich, interview.

20. Carter, interview, April 1995, Atlanta.

21. Millard Fuller, interview, August 1994, Americus, Ga.

22. Carter, interview, April 1995, Atlanta.

23. David Rieff, *Slaughterhouse: Bosnia and the Failure of the West* (New York: Simon & Schuster, 1995); and Roy

Gutman, *Genocide* (Longmead, England: Element Books, 1993).

24. Drew, *Showdown*, 243–55.

25. Roy W. Gutman (*Newsday*) to Douglas Brinkley, January 10, 1998.

26. "Carter Center Jump Starts Peace Efforts in Bosnia-Herzegovina," *Carter Center News*, winter 1995, 1–3.

27. Rieff, *Slaughterhouse*; and Harry Barnes to Douglas Brinkley, January 26, 1998.

28. James Wooten, "Meddler, Moralist, or Peacemaker?" *NYT Magazine*, January 29, 1995.

29. Rosalynn Carter, Bosnia-Herzegovina diary, December 18–20, 1994, Rosalynn Carter Personal Papers, Plains, Ga.; and Harry Barnes to Douglas Brinkley, January 26, 1998.

30. Jimmy Carter, interview, May 1995, Atlanta.

31. Rosalynn Carter, Bosnia-Herzegovina diary.

32. Douglas Jehl, "Carter Heading Off to Bosnia on Broadened Peace Mission," *NYT*, December 18, 1994.

33. Conor Cruise O'Brien, "Bearing the Gift of Peace," *Independent*, December 23, 1994.

34. "Carter Makes Bid for Peace in Bosnia," *San Francisco Examiner*, December 15, 1994.

35. Rosalynn Carter, Bosnia-Herzegovina diary; and Joyce Neu to Douglas Brinkley, January 26, 1998.

36. Jehl, "Carter Heading Off to Bosnia"; and Wooten, "Meddler, Moralist, or Peacemaker?"

37. Jimmy Carter, Bosnia-Herzegovina diary.

38. Rosalynn Carter, Bosnia-Herzegovina diary.

39. Ibid. Also Harry Barnes to Douglas Brinkley, January 26, 1998.

40. Ibid.

41. Jimmy Carter, Bosnia-Herzegovina diary, December 18–20, 1994, Jimmy Carter Personal Papers, Carter Center, Atlanta.

42. Rosalynn Carter, Bosnia-Herzegovina diary.

43. Quoted in Roger Cohen, "Spent

Bosnia Tries to Make Its Peace," *NYT*, December 31, 1995.

44. Rosalynn Carter, Bosnia-Herzegovina diary.

45. Harry Barnes to Douglas Brinkley, January 26, 1998.

46. Rosalynn Carter, Bosnia-Herzegovina diary.

47. Ibid. Also Wooten, "Meddler, Moralist, or Peacemaker?"

48. Jimmy Carter, Bosnia-Herzegovina diary.

49. Rosalynn Carter, Bosnia-Herzegovina diary; and Roy W. Gutman (*Newsday*) to Douglas Brinkley, January 10, 1998.

50. Roger Cohen, "Bosnian Serb Leader Offers His Revisions to Peace Plan," *NYT*, December 21, 1994.

51. Harry Barnes to Douglas Brinkley, January 26, 1998.

52. Rosalynn Carter, Bosnia-Herzegovina diary.

53. Roger Cohen, "Bosnian Foes Agree to 4-Month Truce, Carter Reports," *NYT*, December 21, 1994.

54. Richard Cohen, "In Defense of the Carter Post-Presidency," *Washington Post*, December 27, 1994; and James Wooten, "Meddler, Moralist, or Peacemaker?" *NYT Magazine*, January 29, 1995.

55. Roger Cohen, "Bosnian Foes Agree."

56. Ibid.

57. John Pomfret, "Aw Shucks Diplomacy Pays Off for Carter," *Washington Post*, December 22, 1994.

58. Roy Gutman, "Serbs Being Asked to Renegotiate Peace Terms," *Newsday*, January 27, 1995.

59. Former president Jimmy Carter's testimony on the Bosnian conflict before the Senate Armed Services Committee, June 14, 1995, published in *Carter Center News*, summer 1995.

60. Harry Barnes to Douglas Brinkley, January 26, 1998.

61. Richard Holbrooke, interview, September 1997, New York.

62. Jimmy Carter, interview, January 1996, Jerusalem.

63. Elaine Sciolino, "Accord Reached to End War in Bosnia: Clinton Pledges U.S. Troops to Keep Peace," *NYT*, November 22, 1995.

64. Carter, interview, January 1996.

65. Robert Pastor to Douglas Brinkley, December 31, 1997. Also Anthony Lewis, "Reward for a Job Well Done," *NYT*, October 7, 1994.

66. William Foege, interview, August 1995, Atlanta.

67. Rosalynn Carter, interview, May 1995, Atlanta.

68. Stanley W. Cloud, "Hail to the Ex-Chief," *Time*, September 11, 1989.

69. William Leuchtenburg, *In the Shadow of FDR: From Harry Truman to Ronald Reagan* (Ithaca, N.Y.: Cornell University Press, 1989); and Douglas Brinkley, meeting notes of the Franklin and Eleanor Roosevelt Institute (FERI) Board Meeting, December 1994, New York.

70. Sam Way, interview, May 1995, Hawkinsville, Ga.

71. Jimmy Carter, "Remembering Franklin Delano Roosevelt: Fiftieth Anniversary Commemorative Ceremonies and Presentation of the 1995 Four Freedoms Awards," remarks, FDR's Little White House, Warm Springs, Ga., April 12, 1995.

72. William vanden Heuvel, interview, May 1995, New York.

73. Jimmy Carter, *Living Faith*, 117.

74. Andrew Young, interview, October 1997, Atlanta.

75. Ted Turner, interview, April 1995, Atlanta.

76. Wooten, "Meddler, Moralist, or Peacemaker?" *NYT Magazine*, January 29, 1995.

77. Robert Pastor, interview, August 1997, Atlanta; and Ben Smith III, "A Hard Sell for Carter," *Atlanta Journal & Constitution*, September 15, 1995.

78. "Jimmy Carter to Host Round of Cuba Talks," *Indianapolis News*, September 19, 1995.

79. Carter to Host Talks with Cuban Exiles," *Reuters*, September 19, 1995.

80. Robert Pastor, interview, October 1997, Atlanta.

81. Don Treadaway, "Jimmy Carter Vows to Continue Working for Democracy in Cuba," *Emory Report*, October 2, 1995. Also Marcy Camm, "Pastor Discusses Possibility of U.S.-Cuban Reconciliation," *Emory Wheel*, September 26, 1995; and Larry Rohter, "Clinton and Castro Buy Some Time," *NYT*, May 14, 1995.

82. Rosalynn Carter, Africa diary, March 19–28, 1995, Rosalynn Carter Personal Papers.

83. *Al-Ahram* (Cairo's English-language weekly newspaper), April 6–10, 1995.

84. Rosalynn Carter, Africa diary.

85. Ibid.

86. Chip Carter, interview, May 1995, Decatur, Ga.; and "The Carter Center's Role in Sudan," *Carter Center News*, summer 1995, 4.

87. "INN's Olusegun Obassanjo's Future Uncertain," *Carter Center News*, summer 1995, 10; and Howard French, "Nigeria Accused on a 2 Year War on Ethnic Group," *NYT*, March 28, 1995.

88. Howard W. French, "Repression in Nigeria," *NYT*, November 12, 1995.

89. Jimmy Carter, Africa diary.

90. Rosalynn Carter, Africa diary.

91. Ibid.

92. "USAID Joins Carter Center for Final Assault on Guinea Worm," *Carter Center News*, winter 1995, 9.

93. Rosalynn Carter, Africa diary; and TransAfrica Forum Clippings Files, Washington, D.C.

94. Steven A. Holmes, "U.S. Blacks Battle Nigeria over Rights Issues," *NYT*, June 15, 1995; Michael Marriott, "Brother against Brother," *Newsweek*, May 22, 1995; and Kevin Merida, "Black Americans to Press Nigeria for Democracy," *Washington Post*, March 14, 1995.

95. Wole Soyinka, interview, April 1995, Atlanta.

96. "An Open Letter to Mr. Randall Robinson and the Executives of TransAfrica from Nigerians in the United States," *NYT*, April 20, 1995.

97. Jimmy Carter, interview, December 1995, Washington, D.C. Also see Joshua Hammer, "A Voice Silences," *Newsweek*, November 20, 1995.

98. Jimmy Carter, Africa diary; and "Carter's Clean Water Crusade Visits Sudan," Atlanta Journal & Constitution, July 23, 1995.

99. Warren E. Leary, "With One Disease Nearly Erased, Assault Is Planned on Another," NYT, December 6, 1995; and Richard W. Stevenson, "The Chief Banker for the Nations at the Bottom of the Heap," NYT, September 14, 1997.

100. Jimmy Carter to Douglas Brinkley, March 26, 1997. Also Prime Minister Meles Zenawi to Jimmy Carter, March 24, 1997, Ethiopia File, Carter Center.

101. Elizabeth Kurylo, "African Trip Is His Third One of the Year," Atlanta Journal & Constitution, September 22, 1995; and Jimmy Carter, "Another Urgent Need for International Peacekeepers," Los Angeles Times, September 7, 1995.

102. Jimmy Carter, Sources of Strength (New York: Times Books, 1997), 212–13.

TWENTY-THREE: THE PALESTINIAN ELECTION

1. Barton Gellman, "Israel Prepares to Bury Rabin," Washington Post, November 6, 1995; and Isabel Kershner, "Power to the Palestinians," Jerusalem Report, January 25, 1996, 20–24.

2. National Democratic Institute for International Affairs, Palestinian Elections, January 20, 1996, Pre-Election Report, NDI Archive, Washington, D.C.

3. For a profile of Samiha Khalil see Kershner, "Power to the Palestinians," Jerusalem Report, 24. Also Serge Schmemann, "With Placards and Slogans, Palestinians Prepare to Vote," NYT, January 4, 1996.

4. "702 Register to Run for Palestinian Seats," NYT, December 26, 1995.

5. Jimmy Carter to Douglas Brinkley, February 19, 1997.

6. Jimmy Carter, pre-election Jerusalem statement, January 18, 1996, Carter Center, Atlanta.

7. "Notebook," New Republic, February 12, 1996. Robert Pastor, Harry Barnes, and Kenneth Wollack signed a letter to the New Republic editor, Andrew Sullivan, protesting the characterization of the Carter Center–NDI election-monitoring team.

8. Jimmy Carter, interview, January 1997, Jerusalem.

9. Douglas Brinkley, notes on Jimmy Carter–Shimon Peres lunch meeting, January 19, 1996, Tel Aviv.

10. Douglas Brinkley, notes on Jimmy Carter–Khalil Shaklil human rights meeting, January 19, 1996, Jerusalem.

11. Douglas Brinkley, notes on Jimmy Carter–Yasir Arafat dinner meeting, January 19, 1996, Gaza City.

12. "Arafat Leading with 85 Percent," New Orleans Times-Picayune, January 21, 1996.

13. Douglas Brinkley, notes on Jimmy Carter's election monitoring, January 20, 1996, Gaza (West Bank, East Jerusalem).

14. Serge Schmemann, "Big Vote Turnout for Palestinians," NYT, January 21, 1996.

15. Charles W. Holmes, "Carter Turns Steely as Israel 'Intimidates' Voters," Atlanta Journal & Constitution, January 21, 1996.

16. Jimmy Carter, interview, January 1996, Jerusalem.

17. Jon Immanuel, "Arafat Wins 88% of Vote; 75% of Council to Fatah," Jerusalem Post, January 22, 1996. The best summation of the election is The January 1996 Palestine Election, published by NDI and the Carter Center in 1997. Also see Sterer H. Rowley, "Palestinian Election Judged Fair," Chicago Tribune, January 22, 1996.

18. Serge Schmemann, "Election: A Dawn for Palestinians, Legitimacy for Arafat," NYT, January 22, 1996; Douglas Brinkley, notes on Carter-Arafat meeting, January 21, 1996.

19. Anton Shammas, "The Reality of Palestine," NYT, January 24, 1996.

20. "The Election Festival," Jerusalem Post, January 27, 1996.

21. "Arafat, Peres Bear Heavy Burden in Quest for Peace," USA Today, March 6,

1996; and William Safire, "If Not Arafat . . . ," *NYT*, March 7, 1996.

22. "Arafat's Declarations of War," *NYT*, September 28, 1997 (a full-page compendium of Arafat's anti-Israeli remarks paid for by the Zionist Organization of America).

23. Elizabeth Kurylo, "Arafat Meets Carter Despite Lengthy Detour," *Atlanta Journal & Constitution*, March 6, 1997.

24. Ibid. Also special thanks to Elizabeth Kurylo for sharing with me her many insights about Jimmy Carter.

AFTERWORD: TYRANT FOR PEACE

1. Hendrik Hertzberg, "Jimmy Carter, 1977–1981," in Robert A. Wilson, ed., *Character Above All* (New York: Simon & Schuster, 1995), 172–201.

2. Curtis Wilkie, "The Nation Carter's Memoirs: The Other Version," *Boston Globe*, October 17, 1982.

3. Ted Turner, interview, April 1995, Atlanta.

4. Carter, *Talking Peace*, 34–49.

5. Carter, *Living Faith*, 117.

6. Daniel Schorr, "Peanut Diplomacy in Haiti," *New Leader*, September 12–26, 1994, 3.

7. Carter, *Sources of Strength*, 241.

8. Carol Johnson to Jimmy Carter, August 1, 1988; and Jimmy Carter to Judge Carneal, August 29, 1988, JCPPP, Box 28, JCPL.

9. Robert Pastor, interview, January 1998, Atlanta.

10. Shannon Tangonan, "Elie Wiesel: Carter Suited to Lead U.N.," *USA Today*, April 12, 1995.

11. Jimmy Carter, interview, April 1995; and Lee Michael Katz, "U.N. Head to Announce Reforms in Bureaucracy," *USA Today*, July 16, 1997.

12. Charles Haddad, "Carter Advising Turner on U.N. Project," *Atlanta Journal & Constitution*, October 4, 1997.

13. Kai Bird, "The Very Model of an Ex–President," *Nation*, November 12, 1990, 560.

14. Douglas Brinkley, "Jimmy Carter's Modest Quest for Global Peace," *Foreign Affairs*, November–December 1995; and Carter Center Annual Report (1997), Carter Center.

15. James Bennet, "A Presidential Cold War Begins to Thaw," *NYT*, May 21, 1997.

16. Susan Page *(USA Today)*, transcript of interview of President Bill Clinton, February 25, 1997, Terrence Adamson Personal Papers, Washington, D.C.

17. Ralph Nader, interview, December 1997, Washington, D.C.

18. Andrew Young, interview, October 1997, Atlanta.

19. John Hardman, interview, September 1995, Atlanta.

20. Carter, *Always a Reckoning*, 25.

21. Jimmy Carter Work Build, June 1995, Los Angeles, Press Clipping File, Habitat for Humanity Archive, Americus, Ga. Also Millard Fuller, interview, January 1995, Americus, Ga.

22. Jimmy Carter speech, Carter–Mondale reunion, October 18, 1997, Atlanta (transcript).

23. "At a Glance," transcript, 1997, Carter Center.

24. Douglas Brinkley, "Clintons and Carters Don't Mix," *NYT*, August 29, 1996; and Adam Nagourney, "As One President Nears, Another Stays Away," *NYT*, August 22, 1997.

25. Jessica Lee, "Carter Backs Independent Counsel Call," *USA* Today, October 20, 1997.

26. Ibid.

27. James A. Baker III, interview, October 1997, San Francisco, Calif.

28. *The Former Presidents Quarterly* (January 1999), Volume 6 Number 4.

29. Gerald R. Ford and Jimmy Carter, "A Time to Heal Our Nation," *NYT*, December 21, 1998.

30. Dylan Thomas, *Death and Entrances: Poems by Dylan Thomas* (London: J. M. Dent & Sons, 1946).

BIBLIOGRAPHY

The Jimmy Carter Library in Atlanta, Georgia, is one of ten presidential libraries administered by the National Archives and Records Administration. Like the other libraries, it was built with private funds and then donated to the United States, to be operated thereafter by the government. Architecturally, it is part of the Carter Presidential Center, which includes the Office of Jimmy Carter, the Carter Center of Emory University, and several other private organizations. Most of the primary documents quoted in *The Unfinished Presidency* are housed at the Carter Library, referred to as JCPL throughout the notes. The bulk of the research material relied upon is archived in the Jimmy Carter Post-Presidential Papers (JCPPP)—a collection closed to the general public, but made available to the author by President Carter. This extraordinary collection contains the private correspondence, official documents, travel reports, book manuscripts, random jottings, diary entries, and Carter Center business files of Jimmy Carter since he left the White House in January 1981. The collection is voluminous, containing over 100 boxes of primary source material, cited from for the first time in *The Unfinished Presidency*.

This bibliography is divided into the following sections: manuscript collections; works by Jimmy Carter; books; articles; newspapers and periodicals; and personal interviews.

MANUSCRIPT COLLECTIONS (INCLUDING UNPUBLISHED MATERIAL, TAPE ARCHIVES, THESES, FILMS, AND PERSONAL COLLECTIONS)

Atlanta Federal Records Center, East Point, Georgia (CDC Collection).
Bernard Aronson Personal Papers, Washington, D.C.
Carter Center Archives, Atlanta, Georgia.
Carter Family Newspaper Clippings, Lake Blackshear Regional Library, Americus, Georgia.

CNN Archive, Atlanta, Georgia.
C-SPAN Tape Archive, Washington, D.C.
Global 2000 Archive, Charles Kirbo Building, Atlanta, Georgia.
Governor Richard Snelling Papers, Burlington, Vermont.
Habitat for Humanity Archive, Americus, Georgia.
Hendrik Hertzberg Personal Papers, New York.
Jimmy Carter National Historic Site Papers Collections, Plains, Georgia.
Jimmy Carter Post-Presidential Papers, Jimmy Carter Presidential Library, Atlanta, Georgia (JCPPP).
Jimmy Carter Presidential Papers, Jimmy Carter Presidential Library, Atlanta, Georgia (JCPP).
Jimmy Carter Personal Papers, Carter Center, Atlanta, Georgia.
Jimmy Carter Archive, Emory University, Atlanta, Georgia.
Jimmy Carter Files, Southwest Georgia Branch Experiment Station, Plains, Georgia.
John and Betty Pope Personal Papers, Americus, Georgia.
John H. Patton, "Jimmy Carter and Citizenship: The Communication of Humane Values," unpublished paper presented at the Carter Library Anniversary Conference, February 22, 1997.
MacNeil/Lehrer NewsHour Archive, Washington, D.C.
Maranatha Baptist Church, tape collection of President Carter's Sunday school lectures, Plains, Georgia.
Mary Elizabeth King Personal Papers, Carter Center, Atlanta, Georgia.
Mary Elizabeth King, "Palestinian Nonviolent Resistance and the *Intifada*," unpublished manuscript.
Mary Elizabeth King Collection, Wisconsin State Historical Society, Madison, Wisconsin.
Merck & Co., Inc., Archives, Rahway, New Jersey.
National Democratic Institute (NDI) Archives, Washington, D.C.
Norman Borlaug Personal Papers, College Station, Texas.
Robert Kagan Personal Papers, Washington, D.C.
Robert Lipshutz Personal Papers, Atlanta, Georgia.
Robert A. Pastor Personal Papers, Atlanta, Georgia.
Robert Strong, "Working in the World: Jimmy Carter and the Making of American Foreign Policy," manuscript draft, to be published by LSU Press in 1998.
Rosalynn Carter Symposia Papers, Mental Health Program, Carter Center, Atlanta, Georgia.
Rosalynn Carter Institute for Human Development Papers, Georgia Southwestern University, Americus, Georgia.
Rosalynn Carter Personal Papers, Plains, Georgia.
State Department Archives, Washington, D.C.
Terrence Adamson Personal Papers, Washington, D.C.
TransAfrica Forum Clipping Files, Washington, D.C.
U.S. State Department Archives, Washington, D.C.
Vice Presidential Papers, Bush Presidential Library, Texas A&M, College Station, Texas.
W. W. Rostow and Elspeth D. Rostow, *The Austin Project* (printed privately, 1992), W. W. Rostow Personal Papers.
William Foege Papers, Charles Kirbo Building, Atlanta, Georgia.
YKK Archive, Macon, Georgia.
Zbigniew Brzezinski Personal Papers, Washington, D.C.

SPECIAL DOCUMENT COLLECTION OF THE LATIN AMERICAN AND CARIBBEAN PROGRAM OF THE CARTER CENTER OF EMORY UNIVERSITY, COUNCIL OF FREELY ELECTED HEADS OF GOVERNMENT

"The May 7, 1989 Panamanian Elections." Washington, D.C.: Republican Institute for International Affairs, 1989.

"1990 Elections in the Dominican Republic: Report of an Observer Delegation." Washington, D.C.: National Democratic Institute for International Affairs and Council of Freely Elected Heads of Government, 1990.

"Observing Nicaragua's Elections, 1989–1990." Atlanta: Council of Freely Elected Heads of Government and Carter Center of Emory University, 1990.

"The 1990 General Elections in Haiti." Washington, D.C.: National Democratic Institute for International Affairs and Council of Freely Elected Heads of Government, 1991.

"Report of a Team Sent by the Council of Freely Elected Heads of Government to Witness the Observation of the Elections in Michoacan and Chihuahua, Mexico." Atlanta: Carter Center, July 13, 1992.

"Observing Guyana's Electoral Process, 1990–1992." Atlanta: Council of Freely Elected Heads of Government and Carter Center of Emory University, 1993.

"The International Observation of the U.S. Elections." Atlanta: Council of Freely Elected Heads of Government and Carter Center of Emory University, 1993.

"Electoral Reform in Mexico." Report of a visit by a delegation of the Council of Freely Elected Heads of Government, November 1993.

WORKS BY JIMMY CARTER

Books

Sources of Strength. New York: Times Books, 1997.

Living Faith. New York: Times Books, 1996.

The Little Baby Snoogle-Fleejer (with Amy Carter). New York: Times Books, 1996.

Always a Reckoning. New York: Times Books, 1995.

Talking Peace: A Vision for the Next Generation. New York: Dutton, 1993.

Turning Point: A Candidate, a State, and a Nation Coming of Age. New York: Times Books, 1992.

An Outdoor Journal. New York: Bantam Books, 1988.

Everything to Gain: Making the Most of the Rest of Your Life (with Rosalynn Carter). New York: Ballantine Books, 1987.

The Blood of Abraham: Insights into the Middle East. Boston: Houghton Mifflin, 1985.

Keeping Faith: Memoirs of a President. New York: Bantam Books, 1982.

A Government as Good as Its People. New York: Simon & Schuster, 1977.

Why Not the Best? Nashville, Tenn.: Broadman Press, 1975.

Articles, Op-Ed Pieces, and Speeches

Carter, Jimmy. "Another Urgent Need for International Peacekeepers." *Los Angeles Times*, September 7, 1995.

———. "The Atlanta Project." *Rotarian*, January 1994.

———. "First Step toward Peace." *Newsweek*, December 17, 1990.

———. "From Politics to Poetics." *Washington Post Book World*, July 2, 1995.

———. "Haiti's Election Needs Help." *NYT*, October 1, 1990.

———. "In Perspective." *Carter Center News*, spring 1993.

————. "In Perspective: Panama in Crisis." *Carter Center News*, spring 1989.

————. Introduction to Mary Jane Deeb and Mary King, eds., *Hasib Sabbagh: From Palestine Refugee to Citizen of the World*. Lanham, Md.: University Press of America, 1996.

————. Letter to the editor. *NYT*, April 1, 1990.

————. "Mending the U.S.-China Rift." *Atlanta Journal & Constitution*, August 11, 1995.

————. "The Middle East Consultation: A Look at the Future." *Middle East Journal* 42, no. 2 (spring 1988).

————. "The Need to Negotiate," *Time*, October 22, 1990.

————. "Needed: Middle East Peace Talks." *NYT*, January 2, 1991.

————. "Overview: Options and Recommendations." In Ellen Propper Mickiewicz and Roman Kolkowicz, eds., *International Security and Arms Control*. New York: Praeger, 1986.

————. "The Power of a Project." *Atlanta Journal & Constitution*, October 18, 1995.

————. "Prayer and Civic Religion." *NYT*, December 4, 1996.

————. "Proposed Tobacco Tax Would Raise Money and Save Lives." *NYT*, February 16, 1993.

————. "Rushdie's Book Is an Insult." *NYT*, March 5, 1989.

————. "Text of U.S. Statement on Poland." *NYT*, December 4, 1980.

————. "A Tundra Industrial Complex? NO!" *Los Angeles Times*, December 1, 1990.

————. "The U.S. Needs to Lead in Israel." *NYT*, February 14, 1988.

Carter, Jimmy, and Robert Pastor. "Fear and Confidence: Trade Pact Can Help U.S.-Mexico Ties." *Atlanta Journal & Constitution*, May 19, 1991.

Public Papers of the Presidents of the United States: Jimmy Carter, 1976. 2 vols. Washington, D.C.: Government Printing Office, 1977.

Public Papers of the Presidents of the United States: Jimmy Carter, 1977. 2 vols. Washington, D.C.: Government Printing Office, 1978.

Public Papers of the Presidents of the United States: Jimmy Carter, 1978. 2 vols. Washington, D.C.: Government Printing Office, 1979.

Public Papers of the Presidents of the United States: Jimmy Carter, 1980–81. 2 vols. Washington, D.C.: Government Printing Office, 1982.

BOOKS

Alexander, John R., ed. *How to Start a Habitat for Humanity Affiliate*. Americus, Ga.: Habitat for Humanity International, Inc., 1989.

Allen, Frederick. *Secret Formula*. New York: Harper Business, 1994.

Ambrose, Stephen E. *Nixon: Ruin and Recovery, 1973–1990*. New York: Simon & Schuster, 1991.

Ambrose, Stephen E., and Douglas G. Brinkley. *Rise to Globalism: American Foreign Policy since 1938*. 8th ed. New York: Viking, 1997.

Amler, Robert W., and H. Bruce Dull. *Closing the Gap: The Burden of Unnecessary Illness*. New York: Oxford University Press, 1985.

Ariail, Daniel, and Cheryl Heckler-Feltz. *The Carpenter's Apprentice: The Spiritual Biography of Jimmy Carter*. Grand Rapids, Mich.: Zondervan Publishing House, 1996.

Ashrawi, Hanan. *This Side of Peace*. New York: Simon & Schuster, 1996.

Baker, James III. *The Politics of Diplomacy: Revolution, War and Peace, 1989–1992*. New York: Putnam, 1995.

Barrett, Laurence I. *Gambling with History: Reagan in the White House*. Garden City, N.Y.: Doubleday, 1983.

Beschloss, Michael, and Strobe Talbott. *At the Highest Levels: The Inside Story of the End of the Cold War*. Boston: Little, Brown, 1993.

Bibb, Porter. *It Ain't as Easy as It Looks: Ted Turner's Amazing Story*. New York: Crown Publishers, 1993.

Bill, James A. *The Edge and the Lion: The Tragedy of American-Iranian Relations*. New Haven: Yale University Press, 1988.

Blood, Thomas. *Madame Secretary*. New York: St. Martin's Press, 1997.

Boller, Paul F. Jr. *Presidential Campaigns*. New York: Oxford University Press, 1996.

Bourne, Peter G. *Jimmy Carter: A Comprehensive Biography from Plains to Post-presidency*. New York: Scribner's, 1997.

Brands, H. W. *TR*. New York: Basic Books, 1997.

Brauer, Carl M. *Presidential Transitions: Eisenhower through Reagan*. New York: Oxford University Press, 1986.

Brinkley, Douglas. *Dean Acheson: The Cold War Years, 1953–1971*. New Haven, Conn.: Yale University Press, 1993.

————. *The Majic Bus: An American Odyssey*. New York: Harcourt Brace, 1993.

Brzezinski, Zbigniew. *Power and Principle: Memoirs of the National Security Adviser, 1977–1981*. New York: Farrar, Straus & Giroux, 1983.

Campbell, Colin, and Bert A. Rockman, eds. *The Clinton Presidency: First Appraisals*. Chatham, N.J.: Chatham Publishing House, 1996.

Canon, Lou. *Reagan*. New York: Putnam, 1982.

Carothers, Thomas. *In the Name of Democracy: U.S. Policy toward Latin America in the Reagan Years*. Berkeley, Calif.: University of California Press, 1991.

Carson, Clayborne. *In Struggle: SNCC and the Black Awakening of the 1960s*. Cambridge, Mass.: Harvard University Press, 1981.

Carter, Jimmy, and Gerald Ford, eds. *American Agenda: Report to the Forty-First President of the United States*. Camp Hill, Penn.: Book of the Month Club, 1989.

Carter, Hugh. *Cousin Beedie and Cousin Hot: My Life with the Carter Family of Plains, Georgia*. Englewood Cliffs, N.J.: Prentice-Hall, 1978.

Carter, Lillian, and Gloria Carter Spann. *Away from Home: Letters to My Family*. New York: Simon & Schuster, 1977.

Carter, Rosalynn. *First Lady from Plains*. Boston: Houghton Mifflin, 1984.

Carter, Rosalynn (with Susan K. Golant). *Helping Yourself Help Others*. New York: Random House, 1994.

Carter, Sybil (with Ken Estes). *Billy*. Newport, R.I.: Edgehill Press, 1989.

Christopher, Warren, et al. *American Hostages in Iran: The Conduct of a Crisis*. New Haven, Conn.: Yale University Press, 1985.

Crowley, Monica. *Nixon Off the Record*. New York: Random House, 1996.

Cumings, Bruce. *The Origins of the Korean War*. 2 vols. Princeton, N.J.: Princeton University Press, 1981–90.

de Cuéllar, Javier Pérez. *Pilgrimage for Peace*. New York: St. Martin's Press, 1997.

Dix, Robert H. *The Politics of Colombia*. New York: Praeger, 1987.

Drew, Elizabeth. *Portrait of an Election: The 1980 Presidential Campaign*. New York: Simon & Schuster, 1981.

————. *Showdown: The Struggle between the Gingrich Congress and the Clinton White House*. New York: Simon & Schuster, 1996.

Doctorow, E. L. *Jack London, Hemingway, and the Constitution*. New York: Random House, 1993.

Dumbrell, John. *American Foreign Policy: Carter to Clinton*. London: Macmillan, 1997.

————. *The Carter Presidency: A Re-evaluation*. Manchester: University of Manchester Press, 1993.

Edel, Wilbur. *The Reagan Presidency*. New York: Hippocrene Books, 1992.

Etheridge, Elizabeth W. *Sentinel for Health: A History of the Centers for Disease Control*. Berkeley: University of California Press, 1992.

Fink, Gary M. *Prelude to the Presidency: The Political Character and Legislative Leadership Style of Governor Jimmy Carter*. Westport, Conn.: Greenwood Press, 1980.

Fink, Gary M., and Hugh Davis Graham, eds. *The Carter Presidency: Policy Choices in the Post New Deal Era*. Lawrence: University Press of Kansas, 1998.

Ford, Gerald. *A Time to Heal: The Autobiography*. New York: Harper & Row, 1979.

Frady, Marshall. *Jesse: The Life and Pilgrimage of Jesse Jackson*. New York: Random House, 1986.

Freedman, Robert O., ed. *The Intifada: Its Impact on Israel, the Arab World and the Superpowers*. Gainesville: University Presses of Florida, 1991.

————. *The Intifada: The Middle East after Iraq's Invasion of Kuwait*. Gainesville: University Presses of Florida, 1993.

Fuller, Millard. *Bokotola*. Piscataway, N.J.: New Century Publishers, 1977.

————. *A Simple, Decent Place to Live: The Building Realization of Habitat for Humanity*. Dallas, Tex.: Word Publishing, 1995.

————. *The Theology of The Hammer*. Macon, Ga.: Smyth & Helwys Publishing, 1994.

Fuller, Millard, and Linda Fuller. *The Excitement Is Building: How Habitat Is Putting Roofs over Heads and Hope in Hearts*. Dallas, Tex.: Word Publishing, 1990.

Fuller, Millard (with Diane Scott). *No More Shacks!* Waco, Tex.: Word Publishers, 1986.

Fuller, Millard, and Diane Scott. *Love in the Mortar Joints*. Clinton, N.J.: New Win Publishing, 1980.

Fussell, Betty. *The Story of Corn*. New York: Knopf, 1992.

Garrett, Laurie. *The Coming Plague: Newly Emerging Diseases in a World Out of Balance*. New York: Penguin, 1994.

Garthoff, Raymond. *The Great Transition: American-Soviet Relations and the End of the Cold War*. Washington, D.C.: Brookings Institute, 1994.

Gates, Robert M. *From the Shadows: The Ultimate Insider's Story of Five Presidents and How They Won the Cold War*. New York: Simon & Schuster, 1996.

Germond, Jack W., and Jules Witcover. *Blue Smoke and Mirrors: How Reagan Won and Why Jimmy Carter Lost the Election of 1980*. New York: Viking Press, 1981.

Gillon, Steven M. *The Democrats' Dilemma: Walter F. Mondale and the Liberal Legacy*. New York: Columbia University Press, 1992.

Glad, Betty. *Jimmy Carter: In Search of the White House*. New York: W. W. Norton, 1980.

Goldberg, Robert, and Gerald Jay Goldberg. *Citizen Turner: The Wild Rise of An American Tycoon*. New York: Harcourt Brace, 1995.

Gore, Albert. *Earth in the Balance: Ecology and the Human Spirit*. Boston: Houghton Mifflin, 1992.

Graham, Billy. *Just as I Am*. San Francisco, Calif.: Harper Zondervan, 1997.

Greenfield, Jeff. *The Real Campaign: How the Media Missed the Story of the 1980 Campaign*. New York: Summit Books, 1982.

Gutman, Roy. *Banana Diplomacy: The Making of American Policy in Nicaragua*. New York: Simon & Schuster, 1989.

————. *Genocide*. Longmead, England: Element Books, 1993.

Haig, Alexander Jr. *Caveat: Realism, Reagan and Foreign Policy*. New York: Macmillan, 1984.

Halberstam, David. *The Powers That Be*. New York: Knopf, 1979.

Hargrove, Erwin C. *Jimmy Carter as President: Leadership and the Politics of the Public Good*. Baton Rouge: Louisiana State University Press, 1988.

Hopkins, Donald. *Princes and Peasants: Smallpox in History*. Chicago: University of Chicago Press, 1988.

Jordan, Clarence, and Lane Doulos. *Cotton-Patch Parables of Liberation*. Kitchener, Ontario: Herald Press, 1976.

Jordan, Hamilton. *Crisis: The Last Year of the Carter Presidency*. New York: G. Putnam's Sons, 1982.

Kagan, Robert. *A Twilight Struggle: American Power and Nicaragua, 1977–1990*. New York: Free Press, 1996.

Kantor, Sandford, and Sandra L. Quinn-Musgrove. *American Royalty: All the Presidents' Children*. Westport, Conn.: Greenwood Press, 1995.

Kaufman, Burton I. *The Presidency of James Earl Carter, Jr.* Lawrence: University Press of Kansas, 1993.

Kim Hak Joon. *Unification Policies of North and South Korea, 1945–1991*. Seoul: Seoul National University Press, 1992.

King, Mary. *Freedom Song*. New York: Morrow, 1987.

King, Mary, and Mary-Jane Deeb. *Hasib Sabbagh: From Palestinian Refugee to Citizen of the World*. Lanham, N.D.: University Press of America, 1996.

Klieman, Aaron S. *Foundation of British Policy in the Arab World: The Cairo Conference of 1921*. Baltimore, Md.: Johns Hopkins University Press, 1970.

Kolkowicz, Roman, and Ellen Propper Mickiewicz, eds. *International Security and Arms Control*. New York: Praeger, 1986.

————. *The Soviet Calculus of Nuclear War.* Lexington, Mass.: Lexington Books, 1986.

Kucharsky, David. *The Man from Plains: The Mind and Spirit of Jimmy Carter*. New York: Harper & Row, 1976.

Lash, Joseph, P. *Eleanor: The Years Alone*. New York: W. W. Norton, 1972.

Lee, Dallas. *The Cotton Patch Evidence: The Story of Clarence Jordan and the Koinonia Farm Experiment, 1942–1970*. Americus, Ga.: Koinonia Partners, 1971.

Lefeber, Walter. *The Panama Canal: The Crisis in Historical Perspective*. New York: Oxford University Press, 1978.

Leuchtenburg, William. *In the Shadow of FDR: From Harry Truman to Ronald Reagan*. Ithaca, New York: Cornell University Press, 1989.

Lewis, Finlay. *Mondale: Portrait of an American Politician*. New York: Harper & Row, 1984.

Linowitz, Sol. *The Making of a Public Man: A Memoir*. Boston: Little, Brown, 1985.

Lowenthal, Abraham F., ed. *Exporting Democracy: The United States and Latin America*. 2 vols. Baltimore: Johns Hopkins University Press, 1991.

Makovsky, David. *Making Peace with the PLO: The Rabin Government's Road to the Oslo Accord*. Boulder, Colo.: Westview Press, 1996.

Maraniss, David. *First in His Class: A Biography of Bill Clinton*. New York: Simon & Schuster, 1995.

Martin, William. *A Prophet with Honor: The Billy Graham Story*. New York: William Morrow Company, 1991.

Mazlish, Bruce, and Edwin Diamond. *Jimmy Carter: An Interpretive Biography*. New York: Simon & Schuster, 1979.

McFarlane, Robert C., and Zofia Smardz. *Special Trust*. New York: Cadell & Davies, 1994.

Morgan, David T. *The New Crusades, the New Holy Land*. Tuscaloosa: University of Alabama Press, 1996.

Morley, Morris H. *Washington, Somoza, and the Sandinistas: State and Regime in U.S. Policy toward Nicaragua, 1969–1981*. Cambridge: Cambridge University Press, 1994.

Morris, Benny. *The Birth of the Palestinian Refugee Problem, 1947–1949*. Cambridge: Cambridge University Press, 1987.

Morris, Kenneth E. *Jimmy Carter: American Moralist*. Athens: University of Georgia Press, 1996.

Mosher, Frederick C., W. David Clinton, and Daniel G. Lang. *Presidential Transitions and Foreign Affairs*. Baton Rouge: Louisiana State University Press, 1987.

Muravchik, Joshua. *The Uncertain Crusade: Jimmy Carter and the Dilemmas of Human Rights*. New York: Hamilton Press, 1986.

Nagel, Paul C. *John Quincy Adams: A Public Life, a Private Life*. New York: Knopf, 1997.

Nash, Roderick. *Wilderness and the American Mind*. 3d ed. New Haven, Conn.: Yale University Press, 1982.

Neustadt, Richard E., and Ernest R. May. *Thinking in Time: The Uses of History for Decisionmakers*. New York: Free Press, 1986.

Nielson, Niels C. *The Religion of President Carter*. Nashville, Tenn.: Thomas Nelson, 1977.

Noriega, Manuel, and Peter Eisner. *American Prisoner: The Memoirs of Manuel Noriega*. New York: Random House, 1997.

Norton, Augustus Richard, ed. *Civil Society in the Middle East*. Leiden: E. J. Brill, 1996.

Norton, Howard, and Bob Slosser. *The Miracle of Jimmy Carter*. Plainfield, N.J.: Logos International, 1976.

Oberdorfer, Don. *The Two Koreas: A Contemporary History*. New York: Addison Wesley, 1997.

Ogden, Horace G. *CDC and the Smallpox Crusade*. Washington, D.C.: U.S. Department of Health and Human Services, 1987.

O'Neill, Tip (with William Novak). *Man of the House: The Life and Political Memoirs of Speaker Tip O'Neill*. New York: Random House, 1987.

Oppenheimer, Andres. *Castro's Final Hour: The Secret Story behind the Coming Downfall of Communist Cuba*. New York: Simon & Schuster, 1992.

Orme, William A. *Understanding NAFTA*. Austin: University of Texas Press, 1996.

Pappé, Ilan. *The Making of the Arab-Israeli Conflict, 1947–51*. London: I. B. Tauris, 1994.

Pastor, Robert. *Condemned to Repetition: The United States and Nicaragua*. Princeton: Princeton University Press, 1987.

———. *Integration with Mexico: Options for U.S. Policy*. New York: Twentieth Century Fund, 1993.

———. *Whirlpool: U.S. Foreign Policy toward Latin America and the Caribbean*. Princeton: Princeton University Press, 1993.

———, ed. *Democracy in the Americas: Stopping the Pendulum*. New York: Holmes & Meier, 1989.

Pastor, Robert (with Jorge G. Castaneda). *Limits to Friendship: The United States and Mexico*. New York: Knopf, 1988.

Pendegrast, Mark. *For God, Country, and Coca-Cola*. New York: Charles Scribner's Sons, 1993.

Peres, Shimon. *Battling for Peace: A Memoir*. New York: Random House, 1995.

Pippert, Wesley G. *The Spiritual Journey of Jimmy Carter: In His Own Words*. New York: Macmillan, 1978.

Powell, Colin (with Joseph E. Persico). *My American Journey*. New York: Random House, 1995.

Powell, Jody. *The Other Side of the Story*. New York: Morrow, 1993.

Quandt, William B. *Camp David: Peacemaking and Politics*. Washington, D.C.: Brookings Institute, 1986.

Raeburn, Paul. *The Last Harvest: The Genetic Gamble That Threatens to Destroy American Agriculture*. New York: Simon & Schuster, 1995.

Reagan, Ronald. *An American Life*. New York: Simon & Schuster, 1990.

Rieff, David. *Slaughterhouse: Bosnia and the Failure of the West*. New York: Simon & Schuster, 1995.

Rosati, Jerel A. *The Carter Administration's Quest for Global Community and Beliefs and Their Impact on Behavior*. Columbia: University of South Carolina Press, 1987.

Rosenbaum, Herbert D., and Alexej Ugrinsky, eds. *Jimmy Carter: Foreign Policy and the Postpresidential Years*. Westport, Conn.: Greenwood Press, 1994.

Rubenstein, Danny. *The Mystery of Arafat*. South Royalton, Vt.: Steerforth Press, 1995.

Rubin, Barry. *Paved with Good Intentions*, New York: Penguin, 1981.

Rushdie, Salman. *The Satanic Verses*. New York: Viking, 1988.

Sadat, Anwar. *In Search of Identity: An Autobiography*. New York: Harper & Row, 1978.

Sato, Seizaburo, Keninchi Koyama, and Shunpei Kumon. *Postwar Politician: The Life of Former Prime Minister Masayoshi Ohira*. New York: Kodansha International, 1990.

Schoultz, Lars. *Human Rights and U.S. Policy towards Latin America*. Princeton, N.J.: Princeton University Press, 1981.

Schweitzer, Albert. *Out of My Life and Thought*. London: Allen & Unwin, 1933.

Seale, Patrick. *Assad: The Struggle for the Middle East*. Berkeley: University of California Press, 1990.

Sharp, Gene. *The Politics of Nonviolent Action*. Boston: Porter Sargent, 1973.

Shilts, Randy, *And the Band Played On: Politics, People, and the AIDS Epidemic*. New York: St. Martin's Press, 1987.

Shlaim, Avi. *War and Peace in the Middle East*. New York: Penguin, 1994.

Sick, Gary. *All Fall Down: America's Tragic Encounter with Iran*. New York: Random House, 1985.

———. *October Surprise: America's Hostages in Iran and the Election of Ronald Reagan*. New York: Random House, 1991.

Sigal, Leon V. *Disarming Strangers: Nuclear Diplomacy with North Korea*. Princeton, N.J.: Princeton University Press, 1998.

Smith, Christian. *Resisting Reagan: The U.S. Central American Peace Movement*. Chicago: University of Chicago Press, 1996.

Smith, Gaddis. *Morality, Reason and Power: American Diplomacy in the Carter Years*. New York: Hill and Wang, 1986.

Smith, Richard Norton, and Timothy Walch, eds. *Farewell to the Chief: Former Presidents in American Public Life*. Worland, Wyo.: High Plains Publishing, 1990.

Smith, Tony. *America's Mission: The United States and the Worldwide Struggle for Democracy in the Twentieth Century*. Princeton, N.J.: Princeton University Press, 1994.

Spiegel, Steven L. *The Other Arab Israeli Conflict: Making America's Middle East Policy, from Truman to Reagan*. Chicago: University of Chicago Press, 1985.

Stacks, John F. *Watershed: The Campaign for the Presidency, 1980*. New York: Times Books, 1981.

Stapleton, Ruth Carter. *The Gift of Inner Healing*. Waco, Tex.: World Books, 1976.

Strobel, Warren. *Late-Breaking Foreign Policy: The News Media's Influence on Peace Operations*. Washington, D.C.: United States Peace Institution, 1997.

Suh, Dae-Sook. *Kim Il Sung*. New York: Columbia University Press, 1988.

Sullivan, William. *Mission to Iran*. New York: Morton, 1981.

Thatcher, Margaret. *The Downing Street Years*. New York: Harper Collins, 1993.

Thomas, Dylan. *Death and Entrances: Poems by Dylan Thomas*. London: J. M. Dent & Sons, 1946.

Thompson, Kenneth W., ed. *The Carter Presidency: Fourteen Intimate Perspectives of Jimmy Carter*. Lanham, Md.: University Press of America, 1990.

———. *Morality and Foreign Policy*. Baton Rouge: Louisiana State University Press, 1980.

Thornton, Richard C. *The Carter Years: Toward a New Global Order*. New York: Paragon House, 1991.

Timerman, Jacobo. *Prisoner without a Name, Cell without a Number*. New York: Knopf, 1981.

Troester, Rod. *Jimmy Carter as Peacemaker: A Post-Presidential Biography*. Westport, Conn.: Praeger, 1996.

Turner, Stansfield. *Secrecy and Democracy: The CIA in Transition*. Boston: Houghton Mifflin, 1985.

Updike, John. *Rabbit Is Rich*. New York: Knopf, 1981.

Vance, Cyrus. *Hard Choices: Critical Years in America's Foreign Policy*. New York: Simon & Schuster, 1983.

Victor, Richard H. K. *Energy Policy in America since 1945: A Study of Business-Government Relations*. Cambridge: Cambridge University Press, 1984.

Vogelgesang, Sandy. *American Dream, Global Nightmare: The Dilemma of U.S. Human Rights Policy*. New York: W. W. Norton, 1980.

Walker, Martin. *The Cold War: A History*. New York: Crown, 1994.

———. *The President We Deserve: Bill Clinton, His Falls and Comebacks*. New York: Crown, 1996.

Walker, Thomas W. *Nicaragua: The Land of Sandino*. Boulder, Colo.: Westview Press, 1991.

Wallach, Janet, and John Wallach. *Arafat: In the Eyes of the Beholder*. Secaucus, N.J.: Birch Lane Press, 1997.

Wickenden, Dorothy. *The New Republic: Eighty Years of Opinion and Debate*. New York: Basic Books, 1994.

Wigg, David. *And Then They Forgot to Tell Us Why: A Look at the Campaign against River Blindness in West Africa*. Washington, D.C.: World Bank, 1993.

Wills, Garry. *Lead Time: A Journalist's Education*. Garden City, N.Y.: Doubleday, 1983.

Wilson, Robert A., ed. *Character above All*. New York: Simon & Schuster, 1995.

Witcover, Jules. *Marathon: The Pursuit of the Presidency, 1972–1976*. New York: Viking Press, 1977.

Wooten, James. *Dasher: The Roots and Rising of Jimmy Carter*. New York: Summit Books, 1978.

Wright, Jim. *Worth It All*. McLean, Va.: Brassey's, 1993.

ARTICLES (only by-lined articles are listed below)

Abrams, Irwin. "Nobel Peace Prize." In Bruce W. Jentleson and Thomas G. Petterson, eds., *Encyclopedia of U.S. Foreign Relations*. New York: Oxford University Press, 1997.

Akerman, Robert. "Carter Suit and T.R." *Atlanta Journal & Constitution*, October 25, 1981.

Andersen, Martin. "Argentines Thank Carter for Human Rights Efforts." *Washington Post*, October 11, 1984.

Apple, R. W. Jr. "Carter the Peacemaker Now Turns to Ethiopia." *NYT*, September 8, 1989.

————. "Changing Tack on Haiti." *NYT*, September 17, 1994.

————. "2 Ex-Presidents Advise Bush: Forget Vow and Raise Taxes." *NYT*, November 22, 1988.

Applebome, Peter. "Unofficially, Era of Carter Is Still Here." *NYT*, May 11, 1989.

Babbitt, Bruce. "Poll Position." *The New Republic*, March 19, 1990.

Baker, Russel. "Not to Worry, Jimmy." *NYT*, January 10, 1981.

Bagley, Bruce. "U.S. Foreign Policy and the War on Drugs: Analysis of a Policy Failure." *Journal of Inter-American Studies and World Affairs* 31, summer/fall 1989.

Bailey, Anne Lowrey. "The Controversial Charity of Ryoichi Sasakawa." *The Chronicle of Philanthropy*, June 2, 1992.

————. "Critical Report Leads Jimmy Carter's Atlanta Anti-Poverty Drive to Make Changes." *The Chronicle of Philanthropy*, March 9, 1995.

Barnett, Richard. "An Outsider in Washington." *New Yorker*, January 17, 1983.

Barrow, John C. "An Age of Limits: Jimmy Carter and the Quest for a National Energy Policy." In Fink and Graham, eds., *The Carter Presidency: Policy Choices in the Post New Deal Era*. Lawrence: University Press of Kansas, 1997.

Bassett, Beth Dawkins. "Let Not the Sinuous Worm Strike Me . . ." *Carter Center News*, fall 1995.

————. "Once upon a Time in Newton County." *Emory Magazine* 63, no. 1, March 1987.

Baxter, Tom. "A 'Turning Point' for Carter." *Atlanta Journal & Constitution*, December 13, 1992.

Beasley, David. "Billy's Back." *Atlanta Journal & Constitution*, June 5, 1986.

Beaty, Jonathan, and S. C. Gwinne. "Masters of Deceit." *Time*, April 1, 1991.

Bellafonte, Gina. "Kudos for a Crusader." *Time*, October 29, 1997.

Bennet, James. "A Presidential Cold War Begins to Thaw." *NYT*, May 21, 1997.

Bennetts, Leslie. "Carter Auction Brings $320,000 for New Center." *NYT*, October 8, 1983.

Berke, Richard L. "Inquiry Is Ordered on 1980 Campaign." *NYT*, August 6, 1991.

Bernstein, Jonas. "Carter Earns Mixed Ratings for His Role as a Peace Broker." *Insight*, April 30, 1990.

Biddle, Wayne. "Soviet and U.S. Aides in Atlanta, Trade Accusations on Arms Control." *NYT*, April 14, 1985.

Bierle, Andrew W. M. "Vision of James T. Laney." *Emory Magazine*, special issue, winter 1994.

Binder, David. "U.S. Cautioning on Intervention in Polish Crisis." *NYT*, December 3, 1980.

Bird, Kai. "The Very Model of an Ex-President." *Nation*, November 12, 1990.

Blair, William G. "Carter's Volunteer Group Plans Nicaragua Project," *NYT*, September 9, 1984.

Blatchford, Joseph H. "Another 11th Hour Job for Jimmy Carter." *Los Angeles Times*, September 13, 1994.

Borlaug, Norman. "World Food Security and the Legacy of Canadian Wheat Scientist R. Glen Anderson." *Canadian Journal of Plant Pathology* 14 (1992): 253–66.

Breau, Giovanna, and Susan K. Reed. "The Terminator: Dr. Donald Hopkins Wears Victory in His 15-year Battle to Eradicate a Clipping Parasite, Guinea Worm." *People*, October 30, 1995.

Brinkley, Douglas. "Clintons and Carters Don't Mix." *NYT*, August 29, 1996.

———. "Democratic Enlargement: The Clinton Doctrine." *Foreign Policy*, spring 1997.

———. "The Final Days: Jimmy Carter." *George*, February 1997.

———. "Introduction" in Jimmy Carter, *Why Not the Best?* Paperback reissue. Fayetteville: University of Arkansas Press, 1996.

———. "Jimmy Carter: Poet from Plains." *New Orleans Review* 20, nos. 1–2 (spring–summer 1994).

———. "Jimmy Carter's Modest Quest for Global Peace." *Foreign Affairs* 74, no. 6 (November–December 1995).

———. "The Rising Stock of Jimmy Carter." *Diplomatic History* 20, no. 4 (fall 1996): 505–29.

Brinkley, Joel. "Syria Is Willing to Talk to Israel, Carter Says." *NYT*, March 19, 1990.

Brock, David. "Jimmy Carter's Return." *American Spectator*, December 1994.

Brooke, James. "First Free Elections to Be Held Today in Paraguay." *NYT*, March 19, 1993.

———. "Man with a Plan." *NYT*, October 16, 1987.

Bryant, Nelson. "Outdoors: No Dilettante Angler." *NYT*, September 24, 1984.

Burt, Richard. "Brzezinski Calls Democrats Soft toward Moscow." *NYT*, November 30, 1980.

Camm, Marcy. "Pastor Discusses Possibility of U.S.-Cuban Reconciliation." *Emory Wheel*, September 26, 1995.

Carllie, William H. "Carter Urges Resolution of Arab-Israeli Conflict." *Arizona Republic*, October 9, 1990.

Carothers, Thomas. "The NED at 10." *Foreign Policy*, spring 1993.

Casey, Kathleen. "Carter's Surprise Visit Thrills Edison Church." *Star-Ledger* (Newark), July 30, 1985.

Clendinen, Dudley. "Carter Library Rises Despite Problems with Money and Road." *NYT*, October 10, 1985.

Clifford, Lawrence X. "An Examination of the Carter Administration's Selecting of Secretary of State and National Security Adviser." In Herbert D. Rosenbaum and Alexej Ugrinsky, eds., *Jimmy Carter: Foreign Policy and the Postpresidential Years*. Westport, Conn.: Greenwood Press, 1994.

Clift, Eleanor. "A Man with a Mission." *Newsweek*, October 3, 1994.

Cloud, Stanley. "Hail to the Ex-Chief." *Time*, September 11, 1989.

Clymer, Adam. "The Campaign's Final Week: Basic Themes Stressed." *NYT*, November 2, 1980.

———. "Reagan and Carter Stand Nearly Even in the Polls." *NYT*, November 3, 1980.

———. "3 Ex-Presidents Tentatively Favor Sunday Voting Plan." *NYT*, May 8, 1981.

Cobban, Helen. "The Palestinians and the Iraqi Invasion of Kuwait." In Robert O. Freedman, ed., *The Intifada: Its Impact on Israel, the Arab World and the Superpowers*. Gainesville: University Presses of Florida, 1991.

Cody, Edward. "PLO Sees Possibility of Linking Issues." *Washington Post*, October 3, 1990.

Cohen, Richard. "The Carter Distinction." *Washington Post*, May 11, 1989.

————. "In Defense of the Carter Post Presidency." *Washington Post*, December 27, 1994.

————. "The Lost Dignity in Public Service." *Washington Post*, May 14, 1989.

Cohen, Roger. "Bosnia Foes Agree to 4-Month Truce, Carter Reports," *NYT*, December 21, 1994.

————. "Bosnian Serb Leader Offers His Revisions to Peace Plan." *NYT*, December 21, 1994.

————. "Spent Bosnia Now Tries to Make Its Peace." *NYT*, December 31, 1995.

Coleman, Seth, and Don Melvin. "Carter to Launch National Version of Atlanta Project." *Atlanta Journal & Constitution*, December 14, 1994.

Constable, Pamela. "Haiti: A Nation in Despair, a Policy Adrift." *Current History*, March 1994.

"A Conversation with Sam Nunn." *Georgia Tech Alumni Magazine*, spring 1990.

Cook, Bruce. "Carter Takes His Memoirs on the Road." *USA Today*, October 12, 1982.

Cowan, Edward. "Carter Urges Rises in Military Outlay, Cuts in Other Areas." *NYT*, January 16, 1995.

————. "Reagan Delivers His Budget to Congress with a Warning to Remember 'Our Mandate,'" *NYT*, March 11, 1981.

Cowan, Glenn, and Larry Garber. "The Virtues of Parallel Vote Tabulations." *Journal of Democracy*, April 1993.

Critchfield, Richard. "Grain Man." *World Monitor*, October 1990.

Crittenden, Ann. "Egyptian City is Quiet after Clashes." *NYT*, October 10, 1981.

Cunningham, Rose. "A Day at the Farm with Governor Carter and President Figueres." *Atlanta Journal & Constitution* (Sunday magazine), June 11, 1972.

Cutler, Lloyd. "The October Surprise Made Unsurprising." *NYT*, May 15, 1991.

Curtis, Charlotte. "Mrs. Carter Speaks Out." *NYT*, January 3, 1981.

————. "Nixon Says U.S. Can Use Carter's Help on Mideast," *NYT*, November 14, 1982.

Daly, Emma. "Carter, Arias Disagree on Nicaragua Prospects." *The Tico Times*, December 22, 1989.

Davidson, William D., and Joseph V. Montville. "Foreign Policy According to Freud." *Foreign Policy*, no. 45 (winter 1981–82).

Denniston, Lyle. "The Libel Landmark That Wasn't." *Washington Journalism Review*, January 1982.

de Onis, Juan. "Senate and House Conferees Approve More Aid for Egypt and Israel." *NYT*, November 21, 1980.

————. "U.S. Lifts Carter's Ban on Trade Assistance for Chile," *NYT*, February 21, 1981.

Dewar, Helen. "Nunn's Surprise." *Washington Post*, October 2, 1994.

Dewar, Helen, and Don Podesta. "U.S. Observer Tram Disbands before Nicaraguan Elections." *Washington Post*, February 8, 1990.

DeWitt, Karen, "Carter Welcomes Tsongas to Plains." *NYT*, February 23, 1992.

Dionne, E. J. "Carter Begins to Shed Negative Public Image." *NYT*, May 18, 1989.

————. "Dukakis Says Bush Has Blank Record." *NYT*, May 2, 1988.

Dowd, Maureen. "Ferraro Sharpens Criticism of Reagan's Foreign Policy," *NYT*, September 30, 1984.

————. ". . . And Carter Urges Reagan to Talk." *NYT*, December 10, 1986.

————. "Despite Role as Negotiator, Carter Feels Unappreciated." *NYT*, September 21, 1994.

————. "Man-About Banks Proves Belle of Ball." *NYT*, July 15, 1988.

————. "Star Twinkle amid Glitches in a Show of Unified Strength." *NYT*, July 19, 1988.

Easterbrook, Gregg. "Forgotten Benefactor of Humanity." *Atlantic Monthly*, January 1997.

Eberstadt, Nicholas, Mark Rubin, and Albina Tretyakova. "The Collapse of Soviet and Russian Trade with the DPRK, 1989–1993." *Korean Journal of National Unification* 4 (1995).

Eckholm, Erik. "River Blindness: Conquering an Ancient Scourge." *NYT Magazine*, January 8, 1989.

Eng, Steve. Review of *Citizen Turner: The Wild Rise of an American Tycoon*, by Robert Goldberg and Gerald Jay Goldberg. *Creative Loafing*, July 1995.

Fallows, James. "Plains Talks." *Washington Monthly*, November 1992.

Farah, Douglas. "Nicaragua's Presumptive President, Aleman, Promises to End Sandinista Legacy." *Washington Post*, October 23, 1996.

Farnsworth, Clyde H. "Phosphate Ban Is Ended." *NYT*, April 25, 1981.

Farrell, William E. "Carter Meets P.L.O. Officials in Egypt." *NYT*, March 9, 1983.

———. "3 Ex-Presidents Call on Mubarak and Mrs. Sadat," *NYT*, October 10, 1981.

Fein, Esther. "Carpenter Named Carter Comes to New York." *NYT*, September 3, 1984.

Foege, William H. "Should the Smallpox Virus Be Allowed to Survive?" *New England Journal of Medicine* 300 (1979).

Forest, Stephanie Anderson. "Big Trouble in the Big Easy." *Business Week*, October 16, 1995.

"Former President Carter Wins 1994 J. William Fulbright Prize for International Understanding," *Fulbright Association Newsletter* 1, no. 2 (fall 1994).

Fox, Edward. "Monument to the Man from Plains." *Travel and Leisure*, February 1988.

Foxman, Abraham H. "A Double Standard." *Jerusalem Post*, July 27, 1985.

Franklin, Ben A. "Landmark Designates Are Upheld by New Law." *NYT*, December 14, 1980.

French, Howard. "Haiti Installs Democratic Chief, Its First." *NYT*, February 8, 1991.

———. "In Africa's Harsh Climate, Fruits of Democracy." *NYT*, January 4, 1998.

———. "Nigeria Accused of a 2 Year War on Ethnic Group." *NYT*, March 28, 1995.

———. "Repression in Nigeria." *NYT*, November 12, 1995.

Friedman, Thomas L. "Clinton Rounds Out State Department Team." *NYT*. January 20, 1993.

———. "Rabin and Arafat Seal Their Accord as Clinton Applauds 'Brave Gamble.'" *NYT*, September 14, 1993.

Friendly, Jonathan. "The Bugging Rumor: Carter Raises a Press Issue," *NYT*, October 16, 1981.

Fruhling, Larry. "'Major War' in Mideast is Likely, Carter Tells Storm Lake Audience." *Des Moines Register*, September 26, 1990.

Gailey, Phil. "Carter Intent on Suing *Washington Post* on Rumor." *NYT*, October 15, 1981.

———. "Carter Is Critical of Reagan Policies." *NYT*, October 14, 1981.

———. "Carter May Drop Plans to Sue Paper for Libel." *NYT*, October 24, 1981.

———. "Carter Threatens to Sue for Libel." *NYT*, October 9, 1981.

———. "Memories and Catching Up in Plains." *NYT*, September 2, 1985.

———. "To Build a Library, Some Chairs Go Up For Bids." *NYT*, September 23, 1983.

Galloway, Jim. "Habitat's Founder Hits Road for Housing Funds." *Atlanta Journal & Constitution*, August 4, 1983.

Gelb, Leslie. "Jobs, Jobs, Jobs." *NYT*, November 22, 1992.

———. "Three Past Presidents May Brief Reagan." *NYT*, November 5, 1985.

Gellman, Barton. "Israel Prepares to Bury Rabin." *Washington Post*, November 6, 1995.

Glass, Stephen. "Peddling Poppy." *New Republic*, June 9, 1997.

Goldman, Peter. "Hail the Conquering Hero." *Newsweek*, December 1, 1980.

Goodman, George Jr. "Rush Is On for U.S. Funds in Final Days of Carter Era." *NYT*, December 21, 1980.

Goodman, Joe. "From a Woman Who's Been There, Help for Caregivers." *Barnes & Noble Magazine*, December 1994.

Gordon, Michael R. "Clinton May Add G.I.'s in Korea While Remaining Open to Talks." *NYT*, June 17, 1994.

―――――. "Clinton Offers North Korea a Chance to Resume Talks." *NYT*, June 22, 1994.

Goshko, John M. "Baker Sets Conditions on Nicaragua Relations." *Washington Post*, February 23, 1990.

―――――. "Renewed U.S.-Nicaragua Ties Eyed." *Washington Post*, February 24, 1990.

Gould, Lewis L. " 'Big Bill' and Silent Cal: William Howard Taft and Calvin Coolidge as Former Presidents." In Richard Norton Smith and Timothy Walch, eds., *Farewell to the Chief: Former Presidents in American Public Life*. Worland, Wyo.: High Plains Publishing, 1990.

Greenfield, Meg. "FYI." *Washington Post*, October 14, 1981.

Greer, William R. "Carter Visits Housing Site for the Poor." *NYT*, April 2, 1984.

Griffen, Jeffrey. "Calling the Shots." *Columns*, June 1994.

Griffith, Thomas. "Going Eyeball to Eyeball—and Blinking." *Newsweek*, November 2, 1981.

Gruson, Lindsey. "Noriega Stealing Elections, Carter Says." *NYT*, May 9, 1989.

Gurwin, Larry. "Who Really Owns First American Bank?" *Regardie's*, May 1990.

Gutman, Roy. "Serbs Being Asked to Renegotiate Peace Terms." *Newsday*, January 27, 1995.

Gwertzman, Bernard. "Aid to Zimbabwe Suspended by U.S." *NYT*, July 5, 1986.

―――――. " 'Alive, Well and Free': Captives Taken to Algiers and Then Germany—Final Pact Complex." *NYT*, January 21, 1981.

―――――. "Book of the Times." *NYT*, April 18, 1985.

―――――. "Leaders in Poland Make Urgent Plea For End to Unrest." *NYT*, December 4, 1980.

―――――. "New Administration Says It Will Honor Accord on Hostages." *NYT*, January 23, 1981.

―――――. "Poland's Crisis Puzzle for U.S." *NYT*, October 12, 1980.

―――――. "President Is Expected to Act Today to End Curb on Grain Sale to Soviet." *NYT*, April 24, 1981.

―――――. "Reagan Tells Egypt and Israel He Backs Camp David Process." *NYT*, December 7, 1980.

―――――. "Russians Are Ready for Possible Move on Poland, U.S. Says." *NYT*, December 8, 1980.

―――――. "U.S. Is Cutting Off Aid to Zimbabwe." *NYT*, September 3, 1986.

Haddad, Charles. "Carter Advising Turner on U.N. Project." *Atlanta Journal & Constitution*, Oct 4, 1997.

Haley, Mark. "Carter Writes of Fishing in Spruce Creek." *Altoona Mirror*, August 14, 1988.

Hall, Mimi. "Summit Sends Message That Service Is Money and Time." *USA Today*, April 22, 1997.

Halloran, Richard. "Reagan to Request $38 Billion Increase in Military Outlays." *NYT*, February 10, 1981.

Hammer, Joshua. "A Voice Silences." *Newsweek*, November 20, 1995.

Harris, Art. "Citizen Carter." *Washington Post*, February 20, 1990.

Hartmann, Susan M. "Feminism, Public Policy and the Carter Administration." In Gary M. Fink and Hugh Davis Graham, eds., *The Carter Presidency: Policy Choices in the Post New Deal Era*. Lawrence: University of Kansas Press, 1998.

Heckler-Feltz, Cheryl. "It Was the Most Unusual Postcard from Abroad." *Richmond Times-Dispatch*, July 2, 1994.

————. "Knockout Doc." *Lutheran*, March 1995.

Heller, Karen. "Jimmy Carter: Building a Solid Reputation." *Philadelphia Inquirer*, March 19, 1990.

Helliker, Kevin. "How a Motel Chain Lost Its Moorings." *Wall Street Journal*, May 26, 1992.

Hertzberg, Hendrik. "Actions Restore Carter's Posture as a President." New Republic, May 1989.

————. "The Child Monarch." *New Republic*, September 9, 1991. Reprinted in Dorothy Wickenden, *The New Republic Reader: Eighty Years of Opinion and Debate*. New York: Basic Books, 1994.

————. "Jimmy Carter, 1977–1981." In Robert A. Wilson, ed., *Character above All*. New York: Simon & Schuster, 1995.

Hijazi, Ihsan A. "Carter Says Syria Aids on Hostages." *NYT*, March 17, 1990.

Hochman, Steven H. "With Jimmy Carter in Georgia: A Memoir of His Post-Presidential Years." In Richard N. Smith and Timothy Walch, eds., *Farewell to the Chief: Former Presidents in American Public Life*. Worland, Wyo.: High Plains Publishing, 1990.

Hodgson, Godfrey. "Jimmy Carter's Comeback." *London Independent on Sunday*, June 19, 1994.

Holmes, Charles W. "Carter Turns Steely as Israel 'Intimidates' Voters." *Atlanta Journal & Constitution*, January 21, 1996.

Holmes, Steven A. "U.S. Blacks Battle Nigeria over Rights Issues." *NYT*, June 15, 1995.

Hopkins, Donald R., et al. "Drancunculiasis Eradication: Beginning of the End." *American Journal of Tropical Medical Hygiene* 49, no. 3 (1993).

————. "Eradication of Dracunculiasis from Pakistan." *Lancet* 346 (September 2, 1995).

Hopkins, Donald R., and E. Ruiz-Tiben. "Strategies for Dracunculiasis Eradication." *Bulletin of the World Health Organization* 60, no. 5 (1991).

Hopkins, Sam, and Greg McDonald. "Memoirs from Mrs. Carter, Also?" *Atlanta Journal & Constitution*, January 25, 1981.

House, Karen Elliott. "Korea: Raise Another Desert Shield." *Wall Street Journal*, June 15, 1994.

Hyatt, Richard. "Just Plains Folks." *Columbus Ledger-Enquirer*, March 19, 1995.

————. "Still Keeping the Faith." *Columbus Ledger-Enquirer*, March 19, 1995.

Ifill, Gwen. "Carter, with Clinton at His Side, Praises the Candidate's Qualities." *NYT*, May 21, 1992.

————. "Clinton Recruits 3 Presidents to Promote Trade Pact." *NYT*, September 15, 1993.

Immanuel, Jon. "Arafat Wins 88% of Vote; 75% of Council to Fatah." *Jerusalem Post*, January 22, 1996.

Jackson, Dale. "Millard Fuller's Blueprint for Success." *Reader's Digest*, June 1988.

Jehl, Douglas. "Carter Heading Off to Bosnia on Broadened Peace Mission." *NYT*, December 18, 1994.

―――. "Carter, His Own Emissary, Outpaces White House." *NYT*, June 20, 1994.

―――. "Clinton Is Hopeful Yet Cautious about Carter's North Korea Trip." *NYT*, June 21, 1994.

Kaiser, Robert G. "Wasn't Carter the President Who Said He'd Never Lie To Us?" *Washington Post*, November 7, 1982.

Kaplan, Robert D. "Was Democracy Just a Moment?" *Atlantic Monthly*, December 1997.

Katz, Lee Michael. "U.N. Head to Announce Reforms in Bureaucracy." *USA Today*, July 16, 1997.

Kempe, Frederick. "Noriega Slows Vote Tally to Crawl in Panama." *Wall Street Journal*, May 9, 1989.

Kershner, Isabel. "Power to the Palestinians." *Jerusalem Report*, January 25, 1996.

King, Seth S. "Carter Signs Bill to Protest 104 Million Acres in Alaska." *NYT*, December 3, 1980.

―――. "Environmental Policy Still Being Planned: Reagan Administration Is Hoping to Spur Private Development of Government Property." *NYT*, May 31, 1981.

―――. "U.S. Help to States for Parks May End." *NYT*, February 20, 1981.

King, Wayne. "Carter Redux." *NYT Magazine*, December 10, 1989.

Kinzer, Stephen. "Nicaragua Appeals to U.S. on Pact." *NYT*, September 28, 1984.

Kirkpatrick, Jeane. "Dictatorships and Double Standards." *Commentary*, November 1979.

―――. "Sandinistas Have Stacked the Deck to Retain Power." *Miami Herald*, October 7, 1990.

Kovach, Bill. "Life after the White House." *Atlanta Journal & Constitution*, July 12, 1987.

Kraft, Joseph. "The Post-Imperial Presidency." *NYT*, November 2, 1980.

Krauthammer, Charles. "Peace in Our Time." *Washington Post*, June 24, 1994.

Kurylo, Elizabeth. "African Trip Is His Third of the Year." *Atlanta Journal & Constitution*, September 22, 1995.

―――. "Agreement Is Feather in Carter's Cap." *Atlanta Journal & Constitution*, June 23, 1994.

―――. "Arafat Meets Carter Despite Lengthy Detour." *Atlanta Journal & Constitution*, March 6, 1997.

―――. "Carter Counsels Arabs." *Atlanta Journal & Constitution*, December 7, 1991.

―――. "Carter Culling Mideast Experts for TV Special." *Atlanta Journal & Constitution*, September 11, 1990.

―――. "Egyptian Clergyman Pays Visit to Carter." *Atlanta Journal & Constitution*, October 14, 1989.

―――. "Joining Forces: Emory to Absorb Carter Center." *Atlanta Journal & Constitution*, August 30, 1994.

―――. "Peacemaker Is Redefining the Ex-Presidency." *Atlanta Journal & Constitution*, November 11, 1990.

―――. "Revisiting a Mission to Korea." *Atlanta Journal & Constitution*, July 3, 1994.

―――. "Sasakawa, Philanthropist Who Aided Carter, King Centers, Dies in Japan." *Atlanta Journal & Constitution*, July 21, 1995.

Leary, Warren E. "With One Disease Nearly Erased Assault Is Planned on Another." *NYT*, December 6, 1995.

Lee, Jessica. "Carter Backs Independent Counsel Call." *USA Today*, October 20, 1997.

Lehmann-Haupt, Christopher. "Book of the Times." *NYT*, November 3, 1982.

LeoGrande, William. "The Revolution in Nicaragua: Another Cuba? *Foreign Affairs*, fall 1979.

Leuchtenburg, William E. "Jimmy Carter and the Post–New Deal Presidency." In Gary M. Fink and Hugh Davis Graham, eds., *The Carter Presidency: Policy Choices in the Post New Deal Era*. Lawrence: University of Kansas Press, 1998.

Lewis, Anthony. "One Little Tattler." *NYT*, October 19, 1981.

——. "Reward for a Job Well Done." *NYT*, October 7, 1994.

Lewis, Bernard. "The Search for Symmetry." *NYT*, April 28, 1985.

Lewis, Neil. "A Book Asserts Reagan Solved Hostage Release." *MYT*, November 8, 1991.

——. "House Inquiry Finds No Evidence of Deal on Hostages in 1980." *NYT*, January 13, 1993.

Limbaugh, Rush. "If I Were President." *George*, December 1995–January 1996.

Lippman, Thomas W. "Once Again Carter Plays Peacemaker." *Washington Post*, September 19, 1994.

Longino, Miriam. "Carter's Trailblazers." *Atlanta Journal & Constitution*, February 5, 1995.

Lukacs, John. "Revising the Twentieth Century." *American Heritage*, September 1994.

Madison, Mary. "Meg Greenfield Is Bugged about Her *Post* Editorial." *Palo Alto–Redwood City (Calif.) Peninsula Times Tribune*, October 27, 1981.

Maier, Karl. "Kaunda Swept from Office in Lopsided Zambian Vote." *Washington Post*, November 2, 1991.

Mailer, Norman. "The Search for Carter." *NYT Magazine*, September 26, 1972.

Manegold, Catherine S. "Japan's Emperor Unflappable in Atlanta." *NYT*, June 11, 1994.

Maraniss, David. "Cuban Refugee Uprising Offers View of Clinton's Reaction to Crisis." *Washington Post*, October 22, 1990.

Marriott, Michael. "Brother against Brother." *Newsweek*, May 22, 1995.

Martin, David. "Inside the Rescue Mission." *Newsweek*, July 12, 1982.

Matthews, Christopher. "Jimmy Carter Finds His Place in the Sun." *San Francisco Examiner*, August 19, 1990.

McClellan, Diana. "The Ear." *Washington Post*, October 5, 1981.

McDaniel, Ann, and Vern E. Smith. Interview of Jimmy Carter; excerpts published in *Newsweek*, October 2, 1994.

McDonald, Greg. "Leaders Hear Carter, Ford on Mideast Meeting." *Atlanta Journal & Constitution*, November 18, 1983.

——. "Memoirs Given Blockbuster Hope." *Atlanta Journal & Constitution*, October 7, 1982.

McDowell, Edwin. "Carter, Brzezinski, Writing Books." *NYT*, January 15, 1981.

——. "Carter Hires Josephson as Literary Agent." *NYT*, January 27, 1981.

——. "Carter Sells Memoirs to Bantam Books." *NYT*, March 14, 1981.

——. "Publishing: The President's Researcher." *NYT*, July 17, 1981.

McGill, Lynn Burnett. "Thoughts of Home: The Carter Presidential Living Quarters." *Southern Homes*, July–August 1988.

McMath, Robert C. Jr. "Old South, New Politics: Jimmy Carter's First Campaign." *Georgia Historical Quarterly* 77, no. 3 (fall 1993).

McNulty, Timothy J. "Born Again: Jimmy Carter May Be Our Most Successful Ex-President." *Chicago Tribune Magazine*, July 8, 1990.

Mehren, Elizabeth. "The Couple that Writes Together . . . Fights Together." *Austin American-Statesman*, May 26, 1987.

Merida, Kevin. "Black Americans to Press Nigeria for Democracy." *Washington Post*, March 14, 1995.

Middleton, Harry J. "A President and His Library: My Recollections of Working with Lyndon B. Johnson." In Richard Norton Smith and Timothy Walch, eds., *Farewell to The Chief: Former Presidents in American Public Life*. Worland, Wyo: High Plains Publishing, 1990.

Mitchell, Cynthia. "Deen Day Smith Believes in Giving Back to Society." *Atlanta Journal & Constitution*, January 13, 1993.

Mitchell, Henry. "To Far Away Places." *Washington Post*, September 29, 1976.

Mohr, Charles. "Irate Carter Rebuts Reagan on Military and Security Policy." *NYT*, March 2, 1986.

———. "On Fly Fishing: By Jimmy Carter." *NYT*, January 7, 1982.

———. "Reagan to Send Congress a Note on Awacs Sale." *NYT*, October 14, 1981.

Molotosky, Irvin. "Ex-Nuclear Chairman Whom Carter Ousted Is Named Acting Head." *NYT*, March 3, 1981.

Molyneux, D. H. "Ochocerciasis Control in West Africa: Current Status and Future of the Ochocerciasis Contol Programme." *Parasitology Today* 11, no. 11 (November 1995).

Nagourney, Adam. "As One President Nears, Another Stays Away." *NYT*, August 22, 1997.

Nelan, Bruce W. "Road to Haiti." *Time*, October 3, 1994.

Nelson, Bryce. "Carter Accepts Apology, Won't Sue Post for Libel." *Los Angeles Times*, October 25, 1981.

Nemy, Enid. "Carters Attend Gala Preview of Sotheby Auction." *NYT*, October 5, 1983.

———. "A Small Blue Ridge Pine Cabin Is the Carters' Rustic Treat." *NYT*, July 14, 1983.

Nossiter, Bernard D. "Carter Denounces Policy on Soviet." *NYT*, December 18, 1981.

———. "PLO Observer at UN Praises Carter-Ford Stand." *NYT*, October 13, 1981.

O'Briant, Dan. "Jimmy Carter Stalks the Great Outdoors in His Latest Memoir." *Atlanta Journal & Constitution*, May 22, 1988.

O'Brien, Conor Cruise. "Bearing the Gift of Peace." *Independent*, December 23, 1994.

Offenburger, Chuck. "A Fine Evening with Jimmy Carter at Buena Vista College." *Des Moines Register*, September 27, 1990.

Oldenburg, Don. "For the Carters, Another New Beginning." *Washington Post*, May 23, 1987.

Omang, Joanne. "Ardito Barletta Installed as Panama's President." *Washington Post*, October 12, 1984.

Park, Jae Kyu. "North Korean Policy toward the United States." *Asian Perspectives* 5 (fall–winter 1981).

Pastor, Robert. "How to Reinforce Democracy in the Americas: Seven Proposals." In Robert Pastor, ed. *Democracy in the Americas*. New York: Holmes & Meier, 1989.

———. "The Making of a Free Election." *Journal of Democracy*, summer 1990.

———. "NAFTA: In Whose Interests? To What Effect?" Statement prepared for the NAFTA Summit Conference for Congress, June 28–29, sponsored by the Brookings Institute, the Fraser Institute, and the Center for Strategic and International Studies, Washington, D.C.

———. "The North American Free Trade Agreement: Hemispheric and Geopolitical Implications." Working Paper WP-TWH-21. Washington, D.C.: Inter-American Development Bank and the United Nations Economic Commission for Latin America and the Caribbean, 1993.

———. "Securing a Democratic Hemisphere." *Foreign Policy*, no. 73 (winter 1988–89).
———. "A Short History of Haiti." *Foreign Service Journal*, November 1995.
———. "With Carter in Haiti." *World View* 8, no. 2 (spring 1995).
Pattishall, Roy. "The Trouble in Nicaragua." *Emory Magazine* 64, no. 2 (1987).
Pear, Robert. "Quayle Calls Managua Vote Plan a Sham." *NYT*, June 13, 1989.
Pennington, John. "Grandmother with a Mission." *Atlanta Journal & Constitution*, January 19, 1969.
Perlez, Jane. "With Pride and Economic Pain Ahead, Zambia Swears in New Leader." *NYT*, November 5, 1991.
Peterson, Iver. "Ford and Carter Tell of Difficult Communication in Government." *NYT*, February 11, 1983.
Phillips, B. J. "Carter: Odds Better Than 50–50 for War in Persian Gulf." *Philadelphia Inquirer*, October 22, 1990.
Podhoretz, Norman. "The Reagan Road to Detente." Special issue of *Foreign Affairs*, American and the World 1984, winter 1984–85.
Pollack, Andrew. "Mourning Over, North Korea Has No Coronation." *NYT*, July 9, 1997.
Pomfret, John. "Aw Shucks Diplomacy Pays Off for Carter." *Washington Post*, December 22, 1994.
Pousner, Howard. "The Future of Plains." *Atlanta Journal & Constitution*, March 12, 1995.
Press, Robert M. "Program Plants Seeds of Change." *Christian Science Monitor*, October 16, 1990.
Putzel, Michael. "Legacy of Jimmy Carter." *Atlanta Journal & Constitution*, July 3, 1983.
Raines, Howell. "Carter, Forsaking a 'Moratorium,' Denounces Policies of Successor." *NYT*, July 9, 1981.
———. "Reagan Rejects Revenge on Iran as Unworthy of U.S." *NYT*, January 29, 1981.
———. "Sadat's Successor Invited by Reagan to Visit U.S. in 1982." *NYT*, October 9, 1981.
———. "3 Ex-Presidents in Delegation to Funeral but Reagan Is Not." *NYT*, October 8, 1981.
Randal, Jonathan C. "Arafat Survives Crash Landing." *Washington Post*, April 9, 1992.
Rattner, Steven. "The Economy of the Ballot." *NYT*, November 2, 1980.
Reagan, Ronald. "A New Opportunity for Peace in the Middle East." *Current Policy* (U.S. State Department, Bureau of Affairs), no. 417 (September 1, 1982).
Reif, Rita. "Auctions: Jimmy Carter and His Chairs." *NYT*, September 20, 1983.
Reston, James. "Hart's Fatal Blunder." *NYT*, May 2, 1989.
———. "Jimmy Carter at 57." *NYT*, September 30, 1981.
———. "Lost but Not Defeated." *NYT*, November 7, 1980.
Reinhold, Robert. "Warren Minor Christopher." *NYT*, December 23, 1992.
Rich, Frank. "Springtime for Nixon." *NYT*, December 16, 1995.
Riding, Alan. "Brazil Welcomes Jimmy Carter on Latin Tour." *NYT*, October 9, 1984.
Rimer, Sara. "Ex-Carter Official Calls Reagan's Foreign Policy a 'Disaster.'" *NYT*, November 11, 1984.
Roberts, Steven V. "Senate Votes to Bar Justice Department Suits." *NYT*, November 18, 1980.
Rohter, Larry. "Clinton and Castro Buy Some Time." *NYT*, May 14, 1995.
———. "Clinton May Be Easing Terms with Junta." *NYT*, September 18, 1994.

————. "For Carter, an Old Job in Housing." *NYT*, July 29, 1985.

————. "Scourge, and Sometime Victim, of the Sandinistas." *NYT*, October 23, 1996.

Rosellini, Lynn. "A Reunion for Carter and Colleagues." *NYT*, October 14, 1981.

Rosen, Barry. "The Hostage Crisis." In Herbert D. Rosenbaum and Alexej Ugrinsky, eds., *Jimmy Carter: Foreign Policy and Post-Presidential Years*. Westport, Conn.: Greenwood Press, 1994.

Rosenbaum, David E. "A White House Slumber Party." *NYT*, September 15, 1993.

————. "Splintered on Trade." *NYT*, September 15, 1993.

Rosenberg, Mark. "Carter for Congress." *NYT*, March 13, 1981.

Rosenthal, A. M. "Silence Is a Lie." *NYT*, March 22, 1990.

Rowley, Sterer H. "Palestinian Election Judged Fair." *Chicago Tribune*, January 22, 1996.

Roy, Sara. "Civil Society in the Gaza Strip: Obstacles to Reconstruction." In Augustus Richard Norton, ed., *Civil Society in the Middle East*. Leiden: E. J. Brill, 1996.

Rozell, Mark J. "Carter Rehabilitated: What Caused the 39th President's Press Transformation." *Presidential Studies Quarterly* 23, no. 2 (spring 1993).

Rymer, Russ. "The Mission." *In Health*, March–April 1990.

Sabbagh, Sana. "Honor All." In Mary-Jane Deeb and Mary King, eds., *Hasib Sabbagh: From Palestinian Refugee to Citizen of the World*. Lanham, Md.: University Press of America, 1996.

Safire, William. "Farewell." *NYT Magazine*, February 2, 1981.

————. "History on Its Head." *NYT*, April 9, 1981.

————. "If Not Arafat . . ." *NYT*, March 7, 1996.

————. "Jimmy Clinton." *NYT*, June 27, 1994.

————. "Jimmy Clinton II." *NYT*, September 22, 1994.

Sanger, David E. "Carter Visit to North Korea: Whose Trip Was It Really?" *NYT*, June 18, 1994.

————. "Surprise! Kim Il Sung Smiles for the Camera." *NYT*, June 19, 1994.

————. "Two Koreas Plan Summit Talks on Nuclear Issue." *NYT*, June 19, 1994.

Sayle, Murray. "Closing the File on Flight 007." *New Yorker*, December 12, 1993.

Saxon, Wolfgang. "Ruth Carter Stapleton Dies; Evangelist and Faith Healer." *NYT*, September 27, 1983.

Schmemann, Serge. "Big Vote Turnout for Palestinians." *NYT*, January 21, 1996.

————. "Election: A Dawn for Palestinians, Legitimacy for Arafat." *NYT*, January 22, 1996.

————. "With Placards and Slogans, Palestinians Prepare to Vote." *NYT*, January 4, 1996.

Schmidt, William E. "Carter and Ford Oppose U.S. Strike." *NYT*, November 7, 1983.

————. "Joy over Carter Library Fails to Stop Fight over Parkway to It." *NYT*, October 2, 1986.

————. "Mideast Conference in Atlanta Draws Arab and U.S. Officials." *NYT*, November 9, 1983.

————. "President Praises Carter at Library." *NYT*, October 2, 1986.

————. "With Tourists Gone and Traffic Slow, Plains, Ga., Celebrates Its Centennial." *NYT*, May 18, 1985.

————. "Work Halted on Road to Carter Library in Atlanta." *NYT*, February 23, 1985.

Schonberg, Harold S. "Cultural Leaders Disturbed by Slashes Planned for Arts Agencies." *NYT*, February 20, 1981.

Schorr, Daniel. "Peanut Diplomacy in Haiti." *New Leader*, September 12–16, 1994.

Schwartz, Jerry. "Carter Plan Seeks to Help Atlanta's Poor." *NYT*, October 26, 1991.

———. "Carter Reports Progress in Ethiopia Peace Talks." *NYT*, September 21, 1989.

———. "Peacemaker without Portfolio: Jimmy Carter Goes Where Presidents Fear to Tread." *Atlanta Magazine*, December 1989.

———. "Schwarzkopf on Hussein: Calculating 'Carter Facts.'" *NYT*, October 13, 1994.

Sciolino, Elaine. "Accord Reached to End War in Bosnia; Clinton Pledges U.S. Troops To Keep Peace." *NYT*, November 22, 1995.

———. "Arafat Arrives in U.S. to 'Make Peace.'" *NYT*, September 13, 1993.

———. "Carter and Christopher to Meet in Georgia to Discuss." *NYT*, September 24, 1994.

———. "Christopher Sees a Place for Force." *NYT*, January 14, 1993.

———. "On the Brink of War, a Tense Battle of Wills." *NYT*, September 20, 1994.

———. "U.S. Officials Urge Carter to Cancel a Damascus Trip." *NYT*, March 3, 1987.

Scott, Peter. "Aid for Poor Finally Made '1-Step' Away." *Atlanta Journal & Constitution*, April 19, 1994.

———. "Ex-President Carter Pushes Gun Control in Atlanta Project Visit." *Atlanta Journal & Constitution*, April 30, 1994.

———. "Target 50,000 Households for Peace." *Atlanta Journal & Constitution*, April 28, 1994.

Scowcroft, Brent, and Arnold Kantor. "Korea: Time for Action." *Washington Post*, June 15, 1994.

Shacochis, Bob. "The Immaculate Invasion." *Harper's*, February 1995.

Shammas, Anton. "The Reality of Palestine." *NYT*, January 24, 1996.

Shaw, David. "Writer Identified Source of Confirmation for the *Post's* Ear Item about Carters." *Washington Post*, November 12, 1981.

Shipler, David K. "Carter in Israel, Says Arabs Move toward Peace." *NYT*, March 13, 1983.

———. "Carter Meets with Begin." *NYT*, March 9, 1983.

———. "Israel Rejects Reagan Plan for Palestinians' Self Rule, Terms It 'A Serious Danger.'" *NYT*, September 3, 1982.

———. "West Bank Arabs Protest Carter's Visit." *NYT*, March 10, 1983.

Shipp, Bill. "Georgia's Forgotten Hostage." *Georgia Trend*, September 1992.

Sick, Gary. "Last Word on the October Surprise." *NYT*, January 24, 1993.

———. "The October Surprise: Hear the Case." *NYT*, November 19, 1991.

Sinclair, Barbara. "Trying to Govern Positively in a Negative Era: Clinton and the 103rd Congress." In Campbell and Rockman, eds., *The Clinton Presidency: First Appraisals*. Chatham, N.J.: Chatham Publishing House, 1996.

Smith, Ben III. "A Hard Sell for Carter." *Atlanta Journal & Constitution*, September 15, 1995.

Smith, Gaddis. "Haiti: From Intervention to Intervasion." *Current History*, February 1995.

Smith, Hedrick. "President Concedes." *NYT*, November 5, 1980.

———. "A Turning Point Seen." *NYT*, November 6, 1980.

Smith, R. Jeffrey, and Ann Devroy. "One Small Concession Looms Large." *Washington Post*, June 26, 1994.

Smith, Paul. "Carter Praises Iowa Quality of Life." *Carroll (Iowa) Today*, September 29, 1990.

Smith, Terence. "Carter and Begin Reflect Upon Mideast." *NYT*, November 14, 1980.

———. "Carter Charges Iran Subjected Hostages to 'Acts of Barbarism'; for 52 Haircuts, and Calls Home." *NYT*, January 22, 1981.

———. "Carter Foreseeing Only Limited Role in Rebuilding Party." *NYT*, November 13, 1980.

————. "Carter in Farewell Speech, Cites Peril of Arms Buildup." *NYT*, January 15, 1981.

————. "Carter Saying Defeat 'Hurt,' Pledges Fullest Cooperation." *NYT*, November 5, 1980.

————. "Carter's Veto: A Last Hurrah." *NYT*, December 6, 1980.

————. "Experts See '76 Victory as Carter's Big Achievement." *NYT*, January 8, 1981.

————. "Hometown Plans to Give Carter a 'Festive Welcome.'" *NYT*, January 11, 1981.

————. "Putting the Hostages' Lives First." *NYT Magazine*, May 17, 1981.

————. "A Weary Carter Returns to Plains." *NYT*, January 21, 1981.

Smothers, Ronald. "Carter Sidesteps Mediating Dispute." *NYT*, July 16, 1988.

Sottak, Kevin. "Healing Mission." *Harvard Public Health Review*, fall 1994.

Spaeth, Anthony. "The Split Prize Pair." *Time*, October 21, 1996.

Sperling, Godfrey. "Jimmy Carter Rediscovered." *Christian Science Monitor*, November 14, 1989.

Stanley, Alessandra. "Words of Advice, Bittersweet." *NYT*, January 14, 1993.

Stein, Kenneth. "Syria Now Key Player in Middle East Drama." *Atlanta Journal & Constitution*, July 3, 1983.

Sterba, James. "Carter and Chinese Premier Urge Strong Ties." *NYT*, August 28, 1981.

————. "Carter Ending China Trip, Stresses Taiwan Issue." *NYT*, September 4, 1981.

————. "Carter Finds Chinese Reassured by Reagan on Ties." *NYT*, August 29, 1981.

————. "Carter Leaves Them Puffing at Great Wall." *NYT*, August 27, 1981.

Sternberg, Steve. "Pesticide Gifts Goal: Cut Illness by Killing Guinea Worm." *Atlanta Journal & Constitution*, March 28, 1990.

Stevenson, Richard W. "The Chief Banker for the Nations at the Bottom of the Heap." *NYT*, September 14, 1997.

Stine, Jeffrey K. "Environmental Policy during the Carter Presidency." In Gary M. Fink and Hugh Davis Graham, eds., *The Carter Presidency: Policy Choices in the Post New Deal Era*. Lawrence: University of Kansas Press, 1998.

Stokes, Henry Scott. "Carter, in Japan, Warns of Another Oil Crisis and Assails Khomeini." *NYT*, September 5, 1981.

————. "Outlook Darkens for South Korean Dissident Leaders." *NYT*, November 10, 1980.

Steuck, William. "Placing Jimmy Carter's Foreign Policy." In Gary M. Fink and Hugh Davis Graham, eds., *The Carter Presidency: Policy Choices in the Post New Deal Era*. Lawrence: University of Kansas Press, 1998.

Stuart, Reginald. "Competitors for Carter Library Site Wait for a Cue." *NYT*, February 13, 1981.

Tangonan, Shanon. "Elie Wiesel: Carter Suited to Lead U.N." *USA Today*, April 12, 1995.

Taylor, Paul. "Carter Drops Plans for Suit Against *Post*." *Washington Post*, October 25, 1981.

————. "*Post* Apologizes to Carter for Gossip Column Item." *Washington Post*, October 23, 1981.

Thomas, Evan. "Under the Gun." *Newsweek*, October 3, 1994.

Tolchin, Martin. "From Carter and Ford, an American Agenda." *NYT*, May 24, 1988.

————. "Senators Approve Revenue Sharing; Bill Goes to Carter." *NYT*, December 13, 1980.

Toner, Mike. "Carter Food Projects Yield Hope in Africa." *Atlanta Journal & Constitution*, March 20, 1988.

———. "U.S. Group Starts Drive Opposing 'Star Wars.'" *NYT*, June 20, 1984.

Toner, Robin. "Dukakis Restates Position on Israel." *NYT*, June 11, 1988.

Treadway, Don. "Jimmy Carter Vows to Continue Working for Democracy in Cuba." *Emory Report*, October 2, 1995.

Treaster, Joseph B. "Carter Warns against Withholding Censure of Human Rights Breaches." *NYT*, May 18, 1981.

Trudeau, Garry. "The Fireside Carter." *NYT*, October 2, 1994.

Tully, Shawn. "The Big Moneymen of Palestine, Inc." *Fortune*, July 31, 1989.

Uhlig, Mark. "Carter Applauds Nicaraguans on Election-Monitoring Plan." *NYT*, January 20, 1990.

Vidal, Gore. "Reel History." *New Yorker*, November 10, 1997.

Wald, Matthew L. "Amy Carter Tells Court She Sat in Road to Alter CIA Policy." *NYT*, April 14, 1987.

———. "Amy Carter Today: Causes and Arrests." *NYT*, December 5, 1986.

———. "Amy Is Acquitted over Protest." *NYT*, April 16, 1987.

Walker, Martin. "What's Important to Remember about Jimmy Carter." *Washington Post*, national weekly edition, June 27–July 3, 1994.

Wall, James M. "Jimmy Carter: Finding a Commonality of Concern." *Christian Century*, May 30–June 6, 1990.

———. "Jimmy Carter Doing Work That Speaks for Itself." *Christian Century*, May 16–23, 1990.

Walte, Juan J. "Carter's Coup Could Pay Off with Peace Prize." *USA Today*, September 20, 1994.

Waxman, Sharon. "Carter, Arafat Meet on Middle East Peace Plan." *Washington Post*, April 5, 1990.

Weinraub, Bernard. "Bush Urges Effort to Press Noriega to Quit as Leader." *NYT*, May 20, 1989.

———. "For Bush, Issues of Early 80s Lie." *NYT*, May 1, 1988.

———. "Hart, Risking Party Split, Attacks Carter-Mondale Team as Inept." *NYT*, May 1, 1984.

———. "Mondale's Tightrope Act on the Carter Problem." *NYT*, October 24, 1983.

———. "President Turns Fire on Carter in Southern Drive." *NYT*, October 25, 1986.

———. "White House Staffs Slide by Each Other." *NYT*, January 21, 1981.

Weisman, Steven R. "Carter, in Texas, Outlines His Priorities in a Second Term." *NYT*, November 2, 1980.

———. "President Proposes 83 Major Program Cuts; Tells U.S. Congress Faces 'Day of Reckoning.'" *NYT*, February 19, 1981.

Weller, Thomas. "Medical Research as Measured against the Needs of All." Massachusetts Medical Society, *New England Journal of Medicine* 283, no. 10 (September 3, 1970): 537–39.

West, Paul. "Years Out of Office, Carter Solidifies Spot on World Stage." *Baltimore Sun*, April 24, 1990.

White, Gayle. "Reading Up and Out." *Atlanta Journal & Constitution*, June 18, 1995.

Wicker, Tom. "Whatever Became of Jimmy Carter?" *Esquire*, July 1984.

Wilentz, Amy. "Blood and Guts." *Vibe*, February 1995.

Wilkie, Curtis. "Blessed Is the Peacemaker." *Boston Globe Magazine*, April 12, 1990.

———. "Carter's Image Seen Regaining Luster." *Boston Globe*, July 19, 1988.

———. "Carter's Memoirs, the Other Version: A Handful of Reporters Get the

Private Rundown from the President 10 Days before He Left Office." *Boston Globe*, October 17, 1982.

Wilkinson, Tracey. "Noriega's Party Wins Panamanian Election." *Fort Worth Star Telegram*, May 9, 1994.

Williams, Miller. "Some Words on the Lives and Lines of Jimmy Carter." *New Orleans Review* 20, nos. 1–2 (spring–summer 1994).

Wines, Michael. "As President Claims Victory, Doubts Remain." *NYT*, September 20, 1994.

Wooten, James. "Meddler, Moralist or Peacemaker?" *NYT Magazine*, January 29, 1995.

Young, Andrew. "The United States and Africa: Victory for Diplomacy." *Foreign Affairs: America and the World* 59, no. 3 (1980).

Zakaria, Fareed. "The Rise of Illiberal Democracy." *Foreign Affairs*, November–December 1997.

Zipser, Andy. "Down on His Luck." *Barron's*, June 1995.

NEWSPAPERS AND PERIODICALS

African Journal; al-Ahram (Cairo's English-language weekly newspaper); *Albany Sunday Herald; Altoona Mirror; American Heritage; American Journal of Tropical Medical Hygiene; American Spectator; Austin American-Statesman; Americus Times-Recorder; Arizona Republic; Atlanta Journal & Constitution; Atlanta Magazine; Atlantic Monthly; Baltimore Sun; Barnes & Noble Magazine; Barron's; Boston Globe; Buenos Aires Herald; Bulletin of the World Health Organization; Business Week; Canadian Journal of Plant Pathology; Carroll (Iowa) Today; Carter Center News; Charleston News & Courier; Chicago Tribune Magazine; Christian Century; Christian Science Monitor; Chronicle of Philanthropy; Columbus Ledger-Enquirer; Columns; Creative Loafing; Current Biographer; Current History; Des Moines Register; Ebony; Egyptian Gazette; Emory Report; Emory Wheel; Esquire; Fairfield (Iowa) Daily Ledger; Financial Times; Foreign Affairs; Foreign Policy; Foreign Service Journal; Fort Worth Star Telegram; Fortune; Fulbright Association Newsletter; George; Georgia Historical Quarterly; Georgia Tech Alumni Magazine; Georgia Trend; Harper's; Harvard Public Health Review; Houston Chronicle; Houston Post; Human Rights Insight; Independent; Indianapolis News; Jerusalem Post; Journal of Democracy; Journal of Inter-American Studies and World Affairs; Korean Journal of National Unification; Lancet; Los Angeles Times; Lutheran; Miami Herald; Middle East Journal; Nation; National Review; Negotiation Journal; New England Journal of Medicine; New Leader; New Orleans Review; New Orleans Times-Picayune; New Republic; New York Times; New York Times Magazine; New Yorker; Newsweek; Paper* (University of Georgia College of Agricultural Experiment Stations); *Parade Magazine; Parasitology Today; Peninsula Times Tribune (Palo Alto–Redwood City, Calif.); People; Philadelphia Enquirer; Presidential Studies Quarterly; Reader's Digest; Regardie's; Reuters News Report; Richmond Times-Dispatch; Rotarian; Salisbury (N.C.) Post; San Francisco Examiner; SG2000 Newsletter; Southern Homes; St. Paul Pioneer Press; Star-Ledger* (Newark); *Tico Times; Time; Transitional Law and Contemporary Problems; Travel and Leisure; U.S. News and World Report; USA Today; Vibe; Wall Street Journal; Washington Journalism Review; Washington Monthly; Washington Post; Washington Quarterly; Washington Times; Waycross Journal Herald; World Monitor; World View.*

INTERVIEWS BY AUTHOR
(*ASTERISK INDICATES MORE THAN ONE INTERVIEW CONDUCTED)

Elliott Abrams; Odeh Aburdene; Terrence Adamson*; Andrew Agle*; Raul Alfonsin; Richard V. Allen; Martin Andersen; Patrick Anderson; Cecil Andrus; Yasir Arafat; Daniel Ariail; Bertrand Aristide; Bernard Aronson*; Randall Ashley; Hanan Ashrawi; Brian Atwood; Mubarak Awad; James A Baker III*; George Ball; Harry Barnes*; Tasheen Basheer; Eric Bjornlund; Lindy Boggs; Julian Bond; Eric Bord; Norman Borlaug; Peter Bourne*; Fred Boyles; John Brademas; Ben Bradlee; James Brasher III; Joseph Brodsky; Zbigniew Brzezinski*; George Bush; Joseph Califano; James Cannon; Frank Carlucci; Amy Carter*; Chip Carter*; Hugh Carter; Jack Carter; Jimmy Carter*; Rosalynn Carter*; James Carville; William Chace; Richard Cheney; Bethine Church; Warren Christopher; Ramsey Clark; William Clark; Rev. E. Walter Cleckley Jr.; Lodwrick Cook; Marion Creekmore; William Crowe; Mario Cuomo; Lloyd Cutler; Richard Darman; Morris Dees; Patricia Derian; James Dickey; Faye Dill*; Edward Djerejian; Michael Dukakis; Raven Edge; Stuart Eizenstat; William Foege*; Thomas Foley; Gerald Ford; J. William Fulbright; Linda Fuller*; Millard Fuller*; John Kenneth Galbraith; Robert L. Gallucci; John Gates; Allen Ginsberg; Newt Gingrich; David Hamburg; John Hardman*; Pamela Harriman; Mark Hatfield; Rudy Hayes; Jack Healy; Seamus Heaney; Christopher Hemmeter; Hendrik Hertzberg*; Francis Hertzog; The Reverend Theodore Hesburgh; Walter Hickel; Steven Hochman; Richard C. Holbrooke*; Donald Hopkins; William Hyland; Abdul-Karim Iryani; General David Jones; Hamilton Jordan; Robert Kagan; Mrs. C. B. King; C. B. King Jr.; Mary Elizabeth King*; Charles Kirbo; Paul Kirk; Henry Kissinger; Elizabeth Kurylo; Phil Lader; Anthony Lake*; Bruce Laingen; James T. Laney; Edward Lanpher; Dan Lee; Anthony Lewis; Arthur Link; Sol Linowitz; Robert Lipshutz; Bill Lotz; Lester Maddox; Charles Manatt; Michael Manley; David Maraniss; Christopher Matthews; Eugene McCarthy; George McGovern; Edward Meese; Ellen Propper Mickiewicz*; Mrs. Mills (Nellie Jennings); Frank Moore; John Moores; Edmund Muskie; Ralph Nader; Achsah Nesmith; Joyce Neu; Paul Nitze; Sam Nunn; Don Oberdofer; Kenzaburo Oe; Lisbet Palme; Robert Pastor*; Octavio Paz; Geir Pedersen; Shimon Peres; Mary Prince (formerly Fitzpatrick); Norman Podhoretz; Betty Pope*; John Pope*; Colin Powell; Jody Powell*; George Price; William Quandt; David Rabhan*; Charles Rafshoon; Gerald Rafshoon; Joey Ramone; Maxine Reese; James Reston; Joe Reuben; Randall Robinson; Elliot Richardson; Walt W. Rostow; Catherine Rudder; Dean Rusk; Arthur Schlesinger Jr.; Brent Scowcroft; Bassam Abu Sharif; Gary Sick; Ms. Allie Smith; Jane Smith*; Nicholas D. Snider; Wole Soyinka; Kenneth W. Stein*; Ted Stevens; Gordon Stewart; Bob Strauss; Hal Suit; John Sununu; William L. Swing; Peter Tarnoff; Rob Townes; Paul Tsongas; Ted Turner; Bishop Desmond Tutu; Brian Urquhart; Cyrus Vance; William vanden Heuvel*; Ted Van Dyk; Mrs. Betty Walters; Paul Warnke; Jack Watson; Sam Way; William Webster; Phyllis Wheeler; Garrison Wilkes; Miller Williams; Phil Wise; Kenneth Wollack*; Leonard Woodcok; Judy Woodruff; Sole Woyinka; Andrew Young*; Ahmed Zuaiter.

INDEX